Anton Armstrong and St. Olaf Choir singers
Boe Memorial Chapel, St. Olaf College, April, 1997

Norway Tour, 1913

F. Melius Christiansen, ca. 1910

Popular train stop north of Trondheim
Members of St. Olaf Choir, 1913

Professor Christiansen and two
Choir members, Norway 1913

St. Olaf Choir singing on the "Christianiafjord," 1913

Pausing for a picture, Norway 1913
L. to R.: Mrs. P. G. Schmidt,
Mrs. George Rygh, Caroline
Heltne-Holvick, (unidentified),
J. Jørgen Thompson

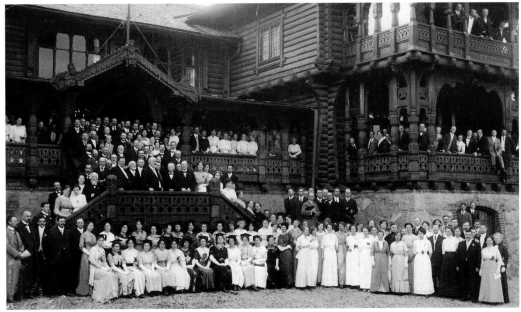

St. Olaf Choir and Norwegian friends at Holmenkollen, near Christiania (Oslo)

Choir reception in Christiania, Residence of American Consul Swenson

Concert sites in Norway

Trondheim
Kristiansund
Molde
Alesund
Bergen
Haugesund
Stavanger
Larvik
Kristiansand

After the final concert, in Copenhagen, Professor and Mrs. P. G. Schmidt and several others traveled to Germany

St. Olaf Lutheran Choir 1920s

Choir lining up by Ytterboe Hall, November 5, 1921

College and Choir leaders by
Hoyme Chapel, ca. 1922
L. to R.: President L. W. Boe,
P. O. Holland, P. G. Schmidt, Martin
Hanson, F. Melius Christiansen

St. Olaf Choir outside Hoyme Chapel, ca. 1922
Impresario Martin Hanson between FMC and PGS

St. Olaf Choir, 1922 at St. John's Lutheran Church, Northfield

F. Melius Christiansen and Ole Rølvaag, 1926

Luther "Luke" Sletten '29, captain-elect of the Augsburg basketball team, transferred to St. Olaf to try out for the St. Olaf Choir. He sang in the Choir his senior year and also participated in the Norway-Germany tour of 1930.

Reunion of St. Olaf Choirs, June 3, 1928

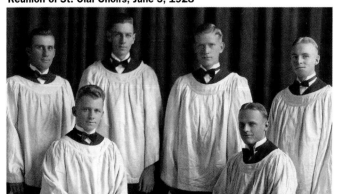

Six St. Olaf Choir men, 1929
Standing L. to R.:
Harris L. Romerein '30,
Frederick Schmidt '31,
Oliver J. Solberg '30,
Carl L. Hagen '29
Seated L. to R.:
Ray Reinholtzen '29,
Carl Norman Giere '29

Leipzig Concert Program, 1930

Fathers of the St. Olaf Choir, FMC and PGS, 1930

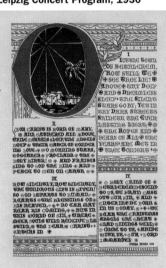

St. Olaf Christmas Festival Program, 1932

F. Melius Chritiansen, his wife Edith, his father Anders, and other relatives in Larvik, Norway, summer of 1930

The St. Olaf Choir, 1933

F. Melius Christiansen, Kirsten Flagstad, famous Norwegian soprano, and Choir members at train station, Springfield, Massachusetts, 1938

St. Olaf Lutheran Choir

1930s

St. Olaf singers at Central Lutheran Church, Minneapolis, Minnesota, 1938. Back: Alvar Sandquist, Gordon Egertson, Halmer Wall. Middle: Leon Hegge, Loiuse Tufte, Joe Running. Front: Margeret Helgen, June Engelstad, Rachel Lunde, Gertrude "Trudy" Roe

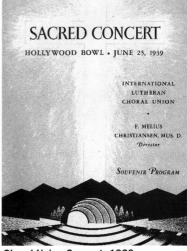

SACRED CONCERT

HOLLYWOOD BOWL • JUNE 25, 1939

INTERNATIONAL
LUTHERAN
CHORAL UNION

F. MELIUS
CHRISTIANSEN, MUS. D.
Director

SOUVENIR PROGRAM

Choral Union Concert, 1939

The St. Olaf Choir, Washington, D. C., 1938

Oscar Overby, F. Melius Christiansen, and Olaf Christiansen, ca. 1945

Olaf C. and F. Melius Christiansen, ca. 1948
The Viking ship before them was a gift to F. Melius from the women of Larvik, Norway

Photo by Jerry L. Hanson

Olaf C. Christiansen, Kalispell, Montana, 1952

Choir in cold car, 1952

Olaf and the Choir, ca. 1955
In front of old Music Hall

St. Olaf Choir, directed by Olaf Christiansen Boe Memorial Chapel, 1960

Recalling Northfield years, Olaf Christiansen, Edel Ytterboe Ayers, Fred Schmidt. A daughter of H. T. Ytterboe who sang under Christy, Mrs. Ayers with her husband Harry entertained the St. Olaf Choir at dinner before the concert in Anniston, Alabama, February 8, 1962.

THE
ST. OLAF CHOIR
A NARRATIVE

THE
ST. OLAF CHOIR

A NARRATIVE

Joseph M. Shaw

Published by
St. Olaf College

DEDICATION

To members of the St. Olaf Choir,
past, present, and future
To Kenneth Jennings and Anton Armstrong
To the memory of F. Melius Christiansen,
Olaf C. Christiansen, and Paul G. Schmidt
To the memory of other St. Olaf Choir members
who are no longer among us

© 1997 St. Olaf College, Northfield, Minnesota

Published by St. Olaf College; printed by Northfield Printing, Inc.

First Printing, 1997. Printed in the United States of America.

ISBN 0-9640020-1-9 (hardcover)

ISBN 0-9640020-2-7 (softcover)

CONTENTS

PREFACE

The purpose of this book is to tell the story of the St. Olaf Choir from its origin in 1912 to the present. As befits a group with such a long history, its story has been told before. In 1921 Eugene E. Simpson wrote *A History of St. Olaf Choir*, published by Augsburg Publishing House of Minneapolis, Minnesota. During preparation of the book, Simpson stayed for a time at the home of Dr. and Mrs. F. Melius Christiansen in Northfield. Paul J. Christiansen, youngest son in the family who became director of the Concordia Choir, remembers his father and Simpson having long talks in the living room about the St. Olaf Choir.

Simpson was a fellow student with F. Melius Christiansen at the Leipzig Conservatory in 1898. With Christiansen's encouragement, he learned Norwegian to increase his access to source materials for the book. Simpson began with the first music activities at St. Olaf College, the coming to St. Olaf of Christiansen as music director, and the birth of the St. Olaf Choir. After chapters on the 1913 tour of Norway and the early career of Christiansen up to the Leipzig years, Simpson told the story of the St. Olaf Choir through the great tour to the east coast in the spring of 1920.

In 1925 Frances Boardman, a reporter for the *St. Paul Pioneer Press*, interviewed Dr. Christiansen for an article. St. Olaf College published the piece in a booklet entitled, "Ideals of St. Olaf Lutheran Choir Explained." Boardman included information on Christiansen's early music training as well as the ideals of the Choir. A promotional booklet published by the Twin City St. Olaf Club in 1931 included a summary of the Choir's achievements since its founding, a biographical sketch of Dr. Christiansen, founder and director, a statement of purpose, and a selection of reviews from the twenties and early thirties.

The next extensive treatment of the St. Olaf Choir after Simpson's volume was *Music Master of the Middle West*: The Story of F. Melius Christiansen and the St. Olaf Choir, by Leola Nelson Bergmann, published by the University of Minnesota Press in 1944. The book developed from Bergmann's graduate study at the State University of Iowa where her Ph. D. dissertation was "F. Melius Christiansen: A Study of his life and work as a Norwegian-American contribution to American culture," submitted in 1942. As a student at St. Olaf College, Class of 1937, the author had been a member of the St. Olaf Choir. Later, in the course of preparing her book, she had the privilege of spending many hours with Dr. Christiansen who was generous with his time and illuminating responses.

Bergmann told how the career of F. Melius Christiansen unfolded as part of the great American epic of immigrants and pioneers pursuing their dreams on the plains of the Midwest. "An immigrant boy became a good and great American." At a small church college in Minnesota, Christiansen trained a group of singers who achieved a quality of a cappella singing that gained national and international admiration.

After Leola Nelson Bergmann came other doctoral theses on choral music, the Christiansens, and the college choirs that carried forward the musical tradition. At Michigan State University in 1969 Robert Lee Jennings submitted a Ph. D. thesis entitled "A Study of the Historical Development of Choral Ensembles At Selected Lutheran Liberal Arts Colleges in the United States." In 1973 Albert Rykken Johnson, St. Olaf graduate, Class of 1955, and a former member of the St. Olaf Choir, presented his Ph. D. thesis to the School of Music in the Graduate College of the University of Iowa. The title of Johnson's thesis was "The Christiansen Choral Tradition: F. Melius Christiansen, Olaf C. Christiansen and Paul J. Christiansen."

As a candidate for the Doctor of Musical Arts degree at Michigan State University, Anton Eugene Armstrong, graduate of St. Olaf College in the Class of 1978 and former St. Olaf Choir member, submitted a thesis entitled "Celebrating 75 Years of Musical Excellence: The Evolution of the St. Olaf Choir." Armstrong received his D.M.A. degree in May of 1987. He was appointed the fourth director of the St. Olaf Choir in 1990.

The St. Olaf Choir occupied an important place in an article by Paul Benson published in 1989 by the Norwegian-American Historical Association: "A Cappella Choirs in the Scandinavian-Lutheran Colleges." Behind Benson's work was a larger, unpublished version of the topic. The college choirs dealt with, in addition to the St. Olaf Choir, were those at Augsburg, Augustana College in Rock Island, Concordia in Moorhead, Luther, and Pacific Lutheran University.

The present work, which has gained much from the earlier studies, is intended to set forth the remarkable story of the St. Olaf Choir in a non-technical way for the enjoyment of the general reader. It was undertaken at the request of the Music Department at St. Olaf College. The idea of a book about the St. Olaf Choir emerged in a series of informal meetings chaired by Bob Johnson, manager of music organizations, and attended by George Aker, vice president for college relations, Anton Armstrong, director of the St. Olaf Choir, Kenneth Jennings, former director of the Choir, and the undersigned. Part of the impetus for this narrative came from the commemoration in 1996 of the 125th anniversary of the birth of F. Melius Christiansen.

It has been my aim to keep the St. Olaf Choir at the center of the story. The four directors receive their due in separate biographical chapters and frequent mention in text and illustrations. Their names will live on as talented and devoted servants of the choral art. It is the Choir, however, that embodies the tradition and provides the historical continuity from 1912, through the rest of the twentieth century, and into the future. May it remain true to its art, and true to its calling, to sing the praises of God with beauty and conviction to coming generations.

Joseph M. Shaw
St. Olaf College
April 21, 1997

CHAPTER 1

THE PURPLE ROBES

St. Olaf Christmas Festival, 1989

On three weekend evenings and a Sunday afternoon in early December, five hundred student singers and instrumentalists present the annual St. Olaf Christmas Festival Concert before some 15,000 appreciative listeners. During the Christmas season, the event is often made available to television viewers throughout the nation. One year, for example, Public Broadcasting Service network stations telecast "What Child Is This?", a 60-minute program made by Twin Cities television station KTCA-TV from a video-tape of the 1983 St. Olaf Christmas Festival. [1]

The Christmas Festival is held in the Skoglund Athletic Center on the St. Olaf College campus in Northfield, Minnesota. The St. Olaf Orchestra, in formal concert dress, is in its accustomed place immediately in front of the platform. It plays the processional as the choirs led by banner bearers enter the auditorium and make their way to the risers on the lighted stage. The entire room is decorated in colors and symbols appropriate to the Advent and Christmas season and expressive of the festival theme.

The Manitou Singers, an ensemble of first year women, process in their white surplices over red choir robes. Their place is at the front on the left side of the wide stage. The Viking Chorus, made up solely of first year male students, and attired in blue robes trimmed in white, are directly behind the Manitou Singers. The St. Olaf Cantorei, a group of men and women singers, wear blue scapulars over white liturgical robes with cinctures at the waist. They are on the right side of the platform. The Chapel Choir, a large mixed chorus, in red robes with white stoles, stands on the highest risers at the back, spanning the entire width of the stage area. Toward the front of the platform on the right-hand side, directly in front of the Cantorei, is the St. Olaf Choir, in purple robes.

Before the music begins, someone in the audience, a St. Olaf student, a faculty or staff member, a Northfield resident, or another veteran patron of the festival, will whisper to their guests, "That's the St. Olaf Choir, the ones in the purple robes." New members of the Choir confess to something like giddiness when first fitted in the distinctive garb in the fall of the year. "We're wearing the purple robes!"

For the last sixty years or so, the purple robes have been the identifying emblem of the St. Olaf Choir. "The purple robed choir has made the name of little St. Olaf college, Northfield, Minn., one to conjure with among lovers of choral music," stated a Milwaukee paper during the choir's 1941 concert tour. Choir members soon discover that putting on the purple robe binds them into a community embracing past, present, and future. "We are part of a bigger history," said Angela Schum '95, a second soprano

Wearing the Purple Robes
Andrea Wollenberg '96 and
Adrienne Redmon '96

from Dallas who joined the St. Olaf Choir as a sophomore. She continued, "We have a responsibility to every person who has worn a purple robe."[2]

St. Olaf Choir singers, 1992, Boe Memorial Chapel

The Standards

The responsibility, simply put, is to live up to the standard of choral music performance set by F. Melius Christiansen, the founder and first director of the St. Olaf Choir, and continued by his successors, Olaf C. Christiansen, Kenneth Jennings, and Anton Armstrong. Each director, each Choir, and each Choir member has understood that the standard is not static but living. F. Melius Christiansen was known for the constant striving toward perfection. "We know that perfection can never be reached," he wrote, "but we have to work toward that goal nevertheless."[3] While on tour with the Choir in 1927, Christiansen wrote to St. Olaf College President Boe: "There are still problems to be solved and improvements to be made with the choir."[4]

Paul G. Schmidt, long-time manager of the St. Olaf Choir and personal friend of F. Melius Christiansen, once described the Choir's disciplined efforts always to improve its skill. "Every composition sung must be accurately committed to memory. There is a continual repetition and drill, phrase by phrase, which to the outsider might seem meaningless or superfluous, but which results in the end in a flexibility of performance and an accuracy in intonation and rhythm which could not be attained in any less laborious manner."[5]

F. Melius Christiansen, ca. 1925

3

Such dedication to the making of music suggests that from its earliest years the St. Olaf Choir established its own standard and continually sought to go beyond it. A music critic for the Cleveland Times expressed this idea as follows: "There are many choirs and choral organizations that are worthy of commendation," he wrote. "But there is a criterion for all of them—for all but one, and that one is the St. Olaf Lutheran Choir, which is the criterion itself."[6] These words were written in 1928, during the second decade of the Choir's activity under F. Melius Christiansen.

When Olaf C. Christiansen took over direction of the Choir in 1943 after two years as associate conductor, friends of

Olaf C. Christiansen, ca. 1942

the Choir naturally addressed themselves to the question of its continuing quality. Albert Goldberg of the *Chicago Daily Tribune* was reassured, as he wrote in the spring of 1944: "As might be expected, the great tradition of the choir, one of the first of American college choruses to seek and merit high artistic recognition, has been faithfully carried on. Obviously there has been no relaxation of standards."[7]

The reviewer for a Buffalo paper heard the Choir in January of 1947 and wrote of Olaf's leadership: "Under his quiet but assured directing, the choir proved there has been no deviation from the high standards set by the founder." After the Choir's 1948 concert in Washington, D. C., Glenn Dillard Gunn wrote that the country's "oldest and most distinguished" specialist in unaccompanied choral art, came to Constitution Hall "to set new standards in their department of the arts, even for themselves."[8]

Olaf Christiansen's tenure as director of the St. Olaf Choir lasted until 1968 at

Kenneth Jennings, 1969

which time Kenneth Jennings was named as his successor. At this point, with someone other than a Christiansen leading the ensemble, the same questions about maintaining the tradition were raised and met with firmly positive answers. "Choir's lofty standards deserve praise," was the headline for a review of a concert in Arizona.[9] As Jennings approached retirement after twenty-two years as director, Curtis Hansen of Curtis Music Press wrote to him, "The technical and musical standards you have set with the St. Olaf Choir are emulated by choral directors the world over, and your expertise and devotion to choral music will be long lasting."[10]

Another admirer was the former music director of the Minnesota Orchestra, Stanislaw Skrowaczewski, who included this statement in a message to Dr. Jennings: "I will never forget the beauty of tone in the works that we did together; for example, in Mozart's *Idomeneo* and Ravel's *Daphnis*. You have spoiled my ear and taste to the point that after collaborating with your choir, no other choir in the world that I work with could give me such satisfaction." [11]

In January of 1990 Anton Armstrong was named the fourth director of the St. Olaf Choir, assuming his duties September 1, 1990. Armstrong had written about the St. Olaf Choir in his doctoral dissertation at Michigan State University, entitling his work "Celebrating 75 Years of Musical Excellence: The Evolution of The St. Olaf Choir."[12] His study had given him a deeper appreciation for this tradition, he said at the time of his appointment. "Yet," he continued, "I also realize that while the past has laid a firm foundation, the focus for this tradition must be to the future as we seek to serve others through the choral art."[13] When the Choir toured the Pacific Northwest in 1992, the *Portland Oregonian* published the

Anton Armstrong, 1990

comment, "Showing musical maturity beyond their years, the group skillfully maneuvered through a program that included works from five different centuries. . . . The group's reputation as the best college choir in the country is safe in Armstrong's capable hands." [14]

The determination to attain a high standard in the presentation of choral music has marked the work of the St. Olaf Choir from the beginning. There has also been a steady drive to move ahead to new attainments in the choral art. The desire for excellence and improvement is to be expected in any sphere of the arts. Noteworthy in the case of the St. Olaf Choir is that the disciplined quest for quality has been motivated by a unique, historical sense of mission.

The Mission of the St. Olaf Choir

The primary mission of the St. Olaf Choir has been to sing as beautifully as possible the great choral music of the world, with special emphasis on music from the Christian tradition. Early on, the Choir committed itself to the renewal of the Lutheran choral heritage, but over the years it has broadened its purpose to sing great religious music from many traditions and to include occasional secular choral works. Therefore the nature of the mission is restated from time to time in statements from the College, in remarks by the directors, and in comments by critics familiar with the Choir's development. One critic spoke for many who have caught the spirit of the Choir's singing, sensing that it involved more than musical skill. Responding to a concert by the St. Olaf Choir given in the twenties, Karlton Hackett wrote:

> It is not an exhibition of technical skill just for vainglorious display, but their rare powers are employed to express the meaning of music. They sing nothing but what is in itself fine and they sing it with an earnestness of purpose that gives it a moving force. They believe in their music and in the meaning it is to convey.[15]

The mission of the Choir is closely related to its origins as a local church choir and to its connection with a college of the Lutheran Church. The fact that the St. Olaf Choir grew out of F. Melius Christiansen's leadership of the choir at St. John's Lutheran Church in Northfield, Minnesota, speaks for itself. The practice of singing sacred music did not change when the St. John's Choir became the St. Olaf Choir in 1912. The Choir's constitution drawn up in 1920 still stated that the purpose "shall be to serve God and the Church by singing at the regular services of St. John's Congregation and by giving such concerts as the organization may decide upon."[16]

The custom of having the St. Olaf Choir sing at the worship services at St. John's continued from 1912 to about 1952, a significant portion of the Choir's history. When St. Olaf students formed their own congregation on the campus in 1952, the St. Olaf Choir took its turn with the other college choirs to provide anthems at the Sunday services. Boe Memorial Chapel, built in 1953, became the site of campus worship. From Olaf Christiansen's

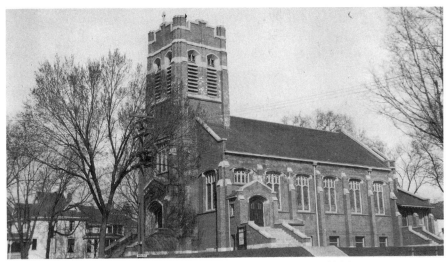

St. John's Lutheran Church, Northfield, Minnesota, ca. 1930

time and forward, the St. Olaf Choir has made at least one annual visit to St. John's Lutheran Church, usually right before its winter tour, to join the congregation in worship and to sing several anthems.

The desire to contribute something of musical value to the people at the College and in the local community is an aspect of the Choir's

St. John's Lutheran Church, Chancel area, ca. 1921

purpose that remained when the ensemble won a wider reputation. Even as President L. W. Boe looked forward to the St. Olaf Choir's extended tour to eastern cities in 1920, he described for readers of the church paper, the *Lutheran Church Herald*, the role of the Choir in its local setting:

> The mission of the St. Olaf Choir is primarily to develop in the students at the college a thorough appreciation of Lutheran church music. It welcomes, however, the opportunity to serve in the larger field. The Choir comes as a representative of the Lutheran congregations of the West with greetings to the Lutherans of the East. It is hoped that through its presentation of our common heritage we may become more conscious of our spiritual ancestry and of our common faith.[17]

For the sake of "Lutheran Church Music of a Better Sort" was how one reporter characterized the plans for the 1920 eastern tour. The appearance of the name "The St. Olaf Lutheran Choir" on printed programs for a period of years was a reminder of the Choir's mission to acquaint listeners with the wealth of chorales and hymns in the Lutheran church.[18]

Without lessening their interest in Lutheran choral music, all four directors have felt free to consider music from other than strictly Lutheran sources. F. Melius Christiansen accepted his Lutheran milieu as a given but was more apt to speak of fidelity to music and to art. "Art itself is above nationality and above sect and denominational considerations" he wrote. "Art stands above and alone."[19]

Lars Wilhelm Boe
St. Olaf College President
1918-1942

When Olaf C. Christiansen took full charge of the Choir in 1943, reviewers were quick to notice a different repertoire. One commented on the appearance of modern English pieces. Olaf introduced music of the sixteenth, seventeenth, and twentieth centuries into his programs.[20] He wrote, "Religious music embraces a wide range of choral literature. It goes beyond any specific church denomination, any particular season of the year, any particular era of history, or even any particular type of emotion."[21] Inclusion in the repertoires of many types and eras of music beyond what may be identified as Lutheran has been characteristic of all the directors.

What has remained constant in the mission of the St. Olaf Choir is its devotion to choral music of a religious nature. The printed programs in the 1960s stated that the Choir strove "to make the religious message the central purpose of the concert."[22] Olaf Christiansen wrote that "the primary motive of the St. Olaf Choir from its earliest days has been to promote great choral music with religious texts."[23] The purpose of the music, he insisted, was to support the meaning of the text.[24] He was once heard to remark, "We have no reason to be concertizing unless we get the text across."[25]

Kenneth Jennings expected Choir members to be "sensitive to the religious values of the texts."[26] Anton Armstrong strongly affirmed the Choir's mission to sing traditional religious music while recognizing the need for new expressions for diverse audiences in the United States and abroad. These directors have shown a common respect for the importance of the texts, religious and secular, by printing them, rather than program notes, in the Choir's concert programs. Following the Christiansen model they also trained their singers in the clean diction which made the texts more easily understood.

Admirable as the concentration on the texts may be, the fact that the Choir so frequently sings in languages other than English draws occasional criticism. Reviewers tend to be impressed by the Choir's ability to sing in Latin, German, Spanish, French, and so on, but some listeners say that they would enjoy the music more if they could understand the words. There are reasons for singing in other languages. Much great church music originated in Latin or German. The Norwegian background of St. Olaf College and F. Melius Christiansen make it natural for the Choir to include folk and Christmas songs in Norwegian. The Choir has surprised and delighted audiences in China and Korea, for example, by singing numbers in their languages.

To summarize, the mission of the St. Olaf Choir continues to be centered on the sensitive performance of great religious choral music. It was inevitable that the Lutheran chorales of the first decades would be supplemented by choral pieces from a variety of other church traditions. Yet several of the old Lutheran favorites made popular by F. Melius in the early years still turn up in recent Choir programs and still evoke an enthusiastic response. In 1995, for example, the St. Olaf Choir sang Bach's "Singet dem Herrn," and Christiansen's arrangements of "Wake, Awake" and "Beautiful Savior." The singing of secular music from time to time, which the Choir has done for decades, does not mean a departure from the organization's main purpose, but allows for musical growth and variety of repertoire.

The Choir on Tour

Consideration of the mission of the St. Olaf Choir leads directly to a few comments about the tours, since a performing group with a purpose will seek to be heard beyond its own community. "The prime motive of the college in sending the choir on concert tours has been and always will be to promote interest in choral singing," stated a Minneapolis paper when it was announced in the late twenties that the St. Olaf Choir was invited to Norway in 1930.[27] Tours are a familiar part of many musicians' lives, but since the St. Olaf Choir was one of the first college choirs to go on tour, there is interest in how this facet of its experience began.

P. G. Schmidt, who at one time managed the St. Olaf Band as well as the St. Olaf Choir, recalls how the first Choir tour came about. Requests came

St. Olaf Choir on tour, 1927

to him from congregations in Kenyon, Holden, Zumbrota, and other southern Minnesota towns "to hear the inspiring rendition of hymns and chorales" by what was then still the St. John's Church Choir. Schmidt continues:

> Quite often, too, when I was out arranging concerts for the band, people would ask me: 'Why don't you take St. John's choir out? Our church people like to hear the band, that is true; but they would be very grateful if they could also hear that choir in sacred concert.' It was therefore decided I should try to arrange a trip for the choir during the Easter recess in 1912.[28]

Schmidt had worked closely with F. Melius Christiansen in the first decade of the 1900s to upgrade the St. John's choir and add more college students to its ranks. He shared with Christiansen and President J. N. Kildahl the belief that the improved choir could better serve the congregation "and at the same time stimulate greater interest in our Lutheran choral heritage."[29] Thus one can identify an early motive for taking the Choir on tour: to demonstrate to other congregations how the Lutheran chorales could be sung.[30] The St. Olaf student yearbook, *The Viking*, published in December of 1912, carried an article about the first tour of the Choir written by Ida Hagen '13, a member of the Choir. She began with

10

these words:

> During the last few years there has been a feeling prevalent
> throughout our Lutheran choir circles that our beautiful old
> church chorales have been sadly neglected, and that something
> ought to be done to reinstate these grand old hymns into favor. It
> was decided, therefore, that the St. Olaf College Choir should
> make a concert trip during the Easter vacation of 1912 to add its
> mite to the good cause. [31]

St. Olaf College Band, 1906
President J. N. Kildahl between F. M. Christiansen and P. G. Schmidt

By 1912 more than one St. Olaf musical organization had already made successful tours. The St. Olaf Band, directed by F. Melius Christiansen, had toured Norway in 1906, and had traveled to the Pacific Northwest in 1909. The St. Olaf Mixed Octet, also directed by Christiansen, gave more than sixty concerts in Minnesota, South Dakota, and Iowa in the summer of 1908.[32] A postcard from Melius to his wife indicates that Cannon Falls, Minnesota, was the first stop.

In the light of such activities, College historian William C. Benson outlined the thinking that would lead to the 1912 tour of the St. Olaf Choir:

> Because [President] Kildahl, Christiansen, and Schmidt had found
> that the band and octet tours had been an effective way of bringing
> the college to the attention of the public, they believed that a choir
> singing the familiar music of the church 'in the manner in which it
> should be sung' might be even more effective. [33]

St. Olaf College in 1912 was a small, struggling institution badly in need of more buildings, a larger and better paid faculty, and improved

Picture postcard:
St. Olaf
Mixed Octet,
1908

The note to Mrs. Christiansen says:
"We have not come very far yet.
This is Cannon Falls. Early tomorrow
we travel 9 miles with horses to Urland
Church where we will sing at 10:30
in the morning.   Melius."

facilities. The Choir tour would promote the College but also serve the congregations by demonstrating how to improve the singing of church music.

The need to help congregations appreciate the Lutheran chorales was elaborated by a member of the 1908 Octet who sought to explain Christiansen's aim in this regard: "Observing that our chorales were not being sung as they should be sung, and that many of the young people in the congregation were getting 'tired of the dragging and monotonous hymns of the old folks,' due to the faulty rendition of the hymns, and that in some places even the light and worthless 'up-to-date' hymns, with a superabundance of 'rhythm' and 'time' were substituted for our dignified and stately choral melodies, Prof. Christiansen decided to try to awaken an interest and an appreciation of our choral music."[34] This analysis, similar to Ida Hagen's in her report of the 1912 Choir tour, suggests how students of the time understood the "good cause" of restoring the old church chorales to new life and favor.

The need to make the small College known was manifest. And the idea of livening up the Lutheran chorales in the congregations was clearly on the minds of Christiansen and his student musicians. Yet the Choir had another motive for going on tour that underlay the other reasons, and that was its need to perform, and thereby to improve itself in the musical art.

At the time when these tours were being planned, before there was radio entertainment, records, and television, any musical performer or organization had to seek out audiences. Music was heard when individuals and groups took their talents to communities beyond their own. In the nineteenth and early twentieth centuries there was a rather amazing amount of musical traffic that brought well-known, even famous, performers to many small towns, where today one would only expect to find them in the large cities. During the 1870s citizens of Northfield, Minnesota, for example, had opportunities to hear such reputable violinists as Camilla Urso and Edouard Remenyi.[35]

Similarly, when the St. Olaf Choir became established, it looked for opportunities to perform. P. G. Schmidt addressed this motive in the 1926-27 *Viking* where he took up the question of the purpose of the Band and Choir tours. They provided some publicity for the school, he conceded, and they rewarded the performers' faithful practice with enjoyable and beneficial experiences. But those were not the main reasons. The primary purpose of the tours was this: "To stimulate the members of the organization to do their best, and to permit the organization to obtain some means of adequate expression."[36]

How Schmidt supported his point is worth examining. Earlier in this article, entitled "Some Reflections on the St. Olaf Band and the St. Olaf Choir," he gave this explanation:

> It is difficult to maintain an organization like our St. Olaf Band or St. Olaf Choir without giving it an opportunity for adequate expression, and this is made possible only by taking the organizations out on a short tour where a number of concerts can be given on consecutive days. It is only after five or six concerts have been given on tour that the organization really finds itself. Without the stimulus of a tour, it is doubtful if either organization could be maintained; surely it would not be possible to maintain either on their present high standards of efficiency.[37]

Going on tour thus serves a basic artistic purpose, which takes precedence over such laudable concerns as publicizing the school, singing the Lutheran chorales properly, and giving the hard-working students the pleasure of a trip. A Pittsburgh reviewer, knowing that the St. Olaf Choir had raised money on its tours to help build a music building, was able to see something deeper at work. He wrote, "Yet for all the choir's concert touring it seeks not prestige nor profit, but to serve an artistic ideal. This it is fulfilling in a noble manner."[38]

The Choir's 1912 tour into Wisconsin and Illinois was followed by numerous domestic and international tours. Only a few need to be

Music Hall, built in 1926

mentioned at this point. In 1913 the St. Olaf Choir went to Norway. The 1920 tour to cities of the east coast was a breakthrough for the Choir, for the first time winning national recognition for its a cappella performance of sacred music. The year 1930 brought the Choir to Trondheim in Norway to celebrate the 900th anniversary of the introduction of Christianity into that northern country. On that tour the Choir also gave concerts in Sweden, Denmark, and Germany.

Tours to various parts of the United States were undertaken through the thirties and forties. War-time travel restrictions limited but did not curtail

St. Olaf Choir, 1930. Aboard "Stavangerfjord"

14

tours in 1944 and 1945. Normal tour practice resumed after the war, with Olaf C. Christiansen as director of the Choir. For years P. G. Schmidt had made the arrangements for all of the Choir's tours, traveling with the Choir as manager and always singing in the bass section. In 1948 he was joined by his son, Frederick A. Schmidt, who first served as his father's assistant but soon took over management of musical organizations at St. Olaf and continued in that position until 1972. With Olaf Christiansen succeeding F. Melius as director of the Choir in 1943 and Fred Schmidt taking over the Choir management a few years later, a second father-son team was serving the College in leading the Choir on its annual tours.

The new Christiansen-Schmidt team took the Choir to Europe in 1955, making a tour of Norway and Germany. It also responded to an unusual request from the State Department to take the Choir to Iceland at Easter time in 1957. The Choir personnel was flown in army planes to represent United States artistic talent before the Icelandic people. The domestic tours assumed something of a repeating pattern: east coast, the southeast, midwest and southward, sometimes as far as Texas, and west coast.

Under Kenneth Jennings the international tours became more frequent. Holland, Germany, Switzerland, and France in 1970; Strasbourg, France, again in 1972; Vienna and Rome in 1975; Norway in 1980; China and Japan

Directors and Managers, ca. 1949. From left: Olaf Christiansen, P.G. Schmidt, F. Melius Christiansen, Frederick Schmidt.

St. Olaf Lutheran Choir, Philadelphia, 1920

St. Olaf Choir, Philadelphia, 1995

in 1986; Korea in 1988. Under Anton Armstrong's leadership, the St. Olaf Choir made another visit to Norway in 1993. The Choir's 1995 tour to New York, Washington, and other eastern cities was the 75th anniversary of the important 1920 tour. With a good sense of history, Manager Bob "B.J." Johnson assembled the 1995 Choir in front of a monument in Phildadelphia near the Museum of Art for a photo, duplicating a similar one taken on the same spot in 1920.[39] Johnson became manager of music organizations at St. Olaf in 1978. In the summer of 1995 he traveled to Australia and New Zealand to make preparations for the first visit of the St. Olaf Choir to those countries in the early part of 1997.

The Robes: Black and White, and Purple

When the St. Olaf Choir goes on tour, the robes are packed in large wooden cases which are placed aboard the bus. Concert appearances on tour require the use of the robes, of course, but the Choir is frequently robed for performances at the College and in Northfield. As was fitting, when King Harald V and Queen Sonja of Norway visited the campus on October 19, 1995, the Choir wore the purple robes when it sang "O Day Full of Grace" at the convocation in Boe Memorial Chapel.

The sound of the St. Olaf Choir is more important than its appearance, everyone would agree. At the same time, a surprising amount of interest attaches to how the Choir is seen on stage, not only by the general public but by the reviewers. Often a reviewer's remark about the Choir's robes will reveal other features of the performance. And within the experience and memory of the Choir members themselves, the robes represent an entire sub-history of life in the Choir, embracing tense or funny episodes known only to them and not always to the director.

First St. Olaf Choir, 1911-1912

The very first garb of the St. Olaf Choir had the women in long, light-colored dresses and the men in business suits, some in bow ties and some wearing four-in-hand ties. Such was the appearance of the 1911-12 choir that made a tour into Wisconsin and Illinois at Easter time in 1912, followed by a June tour to cities in northern Minnesota and North Dakota.

St. Olaf Choir, 1913. Toured Norway

The Choir that traveled to Norway in the summer of 1913 was still not a robed choir. The women wore long white formal dresses and the men had tuxedos with white bow ties for concert appearances. With their street clothes the Choir members on that tour wore black tasseled mortar boards to identify themselves as students from America. Incidentally, both the 1912 and 1913 choirs included several St. Olaf faculty persons and other adult members of St. John's Church. In the picture of the 1911-12 Choir one recognizes P. G. and Mrs. Schmidt, P. M. Glasoe, Nils Kleven, and C. A. Mellby among others. [40] A number of the women were or would become St. Olaf faculty members, including Ida Hagen, Caroline Heltne, Adelaide Hjertaas, Ella Hjertaas, Agnes Glasoe, Evelyn Ytterboe, H. Louise Wright, and Bessie Gulbrandson.

By 1920 the Choir had black robes over which they wore short white satin surplices. On the women, the simple neckline of the black robes was visible above the surplices. The men wore formal white collars with white bow ties. That was the attire on tour. When posing for a photograph at St. John's Church that year the men had white shirts with black four-in-hand ties. Director Christiansen was to be seen in formal attire, white tie and tails.

It was the 1920 Choir that made the first national tour, taking its program of a cappella religious music to the important concert halls of the east coast where it caught the favorable attention of enthusiastic audiences and critics. "The fact that the singers appeared in the severe black and white choir vestments, and sang unaccompanied, an entire hour-and-a-half program of sacred music added to their amazement," wrote a friend and former member about the Choir's impact on hearers at Orchestra Hall in Chicago, Carnegie Hall in New York, and numerous civic auditoriums where the 1920 concerts were held.[41]

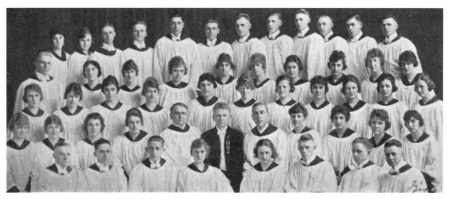

St. Olaf Choir of 1919-20

The Choir's "vestments," as the members called them, remained the same for a number of years. By 1930 they still had black choir robes and white surplices but the men had adopted black bow ties. A reviewer who heard the Choir sing in Savannah, Georgia, in January of 1930, offered this impression of the Choir's appearance. "They group themselves on the stage on a small semicircular tier, changing when necessary to the proper grouping for particular numbers. Each singer is garbed in the regulation black gown and white cotta of choir singers." In Charlotte, South Carolina, the report was, "Clad in conventional black and white garb of Lutheran choirs, the choir held the 1500 or so listeners spellbound from the first note."

In June of 1930 the St. Olaf Choir gave concerts on its way to New York where it would embark for Europe. After a concert in Pennsylvania, a reviewer recorded several observations, including one about the Choir's appearance:

> The accuracy of pitch and the mysterious manner in which the choir obtained this pitch were indeed thrilling to the large audience. The appearance of the choir in their gowns of black and white, from the beginning made a favorable impression upon the audience. Their dynamic director, Dr. Christiansen, seemed to hold an unimaginable power over the choir, standing erect before them and with very few gestures swelling the chorus from a pianissimo of unusual and remarkable fineness to a forte.[42]

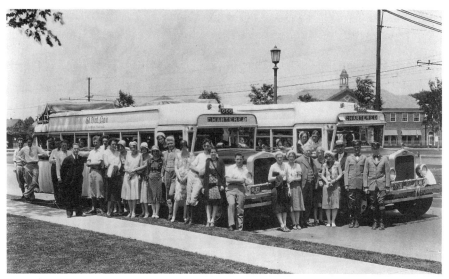

St. Olaf Choir, 1930
On way to New York

According to a letter sent home from Columbia, South Carolina, by Signe Ramseth Johnson, Class of 1933, choir members in the early thirties were responsible for washing and ironing their own "vestments," for which they received a small payment. "We took our vestments home last nite and washed so I'll have to get at my ironing. Ha! I guess we won't get paid the usual $.50 a vestment this year. Money seems to be scarce and things don't seem to be much lower in price either." Later from New York, however, she reported receiving $1.00 for washing the vestments, $.50 each for robe and surplice.[43]

Choir members always wore black shoes with the robes. The women complained of the "clumpy" shoes selected for them, with instep straps and wide, medium-height Cuban heels, but conceded that they were comfortable. As expected, the men wore black trousers, or were supposed to. Finding their wool pants uncomfortably hot, the fellows eliminated all but the bottom twelve inches of the trousers, which were held in place by elastic bands. What was visible to the public eye looked like the standard black trousers. [44]

It was in 1937 that the Choir adopted the new purple robes. Even the director, F. Melius Christiansen, wore a purple robe the first year. Before the Choir left for its January-February 1938 tour that would include concerts in several eastern cities, the new robes were discussed in the College newspaper:

St. Olaf Lutheran Choir, 1930
Toured Norway and Germany

St. Olaf Lutheran Choir, 1938, the first to wear purple robes

Never before has the choir appeared in the eastern states wearing the royal purple robes which were new last year. This year will be the first that Dr. [F. Melius] Christiansen will wear a gown rather than a dress suit. His gown is of royal purple velvet, much the same as those worn by the members of his choir. On his sleeve he will wear six gold chevrons and about his neck will be the cowl [i.e. hood] he received from Muhlenberg College in honoring him as Doctor of Music.[45]

It is not hard to imagine Dr. Christiansen's discomfiture at appearing in public in such overwrought attire. The next year he was back in his usual formal black tails and white tie. Choir pictures show that sometimes, in the warmer months, he would wear a formal white suit.[46]

The new purple robes caught the attention of reviewers as the Choir made its way east, although the comments quickly moved on to the music. Richard S. Davis in Milwaukee had this to say:

> The choir—for the first time, if the reporter's memory can be trusted—was dressed in deep purple robes and this was an added distinction. As always, however, the 60 crusaders were chiefly impressive because of the precision of their work, because of their fidelity to the finest traditions of choral singing and because of the fact that they filled the hall with glorious song.[47]

When the Choir sang in Orchestra Hall, Detroit, on Friday, January 28, 1938, Russell McLaughlin's review the next day took note of "the revered figure of F. Melius Christiansen" standing on the podium "purple robed."

Viewing the Choir in purple robes faced with white silk, and the podium and risers painted white, he commented: "So white and purple were the scheme that adorned a group, famous aforetime for a type of singing with which those colors make excellent harmony."[48]

In Worcester, Massachusetts, an audience of nearly two thousand warmly greeted the "sixty young men and women robed in velvet vestments of royal purple" when they marched on the stage.[49] A reviewer in Lancaster, Pennsylvania, wrote: "The choir members are gowned in purple velvet robes with white satin touches and present a striking appearance." Another regarded the "rich robes of purple velvet" as "befitting such a kingly choir."

When Olaf C. Christiansen succeeded his father as director of the Choir in 1943, World War II was being fought but the St. Olaf Choir still met its annual appointment to sing a "Twilight Concert" with the Minneapolis Symphony Orchestra in Northrop Auditorium on the University of Minnesota campus. On March 29, 1943, Norman C. Houk wrote in the *Minneapolis Morning Tribune*, "Among the choir's purple robes yesterday were several army uniforms, young men who were members of the choir and now are stationed at Ft. Snelling."[50] The war over, a Milwaukee paper noted in the spring of 1946 that the concert in that city was the first since young men started coming back from military service. "Some 60 singers took the platform in their deep purple robes and the director again was Olaf C. Christiansen, son of the man who made both choir and school so famous over America."

Ralph Lewando, critic for the *Pittsburgh Press*, wrote that he could listen to the Choir every day of the year without tiring. "It hews to the line which the Christiansens—father and son—are geniuses in keeping alive. They serve their art with devotion, inspiration and intelligence. They are masters of their craft. . . . The present choir comprises young men and women from 13 states. In their royal purple vestments they please the eye as much as their singing captivates the ear."[51]

About a year later the St. Olaf Choir was in New Haven, Connecticut, where the reviewer for the *New Haven Register* wrote, "Garbed in purple cassocks, the group of 60 singers made a memorable picture on the stage as it responded like a finely-tuned instrument to the sensitive directing of its tall, scholarly-looking conductor, Olaf C. Christiansen."[52]

Much as the members of the Choir adored Olaf and happily gave their best efforts in performances, they were still college students for whom the formal dignity and discipline of the concert stage became an irresistible challenge. During the intermission of a concert in a Baptist church in Macon, Georgia, one of the men picked up a pie tin, tucked it under his robe, and took it with him as the Choir filed up to the sanctuary for the next section. As the Choir sang, the metal plate was passed from singer to singer in the third row until it reached the baritone soloist, who was in no mood for pranks. As he refused to take the pie tin, it fell to the hard wood floor with a loud bang. But the sound did not stop at once because the plate kept spinning, emitting a long series of metallic sounds, "boi-oi-oi-oi-oi-oing!" The Choir members were terrified, fearing that some unspeakable wrath was sure to descend upon them, but according to one, Olaf "did not bat an eye." [53]

Passing objects along from robe to robe or behind the robes during a concert became feats of impressive dexterity. A large book, a guitar, a wet rag, a wine glass, window sash weights, an open bottle of ink, or even a small, unloaded revolver made the trip successfully.[54] In one case it was a heavy, cast-iron pipe joint weighing many pounds that made its way among the basses, baritones, and tenors. Each time the object was received by the next person, the unexpected weight caused a sudden drop of the shoulder on the part of the recipient.[55]

On another occasion a clarinet in its long case was passed along the length of the row. One of the baritones received it just as the section ended and it was time to leave the stage. In his struggle to keep the object concealed, he put it up his sleeve, creating a very odd looking purple lump above his shoulder.[56] It was often the person at the end of the row who had to manage a dignified exit with the item hidden under the robe as the Choir moved off stage.

Each year one of the officers of the Choir has specific responsibility for the care of the robes. Angela Schum was in charge of them during the 1994-95 school year. On the evening of February 5, 1995, during the first part of the concert at the Kennedy Center in Washington, the zipper broke on the robe worn by bass Jeremy Bierlein, due to sing the solo on Jester Hairston's "Mary's Little Boy Chile" during the final set. Angela stayed backstage with Jeremy during the third set, pinning Jeremy's robe back together with safety pins.[57]

In the fall of each year, the Choir member in charge of the robes makes arrangements for all members of the Choir, old and new, to be fitted for their robes by "The Robe Lady." From about 1978 to 1995 the robe lady was Ethel Green, meticulous and experienced in her approach to her task. The fittings took place in Margaret Skoglund Reception Room in the Christiansen Hall of Music. Each Choir member in turn stepped up on a low table, wearing the same shoes that would be worn during concerts. Ethel sat on the floor, legs under the table. Her duty was to ensure that the hem of every robe was exactly the same length from the floor, whether the wearer was short or tall. By an appropriate coincidence going back before Ethel's time, the height desired was exactly the same as the width of the standard St.

Olaf Choir folder. Ethel placed the folder on the table, steadied it with her chin, and had both hands free to work with the hem and pin it at the length where later she would sew it.

When Ethel began her work with the Choir robes, she discovered that from year to year the old hems had never been taken down, but the students or their mothers or roommates had hemmed and re-hemmed them however they could. She found staples, duct tape, scotch tape, and all kinds of pins in the robes. Because the fabric of the robes is velvet, it is fragile and stretches. Hence Ethel insisted on doing the hemming by hand. Moreover, she discouraged anyone from replacing zippers by means of sewing machines because the fabric would be shorter on one side than the other. Actually, she found that it was better to repair the zippers than to replace them.

The triangular white cuffs on the sleeves of the purple robes have been called "flippers" ever since a New York reviewer coined the term in 1976. The writer referred to them as "crumpled flippers," causing Choir members to worry that the cuffs looked dirty.[58] Maintenance of the robes also includes close attention to the "flippers" each year. The seven snaps holding them on often need replacing, sending Ethel down to Jacobsen's in downtown Northfield for fresh supplies of snaps and purple thread. [59]

A new Robe Lady succeeded Ethel Green in 1995. She is Becca Coates, daughter of Jim Coates who sang in the St. Olaf Choir under both F. Melius and Olaf Christiansen in the early forties. Becca quickly proved her value to the Choir through her competence and her conscientious work in fitting the students in their purple robes with the flippers.

"Robe Lady" Becca Coates '74 adjusts Choir robe for Becky Lowe '96

25

Because any movement of the white satin flippers will be noticeable to the audience, Choir members are under strict orders never to raise their hands to their face to suppress a cough or for any other reason. At an outdoor concert in Norway in 1955, during the singing of "Carol of the Drum," a bug flew into the ear of a soprano standing at the end of the row. Instinctively she raised her hand to her ear, flashing the white flipper. The song went on, but Olaf glared his disapproval.[60]

At the inauguration of Mark U. Edwards Jr. as the ninth president of St. Olaf College in October of 1994, the St. Olaf Choir was singing "Alleluia" by Peter Mathews. At the ceremony, held in Skoglund Athletic Center on a beautiful Indian summer afternoon, altos Heather Cleveland and Allison Wedell watched in fascination as a fly first circled Director Anton Armstrong's head, then buzzed Heather and settled on her ear. Knowing the rule, Heather resorted to a quick twitch of her head to discourage the fly. By this time Allison was nearly out of control, at once amused and terrified lest her suppressed laughter should explode and ruin the piece. She struggled to stave off an outburst, squeezing the hands of her two neighbors with such force that they later complained about the pain. The number ends very quietly as the tenors alone let the final line taper down to less than a whisper. Finally it was over and Allison could hold in her hilarity no longer. Fortunately, in the dead silence of that large auditorium, she made her sputtered laugh sound like a sneeze. [61]

The singers are aided in stage discipline by the fact that during concerts all of them hold hands with the persons standing next to them. During the years when Olaf Christiansen was director, only the women held hands, but the practice under both Kenneth Jennings and Anton Armstrong includes the men as well. Choir members attest to the communication and palpable sense of unity that is achieved in this way.

Compared with the robes of the other choirs on the Hill, the purple robes get much more wear because of the tours. Choir members employ a rich vocabulary to describe the aroma the robes achieve by the end of the year. Perspiration of Olympic proportions was produced during the Choir's final concert in Korea in the summer of 1988. The St. Olaf Choir was one of only five choirs in the world invited to the International Choral Festival in Seoul, Korea, held just before the Olympic Games. The temperature in the packed auditorium for its last concert was reported to be 105 degrees, the inevitable result of the enormous crowd and summer heat. The velvet robes were hot and heavy, and the sweating was prodigious. After the Korean appearances, the robes were shipped back to the States. When they were unpacked in Northfield, three inches of water stood at the bottom of the shipping cases.

Summer sun in Australia, February 1997
Photo courtesy Jeff Wright
Choir at St. Peter's College, Brisbane

When the St. Olaf Choir traveled to Australia and New Zealand in January of 1997, it experienced summer heat again. For greater comfort in warm climates, Choir members wore new purple robes of summer weight. And for easier transport of the robes the management acquired new aluminum cases, which are much lighter than the old wooden ones.

Some reviewers have described the robes of the St. Olaf Choir as "royal purple" and in the same vein others have called the group "a kingly choir." Roland Schroeder in the *Niagara Falls Gazette* in January of 1948 wrote that the Choir's performance left little doubt to musician or layman "that this was the peer of peers—royalty—even in purple gowns—of the sacred music groups now so numerous in America." Another plaudit following the "royalty" theme came from Herman Devries of Chicago who wrote in 1941: "The organ is known to be the king of all instruments and it must follow that the St. Olaf Lutheran Choir holds the title of 'King of Choirs.'" [62]

Over the years the directors of the St. Olaf Choir, following the model of F. Melius Christiansen, have taught the singers to respond to such acclaim with grace and modesty. The emphasis is on the importance of the music and their mission to perform it beautifully. Fine art has a significance beyond the praises heaped on the performers. "It matters very little by whom it is produced," F. Melius once wrote. When the audience cheers, it is "because they were gladdened by the spirit of art itself." [63] On another occasion F. Melius stated that all choir members should understand "that they are not working for their own individual honor, but for the honor of something infinitely greater than any human being or organization. You may call it for the honor of God or for the honor of the beautiful which is one of the attributes of God." [64]

27

Those who wear the purple robes discover, at concert after concert, that the spirit of their singing is affected markedly by the glad responses of the listeners. F. Melius Christiansen observed that the inspiration at work between conductor and singer also flows "from the performers to the listeners and from the listeners back to the performers."[65]

Becky Lowe '96, soprano and soloist in the St. Olaf Choir, was caught up in that inspiration when, as a high school junior in Lincoln, Nebraska, she first saw and heard the Choir perform. Thinking back on the experience, she said: "It was their faces that told me what the music was really saying, and they looked so happy to be singing. And then even when the audience was applauding, they were still aware that they were sharing an experience with the audience. They looked out when we were applauding as though to say, 'Well, thanks. Thanks for being here.'"[66]

If others speak of the Choir in the royal purple robes as kingly, the members have the satisfaction of knowing that their intensive efforts are appreciated. They are also reminded that if they are regarded as leaders in the choral field, they must continue to work hard at their music. "We work! and again we work!"[67] In this way F. Melius Christiansen, founder of the St. Olaf Choir, accounted for its success in maintaining high standards in the performance of great choral music.

Notes for Chapter 1 THE PURPLE ROBES

1. *Saint Olaf (SO)* 33 (November 1984), 16.

2. Interview with Angela Schum, March 9, 1995.

3. F. Melius Christiansen, "The Choir," unpublished typescript, 1929, 1. St. Olaf College Archives, hereafter abbreviated as STOARCHIV.

4. Leola Nelson Bergmann, *Music Master of the Middle West*: The Story of F. Melius Christiansen and the St. Olaf Choir (Minneapolis: The University of Minnesota Press, 1944), 153. A reprint of this book, with a new Foreword, was issued by DaCapo Press, 227 West 17th St., New York, NY 10011, in 1968.

5. *The Minneapolis Journal*, December 9, 1928.

6. Cited in *The Minneapolis Journal*, December 9, 1928.

7. Albert Goldberg, "St. Olaf Choir Still Carries on Beautifully," *Chicago Daily Tribune*, April 18, 1944.

8. Theodolinda C. Boris, "High Standards Kept By St. Olaf Choir," Buffalo, New York *Evening News*, January 23, 1947; Glenn Dillard Gunn, *Washington Times-Herald*, February 9, 1948.

9. *The Arizona Republic*, February 8, 1989.

10. Letter from Curtis Hansen to Kenneth Jennings, November 26, 1989.

11. Letter from Stanislaw Skrowaczewski to Kenneth Jennings, December 20, 1980.

12. Anton Eugene Armstrong, "Celebrating 75 Years of Musical Excellence: The Evolution of the St. Olaf Choir," A thesis submitted in partial fulfillment of the requirements of the Doctor of Musical Arts degree from Michigan State University, May, 1987.

13. *SO* 38 (February/March 1990), 25.

14. Cited in *SO* 40 (March/April), inside front cover.

15. Cited in *The 1926-27 Viking*, 115.

16. Eugene E. Simpson, *A History of St. Olaf Choir* (Minneapolis: Augsburg Publishing House, 1921), 29.

17. "St. Olaf Choir Concert Tour," *Lutheran Church Herald* IV (February 17, 1920), 98; cf. Leola Nelson Bergmann, *Music Master of the Middle West*, 126.

18. *Lutheran Church Herald (LCH)* IV (March 2, 1920), 130; cf. Robert Lee Jennings, "A Study of the Historical Development of Choral Ensembles at Selected Lutheran Liberal Arts Colleges in the United States," A Thesis Submitted to Michigan State University in partial fulfillment of the requirements for the degree of Doctor of Philosophy, 1969, 80.

19. F. Melius Christiansen, "To Choir Directors," *LCH* XXIII (January 3, 1939), 30.

20. *La Crosse Tribune*, April 5, 1945; Anton Armstrong, "Celebrating 75 Years of Musical Excellence," 30.

21. Olaf C. Christiansen, "Choral Tradition Lives On," *Music Journal* (March 1968), 36.

22. Robert Lee Jennings, "A Study of . . . Choral Ensembles," 58.

23. Olaf C. Christiansen, "Choral Tradition Lives On," 36.

24. Peter J. Laugen, "Olaf C. Christiansen Retires," *American Choral Review* X (1968), 119.

25. Interview with Frances Williams Anderson, January 23, 1995.

26. Joseph M. Shaw, *History of St. Olaf College 1874-1974* (Northfield, Minnesota: The St. Olaf College Press, 1974), 591.

27. *The Minneapolis Star*, December 9, 1928.

28. Paul G. Schmidt, *My Years at St. Olaf*, A Centennial Decade Publication (Northfield, Minnesota: St. Olaf College, [1967]), 56.

29. *Ibid.*

30. William C. Benson, *High on Manitou*: A History of St. Olaf College 1874-1949 (Northfield, Minnesota: The St. Olaf College Press, 1949), 182.

31. *The Viking '13 '14 '15* (Northfield, Minnesota: St. Olaf College, 1912), 150.

32. *The Viking, Book of the Three Upper Classes '10 '11 '12* (Northfield, Minnesota: St. Olaf College, 1909), 207.

33. Benson, *High on Manitou*, 182.

34. *Viking '10 '11 '12*, 207.

35. Simpson, *History of St. Olaf Choir*, 23.

36. *The 1926-27 Viking*, 126.

37. *Ibid.*

38. Ralph Lewando, *Pittsburgh Press*, January, 1941.

39. *SO* 43 (April/May 1995), 15.

40. Simpson, *History of St. Olaf Choir*, 82; *Viking '13 '14 '15*, 149.

41. Mrs. E. L. Vitalis, "Dr. Christiansen and the St. Olaf College Choir," unidentified newspaper, ca. 1925.

42. *Oil City Derrick* (Pennsylvania), June 18, 1930.

43. Signe Ramseth Johnson '33, 1932 Diary.

44. Letter from Esther Rian Tufte '36 to Bob Johnson, February 18, 1994.

45. *Manitou Messenger* (*MM*), January 18, 1938.

46. *Ibid.*

47. Richard S. Davis, "Chorus Offers Fine Program," *The Milwaukee Journal*, January 26, 1938.

48. Russell McLaughlin, "St. Olaf Choir Sings at Orchestra Hall," Detroit, January 29, 1938.

49. Tyra Lundberg Fuller, "St. Olaf Choir Delights Audience of 2000," *Worcester Daily Telegram*, February 5, 1938.

50. Norman C. Houk, "St. Olaf Choir and Twilight Concert," *Minneapolis Morning Tribune*, March 29, 1943.

51. Ralph Lewando, *Pittsburgh Press*, February 4, 1947.

52. *New Haven Register*, February 1, 1948.

53. Letter from Lars Kindem '55 to Joseph M. Shaw, February 26, 1995.

54. Letter from Don Colton '55 to Bob Johnson, December 11, 1993; letter from Jerry Narveson '57 to Bob Johnson, October 14, 1993; letter from David W. Olson '60 to Joseph M. Shaw, October 19, 1993.

55. Conversation with Lars Kindem, February 15, 1995.

56. Letter from Paul Christenson '55 to Bob Johnson, September 9, 1994.

57. Interview with Angela Schum '95, March 9, 1995.

58. John Rockwell, "St. Olaf Choir Displays Skills," *New York Times*, February 10, 1976.

59. Interview with Ethel Green, May 11, 1995.

60. Letter from Lars Kindem '55 to Joseph M. Shaw, February 26, 1995.

61. Interview with Allison Wedell '96, March 16, 1995.

62. Roland Schroeder, *Niagara Falls Gazette*, January 1948; Herman Devries, *Chicago Herald Examiner*, February 8, 1941.

63. F. Melius Christiansen, "The Listener," *LCH* (July 1, 1930), 907.

64. F. Melius Christiansen, "To Choir Directors," *Lutheran Herald* 23 (January 3, 1939), 30.

65. F. Melius Christiansen, "The Necessity of Concentration in Choir Singing," *LCH* (November 4, 1930), 1548.

66. Interview with Becky Lowe '96, March 29, 1995.

67. *Dubuque Times*, January 2, 1927.

CHAPTER 2

F. MELIUS CHRISTIANSEN

F. Melius Christiansen, ca. 1915

The founder and first director of the St. Olaf Choir was Fredrik Melius Christiansen, born at Smedhaugen in Berger, Norway, on April 1, 1871. That he has always been known as F. Melius Christiansen may be due to the fact that the family distinguished him from an uncle Fredrik who lived near by.[1]

The settlement of Berger with its glass works and smithy knoll (Smedhaugen) is located three miles southwest of Eidsvold, the famous site where Norway's Constitution was signed on May 17, 1814. Adding to the historical luster of F. Melius Christiansen's early surroundings is the fact that the Eidsvold Church, in which he was baptized, once had as its pastor Nicolai Wergeland, father of Norway's eminent poet and patriot, Henrik Wergeland.[2] In addition to valuing young Wergeland's poetry, Christiansen no doubt would have read Wergeland's biography of the great Norwegian violinist, Ole Bull, since he too aspired to become a concert violinist.[3]

Music in the Family

F. Melius was introduced to music at a very early age and from both sides of his family. His maternal grandfather, Jon Braaten, was a capable violinist and organist. He laid down the rule that any young men calling on his daughters must play an instrument. Under this condition, Anders Christiansen, father of F. Melius, gladly accepted help from Jon Braaten and his sons in learning to play several instruments as he pursued his courtship of one of the Braaten daughters, Oleana, whom he married.

Anders developed skills with the cornet, trombone, and the bass viol. When the family moved to the town of Agnes he became the leader of a local factory band, and in Larvik, where they soon settled, Anders was a regular member of the local band. Of Oleana, the mother of F. Melius Christiansen, it is said that she "loved music deeply and was the driving power behind the musical activities of the family. She herself had a lovely voice and, although she had received no formal training, her singing had the beauty and warmth of one who is gifted by nature."[4]

While the family still lived in Berger and made visits to Oleana's parents on the Braaten farm, F. Melius's grandfather would play the violin for him, let him hold the instrument, and show him how to draw the bow over the strings.[5] When he was only three years of age, F. Melius received his first instrument, a small, 3-key clarinet. At age 6, he persuaded his father to let him play in the factory band and proudly played his little clarinet, double stepping along to keep up, as the band marched in the Seventeenth of May parade in the village of Agnes.[6]

Within his family circle, F. Melius steadily gained more experience in instrumental music, though singing was not neglected. Anders, the father, played the trombone, Karl, an older brother, the cornet, and F. Melius the clarinet as the three formed a little band to play marches. A later version of this family ensemble added a younger brother, Kristian, who played the horn. Karl and F. Melius continued on cornet and clarinet, and Anders now played the bass horn, or tuba.[7]

The family of Anders and Oleana Christiansen moved three times while F. Melius was still a young boy. In 1876 they moved from Berger, near Eidsvold, to Sarpsborg in southern Norway, and from there to the village of Agnes where Anders led the band at the local match factory. In 1879 the family settled in Larvik, an industrial seaport near the mouth of the Olsofjord on the western side of the fjord. There Anders Christiansen had work as a mechanic at the Larvik glass works, and there he and sons Karl and F. Melius soon became members of the Larvik Band.

Larvik Band. Oscar Hansen, director   Augsburg Fortress, Publishers
F. Melius, front row far left; Karl, far right; Anders, to left of Director Hansen

In Larvik

F. Melius, with his parents and siblings, lived in Larvik from 1879 until he left for America in 1888. It was a time of change and development for him. His mother Oleana died of tuberculosis in 1885; his uncle Fredrik emigrated to America and settled in Washburn, Wisconsin; Karl, two years his elder, left for America in 1887 to join Uncle Fredrik.

The years in Larvik were immensely important for the education of F. Melius Christiansen. There he lived and went to school from his seventh to his fifteenth year. In church he received instruction from the pastor and was confirmed in 1886 at the age of 15. Perhaps because the words seemed so incongruous for him and his fellow confirmands, F. Melius remembered the pastor issuing this solemn advice: "As you young people go out into the world, there are two things I want to warn you against—Methodism and Socialism." In the Larvik school F. Melius received a good education with thorough instruction from well-trained teachers in reading, Norse literature, history, geography, science, arithmetic, writing, Catechism and Explanation, Bible history, and church history. He did well scholastically and was given high ratings for industry and aptitude.[8]

What proved particulary advantageous for F. Melius at that stage in his young life was the fact that Larvik was a community with thriving musical opportunities. In the town of some 10,000 people his music education was

Larvik Trinity Church, Larvik, Norway

enriched substantially by the presence of a versatile and capable musician, Oscar Hansen. Hansen played the organ at the local church and directed the choir. He was also a pianist, cellist, conductor, and composer. Of Hansen's significance in the musical training of F. Melius Christiansen, Leola Nelson Bergmann, author of a biography of Christiansen entitled, *Music Master of the Middle West*, writes as follows: "To Oscar Hansen must go the credit for initiating Christiansen into the classical tradition of music. Trained in the spirit of the German classics in Leipzig and Christiania, Hansen through his teaching and directing inculcated very early in Christiansen a feeling for the musical style of the great masters."[9]

Hansen was already established as the central musical force in Larvik before the Christiansen family arrived. In addition to providing the music for regular worship services at the local church, Hansen occasionally arranged for the performance of an

Bronze plate on Larvik Church

oratorio or a selection from one. He directed a band at the glassworks where Anders was employed and another at the flour mill. He also led a summer band, three singing societies, and gave numerous private lessons. He organized an orchestra of 20 to 30 talented amateur musicians that gave six or seven concerts a season, offering symphonies of Beethoven, Mozart, and Haydn.

At that time in Norway local orchestras did not, as a rule, have their own music scores on hand. They would rent the manuscript of a symphony or oratorio and copy out by hand the separate parts needed. At one stage F. Melius was able to earn money for lessons in piano, organ, and theory by doing such copying for Director Hansen.[10] Initially his parents had drawn from their limited resources to pay for lessons in piano and organ, a fact that caused the sensitive F. Melius some concern. He even suggested to his father that he take only organ lessons, but his father told him not to worry about the money.[11]

At age nine F. Melius began taking piano lessons from Hansen, whom he feared, admired, and imitated. In her biography Leola Nelson Bergmann describes the relationship. "The handsome, rotund teacher completely captivated the heart of his young pupil and it was not long before Melius' mother noticed with amusement that her son was imitating his teacher in slight mannerisms of speech and even walked with Hansen's characteristic limp."[12]

When the St. Olaf Choir sang in Larvik in 1913, F. Melius Christiansen, responding to a toast at a banquet given at the Larvik Grand Hotel, expressed his gratitude for the inspiration he had received from his old teacher: "When I think of my childhood I have much to be thankful for. First for Organist Oscar Hansen. He did much for me. I cannot but say that I honored and feared him. When I went to his house I often hesitated to go in—I was so seized with fear. But he worked hard with me and was kind, and I played my lessons as well as I could. I have not come far—the way of art is long—but I have sought to do the best I could, and I got my ideal from Oscar Hansen." On another occasion Christiansen said of Hansen, "He was a firebrand!"[13]

For F. Melius the years in Larvik also meant his introduction to the violin, his favorite instrument. He began practicing the violin soon after he started piano lessons. Money for violin lessons, which he took from a Professor Olsen, was provided by a wealthy Larvik citizen, Jørgen Christiansen, not related, who wished to encourage the promising young musician.[14]

Advancing rapidly in competence on the violin, F. Melius reached a gratifying turning point as a twelve-year-old musician when he played a violin solo at a concert in Larvik, accompanied by his teacher, Oscar Hansen. It was a thrill to be asked, and a test of his discipline and poise. He passed the test. Bergmann describes his triumph: "Resounding applause told him he had pleased the audience. He had made his debut as a violinist. A sparkling-eyed boy, carrying a violin case, walked home that night through the foggy March sleet of Larvik."[15]

Another story of going home in the dark was told by F. Melius himself at the banquet in Larvik, as he expressed his pleasure at hearing the old organ again. He recalled practicing on the church organ at night in the company of his younger brother, Kristian, whose task it was to pump the organ. "And that cost something too," he said. "I had to buy for my younger brother 15-øre liver-wurst to get him to pump the organ for me. We remained there until it got dark, and it happened none too seldom that I heard crying in the organ. It was my brother, who had become scared. So I became scared, then we both ran out of the church as fast as we could."[16]

In the light of Christiansen's budding talent, the organ lessons and faithful practice, and his close working relationship with his mentor, it is not surprising that when Hansen went off for half a year of study in Leipzig, the pupil, although only fourteen, was asked to take over the organist's duties at the church and did so.[17] In the years to come, F. Melius would be remembered by the members of St. John's Lutheran Church in Northfield, Minnesota, as their regular organist from 1916 to 1942.[18]

The Larvik years continued to be fruitful for F. Melius Christiansen as a promising, growing musician. In addition to the activities already mentioned, he made his first attempts to compose music, writing pieces for small bands. Once confirmed, F. Melius felt obliged to support himself, securing space for a little studio in the center of the city where he gave music lessons and did further copying work.[19]

Vocal music seems oddly absent in the account of the Larvik years, but the fact is that piano, organ, and violin were F. Melius's chief interests. There is, however, one little glimpse of his response to choral music, reported in an early book on the St. Olaf Choir written by Eugene E. Simpson. He writes that during his years as an orchestral violinist, "probably at the age of twelve, Melius had been once so greatly moved by the choir which the orchestra accompanied that he begged Hansen to allow him to sing in the choir rather than remain in the orchestra."[20] As events proved, it would be some years before F. Melius Christiansen devoted serious attention to the training of choirs.

To America

When Oleana Christiansen died of tuberculosis in 1885, the sad loss had a disintegrating effect on the family that she had held together with her gentleness and love. Karl grew restless and emigrated to America in 1887, as reported, joining his Uncle Fredrik in Wisconsin. Accepting his father's advice to prepare to become a school teacher, F. Melius took some evening classes in mathematics, but his heart remained in music. He continued with music lessons, copying, and some teaching. But as he assessed the prospects of a career as a musician in Larvik, he could see that Oscar Hansen's sons would in all likelihood take over their father's work, so the thought of seeking his fortune in America became more and more appealing. Adding to the motives to leave was his father's approaching re-marriage.[21]

The family in which F. Melius grew up was typical in being exposed to the phenomenon of "America fever," the keen interest in the new world generated partly through letters from those who had already arrived there. For years, letters had arrived from Oleana's relatives. Two of Anders Christiansen's brothers had gone to America, Fredrik to Wisconsin and Hans Petter to Oakland, California. F. Melius also heard about America from two Mormon missionaries who stayed in Larvik for a time. He gave them violin lessons in exchange for instruction in English.[22]

By the late summer of 1888 F. Melius had made his decision to leave for America. His father did not try to dissuade him, but furnished him with money for the trip just as he had done for Karl the year before. On October 4, 1888, young Christiansen received from the assistant to the parish priest the necessary papers, including a permit to leave bearing his vaccination certification, dates of his birth, baptism, and confirmation, and the church's bestowal of God's blessing upon his "prospective journey to California in North America." F. Melius reasoned that there would be more opportunities in a larger city like Oakland for one who hoped to become a professional musician.[23]

The first stage of the journey was by small steamer to Antwerp. There F. Melius visited the Cathedral of Notre Dame, famous for its paintings by Rubens. It was the sound of the organ, however, that captivated him and gave him some momentary relief from the strains of leaving home and coping with the confusion of travel. On the three-week crossing en route to New York he experienced the miseries of sea sickness, making him question his decision to leave Norway. But like countless others he was thrilled at the sight of the Statue of Liberty as the ship approached New York.[24]

By means of a long, sometimes tedious train trip westward, much of it through long stretches of Canada, F. Melius finally arrived in Oakland where he lived a few months with his uncle, Hans Petter Christiansen. The stay in California enabled him to become accustomed to American ways, learn some more English, savor the sights of San Francisco and Oakland, hold menial jobs in a shoe factory and a newspaper office, play a few violin solos, and look for work as a musician. Prospects for a professional career did not open up, however, so F. Melius accepted his brother Karl's gift of sixty dollars for a train ticket to Washburn, Wisconsin.[25]

The journey from California to Wisconsin again took him through Canada. In Winnipeg F. Melius had a memorable adventure. Forced to wait in the train station through most of the night until the 4:00 a.m. train to Minneapolis, he felt menaced by a group of tough-looking vagrants who kept eyeing him and muttering to one another. Suddenly F. Melius had an idea: to amuse them with his violin. He took it out, struck up a lively dance tune, and within minutes they were tapping their feet, dancing, clapping, shouting, and having a good time. In due time the threat was over and Christiansen safely boarded the train for Minneapolis.[26]

He had another adventure in getting from Ashland in northern Wisconsin, where the train deposited him, to the town of Washburn across the bay. He was told that it was five miles shorter to walk directly across Chequamegon Bay on the snow-covered ice. He started out in the direction of Washburn but soon realized that he had lost his way. Night was falling so he sat down in the snow and waited until the lights would be turned on in Washburn. Walking toward the lights, he arrived and climbed up the snowy bank to the town's one street.

Young violinist Photo courtesy Christiansen family

F. Melius recalled the episode:

> When I reached the main street I didn't know where to go or what to do to find my brother, so I walked up and down past the few frost-covered windows, trying to summon up enough courage to go in somewhere. Karl happened to be in the shop of Richardson, the shoemaker, and saw me passing. He couldn't see my face but he recognized me by my stride, which was like my father's. He came running out, slapped me on the shoulder and took me up to his room. I fell down on the bed and cried like a baby, I was so relieved and happy.[27]

In Wisconsin

Despite the shaky beginning in California, F. Melius Christiansen was as determined as ever to pursue his musical aims as he adjusted to a new life in Wisconsin. Karl worked as a mechanic in a saw mill. He organized and directed a Scandinavian band made up of Norwegian, Swedish, and Danish immigrants who worked in the saw mills. Uncle Fredrik played the cornet in Karl's band and F. Melius played the baritone.

In Washburn F. Melius had a pleasant social existence with Karl and other young people who helped him learn the idioms of the language. In the fall he enrolled in the high school but only to study English since his education from Larvik was more than adequate in the other subjects. He advertised for a music position in *Skandinaven*, a Norwegian-American newspaper with a circulation of over ten thousand. He received three offers: to direct a regiment band in Eau Claire, to become conductor of a city band in LaCrosse, and to lead the Scandinavian Band in Marinette in northeastern Wisconsin on Green Bay, directly across the

F. Melius Christiansen, ca. 1888
Washburn, Wisconsin

river from Menominee, Michigan. He chose the Marinette position on the grounds that if it did not work out satisfactorily he could look for work in Menominee.[28]

Christiansen was nineteen years of age when he arrived in Marinette in the late autumn of 1890. His youth surprised the townspeople and the band members, but his ability as a musician soon assured them and quickly opened the way for him to give private lessons in piano, violin, and organ, and to accept the duties of organist and choir director at Our Savior's Lutheran Church.

Begun in 1872 with a membership of Swedes, Danes, and Norwegians, Our Savior's became a strictly Norwegian congregation affiliated with the United Norwegian Lutheran Church that was organized in 1890, the same year that F. Melius arrived in Marinette. In its earlier years the congregation had been part of the group that established Augsburg Seminary and moved it to Minneapolis. The ties with Augsburg continued after 1890, providing a connection that would soon bring about a highly important move in the career of F. Melius Christiansen.[29]

In the meantime, the busy young immigrant musician was doing very well in Marinette. For the first time in his life he could live and work as an independent person, although Karl occasionally came over from Washburn to see how

*Our Savior's Lutheran Church
Marinette, Wisconsin*

he was getting along. According to Bergmann, for a short time F. Melius enjoyed "a mildly bohemian existence after the control and order of his life in Norway." But he was quick to realize that preoccupation with good times was causing his work to suffer, so he returned to his characteristic self-discipline. "It never pays to neglect your work," he would often say.[30]

But the irrepressible personality of F. Melius Christiansen was never fully contained, no matter how successful he was in answering the call of duty. On his first Sunday as organist at Our Savior's Lutheran Church, he displayed the roguish non-conformity that often unsettled people but invariably added color to his reputation. One would assume that F. Melius was familiar with the role of the *klokker* in Norwegian congregations both in the old country and in America. The *klokker* or precentor was a layman whose duty was to offer the opening and closing prayer.

On that particular Sunday in Marinette, however, the *klokker* never got his chance, and from then on his services were discontinued. F. Melius was at the organ playing his prelude when the *klokker* innocently came forward as usual to give the opening prayer. For some reason, perhaps because no one had told him that Our Savior's still followed the old practice, F. Melius did not comprehend what the man was doing there, standing somewhat close to the organ, so he lengthened the prelude, giving him time to sit down. But when the *klokker* remained standing there, F. Melius leaned over and whispered to him, "Sit down." The man simply stood there, waiting, and F. Melius continued to play. Annoyed, F. Melius whispered again, "Sit down." Again, no response from the *klokker*. Bergmann concludes the story: "Exasperated, Christiansen called out in a voice audible to all the startled worshipers, 'Sit down!' Chagrined, the *klokker* obeyed, but it took him a long time to forget his embarrassment and forgive the young organist."[31]

Two decisive happenings in F. Melius's life took place in Marinette, Wisconsin. He met his future wife, Edith Lindem, and he heard about Augsburg Seminary and decided to study there. Edith Signora Lindem was born April 16, 1877, and confirmed at Our Savior's Lutheran Church in 1893. She was only fourteen but a member of the choir, along with her parents, Jacob and Pauline Serine Lindem, when F. Melius first met her.

Jacob Lindem, a carpenter and cabinet maker, was born in Norway in 1845. In Marinette he ran his own sash and door factory. His wife Pauline (Polly) was born in Norway in 1854. The Lindems were a respected family in the town and at least moderately well-off. In later years F. Melius and his family would spend part of each summer at Marinette and at Sister Bay where the Lindems owned 43 acres in Door County.[32]

The young bandmaster, organist, and choir director was a welcome guest in the Lindem home where obviously he was attracted to Edith. While still in confirmation class, Edith, with her stylish clothes and her golden-brown hair done up in the fashion of the day, gave the appearance of being older than fourteen.[33] Edith was the second child in the family of six children and the only girl.

In Marinette F. Melius received his room and board with the prominent Prescott family, well-to-do Methodists. He earned his keep by giving piano lessons to the two small daughters. One of them, Sadie, appeared in one of F. Melius's organ recitals as vocal soloist, and to her he dedicated his first published composition, "Bonny Castle Waltzes," named after the home the Prescotts were building on Lake Superior. As director of the church

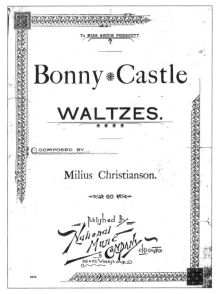

Published in 1892   STOARCHIV

43

choir at Our Savior's, F. Melius was soon composing sacred songs, such as "Et Raab, Et Bud" (A Cry, A Message) and "Kom Barn, Kom Brud" (Come Child, Come Bride). His choir sang "Et Raab" at a song festival of Lutheran singers in Duluth. Interviewed for his 80th birthday, Dr. Christiansen recalled a similar event in Superior, which was the occasion for his first choral composition with a "big solo soprano part" for the young lady in the choir whom he was "stuck on," namely his future wife, Edith.[34]

After two years in Marinette, F. Melius Christiansen moved to Minneapolis to attend Augsburg Seminary. The decision to do so was linked to the visit in Marinette of a male quartet from Augsburg in the summer of 1892. It gave a concert of both sacred and secular Scandinavian melodies at Our Savior's Church. The quartet was organized in 1885 by Theodore Reimestad, a teacher of Latin and Norse at Augsburg. He and three student members toured primarily to popularize the temperance cause, but at the same time to interest young people from rural and small-town communities in the liberal arts program at Augsburg. "How many individual renunciations of strong drink were influenced by the vocalists cannot be determined," writes an Augsburg historian, "but rallies featuring their talent drew larger crowds than a single speaker or two could attract."[35]

Reimestad spoke with F. Melius after the Marinette concert and impressed upon him the need for further education for the sake of his music. Naturally he recommended Augsburg and F. Melius listened. Reimestad assured him that he would probably be able to cover most of his expenses by his music. In September of 1892 the members of the Scandinavian Band of Marinette gave a party to say their fond farewells to their young director, and F. Melius was off to Minneapolis to enroll at Augsburg.[36]

In Minneapolis

It has to be seen as ironic that F. Melius Christiansen, who did so much to extend the reputation of St. Olaf College through the development of the St. Olaf Choir, should have begun his long Minnesota career in music at the institution which in the 1890s was the bitter rival of St. Olaf. The nature of the rivalry will be discussed below. The irony is compounded by the fact that while at Augsburg F. Melius was befriended by Professor Sven Oftedal, one of St. Olaf's severest critics and most adroit and determined adversaries. At the end of the 1892-93 school year, when Christiansen sought Oftedal's counsel in deciding between music and more academic work, the professor did not hesitate to recommend music, saying, "You are a musician by the grace of God."[37]

Music was the major interest for Christiansen during his one year as a student at Augsburg Seminary. His goal was to become a concert violinist.

He showed little enthusiasm for other studies, although he managed to stir things up in geometry class by arguing with the professor about the method for solving a problem. Having suffered a reprimand followed by a lengthy lecture about adapting to the New World, the roguish blond immigrant was seen early the next morning with two other boys as they led a ram into the classroom and sequestered it in a closet at the front of the room. As roll was being called in geometry class that morning, the ram spoke up in his own way from the closet, "ba-a-a-a, ba-a-a-a." A student opened the door to the closet, the ram shot out from his confinement, charged across the room, and butted the professor to the floor.[38]

Professor Sven Oftedal

When Christiansen's talent with the violin was discovered, he was asked to perform at various meetings on and off the Augsburg campus. Before long he was known as the "Ole Bull of Augsburg." He received invitations to play at Norwegian social clubs in the city, where wine and liquor consumption was part of the evening. Christiansen's pious Augsburg friends

Augsburg Seminary
Early campus scene

Augsburg College

45

frowned at his accepting such engagements, but encouraged him to play his violin at temperance meetings, which he did. He gained good experience but little remuneration from appearances at these gatherings.[39]

At heart the young violin player was not the teetotaler that the Augsburg society expected him to be. He welcomed the opportunities to perform at temperance and other meetings, but the schedule of a violin solo nearly every night was wearing him down physically. He found himself in the awkward position of being advised by his doctor to "quit school for six weeks and drink beer." Following a valid concern for his health, for a few weeks he had "to sneak into beer taverns without the faculty's knowing about it." But the faculty did not find out, the liquid prescription worked, and six weeks later he was "fat and rosy."[40]

With practicing, performing, and teaching violin as the core of his musical life at Augsburg, Christiansen also directed the Augsburg Chorus, and taught a class in singing and theory. He did a little composing, setting to music the poems of his friend, Hans Andreas Urseth, who was studying theology at the time and later became a faculty member and dean at Augsburg. The two remained good friends after Christiansen went to Northfield.[41]

Christiansen regarded his time at Augsburg as "a turning point in his life."[42] That evaluation was due as much to gratifying personal associations as to progress in his musical career. Bergmann pictures him with other young

Hans A. Urseth   Augsburg College

Augsburg Seminary Chorus. Director Christiansen in front   Augsburg Fortress, Publishers

Augsburg Seminary

men gathered in Urseth's dormitory room, smoking their pipes and discussing "God and the world," philosophy, theology, and "particularly the relation of art and music to the church and religion." He liked to argue, and was known for taking the opposite point of view. It was through such discussions, Christiansen maintained, that he received much of his education.[43]

One of the controversial issues on the minds of students at Augsburg in the early 1890s was the role that their institution would play in the new church body, the United Norwegian Lutheran Church, created in 1890 through the merger of three smaller bodies. According to the terms of the merger, Augsburg Seminary was to be the divinity school of the new church and St. Olaf its college.[44] This provision was the source of the rivalry between Augsburg and St. Olaf mentioned above.

Professor Sven Oftedal, who had befriended and advised F. Melius Christiansen, and his colleague, Professor Georg Sverdrup, led a movement to "build a wall around Augsburg."[45] They wanted to maintain control of the institution and to preserve its character, not only as a divinity school offering three years of theological study, but a divinity school with its own preparatory and collegiate units. To these two leaders and their followers, the prospect of St. Olaf College being the designated college of the United Norwegian Lutheran Church threatened the existence of Augsburg's preparatory and college departments.[46]

Adding zeal to their opposition to the terms of the merger was the fact that Oftedal and Sverdrup were distrustful of St. Olaf College. In their view,

The Main, St. Olaf College
Northfield, Minnesota

it offered a "Latin School humanism" that fostered intellectualism and elitism. Two different concepts of Christian education faced one another. At Augsburg everything centered on preparing men for the ministry. The institution was essentially a divinity school. At St. Olaf the ideal was a general liberal arts education designed to prepare its graduates, both men and women, for responsible service in many different walks of life, including the ministry.[47] It would not be too much to say that when Christiansen became a member of the St. Olaf faculty, he embraced the very "humanistic" belief in the liberal arts that the Augsburg loyalists deplored. St. Olaf would provide a setting conducive to his flowering as an artist.

The "Augsburg vs. St. Olaf" school issue was eventually resolved when Professors Oftedal and Sverdrup and their followers formed a separate church group, the Lutheran Free Church, with Augsburg as its leading institution. In 1893, at the height of the controversy, the United Church had cut off its support of St. Olaf College, forcing the Northfield school into six painful years of acute financial hardship. Later, in 1899, with Augsburg Seminary having gone its own way, the United Norwegian Lutheran Church re-adopted St. Olaf as its college and pledged to support it.[48]

How much F. Melius Christiansen knew of this controversy or whether he took sides in it is not easy to determine. One is at a loss to explain the statement that "Christiansen had never heard of St. Olaf" when he was first approached by President Kildahl of St. Olaf to consider a position there.[49] Perhaps after an eventful decade, which included his marriage and a two-year stay abroad, Christiansen had simply forgotten the controversy that had

48

provoked discussion back in 1892 and 1893. In any case, given the small size of the Augsburg community and the passion with which the issues were argued, it seems strange that Christiansen would not have heard the name of the "enemy" institution, located a mere forty miles away.

Although information is lacking on Christiansen's involvement with the controversy of the 1890s, one can form a reasonably accurate impression of how he responded to the religious and cultural atmosphere of the Augsburg community. Having been brought up in the staid and somber ways of the Norwegian state church, he was not accustomed to the revivals and prayer meetings that characterized the Augsburg scene. Nevertheless, he respected the fervent religious commitment and genuine personal piety he found among faculty and students.

Nor was he fully at home among those who spoke easily of their personal relationship with God and expected others to do the same. Yet it was a new and bracing experience for him to meet men of his own generation who held strong convictions and were able to express them. Taking a stand and firmly holding it could also be applied to artistic and intellectual matters. As something of a free spirit himself, Christiansen could empathize with his low church Augsburg friends in their distrust of ecclesiastical control from above and their resistance to forms and rituals they perceived as high church and authoritarian.[50]

As a musician, Christiansen was eager to play his violin before various audiences, including the more secularized and convivial Norwegian social clubs, but the prevailing Augsburg attitude, as mentioned above, was to discourage his joining such circles and to urge him to devote his talents to religious and temperance meetings. Similarly, there was a sentiment at Augsburg that preferred things Norwegian and looked with suspicion on anyone who attended such "Yankee" entertainments as the opera, symphony concerts, and recitals by visiting artists.[51] When Christiansen moved on to the Northwestern Conservatory of Music, he was able to break free from the limiting boundaries of the Augsburg milieu.

In the fall of 1893 F. Melius Christiansen began a year of study at Northwestern Conservatory of Music in Minneapolis, established in 1885 and affiliated with the University of Minnesota. He concentrated on violin, piano, harmony, and counterpoint, supporting himself by continuing his Augsburg duties, giving private lessons in violin, and serving as organist and choir director at Trinity Lutheran Church near Augsburg. On the Northwestern faculty were cellist Fritz Schlacter, violinist Heinrich Hoevel, founder of the Hoevel String Quartet, the outstanding pianist Carl Lachmund, and J. Warren Andrews, director of church music, who gave well-attended Sunday afternoon organ recitals at Plymouth Congregational

Church. With musical culture in Minneapolis flourishing, Christiansen was able to attend many concerts and recitals.[52]

Christiansen graduated from the Conservatory in May of 1894, the highest ranking person in the class of seventy students.[53] That month a chorus of twelve Minneapolis Lutheran church choirs sang a "Song of Welcome" that he and Hans Urseth had written for the annual convention of the United Norwegian Lutheran Church.[54] The Augsburg Quartet was in need of a baritone for its summer tour so they invited Christiansen to join them. The quartet visited numerous Norwegian-American communities, lustily singing prohibition songs to old Scandinavian melodies. "Christiansen's contribution as the first bass was not outstanding," writes Bergmann, "but his general musicianship was valuable to the group and his violin solos lent variety to their concerts." The violin was also an instrument for expressing Christiansen's prankish sense of humor, as when he decided to play it for a litter of pigs on a farm in southern Minnesota, sending the frightened creatures rushing to the

Augsburg Quartet, 1894
Christiansen, upper right

other side of the pasture. The Augsburg foursome made twelve hundred dollars on the tour and divided the money equally.[55]

Christiansen was gaining a favorable reputation as a busy, versatile young musician during the 1890s. Recognition came to the Augsburg student chorus he was directing and to his church choir. At Trinity Lutheran Church where he was organist and choir director he took a new step in forming a special chorus, called "Nordlyset" (Northlight), which would be independent of the church choir and "free from any demands other than his own."[56] When the pastor tried to circumvent Christiansen's authority in scheduling the chorus to sing at a function, he soon had to face the ire of the

50

director who flatly refused to let the chorus sing and heatedly told the pastor, "You are not the only one who has bone in his nose!"[57]

The Norwegian-American churches of that era were still inclined to use Norwegian in their worship even though their members spoke English in their daily lives. Thus there was a need for suitable choir music for congregations that still used Norwegian Bibles, Catechisms, and hymn books. Christiansen and Hans Urseth produced a book of songs for church choirs in 1894 and later published a monthly bulletin called *Sangserie* (Song Series). They continued their

Christiansen and Urseth Song Series First Number

collaboration over the next few years. One Christiansen composition from this period was the evangelistic hymn, "Kun et Skridt" ("Only a Step"), later translated by Oscar Overby and given the title, "One Resolve."[58]

In 1897 F. Melius Christiansen was twenty-six years old, determined to pursue further studies in music, and ready to marry the young woman he had

F. Melius Christiansen and Edith Lindem, married July 14, 1897

Photo courtesy Christiansen family

met in Marinette, Wisconsin, Edith Lindem. On July 14, 1897, the two were married in the bride's home. "It was a simple wedding without music, a point upon which Melius had been unyielding," writes Bergmann, but some friends who formed a male quartet succeeded in serenading the couple at the reception with a popular Norwegian song.[59]

Study in Leipzig, 1897-99

The plan was that the newlyweds, accompanied by F. Melius's brother Karl, would spend a few weeks in Norway before going on to Leipzig where Karl would also study music. It was a pleasant summer's stay in Larvik where, among other things, Karl and F. Melius gave a joint cornet and violin recital. After the study period in Leipzig, the Christiansens intended to return to Norway and settle there, but after F. Melius received his diploma in the spring of 1899, they decided to go back to America.[60]

Leipzig as the place for an aspiring musician to study must have been on Christiansen's mind since his fourteenth year when his mentor in Larvik, Oscar Hansen, went to Leipzig to study, leaving F. Melius to take his place at the church organ.[61] Music students were drawn to the German city because of the Royal Conservatory of Music and the institutions related to it: the City Theater and Opera, the *Thomaskirche*, where Johan Sebastian Bach was once the cantor, the *Gewandhaus*, where conservatory students were required to attend concerts, the *Nicolaikirche*, and the *Thomasschule* whose boys' choir regularly sang a motet every Saturday.[62]

Leipzig Conservatory

Christiansen's first concern in Leipzig was to study violin, which he did under Hans Sitt, an excellent teacher. He practiced violin six hours a day. He also put in an hour or two each day on the piano, receiving instruction in that instrument from Alois Reckendorf.[63] For his studies in theory and composition, F. Melius was assigned to Gustav Schreck, cantor of the *Thomasschule*, who gave his classes in the English language. Schreck set such a demanding pace that the number of students dropped from close to thirty at the first meeting of the class to ten at the finish.[64]

Gustav Schreck

The impression must be corrected that these two years with Gustav Schreck were definitive in drawing F. Melius Christiansen into choral work. On the contrary, Christiansen was fully occupied with classes at the conservatory, violin practice and piano work. The violin claimed his first efforts. He showed little or no interest in choral music at this time.[65] Bergmann points out that the atmosphere of the conservatory did not stimulate interest in choral work. "Attention was centered almost entirely on instrumental training; choral study was quite openly snubbed," she writes. There were required classes in chorus drill but in his two years there Christiansen did not attend a single one, and no one objected to his absence.[66]

Which is not to underestimate the profound value of the classes under Schreck. According to Christiansen's St. Olaf colleague, Oscar Overby, the influence of Schreck "helped materially in formulating his philosophy and musical style."[67] Schreck made his significant impact on Christiansen's choral development in 1906-07 when F. Melius went to Leipzig after the St. Olaf Band's 1906 tour of Norway. Under his teacher's guidance, F. Melius examined the influence of folk music on church music and wrote harmonies in contrapuntal style for about seventy familiar chorales.[68]

During the 1897-99 stay in Germany, the benefits gained from contacts with Schreck, Sitt, and other faculty were enhanced by the unusual musical riches of the Leipzig environment. Conservatory students were required to attend all *Gewandhaus* concerts. Thus F. Melius and his brother Karl with other students and an appreciative Leipzig society attended the Thursday night concerts at the *Gewandhaus* where the brilliant conductor was the great Arthur Nikisch.[69] He and Karl would also hear the famous boys' choir, the *ThomanerChor*, on Saturday mornings when it presented a motet and on

Sundays when it sang a cantata either at *Thomaskirche* or *Nicolaikirche*. They could hear such professional chamber groups as the Joachim Quartet or the *Gewandhaus* Quartet, as well as solo recitals and operas.[70]

One hears nothing of Edith's participation in the music life of Leipzig. It is always F. Melius and Karl attending the concerts. One obvious factor is that in the spring of 1898 Edith gave birth to their first child, a boy who was named Elmer. It should also be mentioned that during the Leipzig stay F. Melius gained some acquaintance with Carl A. Mellby, a future St. Olaf colleague, who at that time was studying theology in Leipzig where he earned the Ph. D. degree. Mellby would play tennis with Hans Sitt, Christiansen's violin teacher, who spoke of his "gifted pupil from America."[71]

Through his commendable industry Christiansen was able to graduate from the conservatory in two years, receiving his diploma in the spring of 1899. His previous work at Northwestern Conservatory in Minneapolis apparently had prepared him to make good progress in the theory course, which alone normally took three years.[72]

Return to Minneapolis

The Christiansens returned to America in the summer of 1899 instead of moving to Norway. F. Melius went directly to Minneapolis to resume his career in music, while Edith and the little boy were left in Marinette, Wisconsin, with her parents.

He secured a position on the violin faculty at Northwestern Conservatory where in time he headed the string faculty. His violin expertise also placed him in the violin section of the Philharmonic orchestra. This group came under the direction of a young German musician, Emil Oberhoffer, and in 1903 was incorporated as the Minneapolis Symphony Orchestra. F. Melius appeared in public as violin soloist and, as expected, gave violin lessons, putting him in touch again with a promising pupil he had taught earlier, Adolph Olsen. He was back at the organ of Trinity Lutheran Church, later moving to Bethany Lutheran Church.[73]

Minneapolis, a city of much musical activity, gave F. Melius a variety of outlets for his energies and creativity in performing, conducting, and composing, both for the violin and for choruses. He was made director of the Kjerulf Club, a chorus of twenty-five male voices. A number of these male singing societies, named after the Norwegian composer, Halfdan Kjerulf, were to be found in Norwegian-American circles. Receiving four dollars for each rehearsal, Christiansen soon turned a casual socializing group into a disciplined singing organization. For the Kjerulf Club he wrote, among other pieces, a choral setting for "Ungbirken" (Young Birch),

54

a poem by the Norwegian poet Jørgen Moe. Through the Minneapolis Kjerulf Club F. Melius became acquainted with an extraordinary bass singer named Paul G. Schmidt, and in large part through Schmidt, Christiansen would be invited to teach at St. Olaf College.

Before that invitation was issued, however, Christiansen was busy and productive. One conducting engagement was at the Swedish Tabernacle where he led a chorus of seventy-five singers in a benefit concert for Norwegians who had suffered in a recent storm. A reviewer noted that they sang "with good tone and finish." Another applauded the fact that "Mr. Christiansen had welded the fragments from half a dozen singing societies into the harmonious whole."[74] When Augsburg Seminary dedicated a building on New Year's Day 1900, F. Melius directed the seminary chorus in two numbers and played two violin solos. On April 27, 1900, he led a concert at the First Unitarian Church, conducting the Norwegian Male Chorus and performing the G minor concerto by Max Bruch on the violin. A reviewer for the *Minneapolis Times* wrote:

> F. Melius Christiansen created a most favorable impression as a violinist. He gave a "Concerto" by Max Bruch that was new to the city's musical public. Mr. Christiansen has good technique and considerable spirit and fire.[75]

Christiansen performed as violin soloist on numerous programs and also gave his own recitals. In addition to the Bruch concerto he often played the Concerto in D Minor by Wieniawski, sonatas and other works by Edvard Grieg, and two of his own violin compositions, "Romance" and "Kjølstavisa." He was also composing, examples from 1898 to 1900 include such vocal pieces as "Et Raad et Bud," "Gravsang," "Serenade," "Julen gaar ind," and "Paaskehymne."[76]

The Postcard

In April of 1900, fully expecting to make Minneapolis their permanent home, F. Melius brought his wife and family from Marinette to occupy a rented house in the city. He and Edith now had two sons, Elmer, born in Leipzig, and Jacobi, born in Marinette earlier in 1900. Olaf Christian, a third son, was born August 12, 1901. Sadly, Elmer became ill with spinal meningitis and died in 1902. A daughter, Edith Signora but called "Tulla" by the family, was born in June of 1903.[77]

One evening while Christiansen was leading a rehearsal of the Kjerulf Club in downtown Minneapolis, Paul G. Schmidt appeared and engaged F. Melius in conversation. Schmidt had been invited to join the Kjerulf Club because he was an excellent singer. Moreover, someone must have known that this university student was able to meet the Club's requirement of

F. M. Christiansen family, ca. 1904
Children: Olaf, Jacobi, Edith Signora ("Tulla")

speaking only Norwegian at rehearsals.[78] Schmidt had had considerable exposure to the Norwegian language while attending the academy department of St. Olaf's School from 1886 until his graduation in 1891.[79]

In his book, *My Years at St. Olaf*, P. G. Schmidt tells of his talk with Mr. Christiansen that evening and the rehearsal he observed. "He said he was in need of a low bass and urged me to join." Schmidt continues:

> At the rehearsal of the Kjerulf Male Chorus, . . . I could not help being greatly impressed with both the manner of his directing and the kind of pieces he selected for rehearsal. I noted in particular how he strove to secure certain desired effects. He was not at all satisfied with mediocre results and many phrases were repeated over and over again until the desired fine shade of expression was attained.

From the first rehearsal I attended, I came to have great respect and admiration for Mr. Christiansen. His passionate striving for perfection in his interpretations and presentations gave me a new insight in the power of song. Needless to say, I never missed a rehearsal.[80]

Paul G. Schmidt graduated from the University of Minnesota in June of 1897, having chosen a classical course with such electives as mathematics, physics, and astronomy. He taught at an academy in Minneapolis for a few years, and in 1902 accepted a position at St. Olaf College as assistant teacher of mathematics at $800 per year. Once they had moved to Northfield in the summer of 1902, Schmidt and his wife joined St. John's Lutheran Church and its choir. The president of the College, John Nathan Kildahl, was serving as pastor of the church at the time. Kildahl and the Schmidts would discuss music matters at

Paul Gerhard Schmidt

St. Olaf in the light of the recent action by the United Norwegian Lutheran Church authorizing the president to hire a music director. Writes Schmidt:

Invariably he would mention the problem that was of so much concern to him at the time—whom he could engage as music director at the college. He asked us if we knew of anyone who was capable and who in other respects would be the right man for the place. It was then only natural for me to suggest the man for whom I had learned to have very great respect, my friend in Minneapolis, the director of the Kjerulf Male Chorus, F. Melius Christiansen. President Kildahl did not know him, but agreed to go to Minneapolis to meet him and talk matters over with him.[81]

*John Nathan Kildahl
President, St. Olaf College,
1899-1914*

It was by means of a postcard that President Kildahl first made contact with F. Melius Christiansen. The card found its way to a cottage on Lake

Nokomis in the woods south of Minneapolis where the Christiansen family was living in 1903. In the card Kildahl invited Christiansen to come into the city to meet him in order to discuss a position at St. Olaf College. The conversation led to a train trip down to Northfield to see the College which had been in operation for twenty-nine years.[82]

St. Olaf was still a small but growing college in 1903. It was adopted as the college of the United Norwegian Lutheran Church in 1899, bringing it much-needed financial support, a broadened constituency, and the addition of four teachers and sixty-one students from the college department of the United Church's seminary.[83] The Reverend John Nathan Kildahl, the new president, gave the school the kind of leadership the new day demanded. Enrollment grew from 184 in 1899 to over 300 in 1901, and continued to rise. The size of the faculty increased from thirteen in the 1898-99 school year to eighteen in 1902-03. The following year, when F. Melius Christiansen was listed for the first time in the College catalog, the faculty totaled twenty-two plus seven "instructors."[84]

In 1901 the College introduced a Scientific Course of study to supplement the older Classical Course. Theodore R. Running, who had just completed his Ph. D. at the University of Wisconsin, organized and directed the new course.[85] President Kildahl was eager to put the music program at the College on a sounder footing. Three times he went before the annual meeting of the United Norwegian Lutheran Church to urge that "it would be highly desirable if the convention would sanction the appointment of a

F. Melius Christiansen, 1903

director of music to take charge of all musical activities at the college." The church body accepted Kildahl's proposal in 1903, opening the way for him to secure the services of F. Melius Christiansen.[86]

Christiansen first agreed to a part-time position at St. Olaf. He lived in Minneapolis the first year, reserving two days per week for his violin pupils but giving the larger share of the week to the College. As announced in the Minneapolis *Tidende*, a Norwegian language newspaper, Christiansen was to head the music department, direct the band and the chorus, and teach violin and music theory. His salary would be six hundred dollars a year.[87] While on the

Ytterboe Hall, St. Olaf College, Northfield, Minnesota
Men's Dormitory

campus that trial year he had a room in the men's dormitory, later to be called Ytterboe Hall.

The first year at St. Olaf went well for Christiansen and the new music department. President Kildahl was pleased with the progress made and F. Melius had enjoyed the work. When the 1903-04 school year was over, Christiansen was given the rank of full professor and a salary increase to one thousand dollars. By that time he was ready to bring his family from Minneapolis to settle in the quiet little town of Northfield. He found a house to rent on St. Olaf Avenue and moved his family there in the summer of 1904. The prospect of raising his children in a small town setting appealed to him.[88] Later, there would be opportunity to move elsewhere, but F. Melius Christiansen was content to remain in the environs of St. Olaf College and Northfield for the rest of his life.

Notes for Chapter 2 F. MELIUS CHRISTIANSEN

1. Cf. Leola Nelson Bergmann, *Music Master of the Middle West*: The Story of F. Melius Christiansen and the St. Olaf Choir (Minneapolis: University of Minnesota Press, 1944), 19, 32.

2. Bergmann, 5; Eugene E. Simpson, *A History of St. Olaf Choir* (Minneapolis: Augsburg Publishing House, 1921), 118.

3. Albert Rykken Johnson, "The Christiansen Choral Tradition: F. Melius Christiansen, Olaf C. Christiansen, and Paul J. Christiansen," A thesis submitted in partial fulfillment of the requirements for the Degree of Doctor of Philosophy in the School of Music in the Graduate College of The University of Iowa, July, 1973, 45-46.

4. Bergmann, 6.

5. *Ibid.*, 5.

6. Simpson, 119; Bergmann, 5-6.

7. Bergmann, 6; Simpson, 120.

8. Bergmann, 8-9.

9. Simpson, 120; Bergmann, 11

10. Simpson, 120-21.

11. Bergmann, 12-13.

12. *Ibid.*, 10.

13. Simpson, 107; Leola Nelson Bergmann, "F. Melius Christiansen: A Study of his life and work as a Norwegian-American contribution to American Culture," A dissertation submitted in partial fulfillment of the requirements for the degree of Doctor of Philosophy, in the Department of English, in the Graduate College of the State University of Iowa," July, 1942, 13.

14. Simpson, 121.

15. Bergmann, *Music Master of the Middle West*, 12.

16. Simpson, 107.

17. Simpson, 120-21.

18. Minutes of congregational meetings of St. John's Lutheran Church, Northfield, Minnesota, Entry 131, 25 September 1916; Edna Hong, *The Book Of A Century*: The Centennial History of St. John's Lutheran Church (1869-1969), Northfield, Minnesota, 1969, 91.

19. Simpson, 121.

20. *Ibid.*, 122.

21. Bergmann, *op. cit.*, 15, 19.

22. *Ibid.*, 18-19.

23. *Ibid.*, 19-20.

24. *Ibid.*, 21.

25. *Ibid.*, 23-27.

26. *Ibid.*, 28.

27. Charles M. Sheridan, "Washburn First to Acclaim Musicianship of Eminent Dr. F. Melius Christiansen," *Washburn Telegram*, 1947. F. Melius Christiansen papers, Norwegian-American Historical Association (NAHA) Archives, NAHA MSS. Cf. Bergmann, 29-30.

28. Bergmann, 34.

29. E. Clifford Nelson and Eugene L. Fevold, *The Lutheran Church Among Norwegian-Americans*: A History of the Evangelical Lutheran Church (Minneapolis: Augsburg Publishing House, 1960), I, 200, 206, 218; Thomas Edward Rhude, "The Conference, the LFC and Our Savior's Norwegian Lutheran Church of Marinette, Wisconsin," a paper prepared for Scandinavian Studies 296, the University of Wisconsin at Madison, December 1981, 9. Courtesy of Andreas Jordahl Rhude, Minneapolis, Minnesota.

30. Bergmann, 39.

31. *Ibid.*, 37.

32. Letter from Andreas Jordahl Rhude to Joseph M. Shaw, March 28, 1995; Bergmann, 38; *Peshtigo Times*, September 1, 1993.

33. Bergmann, 38.

34. Bergmann, 39; *St. Paul Sunday Pioneer Press*, Feature Magazine, April 1, 1951.

35. Carl H. Chrislock, *From Fjord to Freeway*: 100 Years - Augsburg College (Minneapolis: Augsburg College, 1969), 108.

36. Bergmann, 40.

37. Bergmann, 52; Chrislock, 109.

38. Bergmann, 48-49.

39. *Ibid.*, 45, 46.

40. *Ibid.*, 41, 47.

41. *Ibid.*, 51; Chrislock, 109.

42. Bergmann, 44.

43. *Ibid.*, 50-51.

44. Nelson and Fevold, *The Lutheran Church Among Norwegian-Americans* II, 24, 28, 31; Chrislock, 47, 49.

45. Chrislock, 69.

46. *Ibid.*, 48.

47. *Ibid.*, 54, 58, 61; Nelson and Fevold II, 41-43.

48. Nelson and Fevold II, 79, 81.

49. Bergmann, 85.

50. *Ibid.*, 43.

51. *Ibid.*, 42, 46.

52. *Ibid.*, 52-53, 56-58; Albert Rykken Johnson, "The Christiansen Choral Tradition," 74-75.

53. Robert Lee Jennings, "A Study of the Historical Development of Choral Ensembles at Selected Lutheran Liberal Arts Colleges in the United States," A Thesis Submitted to Michigan State University in partial fulfillment of the requirements for the degree of Doctor of Philosophy, 1969, 22.

54. Bergmann, 59.

55. *Ibid.*, 60-62.

56. Johnson, 78; Bergmann, 62.

57. Bergmann, 62-63.

58. *Ibid.*, 62, 64-66.

59. *Ibid.*, 71-72.

60. *Ibid.*, 73, 77.

61. Simpson, 120-21.

62. Bergmann, 74; Johnson, 79.

63. Bergmann, 75; Simpson, 128; Johnson, 82.

64. Simpson, 127; Bergmann, 75.

65. Editorial, "In Memory of a Musical Giant," *Lutheran Herald* XXXIX (June 21, 1955), 597.

66. Bergmann, 75.

67. Oscar R. Overby, "Salute to a Giant," *Lutheran Herald* XXXV (April 10, 1951), 359.

68. Bergmann, 105; cf. Paul Benson, *The Empires of Song: A Cappella*

Choirs in the Scandinavian Colleges, Unpublished Typescript, n. d., 25-26. Used by permission.

69. Bergmann, 74.

70. Johnson, 82-84.

71. Bergmann, 76.

72. Johnson, 84.

73. Bergmann, 80-82; Simpson, 124.

74. Simpson, 124-25.

75. Johnson, 89.

76. *Ibid.*, 93.

77. Bergmann, 83-84; Johnson, 93-94.

78. Bergmann, 79.

79. P. G. Schmidt's father, Professor Friedrich A. Schmidt, was a German-born pastor serving in a Norwegian church body who impressed his Norwegian-born colleagues with his acquired facility in their language. Schmidt had learned Norwegian while teaching Norwegian students at Luther College in Decorah, Iowa, Concordia Seminary in St. Louis, and at the Norwegian Synod Seminary in Madison, Wisconsin. He came to Northfield as a theological professor in a small divinity school operated on the St. Olaf campus from 1886 to 1890. Thus his son, Paul G. Schmidt, would have had access to Norwegian at home as well as in school and at church. See Nelson and Fevold, *The Lutheran Church Among Norwegian-Americans* I, 187, n. 131.

80. Paul G. Schmidt, *My Years at St. Olaf*, A Centennial Decade Publication (Northfield, Minnesota: St. Olaf College, [1967]), 21-22.

81. *Ibid.*, 29.

82. Bergmann, 85.

83. William C. Benson, *High on Manitou:* A History of St. Olaf College 1874-1949 (Northfield, Minnesota: The St. Olaf College Press, 1949), 135.

84. Joseph M. Shaw, *History of St. Olaf College 1874-1974* (Northfield, Minnesota: The St. Olaf College Press, 1974), 174; *Catalogue of St. Olaf College* for 1898-99, 5; *Catalogue* for 1902-03, 6-7; *Catalogue* for 1903-04, 6-7.

85. Benson, 134.

86. *Ibid.*, 174.

87. Bergmann. 84, 92.

88. *Ibid.*, 102.

CHAPTER 3

MUSIC AT ST. OLAF

When the St. Olaf Choir was welcomed back to the campus at the conclusion of its remarkably successful tour to the cities and concert halls of the east coast in May of 1920, Director Christiansen was called upon to say a few words. First he obliged with, "I'm mighty glad to be back," but then he spoke, not of the Choir's achievements, but of the setting in which it had been nurtured:

> The choir and band are a natural outgrowth of the culture here.
> They have grown naturally from a little seed way back in history
> and like flowers in the woods, grew under favorable conditions.
> That we were successful was only that the *flavor of St. Olaf* was
> given to the world and they seemed to like it.[1]

The aim of this chapter is to show that a musical culture existed at St. Olaf College from an early point in its history. When F. Melius Christiansen was appointed to the faculty in 1903, he found favorable conditions that allowed his unusual musical talents to flourish and bear fruit.

St. Olaf's School was founded in 1874 by the Reverend Bernt Julius Muus, a Norwegian Lutheran immigrant pastor who had come from Norway in 1859 to serve the rural Holden parish in Goodhue County, Minnesota. Pastor Muus decided to locate the School in Northfield, some twenty-three miles northwest of Holden. Joining Muus in signing the Articles of Incorporation for St. Olaf's School on November 6, 1874, were

Bernt Julius Muus
Holden Pastor, Founder of St. Olaf

Harald Thorson
Northfield merchant

Thorbjørn Nelson Mohn, Principal
of St. Olaf's School

Harald Thorson, a Northfield business man, and three farmers, O. K. Finseth and Knute P. Haugen from Holden in Goodhue County, and O. Osmundson from Nerstrand in Rice County. These five men constituted the Board of Trustees of the School, with Muus as president and Thorson as secretary.

Muus appointed the Reverend Thorbjørn Nelson Mohn as Principal of the Northfield School. When the status and name of St. Olaf's School were changed to St. Olaf College in 1889, Mohn was given the title of President.

Mohn led the little institution through twenty-five years of struggle that involved severe financial hardships and painful church controversies, including the Augsburg controversy of the 1890s mentioned in the previous chapter.

John Nathan Kildahl,
Second president of the
St. Olaf College

Having been made the college of the United Norwegian Lutheran Church in 1899 and receiving an able new president in the person of the Reverend John Nathan Kildahl at the same time, St. Olaf College was beginning to enjoy a measure of stability. The fight to survive during those earlier years left little time or resources for developing a richer academic program. Now it could give more serious attention to the liberal arts, including music, which were intrinsic to the original vision of the founders.

Purpose of St. Olaf College

Appointing a director of music was quite in harmony with the purpose of the Northfield College, which cultivated liberal learning of general interest rather than focusing exclusively on the preparation of future pastors. In this respect St. Olaf's aim was different from that of two other Norwegian Lutheran institutions established earlier. Luther College in Decorah, Iowa, founded in 1861, had as its primary aim the education of ministers, although it would also offer general education. It began as an all-male college, not offering coeducation until 1936.[2] Augsburg Seminary, which eventually found its permanent home in Minneapolis, was established in 1869 explicitly for the training of clergy and only gradually developed a college program. It too began as an all-male institution, becoming coeducational in 1922.[3]

St. Olaf's School, by contrast, was established for the general education of both men and women. The Articles of Incorporation state that the purpose is "to give a higher education to pupils fifteen years of age or over and to preserve them in the true Christian faith as taught by the Evangelical Lutheran church." An early publication announces that the object of the School is "to give the Christian confirmed youth of both sexes a higher education for the practical life than the local schools provide."[4]

After the institution attained college status in 1889, the statement of purpose was expressed in these words: "The general purpose of St. Olaf College is to give young men and women a higher education and to preserve them in the true Christian faith as taught in the Evangelical Lutheran Church."[5] From that time to the present, St. Olaf College has stood for liberal learning applicable to all walks of life, coeducation, and an honored place for the Christian faith in classroom and chapel. While not established for pre-ministerial training, in the course of its history it has sent hundreds of graduates on to theological education and service in the church.

St. Olaf's view of education gave ample room for such cultural pursuits as music. The St. Olaf Catalog for 1889-90 stated that "music is one of the most important elements in modern civilization and culture."[6] Throughout his long career at St. Olaf, Christiansen would be a powerful advocate, in deed and occasionally in pungent word, of an education that encouraged all students to cherish the rich gifts of human culture. "Every student," he wrote in his direct way, "should take voice at least for one semester."[7] At the same time, he knew the worth of general education. "We say that a college education should not consist of professional studies but be of general value," he said in a statement addressed to St. Olaf students. "Even if you do not go into music as a profession, you should at least have a general knowledge of the subject."[8]

Music activity at St. Olaf College took a giant stride forward when F. Melius Christiansen joined the faculty in the fall of 1903. That a totally new era in musical art began with his coming is easily illustrated. In September he appeared as a violin soloist; in November he led the St. Olaf Band in a concert; in early December he conducted the Choral Union in a performance of Schnecker's cantata, "The Fatherhood of God." He lost no time in organizing a music festival held in May of 1904.[8] The student paper, the *Manitou Messenger*, stated in November of 1903:

Front Cover of *The Manitou Messenger* Issue of June, 1890

> Prof. Christiansen came highly recommended, and his work here during the past two months has convinced everyone that he is the man for the place. As a result of the new order of things interest for the art melodious has taken an upward shoot, and our various musical organizations are in a flourishing condition.[9]

The dynamic upsurge of musical activity created by F. Melius Christiansen's appointment should not obscure the fact that there had been a substantial interest in music prior to his coming. P. G. Schmidt, Christiansen's long-time colleague and friend, states that while there was no music department when he came to St. Olaf in 1902, that did not mean "that there was a lack of interest in either vocal or instrumental music. Far from it!" he writes.[10] In fact, the lively participation in music already in evidence helped motivate President Kildahl to recommend at three successive annual meetings of the United Norwegian Lutheran Church (1901-1903) that a director of music be appointed for St. Olaf College.[11]

A review of musical activities at St. Olaf before Christiansen's arrival will show how the ground had been prepared for the work of a talented leader. Musical expressions of some variety, both vocal and instrumental, created a receptivity to the several facets of Christiansen's ability.

First Music Activities

Writing of the pre-Christiansen period, William C. Benson states, "One of the subjects of special interest from the beginning of the institution was music, but no formal courses were offered." Benson mentions piano and voice lessons, required class training in singing in the academy department, and the student musical organizations.[12]

From the beginning there were music teachers on the faculty, piano teachers at first and later some voice teachers. The classes in singing were part of the weekly schedule. The students themselves took the initiative to organize musical groups, including a very early "St. Olaf Choir." And the close relations between the institution and St. John's Lutheran Church had an important bearing on the future work of Christiansen at the College.

While founded on November 6, 1874, St. Olaf's School did not open officially until January 8, 1875. Instruction was given in the old wooden school buildings at the corner of Third and Union Streets in Northfield. A photograph from that year gives evidence that six students from the very first class at the School together with eight adult members of the

St. Olaf student body, 1875
Third and Union Streets, Northfield

St. John's Church Choir, 1875

congregation constituted a St. John's Church Choir. Among the student members of the choir were Marie Aaker, first student to enroll at St. Olaf's School, and Birgitte Muus, daughter of the Reverend Bernt Julius Muus, founder of St. Olaf.[13] This natural combining of students and church members to form a choir was the same pattern that brought into being the St. Olaf Choir in 1912.

A rather striking finding from St. Olaf's very early history is that a "St. Olaf Choir" (*St. Olafs Sangkor*) was organized by students on December 3, 1875. It was to consist solely of St. Olaf students. Personnel included 28

Marie Aaker, first student registered at St. Olaf's School

A.O. Naesset

Mrs. Anna E. Mohn

Miss Ella Fiske

male and nine female student voices. It had a chairman, L. Langen, a secretary, A. O. Naesset, and a constitution that required each member to meet for rehearsals on Saturday afternoons and pay 10 cents per month to the instructor, who is not named. "The choir's object," says the constitution, "is education in Norwegian national and society singing, with the addition of a little religious song." This group did not last long. The reason for its swift demise was that the enthusiasm soon shifted to gymnastics. By April of 1876 Langen and Naesset are named as president and secretary of "Olaf Trygvasons Gymnastikforening," a gymnastics club. Writes Eugene Simpson, "The 'St. Olaf Sangkor' of 1875 had arrived in the world some thirty-seven years before its time."[14]

Information is sketchy, but another source tells of a different early choir, apparently organized a year or so later. Mrs. Anna E. Mohn, wife of the first president, Thorbjørn Nelson Mohn, writes of the organization of a "sangkor" at the beginning of one of the first school years but does not give the exact year. The choir she writes of, unlike the one described above, consisted both of St. Olaf students and of young men and women from the congregation. Moreover, her account identifies the director as Rasmus Støve, a student at St. Olaf. It notes further that the congregation had bought an Estey Organ to enhance the worship and that the first organist was Mons Baker, a Norwegian student at Carleton College. The next organist was Marie Aaker, a student member of the St. John's Church Choir of 1875.[15]

It is of more than passing interest that of the first three faculty members at the School, one was a music teacher, Miss Ella Fiske. She joined Principal Thorbjørn Nelson Mohn

Music Room in the Main

and Prof. L. S. Reque as teachers when classes began in January 1875.[16] As early as the spring of 1876, Miss Fiske and her pupils presented a musical entertainment, the first such ever given at the School. It "was very good," reports Mrs. Mohn, "consisting of vocal and instrumental music."[17]

Although space was obviously at a premium in the crowded quarters of the tiny institution when it was still located in downtown Northfield, two of the six rooms were devoted to music, one for the music teacher, and the other no doubt for practice.[18] Miss Fiske gave lessons on a piano she herself provided, and instruction in singing.[19]

After the School moved to its new campus on Manitou Heights in 1878, one room in the Main building was set aside as a music room.[20] When Principal Mohn proposed that the School purchase a piano for $150, Trustee Harald Thorson said that he thought the music instructor was to provide her own instrument, which apparently Miss Fiske had been doing. Thorson maintained that if the teacher would not supply her own piano, a different instructor should be found. But Mohn persuaded the executive committee to buy the piano, one-third to be paid each year with no interest charge on the unpaid balance.[21]

Choral music figured in two ceremonies related to the building of the Main. After the cornerstone had been laid during a ceremony held on July 4, 1877, a mixed choir of students sang, in Norwegian, "Heaven and earth

Lars E. Lynne

Oluf Glasoe

Vigleik Boe

shall pass away, but Thy Word, O God, shall never be shaken."[22] When the building was dedicated, on November 6, 1878, faculty member Lars E. Lynne directed a chorus of twenty St. Olaf students who sang two anthems, "Prayer" and "Song of Praise." One of the members of that chorus remembered that the rehearsals were long and exacting and that the singing received favorable reviews in the local papers.[23]

Holding an important place among early music activities at St. Olaf's School was the participation of the students and faculty members in the worship life of St. John's Lutheran Church. As noted, in 1875 the St. John's Church Choir included members of the first student body. The practice continued over the next decades, townspeople and students singing together at worship services. The first published catalog, for 1884-85, lists among the faculty Miss Margaret O'Brien as in charge of instrumental and vocal music. Since Miss O'Brien was also organist and choir director at St. John's, she conducted choir rehearsals in the Main on the St. Olaf campus.[24] In October of 1888 the St. Olaf student newspaper, the *Manitou Messenger,* takes note of the fact that "Dr. Egge, Professor Grose, and several of the students constitute the new church choir."[25] Among those from St. Olaf who directed the choir at St. John's, besides Miss O'Brien, were John Dahle, faculty member from 1890 to 1892, Oluf Glasoe, vocal teacher, and Vigleik Boe, a student.

73

Music Faculty and Instruction

Reports submitted to the Norwegian Evangelical Lutheran Church by Pastor B. J. Muus, the chairman of the Board of Trustees, and by Th. N. Mohn, the principal, indicate that during the first year instruction had been given in "singing and music," where "music" means instrumental instruction. Similarly, the principal's report for the second year, 1875-76, again mentions singing, which was taught two hours a week in each of three classes. These reports place singing and music with geography and writing as subjects alongside of or in addition to the main courses.[26]

Ella Fiske has been introduced as the first instructor in music. Lars E. Lynne, faculty member from 1877 to 1881 and an amateur violinist, occasionally played solos accompanied by Miss Fiske. He also added vocal instruction to his other teaching duties and directed the students who sang at the dedication of the Main.[27]

The catalogs and other sources reveal an impressive succession of faculty persons who taught instrumental or vocal music or both. The instrument was the piano, for the most part, but in time organ and violin lessons were offered. Several women who held the position of preceptress were also music teachers, with Lina Koren succeeding Ella Fiske in 1879-80. Next came Margaret O'Brien who seems to have been much admired by both colleagues and students. She is lauded in the first catalog for her musical and social abilities in a section headed "Ladies' Department":

Ladies' Hall, 1888
Margaret O'Brien in center holding fan

74

The Ladies' Hall is in charge of Miss M. O'Brien, an accomplished lady, who takes pleasure in making the Hall as attractive a home as possible for the lady students. Having studied vocal and instrumental music in the East, she is a very competent teacher, and students have an excellent opportunity to pursue musical studies. Should a young lady desire to devote herself exclusively to the study of music she may do so; but as a rule a careful selection of other studies is made by the teachers and a program prepared for the lady students, suited to their requirements; in order to graduate, a young lady must, however, pass a satisfactory examination in all the studies comprising the course.[28]

Margaret O'Brien grew up in nearby Faribault. Her studies "in the East" were at the New England Conservatory in Boston.[29] Even at that early stage, St. Olaf was able to find music teachers with good training.

In June of 1887 an editor of the *Manitou Messenger* wrote that it was "with deep regret that we are compelled to make the announcement that our honored preceptress and musical instructress, Miss Margaret O'Brien, will sever her connection with the institution at the close of this school year. . . . Through her efforts," the editor continued, "the musical department has achieved

Margaret O'Brien

Class of 1893, Agnes Mellby in center,
first woman to graduate from St. Olaf College

marked success." At graduation exercises of the preparatory department that spring, Agnes Mellby, the valedictorian, spoke a fond farewell to Miss O'Brien. "Long have you taught the students of St. Olaf's School the beautiful art of music."[30] Students would also be reminded of Margaret O'Brien by the framed pictures of Mozart and Bach that she and the lady students presented to the musical department.[31]

At that time, with St. Olaf still an academy, two courses of study were available, the English Course for practical business pursuits, aimed at the men, and the Classical Course for college preparation.[32] The notice from the Ladies' Department assumes that the study of music will appeal primarily to the young women, but the School also hoped to lure them into other subjects. In the meantime, general instruction in singing was being given to all students in music classes. Lars Lynne gave such instruction in 1877-78. In the two-year period 1883-85 these classes were taught by A. O. Naesset, who, while a student the previous decade, served as secretary for the short-lived *St. Olafs Sangkor*. Thus there were opportunities in music for the men as well as for the young ladies.

An interesting feature of the St. Olaf catalogs from the first one issued in 1884 and into the 1890s is the proud listing by name of all the students in the "Musical Department." There are 14 names in 1884, 19 in 1885-86, four of them men, and 24 names in 1886-87. The Musical Department has 31 in 1887-88, the year the School took a step forward when it engaged the services of Oluf Glasoe as Instructor in Vocal Music. The number reaches 32 names in 1889-90, the first year St. Olaf was a college, drops back to 22 the next year, but increases to 39, eight of them men, in 1891-92, the year after John Dahle was added to the faculty as Instructor in Vocal Music.

The term "Musical Department" is somewhat misleading and not to be

10   ST. OLAF COLLEGE.

Musical Department.

Anderson, Clara	Houston.
Bredeson, Oline	Northfield.
Bunsness, Anna	Gem, S. Dak.
Egge, John I.	Norway.
Ellefson, Caroline	Granite Falls.
Engebretson, Anton	Grafton, N. Dak.
Engelson, Hannah	Brookings, S. Dak.
Fedje, Martha	Granite Falls.
Gilbert, Ida	Blair, Wis.
Golberg, Sophia	Buttzville, N. Dak.
Hanson, Hjalma	Rushford.
Hanson, Mary	New Richland.
Krohn, Marie	Northfield.
Kvi, Lena	Nerstrand.
Larson, Thea G.	Kasson.
Mellby, Marie E.	New Richland.
Mohn, Nils I. E.	Northfield.
Nelson, L. T.	Hendrum.
Nesheim, Martha	Wangs.
Oie, Maline	Madison.
Rasmussen, Mathilde	Lisbon, Ill.
Rinde, Helen	Nerstrand.
Ringstad, Ivan E. A.	Dundas.
Rude, Erik K.	Holden.
Scanlan, Conrad	Lanesboro.
Stevens, Rebecca L.	Hanley Falls.
Svarstad, Andreas	Bath, S. Dak.
Svarstad, Martha Karine	Bath, S. Dak.
Swennumson, Marie	Park River, N. Dak.
Thoreson, Ole	Woodville, Wis.
Thorstensen, Anna	Hanley Falls.
Vangen, Christine	Cannon Falls.

Page from 1889-90 Catalogue

taken too literally. Since there was no music department as such, the names are of those students taking piano and voice lessons. They may also suggest an early public relations effort by a young institution eager to advertise an attractive pursuit like music. The 1889-90 catalog even went so far as to list "A Course in Music" as a third course of study available after "The English Course" and "The Classical Course." As one reads the description, however, it is clear that the course in music is a supplementary option, not on the same level as the other two courses. The notice of such a course was dropped the next year. Even so, the description is worth quoting for the view of music it sets out and the announced intention to upgrade vocal music at the College:

> Music is one of the most important elements in modern civilization and culture, and this course aims to cultivate a taste for good music, and to give pupils a knowledge of the theory, as well as a thorough training in playing the piano or organ. This course may be taken alone, or in conjunction with studies in the two preceding courses, but it is not regarded as an equivalent for any study in those courses, all of which must be taken in order to graduate. Vocal music is also taught, and it is expected that this department will be extended next year by the appointment of a special teacher of vocal culture.[33]

When the College hired John Dahle in the fall of 1890, it was making good on the above announcement. The student paper expressed pleasure at his coming, hailing his reputation and noting his work in preparing music books and in editing *Musik Tidende* (Music Times).[34]

John Dahle was a leader in church music in Norwegian Lutheran circles before F. Melius Christiansen came on the scene.[35] He assumed a leading role in the Choral Union, an organization that would bring many church choirs together for song festivals. He has been described as "teacher, editor, composer, director and general promoter of excellence in church music and of all that was good and praiseworthy in our heritage of Norwegian song and music."[36]

Dahle and Christiansen had common interests in arranging songs for choirs and promoting the use of better hymns in

John Dahle

St. Olaf Band, June 1892
John Dahle to far left

the Lutheran churches.[37] In his second year at St. Olaf, 1891-92, Dahle taught singing, Norwegian, and organ.[38] He was the first to lead the St. Olaf Band when it was organized in the fall of 1891.[39] When "The United Norwegian Lutheran Singers Union" was organized in Minneapolis in January of 1892, John Dahle was elected its musical director.[40] Dahle left St. Olaf later that year to teach music and Norwegian at Concordia College in Moorhead, Minnesota.[41] At the end of his career he was director of church music at Luther Theological Seminary in St. Paul, Minnesota.[42]

Another part of the music program at St. Olaf in its first decades was instruction in singing given to entire classes. A statement in the catalog for 1887-88 and repeated in successive issues mentions private instruction in vocal and instrumental music (Piano and Organ), practical harmony, and adds the following: "Besides the private instruction, the elements of note reading and singing have been taught, free to all students, twice a week."[43] It is not until 1891-92, however, that "Singing" begins to appear in the official listing of "Courses of Study." There it is listed with other academic courses as given two hours a week all three terms, fall, winter, and spring, and to all classes, both in the College and the Academy.[44]

A few additional music teachers may be mentioned among those who served on the faculty prior to the coming of F. Melius Christiansen. In 1893-94 two new names on the faculty roster are Caroline Annette Finseth, Piano, and Haldor Hanson, Violin and Vocal Music. Again, one must note their special training. Miss Finseth had studied at St. Olaf for two years before taking one year at the Northwestern Conservatory of Music in

Caroline Finseth

Haldor Hanson

Minneapolis where she studied piano under Carl V. Lachmund. Finseth taught at Concordia College for a year, then went to New York for another year of study with Professor Lachmund who had moved to a conservatory of music in that city.[45]

Hanson was a graduate of Luther College with additional study in music in Chicago and Germany. Before St. Olaf he taught music at Willmar Academy and Luther College. While teaching at St. Olaf he lived in Minneapolis where he organized the Bach Choral Association.[46] Hanson's appointment meant adding violin instruction to the music offerings and the re-organization of an orchestra in the fall of 1893.[47]

Mathilda Finseth

In 1896 Mathilda Finseth took over as piano instructor. She continued the next two years, being joined in 1897 by Ditman Larsen as vocal instructor and in 1898 by Vigleik Boe who assumed the vocal duties. Martha Larson began as piano instructor in 1899 and Oluf Glasoe returned to teach vocal music.[48] During the two years before the arrival of F. Melius Christiansen in 1903, the College was increasing the size of the teaching force engaged in music. In addition to Larson and Glasoe one finds such names as Ella Louise Himle and Mary L. Gray, voice

Ditman Larsen

Thonny Felland

culture, Thonny G. Felland and Lizzie Nelson, piano, and A. Onstad, Director of Band.[49]

Thonny Felland, Class of 1906, was the first graduate in the College department of music. Many years later Miss Felland would have Paul J. Christiansen, son of F. Melius, as one of her piano students. It may be noted that the 1902-03 catalog includes among faculty members Paul G. Schmidt, M.A., Mathematics and Greek, the man who played a central role in securing the services for St. Olaf College of F. Melius Christiansen.

Student initiatives: Orchestra and Band

The sketch above of music activity involving faculty and courses of instruction bears out in large part P. G. Schmidt's observation that there was no lack of interest in vocal and instrumental music at St. Olaf when he arrived even if there was no music department. But as he also knew, the interest was not limited to what the College could offer. The students did much on their own to promote and enjoy music. It was true at St. Olaf as at many other small colleges that musical organizations, along with literary societies and athletic associations, "would not have come into existence except for the initiative of the students themselves."[50] Regarding this spontaneous springing up of different types of student music organizations, Carl A. Mellby wrote: "All these were managed by the students themselves and served to bring something of beauty and variety into an otherwise bare and prosaic school routine."[51]

The students tried to start an Orchestra in the beginning of the 1886-87 school year by taking subscriptions and receiving "the proceeds of a sociable." Progress was slow since only two of the members had ever handled their assigned instruments before. After Christmas the second violin player did not return to school. Nevertheless, the student paper reported that "they have acquitted themselves very successfully" and expressed the hope that "the St. Olaf Orchestra will have a very successful future."[52] In the spring of 1888 the Orchestra played a number at the May 17th evening entertainment.

The Orchestra was reorganized with C. J. Rollefson as its leader in 1888. The group played numbers on Foundation Day, November 6, 1889, but lapsed into inactivity for a time. When John Dahle came to teach vocal music in 1890, a *Messenger* writer hoped that he might revive interest in the

Orchestra and wake it "out of its long, but we hope refreshing, stupor."[53] Another reorganization took place in 1892 and the following year Haldor Hanson, teacher of violin and vocal music, assumed leadership.[54]

The 18-piece Orchestra activated in 1894 had E. Molstad as director and Prof. Hanson as its instructor. In the spring the Orchestra served a benefit supper from which it realized about $10.00. Said the *Messenger*: "The orchestra has been making some great strides forward and is deserving of all the encouragement it can get." Among other performances in 1894 the Orchestra played "Hunter's March" by Faust at the Twentieth Anniversary of the founding of the College on November 6, 1894.[55]

After the 1895-96 school year began, the *Messenger* reported: "The Band and Orchestra have both begun practicing and again Manitou Heights resounds with music. The prospects are better than ever, and with a little encouragement we will have some musical organizations of which we may justly feel proud."[57] Despite such hopes and sporadic efforts by various persons, the Orchestra in that era did not reach the stability and popularity enjoyed by the Band.

Orchestra, 1902

By all accounts the St. Olaf Band, organized in 1891 as the St. Olaf College Cornet Band, was the most important of the student-led music organizations. Notice of its founding appeared in the *Messenger* in October, 1891:

> The students here have organized a brass band, styled the St. Olaf College Cornet Band. The band has fourteen members, who practice four times a week. This band should have been started long ago; and now that it is started, all should give it their hearty support.[58]

It is well known that when F. Melius Christiansen came to St. Olaf in 1903 he took as his first project the improving of the Band. Decades later, while serving as guest conductor of the St. Olaf Band, he told its members, much to their delight, that the Band was his first love.[59]

About two months after the initial announcement about the organizing of the Cornet Band, the *Manitou Messenger* reported its progress and expressed hope for further improvement:

> This band was organized at the beginning of this term and has since been practicing regularly, and from the progress made and the music they are already able to render, we feel confident that it will be a success. This is the first effort made to organize a band here, and we hope that it will continue, and if possible improve from year to year. Under the able leadership of Prof. Dahle, we hope that by the time the trees leaf and the flowers bloom we shall have the pleasure of attending open air concerts given by the St. Olaf College Cornet Band.[60]

References to the St. Olaf Band in the student paper are frequent in the decade of the 1890s. An editorial in November 1891 notes that the Band furnished the music for the first part of the November 6th anniversary program. "Bearing in mind that this is our first band, and that it has been organized but a short time, one must admit that the selections were very well rendered."[61] A later article about the Band describes it as "the only permanent musical organization at the school" and "the outgrowth of student enterprise and enthusiasm." Student Ingebret Lee was "the moving spirit" in the organizing but, as implied above, the students asked Prof. Dahle to direct them.[62]

Three faculty persons were "admitted into the band" in the spring of 1892.[63] The Band played at "an entertainment given by the choir of St. John's Church," April 7, 1892, and furnished the music on Decoration Day.[64] Still rehearsing four times a week, the Band gave a concert in the city park in Northfield in the spring of 1893.[65] A unique kind of performance, to be repeated in later years, was the Band's part in getting the *Syttende mai* festivities off to a rousing start in the early morning hours of May 17, 1894. The Band "spent the time between four and six o'clock a.m., in the tower of the college building, flooding the city with sweet music, which brought the people to their feet earlier than usual."[66] In April of 1895 the Band was "quite an attraction" when it practiced its marching on the campus.[67]

A clear sign that "the St. Olaf Cornet Band has become a permanent organization at the institution" was its regular appearance as part of Commencement festivities. Said the *Messenger* in June 1895: "The concert given by the St. Olaf cornet band was the first reminder that Commencement had really begun."[68] With the Band as the leading musical group, Commencements were beginning to assume a pattern in which musical performances were prominent and expected features. One year, for example, Friday evening was given to vocal music and Saturday evening to instrumental music. On Sunday was Baccalaureate with Commencement on Monday morning.[69]

"The band is making great progress," declared the *Messenger* in 1894, "and with a little encouragement we will have a band second to no college band in the state."[70] When the College celebrated its twenty-first anniversary in November of 1895, the *Messenger* announced: "The St. Olaf band, which has become an indispensable feature on all festive occasions at the college, furnished music in the afternoon and evening."[71]

St. Olaf Band, ca. 1898
Andrew Onstad in dark suit

In 1897 it is stated that "the brass band is continuing its work with unabated zeal and success." In the listing of the eighteen members, the first named is Andrew Onstad whose instrument was the Solo B flat Clarinet. The same issue of the student paper states that Mr. Onstad, as usual, made a "hit" with his clarinet, performing "Eighth Air Varie" by Thornton to the pleasure of the audience.[72]

As a student Andrew Onstad directed the Band during the 1898-99 school year,

Andrew Onstad

83

including an open air concert in the park on a Saturday evening in June. In December it was announced that the College had secured Onstad's services as director of the Band.[73] Thus he is listed in the 1900-01 St. Olaf Catalogue among the instructors as "Director of Band." He would remain in charge until 1903, the year Christiansen joined the faculty.[74]

The *Messenger* ran a picture of the Band in the June 1897 issue. It also reviewed the humble beginnings of the organization and the "clamores dissonor" in its first attempts to perform. "In spite of difficulties," said the article, "one of the most serious being the lack of a musical director to take it in charge, the band has grown and improved until we now have a band which is a credit to the institution."[75] Granting that the Band would receive a dramatic new lease on life when F. Melius Christiansen became its director, it is fitting to recall the determined spirit and hard work of the Band members and directors from 1891 to 1903, and to be aware of the enthusiastic support that the organization received from the students during those first dozen years.

Student Initiative: Vocal Groups

"A marked increase of interest in vocal music has been noticed this year," stated the *Manitou Messenger* in February of 1888. "The singers are represented by the Kjerulf Club, a male choir; the Bivrost, a mixed choir; and the Glee Club, all of which are doing well. This is due in a great measure to the efforts of Mr. Glasoe, the able leader of Bivrost and the Kjerulf Club, and Mr. Rollefson, leader of the Glee Club. We hope the interest aroused may be long-lived."[76]

Oluf Glasoe's appointment in 1887 added the services of a voice instructor to the vocal work that previously had fallen to the preceptresses. C. J. Rollefson was a versatile presence on the campus, playing violin solos, reorganizing the Orchestra, and now leading the Glee Club. He was one of the first three persons to receive the Bachelor of Arts degree in 1890 when the first College class graduated.

The students at St. Olaf's School certainly had opportunities for singing in the early decades. The student group that organized in 1875 and actually called itself the "St. Olaf Choir" has been mentioned as an early effort. The singing organizations named above, Kjerulf, Bivrost, and the Glee Club, are the groups most frequently spoken of in the College newspaper in the late eighties and early nineties. But there were others, identified generically as "chorus" or "male chorus" or "the choir," that came and went. At closing exercises in the spring of 1887 "a song by the choir greeted our ears," writes a student reporter, and another song by the choir preceded Agnes Mellby's valedictory.[77]

First College Class, 1890
C. J. Rollefson, A. O. Sandbo, Anton Engebretson

Described earlier as "a male choir," the Kjerulf Club was a double quartet, often named Kjerulf Quartet up to 1890 but thereafter called the Kjerulf Octet. The name "Kjerulf," it may be recalled, is from the Norwegian composer Halfdan Kjerulf (1815-1868) whose repertory of Norwegian songs for male voices inspired the establishing of many amateur singing societies in Norwegian-American communities.[78] While in Minneapolis, F. Melius Christiansen was the director of the Kjerulf Club organized in that city by men who enjoyed the sociability of speaking Norwegian and singing Norwegian songs.[79]

The St. Olaf Kjerulf Club was in existence as early as 1887 when the *Messenger* explained that "Kjerulf Club is the name of the double quartet." The club sang a number on the Sixth of November, Foundation or Founders' Day, 1887.[80] It was heard from again at a musical entertainment February 20, 1888, when it sang "Valdrisvisen" ("Valdres Song") and "'Dans,' raabte felen" ("'Dance,' cried the fiddle"). Inevitably, it was part of the Norwegian Independence Day program on May 17th, singing "Norge, Bedste Vern og Faeste" ("Norway, Best Defense and Stronghold"). Also performing were the Bivrost Club, the Glee Club, and a group of twenty male voices called Orpheus which was "a choir organized for the occasion," ostensibly for the purpose of singing the Norwegian national anthem, "Ja, vi elsker dette landet."[81] Usually the *Messenger* reporters made generous comments about the various singing groups, but in one instance the writer allowed a hint of tedium to slip in. A cantata entitled "The Rainbow" was performed as part of commencement festivities in June 1888 by eight young ladies. Seven of them, representing different hues of the rainbow, "sang severally and in chorus" of how each color beautified God's universe. Then the eighth lady, their mother, had her lengthy role to sing. Wrote the *Messenger*: "The rendering of this piece took over half an hour, yet it was thoroughly appreciated from beginning to end."[82]

Kjerulf Club, 1891
John Dahle fifth from right

The Kjerulf Club performed often on campus. It also went out to the rural Holden parish to take part in an "entertainment" in May of 1890, and in June of 1892, as the Kjerulf Octet, made a tour of Goodhue County. The *Messenger* gave it very high praise in 1892, calling it "the best musical organization at the College" and noting that the Octet, together with the Sunday School Choir, would be representing St. Olaf at a song fest to be held in Minneapolis.[83]

The Bivrost mixed choir had a rather short life, at least under that name, and the same was true of the Glee Club, which was active in the early nineties, seemed to drop out of sight, but was heard from again in the early twentieth century when it was the Senior Glee Club. Bivrost contributed numbers at a musical entertainment in February of 1888. Still directed by Oluf Glasoe, the group sang "Takker vor Gud" ("We thank our God") at graduation exercises for the preparatory department or academy June 20, 1888.[84] As the Bivrost choir disappears in about 1888, other vocal groups step forward with names such as college choir, college male chorus, Ladies'

Ladies' Octette, June 13, 1892

Chorus, and Ladies' Octette. In early 1892 the members of the Bible class organized their own choir of thirty members which they sent to the convention in Minneapolis of the newly-founded United Norwegian Lutheran Singers' Union.[85]

Apparently it was an ad hoc glee club that sang in June of 1887 at an entertainment on the evening of Commencement Day because the next fall a glee club of eight members was organized by C. J. Rollefson. By February of 1888 the Glee Club had increased its membership to twelve singers. It sang "The Young Lover" at a May 17th program in 1888.[86] As suggested, singing groups came and went, with or without specific names. A Ladies' Chorus is mentioned in 1889 and in 1891 the student paper acknowledges The Ladies' Octette with the hearty wish, "May it live and prosper."[87]

But a *Messenger* editorial in 1894 worried that vocal music was on the decline. There seemed to be justification for the concern. A summary of vocal activities earlier in the year, while intending to sound optimistic, spoke only of the Bible Class Choir and "several octettes and society quartettes."[88] The editor noted that whenever special music was needed, a quartette, sextette or octette hastily would be put together, with unsatisfactory results. "We remember the old Kjerulf octette. It used to be the octette of the college." Why cannot there be something similar? The concluding thought was that with the Band and Orchestra flourishing, "something ought to be done to furnish vocal music more frequently."[89]

Students Ditman Larsen and Andrew Onstad took up the challenge. In 1895 Larsen led a male octette and a mixed octette while Onstad was the director of another mixed octette.[90] Two years later the St. Olaf Male Chorus of twelve members and the Orpheus Mixed Chorus are said to be in the charge of Larsen while the Manitou Octette was led by Onstad.[91] The male chorus sang a humorous song at a Washington's birthday observance in 1897. At commencement exercises in June of that year the same group sang "Zions Vaegter" by Phillip Nicolai, a number the St. Olaf Choir would perform year after year as "Wake, Awake," in an arrangement by F. Melius Christiansen.[92]

Two more vocal activities, the St. John's Church Choir and the Choral Union, require only brief mention here since both belong to the beginnings of the St. Olaf Choir, to be discussed in the next chapter. Their relevance for the present chapter is that both contributed to the development of vocal and choral music at St. Olaf College before F. Melius Christiansen joined the faculty.

St. Olaf students worshipped with the St. John's congregation and sang in the church choir under such leaders from St. Olaf as Margaret O'Brien, John Dahle, Oluf Glasoe, and Vigleik Boe.[93] Once settled in Northfield, F. Melius Christiansen would be asked to direct the choir at St. John's.

The Choral Union had its own history among the Norwegian Lutheran churches in the upper midwest before a singing group by this name was organized at St. Olaf College. John Dahle was elected music director of the United Norwegian Lutheran Singers' Union in 1892, and before long F. Melius Christiansen exerted leadership in this endeavor. The Choral Union organized at St. Olaf by Oluf Glasoe in 1899 was destined to play a role in the genesis of the St. Olaf Choir.

The examples above have been offered to indicate the lively activity in music that marked the life of students at St. Olaf College in the years prior to F. Melius Christiansen's joining the faculty in 1903. To this record of participation in musical activities, instrumental as well as vocal, may be added excerpts from two *Manitou Messenger* pieces in which the writers reflected seriously on the importance of music at the College. The first selection is from an article entitled simply "Music" by Ditman Larsen, instructor of vocal music. He wrote of music as the language of the emotions, of music in nature, and music as "a gift of inestimable value" from the Creator. No musical instrument can be compared with the human voice, the noblest instrument of all that is given to nearly all people. "What a great blessing is music to the world. . . . It is our duty to develop our musical faculty and use it for good," wrote Larsen.[94]

St. Olaf Faculty, June 6, 1904. Christiansen third from right in front

The author of the second piece was very likely Michael Stolee '97, chief editor of the *Messenger* during the 1896-97 school year. The thrust of his argument was that music deserves a place in a liberal education. He deplored the materialistic preference for studies designed for success in practical business "while those studies which cultivate and draw out the best sentiments in man's nature do not receive a due attention." He was referring to music and singing which, too often, are regarded as "an educational luxury rather than as a means of education, like any other branch in a school's curriculum." Schools ought to employ salaried teachers to make instruction in music and singing accessible to all. He added that immigrants should enrich the life of America with the musical literature of the countries of their ancestors. "Efforts and expenses contributed for this purpose will pay well for this and probably for coming generations."[95]

Both sets of ideas were in harmony with and prophetic of the musical philosophy implemented by F. Melius Christiansen when he came to St. Olaf a few years later. He would contend for the intrinsic value of music as an art, and in a short time would persuade the faculty to make courses in music a regular part of the St. Olaf curriculum.[96]

1. *Manitou Messenger* (*MM*) XXXIII (May 11, 1920), 1.

2. David Nelson, *Luther College* 1861-1961 (Decorah, Iowa: Luther College Press, 1961), 49, 56-57, 268.

3. Carl Chrislock, *From Fjord to Freeway*: 100 Years - Augsburg College (Minneapolis: Augsburg College, 1969), 27; Eugene L. Fevold, *The Lutheran Free Church*: A Fellowship of American Lutheran Congregatins 1897-1963 (Minneapolis: Augsburg Publishing House, 1969), 158.

4. "St. Olaf's School, en evangelisk luttersk Höiskole i Northfield, Minn.," pamphlet printed in Decorah, Iowa, 1875, inside front cover.

5. *Catalogue of St. Olaf College* for 1889-90 (Northfield, Minn.: Published by the College, 1890), 26.

6. *Ibid.*, 27.

7. F. Melius Christiansen, "The Choir," unpublished typescript, 1929, 3. STOARCHIV.

8. *Ibid.*

9. Cited in Leola Nelson Bergmann, *Music Master of the Middle West*: The Story of F. Melius Christiansen and the St. Olaf Choir (Minneapolis: University of Minnesota Press, 1944), 93.

10. Paul G. Schmidt, *My Years at St. Olaf*, A Centennial Decade Publication (Northfield, Minnesota: St. Olaf College, [1967]), 27.

11. William C. Benson, *High on Manitou*: A History of St. Olaf College 1874-1949 (Northfield, Minnesota: The St. Olaf College Press, 1949), 174; Eugene E. Simpson, *A History of St. Olaf Choir* (Minneapolis: Augsburg Publishing House, 1921), 57.

12. Benson, *High on Manitou*, 139.

13. Simpson, *History of St. Olaf Choir*, 18, 35.

14. *Ibid.*, 27, 31.

15. Anna E. Mohn, "De første aar ved St. Olaf College," *Samband* 98 (June 1916), 487-88.

16. *Ibid.*, 96 (April 1916), 342.

17. Anna E. Mohn, "Reminiscences," *MM* XX (April 1906), 27; cf. Anna E. Mohn, "De første aar ved St. Olaf College," *Samband* 99 (July 1916), 564.

18. *MM* I (March 1887), 6.

19. Anna E. Mohn, "De første aar," *Samband* 98 (June 1916), 487.

20. *Annual Catalogue of the Officers and Students of St. Olaf's School* for 1884-85 (Northfield, Minn., 1885), 16.

21. Benson, 41.

22. Mohn, "De første aar," *Samband* 99 (July 1916), 568.

23. Schmidt, 28.

24. *Catalogue of St. Olaf's School* for 1884-85, 7; Simpson, 35; Oscar R. Overby, "Music in St. John's," *A Brief History of St. John's Lutheran Church* on the occasion of its Seventy-Fifth Anniversary, 1869-1944, (Northfield, Minnesota, 1944), 31-32.

25. Simpson, 35.

26. *Ibid.*, 32.

27. Simpson, 34; Schmidt, 28; Joseph M. Shaw, *History of St. Olaf College 1874-1974* (Northfield, Minnesota: The St. Olaf College Press, 1974), 54.

28. *Catalogue of St. Olaf's School* for 1884-85, 19-20.

29. *MM* XIX (October 1905), 135.

30. *MM* I (June 1887), 1.

31. *MM* I (November 1887), 4.

32. *Catalogue of St. Olaf's School* for 1884-85, 18.

33. *Catalogue of St. Olaf College* for 1889-90, 27.

34. *MM* V (February 1891), 25.

35. Leola Nelson Bergmann, "F. Melius Christiansen: A Study of his life and work as a Norwegian-American contribution to American Culture," A dissertation submitted in partial fulfillment of the requirements for the degree of Doctor of Philosophy, in the Department of English, in the Graduate College of the State University of Iowa," July, 1942, 80.

36. J. C. K. Preus, *The History of the Choral Union of the Evangelical Lutheran Church 1847-1960* (Minneapolis: Augsburg Publishing House, 1961), 7.

37. Bergmann, *Music Master of the Middle West,* 64, 107.

38. *Catalogue of St. Olaf College* for 1892-93, 5.

39. *MM* V (December 1891), 145.

40. *MM* VI (February 1892), 26.

41. *MM* VI (October 1892), 97.

42. Preus, *History of the Choral Union*, 88, 91.

43. *Catalogue of St. Olaf's School* for 1887-88, 24.

44. *Catalogue of St. Olaf College* for 1891-92, 12-14.

45. *Catalogue of St. Olaf College* for 1893-94, 29.

46. Preus, 16.

47. *MM* VII (December 1893), 128.

48. *Catalogue of St. Olaf College* for 1899-1900, 4-5.

49. *Catalogue of St. Olaf College* for 1901-02, 7; *Catalogue of St. Olaf College* for 1902-03, 7.

50. Benson, 150.

51. C. A. Mellby, *Saint Olaf College Through Fifty Years 1874-1924* (Northfield, Minnesota, 1925), 57.

52. *MM* I (January 1887), 6.

53. *MM* V (February 1891), 25.

54. *MM* II (January 1888), 9; *MM* III (November 1889), 98; *MM* VI (February 1892), 25; *MM* VII (December 1893), 128.

55. *MM* VIII (January 1894), 12; *MM* VIII (May 1894), 76, 115.

56. *MM* IX (February 1895), 28.

57. *MM* IX (October 1895), 107.

58. *MM* V (October 1891), 115.

59. Donald Lomen '50, in *St. Olaf Band, 1891-1981 Centennial Reunion Book.*

60. *MM* V (December 1891), 145.

61. *MM* V (November 1891), 128.

62. *MM* XI (June 1897), 113.

63. *MM* VI (March 1892), 42.

64. *MM* VI (April 1892), 59; *MM* VI (May 1892), 71.

65. *MM* VII (March 1893), 34; *MM* VII (June 1893), 92.

66. *MM* VIII (May 1894), 76.

67. *MM* IX (April 1895), 58.

68. *MM* IX (June 1895), 83.

69. *MM* VI (May 1892), 74.

70. *MM* VIII (May 1894), 77.

71. *MM* IX (November 1895), 114.

72. *MM* XI (February 1897), 31, 34.

73. *MM* XIII (June 1899), 98; *MM* XIII (December 1899), 169.

74. *Catalogue of St. Olaf College* for 1900-01, 5; Schmidt, 27.

75. *MM* XI (June 1897), 113.

76. *MM* II (February 1888), 18.

77. *MM* I (June 1897), 2.

78. Albert Rykken Johnson, "The Christiansen Choral Tradition: F. Melius Christiansen, Olaf C. Christiansen, and Paul J. Christiansen," A thesis submitted in partial fulfillment of the requirements for the Degree of Doctor of Philosolphy in the School of Music in the Graduate College of The University of Iowa, July, 1973, 86.

79. Bergmann, *Music Master of the Middle West*, 78-79.

80. *MM* I (November 1887), 10, 4).

81. *MM* II (February 1888), 17-18; *MM* II (May 1888), 65, 75.

82. *MM* II (June 1888), 82.

83. *MM* IV (May 1890), 75; *MM* VI (June 1892), 90-91.

84. *MM* II (February 1888), 17; *MM* II (June 1888), 82.

85. *MM* VI (March 1892), 41.

86. *MM* II (February 1888), 26; *MM* II (May 1888), 75.

87. *MM* V (May 1891), 74; cf. *MM* VI (April 1892), 59.

88. *MM* VIII (June 1894), 83.

89. *MM* VIII (December 1894), 131.

90. *MM* IX (January 1895), 12.

91. *MM* XI (February 1897), 31.

92. *MM* XI (June 1897), 110.

93. Oscar R. Overby, "Music in St. John's," Northfield, 1944, 32-33.

94. *MM* XI (January 1897), 9.

95. *MM* XI (February 1897), 22-23.

96. Benson, 139.

CHAPTER 4

THE CHOIR IS BORN

The St. Olaf Choir had its official beginning in the spring of 1912 when the St. John's Church Choir took the name, the St. Olaf Choir, as it embarked upon its first longer tour, a journey into Wisconsin and Illinois. The year before, the Choir had given a memorable concert in the Congregational Church in Northfield, and some additional concerts in and around Northfield in the spring. The Choir's personnel at the time included, in addition to students, some adult members of St. John's Lutheran Church, most of them St. Olaf teachers and their wives. On May 4, 1911, the members presented their director, F. Melius Christiansen, with a gold watch on which were

Congregational Church, 1910
Third and Union Streets, Northfield

St. Olaf Mixed Octet, 1908
Men, from left: Joseph Tetlie, J. Jørgen Thompson, F. M. Christiansen,
Henry Langum, Oscar Hertsgaard
Women, from left clockwise: Stella Sogn, Mabel Locken, Caroline Heltne,
Gusta Locken

engraved the words, "St. John's Church Choir, May 4, 1911." Once when asked how the St. Olaf Choir began, Christiansen took out this gold watch, opened the back, and displayed the inscription. "This," he said, "was the beginning of the choir."[1]

If members of the St. Olaf Octet of 1908 had been asked about the beginning of the St. Olaf Choir, they would have brought out their inscribed picture of the Mixed Octet on which F. Melius Christiansen, the director, had written the words, "The first St. Olaf Choir." Yet those words do not settle the matter.

Before the Beginning

It is fitting, then, that Christiansen's biographer, Leola Bergmann, should name several strands making up the material from which the St. Olaf Choir was formed. Each will deserve further comment. One was the St. John's Choir which had its own history reaching back at least to 1875.

Another was the series of song services developed and presented by F. Melius Christiansen in collaboration with the president of St. Olaf, John Nathan Kildahl. A third strand was the impact of a tour made by the St. Olaf Octet in 1908. As a fourth Bergmann speaks of Christiansen's artistic growth as composer and director.[2] To these four should be added his leadership of the St. Olaf Band and his involvement in the Choral Union movement.

For a period of some forty years, the St. John's Choir was a mix of St. Olaf students and older members of the congregation, and during those decades it frequently engaged directors who were either students or music teachers at St. Olaf. One recalls such names as Margaret O'Brien, John Dahle, and Oluf Glasoe. P. G. Schmidt, a fine musician though not a music teacher, was the director for a time, being asked at a congregational meeting of St. John's members on October 25, 1904, to continue as leader of the congregation's choir during the coming year.[3]

F. Melius Christiansen did not move his family to Northfield until the fall of 1904.[4] He was taken into membership at St. John's on September 1, 1905, and asked to direct the choir very soon thereafter.[5] The *Northfield News* for October 7, 1905, carried the following information: "Professor Christiansen has just organized a choir of fifty voices for St. John's congregation. The practices are held Sunday morning at 9 o'clock at the church."[6]

According to an item in June of 1906 in the St. Olaf student newspaper, the *Manitou Messenger*, the church choir had thrived under its new leader. It had spent a social evening at the home of the pastor and his wife, the Reverend and Mrs. G. A. Larsen. The article continues: "The choir has done faithful work during the year and the congregation has enjoyed their good singing under the leadership of Prof. Christiansen. The pastor expressed his appreciation of their work and took this opportunity to thank the singers and their able leader."[7] The St. John's Church Choir was the most immediate precursor of the St. Olaf Choir.

Another factor pointing ahead to the birth of the Choir was a unique kind of song service developed by Professor Christiansen and President J. N. Kildahl. These presentations, called in Norwegian *sanggudstjenester*, featured chorales interspersed with sermonic comments by President Kildahl, regarded as one of the most forceful and effective preachers of his day. "By weaving phrases of the hymn through his talk," explains Bergmann, "Kildahl prepared the congregation for the chorale which the choir was to sing."[8]

The surprising impact of the first of these song services was described by P. M. Glasoe, one of Christiansen's faculty colleagues and a long-time

Paul M. Glasoe

partner with him in the Choral Union movement. Glasoe relates that the annual conference of the United Norwegian Lutheran Church of America met on the St. Olaf campus in the spring of 1907, using the relatively new Hoyme Memorial Chapel which seated a thousand persons. A concert was scheduled for Saturday evening, but since the school year was over, the student musical organizations were not available and most of the students had gone home for the summer. But Professor Christiansen was able to put together a chorus of forty voices made up of students and faculty members. He prepared them to sing a program of church hymns, contrapuntally arranged. Glasoe continues:

> There were no new or strange hymns among them—they were the very hymns we sang every Sunday in our churches. After each hymn Dr. J. N. Kildahl spoke briefly, touching upon the text just sung and introducing the theme of the next. Scarcely ever has such a response been registered; the air was tense and electric with feeling.[9]

That was the beginning of the series of *sanggudstjenester* that were printed in pamphlet form and proved to be very popular among the Norwegian-American congregations. The St. Olaf Mixed Octet that toured in the summer of 1908 sang many of the hymns from Song Services 1, 2, and 3. "The effect on the audiences was spontaneous," wrote Dr. Glasoe, "and the result of this trip was to bring a settled conviction into Dr. Christiansen's mind that the Lutheran chorale was choir material that gripped the heart of our people."[10]

These song services were held at the College or at St. John's Lutheran Church from 1907 to 1914. All seven were published, Nos. 1 and 3

First Song Service

in several editions. Here one would find several of Christiansen's well-known arrangements, such as "Beautiful Savior," "Wake, Awake," "Built on a Rock," "O Bread of Life," and "Praise to the Lord."[11]

The first three in the series were in Norwegian. From No. 4 and on each published booklet is called *Song-Service* with the texts of all the musical arrangements in English. There are no printed meditations. In his Preface to No. 4 Christiansen wrote, "The songs in this pamphlet should be supplemented by a short sermon on repentance and the love of God. Two or three hymns sung by the congregation and accompanied by the organ should be added."[12] These pamphlets were the forerunner of the St. Olaf Choir Series that began in 1919.[13] Their reception demonstrated the growing appeal of choral music in Norwegian Lutheran church circles.

Another precursor of the St. Olaf Choir was the St. Olaf Octet that went on tour in 1908, with F. Melius Christiansen as director. At a faculty meeting March 26, 1908 Christiansen had suggested "that something should be done toward making the college better known among the patrons of the school, that, for example, an octet might be organized to visit the congregations during the summer vacation."[14] A mixed octet was selected under the management of J. Jørgen Thompson and trained to demonstrate the singing of the Lutheran chorales. It was also decided to have the Octet raise money for a pipe organ at the College.

The singers gave sixty-two concerts in Minnesota, South Dakota, and Iowa. In Ellsworth, Iowa, the Octet took part in a Choral Union festival at which Christiansen directed a chorus of some 150 voices. It made a very favorable impression when it sang morning and afternoon programs at a

chatauqua in Ames, Iowa.[15] According to the member who wrote up the tour in *The Manitou Messenger*, the Octet appeared before some 20,000 people, singing "the stately old chorales rendered in the light of Prof. Christiansen's interpretation."[16] The net sum raised for the organ was only $400, but the tour was another illustration of how tours could serve both the College and the cause of music.[17]

Christiansen's growth as composer and also as director was another of the intermingling strands that went into "the cloth from which the St. Olaf Choir was cut." As early as his choir directing experience in Marinette, Wisconsin, in

J. Jørgen Thompson

1890-92, he had turned to composing as a necessity since suitable choral music was in short supply.[18] Composing continued during the Minneapolis years. Christiansen and his friend Hans Urseth wrote "Velkomstsang" (Song of Welcome) for the May 17th celebration in 1894. As reported, the two worked together producing and publishing church music. Their collaboration continued after Urseth moved to Rochester, Minnesota.[19]

At St. Olaf Christiansen became prolific with arrangements and original compositions. After leading the St. Olaf Band on its tour to Norway in 1906, Christiansen went to Leipzig for ten months of intensive work during which he wrote new harmonies for some seventy familiar chorales. Back in Northfield he developed the seven Song-Services which included forty-four of his choral arrangements. In them Bergmann sees "a striking progress from a simple contrapuntal style toward the more complex arrangements of his 'developed chorales.'" In 1910 he began publishing a series of "easy lyric-religious songs" which in a few years would number fifty-two original songs for mixed choir.[20]

The Ladies' Chorus, 1909

All the while his growth in confidence and authority as a director was assured by his heavy schedule and his restless drive for self-improvement. At St. John's Lutheran Church he was in charge of the choir. On the campus he directed the Choral Union which worked on such pieces as Cherubini's "Requiem Mass in C Minor" and Josef Haydn's "Creation." He also devoted time to the 1908 Mixed Octet. In 1909-10 Christiansen divided the Choral Union into a 45-voice Ladies' Chorus and a Male Chorus of 50 voices, directing both groups himself.[21]

There was more than enough to do in the choral activity that preceded the official beginning of the St. Olaf Choir, but Christiansen had devoted his first energies on his arrival at St. Olaf to raising the quality of the Band, his "first love."[22] After all, his first job in this country was that of a band director. He had the St. Olaf Band ready for a tour of Norway in 1906, the

The Male Chorus, 1909

first instance of a St. Olaf music organization making a concert tour abroad. The work with the Band expanded his experience as a musician and teacher of young people, preparing him indirectly but significantly for his coming role as director of the St. Olaf Choir.

"We have an organization among us called the Choral Union of the Norwegian Lutheran Church of America," wrote F. Melius Christiansen in 1939. "Its aim is to help the choirs of our congregations to do their work as effectively as possible by the use of good material and by choral concerts for their encouragement and inspiration."[23] Besides giving the purpose of the

The St. Olaf College Band, 1908

Choral Union, this statement indicates that it was still thriving nearly half a century after its beginnings among Norwegian church bodies. Christiansen would serve as director of the Choral Union of the United Norwegian Lutheran Church from 1911 to 1917 and of the Norwegian Lutheran Church of America from 1920 to 1946.[24]

While still living in Minneapolis in the decade of the 1890s, F. Melius Christiansen had contributed his talents to more than one Choral Union song festival as choir singers gathered in places like Eau Claire, Minneapolis, and Mankato to sing the music of the church. Throughout the Upper Midwest were numerous local and regional choral societies whose song festivals attracted thousands of participants. For example, 3,000 people gathered in O. K. Naeseth's grove southwest of Hader, Minnesota, on September 7, 1902, for the annual song festival of the United Singers of Goodhue County. Choirs from Vang, Gol, Holden, Dale, Zumbrota, and Minneola participated plus soloists, a duet, a quartet, and the Kenyon brass band.[25]

In addition to local and church-wide song festivals, the choral union spirit was given further impetus by articles in the church papers. F. Melius Christiansen was a frequent contributor. Of his work in this regard J. C. K. Preus has written:

> As might be expected, the person who contributed articles of most value to choirs and their directors was Prof. F. Melius Christiansen, the man who with unswerving purpose labored mightily to restore the chorale to its historic position of preeminence in the music of the Lutheran church. In time the influence of his work carried over into the program of the American college and high school choirs.[26]

An example of Christiansen's writing on behalf of improved church music appears in the paper *Lutheraneren* in 1904. He begins with a quotation from John Calvin that "the church music be not of a light and effervescent character; but that it be substantial and dignified." Christiansen then continues with his own comments. "Our chorales are the best congregational songs we possess; but they ought to be sung in the tempo of a normal pulse beat; otherwise, they will have a wearying effect." In the straightforward manner for which he was known, Christiansen deplores "the abundance of worthless song books currently in use among us" and appeals for greater use of the "more than three hundred simple religious songs, all of them gems" that are available.[27]

Another Christiansen article sets out three basic rules for good ensemble singing. First, agreement on the meaning of the words. Second, agreement as to the beginning and ending of sentences. The key is that all eyes be on the director. Third, proper balance between the four parts. In this article he also recommends separate practice periods for each of the four parts.[28] Through his leadership in the church-wide Choral Union movement, as writer as well as conductor, F. Melius Christiansen virtually served as music teacher for the entire constituency of the Norwegian Lutheran church bodies years before he founded the St. Olaf Choir.

St. Olaf singers had participated in some of the festivals of the United Norwegian Lutheran Church's Choral Union, but not until 1899 was a Choral Union established on the campus. Credited with organizing and leading the St. Olaf Choral Union was Oluf Glasoe, first hired as a voice teacher for the 1887-88 school year and returning to the faculty in 1900. In 1899, while teaching music at the United Norwegian Lutheran Church seminary in Minneapolis where he started a Choral Union, Glasoe also found time to come to Northfield to organize and train a choral group at St. Olaf.[29]

Oluf Glasoe led various vocal forces at the College until 1902. On Foundation Day 1900 he directed a mixed chorus. At Easter in 1901 he directed a choir that sang anthems with John Eltun as tenor soloist, and on May 24, 1902, a choral group he had trained presented Alfred Gaul's cantata, "The Holy City." The next director of the Choral Union was Carl A. Mellby who prepared and directed the presentation of Gaul's cantata, "The Ten Virgins," on May 18, 1903.[30]

The next one hears about the Choral Union, it is under the direction of F. Melius Christiansen, who joined the faculty in the fall of 1903. In anticipation of a Choral Union concert on December 7, the *Messenger* announced, "The Union has been working diligently under the leadership of Prof. Christiansen and a good entertainment is

Carl A. Mellby

anticipated." How diligently was reflected in the next issue of the student paper by the wry comment: "Members of the Choral Union declare that it is essentially a labor organization."[31] The work performed on December 7, 1903, was Schnecker's cantata, "The Fatherhood of God." During the concert the audience was made aware of the power of Christiansen's conducting. The *Northfield News* wrote of the impression he made as he directed the 90-voice Choral Union:

He not only carefully and ably directs, but is an inspiration to the chorus. It was an agreeable surprise and a gratifying sight to see what control he had over the chorus. Every eye was fixed on the baton.[32]

Scarcely pausing for breath, in January of 1904 Christiansen began rehearsing the Choral Union in Haydn's oratorio, *The Creation*, which was performed at St. Olaf's first annual May music festival May 17-18, 1904. Performers were over one hundred singers of the Union, thirty-five members of the Danz Symphony Orchestra of Minneapolis, and three soloists from the Twin Cities.[33] At the head of the executive committees that arranged this successful festival was none other than Paul G. Schmidt who in years to come would devote his superb managerial talents to the concerts and tours of the St. Olaf Choir.[34] At the

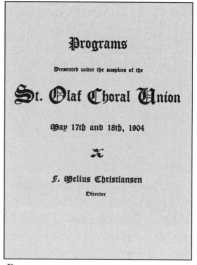

Programs

Presented under the auspices of the

St. Olaf Choral Union

May 17th and 18th, 1904

F. Melius Christiansen
Director

Program cover
May Music Festival, 1904

second May festival, in 1905, the Choral Union was supplemented by choirs from Duluth, Eau Claire, and Decorah and accompanied again by the Danz Orchestra from Minneapolis as it presented *The Messiah*.[35]

St. Olaf Choral Union and Band, Finseth Band Stand, St. Olaf Campus
May 17, 1911

The dividing of the Choral Union into a Ladies' Chorus and a Male Chorus in 1909 did not mean the end of performances by the combined group.[36] For example, it gave a concert with the St. Olaf Band in the Finseth Band Stand on campus on May 17, 1911.[37] Called at times the "Choral Society" or "the second choir," the Choral Union played an important role at the College and continued as a valuable aspect of choral work after it became the St. Olaf Church Choir, directed by Oscar R. Overby. The 1926-27 *Viking*, noting that the Choral Society that year was jointly led by Christiansen and Overby, explains how vital this group was to vocal training on the campus.

> Special emphasis has always been placed on the one most essential feature of ensemble music—intonation. In work of this kind the singer develops a sense of appreciation for the artistic fineness of pure tones, pure harmony and blend. . . . The St. Olaf Choral Society is essential to St. Olaf and exists on its own merits. It is open to a greater number than the choir, and from its constituency are selected the singers for the choir as vacancies occur.[38]

The Choral Union and its smaller successor, the St. Olaf Church Choir, both influenced by the choral principles of F. Melius Christiansen, were valued vocal resources on the campus that were bound to benefit the St. Olaf Choir. The same would be true in the future as such choral groups as the Chapel Choir, the Manitou Singers, the Viking Chorus, and the Cantorei achieved excellence in their own programs and provided the initial training for many students who became members of the St. Olaf Choir.

Choral Union, ca. 1925

The St. John's Church Choir, 1905-1911

The St. Olaf Choir was an outgrowth of the choir at St. John's Lutheran Church where most of the St. Olaf students and faculty members worshiped. As stated earlier, the choir at St. John's had often been directed by faculty members or students from St. Olaf, including P. G. Schmidt who served as director for a year or more in the early 1900s. While Schmidt does not mention this in his book, *My Years at St. Olaf,* he does report the interesting fact that the choir members themselves chose their director. He writes, "The unanimous choice of the choir members was Professor Christiansen and when he was interviewed he gladly accepted."[39]

Old St. John's Lutheran Church
Fourth and Washington Streets

Christiansen began his work with the St. John's choir in the fall of 1905, having become a member of the congregation on September 1, 1905. With his typical drive to improve the choir, he added students from the College to its ranks.

P. G. Schmidt describes how this change came about:

> Soon after he became director, Mr. Christiansen and I quite often conferred about the possibility and advisability of making some rather drastic changes for the choir's improvement. We both felt that, with so much youthful material available at the college, a larger organization of college students could render the congregation better service, and at the same time stimulate greater interest in our Lutheran choral heritage. President J. N. Kildahl, who then also was pastor of St. John's, concurred and gave wholehearted support.[40]

The choir gradually changed, wrote Schmidt, from a small group of fifteen elderly people to a larger organization of fifty young singers. The quality of its singing became known in Northfield and in neighboring towns. Part of its training during these formative years was its role, beginning in 1907, in presenting the important series of song services mentioned above. There were eleven choral numbers in the first service, all sung in Norwegian. Among those not already mentioned were "Lamb of God" and "Behold a Host." The 1908 *Sang-Gudstjeneste* included "O Sacred Head Now Wounded."[41]

Another part of the Choir's ripening process took place through the activity of the St. Olaf Ladies' and Male Choruses since the personnel of these groups was by and large identical with the membership of the St. John's Choir. Their performances at the College and elsewhere meant more experience under the guidance of Christiansen. The Male Chorus combined with the United Church Seminary Chorus in concerts at churches in St. Paul and Minneapolis. During Commencement week in 1910, the Ladies' and Male Choruses joined forces to present one of the Kildahl-Christiansen song-services.[42]

The event of particular significance for the formation of the St. Olaf Choir, however, was the bringing of the two groups together as the St. John's Church Choir for an important concert in the Congregational Church in Northfield on February 21, 1911. The program included organ works performed by Eulalie Chenevert, violin solos by Adolph Olsen, and vocal solos in the choral numbers by baritone Oscar Grønseth, all of the St. Olaf music faculty. The choir sang, in Norwegian, "O Sacred Head now wounded," "Behold a host arrayed in white," "Beautiful Savior," "Praise to the Lord," and "Today there is ringing," among other numbers. Sung in English were Conradi's "Alone with Thee" and "I know that my Redeemer liveth," from the Messiah.[43]

The entire concert was sung a cappella from memory. Among the singers in addition to the students were a few teachers from the College and adults from the congregation.[44] Although this concert took place a year before the St. Olaf Choir officially came into being, it belonged to the shaping of the new choral entity. There were other concerts by the St. John's Choir that spring. This was the choir, one recalls, which gave F. Melius Christiansen the gold watch engraved with "St. John's Church Choir, May 4, 1911."

The choir received requests to sing in nearby congregations. The idea of a tour was already familiar from the earlier Band, Octet, and Quartet tours and the choir's recent trips to neighboring communities. As P. G. Schmidt traveled about arranging concerts for the St. Olaf Band, he was told that people were interested in hearing the St. John's choir.

The St. Olaf Choir, 1912

The official beginning of the St. Olaf Choir is placed in the spring of 1912 when a tour was arranged for concerts in Wisconsin and Illinois. On January 18, 1912, the St. Olaf faculty agreed to "a request presented by the church choir that students belonging be excused from recitations on Thursday and Friday preceding the coming Easter vacation, in order to take part in a series of concerts to be given by the choir."[44] In the student paper,

The Manitou Messenger, the following item appeared in the March, 1912, issue:

> The choir of St. John's Church will make an extended tour during the Easter vacation. This choir was heard in concert here in Northfield last year when it attracted a full house. This year, with increased membership and added enthusiasm due to the prospects of a trip, rehearsals have been held almost daily until at the present time they are in the finest possible condition.[45]

The notice also states that J. N. Kildahl will give an address at each concert, that the itinerary includes Minneapolis, Eau Claire, Madison, and Chicago, and that the home concert will be given in the Congregational Church on March 25th, "and will undoubtedly be of a very high order." In this case, unlike later practice, the "home concert" would be given before the tour began, prompting the *Messenger* writer to urge students to "turn out and give them a good send-off."

The forty-five members in the Choir included both St. Olaf students and some older persons from College and town. Non-students included William C. Benson, Mr. and Mrs. Andrew Boe, Agnes Glasoe, P. M. Glasoe, Nils Kleven, C. A. Mellby, Mrs. G. T. Rygh, and Mr. and Mrs. Paul G. Schmidt.

Students from well-known St. Olaf families included Adelaide and Ella Hjertaas, Ida and Lula Marvick, Anna and John Mohn, and Evelyn Ytterboe.[46]

The tour took place as planned, the Choir boarding a car on the Dan Patch railway line in Northfield for the trip to Minneapolis where the first concert was given in the First Baptist Church on Wednesday, March 27, 1912. The concert program for the 1912 tour opened with "Der ringes paa jord" ("Today there is ringing") by F. M. Christiansen. Second number was "Deilig er jorden" (same tune as "Beautiful Savior"). Then followed three numbers by A. Söderman: "Lamb of God," "He is Blessed," and "Hosanna." After

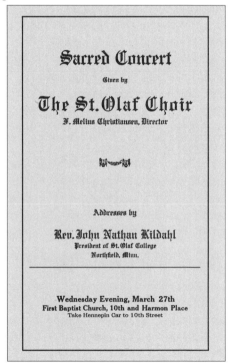

Program for 1912 tour

108

this group President J. N. Kildahl gave the first of two addresses. The Choir then sang "I Know That My Redeemer Liveth" from Handel's "Messiah," "Jeg saa ham som barn" ("I saw him in childhood"), a Norwegian folk song, and "O Jesus se," the English version of which begins with "O darkest woe!"

Kildahl's second address was followed by four anthems to conclude the concert: "O hoved høit forhaanet" ("O sacred Head, now wounded"), "Som sol gaar ned i havet" ("As sinks the sun at even"), by F. M. Christiansen, "Det ringer" ("There is ringing from every tower"), by Kjerulf, and "Lover den Herre" ("Praise to the Lord"). Of the twelve choral numbers, eight were sung in Norwegian, a mark of ethnicity that speaks for itself.[47]

Ida Hagen, Class of 1913, wrote a charming account of the tour which was printed in the student yearbook, *The Viking*. She described the jostling as berths were reassigned on the sleeper after the Eau Claire concert. In Madison she and a few others were entertained by a former St. Olaf student at the Alpha Chi sorority house. On a sight-seeing tour around the city the Choir members saw the Wisconsin capitol under construction. The train took them next to De Forest. "It seemed that everyone had turned out to see the famous St. Olaf Choir, and we were escorted by them all to the opera house where we gave our two o'clock concert. We all remember with pain the inopportune but triumphant crow of a rooster during a critical pause of one of our most impressive songs."[48]

The Choir sang at Sunday morning services at a Lutheran church in Mt. Horeb, "beautifully decorated with Easter lilies and white bunting." Everyone had a good night's rest and slept late in Milwaukee, "except Dr. Glasoe, Prof. Christiansen and a few others, who had gone out to visit the Pabst breweries." There was time for shopping. "Everyone bought a stein or some other souvenir suggestive of Milwaukee. That evening we sang to one of the finest audiences on tour." After the concert, given on April 1st, the Choir had a birthday party for Prof. Christiansen, giving him a silver loving cup. "Then some good rousing cheers for our director, for our hosts and hostesses, and everybody in general."[49]

In Chicago, the "Windy City," the Choir sang for the patients at the Deaconess Home and Hospital. With "Prexy" and local pastor H. B. Kildahl as guides, the Choir members then took the elevated railway into the city where they "had great sport staring at the tops of the sky-scrapers, but, try as we would, we could not play the part of the unsophisticated as well as did Mr. A. Boe and Mr. Wm. Benson, the inseparables and incorrigibles of our party." The evening concert was at Wicker Park Hall. "The house was packed and we had to pinch ourselves to realize that we were to sing to that vast audience which received us so kindly."[50]

Choir Ladies on Train

On April 3rd the Choir left by train for Ottawa, Illinois. "When Prof. Schmidt came to view the flock to see whether or not any were lost, strayed, or stolen, he found only Mykkeltvedt missing, but he joined us later having missed the first train because of an elevated railway accident." In Ottawa they visited Pleasant View Luther College, gave an afternoon concert in a church, and left for Albert Lea, Minnesota, in the early evening. Ida Hagen was captivated by the lovely scenery along the Illinois River at sunset:

> The river had just overflowed its banks so that trees reached up
> here and there from the waters, casting wonderful shadows, pale
> pink, faint lavender, and gold with deep purple tints throughout.
> A few white birches stood out in striking contrast to the other
> dark trees. In the distance rose the hills and cliffs through the
> rifts of which shone the sunset sky in all its glory.

Before the Albert Lea concert in the church, the Reverend Edward Nervig, the local pastor, gave a red carnation and a spray fern to each of the lady members of the Choir, "a courtesy much appreciated." The Choir endeavored to make the last concert their best, and then it was back to Northfield on April 5, 1912. Miss Hagen concluded her account: "The trip of the St. Olaf College Choir was a thing of the past, of memories and pleasant thoughts, to be treasured as an attempt at least to create a love for our old hymns and to sing Christ into the hearts of our Norwegian-Americans."[51]

Within a short time the St. Olaf Choir was out on tour again. It had received an invitation to sing at sessions of the annual meeting of the United Norwegian Lutheran Church convening in Fargo, North Dakota, in June. Additional concerts were given at towns in North Dakota and Minnesota on the way to and from Fargo.[52]

Norway Tour, 1913

The Choir's visit to the Fargo church convention in June of 1912 yielded an important contact that opened the way for the 1913 tour to Norway. The idea of a Choir trip to the motherland must have been on the minds of Christiansen and Schmidt ever since the Band tour to Norway of 1906. Students had been thinking and talking about it. At the Fargo church convention Manager Paul Schmidt took up the possibility with two Norwegian church leaders who predicted a favorable reception for the Choir in Norway. Plans were drawn up, eleven guarantors were secured, and a St. Olaf faculty member, J. Jørgen Thompson, was sent to Norway in March of 1913 to make specific arrangements.[53]

The *Viking* article on the Choir's Norway tour began as follows: "On Friday, June 13, 1913, the St. Olaf Choir left Northfield on its extended tour

to Norway, not with any fear of ill omen which superstition may have attached to this particular date, but with the most joyful anticipation of a sea voyage and of a visit to that country of beauty and freshness which has been described to us from our earliest childhood."[54]

The Choir invited the pastor of St. John's Church, the Reverend T. H. Haugan, to make the trip to Norway with them and to serve as their spokesman at receptions, banquets, and other occasions.[55] It was a happy choice, for Pastor Haugan admirably fulfilled his role. P. G. Schmidt wrote of him, "He was an

Pastor T. H. Haugan

F. Melius Christiansen, T. H. Haugan, P. G. Schmidt

On the "Christianiafjord"
F. Melius Christiansen, J. Jørgen Thompson, P. G. Schmidt

exceptionally fluent speaker in Norwegian and on many occasions the audience was charmed both by his winning personality and by the fine presentation of his message."[56]

There were concerts on the way in St. Paul, in Wisconsin, and Brooklyn, New York. On June 24th the Choir sailed from New York for Norway on the "Christianiafjord." It reached Bergen, Norway, on July 4th and gave the first

Rehearsing aboard ship

concert. Afterwards a banquet was given for the Choir in the Grand Hotel by the Anglo-American Club. When Pastor Haugan was introduced, he expressed thanks on behalf of St. Olaf College for the wonderful reception and won the warm esteem of his listeners when he said:

> We knew that Norway's heart was big and warm but not as big and warm as we have seen and experienced it. We, of course, also realize that mother Norway looks with regret on the many folks that have left her shores to establish homes across the sea. But I want to assure you, my friends, that we cherish all that we have received from our mother country. We will preserve this priceless treasure, our heritage, and we will endeavor to make it felt in the community life of the great country on the other side of the Atlantic. To come back to Norway for many of us is like coming home.[57]

From Bergen the ship took the Choir along the coast with stops at Stavanger and Kristiansand on the way to the capital city, Christiania, later called Oslo. "Our most hearty welcome was felt when we sailed into port at Christiania where thousands of people awaited our coming and three hundred voices sang out their songs of good cheer and brotherhood," wrote K. E. '16, in the *Viking* summary of the tour.[58] The welcome for the Choir was genuine enough, but the size and enthusiasm of the crowd was also related to the fact that the ocean liner "Christianiafjord" was the first ship of the recently established Norwegian-America steamship line and on this occasion was completing its first voyage from America to Norway.[59]

Arrival in Christiania, July 1913

113

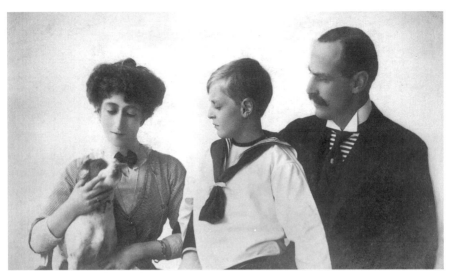

Norwegian Royal Family
Queen Maud, Crown Prince Olav, King Haakon VII

King Haakon and Queen Maude attended the concert at the University Aula in Christiania. Special care was given to having the Choir in place on the platform at 8:00 p.m. Choir member Ida Hagen described the arrival of the royal pair: "They walked leisurely up to their places and we sang 'Gud sign' vor konge god,' ('God bless our good king'), everybody standing until we were through and the king and queen were seated. Our concert was a success, the king and queen smiled their thanks and shook hands with Prof. Christiansen, a thing which Christiania people say the royal pair have never done before."[60]

The itinerary plan followed by the Choir was to travel by train from Christiania northward to Trondheim and from there take the coastal boat "Lyra" southward along the coast and into some of the fjords, giving concerts along the way in coastal towns and cities. They would leave the "Lyra" at Larvik, the town in which F. Melius Christiansen grew up, and return by train to Christiania.[61]

On the way to Trondheim the group stopped at Lillehammer for a boat trip on Lake Mjösa and a visit to Maihaugen, the outdoor museum located on a hill above the city. In Trondheim the Choir sang two concerts in the Nidaros Cathedral and visited the grave of Bernt Julius Muus, founder of St. Olaf College. A wreath was laid at the grave, which is near the Cathedral, and the Choir sang Christiansen's "Som sol gaar ned i havet" ("As sinks the sun at even"). Following the first concert in Trondheim, a review in one of the city's papers had these observations among others:

Choir members in Lillehammer

The renditions were exceedingly beautiful, perfect in all their nuances, and the singing was deeply stamped with the surety which only long and skilled instruction could give. The program was very beautiful and contained some things not hitherto sung here. Grieg's 'Hvad est du dog skjøn' was splendidly sung, likewise 'Lover den Herre' and Söderman's 'Hør os Herre.' It was a great delight to hear 'Deilig er Jorden'; and Conradi's 'Alone with Thee' was given with much intensity and warmth.[62]

The reviewer's reference to "Deilig er Jorden" ("Beautiful Savior") would indicate that it was an optional number, since it does not appear in the printed concert program. The Söderman piece was actually a song cycle of three numbers sung in Latin. In addition to the Grieg,

Grave of B. J. Muus

Nidaros Cathedral in Trondheim

"Lover den Herre" ("Praise to the Lord"), and "Deilig er Jorden," the program offered only two more numbers sung in Norwegian, "Der ringes paa jord" and "Moderens Sang" ("The Mother's Song"), both by F. Melius Christiansen. Other numbers were "O Bread of Life" by Heinrich Isaac, "I Know That My Redeemer Liveth" from *Messiah*, and "Wake, Awake for Night is Flying," by Philipp Nicolai. A Ladies' Quartette sang two numbers: the first was not identified; the second was Christiansen's "The Lord is Full of Compassion."[63]

Coastal Ship "Lyra"

The arrangement of traveling along the Norwegian coast on board the "Lyra" provided both transportation and a comfortable home for the Choir for two busy but enjoyable weeks of concerts and sightseeing.[64] The reviewer in the town of Stenkjaer found the singing of "Deilig er Jorden" ("Beautiful Savior") to be "of overwhelming effect." A writer for Kristiansund's *Posten* reported that the hearers were enthralled.

> We heard singing as never before—singing that was so complete in dynamic shading and with delivery so sincere and moving, that as the tones died away we were left in a state of wonderment that a choir could attain so great skill in the art of singing. And such discipline! It was a great experience merely to watch the conductor's baton, to see how he controlled the 50-voice choir.[65]

Aboard the "Lyra" all was peaceful and quiet between stops. The coastal towns were relatively close together so the ship moved at a leisurely pace. But the atmosphere changed each morning as it approached the landing pier. The captain detonated small bombs in the water announcing the Choir's arrival. Tremendous crowds gathered. There were welcoming speeches, banquets and receptions. Some concert sites were much too small to hold the crowds.

In Haugesund, where this was the case, an unusual impromptu performance took place for an enormous gathering of over 10,000 people who were unable to get tickets for the concert. They gathered in an open square down by the wharf where the "Lyra" was moored and stood silently, as only a Norwegian crowd can do, hoping for a glimpse of the Choir members who had returned to the boat after the concert. P. G. Schmidt depicts the scene:

> Finally, a temporary director's stand was set up on the boat's forward deck, the choir members were called from their state rooms, and in the midnight stillness the choir began to sing to the heart of these people some of the hymns and melodies known to them all, but sung as I am sure they had never heard them sung before. To be privileged to take part in the singing of those half-dozen songs under such circumstances was a thrill never to be forgotten.[66]

The genial "P.G." was not one to forget the hilarious episodes either. The Choir often had to sing in churches in which, so it seemed to them, the windows had not been opened for decades. In such a church in southwestern Norway they removed a rear window for much-needed ventilation and proceeded with the concert. After a couple of numbers, Choir members heard the bleating of some goats far up in the mountain behind the church. First it was a faint "baa, baa." The Choir continued with its singing, louder passages, then softer ones. The goats were listening and coming nearer, and their "baa, baa" was getting louder. By now they were halfway down the mountain. Choir and director were struggling to keep from laughing, but managed, recalled P. G.

> Again the choir sang loud, this time the last number before intermission, and when we finished, the goats, that had now come all the way down were gathered just outside the window which we had removed, gave a veritable concert of their own. Their intonation was something to hear. During the intermission choir boys in evening dress could be seen chasing these pesky critters up the mountain and that too was quite an attraction.[67]

Norway's spectacular scenery drew appreciative responses as the Choir proceeded into fjord country. "We shall always remember the beautiful morning up Geirangerfjord, how we watched the over-hanging mist clear away and reveal to our eager sight the towering peaks and the snow-clad mountain tops. Winding in and out through the irregular course of this fjord we would at times seem hemmed in on all sides when gradually there would appear some opening for escape," wrote one of the students, recalling the experience.[68]

The Choir's visit to Larvik was of particular interest because F. Melius Christiansen had lived there from age seven to seventeen and there received his start as a young musician. At the banquet given in the Larvik Grand Hotel he paid tribute to his organ teacher, Oscar Hansen. The concert in the Larvik church convinced a reviewer that reports about the Choir's singing elsewhere in Norway were not overstated. "It is probable that Norway had never heard singing nearly as fine as theirs. . . . With the very first song the audience was completely won. Christiansen's own beautiful and splendidly arranged numbers held the public, which, with every nerve tense, listened to the great waves of tone that the conductor secured from the choir."[69]

The St. Olaf Choir gave further concerts in Christiania, Eidsvold, and in

King Haakon VII

southern Norway. Its final day in Norway was August 3rd, the birthday of King Haakon. The Choir sent a telegram to the king congratulating him on his birthday and thanking him for the kindnesses it had been shown everywhere in Norway. The king replied in a telegram addressed to Paul G. Schmidt: "I thank the Norwegian-American singers for their good wishes and wish them a happy voyage home."[70] The final concerts were presented in churches in Gothenburg and Malmö in Sweden, and in the City Hall in Copenhagen, Denmark. The return to the United States was made aboard the S. S. "Hellig Olav" which arrived in New York on August 18, 1913.[71]

The Name of the Choir

When the St. John's Church Choir prepared for the 1912 Easter tour into Wisconsin and Illinois, it changed its name to "The St. Olaf Choir" as indicated on the cover of the concert tour program. The same was true when the Choir went to Norway in 1913. Again, the name on the tour program is "The St. Olaf Choir."

It has been stated by some writers that the St. John's Choir became "The St. Olaf Lutheran Choir" in 1912.[72] The evidence is strong, however, for "The St. Olaf Choir" as the original name of the organization. In addition to the evidence of the 1912 tour program, there is an explicit statement by Eugene Simpson, author of the 1921 book, *A History of St. Olaf Choir*. He writes:

> Notwithstanding the home cognomen as a choir of St. John's Church, it is easily understood how desirable it was that upon the first journey away from home the choir should carry the

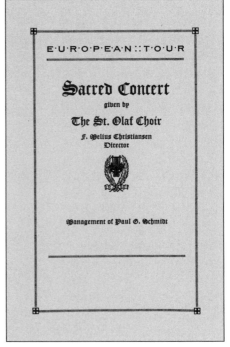

Program for Norway Tour, 1913

name of the educational institution to which all the members owed allegiance, either as students or faculty. Therefore the Easter tour was by The St. Olaf Choir, as was another tour of the following June.[73]

Indeed, the students who submitted reports about the Easter and June tours to the *Viking* both used the phrase, "The St. Olaf Choir," although Ida Hagen alternately used "The St. Olaf College Choir."[74] An even earlier reference to "The St. Olaf Choir" appeared in the student newspaper in February of 1912, the year of the Choir's birth. Reporting on the special services held on the College Day of Prayer, the writer stated: "The St. Olaf Choir assisted in the services by rendering two songs."[75] This item appeared the month before the Choir set out on its Easter tour.

Eugene Simpson also pointed out that the Choir's constitution of 1920 stated unequivocally, "The name of this organization shall be the St. Olaf Choir."[76] Additional early support for this name comes from P. G. Schmidt who wrote a brief piece entitled "History of the St. Olaf Choir" for the 1924-25 *Viking* yearbook. There he stated that "in view of the fact that so many of its members were students and teachers at St. Olaf College, the name was changed to St. Olaf Choir."[77]

In 1920, when the Choir first visited cities on the east coast and became recognized nationally for its excellence in singing sacred music a cappella, the name "St. Olaf Lutheran Choir" was used on the concert program and was often employed by reviewers. It will be recalled that in 1920 it was important to secure the support of Lutheran leaders and churches in eastern cities to make the tour financially possible. Moreover, President Boe had described the mission of the Choir in terms of closer relations among Lutherans: "The Choir comes as a representative of the Lutheran congregations of the West with greetings to the Lutherans of the East."[78]

While the word "Lutheran" appears on the concert program for the important tour of Eastern states in 1920, it is interesting that in the announcement of the tour in the church paper, the *Lutheran Church Herald*, both the heading and the text consistently use "St. Olaf Choir"[79] And on the St. Olaf campus references were made to the "St. Olaf Choir," as under the picture of the 1919-20 Choir in the 1922-23 *Viking*, in the account

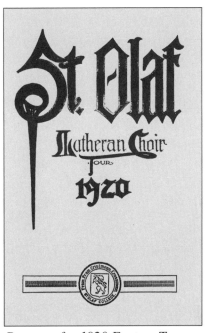

Program for 1920 Eastern Tour

of the eastern tour written by P. G. Schmidt, and in a short article called "The St. Olaf Choir's Mission."[80] Similarly, the *Viking* for 1926-27 also places the heading "St. Olaf Choir" under the Choir's picture.[81]

Critics attending the concerts would be handed the ornate program that stated on the cover, "St. Olaf Lutheran Choir Tour 1920." In his review of the Choir's April 27, 1920, concert in Carnegie Hall, Richard Aldrich of the New York Times entitled his piece, "St. Olaf Lutheran Choir" and used that name in the opening sentence of the review. Reviewers for the *New York Telegraph*, the *New York Herald*, and the *New York Telegram* also referred specifically to the "St. Olaf Lutheran Choir."

This was the name used by the Choir throughout the rest of F. Melius Christiansen's years as director and through Olaf C. Christiansen's entire tenure as leader of the Choir. There was an interesting exception in the 1950s. While the annual tour program for the 1953-54 season carried the name, "St. Olaf Lutheran Choir," another program from that same year identified the ensemble as the "St. Olaf A Cappella Choir." This latter name was also used in 1955 for the annual tour and for the international tour to Norway and Germany.[82] One is reminded that the choir Olaf Christiansen founded and directed at Oberlin was the Oberlin A Cappella Choir. In 1956 the Choir returned to the usage of "St. Olaf Lutheran Choir" which continued through 1968.

When the Choir set out on its first tour with Kenneth Jennings as director, the cover of the concert program announced, "The St. Olaf Choir in Concert—1969." The change back to the original name of the Choir was done quietly and without much discussion. Dr. Jennings felt that it was no longer necessary to add the word "Lutheran" in order to distinguish the College from Roman Catholic institutions. The College itself had never been known as "St. Olaf Lutheran College." Furthermore, other organizations such as athletic teams that represent the College away from the campus do not identify themselves as "Lutheran."

To sum up, the name of the organization is "The St. Olaf Choir."[83] That was the name used when the Choir began in 1912. During the period

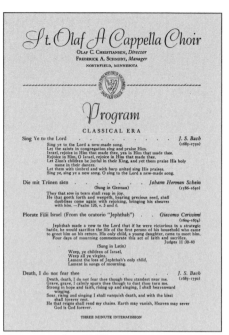

Program for 1955 tour

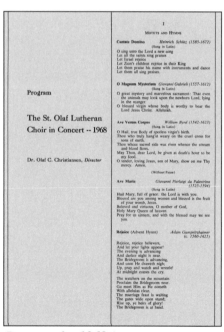

Program for 1968 tour
Last under Olaf Christiansen

122

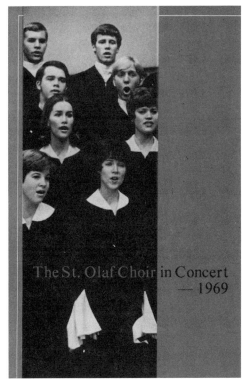

The St. Olaf Choir in Concert — 1969

1920-68 the name used was "The St. Olaf Lutheran Choir," although in common parlance one often heard or read "St. Olaf Choir." In 1969 the Choir resumed its original name and has continued to be known as "The St. Olaf Choir."

Program for 1969 tour
First under Kenneth Jennings

Notes for Chapter 4 THE CHOIR IS BORN

1. Leola Nelson Bergmann, *Music Master of the Middle West:* The Story of F. Melius Christiansen and the St. Olaf Choir (Minneapolis: University of Minnesota Press, 1944), 110.

2. *Ibid.*, 115.

3. *Congregational Minutes of St. John's Lutheran Church*, Northfield, Minnesota, Entry 62, October 25, 1904.

4. *MM (Manitou Messenger)* XVIII (October 1904), 113.

5. *Minutes of St. John's Lutheran Church*, Entry 66, September 1, 1905.

6. Cited by Edna Hong, *The Book Of A Century*, 1869-1969 (Northfield, Minnesota: St. John's Lutheran Church, 1969), 49.

7. *MM* (June 1906), 102.

8. Bergmann, 113.

9. Paul Maurice Glasoe, "A Singing Church," *Norwegian-American Studies and Records* XIII (Northfield, Minnesota: Norwegian-American Historical Association, 1943), 105.

10. *Ibid.*

11. Bergmann, 113-14.

12. F. Melius Christiansen, *Song-Service* No. 4 (Minneapolis, Minn.: Augsburg Publishing House, 1913), Preface.

13. Glasoe, "A Singing Church," 106.

14. William C. Benson, *High on Manitou:* A History of St. Olaf College 1874-1949 (Northfield, Minnesota: The St. Olaf College Press, 1949), 180.

15. Eugene E. Simpson, *A History of St. Olaf Choir* (Minneapolis: Augsburg Publishing House, 1921), 77.

16. Quoted in *The Viking* '10 '11 '12 (Northfield, Minn., 1909), 207.

17. Benson, 181.

18. Bergmann, 39; Simpson, 122.

19. Bergmann, 64.

20. *Ibid.*, 105, 113-14.

21. *The Viking* '10 '11 '12, 206, 208, 210.

22. Bergmann, 98.

23. F. Melius Christiansen, "The Future of our Choral Union," *Lutheran Herald* XXIII (December 12, 1939), 1192.

24. J. C. K. Preus, *The History of The Choral Union of the Evangelical Lutheran Church* 1847-1960 (Minneapolis, Minn.: Augsburg Publishing House, 1961), 38-39.

25. *Ibid.*, 30-31.

26. *Ibid.*, 35.

27. *Ibid.*, 35-36.

28. *Ibid.*, 36.

29. *MM* XIII (November 1899), 148; Simpson, 48, 55.

30. Simpson, 56; *MM* XVII (June 1903), 159.

31. *MM* XVII (November 1903), 223; *MM* XVII (December 1903), 255.

32. Cited by Simpson, 63.

33. *MM* XVII (January 1904), 286; *MM* XVII (February 1904), 312; Simpson, 63.

34. Simpson, 64.

35. *MM* XIX (June 1905), 105.

36. *Viking* '10 '11 '12, 210.

37. *The Viking* '13 '14 '15 (Northfield, Minn., 1912), 157.

38. *The 1926-27 Viking*, 129.

39. Paul G. Schmidt, *My Years at St. Olaf*, A Centennial Decade Publication (Northfield, Minnesota: St. Olaf College, [1967]), 55.

40. *Ibid.*, 55-56.

41. *En Sang-Gudstjeneste*: Tale ved J. N. Kildahl, Musikarrangement ved F. Melius Christiansen (Minneapolis, Minn.: Augsburg Publishing House Trykkeri, 1907, 1916); *Sang-Gudstjeneste* Nr. 2, Tale ved J. N. Kildahl, Musik ved F. Melius Christiansen (Minneapolis, Minn.: Augsburg Publishing House, 1908), 18-19.

42. Simpson, 79.

43. *Ibid.*, 80.

44. *Ibid.*, 81.

45. *MM* XXV (March 1912), 401.

46. 1912 Concert Program, back page.

47. 1912 Concert Program.

48. Ida Hagen, "First Tour of the St. Olaf College Choir," *The Viking* '13 '14 '15, 151-52.

49. *Ibid.*, 152.

50. *Ibid.*, 154.

51. *Ibid.*, 155.

52. A. G. Aker, "The June Tour," *Viking* '13 '14 '15, 155-56.

53. Simpson, 83; Bergmann, 119; Schmidt, 57.

54. *Viking* '16 '17 '18, 219.

55. *Minutes of St. John's Lutheran Church*, Entry 116, May 20, 1913.

56. Schmidt, 61.

57. *Ibid.*

58. *Viking* '16 '17 '18, 220.

59. Schmidt, 59.

60. Ida Hagen, "From the St. Olaf Choir Trip," *The United Lutheran*, letter from Haugesund, Norway, July 23, 1913. Cf. Bergmann, 120.

61. *Viking* '16 '17 '18, 221.

62. Simpson, 102-03.

63. 1913 European Tour Concert Program.

64. Schmidt, 60-61.

65. Cited in Simpson, 104.

66. Schmidt, 62.

67. *Ibid.*, 63.

68. *Viking* '16 '17 '18, 221.

69. Simpson, 107.

70. *Ibid.*, 115.

71. *Viking* '16 '17 '18, 223.

72. Cf. Benson, 182; Bergmann, 117; Schmidt, 56.

73. Simpson, 81.

74. *Viking* '13 '14 '15, 150, 152, 155-57.

75. *MM* XXV (February 1912), 342.

76. Simpson, 29.

77. *The 1924-'25 Viking*, 136. This explanation takes precedence over what Professor Schmidt wrote over twenty-five years later in his book, *My Years at St. Olaf.* See p. 56.

78. Program cover: "St. Olaf Lutheran Choir Tour 1920." STOARCHIV.

79. "St. Olaf Choir Concert Tour," *Lutheran Church Herald* IV (February 17, 1920), 98.

80. *Viking* 1922-23, 133-34, 136.

81. *Viking* 1926-27, 115.

82. Program, "St. Olaf A Cappella Choir," 1955.

83. Program, "The St. Olaf Choir," the 1996 Tour.

CHAPTER 5

TOURS IN THE TWENTIES

"By far the most important tour of the St. Olaf Choir, since the memorable trip to Europe in 1913, was the spring tour of 1920. This afforded an opportunity of realizing a long-cherished desire on the part of both director and manager, namely, to bring the Choir to the larger American cities of the East."[1]. So wrote P. G. Schmidt who played a key role in planning and managing the tour that gained national attention for the St. Olaf Choir and established the practice of annual tours.

The present chapter will review the 1920 eastern tour and treat more briefly a few of the other tours by the Choir in the decade of the twenties. It will also consider the achievement of the Choir in raising money for a new music hall, constructed in 1926.

The reasons for concert tours have been discussed earlier. Among them, P. G. Schmidt gave first place to the artistic purpose. He realized that both Band and

Director and Manager
West Coast Tour 1924-25

Choir had brought the College good publicity; he acknowledged that the trips were both enjoyable and educational for the students; but he concluded that the primary purpose of taking music groups on tour was to stimulate the members to do their best and to provide a needed means of expression.[2] The desire to present the great music of the Lutheran Church continued to be a significant motive, as will be clear from the 1920 tour.

Following the 1913 trip to Norway, the St. Olaf Choir limited its touring to the Midwest the next few years. In 1915 it took the Dan Patch railway to Minneapolis, sang a concert in Our Savior's Lutheran Church, and boarded a Milwaukee train heading west for Montevideo. As usual, a lively esprit de corps infected the Choir when it traveled. The distance to that western

FMC and PGS, 1923

Minnesota town inspired the "Agony Quartette" to sing Ole Larson's latest hit, "It's a long way to Montevideo." Concert sites also included Milan, Sacred Heart, Granite Falls, Cottonwood, Minneota, and Canby. The merriment was quelled at a party for Professor Christiansen. Despite well-meant speeches, songs, and a gift, the surprise birthday party at the pastor's home in Minneota on April 1st received a dampened response from the director, as one student reported. "He told us he did not care for surprise parties; they were such a humiliation."[3] With F. Melius Christiansen on leave during the 1915-16 school year, the Choir made a spring tour in Wisconsin and Minnesota, led by J. Jørgen Thompson. Its final concert took place in Lands Church near Zumbrota on May 17th. To close the program the Choir sang the Norwegian national song, "Ja, vi elsker dette landet" and the American national anthem. "The tour was a success in every way," wrote P. G. Schmidt.[4]

The 1917 tour to some towns in Iowa was remembered for the accident in which the Choir's private car ran off the track. Everyone was shaken up, but the Choir reached Belmond by five o'clock where it "found a high school auditorium packed by a patiently

Lands Lutheran Church

128

waiting audience."[5] A short trip was taken to Austin, Adams, and Hayfield, all in southern Minnesota, in 1918. Because of World War I, no tour took place in 1918-19.

The Eastern Tour of 1920

Under the heading, "St. Olaf Choir Concert Tour," the January 20, 1920, edition of the *Lutheran Church Herald* printed an announcement that began, "Arrangements are being completed for a concert tour of the choir of St. Olaf College, Northfield, Minn., to cover the leading cities east of the Mississippi." The article told of the formation of a Guarantee Syndicate, gave the itinerary, and named Martin H. Hanson, a New York impresario, as the person engaged to manage the tour.[6]

The main weight of the planning fell on the shoulders of P. G. Schmidt. Writing later of his trip to New York in 1919 to speak to officials at the headquarters of the National Lutheran Council, Schmidt admitted: "I believe this was one of the most difficult assignments I have ever had. The men I talked with were very considerate and kind, but I felt they were also more or less skeptical." Schmidt understood their reluctance to help "in bringing to New York an unknown group of singers from the Minnesota prairies."[7]

But Schmidt persevered, noting that there was much publicity at the time regarding the forthcoming tour to the United States by the Sistine Chapel Choir from Rome. "Why should not our people support one of our own American choirs and give it a chance to prove its worth?" argued Schmidt.[8] The plans went forward, but P. G. was about to face a new set of challenges when the tour began in April of 1920.

In the meantime, the *Lutheran Church Herald*, official paper of the Norwegian Lutheran Church of America to which St. Olaf College belonged, kept its readers abreast of further plans for the tour and its rationale. In the February 17, 1920 edition, President Lars W. Boe of St. Olaf restated the desire on the part of the Choir to present the great Lutheran chorales to a larger circle of listeners. His words, cited in Chapter 1, deserve repeating at this point:

> The mission of the St. Olaf Choir is primarily to develop in the students at the college a thorough appreciation of Lutheran church music. It welcomes, however, the opportunity to serve in the larger field. The Choir comes as a representative of the Lutheran congregations of the West with greetings to the Lutherans of the East. It is hoped that through its presentation of our common heritage we may become more conscious of our spiritual ancestry and of our common faith.[9]

FMC, PGS, Martin H. Hanson
New York, 1922

Boe's thinking reveals his awareness of the local function of the Choir to which he adds, with foresight, the ecumenical dimension, viewing the St. Olaf Choir as an agent for a larger Lutheran unity. As suggested earlier, the aim of making known the Lutheran choral tradition would soon be broadened to take in sacred music from a variety of sources.

Looking back on the important and successful 1920 tour, P. G. Schmidt wrote a report in the 1922-23 *Viking* that touched on both the artistic and churchly impact of the tour. "Under most favorable auspices the Choir was heard by the best musical critics of our country and by thousands of Lutherans upon whom the singing of the beautiful Lutheran chorales made a profound and lasting impression."[10]

In preparing his singers for the tour, Christiansen for the first time included a Bach number, or one then ascribed to Bach, "Blessing, Glory and Wisdom," with which the program opened.[11] The other numbers in Part One were Christiansen arrangements of "Praise to the Lord," published by Peter Söhren, "Built on the Rock" by L. M. Lindeman, and "A Mighty Fortress" by Martin Luther. Part Two consisted of three numbers, "The Word of God" by Grieg, "Savior of Sinners" by F. Mendelssohn, and "O God, Hear My Prayer," by A. Gretchaninoff. In Part Three the Choir sang "Father, Most Holy," by Johan Cruger, "Hosanna," a new piece by F. Melius Christiansen, and the latter's arrangements of "Beautiful Savior," and "Wake, Awake" by Philipp Nicolai. "Beautiful Savior" was not yet the traditional closing number of the concert program.[12]

The Choir left Northfield on Easter Sunday, April 5, 1920, and sang its first concert in Orchestra Hall in Chicago to a full and enthusiastic house. Karleton Hackett of the *Evening Post* wrote: "Now in choral affairs we shall date from the visit of the St. Olaf Choir. In my recollection there has been no a cappella choir in America which would compare with these young singers from Minnesota." Herman Devries wrote in the *Herald Examiner*: "It is a group of young people, all of them letter-perfect, pitch-perfect, tone-perfect, text-perfect in the most difficult classic choral music, singing absolutely from

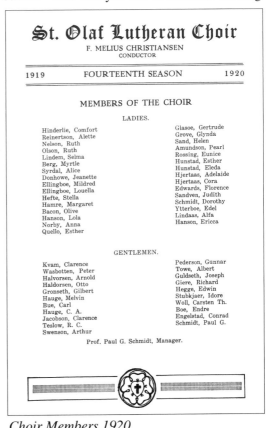

Choir Members 1920
Page from Tour Program

memory and without accompaniment, even without the opening assurance of the diapason or tuning fork. . . . Their concert was one of the rarest expositions of the superlative in choral singing."[13]

The exuberant reactions to the singing were not matched by happy arrangements, unfortunately. The concert manager engaged by the executive committee in New York was to take charge of the tour from Chicago, manage the trip east to New York, and bring the Choir back to Chicago. But there was no one to meet the Choir on its arrival at the depot in Chicago. The taxi drivers had all been sent to the wrong station. The dismal fact was that the concert manager simply was not prepared to handle the arrangements for a large group like the St. Olaf Choir. When he and P. G. Schmidt conferred after the Chicago concert, it was agreed that Schmidt would be in charge of the rest of the tour and the other man would return to New York. "We sat up most of the night going over details," recalled Schmidt. "He gave me an itinerary of places and dates and I jotted down as

much other information as I was able to get."[14] For P. G., it was an abrupt introduction to tour leading, but he proved himself master of the difficult situation.

In a stroke of good planning, copies of the fine reviews gathered in Chicago were sent on ahead to cities yet to be visited. The result was surprisingly good attendance at the concerts, although the crowds were smaller on the way east than would be the case on the return when word had spread of the Choir's excellent singing.[15]

Pleased with the good start in Chicago, the Choir still felt some trepidation, but fully determined to sing well, it proceeded

Paul G. Schmidt

eastward to Fort Wayne, Indiana, where the performance was so well received that a return engagement was requested. A Fort Wayne newspaper spoke of the St. Olaf Choir coming in a chariot of song and "singing their way into the hearts of the people in the most wonderful program of its kind ever heard in this city."[16]

On their way east, the Northfield singers, thirty-two women and twenty men, sang in such cities as Columbus, Pittsburgh, Washington, Baltimore, and Philadelphia, where they had their picture taken in front of a monument near the Museum of Art. After the concert in Washington, D. C., a reviewer for the *Evening Star* wrote: "Its effects were at times like those of a grand organ." The comparison with an organ was often to be repeated.

Inevitably, the excitement mounted as each day brought the Choir closer to its New York concert. On Sunday afternoon, April 25th, it sang at the Academy of Music in Brooklyn. On Monday evening it was in Paterson, New Jersey. And on Tuesday evening, the venue was none other than Carnegie Hall in New York! Leola Bergmann has conveyed the mood of that historic concert:

> Martin Hanson, dapper in tails and pin stripes, watched the box office, saw the lights lower over three thousand listeners, heard the comments of the critics during the intermission, and then rushed backstage with a beaming face. 'The critics are wild, the critics are wild!' Christiansen and the choir had made it. New York had listened and liked it, liked it very much.[17]

Of course not all the reviewers liked everything they heard. Richard Aldrich, writing for the *New York Times* of April 28, 1920, was critical of the tempos in the Bach number and disliked Christiansen's arrangement of Luther's "A Mighty Fortress," but found in the overall performance much that was "of remarkable beauty." Early in the review he wrote:

> It is a body of excellent material, well balanced and trained to a high degree of finish in enunciation, attack and release, phrasing and dynamic shading. It sings with remarkable flexibility under the conductor's beat; there is a plasticity of phrase, a subtlety of accent and rhythmic quality that are unusual, and in these respects it may be numbered among the few 'virtuoso' choirs that have been heard here in recent years.[18]

Carnegie Hall, New York

Words of high praise came from other reviewers, one of whom was H. E. Krehbiel, who wrote in the *New York Tribune*, "Exquisitely balanced, fresh and euphonious in quality. We were made to marvel at the ability of the Choir." Writing for the New York *Evening World*, Sylvester Rawling had this reaction: "Like the life-restoring breeze from the Northwest that sweeps over New York at the close of a suffocating August day after a thunderstorm, the St. Olaf Choir descended upon us at a concert in Carnegie Hall and bestowed upon us in the overwrought dying music season a benison of song."[19]

The Choir had a full day of sightseeing in New York City: lower Manhattan, Fifth Avenue, Central Park, Riverside Drive. In the evening they were entertained at the home of Mr. and Mrs. J. Louis Schaefer. Schaefer was a member of the executive committee that oversaw the tour arrangements. He was a successful merchant and banker who became president of Grace National Bank in 1924.[20]

A disappointment was the failed attempt to make an acceptable recording in a studio in Camden, New Jersey, despite several tries. One version sounded good to the Choir members but "Christy" was not satisfied. Esther Quello '22, Choir member, expressed regret that the fabulous voice of soloist Alpha Lindaas, Class of 1921, was therefore not recorded.[21] On the homeward journey the itinerary through western New York permitted a day at Niagara Falls in addition to the concerts at Rochester and Buffalo.

Alpha Lindaas

Ohio concerts on the return swing were given in Cleveland, Akron, and Toledo. In Akron the Choir enjoyed a buffet lunch and Sunday afternoon visit at the luxurious home of tire company owner Frank and Mrs. Seiberling. The day after the concert in Toledo a Lutheran pastor in that city was moved to write a letter that began: "Dear Brother Schmidt, All day there has lingered in my memory the recollection of the concert last night. It was a foretaste of heaven and strengthens my longing for it. If here singing can be brought to such perfection, what will it be like there? Tell the director that I want to be in his chorus on the other side."[22]

By the time the Choir was traveling west toward Minnesota, word of its earlier concerts had spread from city to city. The crowds grew to the point where many had to be turned away for lack of room in the concert halls and churches.[23]

The reception given the returning Choir in Northfield on May 10, 1920, was unforgettable.[24] On the train station platform awaiting their arrival at 9:08 a.m. that Monday morning were the whole student body, the St. Olaf Band, "clad in duck trousers and gilt-epauletted blue coats," faculty, and townspeople. As the Choir stepped off the train, the Band struck up the popular St. Olaf song, "High on Manitou Heights, St. Olaf College Stands,"

St. Olaf Band, May 10, 1920
Downtown Northfield

Gerhard Mathre scrapbook

and everyone joined in the singing. The Choir members were escorted in a procession up the hill to the campus where a welcoming program was held in Hoyme Memorial Chapel.

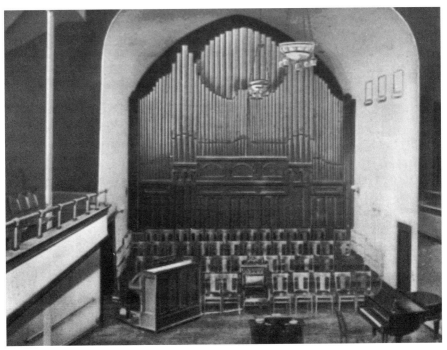

Hoyme Memorial Chapel
Built 1906, burned 1923

In the meantime, Professor Christiansen, who preferred to avoid such noisy receptions, had slipped away and walked up to the campus by himself. At the Chapel program he said, "I'm mighty glad to be back" and shifted the praise from himself to the local culture that had nurtured the Choir. Cited in an earlier context was his gracious reference to the community. "That we were successful was only that the *flavor of St. Olaf* was given to the world and they seemed to like it." [25] P. G. Schmidt complimented the Choir members on the Christian spirit and charming behavior they had displayed on tour. He was also pleased to announce that there was no deficit to be made up by the guarantors.[26]

The 1920 tour was a resounding success in establishing the reputation of the St. Olaf Choir on the national musical scene. The profusion of favorable reviews far outweighed the occasional critical comments. Critics were genuinely impressed by the youth and vigor of the Choir. A New York reviewer wrote: "Mr. Christiansen has trained the choir to veritable virtuosity and it sang with the resilient, irresistible vitality of youth and the intense conviction of a centuries-old tradition."[27]

Also stirred by what they heard and observed were ordinary, untrained listeners. A man from Springfield, Ohio wrote: "Not only the sustained harmony of so many voices but the manifest sincerity, deep Christian devotion, and modesty of these young people all combined not only to make a favorable impression but to bring a real religious message to the people who heard them."[28]

The tour also fulfilled the purpose of letting thousands of people hear the beautiful Lutheran chorales. A professor of hymnology at Augustana Lutheran Seminary, who heard the Choir in Rock Island, Illinois, on its way west, was quite carried away at the prospect of an artistic Lutheran renaissance in America that would mean more singing of Lutheran hymns and a new period of composition of Lutheran music for the church.[29]

On May 14, 1920, shortly after its return to Minnesota, the St. Olaf Choir gave a concert before an audience of over 3,000 persons in the Minneapolis Armory. The editor of the *Lutheran Church Herald* attended and gave his impressions, insisting that they were those of a layman, not a music critic. Also disclaiming sentimentality, he sought to explain why he had been so impressed by the concert. Some of his comments were as follows:

> In the first place there was a complete absence of any effort at any kind of display of stage dress, or stage performance, no smiling solo singer posing for admiration and applause. In a quiet, modest, and orderly manner the vested singers took their places, and as soon as Prof. Christiansen's baton gave the signal,

everything was forgotten except the wonderful melodies and harmonies which he seemed to draw out and modulate as though he were playing on a large pipe organ.

The editor continued by noting that "they all sang with intense devotion and religious feeling." He extended to Professor Christiansen and his Choir the congratulations and thanks of the Church for what they had done to revive classical church music. "In the most effective manner attention has been called to the beauties of the Lutheran chorale, and the result will be a blessing to the whole Church."[30]

Other Tours in the 1920s

The gratifying outcome of the 1920 tour established the idea of an annual tour. The next year the Choir traveled about the Midwest, giving concerts in seven states. The tour began in St. Cloud, Minnesota and continued into western Minnesota and a few towns in South Dakota. By this time the St. Olaf Choir had developed a clear sense of identity with the members providing their own house organ, "The Choir Scream." The *Viking* article about the 1921 tour, signed "G. P.," described the sense of togetherness. "Before a week was past, we felt like a great family." There were jokes, vaudeville songs, whistling, yodeling, declaiming, and other horseplay. Prof. Christiansen was initiated into a secret organization. In an icy cold railroad car without a stove, the aisle and seats covered with snow from a recent blizzard, Choir member "Cora Hjertaas engi-

The Choir Scream Vol. III No. 2 (1922)

neered the construction of an icy slide in the aisle of the coach."[31] "G. P." was most likely Gunnar Pederson, editor of the *Messenger* and student body president.[32]

On an overnight stay in a South Dakota town, a Choir member failed to jot down the address of the family with whom he was to spend the night. He only remembered a brown house on a corner. Walking down the street after the concert, he found one that looked like it, went in, walked upstairs to what he thought was his room, but found it occupied. He had of course entered the wrong house. Embarrassment and explanations followed.[33]

A key concert for which the Choir was poised was in St. Joseph, Missouri, where it appeared at a festival before a huge gathering of 4,000 musicians and music educators. "We outdid ourselves, giving what was perhaps the best concert of the tour," wrote G. P. for the 1922-23 *Viking*. After singing in St. Louis and Chicago, Choir members were aware that they were being "compared favorably with the renowned 1920 choir."

The Choir made its way through Wisconsin, giving concerts in Eau Claire, Madison, and Janesville, and hearing of the glories of that state from the Wisconsin members. The final concert was at the Minnesota State Capitol in St. Paul. The legislators put their business to one side to listen to the Choir. Wrote G. P. of this event: "We sang 'Hosanna' and 'Beautiful Savior' from the visitors' gallery, with Prof. Christiansen directing us from a precarious perch on the rail." The Choir arrived in

Old Main

Northfield after midnight. "The lights on the campus had long since been switched off," wrote G. P., "and the familiar outlines of the Old Main and the pines were made visible only by the stars and a new moon. Climbing the long flight of stairs, we paused at the top and took a deep breath of the sweet air of Manitou Heights. Home again!"[34]

The Choir had accepted an invitation to sing at the State Music Teachers' Convention in Duluth, Minnesota, on June 24, 1921. On its way to that commitment, it gave a series of concerts in Minnesota and the

Dakotas, a tour that was remembered mainly for the unrelenting heat encountered everywhere. But after perspiring through sixteen concerts, the Choir arrived at Duluth where the weather was suddenly cold enough to require the wearing of overcoats. G. P. had this comment: "What with the cold and the sadness of disbanding, one might say there was weeping and chattering of teeth."[35]

On January 3, 1922, the St. Olaf Choir left on its annual tour, again making its way toward the east coast, eager to uphold the standard set by the 1920 Choir. In Milwaukee it was hailed as "the most superb body of singers in the United States, if not in the world." Three famous musicians of the time were guests of the Choir at concerts along the way: Peter C. Lutkin, founder of the Northwestern University A Cappella Choir, Fred J. Wolle, director of the Bach Choir of Bethlehem, Pennsylvania, and at the Metropolitan Opera House in New York, the Norwegian composer Christian Sinding.[36]

Throughout the tour Director Christiansen received accolades for his contribution to choral art, as a wizard of the baton, a man of great vision, a director of the "human symphony." Again reviewers used the image of the Choir as a great organ on which the master played. Among the students in the Choir that year were Olaf C. Christiansen in the back row with the baritones and Gertrude Boe in the front row with the sopranos. [37]

St. Olaf Choir 1924-25
Olaf: back row fourth from right
Gertrude: front row in front of FMC

And again the students were enjoying themselves. Olaf recalled that they all wrote home to report that they had sung at the "Met." The Choir was entertained a second time by the Frank Seiberlings in Akron, Ohio. This time, after the Choir had sung for her, Mrs. Seiberling responded with some vocal selections of her own and was elected an honorary member of the Choir. Other non-concert activities included hearing Wagner's "Die Walkyrie," visiting the Tomb of the Unknown Soldier in Washington, making records in Camden, New Jersey, and amusing themselves on the long train rides. Each issue of "The Choir Scream" was eagerly awaited. One of its features was the "Fresh From the Farm" contest in which the rural and small town Midwesterners poked fun at themselves.[38]

"Scramble for the Scream"
1924-25 Western Tour

With Sinclair Lewis's 1920 novel, *Main Street*, on the minds of Americans in that decade, more than one reviewer borrowed the imagery of "Gopher Prairie" and "Main Street" in commenting about the young singers from rural Minnesota, but in a favorable way. A writer for the *Brooklyn Standard Union* maintained that the Choir's treatment of the classics indicated "that the novelist was wrong, and that Gopher Prairie and its environs are dispensers and not despisers of culture."[39] Similarly, the *New York World* announced, "It was Main Street come to Broadway to show that Main Street itself does not despise, but loves and practices, good music."[40]

The view was gaining ground among critics that the St. Olaf Choir represented the highest level of a cappella singing to be heard in the country. · Leola Nelson Bergmann turned to Deems Taylor, New York critic writing for the *World*, for a representative summary of the Choir's strong points most frequently mentioned in reviews. These features were: "clarity of diction, perfection of attack and release, the discipline of the group, the mystery of the pitch, and Christiansen's complete mastery over the choir."[41]

As each tour was planned and realized, Paul G. Schmidt continued imperturbably and effectively in his vital role as manager of the Choir and anchor of the low bass section. In March of 1923, when the Choir left on a tour of several Midwestern states, P. G. was the sole manager. The College discontinued its connection with Martin Hanson of New York. Moreover, the College administration and the St. Olaf Music Board asked Schmidt to devote the major share of his time to music work, which meant organizing the May Music Festival

FMC, Martin Hanson, PGS

as well as managing the St. Olaf Band and the St. Olaf Lutheran Choir. He would continue to do some teaching in the department of mathematics.[42]

F. Melius Christiansen was always ready to acknowledge his and the Choir's dependence on P. G. Schmidt for the orderly planning and execution of the tours and other concerts. For the student yearbook one year Christiansen paid a worthy tribute to Schmidt in these words:

> With the knowledge of the spirit of the Church and the institution, coupled with his fine presence and even-tempered nature, he is so well fitted to represent St. Olaf among the people with whom he is thrown in contact in carrying out his business. He is a very fine man for looking after details, a quality which is required in laying out routes and making all arrangements for the trip. As a true and loyal member and president of the choir, and manager, he has always been the mainstay in my work during the twenty-odd years we have labored together here at St. Olaf.[43]

Christiansen said repeatedly that Schmidt was as responsible for the St. Olaf Choir as he was. At one point, in order to give weight to his desire to share credit with P. G., F. Melius insisted that on the printed programs for the Choir, the name of P. G. Schmidt should appear in the same size print that was used for his own name.[44]

The spring tour of 1923 was not lacking in highlights, both in performing and sightseeing. There was a visit to the Mayo Clinic in Rochester. A heavy snow storm in Wisconsin had the Choir stranded in its

St. Olaf Choir, 1923
On steps of Old Main

Pullmann for a time, reduced to a temporary diet of milk and crackers. The same snow storm prevented F. Melius, who had spent some extra time with relatives in Marinette, from getting to the concert in Green Bay. P. G. Schmidt recruited a talented student to do the directing. At intermission time P. G. told the audience that the student director's name was Olaf Christiansen, and the crowd exploded in applause.[45]

The 1923 Midwestern tour included some cities in Missouri and Nebraska. In Kansas City Christiansen was interviewed by a reporter from the *Kansas City Post*. In the course of the interview Christy listed his eight maxims:

Olaf Christiansen and Ellen Kjos were married in 1925

142

Kansas City, 1923

"Eat rye bread. Don't sing like graut. Concentrate. Always do your best. Keep things lively. Do not rub off too many edges. Eat oatmeal. Be happy." [46] Of these eight, it was probably "Eat oatmeal" that Choir members heard most frequently from their director. Whenever someone fainted during a program, Christiansen would seek the person out off stage and inquire how he or she was doing. His last word to the victim was always the command, "Eat oatmeal!"[47]

The St. Olaf Choir made its first Western tour, including cities on the Pacific Coast, in 1924-25, leaving Northfield December 18, 1924, and returning after thirty-two concerts in late January, 1925. Because the Choir would be gone at Christmas, P. G. Schmidt made special arrangements with a pastor in Missoula, Montana, to provide a Christmas Eve service and party at the spacious Olson home in that city. Parents of the Choir members had sent presents which were placed under the tree.[48] Arndis Lundeberg, '26, recorded the scene for the yearbook: "As we sang our Christmas songs, sitting on the floor about the tree in the candle-lit room, and the Christmas gospel was read by the Reverend [Conrad] Engelstad—then perhaps more than at any other time on the trip was our 'kindred spirit' awakened and we felt the strength and meaning of our choir unity." And in the humming of "Silent Night," as Mrs. Overby sang the words, they felt the quiet power of the Christmas spirit. [49]

Choir members estimated that they sang to from 75,000 to 100,000 people on the Western tour. In Miles City, Montana, Professor Schmidt obliged when called upon to preach the sermon in the Lutheran church. Among concert sites were Spokane and Everett, Washington. At the luncheon for the Choir in the latter city, the words of welcome were spoken by a Catholic priest. Vancouver, British Columbia, was the scene of the northernmost appearance, and San Diego, California, marked the southernmost point of the Pacific Coast cities. In between came Tacoma, Seattle, Portland, Sacramento, San Francisco, Los Angeles, and Pasadena, with well-received performances and colorful sightseeing at each stop.

In San Francisco the singers discovered that their responses to attention from the press could change from amusement and flattery to sheer distress. They were asked about the cold weather in Minnesota, about St. Olaf College as a legitimate degree-granting institution, and about their home lives. Somehow, the reporters convinced themselves that all of the young singers grew up on farms out

Church in Miles City, Montana
P.G. preached here

Alice Giere second from left
Tia Juana, Mexico, 1925

on the prairie. One young lady, daughter of a St. Paul surgeon, agreed to an interview, happily answered all questions, and posed for a picture. The next day she was aghast and furious to see her picture on the front page of a paper with the preposterous headline: "Miss Alice Giere, champion cow milker of Minnesota, challenges any girl in California to a cow-milking contest." Unhappily, what began as a pleasant visit to San Francisco was ruined for Miss Giere. [50]

Ladies' Quartet, 1921
Gertrude Boe on left

Heading home after the Los Angeles concert, the Choir stopped in Salt Lake City to hear a special recital on the great pipe organ in the Mormon Tabernacle. In Colorado Springs P. G. had arranged a stunning tour of "The Garden of the Gods" which took the Choir up through narrow gorges and awe-inspiring rock formations to an elevation of over 7600 feet where they could visit the famous Cave of the Winds. Additional concerts in Kansas, Missouri, and Iowa brought the singers back home. One day on the train near the end of the tour, Mrs. Gertrude Overby, soprano soloist, was heard to say, "Every time I look at 'P. G.' I want to say 'Thank you!'"[51]

Snapshots on this and previous page from the photo album of Henry M. Halverson, Class of 1925, "St. Olaf Choir Pacific Trip 1924-25"
STOARCHIV

146

A New Music Hall—"Built by Song"

The whole College had good reason to be grateful to P. G. Schmidt. As the 1926-27 *Viking* yearbook noted, "No small share of the credit for the financial success of the musical activities is due to [Schmidt's] untiring efforts."[52] One result of the highly successful 1920 tour to the East had been the earning of enough money to pay back the guarantors, give a generous honorarium to Martin Hanson, and set aside "the first contribution toward the building of a music hall," a respectable sum of $10,000.[53]

What the College had been using as a music hall was an old frame building earlier known as Ladies' Hall and later taken over for music practice. The students, familiar with the variety of sounds, sometimes of strange and unpredictable quality, that daily floated out from the windows, fondly referred to the old house as Agony Hall. It was obvious to all that the building was inadequate, but money for building was scarce in the 1920s. Nevertheless, there was an optimistic spirit at the College that had generated the slogan, "A Greater St. Olaf," and the successes of the St. Olaf Choir contributed to the upbeat spirit. One cannot underestimate the favorable impact of the Choir's 1920 tour to the east coast and the subsequent tours that not only established the Choir's name but brought in significant earnings. Thus the College was able to plan and erect a new music building in 1926, just before the depression set in to curtail further building. Well over a third of the total cost of about $120,000 was met by the earnings of the St. Olaf Choir and other musical organizations, starting with the

Ladies' Hall, built in 1879
Once used as music hall

Proposed Music Building

contribution from the 1920 tour. A brochure about the Choir explained how funds over and above expenses were designated for the music hall and stated: "'Built by song' is the characterization applied to this new building."[54]

The idea of "A Greater St. Olaf" was linked to the introduction of a new and ambitious architectural scheme for the campus. The College engaged the services of the Chicago architectural firm of Coolidge and Hodgdon who proposed a new style for all future campus buildings that became known as the "Norman Gothic" style. Intrinsic to the plan was the decision to use a certain gray limestone, initially quarried in nearby Faribault, Minnesota, as the chief building material.

The new music hall was the third building to appear on campus in the so-called Norman Gothic style and constructed of Faribault limestone. The first had been a new power plant, begun in 1923, and the second was a science and administration building, dedicated in 1925. The latter building would be named Holland Hall in 1949.

The original design for the music hall envisioned an imposing, three-unit structure consisting of a large, church-like recital hall, a seven-story tower with entrance lobby, smaller recital room, band room, classrooms, and studios, and a "working unit" with practice rooms and studios. Because of the strained financial conditions of the depression, the College could afford to build only one of the three units.

Built in 1926 was the "working unit." In its basement and four stories were thirty practice rooms, nine faculty studios, a director's suite, a library, a magazine room, classroom, and social room. The director's suite on the first floor was where hundreds of nervous vocal candidates faced their auditions by F. Melius Christiansen or, in later years, by Olaf Christiansen and Kenneth Jennings. In 1958 the building was named the F. Melius Christiansen Music Hall.

The dedication of the music hall took place on the College's Foundation Day, Saturday, November 6, 1926. The next afternoon the Minneapolis Symphony Orchestra gave a concert on the campus in recognition of the St. Olaf Lutheran Choir and the new music building. This first visit to St. Olaf by the Minneapolis Symphony was the beginning of a tradition of exchange concerts. Again, P. G. Schmidt was the key figure in bringing about this unique development.

While planning another tour to the east coast for 1926, it occurred to Schmidt to compare notes with Arthur J. Gaines, manager of the Minneapolis Symphony Orchestra, then planning a tour into the same part of the country. P. G. mentioned that it had been the practice of the St. Olaf Choir to give a concert in Minneapolis each year at the conclusion of its annual tour. "It was then," wrote Schmidt, "that Mr. Gaines proposed that we trade concerts, the Symphony to give a concert at St. Olaf College, and the choir to give one in Minneapolis under Symphony auspices." Thus began the exchange, the Orchestra coming to St. Olaf in the fall, and the St. Olaf Choir going to Minneapolis for a joint concert with the Symphony in the spring.[55]

Music Hall, built in 1926

Tour Programs

On its concert tours during the 1920s the St. Olaf Choir usually sang a program of eleven pieces, beginning with a Bach number. The 1920 program opened with "Blessing, Glory, and Wisdom," which at the time was ascribed to Johan Sebastian Bach. Subsequent research has questioned whether the piece is a Bach composition. The next two years the opening Bach number was *The Spirit Also Helpeth Us*, used again in 1927. *Be Not Afraid* and *Come, Jesu, Come* were sung respectively in 1923 and 1924. In 1925 and 1926 the opening Bach selection was *Sing Ye* (*Singet dem Herrn*). The same piece appeared on the 1929 and 1930 programs.

While members and friends of the St. Olaf Choir have long been accustomed to a Bach number at the beginning of a concert or early in the program, it is well to recall that it was unusual in the 1920s for any choir to sing Bach unaccompanied. In this respect also, the St. Olaf Choir made a pioneering contribution to choral singing, even as it did both by the frequency and range of its tours.

Dr. Christiansen preferred a three-part program. The heavier, classical numbers came in the first group. In the second and third groups came choral pieces of a more descriptive and romantic sort, including the folk songs he was so fond of. [56] The well-known hymn, "Beautiful Savior," which has become the traditional closing number at St. Olaf Choir concerts, was not always listed on the program through most of the 1920s, although it may have been sung as an encore. It was listed in 1920 as the tenth of eleven numbers and as the final number in 1929. [57]

As a representative concert program from the decade of the 1920s, one may review the numbers from the Pacific Coast Tour of 1924-25. Part I opened with Bach's *Sing Ye to the Lord*. It was followed by "O Bread of Life" by Heinrich Isaac, "Hosanna" by F. M. Christiansen, and "Beautiful Savior." Of the "Hosanna" a critic had written that it was "of lofty conception and was beautifully interpreted." [58] Part II consisted of "Savior of Sinners" by F. Mendelssohn, "How Fair the Church of Christ" from Schumann's

Concert Program
Pacific Coast Tour, 1924-25

150

Gesangbuch, "Welcome," words by N. F. S. Grundtvig and music by F. M. Christiansen, and "Motet for Advent" by Gustav Schreck, with whom Christiansen had studied in Leipzig.

Part III of the 1924-25 program began with "Our Father," by A. Gretchaninoff. Next were "Snow Mountain" by F. M. Christiansen, "In Dulci Jubilo," 14th century melody, and as the final piece, "Wake, Awake" by Philipp Nicolai, set for double choir by F. M. Christiansen.[59] The printed program indicated that four of the twelve numbers were either composed or arranged by Christiansen, but in fact he also arranged four others: "O Bread of Life," "Beautiful Savior," "How Fair the Church," and "In Dulci Jubilo." He preferred that his name not appear too often in the concert programs.

There were always some numbers that the general public never heard. When choirs travel, especially those of college age, the singers perform for their own entertainment. St. Olaf Choir members enjoyed a kind of informal singing that they called "agonizing." Writing about the western tour of 1924-25 for the *Viking*, Arndis Lundeberg '26 described how the Choir relaxed on the train with checkers, cross-word puzzles, rook, and even the throwing of a baseball, but this sport "proved so devastating to the chandeliers, windows, and unknowing heads" that it had to be abandoned. Then she told about the singing:

> Perhaps the most satisfying of all our simple joys, however, and that which will always be a part of the choir, were our sessions of "agonizing" in the observation coach—sometimes to ourselves, sometimes to a group of surprised and delighted travelers, some students like ourselves, others more elderly travelers, but always to those who appreciated our enthusiasm for "Annie Laurie," "The World is Waiting for the Sunrise," "Mandy Lou," and "High on Manitou Heights."[60]

Choir in dining car on Pacific tour, 1927

Choir with Senator Henrik Shipstead
Washington, February 14, 1927

Two visits to the east coast, in 1927 and 1929, are deserving of mention. In 1927 the St. Olaf Choir was greeted by Minnesota Senator Henrik Shipstead on the steps of the Capitol in Washington, D. C. Both years the New York concerts were held in the Metropolitan Opera House and were sponsored by the Inner Mission Society of the Evangelical Lutheran Church in New York City.

A few features of the programs may be noted. The Bach numbers used to open the concerts were *The Spirit Also Helpeth Us* in 1927 and *Sing Ye to the Lord* in 1929. The second part of the 1927 concert included Martin Luther's "From Heaven Above," and two Norwegian folk songs by Grieg, "Hvad est du dog skjøn" ("Behold Thou art fair") and "Guds søn har gjort mig fri" ("God's Son has made me free"). In the third part were two German Christmas songs. The concert closed with the Chorale and Entrance Scene from Schreck's "Motet for Advent."[61]

Following the Bach in the 1929 program was Durante's anthem for two choirs, "Misericordias Domini." Part II had pieces by Edward Elgar, Max

St. Olaf Choir at Minnesota Capitol, 1929

Reger, Georg Schumann, and Arnold Mendelssohn. Part III opened with S. Rachmaninoff's "Glory Be To God" followed by the Norwegian folk melody, "So Soberly." The last two numbers were F. Melius Christiansen's "Clap Your Hands," based on Psalm 47, and "Beautiful Savior," the one and only time in the decade of the twenties that the latter hymn was listed as the final number on the program. [62]

While in New York during the 1927 tour, Christiansen wrote a letter to President Boe back at the College that stressed the importance of his remaining in good physical and spiritual condition for the sake of the choir.

> I am not sentimental when I say that the spiritual condition is very important in this work. We must give genuine expression to those beautiful words and not merely "vain repetitions." May we all be true to our calling. True to our master and true in our work for the master. And may we also be true to Art! The spirit of art is very much like the spirit of Christ. Here, too, truthfulness is essential if it is to reach the hearts of the listeners.[63]

Such reflections on the part of Dr. Christiansen were in keeping with the calling and work of the Inner Mission Society that sponsored the New York concerts in 1927 and 1929. Organized in 1907, the Inner Mission Society of the Evangelical Lutheran Church in New York City had developed an extensive program of social services. Its aim was "to minister in God's name to the indigent, ill, homeless, criminal, fallen and any others in need." Its activities were carried out through institutional ministrations, family and child welfare, Lutheran Hospital social service, and a vacation home for children.

As the Souvenir Program for the 1929 concert stated: "It is by no mere accident that the St. Olaf Choir and the Inner Mission Society are associated in the presentation of a concert. There is an inner harmony of purpose which unites them."[64] It is a point to be remembered, although easily over-looked. While often tucked away in the corner of the concert program or at the end of the newspaper review, the name of the sponsoring organization or the benefit reminded readers of significant ministries that merited their support.

The idea brings one back to the reasons for St. Olaf Choir tours. The artistic purpose emphasized by P. G. Schmidt is seen to be in harmony with the spiritual purpose of which F. Melius wrote. "The spirit of art is very much like the spirit of Christ." And the spirit of Christ finds expression in acts of service to the human family.

FMC Composition

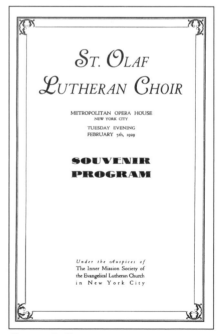

Souvenir Program
New York City, 1929

154

Notes for Chapter 5 TOURS IN THE TWENTIES

1. *Viking 1922-1923*, 133.

2. *The 1926-27 Viking*, 126.

3. *Viking '16 '17 '18*, 216.

4. *Victory Viking '19 '20 '21*, n.p.

5. *Ibid.*

6. *Lutheran Church Herald* IV (January 20, 1920), 33.

7. Paul G. Schmidt, *My Years at St. Olaf*, A Centennial Decade Publication (Northfield, Minnesota: St. Olaf College, [1967]), 66.

8. *Ibid.*

9. Text of the statement partially garbled in *Lutheran Church Herald* IV (February 17, 1920), 98. Correct version in letter from L. W. Boe, President of St. Olaf College, Northfield, Minnesota, Easter, 1920, printed in St. Olaf Lutheran Choir Tour 1920 Program. STOARCHIV. Cf. Leola Nelson Bergmann, *Music Master of the Middle West*: The Story of F. Melius Christiansen and the St. Olaf Choir (Minneapolis: University of Minnesota Press, 1944), 126.

10. *Viking 1922-1923*, 133.

11. Bergmann, *Music Master of the Middle West*, 126.

12. Program: "St. Olaf Lutheran Choir Tour 1920." STOARCHIV. *Viking 1922-1923*, 135; Bergmann, 219-20.

13. Cited in Schmidt, *My Years at St. Olaf*, 67, 68.

14. *Schmidt*, 67.

15. *Ibid.*, 68; *Saint Olaf*, November/December 1989, 4.

16. Quoted in *Lutheran Church Herald* IV (April 27, 1920), 269.

17. Bergmann, 128.

18. Richard Aldrich, "St. Olaf Lutheran Choir," *New York Times*, April 28, 1920.

19. Sylvester Rawling, "St. Olaf Choir Gives Rare Treat," New York *Evening World*, April 28, 1920.

20. "Schaefer, J. Louis," *The National Cyclopaedia of American Biography* (New York: James T. White & Company, 1936), XXV, 236.

21. *Saint Olaf*, November/December 1989, 7.

22. Quoted in *Lutheran Church Herald* IV (May 25, 1920), 318.

23. *Op. cit.*, 317.

24. P. G. Schmidt, "Eastern Tour of Choir 1920," *Viking 1922-1923*, 135.

25. *Manitou Messenger* (*MM*) XXXIII (May 11, 1920), 1.

26. *Lutheran Church Herald* IV (May 25, 1920), 317-18; *Saint Olaf,* November/December 1989, 7.

27. Cited in Bergmann, 128.

28. *Lutheran Church Herald* IV (April 27, 1920), 269.

29. *Lutheran Church Herald* IV (May 18, 1920), 307-08.

30. *Lutheran Church Herald* IV (May 25, 1920), 321.

31. *Viking 1922-1923*, 139-40.

32. *Ibid.*, 65.

33. *Ibid.*, 140.

34. *Ibid.*, 318.

35. *Ibid.*, 141.

36. *The 1924-25 Viking*, 137-38.

37. *Ibid.*, 137.

38. *Ibid.*, 138.

39. *Brooklyn Standard Union*, January 16, 1922.

40. *New York World*, January 18, 1922.

41. Bergmann, 131.

42. Schmidt, *My Years at St. Olaf*, 81.

43. *The 1926-27 Viking*, 127.

44. Paul Benson, *The Empires of Song*: A Cappella Choirs in the Scandinavian-American Colleges, Unpublished Typescript, n.d., 32. Used by permission. Cf. 1930 Tour Program.

45. Letter from Mildred Hoff Anderson '24 to Bob Johnson, January 1994; cf. *The 1924-25 Viking*, 138.

46. Kansas City *Post*, April 11, 1923.

47. *Saint Olaf*, November/December 1989, 4.

48. Schmidt, *My Years at St. Olaf*, 71.

49. *The 1926-27 Viking*, 117.

50. Mrs. E. L. Vitalis, "Dr. F. Melius Christiansen and the St. Olaf College Choir," Unidentified newspaper, 1925.

51. *The 1926-27 Viking*, 121.

52. *Ibid.*, 127.

53. Schmidt, *My Years at St. Olaf*, 70; Bergmann, 131.

54. Booklet: *The St. Olaf Lutheran Choir* (Northfield, Minnesota: The Twin City St. Olaf Club, ca. 1931), 14. This booklet gives the cost of the first section of the music building as approximately $140,000. See p. 11.

55. Schmidt, 71-72; Joseph M. Shaw, *Dear Old Hill* (Northfield, Minnesota: St. Olaf College, 1992), 115.

56. Bergmann, 167.

57. Tour programs 1920-29.

58. Sylvester Rawling, *New York Evening World*, April 28, 1920.

59. Program: "St. Olaf Lutheran Choir, Pacific Coast Tour, December 1924-January 1925."

60. Arndis Lundeberg, "Western Tour, 1924-25," *The 1926-27 Viking*, 117.

61. 1927 Tour Program. STOARCHIV.

62. 1929 Tour Program. STOARCHIV.

63. F. Melius Christiansen to L. W. Boe, February 10, 1927. STOARCHIV. Cited in Bergmann, 134.

64. Souvenir Program: St. Olaf Lutheran Choir, Metropolitan Opera House, New York City, Tuesday Evening, February 5th, 1929, 9.

CHAPTER 6

NORWAY AND GERMANY, 1930

"The musical world has come to know and appreciate the St. Olaf Choir largely through its extensive tours." So declared the St. Olaf student yearbook, the *Viking* for 1930. The tours of the twenties amply confirmed the statement and 1930 gave it added emphasis. That was the year in which the Choir took two outstanding trips, into the southern states in January and February, and to Europe in the summer months. [1]

Trondhjem Festival Brochure

To review the Choir's activities in the thirties naturally means to begin with the southern tour of early 1930. The European tour quickly followed, with memorable experiences first in Norway and then in Germany. Brief mention will be made of domestic tours through the rest of the decade, noting the adoption of the new purple robes and acknowledging the contribution of the Choir's fine soprano soloist, Gertrude Boe Overby. A glance at the 1940 Western tour concludes the chapter.

First Southern Tour, 1930

In St. Olaf Choir lore the year 1930 has come to stand for the eventful trip to Norway and Germany. But members of the Choir who made that trip also remember that in January and February they were singing before an entirely new set of audiences in the South. Even as countless travel and financial preparations were in full swing for the summer tour to Europe, Christiansen, Schmidt, and the Choir were getting ready for a tour into a part of the country where they had not been before, the southern states of

Tennessee, North and South Carolina, Georgia, and Florida. Concerts on the homeward swing would be given in Washington, D. C., Hagerstown, Maryland, Wheeling, West Virginia, Columbus and Dayton, Ohio, Chicago and Rockford, Illinois.

On the way South the Choir sang in Springfield, Illinois, where a reviewer, Clayton C. Quast, observed that it was "one of the very few choice choral bodies now singing before the public." He believed that the Choir did full justice in magnificent style to Bach's motet, "Sing to the Lord." Referring to Grieg's "Guds Søn har gjort mig fri" ("God's Son has made me free"), Quast commented: "The Grieg folk song was of a vital and virile style and withal more in the folk song style and pleased the audience mightily. There was good healthy tone, effectively projected." He also reported the enthusiasm of the audience for an encore number, "Beautiful Savior."[2].

Luther Sletten, Fred Schmidt
St. Augustine, Florida, 1930

Inasmuch as it was twenty below zero when the Choir left Northfield on January 18, 1930, Florida warmth a week later was fully appreciated. After an engagement at the Temple Theatre in Jacksonville, there was an excursion to St. Augustine. The singers were delighted with their visit to the Ancient City and nearby orange groves, said a newspaper report, "and with the drive in what they considered warm sunshine."[3]

The southern audiences were also warm in their reception of the Choir. P. G. wrote home from Savannah: "Radio stations here and elsewhere in the south were broadcasting St. Olaf choir records during each afternoon and evening, and everyone seemed to be talking 'St. Olaf.'" A writer

Gertrude Boe Overby
Choir soloist, voice teacher

160

Choir at Chickamauga Battlefield
Chattanooga, Tennessee, 1930

for a Charleston, South Carolina, paper was much impressed by the singing of the "blonde soprano soloist," not named in the program, Gertrude Boe Overby. "Her clarity of voice is rivaled by its purity, by its sweet lack of affectation. It does not cloy. It enchants." The same writer showed an appreciation of the Choir's dedication. "Perfection in a choir is born of discipline, of confidence, of desire to sink individuality into the pattern of the whole."[4]

In Tennessee a music critic noted that the singers reflected the splendid training they had received from their director. "These 60 earnest, serious-minded students watch their conductor's beat and sing entirely from memory the most intricate part music, coming in at odd intervals, occasionally humming enchantingly, swelling and dying away with every part distinctly audible. . . . The conducting of Dr. Christiansen calls for more superlatives, because it is unostentatious, simple and direct, but tremendously effective." The critic expressed the hope that every choir singer in Nashville was at the concert to learn something.[5]

While in Nashville the Choir visited the Fiske Institute, which had its own famous Jubilee Singers. At a convocation, the St. Olaf Choir was on the stage where it gave a short concert. Then the Jubilee Singers, on the main floor toward the front of the auditorium, sang a number of selections. The audience was invited to join in singing familiar spirituals. At lunch with some of the teachers, Christiansen and Schmidt used the opportunity to enlarge their knowledge of the origin and history of the spirituals.[6]

During the tour the Choir members were learning a few things about race relations. One of the young women in the Choir, 18 year-old Signe Ramseth '33 (Mrs. Signe M. R. Johnson), recorded in her diary some reactions she and others had on seeing blacks or "Negroes." She noted that the audience at the Winston-Salem concert might have been larger, "but as there was only one entrance to the auditorium the negroes could not come." An informal concert at a black high school was arranged and the listeners "were thrilled to pieces." P. G. Schmidt spoke to the audience about the St. Olaf Choir. Then the whole assembly rose and sang the national

Signe M. Ramseth '33

Negro hymn. A young boy handed Choir members copies of the words. "It was very impressive," wrote Miss Ramseth.[7]

On the homeward part of the journey the Choir gave a concert in Mees Hall on the campus of Capital University in Columbus, Ohio. The review mentioned the packed hall, the director's late arrival and the relieved applause that greeted him, the strong fortissimos, the soft phrases, and the fine execution of Bach's motet, "Sing Ye to the Lord," among other things. During the singing of Glinka's "Cherubim Song," which the reviewer especially liked, "people began to notice a powerful agent in the deep diapasonic quality of one particular bass voice. The owner reinforced the bass section like the double basses do the celli in a full orchestra."[8] He could only have been referring to P. G. Schmidt.

The ever-inventive and considerate P. G., always planning ahead, quietly made arrangements to have a special breakfast menu prepared for the diner on the Milwaukee Road train taking the

Choir Menu paa norsk

Choir homeward from Chicago. As the singers sat down for breakfast and were handed the menu, they saw at the top the words, "St. Olaf Lutheran Choir, Dixie Tour 1930," and "Breakfast," but from there on the entire menu was printed *in Norwegian*. P. G.'s clever action for the singers' amusement also anticipated the trip to Norway and Germany scheduled for the summer of 1930.

The 1930 European Tour

The St. Olaf Choir went to Norway in 1930 to represent the Norwegian Lutheran Church of America at festivities in Trondheim to mark the rededication of Nidaros Cathedral and to observe the 900th anniversary of the death of Olav Haraldsson, the medieval king who brought Christianity to Norway.[9] The invitation was extended in 1928 by the Olav's Committee of the International League of Norsemen *(Nordmanns Forbundet)*.[10]

The public was informed of the St. Olaf Choir's impending trip to Europe as early as Sunday, December 9, 1928, when *The Minneapolis Journal* announced on its front page: "Famous St. Olaf Choir to Help Norway Celebrate Christianity Anniversary." Above a picture of the Choir ran the heading: "St. Olaf Lutheran Choir Begins Practice for Norway Concert in 1930." When the Choir went on tour in 1929, the front cover of its concert program carried the following notice regarding the Choir's plans for a tour to Norway the following year:

FRAM, FRAM, CRISTMENN, CROSSMENN
These words formed the inscription on the coat of arms
of King Olaf of Norway, who in 1030 lost his life in
battle, fighting to establish Christianity in his kingdom.

Nine hundred years later, from another continent across the
sea, and from an institution named in honor of this king and
of his cause,—St. Olaf College—, comes a group of young
people with a greeting in songs presenting the great truths
of that religion.

The St. Olaf Lutheran Choir has been invited to participate
in the 900th anniversary which will be observed July 29th and
30th, 1930, in the Old Capital of northern Norway,—Trondhjem,
and the invitation has been accepted.

A note on the cover page explains that the words "Fram! Fram! Cristmenn! Crossmenn!" are on the official seal of St. Olaf College. They are translated, "Forward! Forward! Men of Christ! Men of the Cross!"

After the news had spread that the St. Olaf Choir had accepted the invitation to sing at the great celebration in Norway, College authorities received an invitation from the city of Augsburg to send the Choir to participate in Germany's commemoration of the 400th anniversary of the Augsburg Confession, a document setting forth the core teachings of the faith as accepted by Lutherans all over the world. This invitation was also considered and accepted.[12]

St. Olaf College Seal

With the winter tour into the southern states behind them, the Choir and its leaders began the extensive preparations necessary for the summer tour to Norway and Germany. Again, as in 1913, Professor J. Jørgen Thompson was sent to Norway in the spring to make arrangements. He was also to schedule concerts in Sweden, Denmark, and Germany. Contacts were made with the League of Norsemen in Norway and with the German Festival committee in Augsburg, Germany, for assistance in arranging travel and concerts. Much of P. G. Schmidt's planning was done in collaboration with the Trønderlag, an organization of Norwegian-Americans who had emigrated from the district in which the city of Trondheim was located. Many members of this group planned to travel to Norway. P. G. was suddenly in the travel business, booking passage for the Choir, first of all, but also for friends of Choir members and many others. He became involved in promoting three separate sight-seeing tours in Europe in addition to his numerous responsibilities related directly to the Choir. One must not forget that, as one of the singers, he also had to attend choir rehearsals and memorize the new numbers.[13]

CITY	DATE	Hotel	Place of Concert
St. Paul	June 3rd	St. Paul	Auditorium
Eau Claire, Wis.	June 4th {Mat. and Eve.	Private Homes	City Auditorium
Madison, Wis.	June 5th	Park	University Armory
Milwaukee, Wis.	June 6th	Martin	City Auditorium
Janesville, Wis.	June 7th	Monterey	H. S. Auditorium
Elgin, Ill.	June 8th Mat.		Masonic Temple
Oak Park, Ill.	June 8th Eve.	La Salle, Chicago	United Luth. Ch. Ridgeland & Greenfield
Chicago, Ill.	June 9th		Orchestra Hall
Grand Rapids, Mich.	June 10th	Pantlind	Armory
Lansing, Mich.	June 11th	Olds	Prudden Auditorium
Mansfield, Ohio	June 12th	Leland	Sen. H. S. Auditorium
Cleveland, Ohio	June 13th	Cleveland	Music Hall Public Auditorium
Canton, Ohio	{June 14th {June 15th	Northern	City Auditorium
Jamestown, N. Y.	June 16th	Jamestown	First Luth. Ch.
Oil City, Pa.	June 17th	Arlington	Latonia Theatre
Kane, Pa.	June 18th	New Thomsen	Temple Theatre
Altoona, Pa.	June 19th	Penn Alto	Rooseveldt Jr. H. S.
Clearfield, Pa.	June 20th	Dimeling	
Binghamton, N. Y.	June 21st	Carlton	Central H. S.
Syracuse, N. Y.	June 22nd	Syracuse	Kendricks Chapel Syracuse University
Scranton, Pa.	June 23rd	Casey	Central H. S.
Wilkes-Barre, Pa.	June 24th	Sterling	Irem Temple
New Haven, Conn.	June 25th	Taft	Woolsey Hall
Brooklyn, N. Y.	June 26th	St. George	Elks Auditorium
	June 27th		Ritz Theatre Staten Island

Concerts en route to New York
Summer, 1930

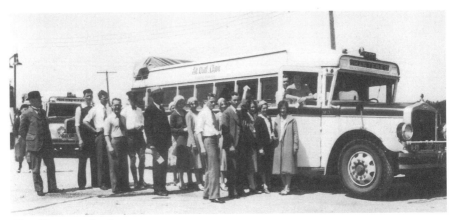

Heading east by bus

The European tour was an extremely ambitious and extensive enterprise. The itinerary called for twenty-six concerts on the way to New York, the Atlantic journey on the "S. S. Stavangerfjord" from New York to Trondheim, then called Trondhjem, where the first concerts were given, and a heavy schedule of twenty concerts in Norway alone. The tour would continue into Sweden and Denmark on the way to a demanding series of performances in Germany, where concerts were presented in such cities as Nordlingen, Augsburg, Naumburg, Frankfurt, Wittenberg, Eisenach, Leipzig, Berlin, and Hamburg. During its three months of travel the St. Olaf Choir sang some

Bus drivers and wives on the "Stavangerfjord"

"S.S. Stavangerfjord"   *Captain Irgens, P.G. Schmidt*

sixty concerts, having left Northfield June 3 and returning to a tumultuous welcome at Union Station in St. Paul on September 1, 1930.

On the way to New York the Choir traveled in two chartered buses. In New York they stayed at Hotel St. George where they had the excitement of spotting fellow guest Rear Admiral Richard Byrd. At the hotel members also enjoyed "the most luxurious swimming pool in history." The last of the twenty-six concerts given in the States was at the Ritz Theatre, Staten Island.[14]

On June 28, the day of departure from New York, the buses brought the Choir from the hotel directly to the pier where the "Stavangerfjord" was tied up. In a gesture typical of P. G. Schmidt's unfailing thoughtfulness, the bus

Playing shuffleboard

166

drivers and their wives were invited aboard the ship to be guests of the Choir at a bountiful smorgasbord.[15]

Crossing the Atlantic aboard the "Stavangerfjord," the Choir had a good time playing, eating, rehearsing twice a day, and singing at a special July 4th service at which Dr. J. A. Aasgaard, president of the Norwegian Lutheran Church of America, was the main speaker. Captain K. S. Irgens, gracious skipper of the "Stavangerfjord," endeared himself to all his passengers with his hospitality and courtesy. He amiably accepted the fact that Miss Ella

Sighting land
FMC on "Stavangerfjord"

Hjertaas declined cigarettes on behalf of the ladies in the Choir. "When you can't take a cigarette you take a song instead, and that is very fine," he commented.[16] The good captain "seemed a bit worried," however, recalled P. G. Schmidt, when told that Choir members would not be permitted to join in the dancing that was a regular part of the entertainment on board. P. G. assured him that the students would be able to arrange their own entertainment.[17]

Elizabeth Day '31 (Mrs. Elizabeth Day Wee) recorded in her diary how she exulted in the fun of speaking Norwegian with the waiters, the grand food, the beauty of the sea, the

Elizabeth Day '31

singing, and other delights of the ocean voyage. "We wore full evening dress for the captain's dinner the last night. We are sailing up Romsdalfjord, beautiful beyond words."[18]

The central focus of the tour was Trondheim and the great Nidaros Cathedral where the 900th anniversary of the coming of Christianity into Norway was observed officially July 29 and 30, 1930. The Choir first arrived in Trondheim July 8, the "Stavangerfjord" departing from its usual route by sailing directly to Trondheim.[19] During the three-week interval the

Nidaros Cathedral
Trondheim, Norway

At grave of B. J. Muus: Birgitte Muus
Klüver and Dr. J. A. Aasgaard

Choir and crowds, Trondheim, Olav Tryggvason Square, July 8, 1930

Choir would visit other Norwegian cities and return to Trondheim for the anniversary later in the month.

On its initial arrival in Trondheim, the Choir was nearly overwhelmed by the welcomes it received. One of these took place at the square where a statue of Olav Tryggvason overlooks the city. A throng of 40,000 people had assembled for another welcoming program of speeches, band music, and singing. Carrying flags and shouting Hurrahs, the crowd followed the Choir in a huge procession that made its way to the grave of Bernt Julius Muus close by the Cathedral. At the grave Dr. Aasgaard gave a short talk and offered a prayer. Birgitte Muus Klüver, daughter of B. J. Muus, spoke briefly after which the St. Olaf Choir sang, "So Soberly and Sweetly the Seasons Tread Their Round," composed by F. Melius Christiansen to a Norwegian folk melody.

At a program held at the Bishop's Court near the Cathedral, a Trondheim choir sang "The Star Spangled Banner" and the St. Olaf Choir sang "Ja, vi elsker dette landet." There was more singing; a band played; the crowd shouted more Bravos and Hurrahs; and there were more speeches. One Norwegian speaker was roundly booed for delivering his interminable speech in *landsmaal,* a language then being promoted but disliked by many. At yet another reception Choir members could only be amused as their hosts were drinking their health in wine while they, the guests, had to respond to the "skaals" with water. "It was so comical we could scarcely contain ourselves," recalled Signe Ramseth.[20]

Church in Melhus, Norway

As the Choir proceeded south by train toward Oslo, it stopped to give a concert in the small village of Melhus. Two features of the Melhus visit stand out in the memories of the Choir of 1930. First, the extreme solemnity on the part of the local people who lined the road as the Choir walked up to the church. Wrote Norma Lee '30 (Mrs. Norma Lee Simso), "Nobody seemed to talk, and it was almost painfully quiet." Elizabeth Day recalled, "The atmosphere was dreadfully sober and therefore depressing at first."[21] A full worship service including a long sermon took place before the Choir gave its concert. The church was

Norma M. Lee '30

completely filled, with scores of people standing outside. "Old men and women stood perfectly still except for wiping the tears out of their eyes occasionally."[22]

The other association with Melhus had to do with a Norwegian delicacy called *rømmegrøt*. Made of rich cream and milk, it was served to the Choir after the concert as a special treat, a sample of a unique Norwegian dish for festive occasions. The problem was that the Choir members had not eaten for about eight hours and were understandably hungry, but no meal provision had been made for them other than the *rømmegrøt*. To compound the matter, after consuming more of this substance than would be good for anyone, they munched on chocolate bars, oranges, and cookies, and entertained themselves by climbing up the mountain to romp about in the new-mown hay.[23]

Clearly a disaster of sorts was in the making. Boral Biorn '30 recalled the acute physical discomfort—"internal and external activity"—he and the others experienced as the Choir assembled at the station to wait for the train to Oslo. Boral himself wandered off to a lumber yard where he suffered in isolation and struggled to get some sleep on a stack of lumber.[24] After a long wait, they finally boarded the spacious sleepers which, under normal circumstances, would have rocked the tired singers gently to sleep. Instead, by the time the train reached Hamar the next morning, at least seventeen Choir members were sick.

The effects of the Melhus *rømmegrøt* trailed the Choir to Oslo where it sang a concert at the University Aula with King Haakon and Crown Prince Olav in attendance. Because of illness a number of the singers had to leave the platform during the first group. Nevertheless, it was a successful concert, opening with a special number invoking God's blessing on the king, and closing with "Ja, vi elsker dette landet," Norway's national anthem.

At Eidsvold, Norway

Three bouquets of flowers were presented to the Choir. As to singers leaving the stage, the audience assumed that the program was so planned that some Choir members would rest during certain numbers. The next day the critics had generous words for the Choir and Dr. Christiansen.[25]

In Eidsvold, where Norway's Constitution was signed in 1814, the Choir sang in the church in which Christiansen had been baptized. During free time in Eidsvold, reported Elizabeth Day, "I had a swell ride with Freddie Schmidt on a girl's bicycle." As it had done in 1913, the St. Olaf Choir made good use of a chartered coastal ship to transport it from one engagement to the next. This time, for a little over two weeks, the Choir lived and traveled aboard the "Zeta," which was "much to our liking and larger than we thought," according to Miss Day.[26]

The "Zeta"

On July 19, 1930, the boat portion of the Choir's trip began, the first stop being Larvik, the town where F. Melius grew up and where his father still lived. Stretched high across the length of the pier was a sign with huge letters: VELKOMMEN HJEM, LARVIK GUTTEN (Welcome Home, Larvik Boy).[27] Norma Lee described the arrival at Larvik. "Hundreds of people were at the dock, and Christy's father was with the silk-hatted committee. They gave us a royal 'velkommen.' The band, of course, plays as we land and motor boats surround us, the people yelling and waving Norwegian flags."[28] The concert was in the church where F. Melius had been confirmed and where he often played the organ. Interest in the Choir was so great that those who were unable to find places inside stood outside all around the church, despite a hard rain.[29]

FMC, his father Anders, and his wife Edith

One colorful arrival and departure followed another as the "Zeta" took the St. Olaf Choir around the coast of Norway. There were concert stops at such cities as Arendal, Kristiansand, Stavanger, Haugesund, Bergen, Aalesund and Molde as the group made its way back to Trondheim for the festivities scheduled for July 29 and 30. Part of the Bergen experience was a trip out to Troldhaugen, the home of Edvard Grieg. Wrote Norma Lee: "No wonder he was inspired to write music; his home and surroundings looked like a dreamland. He wrote all his music in a one-room hut on the shore of a beautiful lake. His piano and furniture are still there just as he left them."[30]

The beauty of Norway's coast and fjords filled the students with a mixture of strong feelings. After seeing the Geirangerfjord and the famous

Edward Griegs's studio
Troldhaugen, Norway

Geirangerfjord

Seven Sisters waterfalls, Elizabeth Day declared it "the most beautiful nature I have ever known." She reflected further: "Everything is so roughly, strongly, majestically beautiful that I can appreciate it just so much and then it hurts me and I'm so lonesome I could scream!" The next day she wrote in her diary: "I stood on deck early and thought, 'My Lord, what a morning!'"[31]

Arriving in Trondheim on July 29th, the Choir traveled up the Trondheimsfjord to give a concert that evening in Levanger. The next day, the 30th, was the great festival day at the Nidaros Cathedral. First the Choir participated in the Norwegian-American worship service that began at 12:30 p.m. It was part of the grand processional consisting also of priests, bishops, and archbishops from Norway, Sweden, Denmark, and Germany. Signe Ramseth remembered the thrill the Choir felt as it formed "in Bach order" and marched in twos the entire length of the Cathedral, "parting at the American altar to rejoin under the massive organ which was 'toning' magnificently."[32]

Nidaros Cathedral July 30, 1930

Dr. J. A. Aasgaard, president of the Norwegian Lutheran Church of America, preached at the service and the St. Olaf Choir sang a "Hymn of Greeting to Norway" composed specifically for the occasion. The words were by the Reverend D. C. Jordahl and the music by F. Melius Christiansen. In Norwegian the first stanza began with the words, "Nu runden er den saele stund vor fot betraeder faedres grund." In an English translation by Olav Lee of the St. Olaf faculty, the opening stanza proclaims:

At this most happy hour we stand
Upon our fathers' native land.
Here mother lived when young at heart,
Here father from his friends did part,
    In faith and hope.

The final stanza had these words:

For Gospel's rod and staff they gave,
For light of grace at death and grave,
For saving faith our thanks we bring
With greetings warm and gladly sing
    In praise of God. [33]

The Choir also sang "Deilig er jorden," the Norwegian version of "Beautiful Savior." The vast crowd in the Cathedral was powerfully moved by the singing. [34] With understandable pride, Oscar Overby, who was with his wife and the Choir on the tour, wrote of the moment: "Our hearts swelled as Gertrude's voice rose in solo to the heights of the Dome and floated away to the far ends of the vast cathedral. The acoustics were perfect for the song."[35]

The long service lasted more than three hours. A few Choir members sneaked out in search of something to eat, hailed a taxi, but it ran out of gas.[36] Somehow they and the others found nourishment and returned to the Cathedral for the full concert which the Choir gave at 8:00 p.m. Again, the huge church was packed. Only a fifth of the

Gertrude and Oscar Overby

people who sought admission could get in. The honored guests were King Haakon, Queen Maud, Crown Prince Olav, Crown Princess Martha, and the president of the Storthing, the Norwegian parliament.

Royal Family in Trondheim
Crown Prince Olav, Queen Maud, King Haakon VII

The program for this historic concert opened with Bach's motet for double choir, "Sing Ye to the Lord." Then followed "Cherubim Song" by M. Glinka, and "Benedictus Qui Venit" by Franz Liszt. The second part consisted of the hymn greeting, "Nu runden er den saele stund," music by F. Melius Christiansen, "O Hoved høit forhaanet" ("O Sacred Head now wounded") by H. L. Hassler, "How Fair the Church of Christ Shall Stand" from Schumann's *Gesangbuch*, and "Deilig er jorden" ("Beautiful Savior"). The third part of the program began with Gustav Schreck's "Motet for Advent" (Psalm 47). Next the Choir sang "I Himmelen, i Himmelen," "Lost in the Night," Finnish folk melody, and concluded with "Wake, Awake" by Philipp Nicolai.[37] The king sent word to the Choir afterwards that he and his party were never so inspired in their lives. [38]

But the long and eventful day was not over. After a short rest the Choir assembled again in the Cathedral at 10:45 p.m. to sing three numbers over the radio in a transoceanic broadcast to America. Telephone wires took the broadcast to Southampton, England, and from there a short wave transmitter carried it to Long Island, New York and a nationwide network. It was reported that national baseball games were interrupted to let the crowds listen to the St. Olaf Choir singing in Norway. [39]

Trinity Church
Trefoldighetskirken
Oslo, Norway

For this special broadcast the Choir sang the "Star Spangled Banner," "Ja vi elsker dette landet," and "Wake, Awake." Cablegrams received from America the next day assured the Choir that its singing had been heard at home in such places as Northfield and Fergus Falls.[40] Norma Lee wrote to her parents, "I was so thrilled I could hardly stand it when I thought you might be listening."[41]

On July 31 the Choir was back in Oslo for another concert, singing in Trefoldighet (Trinity) Church. On this occasion Dr. Christiansen became ill and had to leave the podium during the first movement of the Bach number, the Choir finishing without him. Edna ("Eddie") Olseth, one of the students, directed the rest of the program "and it went just fine," reported Elizabeth Day. [42]. Olseth '30 was a music major from St. James, Minnesota, who sang in the first soprano section.

Edna Olseth '30

On to Germany

After a second concert in Oslo, the Choir gave concerts in several cities in southern Norway and traveled to Gothenburg and Malmö in Sweden to sing in those cities. By ferry the Choir traveled to Copenhagen where it sang in the cathedral, "The Church of Our Lady," standing right in front of the famous Thorwaldsen statue of Christ with outstretched arms. Everyone enjoyed Copenhagen with its Tivoli Park and the Glyptotek Art Museum [43]

Church of Our Lady (Vor Frue) *Copenhagen, Denmark*

The first German city on the itinerary was Berlin, but the first concert was given in Nordlingen, a city north of Augsburg. In Oberammergau the Choir attended a day-long performance of the famous Passion Play and were

En route to Oberammergau

St. Anna Church
Augsburg, Germany

housed in the homes of townspeople who took parts in the play. For example, Norma Lee and five others stayed with Andreas Lang, who played the part of Matthew, and Dr. and Mrs. Aasgaard stayed in the home of the young girl who was Salome in the play. In Augsburg on a Sunday the Choir sang an anthem and Dr. Aasgaard preached the sermon in the St. Anna Church, where Luther had once preached. The chance to view original works by Albrecht Dürer made Norma Lee especially grateful for the history of art course she had taken from Dr. C. A. Mellby. The service and the concert the next day in the Church of the Barefoot Monks were part of the 400th anniversary of the Augsburg Confession.[44]

On August 14, in Eisenach, the Choir visited the home of J. S. Bach and had the thrill of seeing the original manuscript of the Bach number on the program, "Sing Ye to the Lord." The next night, after singing a concert in the large and beautiful cathedral in Naumburg, Choir members hurried back to their rooms and put on their best clothes to attend a surprise party they had arranged, with Ella Hjertaas's help, in honor of P. G. Schmidt. A splendid meal began the party. There were funny speeches in German and English, several songs, and humorous toasts in both German and Norwegian, Christy teaching the crowd a German toast. Of course these were all non-alcoholic toasts. A local paper the next day observed that the young Americans had enjoyed a wonderful evening without the use of intoxicating drinks.[45]

The Choir was in Martin Luther's home town of Wittenberg on a cold, rainy Sunday. It made a pilgrimage to the Castle Church where Luther nailed the Ninety-Five Theses to the door. Inside the church the singers gathered around Luther's grave near the pulpit; they also saw where Luther's colleague Philip Melanchthon was buried. The Wittenberg concert was not held in the Castle Church but in the State Church where the American visitors took note of a number of paintings by Lucas Cranach.[46]

In Leipzig the Choir sang in the St. Thomas Church. During a tour the students were shown the room in the Conservatory where Dr. Christiansen had studied with Gustav Schreck. At the grave of

*Luther's Pulpit and Grave
Castle Church, Wittenberg*

Bach in the Johanneskirke everyone in the group gathered around for a moment of silent meditation. Of the Leipzig concert Wilhelm Jung of the Leipzig Conservatory wrote, "This was a most illuminating and inspiring concert, which did not only testify to a choral training of the highest order; but also proved that a cappella singing is steadily winning a prominent place in the musical activities of the New World."[47]

Laudatory reviews in German newspapers appeared wherever the Choir went. The Choir was anticipating its stay in Berlin. The weather turned favorable, and all enjoyed shopping and sightseeing in the beautiful city. There it faced a large and appreciative audience as it sang from one of the

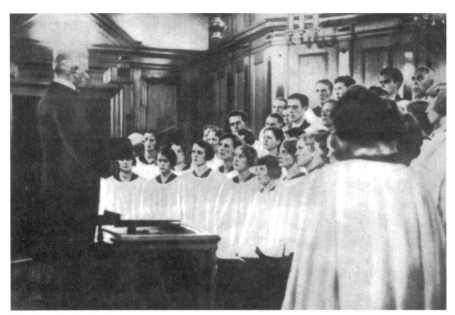

Berlin Cathedral
August 18, 1930

balconies in the magnificent Dom. The Berlin critics were impressed by what they heard. Wrote the reviewer for the *Deutsche Allgemeine Zeitung*: "We in Berlin are undoubtedly accustomed to a very high standard in regard to choral singing, but the impression made by this choir, which could as well be called German as American, exceeded all expectations. The first surprise were the glorious vocal resources of the group, in which soft and soaring Sopranos contrasted with fundamentally deep Basses and dark colored Altos joined with warm and glowing Tenors. Joined to this there was revealed an artistic schooling such as is to be found only in choral societies of the very highest type. The union of these excellencies of material and technique is the rare and striking quality which makes the St. Olaf Choir an outstanding organization."[48]

For the *Deutsche Tageszeitung* Prof. Dr. Herman Springer wrote, "This chorus of sixty voices has gained an amazing purity of voice production and mobility of technique. Such clarity in full chorus, such perfection in the mechanics of singing, such fine elaboration of detail in interpretation are very rarely heard anywhere. . . . The credit for the high development of the choir belongs to the director, F. Melius Christiansen, who leads his singers with restraint and dignity." Another Berlin critic included these comments in his review: "The sustained and soaring harmonies; the accurate attack, the full bodied unison involuntarily recall orchestral effects. Astonishing also is the unusually developed art of breath control upon which the whole artistic delivery is built up."[49]

The final concert on the European tour took place in Hamburg in the St. Michael Cathedral. The evening was packed with emotion, for the listeners as well as the Choir members. P. G. Schmidt had the local pastor express the Choir's gratitude to the immediate audience and to all the people in Germany who had shown such grand hospitality. During the singing the Choir members struggled to hold off the sad thought that this particular family of singers would never sing together again. "Even Christy seemed sad," wrote Signe Ramseth. For her the thought "that all that grand sound would pass off into space" was an appalling one.[50] P. G. Schmidt remembered the unusual response of the audience after the concert:

> There was no cheering in the church but when the concert had ended and the choir members had put away their robes and had come out into the street, they found the entire audience waiting for them, clapping hands and cheering. It was a wonderful "good-bye."[51]

The 1930 European tour was also memorable for the extraordinary public welcome the St. Olaf Choir received at the Union Depot in St. Paul, Minnesota, when it arrived there by train on September 1, 1930. A crowd of 1500 alumni, faculty and friends awaited the singers, Dr. and Mrs. Christiansen, Professor and Mrs. Schmidt, and Dr. and Mrs. Aasgaard. A telegram from President Herbert Hoover was read: "I cordially congratulate members of St. Olaf choir upon the splendid reception given them in Europe and tender my congratulations upon your happy return to the community and people whom you have so well represented in the field of musical art."[52]

Minneapolis Mayor William Kunze, St. Olaf President L. W. Boe, and Arnold Flaten '22, chairman of the welcoming committee, gave speeches. Greetings sent from Governor Christianson and St. Paul Mayor Gerhard Bundlie were read to the celebrating throng. Dr. J. A. Aasgaard told the crowd, "You people have every reason to be proud of this choir which represents the best interests of the northwest." After the speeches O. I. Hertsgaard, Class of 1908, directed a rousing rendition of "High on Manitou Heights." As he watched the crowd disperse, F. Melius remarked, "This is the greatest reception home the choir has received in any year."[53]

Domestic Tours

It happened that the 1930 St. Olaf Choir had an opportunity to be together again at the first reunion of former Choir members held during Commencement in June of 1938. Several hundred choristers came to the campus to celebrate the twenty-fifth anniversary of the Choir's first

European trip.[54] The Choir of 1913 sang two numbers. As its part of the reunion concert the 1930 Choir sang "In Heaven Above."

In the early thirties the St. Olaf Choir gave an annual concert for the students and faculty of Carleton College. At the request of *The News*, a Northfield paper, Dr. T. O. Wedel, a Carleton professor, wrote "An Appreciation" of the Choir after its concert in Skinner Memorial Chapel on April 13, 1933. His main observation was that Director Christiansen was wise in limiting himself to religious music. Music, the language of the emotions and of the will, touches the

Skinner Chapel
Carleton College

core of our being, he wrote. Religious music, expressing human feelings of awe and reverence before the mysteries of an eternal world, "is art put to its noblest use." [55]

Other choral groups at St. Olaf also concentrated on religious music. One thinks of the Choral Union and of the Church Choir, directed by Oscar

St. Olaf Viking Chorus, 1936

R. Overby. In 1935, another group made its appearance. The Viking Male Chorus was founded by students, with Luther Onerheim '37 its leading spirit and first director. Onerheim also sang tenor in the St. Olaf Choir and played in the St. Olaf Concert Band. The Chorus went on several weekend trips and, according to the yearbook, "cast reflected glory on St. Olaf musical organizations through its fine interpretation of religious songs."[56] Luther Onerheim took his taste for religious music with him when he entered the U. S. Army during World War II and transmitted it to a fellow soldier also interested in music, Kenneth Jennings.

Luther Onerheim, Director

On its annual tour in 1936 the St. Olaf Choir gave concerts in several midwestern states. Included that year were appearances on six university campuses: Purdue, Drake, Wisconsin, Indiana, Illinois, and Iowa State.[57]

The following year the Choir went on a three-week tour to the Pacific Coast, singing in such cities as Seattle, Tacoma, Spokane, Portland, San Francisco, Oakland, San Diego, and Los Angeles. During an interview in San Francisco, F. Melius Christiansen, with typical modesty, explained the success of the St. Olaf Choir. "It happened," he said, "that this country had had too much flimsy church music. We came along at the psychological moment with the right kind of church music sung in the right way. If the time had not been particularly right we should not have been so lucky."[58]

During that trip a western newspaper carried a story about the Choir with the headline, "Almost Lost Christy." After a concert, Dr. Christiansen had wandered off, saying he was going "to get some groceries." He was gone for some time, the Choir was ready to leave, and P. G. Schmidt was getting worried. Schmidt started hunting for Christy in the restaurants. Finally he found him, leisurely enjoying a snack of sandwiches, pie, and coffee to which he had treated five of the Choir fellows. When the director returned to the waiting bus and innocently climbed aboard, P. G. administered the mildest of reprimands. "Consider yourself spanked," he said.[59]

The St. Olaf Lutheran Choir of 1937-38 had a very productive year including a successful tour to the east coast. That was the first Choir to appear before the public in the purple robes that have become its regular concert dress. Said the *Brooklyn N Y Eagle* after the concert in the Brooklyn Academy of Music, "Appearing last night in their rich purple gowns, the

183

Awaiting the Choir in Northfield, 1937

choir made a notable impression before a good-sized audience which was most enthusiastic in its applause."[60]

The concert program began with Bach's motet for double choir, "Sing Ye to the Lord." Gustav Schreck's "The Twenty-Third Psalm" was sung in German, and there were songs in Latin and Norwegian. For the second year in a row, the Choir sang Canadian composer Healey Willan's piece, "An Apostrophe to the Heavenly Hosts." New numbers were "Beauty in Humility," by F. Melius Christiansen, and a composition called "Autumn Woods," by Paul Christiansen, youngest son of F. Melius. Gertrude Boe Overby continued to please audiences with her soprano solos in "Lost in the Night," "The Three Kings," and "Beautiful Savior." Other soloists that year were Adelaide Thovson, alto, Gordon Egertson, tenor, and Alvar Sandquist, bass. [61]

The value of Gertrude Boe Overby's singing in the St. Olaf Choir cannot be overestimated. With P. G. Schmidt anchoring the low basses and Mrs. Overby supplying her "rare combination of an ensemble voice and a solo voice"[62] in the upper ranges, F. Melius Christiansen could face each year's task of building the Choir in the secure knowledge that he could rely on those two superb singers.

184

Born September 21, 1900, in Minneapolis, Gertrude Boe was the daughter of the Reverend and Mrs. Vigleik Boe. Her father had directed the St. John's Church Choir from 1897 to 1899 while a student at St. Olaf College and enjoyed music throughout his adult life. [63] Gertrude enrolled in Concordia Academy in Moorhead, Minnesota, in 1916, and entered St. Olaf College in the fall of 1920. She and her roommate, Klara Overby, sister of her future husband, Oscar R. Overby, had a private audition at Professor Christiansen's home and were admitted to the St. Olaf Choir.

As a student, Gertrude sang in the Choir for three years, graduating in June of 1923. She married Oscar R. Overby, a member of the music faculty, in August of 1923. The newlyweds spent a year in New York studying music and performing. They returned to Northfield and St. Olaf College in the fall of 1924. That year Gertrude was invited to go on tour with the St. Olaf Band as vocal soloist and resumed her singing in the St. Olaf Choir.[64]

Gertrude Boe as student
Early WCAL broadcast, 1922

The appealing quality of Gertrude Boe Overby's voice, hailed by scores of critics over a period of more than twenty years, was ably described by Clifford Bloom in the *Des Moines Register* in 1939: "She sings with a voice of warm beauty, richly resonant tones, meticulous phrasing and clear enunciation." Her musician husband, Oscar Overby, wrote of "the flexible, lyric and personal qualities of singing which have endeared her to audiences far and wide." [65]

F. Melius Christiansen expressed his admiration for Mrs. Overby at concerts, in poems and inscribed photos, and in public statements. A columnist in Chicago told of a concert in Orchestra Hall in 1934 when the director time and again stepped aside to let the soloists, especially Mrs. Overby, receive their deserved applause. Above his signature on a photo

Oscar and Gertrude Overby ca. 1940

presented to her F. Melius wrote, "With appreciation of the many thousand beautiful tones you have produced to lift our spirit." On another he wrote, "In singing to the Lord, you sang Him down to us."[66]

At a May Music Festival at St. Olaf in 1945, when called upon to make a little speech to honor P. G. Schmidt on his birthday, F. Melius also used the occasion to express his thanks to Mrs. Overby. Even before reaching the microphone the puckish director emeritus teased the crowd about not clapping so much for him, thereby provoking loud applause. He proceeded in his delightful, informal way, starting with a story about buying five-year-old Ole a milkshake, commending his son and the Choir, and making droll comments about the girls pumping their instruments at the Band concert. There were delighted peals of laughter as he rambled on, eventually to express his thanks to P. G. Schmidt. But he also had someone else in mind.

Gertrude Boe Overby

"We've had a little girl singing in the Choir for many years," began F. Melius. "Gertrude." His unexpected use of her first name caused a chuckle to ripple across the audience. F. Melius always referred to her formally as "Mrs. Overby." He continued: "And she has done a great deal to promote the Kingdom of God through her singing. And when I stand before the Choir and she is to sing, a moment before she starts there is a revelation over her face. And I'm gripped by it. And that beautiful tone comes out, and it is wonderful, beautiful, and I want to express my thanks to her for all the beautiful moments she has made for thousands of people in the United States, and in Europe too. Now you can clap!" An enormous cascade of applause thundered across the old gymnasium and all eyes were on Gertrude Boe Overby.

The tribute paid to P. G. Schmidt on that occasion will be taken up in a later chapter, but part of it deserves mention here. Recalling something Dr. Granskou had said when he came to St. Olaf as president in 1943, F. Melius applied the thought to P. G. Schmidt: the happy person is the one who does not need to claim credit for what he or she does. Said the speaker, "Happy is the man who is not an egoist. And Professor Schmidt has been such a happy man." He has used his talents and they have multiplied. He has been a great singer with an extraordinary bass voice. F. Melius continued:

Professor P. G. Schmidt

> And that voice we've had in the St. Olaf Choir. And it's been the steadying voice and the steadying power for all these years. We appreciate all of this, Professor Schmidt, and we want to thank you, not from me, particularly, but from the *Lord*, who is the *King* in the vineyard in which you and I have been working together.[67]

The last concert tour to be mentioned is the one undertaken in January and February of 1940. P. G. Schmidt also helped make this trip a memorable one for the Choir. The singers left on January 19th. The destination was the Pacific Northwest. The program that year began with Tschaikowsky's "O Praise Ye God." It was followed by the 16th century Italian composer Marc Antonio Ingegneri's "Tenebrae Factae Sunt" and Benjamin Edwards' "Restoration." In addition to such familiar pieces as Schreck's "Motet for Advent" and the Finnish Folk Song, "Lost in the

Night," the Choir sang two anthems by Paul Christiansen, "As a Flower" and "Sing to God," and F. Melius Christiansen's "From Grief To Glory," a chorale suite in four movements with words by Oscar R. Overby.

The *Viking* yearbook summarized the tour in this fashion:

> Through the wastelands of North Dakota, across mountainous Montana, over the Rockies, down the lush slopes of Washington, Oregon, and California, and then back across the deserts to the cornfields of Iowa and the finale in thriving Chicago, the musical enchantment from Northfield spread its fervor into the hearts of all who heard.[68]

The reviewer for the *Sacramento Union* was among those enchanted. Paul Tanner characterized the Choir's singing as "of almost ethereal beauty." He described the reaction of the audience: "People sat spellbound through the program of a dozen sacred choruses plus half as many encores and refused to leave their seats until the dimming of the stage lights proclaimed there would be no more music." [69]

Before heading back toward Chicago and home, Choir members enjoyed the sightseeing tours in Los Angeles. Three days before the Choir performed in Chicago, the "S.R.O." sign was posted at Orchestra Hall. The

Paul J. Christiansen, Composer Conductor of Concordia Choir

concert was sponsored by the Chicago Bible Society, observing its Centennial Year in 1940. A matinee performance was added to accommodate interested patrons.

In Chicago, too, the Choir received a highly favorable response. Cecil Smith, writing for the *Chicago Daily Tribune*, said that the Choir apparently never has an off season, and that its technique is a source of joy. "Every note is in the right place at the right time with just the volume and color Dr. Christiansen wishes for his interpretative purpose. The pitch is uncannily exact; it is not too much to call the intonation of the St. Olaf Choir the most perfect in America."[70]

St. Olaf Choir, 1940

Before the Chicago performance, aboard the train bringing them back to the Midwest, Choir members were reminded that in "mountainous Montana" they had received an introduction to western ways. During the stay in Billings, the students had been out shopping. Three of the men in the Choir returned to the hotel lobby sporting large ten-gallon western hats. They made themselves comfortable on one of the sofas and happily displayed their new purchases, enjoying the attention from Choir members and others.

Presently two tall, rangy local men, also wearing ten-gallon hats, strode into the hotel and walked slowly past the three Oles on the sofa, carefully looking them over. The taller one, a full 6' 8", was the local sheriff and the other was his deputy. They stopped a short distance away and conferred with one another in whispers. Then they came back to where the Choir members were clustered and approached the three new hats whose owners began to slide lower and lower on the sofa. There was a measure of tension in the air.

In a typical Montana ranch drawl, the sheriff inquired of the three guys whether they had their licenses so he could check their identity. "What licenses?" "The Ten Gallon Hat license," said the sheriff. "Out here you need a license to wear one of them hats." Some kind of identification was produced and the sheriff seemed satisfied. He got out his pad, made a notation, and announced that they were now eligible for membership in the Ten Gallon Hat Brotherhood and that the charge would be $5.00 from each of them. Somehow the three managed to come up with the money and handed it over. The atmosphere in the hotel lobby suddenly eased. Now there was good-natured back slapping and hand shaking among the boys, the sheriff, and the deputy. And so it was over. The sheriff and the deputy left.

Some days later, its concerts in the west completed, the Choir was on the train heading back toward the Midwest and Chicago. Everyone was assembled in one of the special cars on the train. P. G. asked the three members of the Ten Gallon Hat Brotherhood to step forward. They did so, and he handed each of them his $5.00 "license fee." Not until that moment did they realize that they had been the unsuspecting victims of a brilliant stunt executed to perfection by none other than their beloved manager, P. G. himself![71]

Notes for Chapter 6 NORWAY AND GERMANY, 1930

1. *The 1930 Viking*, 100.

2. Review in unidentified Springfield newspaper, January 21, 1930. From a scrapbook compiled by Choir member Elizabeth Day '31 (Mrs. Elizabeth Day Wee) who sang in the alto section. Further references will be to Eliz. Day Scrapbook. As is often the case with newspaper clippings in scrapbooks, names of newspapers and specific dates of the reviews are not noted. The Choir's southern tour was from January 18 to February 12, 1930. Mrs. Wee also made available her tour diary, to be referred to as Eliz. Day Diary.

3. "Choir Jumps from Twenty Below to Florida Sunshine," unnamed Jacksonville newspaper, Eliz. Day Scrapbook. The Jacksonville concert was on January 26, 1930.

4. "St. Olaf's Choir is Incomparable," Charleston, South Carolina paper, Eliz. Day Scrapbook. The Charleston concert was on January 29, 1930.

5. Alvin S. Wiggers, "Work of St. Olaf Choir Impresses," *The Tennessean*, Nashville, Tennessee, Eliz. Day Scrapbook. The Nashville concert was on January 22, 1930.

6. Paul G. Schmidt, *My Years at St. Olaf*, A Centennial Decade Publication (Northfield, Minnesota: St. Olaf College, [1967]), 101.

7. Signe Ramseth Diary for 1930. Signe Mildred Ramseth '33 (Mrs. Signe M. R. Johnson), sang alto in the Choir. She was one of five first year students to join the Choir in 1929-30 and thus one of the youngest members. She kept diaries on Choir tours from 1930 to 1933. Mrs. Johnson also made available clippings and programs from the Norway and Germany tour. See also Schmidt, 101-02.

8. Review in Columbus newspaper, ca. February 10, 1930, Eliz. Day Scrapbook. The Choir sang two concerts at Capital University on February 9, 1930.

9. *The 1930 Viking*, 101.

10. William C. Benson, *High on Manitou*: A History of St. Olaf College 1874-1949 (Northfield, Minnesota: The St. Olaf College Press, 1949), 255.

11. Editorial: "Norway Tour of the St. Olaf Choir," *Lutheran Church Herald* XIII (September 10, 1929), 1303. Further references to the Church publication, *Lutheran Church Herald*, to be listed as *LCH*.

12. Schmidt, 80-81.

13. *Ibid.*

14. Norma Lee, "The St. Olaf Choir," *LCH*, July 29, 1930. Norma Lee '30 (Mrs. Norma Lee Simso), Minneapolis, a soprano in the Choir, wrote letters home to her parents unaware that they would be published. Her father, Dr. G. T. Lee, Editor-in-Chief of the *Lutheran Church Herald*, official organ of the Norwegian Lutheran Church of America, edited the letters and printed them in the *Herald* as a series called, "Young America Abroad." He explained to readers that he used the material because it contained "reactions and impressions of a member not spoiled by the idea that the product was to be printed." ("The St. Olaf Choir Back from Europe," *LCH* XIV [September 9, 1930], 1284). In a personal note to Editor Lee in 1930, F. Melius Christiansen wrote in a postscript: "Please bring my thanks to your fine daughter for those articles in the *Herald*. F. M. C."

15. Schmidt, 83.

16. Signe Ramseth Diary, 1930.

17. Schmidt, 83.

18. Eliz. Day Diary.

19. Schmidt, 84.

20. Signe Ramseth Diary.

21. Norma Lee, "Young America Abroad," *LCH* XIV (August 12, 1930), 1130; Eliz. Day Diary.

22. Lee, "Young America," *LCH* XIV (August 12, 1930), 1130.

23. Signe Ramseth Diary.

24. Letter from Boral R. Biorn to Robert Johnson, November 17, 1993.

25. Schmidt, 86.

26. Eliz. Day Diary; Schmidt, 86.

27. Oscar R. Overby, *The Years in Retrospect*, Unpublished Typescript (Northfield, Minnesota, 1963), 89. STOARCHIV.

28. Norma Lee, "Young America," *LCH* XIV (August 26, 1930), 1204.

29. *Ibid.*

30. *Ibid.*, 1205.

31. Eliz. Day Diary.

32. Signe Ramseth Diary. The "American altar" to which Signe Ramseth refers was the main altar of the Cathedral over which was placed a large, silver crucifix, a gift from Norwegian-Americans. Cf. "St. Olav Festivities in Nidaros-Trondhjem," *LCH* (September 9, 1930), 1269.

33. *LCH* XIV (June 10, 1930), 811.

34. Lee, "Young America Abroad," *LCH* XIV (September 9, 1930), 1275.

35. Oscar R. Overby, *The Years in Retrospect*, 93.

36. Signe Ramseth Diary.

37. Concert Program: "St. Olaf Korets Festkonsert, Olavsjubilaeet, Domkirken, 30. Juli 1930." Courtesy of Signe Ramseth Johnson.

38. Lee, "Young America," *LCH* XIV (September 9, 1930), 1275.

39. Schmidt, 87.

40. Signe Ramseth Diary.

41. Lee, "Young America," *LCH* XIV (September 9, 1930), 1275.

42. Eliz. Day Diary; Gladys Edwardson Rice Diary, edited by Boral R. Biorn. Gladys Edwardson '31 sang soprano in the St. Olaf Choir. On the Norway tour of 1930 she roomed with soprano Gladys Querna '31 who married fellow Choir member, bass Boral R. Biorn '30.

43. Schmidt, 89-90; Eliz. Day Diary.

44. Schmidt, 92; Lee, "Young America," *LCH* XIV (September 9, 1930), 1275; *Ibid.*, (September 16, 1930), 1308.

45. Signe Ramseth Diary; Schmidt, 92-93.

46. Schmidt, 93.

47. Wilhelm Jung, *Kirchenchor*, No. 9. Quoted in Schmidt, 130.

48. Schliepe, *Deutsche Allgemeine Zeitung*, Berlin, August 19, 1930. Quoted in Schmidt, 131.

49. Herman Springer, *Deutsche Tageszeitung*, Berlin; Hans Pasche, *Signale*, Berlin, August 20, 1930. Quoted in Schmidt, 129.

50. Signe Ramseth Diary.

51. Schmidt, 95.

52. Unidentified Twin City paper, September 2, 1930.

53. *Ibid.*

54. *The 1938 Viking*, 125.

55. T. O. Wedel, "An Appreciation: The St. Olaf Choir," *The News*, Northfield, Minnesota, April 13, 1933.

56. *The 1936-37 Viking*, 92.

57. *Ibid.*, 89.

58. Letter from Mrs. Victor H. Quello (Sigrid Horneland '37) to Manager of the St. Olaf Choir [B. J. Johnson], January 1994.

59. *Ibid.*

60. *Brooklyn N Y Eagle*, February 8, 1938.

61. *The 1938 Viking*, 125.

62. Leola Nelson Bergmann, *Music Master of the Middle West*: The Story of F. Melius Christiansen and the St. Olaf Choir (Minneapolis: University of Minnesota Press, 1944), 135.

63. Oscar R. Overby, "Music in St. John's," *A Brief History of St. John's Lutheran Church*, Seventy-Fifth Anniversary, 1869-1944, 33; Eugene E. Simpson, *A History of St. Olaf Choir* (Minneapolis: Augsburg Publishing House, 1921), 43, 53.

64. Oscar R. Overby, *The Years in Retrospect*, 54, 65, 79.

65. *Ibid.*, 65.

66. *Ibid.*, 73, 79.

67. Tape recording of remarks made at May Music Festival, St. Olaf College, May 1945.

68. *The Viking 1940*, 114.

69. Paul Tanner, *Sacramento Union*, February 2, 1940.

70. Cecil Smith, *Chicago Daily Tribune*, February 13, 1940.

71. Letter from Paul G. Peterson to Joseph M. Shaw, March 15, 1994. Cf. *The Viking 1940*, 114: "Comedy broke the spell in spots. At Billings, the cleverness of P. G. Schmidt, manager of all choir tours, forced several members to take out licenses for the ten-gallon hats which they had purchased there."

CHAPTER 7

THE F. MELIUS MODE

"The St. Olaf Choir is Christiansen," wrote a reviewer in 1923. "Dr. F. Melius Christiansen is the heart and soul of this organization," said another.[1] Wherever the St. Olaf Choir went, and whenever a journalist wrote about it, sooner or later the director himself came in for more than conventional admiration as the able leader of an accomplished a cappella chorus. "Throughout the program," wrote a Pennsylvania reviewer, "the guiding spirit of Christiansen stood out." Critics and audiences alike were fascinated by the man, his appearance

F. Melius Christiansen, November 1927

and personality, his method of conducting, and his reputation as the one who had revitalized choral singing in America.

When the St. Olaf Choir was in Germany in the summer of 1930, Walter Krieger wrote at length about the Choir's virtuosity after the concert in Naumburg. Commenting on the features of the Choir that impressed him, such as flexibility of voices, balance of parts, and fine sense of pitch, he went on to say that these characteristics depended on the personality of the director.

The results attained point to a quite unusual musical endowment and a tonal genius in Dr. F. M. Christiansen.. . . The whole personality of this talented director is most sympathetic and attractive. The restraint and dignity of his manner of directing, which scorns any theatrical effects, but which can inspire his singers to the highest achievements with the simplest means, gives evidence of the immense power of this gifted artist.[2]

In 1922 a writer for *The Dearborn Independent* noted that "many have asked how Professor Christiansen obtains his unusual results. The answer, of course, is Christiansen."[3] A simple statement of how the desired results are gained was the headline in a midwestern paper in the thirties. "St. Olaf Choir's Fame Rests on Its Director's Exacting Thoroughness." F. Melius himself had an even simpler, shorter explanation, "We work! and again we work!"[4]

After spending part of a day with Christiansen in Northfield, Frances Boardman of the *St. Paul Pioneer Press* wrote an article entitled, "Ideals of St. Olaf Lutheran Choir Explained." Taking as axiomatic that a successful musical director must be a thorough musician, and have a magnetic quality that commands voluntary respect, Boardman added what she described as "vast technical patience; a certain inexhaustible interest in the analytical side of his work, and indefatigable zeal in adapting it to the best interests of the choir."[5]

St. Olaf Choir in rehearsal, Dr. Christiansen at piano, January 1936

Frank A. R. Mayer, another journalist, had attended a rehearsal of the Choir on the St. Olaf campus. At one point, he observed, the director's blue eyes were sad. "'The altos should be ashamed of themselves,' he mused. Then he rushed on impetuously: 'They sang that phrase like it was a rubber hose. It should be a bar of steel.' The baton went heavenward and the blue eyes flashed fire." The article went on to emphasize that every practice session called for the hard work of perfecting phrases, singing them again and again. The director was not punishing the singers for mistakes. "Instead, he was patiently, tediously polishing every note, every breathing space between phrases in a drive for ultimate beauty." As Mayer discovered, "Work is the very essence of Dr. Christiansen's philosophy of singing sacred music."[6]

The hard work on the part of director and singers had the specific purpose of freeing the instrument to express itself. In 1930 Christiansen wrote: "We must learn to like our work and we must be willing to work hard on the perfection of our means of expression in order that the spirit may be set free and given the fullest liberty and power." In a letter to his son Olaf, then at Oberlin, Christiansen commented on "the relation of the science of music to that of the art of music—the necessity of hard work to perfect the locomotive and make it perfect mechanically before they put fire under it."[7]

The Soul of the Choir

Recalling her visit with Dr. Christiansen in the living room of his home on St. Olaf Avenue, Frances Boardman described him as "a rather short, thickset man with gray hair and a kindly face which assumes a smile with the greatest possible ease." Noting that there were other Scandinavian-American schools and singers with a capacity for hard work and discipline, but only one St. Olaf Choir, she concluded that the credit obviously belongs to the conductor.[8]

As a man whose genuine modesty co-existed with a quiet self-assurance, F. Melius was at ease with the knowledge that he was the key figure in the life of the St. Olaf Choir. One afternoon in April of 1936 a reporter interviewed Christiansen as he puffed on his pipe in the Russell-Lamson Hotel in Dubuque, Iowa. The writer had this impression of the director: "While he is genial and modest in relaxation, he has a sturdy, vigorous body, a voice that changes in an instant from good-natured banter to imperious commands, and bright blue eyes that shift in a flash from sparkling smiles to glinting steel." When Christiansen commented that children in school can go as far as the teacher can go, the interviewer was quick to apply the point to the director and the St. Olaf Choir. "Even if one

St. Olaf Choir in concert, February 1941

were to judge Dr. Christiansen by his physical appearance alone, one might conclude that the St. Olaf choir has gone far because its teacher could go far."[9]

F. Melius understood his central role with the Choir in a professional, objective way. "The conductor is not only to beat time," he wrote, "but he is mainly a center or focus-point of thought and feeling to which the singers look for inspiration and encouragement." As F. Melius wrote to Olaf, "A choir is as good as its master."[10]

To be at once the center of energy and the agent of a common spirit, the Choir's leader had to cultivate both his health and inner attitude. One may refer again to a letter Christiansen wrote to President Boe from New York in 1927: "It is important that I am in good physical and spiritual condition because the singing of the choir is so dependent on how I feel. I am not sentimental when I say that the spiritual condition is very important in this work. . . . May we all be true to our calling. . . . And may we also be true to Art! The spirit of art is very much like the spirit of Christ. Here, too, truthfulness is essential if it is to reach the hearts of the listeners."[11]

"Truth" and "truthfulness" carried much weight for F. Melius, a man not given to wordy philosophizing. Even as truthfulness was required in the spiritual realm, it simultaneously served aesthetics as well as ethics. The

198

Inscribed for Willis Miller

disciplined, demanding work of repeating and polishing a single phrase led to the desired artistic and spiritual results. As one Choir member put it, recalling the intensive rehearsals and the concentration required of the singers, "Christy preached that perfection was TRUTH which became BEAUTY and inspiration to the listener."[12]

Choir members who sang under F. Melius were totally devoted to him and happily accepted the intensive discipline. Willis Miller '40 recalled the Choir spending an entire rehearsal on a certain phrase. When the director's standard was finally reached after an hour of drilling, Christy would say, "I knew you could do it." F. Melius was an uncompromising perfectionist and a constant taskmaster, wrote Miller, but the singers were fiercely loyal to him. "As students and singers in the choir, all of us were keenly aware that we were in the presence of genius. We accepted his word for law and sang our hearts out for him."[13]

FMC has coffee with colleagues Ella Hjertaas and Charlotte Donhowe

Recollections of Christy by former Choir members invariably bring out the engaging warmth of the man and the profound affection they had for him. By the simple action of walking through the railroad coach where the singers were relaxing, F. Melius could create a wave of good feeling. Having described such a scene as indicative of the Choir's "quiet affection" for Christy, Richard Tetlie '43 wrote, "Throughout the trip one could not but notice how the choir reflected his every mood. And his chuckle and famous ear-to-ear grin, how infectious they are!"[14]

The Try-outs

Once they became members of the St. Olaf Choir under Dr. Christiansen, students had the opportunity to savor their director's personality, finding charm in the same traits that had once intimidated them. One of them wrote that on tour "we were able to experience and enjoy the fascinating and sometimes mischievous side of our director."[15] It is safe to say, however, that former Choir members and hundreds of other St. Olaf students were stricken by varying degrees of terror when they first appeared before the maestro to audition for the Choir. Their stories are packed with drama, fear, humor, and occasionally some anger.

In the early years, students went to Professor Christiansen's home on St. Olaf Avenue to audition for the St. Olaf Choir. After 1926, auditions took place in the director's studio on the first floor of what was then the new music hall.

Hazel Baker

Hazel Baker Tudor '41, came to St. Olaf with "a burning desire to be a 'purple-rober'" and sang in the St. Olaf Choir from 1937 to 1941. She has provided a choice account of an unforgettable tryout experience:

I successfully endured the two routine try-outs, and suddenly the third and last test was upon me. As the numbers ahead of me diminished, I found my legs turning to rubber, and my throat dry and parched. Then I was eyeball to eyeball with those piercing blue eyes. Christy asked me to sing the arpeggio from middle C to high C. I opened my mouth, and was utterly appalled when all I could muster was a disastrous gasp. Christy just threw his silver head back and guffawed in my face.

This really riled my normally placid Norwegian temperament. So I stoically planted my two sturdy feet a foot apart, ballooned

Betty Ann Donhowe

up my lungs, and soared up to high C. Christy's blue eyes sparkled, and he gave me a healthy pat on my back.

When at long last the last contestant had finished,Christy slowly eye-balled each co-ed down the line again. When he approached me, my feet still solidly planted, he winked and tugged the front of my blouse. "I vill take you"—and then did likewise to Betty Ann Donhowe (Ramseth) '41, who was next in line. We had been clasping our perspiring hands together; and with that verdict, we hugged each other deliriously.[16]

Some former Choir members relate stories of their failure to qualify for the St. Olaf Choir on the first try. Students would form a long line outside the music hall waiting their turn to try out for various music organizations, most of them hoping to be admitted to "the first choir." On her first try-out, Esther Tufte (Rian) '36 sang the pitch and rhythm patterns that Dr. Christiansen played on the piano. "He was kind and gentle," she recalled, asking her if she had done much singing. She sang around the house, she replied. He said, "Keep it up. Now go over and see Mr. Overby." "So I became a member of the Church Choir, which we called Second Choir."[17]

Esther Tufte

Prior to the try-outs, students would fill out a slip indicating what instrument they played. Sanford Egge '37 played the trombone, but was hoping, as he stood in the long line, to get into the St. Olaf Choir.

> My turn finally came and with fear and trepidation I went into the tryout room. . . . As I entered the room Dr. Christiansen was sitting at his desk and Professor Oscar Overby was at the piano. The tryout consisted of singing two or three runs. After a short pause, Dr. Christiansen looked at me and said, "Val, I think you should bring your trombone over to band."[18]

Sanford Egge

201

The following year Egge tried out for the Choir again. Twelve tenors reported for three openings. "All of us were petrified," Egge recalled. When it was over, he was one of the fortunate three. "What a wonderful feeling."[19]

The story is told of a very self-assured young woman from Minneapolis who came to Northfield and secured an audition for the St. Olaf Choir. When it was over, she asked Dr. Christiansen, "Do you think you could use my voice?" "Oh yes," he replied, "In case of fire."[20]

One singer was admitted to the Choir on his second try when he yielded to Christy's terse assessment. "When I first auditioned for the Choir during the fall of 1939," reports Keith Textor '43, "F. Melius said to me, 'You're a tenor.' 'I'm a baritone,' I replied. A year later the conversation went like this: 'You're a tenor.' 'I'm a tenor,' I replied, and with that three-word sentence I joined the St. Olaf Choir. Second tenor really *was* too high for me, though, and after another year I was graciously allowed to join the baritones." [21]

In her interview with Director Christiansen in 1925, Frances Boardman learned that members of the St. Olaf Choir were chosen for one year at a time. They were all required to submit their resignations at the end of the school year to give the director a free hand in forming the new Choir in the fall. Qualifications for membership were (1) a good voice; (2) a good ear; (3) rhythmical perception; (4) ability to sing at sight; (5) knowledge of the rudiments of music; (6) good pronunciation; (7) educated taste; (8) musical

St. Olaf Male Quartet, 1941
Dayton Smith, Keith Textor, Burnett Engen, Harold Jensen

temperament; (9) experience in choral singing; (10) a spirit of willingness to sacrifice self-interest for the general welfare of the choir. Membership in the Choir was forfeited after three unexcused absences from rehearsal.[22]

In some of his writings Dr. Christiansen has discussed what he was looking for in choir singers. In one article he stated: "It is fine to have good voices in the choir, but it is still finer to have people of good character and fine moral sense and natural musical feeling combined with their good voices." [23] In interviews F. Melius often insisted that character and personality counted for as much as the excellence of the voice. The two went together, he explained to a reporter: "We pick our singers by their character, as revealed in the color of their voices. Nothing is so personal as the human voice. It reveals one's true nature."[24]

In April of 1929 Christiansen gave two chapel talks about the St. Olaf Choir and the St. Olaf Band. In discussing the Choir he began with the statement that "the St. Olaf Choir is an expression of the spirit of the institution." Its existence depends on the singing of the chorale, the a cappella style of singing, and the ability of the student body to continue to furnish singers. He appealed to students to try out even if they thought they could not get into "the first choir." Said Christiansen:

> It is important that a candidate for the choir has a good musical ear and a good voice, but still more important that they have a good scholastic standing, that they are physically fit and that they have a strong personality with a determination to succeed, that they love the ideals of religion and religious singing.[25]

Small group rehearsing with Christy, 1938
Front: FMC, Betty Ann Donhowe '41, Velva Mae Grose, '40, June Engelstad '39, Margaret Donhowe '40. Back: Rudy Ramseth '39, John Tetlie ex-'41

"When we organize choirs, we try out *ears* as well as voices!" said Christiansen. He would check the ear for accuracy of pitch. "I play a scale for the singer, to see if the ear is fine enough to sing pure distances, and usually if I stop the singer at A he is below the pitch."[26] A Baltimore reviewer, among others, expressed astonishment at the Choir's "command of absolute pitch" which he ascribed to painstaking drilling on the part of the director and "tremendous enthusiasm as well."[27] Some have believed that Christiansen himself had what is sometimes called "absolute pitch." Perhaps that was the case. He wrote that "there is no such thing as absolute pitch" and suggested that string players in an orchestra are the musicians who come nearest to having "perfect pitch" because they must tune their instruments so much. Christiansen valued the ability to sing difficult intervals as a much more useful gift.[28]

As to what constituted a good voice, it is well known that Christiansen favored a straight voice free of tremolo. Leola Bergmann comments, "The smooth tone that Christiansen tried to develop in all sections was dependent on the straightness of each individual voice; wavering of tone from one pitch to another made pure intonation an impossibility."[29]

"One of the most difficult things to deal with is the tremolo voice," Christiansen had written.[30] Candidates for the St. Olaf Choir were aware of Christiansen's preference. When Margaret Lunder (Sloane) '40 tried out for the Choir in her first year, "Dr. Christiansen told me in a kindly way that I had a 'slight corduroy' in my voice. We all knew he couldn't tolerate a tremolo voice."[31] A less kindly response to another owner of a tremolo was the blunt comment: "You sound like a Ford car bumping over a corduroy road."[32]

Margaret Lunder

The constant effort to weed out "curly voices" brought results. Christiansen's success in achieving the right tone was noted by reviewers. "The disciplined art of the choir," wrote "J.L.B." in the Philadelphia *Evening Bulletin* in 1941, "is effective in a style all its own. The vocal tone is shorn of all vibrato. . . . This makes for a collective instrument that yields to the most exact control of tonal values."

A few years after his retirement, F. Melius and Mrs. Christiansen visited Washburn, Wisconsin, where he had begun his American musical career in 1888. In an interview with a local reporter Dr. Christiansen described succinctly how he had trained the St. Olaf Choir: "We revived and practiced a certain principle of ensemble singing that the world had forgotten. This consisted of dispensing with the tremolo voice and singing straight tones for the purpose of good intonation."[33] Christiansen brought to the American scene a style of singing long known in northern Europe and still practiced in Germany and the Scandinavian countries.

For F. Melius, a good voice was one that could blend with the others. In his book, *School of Choir Singing*, he wrote, "In ensemble singing, as for example in a choir, no individual voice should stick out from the rest of the voices in the choir. The best choir singer is the one who can produce the strongest tone without being heard above the rest."[34]

After the initial try-outs came the "recalls" when he would listen to how the new candidates sounded as they sang with current members of the Choir. "Blending of tones was vital," wrote Esther Tufte (Rian) '36. "He would start with a note from a single, clear, straight voice, add another voice, then another, and then us neophytes, one by one, until the sound came as if from one throat."[35] William H. K. Narum '43 pictured Christy at work during the recall session. "He wanted to hear how your voice blended with others and so he'd insert you between a couple of the older ones. He would stick his head right between us and listen. Then he'd go to the other one and listen."[36]

Once at a rehearsal Christiansen complimented one of the sopranos by telling the Choir, "You know, Miss Mason is different from so many of you; she has the ensemble attitude."[37] Clearly he meant both quality of voice and personality. His comment was in keeping with his well-known reservations about soloists and "stars." "Soloists are what ruin choirs," he once said. "The boys and girls who come into this choir must be prepared to sacrifice individual glory. If they aren't, we don't want them. That is the only way to build a choir."[38]

Yet Dr. Christiansen made use of a succession of soloists, prominent among them being Gertrude Boe Overby, soprano, long remembered for exquisite solo work on such St. Olaf Choir favorites as "Beautiful Savior" and "Lullaby on Christmas Eve." Mrs. Overby sang with the St. Olaf Choir more than twenty years, beginning as a student in 1920 and continuing after her marriage to Oscar Overby, faculty member in the St. Olaf Music Department. "In her singing," writes Leola Bergmann, "Christiansen found a rare combination of an ensemble voice and a solo voice."[39] A reviewer for the Charleston, South Carolina paper, *The News and Courier*, wrote of "the blonde soprano soloist" who was not identified in the program: "Her clarity of voice is rivaled by its purity, by its sweet lack of affectation. It does not cloy. It enchants."[40]

The search for suitable voices also embraced considerations of color, smoothness of tone, range, and flexibility. Preferably, sopranos should have a small, reedy voice but some fluty voices were needed. In the altos

Christiansen wanted voices of cello-like quality, rich and colorful. Tenors should have smooth, reedy-toned voices. Basses should be able to sing a low D without "scraping the bottom of the kettle."[41] Paul G. Schmidt, the singing manager of the St. Olaf Choir, had a bass voice of legendary richness and range. Of him F. Melius said, "No matter how deep the ocean, P. G. can always hit bottom."[42]

P. G. sang in the St. Olaf Choir when it began in 1912 and continued to sing with it until 1953. A story told by Albert Rykken Johnson '55 in his doctoral dissertation, "The Christiansen Choral Tradition," dramatically confirms all the reports of P. G.'s fabulous bass voice. Johnson relates an incident from a rehearsal in 1953 when he and the other basses succeeded in coaxing P.G. into a contest among the low basses. One by one they sang their way down the scale until the last challenger had reached low C.

> While everyone was waiting for the great "basso" to make with his full and vastly superior low C, he instead dropped down a perfect fifth to F below low C. Since there may be those who would question the resilience and strength of this tone, it may be worth mentioning that although there were maple boards in the flooring, one vibrated vigorously under this writer's foot, slapping firmly against the sole of the shoe. This writer was seated six chairs away in the back row of the choir.[43]

As a talented singer but a non-soloist, P. G. Schmidt was the model of one who always put the good of the Choir above self-interest. As F. Melius wrote in a 1930 article, "'We' is the word to use in talking about choir matters, not 'I.' The choir-master can not say: I did this or that. He is helpless without his choir and so is any other single member of the choir. They all are dependent on each other in the organization."[44]

Rehearsals

Choir members who sang under F. Melius Christiansen have vivid memories of the rehearsals just as they do of the try-outs and recalls. Wrote Jean Malmquist Schuler '39: "Rehearsals were intense and inspiring to hear the progress. F. Melius had a unique ability of keeping us from getting too serious or maybe taking ourselves too seriously. He did have a light touch— almost a mischievous side. But he also liked to challenge us. What an inspiration!"[45]

It says much for Christiansen's ability to inspire that singers could look back on the hard work of practicing "with great pleasure." Rehearsals were held five days a week, including time for sectional rehearsals or "part practices," the latter conducted by experienced members of the Choir. For a time rehearsals of the whole Choir were in the late afternoon with sectionals

Holland Hall

at noon. Another scheme placed rehearsals from 8:50 to 9:40 a.m., Monday, Wednesday and Friday, with sectionals on the other days. Wrote Sanford Egge '37, "At rehearsals we would work hard to achieve the best intonation, balance, chords in tune and a response to direction as good as a human being could produce."[46]

The place of the rehearsals changed over the years. At times they were held in a basement room, once a primitive gymnasium, in Ytterboe Hall, the men's dormitory. One also finds references to practice sessions in a large studio in the campus radio building. While sectionals were held in the basement of the Music Hall and elsewhere, the usual site for rehearsals of the entire Choir became the chemistry lecture room, No. 501, in the building now known as Holland Hall.

Esther Tufte Rian '36 has provided a word picture of Christy in action with the Choir in Room 501:

> Rehearsals were efficient and demanding, but a joy. We met in the chemistry lecture-lab, with its raised tiers of seats, Christy standing just in front of the built-in table of sinks and faucets. Sometimes he was business-like, sometimes smiling, and once in a while he would kick out exuberantly. He enjoyed.[47]

Dr. Christiansen was the kind of disciplinarian who could get sixty college students to tend strictly to business without having to raise his voice.

He controlled the situation by a quiet, dignified authority and by his workmanlike demeanor. He never had to contend with chattering or other distractions during rehearsals. There was no loss of time between numbers. Complete attention to the musical task at hand was achieved without threats or appeals. "He wielded his baton with authority;" wrote Willis Miller '40, "discipline was the key word of the organization."[48]

Many of the colorful F. Melius sayings had their origins in rehearsal sessions. He could unleash scathing remarks, usually tempered by droll humor. To get the sopranos to sharpen up their attacks he told them, "Your approach reminds me of a man throwing a bucket of water up against a wall!"

And in saying so he acted out the motion. He might respond to sounds that displeased him by snorting, "You must have a mouth full of hot mashed potatoes." In his demand for crisp, unified releases he would say, "They must be like the end of a sawed-off log! Clean!"[49]

Lillian Bengston Eliasen '40 (BM '41) accomplished the daring feat of recording verbatim dozens of FMC sayings she heard during her two years in the St. Olaf Choir.

Lillian Bengston

The fourteen typed pages are crammed with F. Melius's colorful remarks and his lively, original metaphors. "I'm trying to look pleased but I can't," he said during the rehearsing of Liszt's "Benedictus." "Have you ever blown

Studio rehearsal, 1940
Genevieve Hendrickson, Jean Berg, Lucille Grong

soap bubbles? As a fine one falls, that's the way this chord must sound." During a December rehearsal: "You can't go home for Christmas if you don't learn these songs." His comment about a certain phrase: "That shouldn't have been given to the basses. They're elephants and we want cats." A warning to the tenors: "Don't slide. I can already hear you slide, tenors. I caught you that time."

F. Melius was sparing in compliments but he could give them on occasion. Regarding Gen Hendrickson he said, "Life is worth living when you have an alto like that. She's good and we praise the Lord for her." Some of the men needed to lighten their attitude. "Hoiness, don't look so serious. Peterson and Engen, you look so tremendously earnest that you got old last night. You have so many ruts in your forehead." The sopranos received their orders: "Sopranos, hit that second high G on the head. I know you're messy but not that bad. You ate a sandwich in between that. Don't stub your toe on that note."[50]

Choir directors invariably conduct with their eyes and face as well as with hands and arms, but every indication from his singers is that F. Melius had an unusually expressive face which reflected every nuance and emotion of the number being practiced or performed. Leola Bergmann, a member of the St. Olaf Choir as well as Christiansen's biographer, has written an especially effective paragraph about Christy's facial eloquence:

"His entire face listened"

> His entire face listened, alive to every part, yet in perfect control of the whole. A sharp twist would cross his face when a note faltered or was impure, but as he held it until it gradually blended, his face would relax into a smile. Once, lingering over the beauty of a fifth perfectly in tune at last, he said after releasing it, "I would like to die in moments like that."[51]

Leola Nelson '37

Christiansen himself once wrote: "The face of the conductor is an open book to be read by all. It expresses all the different emotions of the composition."[52]

The rehearsals were strenuous, but Choir members actually looked forward to them. While Dr. Christiansen drove them hard, he was wise to know the limits, alert to offer words of encouragement at strategic times, and skillful to supply the occasional necessary change of pace. Shortly before

Christmas break one year he said: "You've worked so hard before Christmas so go home and have a Merry Christmas and forget all about the choir and come back with a fresh interest."

Everyone knew that Dr. Christiansen's birthday was April First, so the date was often observed by a Choir party at the Christiansen home on St. Olaf Avenue. At the end of the party Christy would give a little talk about the responsibilities of Choir membership and the proper motive for being a member, namely, wanting to preserve fine art and be willing to sacrifice to that end.[53]

On April 1, 1940, Christy was sixty-nine years old. The Choir had gathered for its daily rehearsal in the basement of Ytterboe Hall. Before Christiansen arrived, P. G. Schmidt announced that since it was the director's birthday and April Fool's Day, the Choir would surprise him. When Dr. Christiansen went to the piano to begin the rehearsal, the Choir would sing "Happy Birthday" instead of the first anthem on the schedule. Willis Miller has recorded the scene:

> Precisely at the starting time, the revered and beloved maestro entered the rehearsal room and walked briskly to the conductor's stand. There he bowed ceremoniously to the members of the choir, and turned and sat down at the piano.
>
> With two thundering chords, Christy started to play the piano. The tune reverberated through the room. It was "Happy Birthday to you . . . ." The choir gasped and then broke into a hearty applause. Christy had pulled an April fool's joke on them![54]

Christy on Stage

When the St. Olaf Choir sang in Hagerstown, Maryland, in February of 1938, a reviewer hailed F. Melius Christiansen as "one of the great choral directors of modern times" and commented on the conducting:

> His control of the singers is so complete that even slight changes of facial expression, the movement of a finger and the tilt of his head bring remarkable response. Certainly his results are as complete and as definite as those achieved by the conductor of a symphony orchestra.

While traveling with the Choir during its Norway tour of 1930, Oscar R. Overby observed his esteemed colleague in action at concert after concert. Later Overby reflected on the nature of Christiansen's gift. "In trying to pinpoint the source of his power, his secret in directing his choir to its unique peaks of performance, I found myself coming back again and again to his never static way of interpreting the individual *musical phrase*. He made it literally come to life in a way which only the Lord can explain. That was the core of his genius." [55]

From the viewpoint of the singers, F. Melius exuded a princely aura as he stood before them. "He was an incredibly handsome, imposing figure on stage with an ability to inspire each of us beyond our individual abilities," recalled Jean Malmquist Schuler '39.[56] Richard Tetlie recorded his impression of Christy in an article published in 1941:

> What a magnificent picture he presents while on the podium! It is hard to suppress a smile of pride in watching him. Here is the ideal conception of the great musician: his white hair, his twinkling eyes, and the hands so graceful as they weave a spell of enchantment over his singers and the audience. What power and authority emanate from him as he stands there![57]

In his conducting as in the rest of his work as a musician, F. Melius was modest, unaffected, and interested primarily in the music. He once wrote: "I am the servant of the musical spirit—the spirit of the composer—the spirit of the music which has become my vehicle upon which I ride to an ideal world." In a similar vein he wrote to choir directors: "When you are directing your choir, it is not you that is directing. It is the beauty of the music which directs you. You are only a servant of the spirit of music."[58]

Where many directors capture attention by the exuberance of their movements on the podium, Christiansen mesmerized audiences precisely by his restraint. "The conductor who lets the music lead him is a true interpreter," he wrote. "Empty motions are of no avail."[59] It was against his philosophy and temperament to indulge in theatrical gestures. Leola Bergmann describes his conducting:

> It was vigorous and forceful, but without mannerism and without frenzy; there was no bending, no podium cavorting, but crisp, economic motions of the arm. He agreed with the majority of conductors in a sparing use of the left hand. Although the outstanding characteristic of his directing was dynamic energy, he was equally skillful in smooth-flowing legato and lyric passages.[60]

Through the 1920s, the 1930s, and into the 1940s, there was widespread mystification as to how the St. Olaf Choir obtained the pitch for each number. There was no accompaniment, of course. The audience never saw a tuning fork or a pitch pipe in use. Yet, apparently without any technical assistance and as if each Choir member had perfect pitch, the first note would burst forth in perfect tune.

A writer for the *Buffalo Express* in 1922 addressed this apparent mystery: "A most marvelous feature of the St. Olaf Choir is its ability to attack the different numbers, often in the most remotely related keys, with unerring surety and a precision beyond criticism, without aid from instrument, pitch pipe, or voice. It is veritably uncanny."[61] After the Choir's 1941 appearance in Symphony Hall, a Boston reviewer began with the observation:

> This body of some 60 stalwart young men and comely young women once more exhibited its extraordinary collective sense of pitch by starting always on the key without any external aid, even that of a tuning fork or a pitch pipe.[62]

A reporter for the *Youngstown Telegram* thought he had solved the "pitch mystery." His theory was that the singers brought the pitch for the first number with them when they came on stage. As soon as the piece ended, each member was able to find the interval to the first chord of the next number.[63]

All such speculation was pointless. Christiansen had never intended to impress or baffle anyone about getting the pitch. He simply distributed a few single-tone pitch pipes throughout the Choir, one for each pitch that

Getting the pitch, ca. 1951. Mary Stegner, Barbara Strand, Rolf Charlston, Ramona Halverson, Yvonne Overby

would be needed in the program. During the applause the pipe was blown softly and the pitch hummed quietly throughout the Choir. Sounding and spreading the pitch only took a few seconds. By the time the applause had ended, the Choir was ready to begin the next number.[64]

As curiosity about getting the pitch persisted, despite the growth of a cappella singing and wider familiarity with Christiansen's techniques, it was probably inevitable that Christy's impish humor would be brought into play about this supposed "secret." On one occasion, it is claimed, he replied to the question with the revelation, "We chew tobacco."[65]

Better documented is the story of how wickedly he toyed with the demand of an aggressive woman critic in Detroit. She had pushed her way past P. G. Schmidt before the concert to wrest the secret of the pitch from Dr. Christiansen. He smiled warmly and said, "Watch my baton. The secret of our pitch is in my baton." After both the first and second groups the music critic was back stage again, complaining that she had in fact watched the baton but still could not understand how the Choir got its pitch. Again Christy smiled and repeated the advice to watch the baton. The concert ended, and the woman appeared again, very upset because she still had not unlocked the secret. As reported by Howard J. Glenn '41, "Christy told her, still with that warm smile. 'The secret of pitch is in my baton. It is made of soft pine, and everyone knows that soft pine is full of pitch.'"[66]

Season after season, concert after concert, the St. Olaf Choir got its pitch from the discreetly placed pitch pipes, and the audiences thrilled to the magnificent singing. But there were at least a few times, it must be said, when something went wrong and the Choir's beginning notes were anything but precise and confident. One such instance happened in Orchestra Hall in Chicago in 1942. By this time Olaf C. Christiansen, son of F. Melius, had been named as assistant director. He conducted the first two groups of the concert program that year and his father, soon to retire, conducted only the last group.

Under the mature conducting of the older man, the Choir had turned in a fine performance of "Beauty in Humility," a composition by F. Melius with words by Ellen Hilleboe. The audience responded with prolonged and enthusiastic applause during which time the Choir was humming the pitch for "Beautiful Savior." Christy took his bow, turned to the Choir with upraised baton, and said, to everyone's stunned astonishment, "Sing it again!" Quickly, someone sounded the pitch for "Beauty in Humility" but not everybody heard it. Half were still ready to sing "Beautiful Savior." It was a moment of confusion and panic.

F. Melius gave the downbeat but when the baton came up, two pitches were heard and the first line of "Beauty in Humility"—"How tardily in life we tend to learn"—came out, as one of the male singers remembered, "as a mushy mumble." Christy cut the Choir off. There was an awful silence. Christy then did something unprecedented: he attempted to hum the pitch himself.

The result was disastrous. It was impossible to find the right pitches from his "low, trembling growl." When the baton moved again, only "a miserable dissonance" was heard. But Christy kept things going and the women's voices came in, struggling to produce something like the anthem. Finally, the agony was over. Christy's face was red and the Choir members also were blushing furiously, but amazingly, the audience responded with more enthusiastic applause.[67]

In addition to the matter of getting the pitch accurately but unobtrusively, another feature of St. Olaf Choir performances under F. Melius Christiansen that elicited comment was the delayed attack. "After the initial upbeat, there was a pause before the choir attacked the chord," explains Leola Bergmann. It was a sign of the Choir's marked sense of unity. Until the singers felt that complete unity, they would not sound the chord. [68] When Dr. Christiansen's baton came up to signal the Choir to begin, nothing would happen for a second or two! He might even repeat the motion. "Then suddenly," in the words of Esther Tufte Rian '36, "an explosion of glorious sound!" F. Melius and his son Olaf both trained their choirs in perfecting the delayed attack for the purpose of achieving unity in the group.[69]

When students became ill during a number, their instructions were to sit down on the risers, let the others close up the gap, and to leave the stage when the group was completed. F. Melius and P.G. were always solicitous about the indisposed person and inquired about them backstage. An alto was very touched by Christiansen's tender thoughtfulness when, taken ill, she received permission at intermission to stay out and rest. She found three chairs backstage, sat down on the middle one and rested her shoulders on the next one. The Choir was already back on stage for the next group, the applause had subsided, and the audience was awaiting Dr. Christiansen's entry. As he was about to return to the stage, Christy spotted the miserable young woman, came over, and gently lifted her feet and legs up on the third chair to make her a little more comfortable. Then he hurried out on stage.[70]

Choir memories include episodes when Dr. Christiansen had to leave the platform because of illness and a student had to take over the conducting to complete the program. Once in Norway he explained amiably that he had "smoked too many cigars." In Grand Rapids, Michigan in 1941 the onset of the flu forced him to lie down backstage during the second group while student Dayton Smith ably took charge. The Choir itself joined gratefully in the applause when Christiansen was able to return to the stage for the final group of numbers.

More interesting, however, were the times when he deliberately walked off in the middle of a number and let the Choir fend for itself. In the stories told of such incidents, the number being sung is always a Bach motet for double choir. One instance was at a school convocation in Iowa. Christy left the podium and sat down in the audience. As Trudy Roe Anderson relates the incident, "Our shock turned to pride with determination to finish without a director." After a little hesitation, all

Gertrude "Trudy" Roe '38

eight parts came together and the undirected Choir finished the number with gusto. "Christy, with a glint in his eye, came back to the podium and commented, 'That's more like it.'"[71] Apparently Christiansen had sensed a flagging in the Choir's alertness and attentiveness.

While initially startled, the singers knew that Christy had a purpose with what seemed like an impulsive action. Once it was toward the end of a tour and everyone was tired. Christy walked off the stage during the Bach number and sat down in the middle of the front row, "grinning away at us."

On reflection, the narrator of this episode rightly asked, "How did there happen to be one empty seat available to him in the center front row of a packed house?"[72] Again, it was not a stunt to impress an audience but a device to quicken the Choir's energies.

Building the Program

Throughout his career, F. Melius Christiansen devoted much time and effort to locating suitable choral music, the lack of which prompted his prolific composing. He regarded program-making as one of his most difficult tasks. "This has been my bugbear, my greatest worry and work. If I helped lay the foundation for a cappella singing in this country, program-making has been the hardest and most important work I have done," he said.[73]

He spent summers searching libraries and publishing houses. In 1923 he was in Boston for three weeks at the City Library. He spent the summer of 1926 in England, Germany, and Norway. Each year he was faced with the new challenge of constructing a concert program of the best sacred music. He had to take into account what the new Choir would be like, its capabilities, temperament, and solo voices, and his own aims and mood.

The concert programs Christiansen directed presented works by German and Russian composers of the nineteenth and twentieth centuries. A favorite selection from the Eastern church was Tschesnekov's "Salvation is Created." He used some but not many Italian compositions and relatively few from the modern English school, much as he was impressed by Edward Elgar, Gustav Holst, Martin Shaw, Vaughn Williams, and others. Christiansen incorporated his own compositions into programs and it is well known that he liked the folk song and the nineteenth-century romantics.[74]

F. Melius preferred a three-part program. When his time came, his son Olaf would develop a pattern of four-part programs. In the general scheme of F. Melius, the heavier numbers should come early in the program and the lighter ones toward the end. A typical program of three groups and a total of twelve numbers, as he outlined it, would look like this:

Group I. 1. Short majestic opening
2. The heaviest and longest
3. A smaller lyric
4. Bright objective
Group II. 1. Strong objective
2. Lyric
3. Lyric
4. Light
Group III. 1. Lyric
2. Light
3. Lighter
4. Strong objective but short[75]

Christiansen's choice of music for concerts occasionally drew criticism. The *Boston Herald*'s reviewer thought that "a more interesting program could be arranged" after hearing the St. Olaf Choir in Symphony Hall January 28, 1941. But when the same program was sung in Washington's Constitution Hall, it was described by Alice Eversman as "dignified in character and superbly presented." Christiansen was not surprised by critics reacting differently to what they heard, having said as much in an article he had written in 1930. He recognized the purpose of the critic's task, "to encourage whatever he thinks is of value to the world," but refused to take criticisms as absolute truth. While students were eagerly reading reviews of the previous night's concert as the train rolled toward the next city, Christiansen would be settling down to work on a crossword puzzle.[76]

Since the concert tour of 1941 was the last one on which F. Melius was sole director before his son Olaf joined him as assistant, the program of that season is of interest. It opened with the Brahms motet, "O Savior, Throw the Heavens Wide." Second number was Hassler's "O Sacred Head," arranged by F. Melius Christiansen. The other pieces in order were "We Have No Other Guide," by Schvedof, "The Lord Reigneth," by Paul Christiansen, "Savior of Sinners," by Felix Mendelssohn, "Thanksgiving Motet," by Arnold Mendelssohn, "Come, Guest Divine," by Georg Schumann, "Faith Victorious," by Gretchaninoff, with words by Oscar R. Overby, "When Curtained Darkness Falls" and "Beauty in Humility," both by F. Melius Christiansen, "Sing Unto Him" by Morten Luvaas, "Lullaby on

Tour Program 1940-1941

Christmas Eve" by F. Melius Christiansen, and "Doxology," by Bourgeois.[77]

Some have expressed the view that Christiansen should have chosen more works by sixteenth and seventeenth century composers which, indeed, is what Olaf C. Christiansen would do.[78] Critics and admirers alike agreed with F. Melius's principle that it is better to have the Choir trained to perform fewer pieces well than to sing a larger selection of musical literature in mediocre fashion.[79]

F. Melius believed that one hour and fifteen minutes was a good length for a choir program. He was firmly opposed to diluting a choir concert with distractions of any kind. "If you have a choir concert, let it be a choir concert." He was particularly intolerant of announcements, speeches of welcome, speeches of thanks, and the like. Such "monstrosities" defeated the purpose of the program, which was that "of transporting the listener to a better clime, to an ideal perfection for which we as humans long and to which the art of music is able to lift us."[80]

The Contribution of F. Melius Christiansen

When F. Melius Christiansen reached his eightieth birthday on April 1, 1951, he received a letter of congratulation from Leopold Stokowski who wrote, "The whole world is indebted to you for what you have done for American choral music."[81] What he had done was to raise the standards of choral music, especially in the revitalization of a cappella singing. In the words of Glenn Dillard Gunn of the Washington *Times-Herald*, "If the great and ancient art of unaccompanied choral song has known a rebirth in this country, Dr. Christiansen is responsible for that fortunate result."[82] As early as 1923, Peter Lutkin, founder of the Northwestern University A Cappella Choir, referred to Christiansen as "that prince of choirmasters."[83]

The impact of Christiansen's work was heightened by the fact that he, unlike Lutkin at Northwestern, took his choir on national tours, a practice then in its infancy and quite unique for choirs. Even more bold was the develpment of what Kenneth Jennings has called "the format of the sacred concert." The homily or address by the College president that was part of the earliest St. Olaf Choir concerts quickly dropped away, and the program of sacred choral music was left to stand on its own. This too was a unique feature in the Choir's evolution and a key part of the F. Melius Christiansen legacy to musical life in the country.

In evaluating Christiansen's contribution, due weight should be given to the maestro's comment on what he had achieved with the St. Olaf Choir. On a visit to Washburn, Wisconsin, mentioned earlier in this chapter, he spoke of reviving and practicing a forgotten principle of ensemble singing, namely, removing the tremolo and singing straight tones to make good intonation possible. Over the years some have criticized F. Melius Christiansen for his "straight tone," but it was not his invention. He brought to this country a north German style of singing that insisted on a controlled vibrato in sacred music, singing in the center of the pitch, and getting the tuning as accurate as possible. It was a way of singing that stood in contrast to the more effusive operatic style popular in southern Europe.

The value of Christiansen's work has often been viewed within the setting of American college life, where he was credited with lifting ensemble singing beyond the glee club. John K. Sherman stated the matter in these words: "Christiansen in his long service to music took the sloppiness out of choral singing, helped to speed the decline of the oldtime glee club booming and humming, and made strictly professional—and important—what had hitherto been regarded as unavoidably amateur, and mostly social."[84]

His achievements centered in the founding and directing of the St. Olaf Choir, but his compositions were also a major contribution. He composed or arranged over 600 numbers, more than

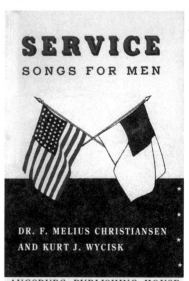

Popular collection, published in 1943

218

250 of them known to the wider public through the *St. Olaf Choir Series*, published by Augsburg Publishing House of Minneapolis beginning in 1919. He also compiled volumes of music for women's voices, for men's voices, and for organ.[85] Many of Christiansen's arrangements were first sung from the balcony of St. John's Lutheran Church in Northfield where Dr. Christiansen was organist and where the St. Olaf Choir, or the St. Olaf Chapel Choir, directed by Oscar Overby, often sang the anthems.

Oscar Overby has told a moving story related to Christiansen's setting of "Lamb of God." While the piece was still in manuscript form, Overby took the liberty of making copies and teaching the number to the Chapel Choir, which sang it at a church service one Sunday. After the service, Overby summoned his courage to approach Christiansen at the organ bench to congratulate him on the wonderful new anthem and to apologize for having the Chapel Choir sing it first. He was not prepared for the response:

> I found the master stooped over at the organ, unable to speak; his face was wet with tears—the only time I saw him weep and shed tears visibly. I stood helpless during the silent moments that followed; I felt as if I stood on sacred ground. He finally regained his composure and muttered softly under his breath: "Thank you! Did *I* write that?"[86]

Year by year through his compositions and in his teaching at St. Olaf College, he spread the gospel of fine sacred music and how to express it beautifully. Christiansen's course in Choir Conducting was a particularly effective platform. About this course Professor Overby wrote: "In this, as in all his work, he stressed good musical taste and high art standards, both in choice of music and in performance."[87]

Not only at the College but in much wider circles Christiansen taught the importance of high standards in performance and repertoire. He demolished the notions that the public will shy away from Bach and that it will need constant relief in serious programs. As he held firmly to his standards, people flocked to the concerts and other directors were encouraged by what he had demonstrated.[88]

"Lamb of God" St. Olaf Choir Series

219

Through his founding and conducting of the Christiansen Choral Schools, which began in 1935 and in which his sons Olaf and Paul shared leadership, he passed on the "St. Olaf sound" to hundreds of church and college choir directors. Additional circles of the Christiansen musical influence spread out from the work of Olaf as director of the St. Olaf Choir and Paul as director of the Concordia College Choir. Both sons taught hundreds of students in their Choir Conducting courses at the two colleges.

F. Melius Christiansen directly influenced the founder of the Westminster Choir, John Finley Williamson. At a reception for the Westminster Choir at St. Olaf in 1954, Williamson credited F. Melius Christiansen, P. G. Schmidt, and the St. Olaf Choir with inspiring him to take the first steps in establishing the Westminster Choir School.[89] Both F. Melius and Olaf Christiansen had personal contacts with Williamson over the years. When it happened that both choirs were scheduled for concerts the same night in Sacramento, California, Dr. Williamson immediately canceled the Westminster concert and took his choir to hear the St. Olaf Choir.[90]

John Finley Williamson   Prestige Publications, Inc.

Trained to emphasize power of tone, the Westminster Choir became the primary vocal ensemble for a number of prominent American orchestras, such as the New York Philharmonic, the Philadelphia Orchestra, the NBC Symphony, and the Cincinnati Orchestra.[91] The Westminster Choir sang at St. Olaf again in 1955, when F. Melius was in failing health. After the concert Dr. and Mrs. Williamson called on Dr. Christiansen at his home, and the Westminster Choir, assembled on the lawn, sang Peter Lutkin's "Benediction."[92]

While F. Melius Christiansen's influence extended well beyond his state and region, one must still recognize the importance of the heading used by the editor of the church paper, the *Lutheran Herald*, when he reflected on the revered musician's work after his passing in 1955: "He taught our Church to sing."[93] From his first job in Washburn, Wisconsin, to his retirement years in Northfield, Christiansen attended to the writing and performing of music that would add beauty and joy to the life of the Church.

The composer at work

F. Melius Christiansen knew the importance of art on the local level. Willingly and energetically over decades he devoted his musical skills to the local needs of College and Church. When national and international recognition came to him and the St. Olaf Choir, it was because he remained true to his calling and to the spirit of art. As he approached retirement age, he was hailed as the ablest man in his field. "Certainly no man," wrote Richard S. Davis, "has done more to raise the standards of choral music. For generations to come the effect of his devoted service will surely be felt."[94]

A few days after F. Melius Christiansen died, John K. Sherman wrote of him in the *Minneapolis Sunday Tribune*, "What he built has become a part of our permanent cultural heritage." Sherman rightly traced the sweep of Christiansen's influence when he added, "There's hardly a child singing in the public schools today who is not singing better—and singing better music—because of Christiansen."[95] The reference to young people was fitting. Always true to his art, F. Melius Christiansen modestly and patiently built for the future.

1. *Rochester Daily Post*, March 26, 1923.

2. Walter Krieger, Naumburg, Germany, quoted in Paul G. Schmidt, *My Years at St. Olaf*, A Centennial Decade Publication (Northfield, Minnesota: St. Olaf College, [1967]), 131.

3. Earl Christmas, *The Dearborn Independent*, August 19, 1922.

4. *Dubuque Times*, January 2, 1927.

5. Frances Boardman, "Ideals of St. Olaf Lutheran Choir Explained," *St. Paul Pioneer Press*, July 5, 1925, 3.

6. Frank A. R. Mayer, "St. Olaf Choir's Fame Rests on Its Director's Exacting Thoroughness," Unidentified Twin Cities newspaper, ca. 1935.

7. F. Melius Christiansen, "The Energizing Power of Thought in Singing and Chanting," *Lutheran Church Herald* (*LCH*) XIV (April 1, 1930), 445. Letter from F. Melius Christiansen to Olaf C. Christiansen, n.d., ca. 1930.

8. Boardman, "St. Olaf Choir's Ideals," 3.

9. Unidentified Dubuque, Iowa newspaper, April 7, 1936.

10. F. Melius Christiansen, "The Necessity of Concentration in Choir Singing," *LCH* (November 4, 1930), 1548. Letter from F. Melius Christiansen to Olaf C. Christiansen, n.d., ca. 1930.

11. Letter from F. Melius Christiansen to L. W. Boe, February 10, 1927. STOARCHIV. Also cited in Leola Nelson Bergmann, *Music Master of the Middle West*: The Story of F. Melius Christiansen and the St. Olaf Choir (Minneapolis: University of Minnesota Press, 1944), 134.

12. Letter to Bob Johnson from Gertrude "Trudy" Roe Anderson '38, January 15, 1994.

13. Willis H. Miller, "Memories of a Choir Member," *The Lutheran Journal* 54:2 (1987), 21.

14. Richard Tetlie, "A Great Man," *Lutheran Herald* XXV:13 (April 1, 1941), 335.

15. Letter from Hazel Baker Tudor to Bob Johnson, n.d., ca. 1993.

16. *Ibid.*

17. Letter from Esther Tufte Rian to Bob Johnson, February 18, 1994.

18. Letter from Sanford Egge to Bob Johnson, December 18, 1993.

19. *Ibid.*

20. Interview with Frederick and Lenore Schmidt, April 17, 1991.

21. Letter from Keith Textor to Bob Johnson, December 6, 1993.

22. Boardman, "St. Olaf Choir's Ideals," 8; Schmidt, *My Years at St. Olaf*, 110.

23. F. Melius Christiansen, "Necessity of Concentration," 1548.

24. Unidentified Dubuque, Iowa newspaper, April 7, 1936. Cf. MUSIC: "At St. Olaf," *Time*, May 22, 1939, where Christiansen is quoted as saying, "If it comes to a choice between character and exceptional voice, I choose character."

25. F. Melius Christiansen, "The Choir," Unpublished Typescript, 1929, 2; cf. *Manitou Messenger*, April 23, 1929.

26. Bergmann, *Music Master of the Middle West,* 145.

27. *Baltimore American*, January 21, 1922.

28. F. Melius Christiansen, "Pitch Variations," *LCH*, November 1929, 1584.

29. Bergmann, 145.

30. F. Melius Christiansen, *School of Choir Singing* (Minneapolis: Augsburg Publishing House, 1916), 62.

31. Letter from Margaret Lunder Sloane to Bob Johnson, n.d., ca. 1993.

32. Bergmann, 146.

33. *Washburn Telegram*, 1947. Norwegian-American Historical Association (NAHA) Archives.

34. F. Melius Christiansen, *School of Choir Singing*, 62.

35. Letter from Esther Tufte Rian to Bob Johnson, February 18, 1994.

36. Interview with William H. K. Narum and Genevieve Hendrickson Sovik, December 6, 1994; cf. Bergmann, 148-49.

37. Signe Ramseth Johnson 1932 Diary.

38. *The Minneapolis Journal*, December 9, 1928.

39. Bergmann, 135.

40. *The News and Courier*, Charleston, South Carolina, January 29, 1930.

41. Bergmann, 147-48.

42. Letter from Paul Lavik to Bob Johnson, November 28, 1993.

43. Albert Rykken Johnson, "The Christiansen Choral Tradition: F. Melius Christiansen, Olaf C. Christiansen and Paul J. Christiansen," A thesis submitted in partial fulfillment of the requirements for the degree of Doctor of Philosophy in the School of Music in the Graduate College of The University of Iowa, July, 1973, 322, note 40.

44. F. Melius Christiansen, "The Necessity of Concentration in Choir Singing," *LCH*, (November 4, 1930), 1548.

45. Letter from Jean Malmquist Schuler to Bob Johnson, January 27, 1994.

46. Letter from Sanford Egge to Bob Johnson, December 18, 1993.

47. Letter from Esther Tufte Rian to Bob Johnson, February 18, 1994.

48. William H. K. Narum interview; Willis H. Miller, "Memories of a Choir Member," 21.

49. Paul Lavik letter; letter from Jean B. Ellison '41 to Bob Johnson, January 27, 1994; Bergmann, 160.

50. Lillian Bengston Eliasen, "Bits from 'Christy,'" (1939-40; 1940-41), Unpublished typescript sent to Fred and Lenore Schmidt, April 20, 1960. Used by permission.

51. Bergmann, 162.

52. F. Melius Christiansen, "Conducting," *LCH* (August 5, 1930), 1085.

53. Bergmann, 136.

54. Willis H. Miller, *Hudson Star Observer*, April 1, 1971.

55. Oscar R. Overby, *The Years in Retrospect*, Unpublished Typescript (Northfield, Minnesota, 1963), 92. STOARCHIV.

56. Jean Malmquist Schuler letter.

57. Tetlie, "A Great Man," 335.

58. F. Melius Christiansen, "Inspirational Leadership," *Choral News*, ca. 1947; F. Melius Christiansen, "To Choir Directors," *Lutheran Herald* XXIII (January 3, 1939), 31.

59. "Inspirational Leadership."

60. Bergmann, 159.

61. *Buffalo Express*, January 13, 1922.

62. Unidentified newspaper, Boston, Massachusetts, January 29, 1941.

63. *Youngstown Telegram*, January 27, 1922.

64. Bergmann, 157-58; Anton Eugene Armstrong, "Celebrating 75 Years of Musical Excellence: The Evolution of the St. Olaf Choir," A thesis submitted in partial fulfillment of the requirements of the Doctor of Musical Arts degree from Michigan State University, May, 1987, 18.

65. *Minneapolis Tribune*, n.d., 1948.

66. Letter from Howard J. Glenn to Bob Johnson, January 7, 1994.

67. Letter from Neal Johnson '44 to Bob Johnson, n.d., ca. 1993; cf. Jean B. Ellison letter, January 27, 1994.

68. Bergmann, 159-60.

69. Esther Tufte Rian letter. Cf. F. Melius Christiansen, "Conducting," LCH (August 5, 1930), 1085.

70. Esther Tufte Rian letter.

71. Trudy Roe Anderson letter.

72. Esther Tufte Rian letter.

73. Bergmann, 165.

74. *Ibid.*, 164-65.

75. F. Melius Christiansen, "Program Making," *LCH* XIII:27 (July 2, 1929), 952.

76. F. Melius Christiansen, "The Listener," *LCH*, July 1, 1930, 907; Bergmann, 164.

77. Program, St. Olaf Lutheran Choir Annual Tour, 1940-41.

78. Bergmann, 167.

79. Armstrong, "Celebrating 75 Years of Musical Excellence," 20, A. R. Johnson, "Christiansen Choral Tradition," 222-23.

80. F. Melius Christiansen, "Program Making," 952.

81. Letter from Leopold Stokowski to F. Melius Christiansen, April 2, 1951. STOARCHIV.

82. Glenn Dillard Gunn, *Times Herald*, Washington, D. C., January 31, 1941.

83. Quoted in Johnson, 17.

84. John K. Sherman, "Choir Became 'Celestial' under Christiansen's hand," *Minneapolis Sunday Tribune*, June 5, 1955.

85. Editorial, "He Taught Our Church to Sing," *Lutheran Herald* XXXIX:25 (June 21, 1955), 601.

86. Overby, *Years in Retrospect,* 75.

87. Oscar R. Overby, "Salute to a Giant," *Lutheran Herald* XXXV:15 (April 10, 1951), 359.

88. "St. Olaf Lutheran Choir," Concert Program, Baptist Temple, Philadelphia, January 31, 1947.

89. Johnson, 16.

90. Letter from Howard J. Glenn to Bob Johnson, January 7, 1994.

91. Paul Benson, *The Empires of Song: A Cappella Choirs in the Scandinavian-American Colleges,* Unpublished Typescript, n.d., 38. Used by permission.

92. Ray Robinson, *John Finley Williamson: A Centennial Apprecition* (Princeton, New Jersey: Prestige Publications, Inc., 1987), 20.

93. "He Taught Our Church to Sing," 600.

94. Richard S. Davis, *Milwaukee Journal*, January 1941.

95. Sherman, "Choir Became 'Celestial,'"

CHAPTER 8

OLAF C. CHRISTIANSEN

On the morning of August 12, 1947, Olaf C. Christiansen had work to do. There were only three more working days left of the two-week session of the Christiansen Choral School meeting at Lake Forest College in Illinois. When he raised his baton to begin the class in choral technique, the 210 voices broke into "Happy Birthday, dear Olaf." Olaf was surprised and delighted. It was his forty-sixth birthday.[1]

Olaf Christiansen enjoyed the same affection and respect from his singers that prompted St. Olaf Choir members to honor F. Melius Christiansen on April 1st each year. But with an August birthday, Olaf was seldom with his college singers, whether at Oberlin or at St. Olaf, on the date. There is no doubt, however, that he was held in high esteem by both students and faculty colleagues during his Oberlin years. When Paul J. Christiansen, Olaf's younger brother, attended the Oberlin Conservatory, he found that Olaf commanded the same kind of respect at Oberlin as their father, F. Melius, had received at St. Olaf.[2] The same was also true when Olaf moved to St. Olaf College. There too, he was held in highest regard, not simply because he was the son

*Olaf C. Christiansen, 1932
At Oberlin Conservatory*

of the famed F. Melius, but because he won the affection of the community with his sterling character, warm personality, and masterful musicianship.

The career of Olaf C. Christiansen occupies a unique place in the story of the St. Olaf Choir. Succeeding his father as director of the Choir, he carried the tradition of sacred choral music forward into new realms of excellence. He came to St. Olaf from Oberlin in 1941 to serve as associate with F. Melius Christiansen and soon to assume sole responsibility for the Choir. That important transitional period will be treated in the next chapter. Here it is fitting to look at some biographical data about Olaf's life and work prior to his joining the St. Olaf faculty in 1941.

Born in Minneapolis, Minnesota, in 1901, Olaf Christiansen was the third son in the family. During his early childhood years, his father went through the career changes that led him to develop a music program at St. Olaf College. At the same time, the Christiansen family also lived through experiences of change, some of them marked by sadness. Olaf was born at a time when the household was enlarged by the presence of F. Melius's brother Karl who made his home with the family while he studied engineering. A year after Olaf's birth, four-year-old Elmer died. In 1903 F. Melius and Edith received into their home from Norway his brother-in-law and two small children. That June the already-busy Edith gave birth to a daughter, affectionately called "Tulla."[3]

Olaf was two years of age in 1903 when his father accepted the position of music director at St. Olaf College in Northfield. As noted previously, F. Melius left his family in Minneapolis during his first year at St. Olaf. He devoted the greater share of his time to the College in Northfield but continued to teach his pupils in Minneapolis. In the summer of 1904, at the conclusion of the trial year, he moved his family to Northfield where he rented a house on St. Olaf Avenue.

Olaf's Youth and Education

As the son of a young college teacher in a small town, Olaf Christiansen had a happy childhood that offered him a loving home situation, sports, and music. His mother was a strong, capable woman devoted to her family. Occupied with multiple duties at the College, his father was not able to spend much time with the children, but he was a steady and affectionate force in their lives.[4]

When Olaf was seven, his sister Tulla, age five, died from peritonitis, the second time within six years that death had visited the Christiansen family. Tragedy would strike again when Olaf was of college age. A ten-year-old younger brother, Carl, was fatally injured in a car accident in August of 1921. In the period of grief following Carl's death, F. Melius Christiansen composed his powerful *Psalm 50* that included the text, "Offer unto God the sacrifice of thanksgiving."[5] Undoubtedly Olaf and his older brother

Helping Dad mow, 1930
Elsa, Paul, and FMC

Jacobi ("Jake") were also affected in their own ways by these deaths in the family.

As young boys growing up in Northfield, Jake and Olaf were soon active in music, but not because of any special urging on the part of their father. Olaf, like his father, started playing on a small E-flat clarinet. Jake played the B-flat clarinet. During their practice sessions in the basement during the summer months they would often get some pointers from their father. From time to time the boys sneaked out of the basement to play ball. Yet they loved music and rhythm. When F. Melius was rehearsing the St. Olaf Band on campus, Jake and Olaf would be outside the windows beating accurate time with sticks on tin pans and tubs. [6]

There was considerable natural athletic ability in the Christiansen family. F. Melius encouraged his boys in their baseball, football, basketball, swimming, skating, and skiing. Although the father was too absorbed in music

St. Olaf Ski Jump

229

to engage in sports himself, his sons remember seeing him walk around the house on his hands. When a new ski jump was built on the St. Olaf campus for collegiate competition, Olaf was the first of the local daredevils to try it out, followed very soon by Jake. And it was Olaf who once made a high dive into the Cannon River from the top of the steel girders of the bridge.[7]

Sports would figure quite heavily in the lives of both Jake and Olaf in the years that lay ahead. Jake spent the major part of his career as director of physical education and head football coach at Concordia College in Moorhead, Minnesota. At age nineteen, Olaf would take a job at a teachers' college in Mayville, North Dakota, where his several duties included those of athletic director and coach. St. Olaf Choir members who sang under Olaf's direction have vivid memories of his remarkable athleticism. They tell of seeing him chin himself with one hand and of doing push-ups with one hand held behind his back.

Olaf Christiansen was a multi-talented young man in high school and college. He played the clarinet in the St. Olaf Band while still a student in the Northfield High School. When F. Melius had a sabbatical in Minneapolis, Olaf attended Central High School where he played the piccolo and joined the gymnastics team. Becoming interested in other band instruments, he also learned to play the baritone horn with which he made a few dollars performing at barn dances. But athletics were not neglected, high-jumping and pole-vaulting being his favorite track sports. A different sort of outdoor testing also came his way. When he was about fifteen, with only a wooden flute and a dog for company, he herded sheep on a ranch in South Dakota. He recalled getting help from a kind old Indian after a storm had blown down his tent and soaked his bedding.[8]

In addition to his manifest ability in music and athletics, Olaf displayed some promise in painting, an activity that his mother had enjoyed before she was married. Olaf took a correspondence course from the School of Commercial Designing in Minneapolis in 1918-19. Oil painting remained one of his interests.

Olaf C. Christiansen
In his twenties

230

Olaf entered St. Olaf College in the fall of 1919, trying to decide whether his future would be in music, athletics, or art. He had a chance to try himself out in two of these pursuits when he took the job at Mayville Normal Teachers College in North Dakota for which his father had recommended him. It required starting and directing a college band, having charge of athletics, and serving as dean of men.

Thus in 1920, at the age of nineteen with but one year of college behind him, Olaf went out to Mayville, North Dakota, to take on the position. As he thought back on the experience, he said, "We developed a fair band and church choir, but I lost all but one basketball game! That year provided the needed source of inspiration!" The year in North Dakota was important in more than one way. He solidified his decision to go into music, and he met his future wife, Ellen Beatrice Kjos.[9]

At St. Olaf College

Olaf resumed his college education at St. Olaf in the fall of 1921. His aim now was to take the prescribed courses leading to the Bachelor of Music degree in composition and voice. He was the principal clarinetist in the St. Olaf Band, then directed by J. Arndt Bergh. During his college years he was choir director at the Congregational Church in Northfield. He participated in gymnastics, tennis, swimming, track, and golf. During his junior and senior years he served as captain of the gym team.

*J. Arndt Bergh
Director, St. Olaf Band*

St. Olaf Band, 1922, Olaf to right near drum

St. Olaf Gym Team, ca. 1922
OCC in center, bottom row

And for four years, beginning with the 1921-22 school year, Olaf sang in the St. Olaf Choir, directed by his father. Sectional rehearsals for the basses were held at the home of Professor and Mrs. P. G. Schmidt on Sunday afternoons, but it was Mrs. Schmidt, not P.G., who was in charge of these rehearsals.[10]

Olaf was with the Choir on its 1922 tour to such eastern cities as Cleveland, Albany, New York, and Washington. In the spring of 1923 the Choir made a midwestern tour, giving concerts in Minnesota, Wisconsin, Illinois, Indiana, Missouri, and

Olaf as Choir member
With FMC, 1924

Nebraska. On this tour Olaf was called upon to direct the concert in Green Bay. Summarizing the tour for the *Viking* yearbook, Grace Riggle '23 wrote of "the excitement when 'Christy' failed to appear at Green Bay, and 'Ole' had to direct us."[11]

Additional details of this incident, mentioned in an earlier chapter, have been supplied by Mildred Hoff Anderson '24. She remembered that it was not until the break before the final group that P. G. Schmidt told the audience, "The director you have seen this evening is not F. Melius

Christiansen but his son Olaf." P. G. explained the reason for the change and "a storm of applause followed."[12] Olaf himself recalled the incident in a 1967 interview:

> Everyone was primed and eager, so all went well, except that I had not been coached in stage decorum: timing between numbers, bowing, and so forth. So I would jump off the podium [hurriedly]. It was an exciting performance that ended a half hour early.[13]

Among the other glimpses available of Olaf's college days are his Junior and Senior recitals. For his Junior recital, May 29, 1924, he shared the program with J. O. Edwards, an organist. The printed program for the Senior recital on May 21, 1925, lists Olaf C. Christiansen as a baritone. His accompanist was Miss Gladys Grindeland. The first number was the Prologue from Leoncavallo's opera *Pagliacci*. It was followed by three numbers in German by Franz and Schumann and a Schumann piece sung in English. Then followed a series of folk songs, Italian, Welsh, Swedish, German, and Russian. The recital ended with F. Melius Christiansen's "Yearnings of the Norwegian Emigrant," a selection from the Centennial Cantata composed for the observance of the 100th anniversary of the first Norwegian emigration from Norway to America. It was the first public performance of the composition.[14]

As a member of the graduating class of 1925, Olaf was pictured in the *Viking* yearbook for 1924-25. His college activities listed were Pi Sigma Alpha, a literary society, Choir, Band, Track, and Gym Team.[15] St. Olaf societies were local organizations unrelated to national Greek letter fraternities and sororities. Pi Sigma Alpha had been founded at St. Olaf in 1911. Its motto was "Frankness with truth." During Olaf's student years his society was proud of the number of "great and near-great athletes" who belonged to its roster.[16] One of these fine athletes was Olaf's long-time friend and colleague, Carl "Cully" Swanson '25, St. Olaf baseball coach and Dean of Men.

Olaf Christiansen also belonged to the St. Olaf Music Club, organized in 1924 to develop true appreciation of good music and to encourage its members to perform in public. The genesis of the Music Club is credited to a group pictured in the 1926-27 yearbook as "post graduates, 1924-25." Olaf, his future wife, Ellen Kjos, class of 1923, O. Matthew Lyders, Gunnar Malmin, Gladys Grindeland, Obed Grinder, Kenneth Onsgard, and Waldo Furgason were the eight who took advanced work in the School of Music. Among their many music activities, these eight were members of the St. Olaf Choir. As the *Viking* said, "The musical activities of the college were much enriched by the presence of these special talents."[17]

Top: Ellen Kjos, O. Matthew Lyders, Gunner Malmin, Obed Grinder. Bottom: Kenneth Onsgard, Gladys Grindeland, Olaf Christiansen, Waldo Furgason

Three other Club members may be mentioned: Margaret Hoigaard, Neil Kjos, and Alvin Snesrud. Margaret Hoigaard '25, a classmate of Olaf's was, with him, the recipient of one of four Bachelor of Music degrees granted in 1925. She is honored on the St. Olaf campus by the Margaret Hoigaard Skoglund Reception Room, a beautiful room in Christiansen Hall of Music, a surprise anniversary gift from her husband, Howell P. Skoglund '26, one-time chair of the St. Olaf Board of Regents. The room is in frequent use for

Margaret Hoigaard Skoglund
Howell P. Skoglund

social activities related to musical events. There one finds the marble bust of F. Melius Christiansen created by Arnold Flaten, and the oil painting of Olaf C. Christiansen executed by James Ingwersen.[18]

Neil Kjos '24, brother of Ellen Kjos and Olaf Christiansen's future brother-in-law, played in the Band and the Orchestra. After graduation he established and managed a music publishing firm in Chicago that brought out several of Olaf Christiansen's compositions. Kjos worked with Olaf and F. Melius in the Christiansen Choral School, serving as manager and registrar. The Neil A. Kjos Music Company, later moved to California,

Arnold Flaten and bust of F. Melius Christiansen

Olaf's Portrait Unveiled, 1979. OCC, Mary Ann Johnson, James Ingwersen

235

would also publish compositions by Olaf Christiansen's successor, Kenneth Jennings.[19]

Neil Kjos

Alvin A. Snesrud sang in the St. Olaf Choir in 1923-24. He became an ordained minister and gave significant leadership, in association with F. Melius Christiansen and others, to the thriving Choral Union movement in the 1930s. He organized and managed the highly successful Choral Union Festival Concert held in Chicago Stadium in 1931 when F. Melius directed a choir of 3,000 voices.[20] It was Snesrud who organized the Choral Union of Southern California that resulted in a series of Choral Union concerts in the Hollywood Bowl. In the spring of 1939, for example, Snesrud directed the Lutheran Choral Union of Southern California at an Easter sunrise service held in the Hollywood Bowl attended by over thirty thousand persons. In June of that year, when F. Melius Christiansen directed 2,000 voices in the Hollywood Bowl Choral Union Concert, Snesrud directed the Children's Choir of 1,000 voices.[21]

The other two Bachelor of Music graduates in 1925 were Odvin Hagen and Gunnar J. Malmin.[22] Hagen carried on the Christiansen choral tradition as director of the Waldorf College Choir. Gunnar Malmin gained a name for himself and the Choir of the West at Pacific Lutheran University in Parkland, Washington. O. Matthew Lyders '25, after receiving the master's degree in music at Northwestern University, taught music and led choirs in Rochester, New York. One has to conclude from the talents and subsequent careers of Olaf's college friends and classmates that they benefited from the strong and promising musical culture that had been developed at the school.

Hollywood Bowl
Site of Lutheran Choral Union Concert, 1939

Photo courtesy Frances Anderson

Olaf C. Christiansen, professional musician

In one sense, Olaf Christiansen's professional career began in 1920-21 when he directed a band and church choir at Mayville Normal Teachers College.[23] And directing the choir at the Congregational Church in Northfield during his student years pointed ahead toward a career in music.

Wedding, September 2, 1925
Maid of Honor, Hedwig Ylvisaker, Best man, Clarence Kjos

On September 2, 1925, Olaf Christiansen and Ellen Kjos were married. They went to New York where Olaf studied voice and gained further choir conducting experience. Twice a week he took voice lessons from an outstanding professional teacher, Paul Parks, who trained him in Italian song. Olaf remembered that Parks had particularly stressed "the value of pure vowels for the clarity of words."[24] St. Olaf Choir members from Olaf's time readily vouched for his zeal in perfecting the vowel sounds.

While living in the New York area in 1925-26, Olaf directed two choirs at Zion Lutheran Church in Brooklyn. One sang at the English worship service and the other at the Norwegian. Ellen Christiansen played the organ at the Norwegian service. Olaf and Ellen attended operas in New York where they heard world-famous singers. With his voice study Olaf was aiming at a career in opera, but choral directing had its own appeal. "It was easier to make music with my back to the audience," he said. [25]

Evidently Olaf kept his father posted on his various directing duties. Among items received from F. Melius was a hand-written list of "The problems of a church choir conductor" in the form of rather loaded questions. For example: "Will he be permitted to work unhampered in selecting the music and the singers?" "If the choir conductor aims to build up the congregation with spiritual songs of a fine order, does the minister counteract his work by selecting hymns with small dance tunes for the congregation to sing?"[26]

Writing to "Dear OleEllen" on a Sunday evening, F. Melius reported that the St. Olaf Choir had sung a Liszt number that morning in church. "It ends with a couple of notes as an echo sung from the sacristy, but while they sang them a baby hollered out at the same time and spoiled it. Such is life! Or What a life! or something else, for instance: For crying out loud!"[27]

Olaf and Ellen would continue to receive instructive and amusing letters from "Your Pa" when they lived in Flint and Oberlin.

As with many student couples, money was a problem. A gift from his grandfather in Norway, Anders Christiansen, enabled Olaf and Ellen to get through the rest of the year of work and study and return to Minnesota for the summer. In the fall of 1926, Olaf took a job in Flint, Michigan. Ellen was in Northfield for a time, giving birth to their first child, Sylvia Ellen, in October.[28]

The first of Olaf's three years in Flint was spent teaching in Emerson Junior High School where he gained useful experience in dealing with young people and testing the different levels of their musical aptitude. During the next two years he taught at Flint Junior College. There he had an uncommonly full schedule, teaching theory, madrigal, and public school vocal music methods. He also had to direct a high school band, teach choral classes, and

Anders Christiansen STOARCHIV

238

coach gymnastics and golf. Moreover, it was also his responsibility to direct the a cappella choir and to plan and direct the annual opera.[29]

Energetic and community-minded, Olaf Christiansen lent his talents to musical activities in Flint outside of the Junior College. He was soloist with the Civic Chorus in a Christmas performance of Handel's *Messiah* and sang in performances of Verdi's *Aida* and Mendelssohn's *Elijah*. When needed, he played bass clarinet in the Flint Civic Symphony Orchestra.

Not surprisingly, he also directed church choirs. At Central Methodist Church he was fortunate to have the participation of a thirty-piece church orchestra on hymns, preludes, postludes, and offertories. On Sundays there were evening as well as morning worship services at Central. The two choirs Olaf directed rehearsed together on Friday evenings. This arrangement was necessary because many of the choir members were factory workers who could sing at one but not both services.[30]

The Olaf Christiansen family lived in Flint for three years, from 1926 to 1929. In March of 1929, their second child was born, Fredrik Melius II. During the third year in Flint Olaf was interviewed by two faculty members from the Oberlin College Conservatory of Music in Oberlin, Ohio. One was Frank Shaw, Dean of Music or Director of the Conservatory; the other was Charles Adams, a member of the voice faculty. On their visit to Flint they also listened as Olaf directed the a cappella choir. An offer was made and accepted with the result that Olaf and Ellen and their two children moved to Oberlin, Ohio in 1929.[31] Olaf was twenty-eight years old when he began his work at Oberlin in the fall of 1929.

In Oberlin, ca. 1932
Children: Sylvia and Fredrik

Olaf C. Christiansen at Oberlin

The director who hired Olaf, Dr. Frank Holcomb Shaw, had been appointed to his position in 1924. Times were changing in the realm of music institutions. The Oberlin Conservatory was an established, outstanding school of music, but it could not afford to be complacent in view of challenges posed by the younger Eastman, Curtis, and Juilliard schools. Economically as well, the twenties and thirties constituted a difficult period. The new director had to shape Oberlin to meet the tests.

A 1907 graduate of Oberlin, Shaw had spent the previous ten years as Director of the Conservatory of Music at Cornell College in Iowa. As soon as he came to Oberlin he proceeded to shake things up. He set a good example for the rest of the faculty in the industry and excellence of his piano teaching. The author of a dissertation on the Oberlin Conservatory wrote of him:

> Frank Shaw ruled the Conservatory with a firm hand, doing the work of two men, and giving his entire life to the furtherance of music in Oberlin. There is no question of the high respect he won from his colleagues and associates.[32]

An assessment of how Olaf Christiansen's work contributed to the renewal at Oberlin is seen in a chapter of the Oberlin centennial history. Following a brief discussion of orchestra and band developments, the author turns to choral music.

> Another musical organization that was flourishing strongly in 1936 was the A Cappella Choir. In 1929 Olaf C. Christiansen, son of F. Melius Christiansen, leader of the famed St. Olaf's Choir, came to the Conservatory to re-establish a strong choral program. He did this by opening choral classes to all Conservatory and College students. . . . He also taught choral conducting, led a madrigal group, the Musical Union, and the select sixty-voice A Cappella Choir, which was probably Oberlin's most polished performing group up to that time.[33]

It should be underscored that Olaf Christiansen founded the Oberlin A Cappella Choir, doing so in 1929, his first year.[34] An Oberlin faculty publicity release issued in the 1930s stated that the A Cappella Choir

The Director

The Oberlin A Cappella Choir
OF THE OBERLIN CONSERVATORY OF MUSIC
Touring Ohio Pennsylvania New York-- April 2 to 12

was Olaf's "outstanding achievement" at Oberlin. The sixty voices included "some of the best vocal material in both the Conservatory and the College." The release continued with the comment: "The aim of this young choir is toward spiritual expression as well as musical, and it is this combination that gives it the quality peculiar to it. As director, Mr. Christiansen never lowers his standard of perfection."[35]

When F. Melius heard about Olaf's success at Oberlin, he wrote in the teasing way that was typical among the Christiansens. "Dear children: Thanks for letters. I am glad everything is going good and that the Oberlin a capella Choir is going to beat St. Olaf Choir or any other Choir in the universe to a standstill. Let the universe stand still and listen!"[36]

On the Oberlin campus the A Cappella Choir, later known as the Oberlin College Choir, became part of a larger Chapel Choir to sing for chapel services two days a week. Before the spring tour, Olaf would try out all seventy-seven members of the Chapel Choir to establish the smaller ensemble to take on tour. Concerts were in churches selected for location, good acoustics, and the congregation's willingness to sponsor the Choir's appearance. "We sang music that had a message of consequence and was good for all churches, regardless of denomination," said Olaf.[37]

In 1932, when the A Cappella Choir was in its third year, the Oberlin alumni magazine ran a brief article, accompanied by a picture of Olaf C. Christiansen, entitled, "Choral Singing in Oberlin." The writer noted that the student body had been dubious in its initial reception of the Choir, but that the Choir had won its enthusiasm and respect. A clear mark of the Christiansen approach appeared in the next statement: "The Choir, in itself a fine organization, has brought to Oberlin audiences an entirely new conception of the voice as an ensemble instrument—a conception that is bound to have a tremendous influence on popular appreciation of any kind of choral singing."[38]

Other teaching and directing duties at Oberlin kept Olaf an extremely busy man. He had a teaching load of from forty to sixty students in private voice. He taught classes in choral singing and choral conducting. He revived the Musical Union, an oratorio society, meeting it for rehearsals each Monday night. On December 17, 1931, the Musical Union performed the *Messiah* under Olaf's direction before an audience that overflowed Finney Memorial Chapel. Another year this group offered the first performance with orchestra in this country of Gabriel Fauré's *Requiem*.[39]

A third choral group in Olaf's charge was the Elizabethan Madrigals, which met on Tuesdays for rehearsals. It was a small group of six students whose singing set forth "the exquisite finish of the smaller vocal ensemble, in the charmingly social music of the 16th and early 17th centuries."[40]

In addition to this heavy schedule at the Conservatory and College, Olaf took on the directing of the choir at First Church in Oberlin, a group whose history extended back to 1837. It had 120 singers and a long waiting list of those wanting to join. Olaf rehearsed the Choir once a week and conducted its singing in church every Sunday.[41]

In the meantime, wisdom and humor arrived in the mail from Northfield. The correspondence between F. Melius and his son Olaf dealt often with matters of choral work: singing Bach for vocal agility, the relation of the science of music to its art, concert programs in preparation, pronunciation of vowels in such words as "sabaoth" and "Savior," rating voice candidates as (1) splendid (2) possible and (3) impossible, and memorizing music. Regarding a Christmas program Olaf was preparing, F. Melius wrote: "Sing something Rye Bread too to offset the sweet things."

The father's advice to the son was blunt and to the point: "Don't dwell upon the past successes or failures, but think always how you can improve in the future." "Learn to say no!" "One thing! Do one thing so well that whatever faults you may have will be forgiven on account of this one thing." "Don't theorize much with the Choir—sing, sing, sing till you don't know that the time is up." "More rehearsing and interesting and inspiring rehearsals are what is needed and it is all up to you—you and nobody and nothing else." [42]

"Under the leadership of Olaf Christiansen the future of Oberlin choral music looks bright," wrote D.H. in the Oberlin alumni magazine.[43] The statement proved to be correct. The Oberlin College Choir that Olaf founded and directed until 1941 won additional fame when it came under the talented leadership of Robert Fountain in the 1950s. After successful appearances in New York, one of its high points was the tour of the Soviet Union under State Department auspices in the spring of 1964.[44]

While still caught up in his multiple duties at Oberlin, Olaf was putting his summers to good musical advantage for himself and those he taught. During five summers and a sabbatical, the 1939-40 school year, he studied voice privately with Marshall F. Bryant. In the early thirties he taught in university summer sessions at Missouri and Iowa. In the summer of 1940 he taught at Michigan. Later he would do a similar stint at Southern Methodist.[45]

Olaf was co-founder with his father of the Christiansen Choral School. It was advertised as "A Master Course for Choral Directors of College, Church & School." Beginning with the first two-week summer session in 1935, Olaf gave part of each summer to the Choral School for several years. In 1939, for example, one session was held in Los Angeles and a later one in Chambersburg, Pennsylvania. That year the faculty consisted of F. Melius

Christiansen, Carol M. Pitts, an expert in the training of high school voices, and Olaf C. Christiansen. [46]

During the 1939-40 school year Olaf was granted a sabbatical leave from Oberlin. He studied church music at Union Theological Seminary in New York as a candidate for the Master of Sacred Music degree, awarded in 1940. His master's thesis was entitled, "Congregational Singing." The year at Union was intensive. In addition to pursuing his regular course work toward the master's degree, normally a two-year effort that Olaf completed in one year, he taught a course in church choir techniques and filled in for one of his instructors, Clarence Dickinson, both in the classroom and in choir conducting at

Brochure for Christiansen Choral School Session for summer of 1940

Brick Church. He was also studying voice with Marshall Bryant and Douglas Stanley.[47]

If one counts the sabbatical year at Union Theological Seminary, Olaf spent a total of twelve years associated with Oberlin Conservatory and College. He began at Oberlin in 1929 and left to accept a position at St. Olaf College in 1941. Because of his excellent work with the A Cappella Choir, the Musical Union, and the Elizabethan Singers, he had indeed given Oberlin a bright future in choral music, as the alumni writer had said.

The same writer, identified only as "D. H.," had a valuable comment about the wide appeal of choral music, observing that "choral music comes nearest to the common kind." That is, many people sing hymns, Christmas carols, and patriotic songs, and many can enjoy such performances as the *Messiah*. These are common experiences available to all. "Deep down we have the feeling that choral music is not foreign or impossible to us; that we might have participated, that we, too, might have helped to make that music." [48]

The thought would have received ready endorsement by both F. Melius and Olaf Christiansen and their successors. St. Olaf Choir concerts gave the listeners a sense of being participants. And at the College, choral music was available to all, not just Choir members. As Olaf would tell the St. Olaf chapel crowd at the Wednesday hymn sings he often conducted, "At St. Olaf, everybody sings!"

St. Olaf Hymn Sing
Boe Memorial Chapel, ca. 1965

Olaf C. Christiansen Comes to St. Olaf

That Olaf Christiansen succeeded his father as director of the St. Olaf Choir may seem, in retrospect, the most natural course to expect. Moreover, Olaf's signal success in directing the St. Olaf Choir from 1941 until his retirement in 1968 only underscored how appropriate it was that he took over the leadership of the Choir at his father's retirement. The actual sequence of events, however, indicated that Olaf's appointment should not be perceived as inevitable.

In looking at Olaf Christiansen's situation in 1940, the year before he came to St. Olaf, one finds a highly successful, proven, professional musician with a secure position at one of the nation's leading music conservatories. His faculty colleagues supported the changes he brought to the music program and his students were very fond of him. Olaf had moved steadily up the academic ladder at Oberlin, having been promoted to associate professor in 1940 with every prospect of being named full professor within a reasonable time.

His family was well settled in Oberlin. A third child, Sigrid Edith, was born in November of 1934. Oberlin was a good place to live while raising children. One of Olaf's friends and colleagues was the composer Normand Lockwood. Olaf and Ellen had many friends among the faculty couples and enjoyed a lively social life with them. Every week faculty members would entertain students in their homes. All in all, it was a good and satisfying life for the Christiansens in Oberlin. [49]

What Olaf had achieved at Oberlin in the creating of the A Cappella Choir and his many other services was impressive and was recognized by the president of Oberlin College, the director of the Conservatory of Music, his colleagues, and his students. Olaf had also established a favorable reputation beyond Oberlin through his work in the Christiansen Choral School, editing, directing festivals, and teaching summer sessions at midwestern universities.

At thirty-nine years of age in 1940, Olaf Christiansen was at the peak of his career with attractive opportunities before him. One strong option was to remain at Oberlin where he was happy, fully immersed in the kind of work he enjoyed, and well appreciated. Another was at the University of Michigan at Ann Arbor where he had taught summer school in 1940 and from where he received an offer in early 1941. While fully aware of his father's approaching retirement, he was too engaged in productive, satisfying work to be lingering at his mailbox waiting for a summons from St. Olaf College.

At St. Olaf College, in the meantime, President L. W. Boe was aware that "Kong Kristian," his affectionate term for his respected friend and colleague, Dr. Christiansen, would soon want to be relieved of the heavy demands of his position, including the leading of the St. Olaf Choir. But Boe preferred to say nothing until F. Melius himself would bring up the subject and make a suggestion. [50]

F. Melius Christiansen would be seventy years of age on April 1, 1941. Obviously he had to be thinking of retiring and finding a successor. In January of 1941 the St. Olaf Choir was on winter tour in the eastern part of the country. Olaf came up from Oberlin to hear the Choir in Cleveland.

P. G. Schmidt and L. W. Boe

There he told his father that he might take the position at Ann Arbor that had been offered. In the light of this information, F. Melius lost little time in getting word to President Boe. After the Choir's concert in Buffalo, F. Melius wrote to Boe:

> I wish you would make arrangements with Olaf to become my assistant for next year. I feel that should be done for the security of the Choir and my other work. Ole feels that he should make a change for the sake of his children at this time and now would be the time to approach him on the subject. . . .

Although he was considering the Ann Arbor offer, Olaf "would much rather come to St. Olaf for less," wrote his father. "He feels more at home with his own people (Norw. Lutherans)." And F. Melius was concerned about the future welfare of the St. Olaf Choir.

> I don't want the Choir to die with me—not even sag. The sagging process is apt to begin next year—the way I feel on this trip. If you feel like doing anything with this proposition, please act in time.[49]

President Boe immediately wrote to Olaf: "Before you come to any decision about Ann Arbor, I want to have a talk with you and I was wondering if matters can drift along until you and I and your father could meet, either before or after the Choir concert in Chicago."[51]

A breakfast meeting was arranged for Saturday, February 8, 1941, in the Congress Hotel in Chicago. An offer was made which Olaf and Ellen discussed over the next several days. On February 18, 1941, Olaf wrote to Dr. Boe: "After careful consideration we feel that it is God's will that I

246

accept your proposition to come to St. Olaf. We shall be very happy to be associated with St. Olaf and to help carry on her ideals." They would be sorry to leave their good friends in Oberlin but looked forward to renewing friendships in Northfield. "And of course it will be a pleasure and privilege to work with father," wrote Olaf.[52]

A number of details were worked out through further letters exchanged in the spring and summer of 1941. Olaf would be his father's associate, wrote Boe. "In reality, you will be co-conductors of the Choir, to see if we can pass over all the goodwill that your father has built up these many years." Teaching arrangements and personnel were discussed. Boe informed Olaf that his salary would be $2,500 plus 70% of the fees from the private lessons he would give.[53] Ten years earlier, as assistant professor at Oberlin, Olaf's salary had been $3,000. He received another $500 for directing the choir at First Church. By 1940 it was proportionately larger, so he was indeed coming to St. Olaf for a markedly lower salary.

The correspondence covered most of the terms of Olaf's position at St. Olaf, but the matter of his academic rank had not been settled. On July 28, 1941, Olaf wrote to President Boe from the family's summer home in Sister Bay, Wisconsin, setting forth his understanding. Citing his eagerness to

The Christiansens at Sister Bay, 1938
Back: Olaf, Elsa, Paul; front: Jake, Edith, F. Melius

accept the challenges at St. Olaf, his years at Oberlin, the advancement he expected to receive there, and what his father had said on the subject of rank, Olaf warmly contended that he expected to be appointed full professor.

His father had told him that "I would be ranked with him as co-director and full professor," he wrote. Olaf felt strongly enough about the matter to suggest that he would not have considered the call to St. Olaf without a clear understanding that it was a full professor appointment. He wanted to make sure that President Boe understood his motivation. "If you think it is a matter of *personal* pride that leads me to expect full professorial ranking, you misjudge me. This is a matter of *professional* pride and respect for my job."[54]

There was no mention of salary in Olaf's letter. He was willing to come to St. Olaf at a large reduction in pay, clearly making a financial sacrifice. Apparently Boe had hedged on promising Olaf the rank of professor because of possible jealousy on the part of some already in the music department. Olaf deftly responded to the jealousy issue by suggesting that making him full professor might be the way to eliminate future discord. He also noted that there were no full professors on the music faculty. Yet Olaf was not inflexible. He was willing to be named co-director and leave the matter of rank undetermined for the time being.

President Boe's unusual response, shrewd and generous at the same time, was to tell Olaf that he was leaving it up to him "to decide whether you want to have the rank of full professor, or associate, or assistant." Boe's personal hope was that Olaf would choose to come as associate professor. By so doing, he would be "carrying out on the ranking proposition what you are doing when it comes to salary, taking less than you reasonably could expect, but advisable in view of what others are getting."[55]

The resolution of the question was in Olaf's favor. The first time he is listed among the faculty in the St. Olaf College Catalog it is as "Professor of Music." One notes that the same catalog now lists Oscar R. Overby as "Professor of Music." The previous year Overby had been Associate Professor.[56]

Oscar R. Overby was a graduate of the Northwestern Conservatory of Music in Minneapolis and the recipient of the Bachelor of Music degree from St. Olaf in 1921. Overby had also studied at the New England Conservatory and at Columbia University. As a member of the St Olaf music faculty, he taught theory, public school music, music appreciation, composition, and other courses. He was the director of the St. Olaf Church Choir, a mixed ensemble of seventy-five voices. Overby was a versatile, energetic, and creative musician who among other things wrote poems that F. Melius Christiansen set to music. He had begun teaching at St. Olaf in

1921 and was thus due for promotion. It appears that Olaf Christiansen's words to Boe about full professor status also served to benefit Overby.

The exchanges between Olaf Christiansen and President Boe offer a glimpse into the academic sparring between a confident candidate and a president of a small college who must stretch the dollars and keep peace in the faculty. They confirm that the steps whereby Olaf Christiansen succeeded his father were not automatic and predictable. They also illustrate how Olaf, his father, and President Boe had somewhat different readings of the situation.

Oscar R. Overby

Olaf had other options, as noted above. His leaving Oberlin for St. Olaf was not a foregone conclusion. In a sense, St. Olaf College needed him more than he needed St. Olaf. As F. Melius saw the situation, it was important that Olaf should come "for the security of Choir." The father is also the source of the view that Olaf wanted a change and preferred to be "with his own people." Therefore, in the view of F. Melius, the president of the college should make the necessary arrangements. To Olaf and Ellen, however, the situation was not that clear-cut. There were good reasons to stay in Oberlin where they enjoyed both professional opportunity and personal contentment. Thus President Boe, the administrator, saw that he had a negotiating task on his hands. He carried it through and was pleased that Olaf agreed to come to St. Olaf.

Olaf's appointment meant more than filling an important position; it also provided a way for F. Melius to retire with grace and dignity. Boe, who always retained his pastor's heart, had a genuine concern for the well-being of the father. In one of his letters to Olaf, Boe said, "I thank God for the solution that we have found, making it possible for him (F. Melius) to go on until traveling days are o'er." Boe's personal solicitude for F. Melius was combined with a knowing appreciation of the treasure that the elder Christiansen was in the community. Therefore he sought to convey to Olaf that he, the loyal son, was the key person to "draw out of your father every ounce of inspiration and leadership there is left."[57]

Working together, ca. 1942

The decision to accept the offer at St. Olaf was a difficult one. It speaks well of Olaf that he was willing to come back to his alma mater at a marked decrease in salary, to permit his very promising career to take a different turn, and to enter a situation where it was inevitable that he would be living and working in the shadow of a famous, beloved father. Yet for Olaf, the thought of working with his father "for a common ideal" was, as he put it, "most uplifting."

Through the entire process of arriving at his decision, Olaf was looking at the larger picture, "the many favorable qualities of St. Olaf, the various opportunities for service to the church and to education which few other schools can offer." Olaf acted from a sense of mission. His main motivation in accepting the offer from St. Olaf was to step in where he was needed and do something worthwhile. He would continue the work with the Choir and make the needed improvements in the music department. That was the challenge. But it was not his role merely to help St. Olaf "to hang on," as he wrote to President Boe. "I am still young enough (40) to want to see progress." [58]

From his arrival at St. Olaf College in 1941 to his retirement in 1968, Olaf C. Christiansen would create and see progress. As head of the music department and director of the St. Olaf Choir, he showed himself to be an agent of change and always a model of the musician as educator and servant. He would leave his own distinctive mark on the world of choral music.

Notes for Chapter 8, OLAF C. CHRISTIANSEN

1. Lake Forest College News Release, Lake Forest, Illinois, August 12, 1947.

2. Albert Rykken Johnson, "The Christiansen Choral Tradition: F. Melius Christiansen, Olaf C. Christiansen, and Paul J. Christiansen," A thesis submitted in partial fulfillment of the requirements for the degree of Doctor of Philosophy in the School of Music in the Graduate College of the University of Iowa, July, 1973, 308-09.

3. Leola Nelson Bergmann, *Music Master of the Middle West*: The Story of F. Melius Christiansen and the St. Olaf Choir (Minneapolis: The University of Minnesota Press, 1944), 83-84.

4. Cf. *Ibid.*, 84, 103.

5. *Ibid.*, 130.

6. *Ibid.*, 103; Johnson, "Christiansen Choral Tradition," 286.

7. Bergmann, 104; Johnson, 286-87.

8. Johnson, 287-89.

9. *Ibid.*, 290.

10. Frederick Schmidt, "Former St. Olaf Choir manager fondly recalls the group's early days," *Northfield News*, March 4, 1992; Johnson, 296, from an interview with Olaf C. Christiansen.

11. Grace Riggle, "St. Olaf Choir Tour—1922-1923," *Viking* 1924-1925, 138.

12. Letter from Mildred Hoff Anderson to Bob Johnson, n.d., ca. 1993.

13. A. R. Johnson interview with Olaf C. Christiansen, in Johnson, "Christiansen Choral Tradition," 296.

14. Senior Recital Program, in Johnson, 294.

15. *Viking* 1924-1925, 59.

16. *Viking* 1926-1927, 147.

17. *Ibid.*, 127, 164.

18. Joseph M. Shaw, *Dear Old Hill*: The Story of Manitou Heights, The Campus of St. Olaf College (Northfield, Minnesota: St. Olaf College, 1992), 232-33.

19. Brochure, "Christiansen Choral School," Chicago, 1939. Neil A. Kjos, Jr. is now President of the Neil A. Kjos Music Company, Publisher, located in San Diego, California.

20. J. C. K. Preus, *The History of the Choral Union* of the Evangelical Lutheran Church 1847-1960 (Minneapolis: Augsburg Publishing House, 1960), 102.

21. *Lutheran Church Herald* XXIII:20 (May 16, 1939), front cover; Preus, 102-03.

22. *St. Olaf College Bulletin* XXII:1 (March 1926), 84.

23. Robert Lee Jennings, "A Study of the Historical Development of Choral Ensembles at Selected Lutheran Liberal Arts Colleges in the United States," A Thesis submitted to Michigan State University in partial fulfillment of the requirements for the degree of Doctor of Philosophy, Department of Music, 1969, 43.

24. Johnson, "Christiansen Choral Tradition," 298.

25. *Ibid.*, 299.

26. F. Melius Christiansen letter to Olaf and Ellen Christiansen, n.d. This and other FMC letters cited in this chapter made available to the writer by Sylvia Christiansen Buselmeier in August 1996 and used by permission.

27. Letter from F. Melius Christiansen to Olaf and Ellen Christiansen, September 19, 1925.

28. Johnson, 299-300.

29. *Ibid.*, 300-02.

30. *Ibid.*, 303.

31. *Ibid.*, 303-04.

32. Richard Skyrm, cited in Willard Warch, *Our First 100 Years*: A Brief History of the Oberlin College Conservatory of Music (Oberlin, 1966), 42.

33. Warch, 45.

34. *Ibid.*, 62.

35. Oberlin Faculty Publicity, Olaf C. Christiansen, ca. 1932.

36. Letter from F. Melius Christiansen to Olaf Christiansen family, n.d.

37. Johnson, 305.

38. D. H., "Choral Singing in Oberlin," Oberlin Alumni Magazine, January 1932.

39. Johnson, 305-06; "Choral Singing in Oberlin."

40. "Choral Singing in Oberlin."

41. Oberlin Faculty Publicity, ca. 1932; Johnson, 306.

42. Letter from F. Melius Christiansen to Olaf Christiansen family, n.d.

43. "Choral Singing in Oberlin."

44. Warch, 62-63.

45. Jennings, 42-43.

46. Brochure, "Christiansen Choral School," Chicago, 1939.

47. Johnson, 309.

48. "Choral Singing in Oberlin."

49. Interview: Joseph M. Shaw and Betty Stromseth with Fred and Mary Christiansen, May 16, 1996.

50. Letter from L. W. Boe to F. Melius Christiansen, January 29, 1941.

51. Letter from F. Melius Christiansen to L. W. Boe, ca. January 26, 1941. F. Melius Christiansen Papers, STOARCHIV.

52. Letter from L. W. Boe to Olaf C. Christiansen, January 29, 1941.

53. Letter from Olaf C. Christiansen to L. W. Boe, February 18, 1941.

54. Letter from L. W. Boe to Olaf C. Christiansen, March 21, 1941.

55. Letter from Olaf C. Christiansen to L. W. Boe, July 28, 1941.

56. Letter from L. W. Boe to Olaf C. Christiansen, August 6, 1941.

57. *Catalog of St. Olaf College*, Sixty-Eighth Year, 1941-42, 15; *Catalog of St. Olaf College*, Sixty-Seventh Year, 1940-41, 16.

58. Letter from L. W. Boe to Olaf C. Christiansen, June 5, 1941.

59. Letter from Olaf C. Christiansen to L. W. Boe, July 28, 1941.

CHAPTER 9

TRANSITION YEARS

St Olaf Choir, 1941-42

The decade beginning with 1941 marked an important transition for the St. Olaf Choir as its leadership passed from F. Melius to Olaf Christiansen. The Choir's formal picture in the 1942 yearbook, showing the younger and older directors with P. G. Schmidt between them, vividly illustrates the change. St. Olaf College itself was also in transition. It lost its dynamic president, L. W. Boe, who died in late 1942, adapted to the circumstances of World War II, and readjusted itself to post-war conditions after 1945. Enrollment declined gradually at the beginning of the decade, but more dramatically after the United States entered the War.

War conditions inevitably affected the life of the St. Olaf Choir. Beginning with the 1941-42 concert tour and continuing for the next three years, the Choir opened every concert with "America," inviting the audience to stand and join in the singing "of this prayer for our country." There were fewer men available for the Choir, of course, and the extent of touring had to be reduced. Nevertheless, the work of the Choir went on, now given new energy and purpose through the presence of the new member of the music faculty and Associate Director, Olaf C. Christiansen. Said the *Kansas City Times* of the Choir, after a concert in January of 1942 led jointly by F. Melius and Olaf, "Its established excellence has not yet been impaired by the vicissitudes of war and calls to service."[1]

St. Olaf College 1941-1946

The years of World War II and the next year when many veterans enrolled were also the first five years of Olaf Christiansen's tenure as director of the Choir. Working in close collaboration with his father the first two years and continuing on his own from 1943, Olaf trained and directed Choirs of accomplishment during difficult years when the pool of male singers was shrinking. The 1945 yearbook credited him with moulding and maintaining the male section, despite losses in the middle of the year, "to a standard comparable to that of male sections of pre-war days."[2]

When Olaf joined the St. Olaf faculty in the fall of 1941 there was still an enrollment of 1,122, down somewhat from the year before but healthy in comparison with what was to come. A marked drop appeared in the 1942-43 school year when scores of students left for military service. Over 1,000 students registered in the fall, but as the second semester began in February of 1943, there were 927 enrolled, 532 women and 395 men. The decrease in the number of male students was even more perceptible in the 1943-44 school year when the total enrollment of 707 consisted of 597 women and 110 men.[3] For the College the unavoidable drop in enrollment meant a loss of tuition income that was offset, in large part, by the Navy programs

Lars Wilhelm Boe
President, St. Olaf College,
1918-1942

conducted on the campus from 1943 through 1945. At the end of the war enrollments would go up, soaring beyond pre-war figures.

In 1941 and 1942, even as the men were volunteering or being drafted for military service, the College community was concerned about the health of President Boe. When Olaf Christiansen wrote to Boe in the summer of 1941, he expressed his respect for him and stated that he looked forward "to many years of friendship and cooperation with you."[4] Unfortunately, Boe had little time left. Ill with cancer, he was granted a six months' leave of absence by the Board of Trustees in the spring of 1942. The leave was extended to a year, but the president's strength ebbed away and he died December 27, 1942. The St. Olaf Choir sang at the memorial service held for Dr. Boe at the College on January 6, 1943, after the students returned from their Christmas vacation.[5]

Lars Wilhelm Boe is credited with leading St. Olaf College from its struggling pioneer decades into maturity as a reputable liberal arts college closely related to the Lutheran Church. According to his vision of the College, the academic and spiritual life of the institution should be placed in the service of a larger constituency. With that view in mind, he early became one of the St. Olaf Choir's strongest and most effective supporters, maintaining a warm and long-standing friendship with "Kong Kristian," as he affectionately addressed F. Melius Christiansen.

Prexy Boe's encouragement of the Choir was related to his vision of closer Lutheran unity. Prior to his election to the presidency of St. Olaf in 1918, Boe served as secretary for all Lutheran war charities. This work had brought him into contact with Lutheran leaders in the eastern part of the United States. With them he was part of a joint Lutheran effort in caring for soldiers and sailors that led to the formation of the National Lutheran Council with offices in New York City. On the basis of this record of Lutheran cooperation, it occurred to Boe "that the great common heritage in Lutheranism, the vast literature of Lutheran music, might prove to be the one most likely force of unity" to carry forward the good relations established among the different Lutheran groups.[6] Thus when Paul G. Schmidt went to New York in 1919 to secure support for the St. Olaf Choir's eastern tour of 1920, he began by visiting the headquarters of the National Lutheran Council.[7] The acquaintances made there led to others that eventually provided the needed guarantors for the successful tour.

J. Jørgen Thompson
Acting President, 1942-43

During the last months of Boe's illness and into the middle of 1943 when the new president began work, the leadership of the College was in the hands of an acting president, Dean of Men J. Jørgen Thompson. It happened that Dean Thompson had done some important things for the cause of music at St. Olaf over the years. As a student he had been manager and member of the St. Olaf Octet of 1908, a predecessor of the St. Olaf Choir. Later, as a staff member at the College, he went to Norway in 1913 and again in 1930 to make arrangements for the Choir's European

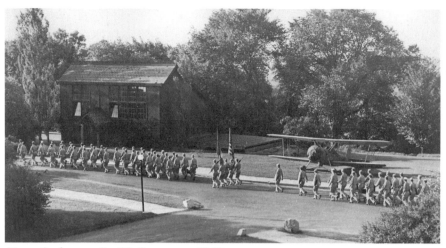

Navy Cadets on St. Olaf campus, 1943

tours. He even directed the St. Olaf Choir in 1915-16 when F. Melius Christiansen was on leave.

One of Thompson's major tasks as acting president was to oversee the establishment on the St. Olaf campus of two Navy training programs. One was a Naval Pre-Flight School that trained 3,510 cadets between January 1943 and October 1944. The other was a Navy Academic Refresher Unit that was in operation from summer 1944 until December 1945. The sights and sounds of Navy cadets marching and training on campus made explicit the reality of war-time conditions. Appropriately for St. Olaf, a Navy choir was organized and participated in campus life, singing over radio station WCAL.[8]

Betty Halvorson '46
Student Body President

The academic program at the College went forward as normally as possible during the war years. Student life continued in its vigor and variety, affected by but not dominated by the Navy presence. Women students quickly and naturally assumed positions of leadership as editors and student body officers. At St. Olaf and elsewhere, the number of women attending college rose significantly during the war period. From 564 women in 1942, the numbers went to 597 in 1944, 682 in 1945, and 727 in 1946.[9] In a stroke of good timing, St. Olaf College was able to add a new library to its campus just before war restrictions ruled out further building. Fifteen years earlier, similar good fortune had made possible the building of a music hall before the depression stopped all construction.

Construction of the much-needed library had begun in early 1941 at the very time that President Boe was corresponding with F. Melius and Olaf Christiansen about Olaf's coming to St. Olaf. In a letter to "Kong Kristian" in February of 1941, Boe mentioned that he had been moved into a different office from which he could see the digging for the new library. "It is going to be fun to watch this building grow out of the ground," Boe wrote, adding that "things are growing at St. Olaf."[10] President Boe lived to see the building completed but it was his successor, Clemens Granskou, who stood on the library steps when Dr. J. A. Aasgaard, president of the Norwegian Lutheran Church, dedicated the building on October 14, 1944.[11]

Rølvaag Memorial Library

Dr. Clemens M. Granskou, the new president of St. Olaf College, began work July 1, 1943. He came to his new position under doubly difficult circumstances. He succeeded the very able, colorful, and beloved Prexy L. W. Boe, and he began his duties in the middle of a world war. Many years later, President Granskou recalled the unusual phone call he received from F. Melius Christiansen in August of 1943. When Granskou picked up the receiver, he heard a distinctive voice on the other end of the line. "Hello," said the caller. "This is Christiansen. I just wanted to say, 'I love you.'"[12] Perhaps more than others, Christiansen sensed that the new president could use a friendly word of encouragement.

Dedication of Library,
October 14, 1944, J. A. Aasgaard,
Dr. Granskou, F. H. Knubel

259

It was not the first time F. Melius had extended a reassuring word to Clemens Granskou. Like Lars Boe, Granskou was an alumnus of the College, Class of 1917. As a freshman, he played last chair in the clarinet section of the St. Olaf Concert Band. One day, he recalled, he was walking down the avenue with the director, who asked how he was getting along. Granskou explained his humble position in the clarinet section, but said at least he was in the Band. F. Melius stopped, faced the young first year student, and said with a twinkle in his eye, "You know, the soloists in the band don't sound very good unless they are backed up by those who play ump-pa-pa, ump-pa-pa."[13]

Clemens Matthew Granskou President, St. Olaf College, 1943-63

Elected by the Board of Trustees in 1943, Dr. Granskou became the fifth president of St. Olaf College. He chose to be inaugurated on Homecoming weekend in 1944 when the College dedicated the Rolvaag Memorial Library. The St. Olaf Choir sang at the inauguration. For a school like St. Olaf, a liberal arts college of the church, having this key building in place meant a reaffirmation of the liberal arts at a time when there was concern that post-war education would be heavily technical and professional.[14]

As a staunch defender of the liberal arts curriculum, President Granskou wisely distinguished between the training needed for conducting a war and the education appropriate for the pursuits of peace. "Building a war machine and teaching men to think creatively and act intelligently in a free world are two different things," he wrote. "If the culture we cherish is to survive, we need to recover again the mind that is educated for reflective thinking. That is the job of Christian higher education."[15]

What actually happened was that the veterans proved eager to embrace the liberal arts as well as other educational options. Moreover, having had opportunity to ponder issues of life, death, and meaning while in the military, many of them found the church college to their liking. St. Olaf's effort to link cultural and intellectual life with Christian insight exerted an appeal on veterans and others. Soon the College found itself trying to cope with unprecedented numbers of students, among them men and women eager to become part of the well-known music tradition of the school.

The first sign of the return of the veterans was the appearance on campus of 41 former service personnel in the fall of 1945. Among them was

Andrew Lindstrom, heavy bomber pilot, who had sung solos in the St. Olaf Choir in 1942 and 1943.[16] Lindstrom rejoined the Choir, and again he was heard as tenor soloist in Herbert Howells' "A Spotless Rose." He also did solo work on "I wonder as I wander." A larger group of 259 registered for the second semester in February of 1946, bringing total enrollment for the 1945-46 school year to 1,114. At the opening of the 1946-47 school year, St. Olaf College suddenly had a nearly overwhelming enrollment of 1,660. It would rise to 1,703 by the fall of 1948.[17]

Andrew Lindstrom '46

The dramatic increase in the size of the student body cried out for a larger faculty, emergency housing measures, and more teaching facilities. A number of faculty members who had been in military service had now returned. There had been 61 full-time teachers in 1943; by 1948 there were 91. Male students were jammed into every available space in Ytterboe Hall, the only men's dormitory, including

Ytterboe Hall

basement and attic. The women were slightly better off, having old Mohn Hall and Agnes Mellby Hall, but a great amount of off-campus housing had to be found for both male and female students.

Until suitable, permanent facilities could be constructed, the College in 1946 acquired a set of "temporary" buildings from the Federal Works Administration. Prefabricated barracks for both married and single veterans were placed below Old Main Hill and called "Viking Court." Other frame structures were placed strategically about the campus to provide

Agnes Mellby Hall

Old Mohn Hall

261

supplementary administrative and classroom space. One of them was the Music Hall Annex, located west of the old gymnasium on the site now occupied by the Christiansen Hall of Music.[18] It supplemented the functions of the music hall built in 1926, providing six practice rooms, six studios, and one class room.

Music Annex, 1948

The Music Annex was occupied primarily by instrumental students and their teachers, Donald Berglund, flute instructor and director of both Band and Orchestra at the time, and Beatrix Lien, violin teacher and concertmistress of the St. Olaf Orchestra.[19]

Beatrix Lien   *Donald Berglund*

The Music Department

In the fall of 1941, Olaf Christiansen's first year at the College, the music faculty consisted of twelve teachers for a student body of 1,122. Such a force was none too large to teach the many courses needed by candidates for the Bachelor of Music degree and by those choosing a major in music, to accommodate the number of students taking private music lessons, and to handle the separate music organizations. In keeping with a long-standing belief that music at St. Olaf should be available to everyone, the 1941-42 catalog carried the notice, "All regular students of the College are eligible to try out for membership in the music organizations." Music groups listed were the St. Olaf Lutheran Choir, the St. Olaf Second Choir, the Viking Male Chorus, the St. Olaf Girls' Chorus, the St. Olaf Band, and the St. Olaf Orchestra. [20]

Given the teaching loads implied by these activities, one might assume that Olaf Christiansen would represent an addition to the staff, but Boe found it necessary to release a voice teacher in 1941, anticipating that Olaf would be giving private lessons. In addition to working with his father and the Choir, Olaf would take over "some of Overby's work as he has had too much," according to Boe.[21] The 1941-42 College catalog, the first to list Olaf as a faculty member, stated that he was responsible for "choir, theory, and voice." Specifically, he served as Associate Director of the St. Olaf Lutheran Choir, taught courses in simple counterpoint, composition, and choir conducting, and gave private voice lessons. [22]

O. Overby   G. Overby   Engstrom   Hjertaas   C. Woll

Abrahamson   E. Woll   Donhowe   Bergh   Lien

When Olaf joined the music department, his father was named in the catalog as "Director" with Oscar Overby as "Curriculum Adviser." These designations continued for some years. In 1946 Olaf's name was added to the leaders with the title "Chairman." [23] Olaf would have known many of his colleagues in addition to his father and Overby, who was also Director of the Second or Church Choir. Others in the department at the time were voice teachers Gertrude Boe Overby, Adolph Engstrom, Ella Hjertaas, and Carsten Woll, piano and organ teacher Carl Abrahamson, piano instructors Esther Woll and Charlotte Donhowe, Johan Arndt Bergh, Director of Band and Orchestra, and M. Beatrix Lien, who taught violin and theory.

Other music faculty members joined the department or returned to it later in the decade. Among them were Jennie Skurdalsvold, voice teacher, Lewis Whikehart, who led the Chapel Choir, Joseph Running, piano and organ, Louise Wright Drake and Ellen Herum Bjork, piano instructors, Helen Luvaas, director of a first year women's chorus, Donald Berglund, flute, Band and Orchestra, Paul Ensrud, organ teacher and director of the Chapel Choir, Sigurd Fredrickson, voice, Donald Hoiness, voice, Marian Walker, theory, and Pauline Seim, voice. Most of the music teachers in this group were hired by Olaf Christiansen. In this way also Olaf contributed to the strengthening of the music department, with other outstanding appointments still to come. One thinks, for example, of Alice Larsen and Kenneth Jennings in vocal and choral work, and Miles Johnson, director of the St. Olaf Band.

Paul G. Schmidt, manager of music organizations, must also be mentioned among Olaf's colleagues. He continued to sing as a member of the Choir until 1954, when he was 77 years old. In 1948, Frederick A. Schmidt, the son of P.G., joined the staff as his father's assistant and soon took over the responsibility of arranging tours and managing the musical organizations. The uniqueness of a second generation Christiansen-Schmidt team was duly noted by news reporters, as in the *St. Paul Pioneer Press* headline, "Chips Off Two Old Blocks at St. Olaf."[24]

In addition to the performing groups under faculty direction were those led by student directors. In 1941-42 Mary MacCornack directed The St. Olaf Girls' Choir, Paul G. Peterson led The Viking Male Chorus, and Johan Thorson directed The Norse Choir, which sang anthems in Norwegian for the church services in that language broadcast over the College radio station, WCAL. [25] MacCornack, Peterson, and Thorson were all members of the St. Olaf Choir. Leadership of these student performing groups changed from year to year.

The Passing of the Baton

At the College and beyond, unusual interest centered on the leadership of the St. Olaf Choir when Olaf Christiansen entered the picture. "This year we record an important milestone in the history of the St. Olaf Choir," stated the student yearbook for the 1941-42 school year, "the coming of Olaf Christiansen from Oberlin as assistant director to his father." The comment appeared next to a picture showing F. Melius and Olaf Christiansen looking at a piece of music together. The writer continued, "Our sentiments are best voiced by the words

Olaf and F. Melius Christiansen

of Herman Devries, dean of American music critics, who said, 'He is a worthy son of a famous father.' We welcome him and look forward to a continuation of the great musical tradition at St. Olaf."[26]

Inevitably, reviews of St. Olaf Choir concerts in the forties would speak of the father-to-son succession in the image of passing the baton. For example, when the Choir made its 1945 "Twilight" concert appearance with the Minneapolis Symphony Orchestra at the University of Minnesota, Frances Boardman wrote of the debut on the Northrop Auditorium stage of "Olaf C. Christiansen, heir to baton of his father, Dr. F. Melius Christiansen, who founded the famous choir and directed it until recently."[27]

One might pause a moment to consider "the baton" in the literal, practical sense. F. Melius Christiansen nearly always used a baton in his conducting. Moreover, he had some emphatic things to say about it in a 1930 article entitled "Conducting." He wrote:

> Some of our modern a cappella choir conductors have discarded the baton and use only their empty hands in conducting their choirs. When I see such performances I thank Providence for the traditional baton. The clawing of the air and the sprawling of the fingers certainly do not give an esthetic impression. To hold a baton in the right hand, the butt end hidden in the palm, the thumb on top and the fingers grasping the stick, is the better way.[28]

News photos of F. Melius conducting show him with baton in hand. Former Choir members treasure among their keepsakes a baton received from Christy or the one they used as a student in his choir conducting class. The batons were made on campus by John Berntsen, superintendent of grounds and buildings. Each baton had the letters "STO" stamped on the end of the handle.[29] More than a few times F. Melius would break batons. Once during rehearsal he gave a beat with such force that the baton snapped in two. He retained the knob in his right hand but the rest of the stick flew off and lodged in the hair of one of the altos, to his considerable amusement. At concerts, Gertrude Boe Overby would have the baton hidden up her sleeve and would slip it to Christy before the first number.[30]

F. Melius conducting

Dimitri Mitropoulos with PGS and FMC

As conductor of the St. Olaf Choir, Olaf Christiansen did not, as a rule, use a baton. Neither did his brother, Paul J. Christiansen, director of the Concordia Choir. In this respect and others, Paul took as his model Dimitri Mitropoulos, one-time director of the Minneapolis Symphony Orchestra. Asked about his father's use of a baton, Paul commented that it was the customary thing to do in F. Melius's time.[31]

The striking picture of Olaf Christiansen that graces the cover of earlier St. Olaf Choir record albums shows him in characteristic conducting pose,

arms upraised, expressive fingers poised, but no baton. After the St. Olaf Choir had given a Sunday evening concert in Ellsworth, Wisconsin, in April of 1946, the reviewer wrote: "Director Olaf C. Christiansen presented an impressive figure as he conducted the choir through innumerable intricate passages without baton."[32]

With or without baton, Olaf C. Christiansen worked alongside of his father for two years, taking over the leadership of the St. Olaf Choir by stages. By agreement between father

Olaf Christiansen conducting   and son, during the 1941-42 school year and concert season, Olaf conducted the first of the three groups and F. Melius conducted the second and third groups. On one occasion, F. Melius proposed that they trade sets, and Olaf agreed. During the conducting of the Finale from Healey Willan's "An Apostrophe to the Heavenly Hosts," the elder Christiansen lost his place, but the Choir's ability to adapt quickly saved the situation. The experiment was not repeated.[33]

The tour in 1942 took the Choir into the South, where they performed in such cities as Corpus Christi, Texas, and St. Louis. They also sang at the Great Lakes Naval Station and gave two "Standing Room Only" performances in Chicago's Orchestra Hall.[34]

At Great Lakes Naval Station, February, 1942

Critics observed closely as the two directors shared conducting duties. A writer for the *St. Louis Globe Democrat* gave the opinion that the younger Christiansen lacked the authority and subtlety of his father. "But his beat is virile, his reading presents firmly the polyphonic structure, and one of the most beautiful of the evening's offerings was from his baton as the choir sang Vittoria's 'O Magnum Mysterium.'"[35] A reviewer for the *Chicago Daily Tribune* also liked the Vittoria piece and with it the works by

267

Sweelinck and Bach that opened the program. That was the group directed by Olaf.[36]

The next year, 1942-43, Olaf conducted the Choir in the first two groups and F. Melius conducted only the last group. Plans made for a tour to the east in early 1943 had to be canceled and a shorter tour to a few cities in Wisconsin, Illinois, and Minnesota was taken instead.[37] The program of "religious music old and new" was well received in the Milwaukee Auditorium where the listeners displayed "huge enthusiasm for the gloriously youthful singing of the purple robed and solemn choristers." The reviewer, Richard S. Davis, commented on the division of directing duties.

> Two-thirds of the program was under the direction of Olaf C.
> Christiansen and the other third in the keeping of F. Melius
> Christiansen. Thus the gray haired son and the white haired
> father, equally erect and equally positive, demonstrated how firm
> is the Christiansen tradition at St. Olaf and how prized. [38]

That was the last tour F. Melius Christiansen made with the St. Olaf Choir. He retired officially in the spring of 1943 at the end of the school year. Nevertheless, the 1943-44 concert program was planned so that he might conduct the final group, as he had done the year before. But when rehearsals began in the fall of 1943, F. Melius decided that his health would not permit him to continue. As a result, audiences attending concerts on the Choir's midwestern tour in the spring of 1944 received a note with their programs explaining that because of his age the Choir's founder, Dr. F. Melius Christiansen, was "unable to be with the St. Olaf choir on its annual tour this year."[39] Thus Olaf did all the conducting on the tour and from that season on was the sole director of the St. Olaf Lutheran Choir.

A couple of anecdotes shed additional light on F. Melius's decision to step aside from further direct participation in the work of the St. Olaf Choir. He reached the age of seventy-two on April 1, 1943, but it had been understood, first by President Boe and also by President Granskou, that he should continue with the Choir as long as

Edith and F. Melius note another birthday

268

St. Olaf Choir, 1944, Director: Olaf C. Christiansen

he chose to do so. Dr. Granskou told of a conversation in the early fall of 1943 in which Dr. Christiansen spoke of stepping aside and the president tried to dissuade him.

> [Dr. Christiansen] came up to the office with the intent of turning over the reins to son Olaf. As we remonstrated with him, he responded: "Olaf is good, and I am good too!"

The remark was typical of F. Melius, brief, humorous, and to the point. Having told this story in his tribute at the memorial service for F. Melius on June 3, 1955, President Granskou added this observation: "Thus he went out of the picture as active director of the Choir as magnificently as he had entered the scenes of his labours."[40]

A second anecdote hints at the tension inherent in the co-directing of the St. Olaf Choir from 1941 to 1943. A Choir member, Violet Wekseth Risch '45, recalled that one day at rehearsal F. Melius announced that he was turning over the full responsibility to Olaf. In explaining the decision he said something to this effect: "When the retiring pastor remains in the same town, it is difficult for the new pastor to do his job."[41] Years later, when Mrs. Risch told Professor and Mrs. Oscar Overby what F. Melius had said, Overby was very moved by the account because in one of his many conversations with F. Melius he had once offered exactly the same observation, but had not known until that moment that it might have been a factor in Dr. Christiansen's decision to retire. The comparison seemed to be F. Melius's way of acknowledging that he and Olaf had their differences in how they trained the Choir.

Some Choir members who sang under both men thought the transition was a smooth one and counted it a privilege to sing under the two Christiansens. It was "truly an awesome experience," wrote Donald Flom '45.[42] Others recalled some problems. As one of them put it, "When we rehearsed with Christy, the vowels were dark. With Olaf, probably the following day, the vowels were to be bright. The choir kept making adjustments to each director, and as a result, did not make a lot of progress."[43] Another Choir member, who remembered F. Melius introducing Olaf to the group, stated that the Choir didn't understand what Olaf wanted. He came across as remote and objective in his approach in contrast to Christy's emotional feeling for the music.[44]

The transition, which seemed so orderly to the general public, had not always been easy for the singers nor for Olaf himself. One Choir member, close to the scene, wrote the following of Olaf: "He was determined to make his own way and that meant stepping on some toes. We who remained with him through those first years learned to have a deep respect for this man."[45]

Another student who sang under both Christiansens wrote of loyalties related both to the directors and the repertoire they preferred. Olaf's interest in sixteenth century works was resisted by some members who liked the Romantic repertoire of F. Melius. For the latter the Choir had developed the "covered tone" that suited the Baroque/Romantic music favored by F. Melius. "Olaf, on the other hand, in favoring selections from the Pre-Bach period, sought a more brilliant tone." [46] By tour time, however, the loyalty tensions had melted away.

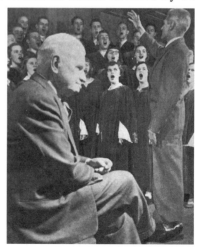

Singers remember the two directors conferring with one another in front of the Choir during rehearsal. A. B. "Bud" Engen '42 recalled that he and the other music majors in particular strained to listen in on these discussions in which differences in the interpretation of a piece would come to light. Finally, Christy would be heard to say, "Vell, I guess there are two good vays to do it."[47]

Choir and directors

270

Quite apart from the differences between the two directors but still a factor affecting the Choir was the war, which meant loss of male voices and limited travel. The *Viking* yearbook recognized the problem and cheered the Choir on, reporting in 1943: "Before the end of the school year a majority of the men of the choir were called to active duty in the armed forces. However, in spite of this great handicap, the aims and purposes of the St. Olaf Choir will be perpetuated."[48] The Twilight Concert with the Minneapolis Symphony Orchestra in March of 1943 was a moving experience for Choir members because several of the basses and tenors sang with them for the last time, dressed in their military uniforms.[49]

The somber realities of the war posed problems of conscience for Olaf, a man of pronounced pacifist leanings. He was rightly concerned for the young men who had to leave St. Olaf when drafted into the armed forces. On the other hand, he offered little encouragement to the ones who chose to enlist. He was not against serving the country but drew the line at carrying a gun and killing. Reverence for life meant that he and members of his family never cared for hunting.[50]

Yet despite the mental and physical pains associated with the war and its disruptions, directors and singers concentrated on the tasks at hand, which were to rehearse diligently and sing the great music of faith wherever they could. Thanks to the resourcefulness of Manager P. G. Schmidt, the Choir was able to make a twelve-day trip in April of 1944 that included concerts at the Great Lakes Naval Station and Orchestra Hall in Chicago, where the large crowd left an "overflow of late comers in the lobby."[51] Reflecting on the Choir's year, the student yearbook offered this summary:

The St. Olaf Choir brought its message to hundreds of people again this year, despite wartime shortages of manpower and transportation. Many hours of practice brought this year's choir up to par, although the tenor and bass sections were at the mercy of a dozen draft boards. How many tenors there would be 'by next week' was often a matter of speculation, but persistent work and real choir spirit won out. And to the director, Prof. Olaf C. Christiansen, is due a large share of the credit. In his first year as sole director, Professor Christiansen has gained the confidence and respect of every member, inspiring each one to enthusiastic effort.[52]

Olaf Christiansen, 1944

Sole Director

In assuming full responsibility for the St. Olaf Choir, Olaf Christiansen made good on the prediction that the aims and purposes of the St. Olaf Choir would be perpetuated despite the loss of men to active duty in the armed forces. The reviewers of the Choir's March 1945 Twilight Concert at Northrop Auditorium had good words for the Choir's adjustment to wartime conditions, praise for Olaf, "on whose shoulders the mantle of his distinguished father, the founder of the choir, has fallen," and a measure of nostalgia for how F. Melius would have interpreted the numbers. Frances Boardman commended the Choir for making the best of wartime shortage in the tenor and baritone sections and, under Olaf Christiansen, for maintaining "the traditional standards of musicianship that carry the singers triumphantly through the truly formidable contrapuntal hazards of such undertakings as the Bach motet for double chorus, 'Sing Ye to the Lord,' and the beautiful but also formidable Brahms motet, 'O Savior, Throw the Heavens Wide.'"[53]

There was much to be admired in the concert, wrote Grace Davies of the *Minneapolis Tribune*: "the same infinite pains in preparation, the same precision, sensitive feeling for nuance—more than color—and refinement." But it was the last point that bothered Davies; it seemed like "over-refinement." She felt that "F. Melius Christiansen's secret for giving each composition an individual profile was lacking." The young conductor could have "overemphasized a few points" and "captured more of the sentiment of the text and diction." Nevertheless, she thought that Olaf would meet the challenge.

> It would be a difficult task for any man to follow in the steps of the great founder of the choir who has closed an important chapter in the history of American music. It is now up to Olaf to disprove the statement that "there is only one F. Melius" and we believe he may yet do it.[54]

When the Choir gave its concert the next month in the Vocational School Auditorium in La Crosse, Wisconsin, the reviewer began with a resounding endorsement of the new director. "The many admirers of Dr. F. Melius Christiansen need have no fear for the future of the St. Olaf college choir as long as it remains in the capable hands of his talented son, Olaf Christiansen."[55]

Those capable hands assumed firm charge of the Choir, and in a relatively short time any reservations concerning Olaf's succession simply evaporated. F. Melius was still the grand old man, revered and honored in his retirement and still mentioned with respect by reviewers. But he readily added his voice to those expressing full confidence in Olaf. In a brief speech after a spring festival concert on the St. Olaf campus in May of 1945, F. Melius said in his direct and winsome way, "I'm proud of him. I think the Choir is doing very fine."

Now it was Olaf's duty and privilege to set the tempo for the future. He was responsible, said the 1946 yearbook, "for maintaining [the Choir's] reputation of excellence." That year the Choir made a sixteen-day tour into Wisconsin, Michigan, Iowa, Illinois, and Indiana. Favorites among both concert audiences and Choir members were Bach's *Sing Ye to the Lord* and the *Fiftieth Psalm*, arranged by F. Melius Christiansen.[56] Wartime conditions produced a "brownout" in Kintner Gym in Decatur, Illinois, in May of 1946. A newspaper ad announced that the gym would have battery-operated, generator-operated lights, and urged patrons to "BRING YOUR OWN FLASHLIGHTS." The concert drew 1,400 listeners. A reviewer admired "the grace in direction and perfect control of the silver-haired, distinguished director over the 60 voices" and commented favorably on "the excellent bass section" which was impressive in Palestrina's "Tu es Petrus."

The availability of mature male voices, many of them veterans two or three years older than their non-veteran classmates, was a strong feature of the Choirs led by Olaf in the late forties. Building on a rock-solid bass section was a fundamental trademark of the choirs of both Olaf and his father. If there was resonance, good intonation, unified vowels, and blend in the low voices, it would establish a framework within which the aligning and balancing of the upper voices would be enhanced.[57]

Reviewers who appreciated how a choral ensemble could be so superbly trained and balanced often compared the Choir with such top instrumental groups as the Chicago Symphony and the Eastman Wind Ensemble. Non-trained listeners were also pleased by the fine quality of the bass and tenor voices. But a reviewer in Chicago suspected that the presence of returned G.I.'s among the tenors and basses caused a "dynamic disbalance between male and female voices" and made the younger ladies sound thin by comparison.[58]

For the most part, however, listeners and reviewers considered the sturdy male voices a boon to the Choir. In 1946 a reviewer in Milwaukee complimented the Choir for the "richness in the bass and tenor sections." "The men's voices, the basses particularly, are excellent," was the opinion expressed by a Buffalo reviewer. In 1948 Alice Eversman in the *Washington Evening Star* wrote of the "remarkable sonority present in the lower men's voices."[59]

Olaf himself savored the added power in the men's sections, even though he could not always count on docile behavior from the veterans. Said a soprano who sang in the late forties, "It's never sounded quite the same because of these older men. So it was really quite exciting for Olaf to have these men who could rumble along and of course they were not as much in awe of everything at that time." Unknown to audiences but heard by the women singers in front of them were the outrageous words the men sometimes substituted for the standard texts. For example, instead of the usual words for a stanza of Martin Luther's Christmas anthem, "From heaven above to earth I come," the solemn-faced women in the first two rows would hear voices behind them intoning, "Oh, were the world ten times as wide, then I could park my car outside." In another variation, as the women were singing, "O beautiful Yuletide, so festive and fair," the incorrigible males were crooning, "O, boozeyful Yuletide, so festered and sore."[60]

The women could be relied on to sing the right words. Moreover, their voices won the praise of critics, as when the sopranos were called "ethereal" and the altos commended for "richness of tone." Yet some critics were not entirely pleased with the quality of sound from Olaf's singers. One detected rigidity and "a feeling of stiffness." One thought the tonal color was limited "to a somewhat unnatural whiteness."[61] Alice Eversman of Washington, D.C., singled out the sopranos. They are "firm, true and clear," she wrote, but "that cool, rather hollow tone" made for a monotonous effect. Eversman remembered a warmer and more vital tone from the choirs led by F. Melius Christiansen compared to "the finely thought out and restrained singing" she heard at the concert in Constitution Hall in 1948. [62]

Although Olaf was unequivocally in charge of the St. Olaf Choir, it was part of the transition that when critics had their say about his work, they would compare it to that of his esteemed father. The "cool" tone they associated with Olaf's Choir might better be termed "controlled." The warmer, more emotional feel for the music linked with F. Melius owes much to the Romantic literature he favored. Such observations remind one of comments made by Choir members of the early forties who sang under both directors.

Yet the audiences and critics filling the concert halls were increasingly under the spell of the younger Christiansen, a lithe, athletic figure, taller than his father and fully as handsome, making his dramatic entrance from the wings with long, quick, authoritative strides. After the Choir had sung in New Haven a reviewer stated: "There can be no doubt of the genius and energy of Olaf C. Christiansen, director, who shaped the performance of this group through many months of sustained, coordinated effort." In Cleveland a reporter remarked on how the Choir put passion into its work and that it adored its conductor.[63]

When the Choir sang in Toledo in January of 1947, Frederick Kountz wrote his impression of Director Christiansen and "an afternoon of

Olaf directing, ca. 1948

uncommonly lovely singing":

> Mr. Christiansen is a lean, gray, powerful looking man. He
> directs powerfully. And the masses of tone which his singers
> produced were on occasion immense beyond comprehension.
> But they were more than simply tonal masses. For they were
> incisively lined. . . . The songs were finely delineated but always
> toward a unity, toward a common, a complete realization of their
> spirit and their text.

Olaf's manner of conducting appealed to Kountz. "Mr. Christiansen's
directing was straightforward. There was no hokum about it, no striving for
effects at the expense of the songs. He began and ended precisely and there
were no ragged edges in phrasing."[64]

About a year later, when the Choir performed in Battle Creek,
Michigan, on a second trip east, another reviewer studied Olaf's conducting
style, characterizing it as "fluent yet suppressed." The comments continued:
"He did not follow some of the accepted rules for conductorship. For
example, the choral attacks came on the upsweep of his hands, rather than
on the downsweep. He used no baton and he resorted to no gymnastics, but
he had the singers at his finger tips in every number."[65]

275

Commentary on the appearance and style of such a handsome, commanding, yet sensitive conductor was to be expected. What Olaf himself always wanted was that everything should be concentrated on bringing the music and the texts to the listeners. Thus the review from the Choir's 1947 appearance at the Opera House in Chicago would have been to his liking. The reviewer praised the Choir for bringing sincerity and artistry together, suggesting that the zeal of the singers might be traced to their youth. "Whatever its origin," wrote the critic, "earnestness is a part of these young men and women, and because they believe what they sing, they transmit that belief to their hearers—a particularly admirable quality in such music."[66]

Concert reviewers in the late forties began to pay close attention to the solo voice of Winnifred Greene, soprano from Bainville, Montana, who sang with the Choir in 1946-47, 1947-48, and again, as Winnifred Alberg and voice teacher, in 1949-50. She came to be associated in a special way with F. Melius Christiansen's "The Christmas Symbol" with its simple, tender text:

> Only a manger, cold and bare, Only a maiden mild, Only some
> shepherds kneeling there, Watching a little child.
> And yet that maiden's arms enfold, The King of heaven above;
> And in the Christ-Child we behold
> The Lord of life and love.

Winnifred did solo work on several other numbers, including "The Song of Mary" and "Beautiful Savior." After the concert in Milwaukee in January of 1950, Richard S. Davis wrote:

No review of the concert could be adequate without mention of the singing of the soprano, Winnifred Alberg. The warmth, clarity and unaffected grace of this voice must gladden everyone who hears it. The way Miss Alberg sings is the right way to sing and it is indeed a pleasure to discover such talent — and intelligence.[67]

Winnifred Greene Alberg
Soprano soloist 1946-48, 49-50

Pauline Seim, Winnifred's friend and contemporary, also received extremely favorable reviews. A New Haven reviewer wrote, "Miss Pauline Seim, contralto soloist in 'My Heart is Longing,' performed outstandingly." After the Choir sang in Reading, Pennsylvania, a review in the *Reading Times* had these comments: "Pauline Seim . . . sings with strength and clarity that many a more publicized singer may well envy. Miss Seim has an exceedingly fine voice, rich in texture and sure of tone. She deserves a wider hearing than even this famous choir can possibly give her.'

The number referred to, "My Heart is Longing," was composed by Sune Carlson and translated from the Swedish by St. Olaf voice teacher Ella Hjertaas. As sung with powerful but controlled feeling by Pauline, the composition created a hush of devotional quiet over the audience. The song begins with these words:

Pauline Seim, 1948
Mezzo Soprano soloist,
1946-48

My heart is longing day and night,
Tho' not for treasures here below,
All earthly joy soon fades from sight;
'Tis higher realms my soul would know.[68]

Transition Completed

It does not seem necessary to determine a precise time when "the transition years" ended for St. Olaf College or the St. Olaf Choir. The editors of The 1946 *Viking* yearbook could well characterize that year as "A Year of Transition." World War II ended in August of 1945 but the enrollment increases brought about by the return of veterans to civilian life did not occur until 1946 and 1947, as indicated earlier in this chapter. A startling increase of 546 took place in one year, from the 1945-46 school year to 1946-47, yielding an enrollment in the fall of 1946 of 1,660.

As far as the Choir was concerned, those who became members in 1945 and after would have regarded the transition as already in the past. It is natural to associate World War II veterans with the transition, but only a handful of them in the period from 1946 to 1950 would have had any singing experience under F. Melius Christiansen. For the most part, the men whose mature voices elicited favorable comment in the post-war years were trained and molded by Olaf Christiansen. The central idea of the transition was that the Choir had received a new leader.

The fact that the St. Olaf Lutheran Choir was under the full direction of Olaf C. Christiansen was brought home to the general public through the tours. A larger circle was made aware of the new leadership during the eventful 1948 tour of the Choir, the first trip to the east coast since the end of the war. It began in Northfield January 22 and ended with the return to the campus on February 18, 1948. Among the cities in which concerts were

277

St. Olaf Choir in New York, 1948

given were Chicago, Detroit, Cleveland, Boston, Philadelphia, New York, Washington, and Pittsburgh.

Highlights were the performances in New York's Carnegie Hall and in Constitution Hall, Washington, D.C. Of the Carnegie Hall concert heard on February 7, 1948, the *New York Times* said: "From the opening notes it was clear that the group was superbly trained and musicianly. Not only in contrapuntal passages but even in blended harmonies, one enjoyed the rare pleasure of hearing all the notes." John Hall Jr. of the *Brooklyn Daily Eagle* gave credit to Northfield, Minnesota, for producing a choir "which can assemble on the stage of Carnegie Hall, in New York city, and show our metropolis how things are done out their way. This choir looks better, sounds better, and is better than any group we know." *The New York Herald Tribune* regarded as outstanding the Choir's combination of "the spirit of the inspired amateur who sings because he has to sing and the developed skill of the professional." Its reviewer characterized Olaf Christiansen as "a musician of deep musical culture."

Critics who heard the Washington concert were equally impressed. Glenn Dillard Gunn of the *Washington Times-Herald* declared that the Choir's appearance meant "that the season's greatest choral art has been presented." Paul Hume, writing for the *Washington Post*, stated that the concert "demonstrated once more the technique of impeccable control for which this group has been famous for more than a generation." The singers had no difficulty, he observed, in turning from the scores of Bach and Carissimi to the contemporary works of Milhaud, Willan and Georg Schumann. "Diction, intonation, and the mechanical side of singing is to them an open book."[69] Comparable words of praise could be cited from reviews in Milwaukee, Cleveland, Boston, New Haven, Philadelphia, Pittsburgh, and other cities.

Interspersed with copies of glowing reviews in Choir members' scrapbooks are items reminding them of tour incidents that were memorable but not necessarily glorious. "60 in Choir Unhurt as Stand Collapses at City Concert" was a headline in the *Wilmington Morning News* on February 4, 1948.

The article explained that the risers gave way just as the director was nearing the center of the stage and the applause was beginning to die down. "The only warning given the singers was a loud crackling of wood." In good Nordic fashion, they stayed calm. "Silently and orderly the singers moved to the side of the collapsed stand and, apparently unshaken, proceeded with the concert." But the newspaper account failed to mention that the platform supporting the risers had been weakened the week before when the armory had been used by a visiting circus, including two elephants.[70]

An incident not recorded by reviewers but vividly remembered by Choir members from the 1948 tour was a remarkable lapse that occurred in the Boston concert. The final number in the second section of the four-part concert was Healey Willan's "Apostrophe to the Heavenly Hosts," arranged for double choir. The choirs sang alternately and as a single unit, with similar entrances, some soft and others *forte*. The singers, their eyes and full attention fixed on Olaf's directing, were awaiting the next entrance, a soft one. But they could tell from Olaf's arm movements that he was cueing them for a big, double *forte* entrance. Instantly, the whole Choir read his mind. They realized that he had forgotten the section beginning with the subdued entrance. Responding to his preparatory gesture, they skipped over that section and came in on "Hail, Michael, Prince of Heav'n" with exactly the force he called for. Recalling the moment, a Choir member said, "It was a miracle." It was an uncanny display of Choir responsiveness, possible only through singular discipline.[71]

The number finished, the Choir filed off stage for a ten-minute intermission. Everyone was curious about what had happened. They waited for an explanation, but none was given. Olaf said nothing about it. The incident went unexplained the rest of the tour and the rest of the season.

Sylvia Christiansen, Olaf's daughter, was a member of the Choir that year. Years later, in an exchange with her father at their home in Northfield, she asked him if he remembered the unique incident in Boston. No, he didn't. So she told him what had happened. As she finished, Olaf said, "My hands and feet are sweating!"[72]

Sylvia and Olaf Christiansen, 1949

More than one story is told of the Choir continuing a number when the lights in the concert hall went out. Such was the case one year in the late forties when the St. Olaf Choir was giving a concert in Skinner Chapel on the campus of Carleton College. According to one version, Choir members were able to see a bit of white on the cuff of Olaf's shirt, and that enabled them to keep the rhythm. In another version, when the power went out "Olaf just kept snapping his fingers and we kept right on going and the applause was tremendous when we got through."[73] Olaf himself also related the incident, supplying the added detail that he used his white handkerchief to signal the final release. One of the front row altos later told him that while she couldn't see very well, she literally felt the breeze from his handkerchief for the ending cue.[74]

The reference to the applause is of interest in this case because during the earlier part of the concert, before the lights went out, the Carleton audience seemed unimpressed by the singers from the other side of town. The Choir's feat of singing in the dark apparently started a warming trend among the chilly hearts on the east side of the mighty Cannon River, because twenty years later Carleton College bestowed the honorary degree, Doctor of Music, on Olaf Christiansen.

Olaf Christiansen family, ca. 1950
Sylvia, Fredrik, Sigrid, Ellen, Julie, Olaf

280

Notes for Chapter 9 TRANSITION YEARS

1. *Kansas City Times*, January 27, 1942.

2. *Viking* 1945, 94.

3. Joseph M. Shaw, *History of St. Olaf College 1874-1974* (Northfield, Minnesota: The St. Olaf College Press, 1974), 344, 367.

4. Letter from Olaf C. Christiansen to L. W. Boe, July 28, 1941.

5. Shaw, 357; *Viking* 1943, 87.

6. Eugene E. Simpson, *A History of St. Olaf Choir* (Minneapolis: Augsburg Publishing House, 1921), 153.

7. Paul G. Schmidt, *My Years at St. Olaf* (Northfield, Minnesota: St. Olaf College, [1967]), 66.

8. *Viking* 1944, 137-38.

9. Shaw, 392.

10. Letter from L. W. Boe to F. Melius Christiansen, February 3, 1941.

11. Joseph M. Shaw, *Dear Old Hill*: The Story of Manitou Heights, the Campus of St. Olaf College (Northfield, Minnesota: St. Olaf College, 1992), 147-48.

12. Clemens M. Granskou, "F. Melius Christiansen," Tribute at Memorial Service for Dr. F. Melius Christiansen, Boe Memorial Chapel, June 3, 1955.

13. *Ibid.*

14. William C. Benson, *High on Manitou*: A History of St. Olaf College, 1874-1949 (Northfield, Minnesota: The St. Olaf College Press, 1949), 316-17.

15. *Ibid.*, 315, 317.

16. Shaw, *History of St. Olaf College* 1874-1974, 391.

17. *Ibid.*; Benson, 318.

18. Shaw, *Dear Old Hill*, 151.

19. Shaw, *History of St. Olaf College 1874-1974*, 400.

20. *St. Olaf College Bulletin* XXXVIII (April 1942), Catalog Number 1941-1942, 100.

21. Letter from L. W. Boe to Olaf C. Christiansen, March 21, 1941.

22. *St. Olaf College Bulletin* XXXVIII (April 1942), Catalog Number 1941-1942, 102-105.

23. *St. Olaf College Bulletin* XLII (April 1946), Catalog Number 1945-1946, 81.

24. *St. Paul Pioneer Press*, January 23, 1949; Shaw, *History of St. Olaf College 1874-1974*, 410.

25. *Viking* 1942, 125, 128-29.

26. *Ibid.*, 123.

27. Frances Boardman in *St. Paul Pioneer Press*, March 25, 1945.

28. F. Melius Christiansen, "Conducting," *Lutheran Church Herald*, August 5, 1930, 1085.

29. Letter from Conrad Thompson '39 to Joseph M. Shaw, October 13, 1993; interview: JMS with James Coates '41, February 29, 1996.

30. Interview: JMS with A. B. "Bud" Engen '42, July 19, 1995.

31. Interview: JMS with Paul J. Christiansen '34, November 16, 1994.

32. S. E. Doolittle in *Pierce Co. Herald*, Ellsworth, Wisconsin, April 18, 1946.

33. Olaf C. Christiansen in conversation with Lyndon Crist. Letter from Lyndon Crist to JMS, June 12, 1996.

34. *Viking* 1942, 122.

35. *St. Louis Globe Democrat*, February 13, 1942.

36. *Chicago Daily Tribune*, February 17, 1942.

37. *Viking* 1943, 87.

38. Richard S. Davis in *Milwaukee Journal*, January 13, 1943.

39. *Appleton Post-Crescent*, April 14, 1944; *The Manitowoc Herald-Times*, April 15, 1944.

40. Clemens M. Granskou, Tribute to F. Melius Christiansen, 1955.

41. Letter from Violet Wekseth Risch '45 to Bob Johnson, January 20, 1994.

42. Letter from Donald G. Flom '45 to BJ, January 5, 1994.

43. Violet Wekseth Risch letter.

44. Interview: JMS with June Anderson Swanson '42, October 17, 1994.

45. Violet Wekseth Risch letter.

46. Letter from Paul G. Peterson '42 to JMS, March 15, 1994.

47. Letter from A. B. "Bud" Engen to JMS, June 1, 1995.

48. Viking 1943, 87.

49. Letter from Phyllis Hardy Blodgett '43 to BJ, January 27, 1994; letter from Harold Heiberg '43 to BJ, January 23, 1994; cf. *Minneapolis Morning Tribune*, March 29, 1943.

50. Cf. Violet Wekseth Risch letter; Paul G. Peterson letter; letter from Sylvia Christiansen Buselmeier to JMS, July 16, 1996.

51. *Chicago Daily Tribune*, April 18, 1944.

52. *Viking* 1944, 102.

53. Frances Boardman in *St. Paul Pioneer Press*, March 25, 1945.

54. Grace Davies in *Minneapolis Tribune*, March 25, 1945.

55. *La Crosse Tribune*, April 5, 1945.

56. *Viking* 1946, 100.

57. Letter from Lyndon Crist to JMS, August 12, 1996.

58. *The Chicago Sun*, February 7, 1947.

59. RSD in Milwaukee paper, April 28, 1946; TCB in Buffalo paper, January 23, 1947; Alice Eversman in *Washington Evening Star*, February 10, 1948.

60. Interview: JMS with Winnifred Greene Alberg, March 24, 1995.

61. RSD, Milwaukee paper, April 28, 1946; Albert Goldberg in *Chicago Daily Tribune*, April 18, 1944.

62. Alice Eversman in *Washington Evening Star*, February 10, 1948.

63. *New Haven Journal-Courier*, February 2, 1948; *Cleveland Plain Dealer*, January 27, 1948.

64. Frederick Kountz in *Toledo Times*, January 20, 1947.

65. Battle Creek, Michigan paper, ca. January 24, 1948.

66. *Chicago Journal of Commerce*, February 7, 1947.

67. Richard S. Davis in *Milwaukee Journal*, January 23, 1948.

68. St. Olaf Lutheran Choir, Annual Tour Program 1947-1948.

69. Paul Hume in *Washington Post*, February 10, 1948.

70. Interviews: JMS with Ronald '49 and Betty Lou Oleson Nelson '49 and Lois Jacobson Nelson '49, May 5, 1995; with Winnifred Greene Alberg '48 and Marilyn Swanson Haugen '48, March 24, 1995; letter from Ronald and Betty Lou Nelson to BJ, January 28, 1994.

71. Alberg and Haugen interview; Ronald and Betty Lou Nelson letter.

72. JMS conversation with Sylvia Christiansen Buselmeier '50, June 19, 1996.

73. Marilyn Haugen interview, March 24, 1995; Lois Nelson interview, May 5, 1995.

74. Olaf C. Christiansen, conversation with Lyndon Crist; letter from Lyndon Crist to JMS, July 19, 1996.

CHAPTER 10

ON TOUR WITH OLAF AND FRED

The St. Olaf Choir first received national and international acclaim because of its tours. When Olaf C. Christiansen became sole director of the Choir in 1943, he was well posted on the Choir's previous history of touring. As a student at St. Olaf in the early twenties he had been a member of the Choir when the triumphant tour to the east coast of 1920 was still a fresh memory. Singing in the baritone section under his father for four years, Olaf was part of the 1923 midwestern tour when he was called upon to conduct at the Green Bay concert. During Olaf's senior

Olaf C. Christiansen

year, the Choir made its first tour to the Pacific coast, leaving Northfield in December of 1924 and returning in late January of 1925. The largest audience was in Denver, where 8,000 were "held spellbound" by the St. Olaf Choir.[1]

St. Olaf Choir of 1922-23, Olaf Christiansen in back row

Although limited by war-time conditions, Choir tours continued the first years after Olaf joined the St. Olaf faculty in 1941. A trip southward to Texas and New Orleans was possible in 1942, but for the next three years travel was limited to swings through the nearby midwestern states. Even without traveling far from Northfield, the Choir still gained national attention. Its singing at a national church convention in Minneapolis in 1944 inspired this comment from the *Christian Century*: "When the St. Olaf Choir had finished its last lovely note, it would have taken only a move of the hand to brush the veil of temporality aside and admit that huge scarcely breathing audience into the presence of the choir eternal."[2]

Olaf and Fred

The expert managing services of P. G. Schmidt continued without interruption when Olaf Christiansen joined his father in leading the St. Olaf Choir. One recalls that P. G., attired in his Choir robe, was shown standing between Olaf and F. Melius in the Choir's formal picture in the 1942 yearbook.[3] Choir member Marion Voxland '49 wrote that Olaf and P. G. Schmidt "were an exceptional team on tour. I recall how impressed I was with their 'fatherly' care for us during travel and how calm they always were in all situations."[4]

P. G. and Olaf

P. G.'s singing days were not over, but a change in managing duties would take place before the decade of the 1940s had ended. At the beginning of the 1948-49 school year, Frederick A. Schmidt, son of P. G., became a member of the St. Olaf staff as assistant to his father in managing the St. Olaf Choir and the other musical organizations at the College. Within a short time, as planned, Fred assumed full responsibility as his father's successor. Olaf Christiansen and Fred Schmidt constituted the

Coffee at the Christiansens, 1949
Olaf Christiansen, P. G. Schmidt, F. Melius Christiansen, Frederick Schmidt

second father-son combination that was responsible, as Willmar Thorkelson wrote in *The Minneapolis Star*, "for putting the St. Olaf Choir on the music map."[5] A photo taken in 1949 shows the two Christiansens and two Schmidts having coffee together at the home of F. Melius Christiansen.

Fred Schmidt had both personal and professional background working to his advantage as manager of the St. Olaf Choir, director of public functions, coordinator of the Artist and Lecture Series, and manager of the other musical organizations at the College. As a student at St. Olaf College, Class of 1931, he sang in the Choir under F. Melius Christiansen for four years. His bass voice was such a known quantity that when he was a high school senior, F. Melius asked P. G. Schmidt to bring Fred up to the College to sing with the St. Olaf Choir at rehearsals. By the time Fred became a

student at St. Olaf, his membership in the Choir was virtually taken for granted. He never had an individual try-out with F. Melius, but he remembers going with several other basses to sing for him.[6]

As a student, Fred was a member of the St. Olaf Choir on its 1930 tour to Norway and Germany. His name appears in diaries, scrapbooks, and newspaper articles in connection with outdoor sports and swimming. Whenever the Choir had a chance to go swimming, Fred would be among those participating. A snapshot shows him in swim

Frederick A. Schmidt '31

suit aboard the Norwegian coastal boat, "Zeta." Another catches him in mid-air as he dives from the boat. During the Choir's Southern tour in early 1930 before the Norway trip, Fred was identified in a Jacksonville newspaper as the backstroke champion of Minnesota for the last two years; he was also the state's breast stroke champion.[7]

During the Choir's 1931 Southern tour, a reporter for a paper in Wichita, Kansas, wrote of Fred's swimming prowess as evidence that the students from St. Olaf were "typical college boys and girls" and not "staid" because they sang religous music. The account described Fred as "a tall, strapping fellow who is breast-stroke

Fred in high dive
Norway 1930

swimming champion of the state of Minnesota."[8] Fred's golfing skill also received mention. A New Orleans paper stated that he "made a 76 in 18 holes of golf just the other day on a strange Texas course."

As the son of P. G., Fred was expected to be a good singer, to which his four years in the St. Olaf Choir bears convincing witness. Like his father, Fred was modest about his singing ability, but others would attest that "his voice was just like his dad's." But unlike his dad, Fred had had special training in music. He took graduate study in music at the University of Wisconsin in Madison and at the University of Iowa, where he received the master's degree. He was chair of the music department at the University of Wisconsin in Whitewater. Later he was appointed director of the music system in the Austin, Minnesota, public schools and was enjoying a successful career in that position when the St. Olaf offer came.

In some ways it was a difficult decision for Fred to leave teaching for an administrative position, but his love for the College and the Choir was such that he accepted President Clemens M. Granskou's invitation to take over his father's work at St. Olaf College.[9] He received the unusual honor of being given his father's faculty rank of full professor, and the same salary his father had been receiving. But in accepting the offer, Fred took a salary reduction of several hundred dollars, just as Olaf Christiansen had done when he came to St. Olaf College in 1941.

Fred Schmidt was a few years younger than Olaf Christiansen, but they had known one another since childhood, both growing up in Northfield as the sons of the two men who had made the St. Olaf Choir famous. Fred

288

Manager and Director, 1951

remembered Olaf's athletic as well as musical ability, characterizing him as a "splendid gymnast, ardent skier, and devoted golfer." One night the Choir was to give its concert in a high school auditorium where the gym with its equipment was right behind the stage. After watching some of the men chin themselves on the horizontal bar, Olaf asked them, "How many can do this?" Then, wearing his formal concert dress suit, Olaf jumped up, caught the bar with one hand, and began chinning himself *with one hand.*[10] As a rule, however, Olaf did not put his athletic ability on display.

"Our associations over the years were very enjoyable," wrote Fred of the years he worked with Olaf. He described some of their common leisure activities while on Choir tours:

> Riding on trains we spent many a happy hour over the cribbage board. . . . The early choir tours were from three to four weeks long, and we always planned one free day in the middle of the tour to give the director and the students a rest. I had occasion on the tours to the West, South and Southeast to plan this free day where the two of us could spend the day on a golf course. We've played some fine courses along the way, including Pebble Beach in California.[11]

Fred and Olaf worked together from 1948 until Olaf retired in 1968. Fred's initiatives secured such new concert sites for the Choir as Philharmonic Hall at Lincoln Center in New York and the Dorothy Chandler Pavilion of the Music Center in Los Angeles.[12] After Kenneth Jennings became the director of the St. Olaf Choir, Fred continued as manager until 1972, having arranged for the Choir to open the Strasbourg Festival that year with the presentation of the *Mass in B Minor* by Johann Sebastian Bach.

By Train and Bus—Domestic Tours

In the St. Olaf Choir's earliest years, there were instances of travel by horse-drawn vehicles of various kinds and early gasoline buggies, at least for local jaunts. Regarding local transport, Choir members who regularly sang at St. John's Lutheran Church in Northfield would point out that they logged many miles on foot as they walked from the campus to the Church and back Sunday after Sunday in all seasons. Such was still the practice during the first dozen years or so of Olaf Christiansen's tenure as director.

But the major means of transportation used by the St. Olaf Choir from its beginnings until well into Olaf's time was the train. Train travel was ideal for the long distances of a western tour, for example, and the students from the era of train travel regarded it as the preferable way to go. They recalled with pleasure the nice trains and the camaraderie of relaxing in their own private car. There was ample opportunity for reading, snoozing, knitting, chatting, card playing, and clowning. When mealtime came, they enjoyed the ease and luxury of getting their meal allowance from P. G. or

Choir Travels via Great Northern
Whitefish, Montana, 1957

290

In the dining car,
1949

Relaxing on
the train

Nice hats

Fred, then proceeding into the pleasant dining room with white tablecloths and fresh flowers on the tables and uniformed waiters to take their orders.

Train travel had its drawbacks, however. Pullman cars were sometimes cold and the berths less than ideal for restful sleep, especially when some doubling up was required. Trains lacked the convenience buses provided for moving the Choir members about once the next concert city had been reached. Fred Schmidt described some of the limitations:

> In each city we would arrange for buses or taxis to take the group from the depot to the hotel, then from the hotel to the concert hall and return and back to the depot the next morning. I remember that whenever we had our private cars attached to the train, we were the farthest removed from the depot because our cars were at the rear of the train.[13]

Among Choir members Fred became known for his trademark practice of rallying the forces by calling out "Um-Ya-Ya" whenever the Choir needed to be assembled or an announcement had to be made. On one trip, when the Choir was changing trains in Grand Central Station in New York, Fred made use of the station's loudspeaker. Suddenly throughout Grand Central there rang out Fred's "Um-Ya-Ya" that brought sixty-five students from all parts of the station to pick up their suitcases and board the train.[14]

With buses, the Choir had almost complete mobility, for the long distances and for transfers between hotel and concert hall. The bus drivers came in for much friendly give and take with Choir members, but also earned a great deal of admiration as they jockeyed the buses through heavy city traffic and succeeded in finding their way along dark, unknown streets to churches and other concert sites. The Choir would travel in two buses, the director in one and the manager in the other. At one time the bus on which Olaf Christiansen rode was called "the morgue" because Olaf asked

Boarding the buses

"I always take my pillow."

the students not to sing in order to save their voices. One learns also of "smoking" and "non-smoking" buses, the latter sometimes called the "presem" bus on the shaky assumption that students planning to attend theological seminary were non-smokers.

Buses allowed less moving about during the ride. Directors and managers used various measures to encourage times of rest and quiet. Choir members became adept at twisting their bodies into amazing shapes and positions as they and the seat partner contrived to get some sleep as the bus rolled along. Nature's call had to be respected, which meant rest stops along the way and an occasional unscheduled stop. Buses in more recent times were equipped with an on-board facility, one label for it being "The Blue Soup."

When Fred Schmidt began his work in the fall of 1948, his father had already planned the tour of the St. Olaf Choir to the west coast that began January 29 and ended February 23, 1949. P. G., "our guardian and protector," accompanied the Choir on this tour with Fred joining the group in Portland for the rest of the journey. The trip west involved the use of several railway lines. From

Sleeping on the bus

293

Minneapolis the Choir took the Great Northern railroad to Spokane, the Southern Pacific along the west coast as far as Los Angeles, the Santa Fe down to San Diego and back, the Union Pacific from Los Angeles to Omaha, and the Rock Island from Omaha to Des Moines and Northfield.[15]

P. G., Fred, Olaf, Western tour, 1949

The Choir received an enthusiastic welcome in Fargo. The Concordia Choir met them with a 50-piece band and later hosted them at a reception where the Concordia singers presented a take-off on choir try-outs and the two Christiansen directors. "Paul and Olaf laughed the loudest and longest." The concert at the Moorhead Armory was well-received. John Strohm nearly walked out on the stage without his pants, but Maurice Schmidt noticed the situation in time to stop him. The next day the St. Olaf singers joined the Concordia Choir at its rehearsal. Together the two choirs sang "A Joyous Christmas Song" ("Jeg er saa glad") and "Beautiful Savior," with Pauline Seim doing the solo on the latter number. The Concordia Choir sang several numbers for their Ole counterparts, prompting a St. Olaf student to write back to the *Messenger*, "They're good!"

As the Great Northern's "Oriental Limited" carried the Choir across the sub-zero plains of North Dakota, the heat in the train went out, requiring the students to pile on every available piece of clothing for warmth.[16] On the approach to Seattle the train was stalled in a snowbank, cutting down on the time needed to get ready for the concert in a Presbyterian church. The crowd was already in place as the risers were being put up, but the concert went very well. So enthusiastic was the audience

Paul J. Christiansen
Director, Concordia Choir

294

that the Choir had to sing "A Joyous Christmas Song" three times.[17]

The singing of Pauline Seim drew adulation from teenage listeners and others who surrounded her after concerts and asked for autographs.[18] In addition to her solo in "Beautiful Savior," Pauline sang the soprano part in the Entrance Scene of the well-known "Motet for Advent" by Gustav Schreck.

Soloists and director
Winnifred Greene, Betty Lou Oleson,
OCC, Pauline Seim, Charles Rosenthal

Other solo voices heard were Betty Lou Oleson, alto, Charles Rosenthal, tenor, and Eugene Nelson, bass. Seim and Rosenthal received ovations for solo work in Milhaud's "Cantata of Peace" and Paladilhe's "Benedictus." In Tacoma, the St. Olaf Choir was hosted by members of the Choir of Pacific Lutheran College whose director, Gunnar Malmin, conducted both choirs in the Schreck motet.

In the meantime, back on campus, the *Manitou Messenger* published a Choir journal with day-by-day reports sent back by Choir members. After the Tacoma visit the Choir headed for Portland. "We're really West now," wrote one of the Choir correspondents, and added: "And as Arline Heen said today as she looked at her calendar, 'We only have two and a heef wacks left.'"

It was a long tour, and a very good one, but not without its low moments. The concert in Portland, according to a letter from one Choir member to her parents, was a "flop." Even so, the audience was enthusiastic and the review was good, she wrote. "But we all were *so* tired we didn't have any *life* whatsoever! Olaf tried to give us a pep talk just before the last section but it didn't work." The disappointment was alleviated by the cheerful enthusiasm of Mrs. Edith Charlston, sister of Ella Hjertaas, who was overjoyed that the "King of Choirs" had come to the city.[19]

Arriving in Salem, Oregon, Choir members had scarcely an hour before

Mary Stegner making hamburgers

295

the concert to find something to eat. About thirty of them chanced upon a small restaurant-grocery store whose one waitress despaired over handling their orders for hamburgers, sandwiches, malted milks, coffee, and tea. So the Choir members went into action. According to the *Messenger's* account:

Salem Restaurant, 1949

> Within three minutes Hazel Olson was whipping up malted milks, Janet Anderson was selling donuts, Audrey Overson was pouring coffee, Mary Stegner was bustling about in the kitchen fixing hamburgers, and Pauline Seim was selling Oxydol and cigars to a very astonished customer.

The frenzied but successful meal episode was over in half an hour. The waitress was happy because business had been good and the Choir members had handled their impromptu duties with great dispatch. The next day the Choir sent the waitress and proprietress, Dorothy Gottfried, a dozen red roses. Several days later they received a letter of thanks from her and a request for a picture of the Choir.[20]

Unfortunately, illness smote the Choir for a number of days from Oregon to California to Salt Lake City. One even had a malaria attack, but most were afflicted by the flu. The fainting during concerts became alarming but at the same time somewhat comical. One evening, in Klamath Falls, Oregon, P. G. Schmidt called out, "All those who can line up, line up." Ronald Nelson '49 remembered that Olaf wasn't sure he would have enough singers to finish the concert:

> From the beginning of the concert, heads began disappearing as singers felt faint and had to sit down. At times in the second group the first row found it hard to close ranks enough to cover all the "sitters." Finally, at the end of Group III, Olaf went right into Group IV without letting us leave the stage. He was taking no more chances![21]

Nurse "Inky" Engebretson

But the hardy students, with the help of their nurse, Elida "Inky" Engebretson, were able to bounce back and keep singing. One of the many outstanding performances of the Choir took place in Sacramento where the reviewer, Merril Osenbaugh, commended the singers "for consistently true intonation, self-reliance and pitch." He thought the entire program "glistened" but singled out Schreck's "Motet" and Healey Willan's "Apostrophe to the Heavenly Hosts" for the unusual contrapuntal passages. He credited the director for welding the voices into a marvelous singing unit. He also liked Olaf's style of conducting:

> One refreshing recommendation of Conductor Christiansen is that he does not go into a lather of gyrations like some directors. He is calm, suave, with no gymnastics to attract attention to himself instead of the fresh, young eager students who face him attentively.[22]

The quiet director

On the train the next day it became evident that the favorable review had circulated among the Choir. To everyone's amused astonishment, the genuinely modest director, Olaf himself, came strutting down the aisle, thumbs under his suspenders in a parody of self-importance. The president of the Choir immediately caught on and asked, "You've read it, huh?" In relating the episode in a letter home, Alice Larsen '51 explained that it was so funny because "He's really quiet and humble most of the time. . . . Everyone thinks the world of him. People have told us after concerts that we look like it, too, when we sing."[23]

Alice Larsen, Edel Tetlie, Pat Lace, Jay Schroeder

Alice Larsen

St. Olaf Choir, 1949

The students were excited to learn that the composer Darius Milhaud would be in the audience for the February 10th concert in the Scottish Rite Auditorium in Oakland. They spotted him and sang his "Cantata of Peace," as one of them said, "with a vengeance." After the number Olaf motioned to Mr. Milhaud, who stood up, bowed, and pointed appreciatively at the Choir.

Milhaud, a large man unable to walk without difficulty, could not come backstage but Mrs. Milhaud came to greet Olaf and the Choir.[24]

Thanks to P. G.'s arrangements, the Choir toured China Town in San Francisco and had a meal there. The next day was a more complete tour of the environs of the city,

San Francisco, 1949

including cable car rides. In Los Angeles the Choir stayed at the Alexandria Hotel and sang before a packed house in the Philharmonic Auditorium. "And how we sang! The thunder of that applause was music to our ears," wrote a Choir member. The next morning the Choir met at Warner Brothers Studio in Hollywood to make recordings for Vonna Productions, Inc., to be issued by the College, the first commercial recordings since the twenties.

Heading east toward home, the Choir gave concerts in Salt Lake City, Denver, Cheyenne, Omaha, and Des Moines. In Salt Lake City, Sylvia Christiansen, Olaf's daughter, passed out as her father was bowing to the audience at the end of the last piece in a group. In Denver, the crowd began stomping and cheering before the final chord of "Beautiful Savior" had ended. A reviewer in Omaha, where the concert was in the Technical High School, wrote of the Choir's "technical perfection" and commented on the types of music offered in the program:

> Contrasts of schools was shown in the severity of Palestrina and Corsi, the incomparable musical oratory of Bach, the modernity of the contemporary Frenchman, Milhaud, the exalted beauty of Healey Willan's "Apostrophe to the Heavenly Hosts," a splendidly written setting of "The Fiftieth Psalm," by Melius Christiansen and other music by Schreck, Tschesnokoff and Grieg[25]

As soon as the Rock Island train bearing the singers crossed the Missouri River and entered Iowa, the Iowa members of the Choir assembled and welcomed the others by singing the Iowa Corn Song. At the Des Moines concert the Choir put everything they had into their last concert before returning to Northfield. They were not prepared for the exuberant reception when the train pulled into the Northfield station where the Band and a crowd of friends greeted them. The *Manitou Messenger*, which had published reports from the western tour, announced in a headline: "Band Blares, Crowd Cheers, Choir Returns Triumphant."

Iowa "Fat Farmer" by Ding

Choir at Des Moines depot, 1949

The tour of 1950, taking the Choir east, was also by train. Between Minneapolis and Milwaukee fellow passengers included the Minneapolis Symphony Orchestra, "complete with long hair, instruments, and Dorati," according to Mary Stegner and Dave Hesla who sent reports back to the *Messenger.* At one point, one of the Choir fellows came through the car to announce: "Antal is taking a nap."[26]. The Choir concert in Milwaukee went well, being the first tour appearance with many new members in the ensemble, but Olaf was faced with a problem of a somewhat different odor. Many singers had gone out to dinner at a German restaurant where the food was highly seasoned. "Every note we sang contained a mixture of onion and garlic aimed right at Olaf."[27]

In Sheboygan, Wisconsin, Winnifred Greene Alberg won the crowd's approval and a huge bouquet of carnations with her solos in "Lost in the Night" and "Lullaby on Christmas Eve." After graduating from St. Olaf in 1948 with the Bachelor of Music degree, Mrs. Alberg taught voice at Augustana College in Sioux Falls for one year, then returned to St. Olaf as a member of the music faculty.[28] Roland Johnson's birthday was on February 2, 1950. Fred Schmidt had wired ahead to the restaurant where the Choir stopped for dinner with the result that a speechless Roland was presented with a 20-inch decorated cake with 19 candles.[29]

Two concerts were sung in Madison, one of them broadcast over nine FM radio stations. The review in a local paper stated: "The choir maintained the music stature which the Christiansens have given it, with a tonal beauty that few such groups equal." In Springfield, Illinois, a critic wrote that the "earnest young people in this choir sing with their hearts as well as their voices and are as responsive as a beautifully tuned instrument."

300

There was also praise for the "virility of the men's voices," but uniquely gratifying was the comment: "As long as St. Olaf choir exists there will be beauty in the world."[30]

When the Choir set out for the east coast in 1951, anticipation centered on performing in certain famous halls, including Carnegie Hall in New York. In Cleveland, the Choir sang in Masonic Hall, where there was standing room only despite a storm. Music critic Arthur Loesser thought the climax of the program came with Bach's motet, *Jesus, Priceless Treasure*. Loesser itemized what he called the St. Olaf virtues: "the purity and steadiness of intonation, the blend of the voices, the distinct articulation of the rapid passages, and the profound security of delivery and ensemble which can come only from the most intensive practice and the most thoroughgoing knowledge."[31]

Special interest was also directed at the concert in Buffalo because the Kleinhans Music Hall was reputed to have the finest acoustics of any hall in the country. While the Choir was in Buffalo, looking forward to the concert in New York and its other appearances in the area, it heard rumors of an impending rail strike. At the hotel in New York, Fred Schmidt left word that he was to be awakened if the trains went on strike. After midnight the message came that the strike was on, so Fred got up, dressed, hailed a cab, and started making the rounds of bus companies. By working all through the night, he managed to charter three small commuter buses that transported the Choir to its concerts the next few days until the strike was over and rail service was restored.[32]

The Choir's appearance at Carnegie Hall that year was made possible when a symphony orchestra relinquished its prior right to the date. After the concert a New York critic wrote: "The St. Olaf Choir is a first-rate amateur chorus. Its pitch is clean, its tonal color rich and warm, and the high-voice-low-voice balance is everywhere just and delicate. The group's conductor, moreover, is obviously a musician of rare sensibility. . . . Mr. Christiansen is able to draw from his ensemble shades of sound whose expressive ring is always appropriate and never less than deeply sincere."[33]

Minnesota Senator Edward Thye invited President and Mrs. Harry Truman to attend the Washington concert in Constitution Hall. President Truman wrote in reply: "Mrs. Truman and I would certainly like to attend and if nothing unforeseen takes place we will be present."[34] As things turned out, the Trumans were unable to attend the concert. Critic Paul Hume was in attendance, however. According to the Choir scribes who kept a diary for the *Manitou Messenger*, "Hume didn't agree with our method of saying vowels, but Olaf says that he's still young." It was one of the best concerts and the crowd was very responsive. Olaf received five curtain calls.[34]

Constitution Hall, Washington, D. C., February 12, 1951

Readers of the *Messenger* received an inside view of Choir adventures on the road. In one issue they saw a photo of Choir members Edel Tetlie and Gordy Hafso in aprons helping serve their comrades at a small restaurant whose resident staff could not handle the invasion of hungry Oles.

Servus servorum   *Yoshiteru Murakami '51*

Another memorable food incident was the lavish luncheon provided for the Choir in the Waldorf-Astoria by Norwegian whaler Lars Christensen and Mrs. Christensen. The latter was incredulous when courteous Yosh Murakami '51 stepped up and thanked her in Norwegian![35]

Train travel was not always comfortable. Sometimes two students had to share one crowded berth. At one point singers complained that they had been placed in a refrigerator car instead of a coach. The resulting colds added a new song to the repertoire: "O Cub Led Us Sig a New Sog." This piece took its place alongside such numbers mentioned in reviews as "O Harry Bethlehem" and "Jesus, Priceless Treasurer." Riding trains made it difficult to keep clothes clean. Chandeliers, lamp shades, and door knobs in hotel rooms became favorite clothes lines. Rolf Charlston '53 washed his new nylon shirt one evening and Ramona Halverson '53 agreed to iron out the wrinkles. "The only trouble was she took out more than the wrinkles—in fact, about a 5 by 5 inch hunk of what used to be shirt." Ramona turned several shades of red and wrote in her journal, "Never will I forget that!!"[36]

Rolf Charlston '53

The touring experience always meant reviews, in which critical comments might appear along with copious paragraphs of laud and admiration. So it was in Toledo, where the concert was in the Peristyle of the Museum of Art. Frederick J. Kountz acknowledged that "the reviewer treads a tortuous path" in the light of the St. Olaf Choir's accurate pitch, articulation, balance, and clarity of execution.

Ramona Halverson '53

What Kountz found missing was poetry and plasticity in Bach's *Jesus, Priceless Treasure*, and more spontaneity and joy of feeling in Berger's "Brazilian Psalm." And in Chicago, Claudia Cassidy missed the "clinging beauty of a voluminous, almost mystical tone" she remembered from the Choir "in older days." What she heard was "strong, almost blunt, singing erected in blocks of tone on a rock of musicianship. Some of the high tone was white with strain, some of the low tone developed the drone of motor drive." What Cassidy liked most in the concert was the F. Melius arrangement of "Praise to the Lord."[37]

At the homecoming concert, Olaf explained to the crowd that the cause of peace had been the theme of the tour. Jean Berger's "Vision of Peace" and Morten J. Luvaas's composition, "The Cry of God," were chosen to express the theme. The reporter for the *Manitou Messenger* ended his review with the comment: "Our college is proud to have a Choir singing the message of the triumphant Christ, the Prince of Peace."[38]

Happy 80th Birthday to F. Melius Christiansen

Not long after the Choir returned from its 1951 eastern tour it was time to prepare for the events planned in honor of Dr. F. Melius Christiansen on the occasion of his 80th birthday. The actual date was April 1, 1951, but in Minnesota and elsewhere there would be observances throughout the month of April. Choirs in 5,000 Protestant congregations sang one of F. Melius's compositions on April First.

On the afternoon of April 7, 1951, the St. Olaf Choir broadcast a special program over CBS that originated in the WCAL studios on the campus. The St. Olaf Band gave a special concert. On Sunday, April 28th, the St. Olaf Chapel Choir and

F. Melius Christiansen

Orchestra, under the direction of Dr. Paul Ensrud, presented F. Melius Christiansen's cantata, *The Prodigal Son*.

F. Melius Christiansen, 1951

Articles saluting the maestro on his 80th birthday appeared in Minneapolis, St. Paul, Milwaukee, and other newspapers. Congratulatory letters were sent. One came from Leopold Stokowski who wrote, "The whole world is indebted to you for what you have done for American choral music." Senator Hubert H. Humphrey wrote: "In our present world of trouble and doubt you have done a wonderful service in teaching the people of America to sing and to love fine singing."[39]

The birthday observance that probably received the widest participation and publicity was the Recognition Concert given by the St. Olaf Choir in Northrop

Recognition Concert
BY THE
ST. OLAF CHOIR
OLAF C. CHRISTIANSEN, DIRECTOR

NORTHROP MEMORIAL AUDITORIUM
MINNEAPOLIS, MINNESOTA

FRIDAY, APRIL 13, 1951 • 8:30 P.M.

IN HONOR OF THE 80TH BIRTHDAY OBSERVANCE OF

Dr. F. Melius Christiansen

INTERMISSION SPEAKERS
Luther W. Youngdahl
Governor of the State of Minnesota
James L. Morrill
President of the University of Minnesota
Clemens M. Granskou
President of St. Olaf College

PRESENTED BY
THE UNIVERSITY OF MINNESOTA ARTISTS COURSE IN COOPERATION WITH THE
MINNEAPOLIS SYMPHONY ORCHESTRA AND THE TWIN CITY ST. OLAF CLUB

80th Birthday Concert

Auditorium in Minneapolis on Friday, April 13, 1951, before an audience of 3,600. Directed by Olaf C. Christiansen, the Choir sang a full concert, opening with Palestrina's "Hodie Christus Natus Est" for double choir. Other numbers included "Praise to the Lord," arranged by F. Melius Christiansen, Bach's *Jesus, Priceless Treasure*, Jean Berger's "Vision of Peace" and "Brazilian Psalm," Alexander Gretchaninoff's "Our Father, "The Cry of God," by Morten J. Luvaas, "Sing Unto the Lord," by Paul Christiansen, and "Beautiful Savior."

In the intermission, between Parts II and III of the program, greetings to Dr. F. Melius Christiansen were spoken by St. Olaf president Clemens M. Granskou, University of Minnesota president James L. Morrill, and Governor Luther W. Youngdahl. At the close of his talk, the governor led the audience in the "Happy Birthday" song and a standing ovation for the guest of honor.

The drama and emotion of the occasion were given fitting expression by John K. Sherman the next day in the *Minneapolis Tribune*. "The big moment . . . came at the end," he wrote, "when the stocky, snow-haired founder of the famous choir rose from his seat . . . , made his way to the stage, and took over." Sherman's account continued:

Rehearsing "Beautiful Savior" April, 1951

306

Not for many years has Minneapolis seen the grand old man of Minnesota music, the patriarch of American choral singing, mount the platform and assume his old role. The occasion was an affecting and memorable one. The last song was his, the one so long associated with him and the choir—"Beautiful Savior."[40]

The week before the birthday concert F. Melius had rehearsed "his" number with the Choir. One day, when he failed to appear, the Choir was worried about the coming performance. Olaf reassured them by saying, "Just watch his eyes!"[41] Ole Winter '51, a member of the tenor section, recalled the emotional, nervous awe of the Choir on the Northrop stage as the venerable maestro slowly came up the steps to direct and the audience applauded wildly. Before leading the Choir in "Beautiful Savior," F. Melius stepped up close to the singers, looked up and around at all of them, and said, "Take it easy, kids. Let's sing!" One of the "kids" was Olaf Christiansen who nimbly climbed up into the baritone section to sing one more time under his father's direction.[42] The solo stanza was sung by Pat Lace '52.

In describing the conducting of F. Melius, Sherman wrote fondly and knowingly of "the same calm vigor and authority we all remember—the close-in arm work, the little elbow jerk, the come-on gesture (never frantic) by which he summons the big organ and trumpet tones of the final measures." Sherman did not neglect the Choir itself, stating his admiration for "the clear, cool tone; controlled dynamics and shading; the usual unanimity in attack and releases and in phrasing, with never a hitch in polyphonic passages."[43]

When the St. Olaf Choir next hit the road, it was aboard the "Western Star," a train heading for the far west in January of 1952. A major blizzard caught them in Kalispell, Montana, making doubtful their reaching Spokane for the next concert. But they made it. Fred Schmidt got Great Northern to send the Choir on a special train, consisting of engine, coal car, baggage car, and two passenger cars. Choir members recall the unique experience of holding a rehearsal en route in the baggage car.[44]

Heading west, 1952

During intermission at Pacific Lutheran College in Tacoma, Washington, Olaf Christiansen was awarded an honorary doctor's degree. Choir members watched the presentation from offstage by peeking out from behind the curtains. Traveling overnight from Oregon to California, the midwestern singers were thrilled to wake up and see palm trees and flowers.[45]

Among the reviews of concerts on the western trip was one by Alfred Frankenstein after the Choir's performance at the Opera House in San Francisco on February 3, 1952. He compared the work of F. Melius and Olaf: "In the days of Melius Christiansen the St. Olaf Choir was especially well known for its elaborate palette of orchestral effects. Olaf Christiansen seems to think that the human voice is a sufficiently colorful instrument in itself, and he proves that point to the hilt."[46]

Judging from the broad smiles displayed in the 1952 yearbook, the St. Olaf Choir of that year must have been a happy aggregation. In its ranks was Gordon Hafso '52 who had collaborated with Larry Christenson '52 the year before in writing the original and highly successful operetta, "The

"The Heartless Troll" Minneapolis Performance

308

Christenson and Hafso

Rodney Eichenberger '52

Heartless Troll." Among other Choir members in the musical was tenor Rodney Eichenberger '52, who played the part, as he described it, of "the vocally-frazzled, cowardly mountain troll 'Crumbleefub.'" One day in Choir rehearsal, aware of Rod's role in the production, Olaf coolly called out, "Too much *troll* in the tenor section!"[47]

The same *Viking* carried a picture of P. G. and Fred Schmidt looking at a scrapbook together as P. G. savored memories of singing in the St. Olaf Choir for fifty years.[48] In April of 1952 the Choir gave a concert at Central Lutheran Church in Minneapolis to honor P. G. Schmidt for his half-century of singing in the Choir and serving as its manager most of that time.[49] P. G. sang in the Choir in 1952-53 when it went "to towns large and small in the Midwest."[50]

That was the year of the friendly contest in rehearsal when P. G. dropped down to F below C. The remarkable "basso" reached the age of 78 in May of 1954. The *Viking* showed him in his usual place among the singers, but illness prevented him from going on tour with the Choir that year. True to his steady personality, P. G. was philosophical about missing the tour. "It had to come sometime," he said.[51]

P. G. and Fred Schmidt

By Ship and Plane—the Choir Goes Abroad

Twenty-five years had elapsed since the St. Olaf Choir had traveled abroad. In 1930 it had made a successful tour of Norway and Germany. In the mid-fifties two trips out of the country were made in relatively quick succession. The Choir went back to Norway and Germany in 1955. In 1957 it made a special Easter visit to Iceland.

St. Olaf Choir, 1955

On a warm day in May of 1955 the St. Olaf Choir gathered on the front lawn of the Christiansen home at 812 St. Olaf Avenue to sing for the aging founder of the Choir before leaving on its trip to Norway and Germany. F. Melius, looking quite frail, sat on the front porch and listened.[52]

Dr. F. M. Christiansen suffered a stroke, lapsed into a coma, and died on June 1, 1955. The Choir, set to leave for the east coast and Europe on Thursday, June 2, 1955, went by bus to sing its scheduled first concert in Lanesboro, Minnesota, but returned to Northfield for the Memorial Service on Friday. Kenneth Jennings, assistant director, conducted the Choir at the first concert, at the Memorial Service, and at the second concert of the tour, held in Whitewater, Wisconsin. Olaf Christiansen joined the Choir and assumed his conducting duties in Cicero, Illinois. More will be said in the next chapter about the Memorial Service held in Boe Memorial Chapel on the St. Olaf campus on Friday, June 3, 1955.

For Olaf and Ellen Christiansen, Fred and Lenore Schmidt, and all the members of the Choir, the sadness of saying Goodbye to the beloved maestro was alleviated in part by the excitement of embarking on the Choir's first trip abroad in a quarter century. Olaf, who mourned and buried his father in Northfield before leaving on the tour, would soon find himself accepting the happy role of "father of the bride" in Oslo, Norway, when two

Off to Europe, June 1955

Choir members were married in the Cathedral Church in that city. The music, of course, would be furnished by the St. Olaf Choir.

But before the Choir boarded the "Stavangerfjord" for the trip across the Atlantic to Norway, it had a very demanding schedule of nightly concerts between the Lanesboro concert on June 2nd and the concert in Brooklyn's Academy of Music on June 21st. During the Brooklyn performance, the lights went out but the Choir, which sometimes practiced with eyes closed, was able to continue its singing without faltering.[53] In the Brooklyn audience that evening was Jean Berger, composer of "Vision of Peace" and "Thy Kingdom Come."

The weather was perfect and the sea calm for the crossing from New York to Oslo. Social life on board was enlivened by the presence of some 150 American students on their way to the Oslo Summer School. Rehearsals were held on board, sometimes on the open deck, but usually in the tourist class dining room. Since the Norwegian crew members often paused to listen to the Choir rehearse, it was decided to give a concert for them. The crew assembled, removed their caps, and stood at attention as the Choir began with the "Star Spangled Banner" and "Ja, vi elsker dette

On the "S. S. Stavangerfjord," June 1955

Arriving in Oslo

landet." Already stirred by hearing the Norwegian national anthem, they were visibly moved when the Choir sang Edvard Grieg's "Til Norge."[54]

On arriving in Oslo on July 2, 1955, the Choir met its host families. The next day it gave concerts in Kongsberg and Drammen, southwest of Oslo, and returned that evening. On Monday, the Fourth of July, the Choir attended a reception at noon, an Independence Day ceremony at the Lincoln Monument in Frogner Park at 3:00, and Open House at the American Embassy at 4:00 p.m. That evening at 8:00, the Choir sang in the University Aula, the festive hall with its brilliant murals by Edvard Munch.

The concert program for the European tour began with Bach's *Sing Ye to the Lord*, followed by "How Fair the Church of Christ shall stand," arranged by F. Melius Christiansen, "Plorate Filii Israel," ("Weep, ye children of Israel") by Giacomo Carissimi, and "Death, I do not fear thee," by J. S. Bach. The second group consisted of Jean Berger's "Vision of Peace" and "Thy Kingdom Come," and Edvard Grieg's "Hvad Est Du Dog Skjøn" and "Guds Sønn Har Gjort Mig Fri" ("God's Son has made me free").

In the Aula, Oslo 1955

The third part of the program offered folk melodies from many lands. Two items from the United States led off this group: "What Wondrous Love," a southern hymn arranged by Olaf Christiansen, and "Deep River," arranged by H. T. Burleigh, the one and only spiritual Olaf ever included in a program. Next was Olaf's arrangement of the Danish song, "Deilig Er Den Himmel Blaa" ("O How Beautiful the Sky"). Representing Poland was "Lowly Shepherds." The Norwegian Christmas song, "Jeg Er Saa Glad," arranged by M. Haakansen came next, and the third part closed with "Carol of the Drum" by Katherine K. Davis.

Concert program for Norway

The final part of the concert program was given over to four optional encore numbers: "Wake, Awake," by Philipp Nicolai, "Alleluia," a composition by St. Olaf faculty member G. Winston Cassler, "Our Father," by Alexander Gretchaninoff, and "Beautiful Savior," arranged by F. Melius Christiansen.[55]

Reviews of the Aula concert contained warm compliments and some reservations. Hans Jørgen Hurum wrote that "the St. Olaf Choir is truly an elite choir. It bursts with fresh and youthful joy in singing. A veritable store of energy has gone into such a thoroughly prepared concert tour." The opening Bach number for two choirs was "a convincing introduction to the concert, a shining, fresh sound, admirably pure in every sense." Yet the strongly accented syllables and changing voice coloring spoke of a Bach style that broke with European tradition. Hurum regretted that the director had omitted the middle part of Grieg's "Guds Sønn Har Gjort Mig Fri" which, in his view, gave the number its perspective. Other reviewers would make the same point, that cutting away that portion did violence to one of Grieg's finest choral compositions.[56]

Pauline Hall began her review by noting the sold-out house and the enormous enthusiasm of the crowd. She observed that the different voice parts knew their role within the whole ensemble, a sign of an advanced musicality that is not attained simply by drilling. The directing was done with supple but at the same time distinct gestures. "He never threatens, but coaxes forth the sound he wants." Hall was impressed by Jean Berger's "Vision of Peace" with its "wonderfully relevant text from the prophet Isaiah, composed in the style of our own time and with many difficult modulations and harmonies which the Choir mastered with ease." She sensed the reflection of Southern culture in the hymn, "Wondrous Love," and thought the Christmas songs at the end deservedly brought a shower of gifts and flowers to the Choir.[57]

The theme of romance followed the Choir throughout its Norway itinerary. Choir members Edwin Gass and Louise Horchler had hoped to be married in New York before the "Stavangerfjord" sailed, but the law's requirement of a waiting period thwarted their plans. Next, they appealed to the master of the Norwegian ship, Captain Leif Hansen, who told them it was only in the movies that couples were married by a ship's captain. "I could bury you," he said, not without sympathy, "but I can't marry you." [58] Under international law, he was not authorized to perform the ceremony.

After resigning themselves to waiting until their return home, they learned on their arrival that the wedding could be held in Norway. Thanks to Fred Schmidt's appeal to the U. S. Embassy and the intervention of the Choir's patron, *Nordmanns Forbundet*, Norwegian legalities were cleared away so that Ed and Louise would be married in the Oslo Cathedral on July 22, 1955, at the end of the Norway tour. With that happy prospect awaiting them, they bought material for the wedding dress and a pattern, and at every place along the way Louise was housed with a family that owned a sewing machine. Snatching such bits of time as she could, Louise kept working on her wedding dress throughout the tour.

An early concert was given in Larvik, where F. Melius Chrisitansen had grown up. The Choir traveled from Fredrikstad to Larvik in glorious summmer sunshine aboard the boat "Peter Wessel." It was Olaf Christiansen's first visit to the town his father had often told him about. Hundreds of people were on hand to greet the American singers. "Larvik Guttemusikk," a local boys' band, played the "Star Spangled Banner" and the Choir responded by singing, "Ja, vi elsker dette

Ed and Louise Gass

landet," the Norwegian national anthem. Seeing the boys' band remained in Olaf's memory. Later he recalled the scene.

> As we walked down the gangplank, I noticed a boy about 9 years old in a blue uniform, playing clarinet in the front row. When I saw that little guy, I thought of Dad as a boy there in Larvik 75 years ago. So I leaned over, and winked at him. And the little guy winked back —right in the middle of an eighth note!—and kept right on playing.[59]

In Larvik Olaf was also moved by the opportunity to play the same piano that his father had practiced on as a boy. The concert took place in the church where F. Melius had played the organ. Olaf had tears in his eyes as he directed the Choir in "Beautiful Savior." In a brief speech to the audience he said, "As we grow older, we become more conscious of the questions of where we come from, why we are living, and where we are going." Then the Choir and the listeners joined in the singing of "Praise to the Lord." On the church steps a few minutes later, the Choir sang Grieg's touching hymn, "To Norway," which begins with the words, "You are my mother, I love you."[60]

As the tour continued, the Choir came to Henrik Ibsen's birthplace, Skien, where Olaf had to stop the Choir twice before it got in tune with the first chord of

OCC, Norway 1955

"Deep River." A memorable part of the Kristiansand visit was that the famous opera singer Kirsten Flagstad was in the audience and greeted the Choir after the concert.[61]

The Choir made its way from Stavanger to Haugesund and Bergen, part of the journey on a fjord steamer. They were welcomed wherever they went. "The Norwegians were so good to us, so hospitable and kind, they really spoiled us with their attention and efforts to make us feel at home," wrote Carla Schimmel. There were receptions, speeches, dinners, and more than

Choir in Our Savior's Church, Haugesund

enough *smørbrød*, the delicious and ubiquitous open-faced sandwiches. Carla aptly summarized the sights they encountered along the way:

Such scenery we saw; high mountains and waterfalls every few yards; thick forests and little snuggled valleys. The towns were small and comfortable—flowers everywhere. The colors all over were beautiful, for they use red tiled roofs and paint the homes different colors—a pretty picture wherever you looked.[62]

The Choir's itinerary naturally included a concert in the great Nidaros Cathedral in Trondheim where it sang on July 19th. On arrival at the train station the night before, Olaf told a reporter that he and the Choir looked forward to the concert in the Cathedral as the high point of the entire tour. The performance was very favorably received. A reviewer stated that a superb, confident, musical quality characterized everything the Choir undertook. There was special admiration for the sopranos and basses, and perceptive notes of appreciation for the Jean Berger numbers, the Grieg songs, and the folk melodies. An enthusiastic audience filled the huge church. The reviewer felt that the common values uniting Norwegians on both sides of the Atlantic accounted for the emotional response to "Deilig er den himmel blaa," arranged by Olaf Christiansen, and the charming

In Nidaros Cathedral

Christmas song, "Jeg er saa glad hver julekveld." But an honest question was raised: "Why sing 'Beautiful Savior' so slowly?"[63]

The trip from Trondheim to Oslo was made by train, with a stop at Lillehammer for an outdoor concert at the Maihaugen Museum. The Choir's agenda for Friday, July 22, 1955, in Oslo began with an early arrival, final preparations for the marriage of Edwin Gass and Louise Horchler in the Oslo Cathedral, the wedding itself at 1:00 p.m., and the 7:00 p.m. concert at the University Aula. The wedding dress was almost ready. Louise had put the finishing touches on it during the train ride from Trondheim, and each of the Choir women had taken a stitch in the beautiful gown. But all the handling meant it required cleaning, so Louise and a couple of friends stayed up most of the night to wash and iron the gown.[64]

The entire Choir and entourage participated in the wedding. Olaf and Ellen Christiansen took the role of parents of the bride, Olaf escorting

Louise down the aisle of the Cathedral Church. Fred and Lenore Schmidt served as parents of the groom. Lenore was Louise's voice teacher..[65]

Before the ceremony, the St. Olaf Choir sang Gretchaninoff's "Our Father," directed by Kenneth Jennings. The marriage ceremony was performed in English by a Norwegian pastor, the Reverend Sverre Eika. Next the Choir sang "Beautiful Savior" and Marie Biorn chanted the Lord's Prayer. After the service Choir members hurried outside to throw rice on the newly-married couple, an action that drew some disapproving stares from Norwegian onlookers who thought it wasteful.[66] A photographer for the Oslo newspaper *Morgenbladet* snapped a photo of the couple coming down the aisle after the vows. Within an hour after the wedding, Ed and Louise found a framed print of the

Mr. and Mrs. Edwin Gass

photo and a bouquet outside their hotel room door, courtesy of the paper. The reception for the Choir following the concert in the Aula also served as a wedding reception for Mr. and Mrs. Edwin Gass.

Wedding reception in Oslo
Louise Gass, Fred and Lenore Schmidt

More adventures lay ahead as the Choir headed for Sweden and Germany. There was only one concert in Sweden, held in the ancient Romanesque cathedral in Lund. Choir members changed into their robes by candlelight in a dank, dark crypt where generations of bishops were buried. Six of the Choir members took up the offering, manipulating bags attached to long poles. Only one hat was knocked off.[67]

Because of the six-second reverberation time in the cathedral, Olaf instructed his singers to be ready for a much slower tempo, especially in Bach's *Sing Ye to the Lord*. It was a thrill to hear the final, triumphant "FREE" of Grieg's "God's Son Has Made Me Free" as it "rolled in waves down the church and hung under the dome."[68]

When the group reached "Wonderful Copenhagen," Fred Schmidt was thoughtful enough to cancel a radio appearance to let the singers have maximum enjoyment during their two well-earned free days. They rented bicycles and saw the sights of the city.

Dr. Christiansen made a few changes in the program for the concerts in Germany, replacing three contemporary American anthems with Gretchaninoff's "Our Father" and three German songs, "Die mit Tränen säen" by J. H. Schein, "Psalm Ninety-Two" by Georg Schumann, and the carol "Auf dem Berge," arranged by Kranz. The Grieg piece, "God's Son Has Made Me Free" was sung to

Choir poster, Hamburg

German audiences in English instead of in Norwegian. The crowd in Hamburg was small but enthusiastic and noisy, stamping its feet and cheering in delight at the end of the concert. Traveling from Hamburg to Hanover and other German cities, the Choir took note of the impressive rebuilding that had already been done after the end of World War II.

In Hanover, where Bishop Hans Lilje was their host at a reception, Choir members saw the effects of the war's destruction, and the half-destroyed cathedral left as it was as a war memorial, "just the walls and tower standing, the huge cross on the altar stark against a pile of brick and rubble." But Göttingen, with its appearance of a medieval town, was untouched by the war. There the Choir sang in the Johanneskirche. The local paper praised the choristers for their "oneness in singing that can only come from a unity of spirit."[69]

For the trip from Göttingen to Munich, Fred had everyone up and aboard the two chartered buses for an early start. The first bus, carrying the robe trunks and risers, three German tour managers, assistant director Kenneth Jennings, and about a dozen singers, proceeded as fast as it could for the evening concert in Munich, saving time by eating sandwiches en route. Even so, it reached Lukaskirche in Munich about a half hour late, but the crowd was waiting patiently. In the meantime, the other bus, with Olaf and Fred and the rest of the Choir, experienced one breakdown and delay after the other. The driver made some repairs himself, enough to get the bus to a garage where further repairs took several hours. Word was sent to the church in Munich to change the time of the concert. Once on the road again, the bus was delayed at railroad crossings and by a road-block.

In Munich, Jennings and a small cadre of singers stalled as long as they could. Finally they decided to reward the patience of the audience by singing some of the lighter numbers. As soon as the first women filed on to the risers, the American military men in the audience let out unbridled whoops and cheers, much to the chagrin of the proper Germans who

Marktkirche, Hanover, Germany
Dick Hanson, Tom Herbranson,
Tom Twaiten, Paul Peterson

Choir in Marktkirche, Hanover

tried to shush them into churchly decorum. There was only one tenor, so Jennings asked Lars Kindem to switch from bass to tenor. The partial Choir began with the always popular "Carol of the Drum," and again the American G.I.'s went wild, angrily shushed again by the Germans.[70]

Lars Kindem '55

Jennings and the small Choir did two groups, singing numbers that called for four parts and avoiding the more complex eight-part pieces. The strategy was to sing three numbers, leave the stage to take a break, draw it out as long as possible, look for the other bus, go on to sing three more numbers, and take another long break. By this time the little group was running out of concert pieces they could manage, and was actually thinking about resorting to college songs for a third group, but then the other bus arrived.[71]

The time was about 10:00 p.m. or later. Hurriedly the singers threw on their robes, not taking time to change shoes. When the full Choir filed out to take their places and Dr. Christiansen made his entrance, the American servicemen were completely uninhibited in their clapping and yelling. The crowd, which had been waiting since 6:30 that evening, gladly sat through the entire concert, which ended around midnight. Later it was reported that only four persons asked for a ticket refund.[72]

Arriving in Minneapolis

The memorable European tour of 1955 ended with a final concert in Düsseldorf on August 2nd. Some remained in Europe for further travel while others flew from Amsterdam to New York on Royal Dutch Airlines and by another flight to Minneapolis.

Iceland Tour, 1957

The St. Olaf Choir flew to Iceland in April of 1957 where it spent Easter vacation singing at the U. S. Air Force base in Keflavik and at other sites. Planning for the trip had been underway for over a year when the tour was announced in January of 1957.[73] During the week in Iceland the sixty singers were guests of the Iceland Choral Association and the U. S. Air Force.[74]

Leaving for Iceland

Behind the sending of the St. Olaf Choir to Iceland was a matter of foreign relations, as became clear through Fred Schmidt's communications with the State Department. The United States wanted to renew its contract with Iceland to operate the air base at Keflavik. The Russians, eager to lease the strategic site, had been cultivating favor in Iceland by sending the Red Army Chorus, the Russian Ballet, and other artists to perform for the people. The Soviet cultural propaganda worked at first, moving the Icelanders to ask for the removal of the United States air base. But when the Soviets brutally repressed the revolt in Hungary, Iceland decided to renew the contract with the U. S. and keep the base as before.[75]

The people of Iceland now wanted to see and hear some American artistic talent. The Association of Church Choirs of Iceland asked the commander of the air base to have the St. Olaf Choir come to Iceland and do a series of concerts. The Choir shared with the Icelanders a common Nordic and Lutheran background. The request went from the air base to the State Department in Washington, and from there the invitation was extended to the St. Olaf Choir.[76]

Since the Choir had already been on its annual tour, the College had to approve additional days away from the classrooms. Rehearsals included hurried lessons in pronouncing Icelandic words, coached by a prominent Minnesotan of Icelandic descent, Val Bjornson, State Treasurer, who knew the language well. By a lucky coincidence, Olaf Christiansen had recently arranged an Icelandic number for choir, and its performance would be met with tremendous enthusiasm.

The Choir left Minneapolis on Wednesday, April 17, 1957, on two Military Air Transport Service planes and arrived in Iceland the next morning. Thanks to a prior request for the necessary music by St. Olaf graduate Lieutenant Colonel Clarence "Ace" Eliasen '39, when the Choir arrived the post band greeted it with the playing of the St. Olaf College Song.

It was a very busy week, beginning with concerts in churches and city halls on Good Friday and Saturday. On Easter Sunday the Choir sang at a 7:00 a.m. service at the American Air Base and again that evening when the auditorium was filled to overflowing. Noting the response, St. Olaf grad and

Concert in Reykavik Cathedral
Iceland, April 1957

324

Chaplain Paul Roe '51 remarked, "Well, you can be proud. You outdrew Bob Hope."[77] Smaller groups flew to outlying communities. After the Easter sunrise service on the base, one group of eight singers traveled by small plane, open boat, and truck to reach an isolated radar station where the crew of American service men were lined up to greet them.

The main concert was given in the Cathedral in Reykavik, the capital city, on April 22. Two concerts were also given in the National Theater. During sightseeing in the city the Choir sang the Icelandic national anthem on the steps of the university.[78] So well had the Choir mastered the Icelandic sounds that people hearing the national anthem over the radio thought it was an Icelandic choir.[79]

On its tour to Iceland the St. Olaf Choir represented both the nation and the church. The *Viking* yearbook had this comment on the significance of the trip: "Our government felt it necessary to show these Icelandic young people some American youth—youth whose vitality for life is not confined to a rock-and-roll demigod, but combines spiritual earnestness with a rooted belief in democratic principles."[80]

The Icelandic people were charmed by the young singers and their handsome director, and were especially touched by the numbers sung in the Icelandic language. Similarly, the Air Force troops, instead of being uninterested, as one officer had assumed, were captivated by the singing, filling the hall to overflowing and calling for encores.[81] The Choir felt amply rewarded for its Easter mission to Iceland.

Singing at University in Reykavik, Iceland, April 1957

1. 1926-27 *Viking*, 119.

2. *The Christian Century*, November 8, 1944, cited in *Viking* 1945, 94.

3. *Viking* 1942, 122-23.

4. Letter from Marion Voxland '49 to Joseph M. Shaw, June 7, 1996.

5. Willmar Thorkelson, "Father-Son Teams Put Choir on Map," *The Minneapolis Star*, April 4, 1968.

6. Interview: Joseph M. Shaw '49 and Betty Stromseth '53 with Fred '31 and Lenore Schmidt '31, December 26, 1994.

7. Snapshots, clippings from scrapbooks of Norma Lee Simso '30 and Elizabeth Day Wee '31.

8. *The Wichita Beacon*, January 1931; Signe Ramseth '33 Johnson Diary, 1931.

9. "Former St. Olaf Choir manager fondly recalls the group's early days," first segment of five-article series by Fred Schmidt in *Northfield News*, March 4, 1992.

10. "Christiansen surprises choir with athletic prowess less well known than musical talents," fifth segment of five-article series by Fred Schmidt in *Northfield News*, March 25, 1992.

11. *Ibid.*

12. Willmar Thorkelson, "End of an Era," *Lutheran Bond* (May 1968), 10.

13. "St. Olaf Choir depended on rails," second segment of five-article series by Fred Schmidt in *Northfield News*, March 6, 1992.

14. "St. Olaf Choir rallies to 'Oom-ya-ya!' and delights Icelanders," fourth segment of five-article series by Fred Schmidt in *Northfield News*, March 18, 1992.

15. Itinerary, "St. Olaf Choir Tour, January 29 to February 23, 1949." Alice Larsen '51 scrapbook.

16. Letter from Ronald '49 and Betty Lou Nelson '49 to Bob Johnson, January 28, 1994.

17. *Manitou Messenger (MM)*, February 1949; letter from Alice Larsen to her parents, Dr. and Mrs. M. W. Larsen, February 4, 1949.

18. *Ibid.*

19. Letter from Alice Larsen to her parents, February 7, 1949.

20. *MM*, February 1949; letter from Dorothy Gottfried to St. Olaf Choir, February 19, 1949; 1949 *Viking*, 79.

21. Ronald and Betty Lou Nelson letter.

22. Merril Osenbaugh, unidentified Sacramento paper, ca. February 10, 1949.

23. Letter from Alice Larsen to her parents, February 10, 1949.

24. *MM*, Choir Journal item for February 10, 1949; Alice Larsen letter, February 10, 1949.

25. Martin W. Bush, unidentified Omaha paper, February 22, 1949. Alice Larsen scrapbook.

26. Letter from Nordis Evenson Christenson '51 to JMS, July 19, 1996.

27. *MM*, February 10, 1950.

28. *MM*, November 3, 1950.

29. *MM*, February 10, 1950.

30. Cited in *MM*, February 10, 1950.

31. Arthur Loesser, *Cleveland Press*, February 1, 1951.

32. "St. Olaf Choir depended on rails," second segment of five-article series by Fred Schmidt in *Northfield News*, March 6, 1992.

33. JSH in *New York Herald Tribune*, ca. February 5, 1951. Edwin Gass '52 scrapbook.

34. *MM*, February 2, 1951; February 16, 1951.

35. *MM*, February 9, 1951.

36. *MM*, February 16, 1951. Ramona Halverson scrapbook.

37. Frederick J. Kountz, "St. Olaf Choir Is Full-Voiced and Pleasing," in *Toledo Times*, February 16, 1951; Claudia Cassidy, "St. Olaf Choir Rears Some Triumphant Towers in Blocks of Tone," in *Chicago Tribune*, February 21, 1951. Ramona Halverson scrapbook.

38. *MM*, ca. February 23, 1951. Edwin Gass scrapbook.

39. F. Melius Christiansen Papers, STOARCHIV.

40. John K. Sherman, "St. Olaf Choir Pays Tribute to 'F. Melius,'" *Minneapolis Tribune*, April 14, 1951.

41. Interview: JMS with Edwin '52 and Louise Gass '56, March 12, 1996.

42. Letter from Ole Winter '51 to JMS, May 25, 1996; letter from Nordis Evenson Christenson to JMS, July 19, 1996.

43. Sherman, "St. Olaf Choir Pays Tribute."

44. Letter from Jerry L. Hanson '54 to BJ, October 25, 1993; letter from Louis Banitt '54 to BJ, January 5, 1994.

45. Nordis Evenson Christenson letter.

46. Alfred Frankenstein, "St. Olaf Lutheran Choir Sings," in *San Francisco Chronicle*, February 4, 1952.

47. Letter from Rodney Eichenberger '52 to BJ, November 7, 1993.

48. *Viking* 1952, 91.

49. *Minneapolis Sunday Tribune*, April 13, 1952.

50. *Viking* 1953, 74-75.

51. *Viking* 1954, 55; *Northfield News*, January 28, 1954, cited in Joseph M. Shaw, *History of St. Olaf College 1874-1974* (Northfield, Minnesota: The St. Olaf College Press, 1974), 411.

52. Interview: JMS with Charlotte "Shoonie" Donhowe Hartwig '57, November 10, 1995.

53. Carla Schimmel '56, "Choir Sees Europe for a Song," *MM*, September 23, 1955.

54. Letter from Lars Kindem '55 to JMS, February 26, 1995.

55. Tour program: "St. Olaf A Cappella Choir. Europe-Turne, Sommeren 1955."

56. Hans Jorgen Hurum, "St. Olaf-koret," *Morgenbladet*, Oslo, July 5, 1955. Edwin and Louise Gass scrapbook.

57. Pauline Hall, "St. Olaf-koret," *Dagbladet*, Oslo, July 5, 1955. Edwin and Louise Gass scrapbook.

58. "St. Olaf Choir's first tour to Europe full of surprises," third segment of five-article series by Fred Schmidt in *Northfield News*, March 11, 1992.

59. "Conductor's Career in Tune With Father's," *The Minneapolis Star*, December 9, 1960.

60. Audrey Johnson in *Northfield Independent*, n.d., summer 1955. Edwin and Louise Gass scrapbook.

61. Interview: JMS with Paul E. Peterson, February 13, 1996; Audrey Johnson in *Northfield Independent*, n.d., summer 1955.

62. Carla Schimmel, "Choir Sees Europe for a Song."

63. "St. Olaf A Cappela Choir," unnamed Trondheim paper, ca. July 20, 1955. Edwin and Louise Gass scrapbook.

64. "St. Olaf Choir's tour to Europe," *Northfield News*, March 11, 1992; JMS interview with Ed and Lou Gass, March 12, 1996.

65. "St. Olaf Choir's tour to Europe"; *Northfield News*, July 29, 1955.

66. Lars Kindem in *Northfield News*, July 21, 1955; Ed and Lou Gass interview.

67. Carla Schimmel, "Choir Sees Europe for a Song."

68. Letter from Paul Christenson '55 to BJ, September 9, 1994; Audrey Johnson in *Northfield Independent*, summer 1955.

69. Audrey Johnson, "Choir Turns Homeward Saturday, Impressed by Stay in Germany," *Northfield Independent*, summer 1955.

70. Lars Kindem letter to JMS, February 26, 1995.

71. JMS conversation with Kenneth Jennings, June 27, 1996.

72. Lars Kindem letter; Carla Schimmel, "Choir Sees Europe for a Song."

73. *Minneapolis Sunday Tribune*, January 20, 1957; *St. Paul Pioneer Press*, January 20, 1957; St. Olaf *Alumnus*, January 1957.

74. *St. Paul Sunday Pioneer Press*, May 19, 1957.

75. St. Olaf College News Bureau, n. d. 1957.

76. *Ibid.*; "St. Olaf Choir . . . delights Icelanders," *Northfield News*, March 18, 1992.

77. *Northfield News*, March 18, 1992.

78. *St. Paul Sunday Pioneer Press*, May 19, 1957.

79. *Northfield News*, March 18, 1992.

80. *Viking* 1957, 83.

81. *Northfield News*, March 18, 1992; *St. Paul Sunday Pioneer Press*, May 19, 1957.

CHAPTER 11

SING TO THE LORD A NEW SONG

The years of the Norway-Germany and Iceland tours, 1955 and 1957, were also the years during which the two great pioneers of the St. Olaf Choir passed away. F. Melius Christiansen died on June 1, 1955, and Paul G. Schmidt on July 26, 1957. The Choir under their successors extended its reputation, at times acknowledged in surprising quarters. The Golden Anniversary of the Choir was observed in 1962. One successful tour followed another through the sixties, and suddenly friends of the Choir heard that Olaf Christiansen was retiring and that his final tour would be in 1968.

Consideration of Olaf's retirement invites reflection on his techniques as a choral leader and the nature of the repertory he developed. Finally, something must be said about the goals he pursued during his twenty-seven years as director of the St. Olaf Choir.

St. Olaf Choir, 1967-68, in Boe Chapel

Reidar Dittmann and FMC

The Passing of the Fathers

Both F. Melius and P. G. remained active in Northfield and were seen on the St. Olaf campus from time to time after they retired. At his home F. Melius gave private tutoring in composition to Reidar Dittmann '47, Ronald Nelson '49, and a few others. Christy even directed the St. Olaf Orchestra during the 1943-44 school year, inspiring trumpeter Helen Drovdal '44 to hit the high B-flat in a performance of "Landsighting." During rehearsal he walked over and told her, smiling confidently, "You can do it!" And she did![1]

F. M. Christiansen, Portrait, 1949

Paul G. Schmidt, Portrait, 1949

332

St. Olaf College observed its Diamond Jubilee in the fall of 1949. As part of the celebration, portraits of F. Melius Christiansen and Paul G. Schmidt were unveiled, with both men present for the occasion. The portraits, by Minneapolis artist Theodore Sohner, were presented to the College by a group of alumni.[2]

The major event of the Seventy-Fifth Anniversary was the presentation on November 3rd and 5th, 1949, of the historical pageant, "An Adventure in Faith." One of the St. Olaf Choir's roles in the pageant was to don white surplices and take the stage as "the old St. Olaf Choir." The singers stood in readiness under the spotlight in the darkened gym. It was an unforgettable moment when white-haired F. Melius Christiansen stepped into the spotlight and directed the Choir in the singing of "Beautiful Savior," with Gertrude Boe Overby singing the solo.[3]

FMC and 1949 Choir, Anniversary Pageant

P. G. Schmidt continued to sing in the St. Olaf Choir until he retired from the faculty in the spring of 1954. Although he missed the tour, he took his usual place at the Commencement concert, completing fifty-two years of singing with the Choir with which he had been intimately associated since its founding. During the Choir's 1952 tour to the west coast, P. G. approached Director Olaf Christiansen about stepping aside and letting a student take his place. Replied Olaf, "If you were to step aside, I would need a multitude to replace you."[4]

Having seen his son Fred settle into the Choir managing role, P. G. still busied himself with young people and travel. He coordinated bus travel, tours, and housing for midwestern youth attending a Luther League convention in San Francisco in 1955. He represented Jefferson Lines in Northfield and organized summer tours to Europe. In 1956 he was looking forward to a reunion of the 1906 St. Olaf Band that went to Norway.[5]

F. Melius Christiansen died the day before the St. Olaf Choir was due to leave on the 1955 tour that took it across the country to New York, and across the Atlantic to Norway, Sweden, and Germany. Knowing of his passing before leaving Northfield, the Choir returned to campus from its first concert to sing at the Memorial Service in Boe Memorial Chapel on Friday, June 3, 1955. It was a relatively simple service, with a tribute by President Clemens M. Granskou but no sermon. Granskou said that Dr. F. Melius Christiansen was loved as "the man who by his genius and devotion put the stamp of his personality upon St. Olaf College. . . . We knew him as a man who chose to be different. He refused to yield to mediocrity, triviality, and the commonplace."[6]

The congregation sang "In Heavenly Love Abiding" and the St. Olaf Choir, conducted by Kenneth Jennings, sang "Asleep in Jesus" and "Beautiful Savior." Paul Christenson '55 recalled, "It was difficult to sing through tight vocal chords and teary eyes, saying our farewells to the one who had made our experience possible."[7] Officiating at the memorial service and at the committal service at Oak Lawn Cemetery in Northfield was the Reverend Boral R. Biorn '30, pastor of St. John's Lutheran Church and a St. Olaf graduate who had sung under F. Melius when the St. Olaf Choir traveled to Norway and Germany in 1930.[8]

Paul Gerhard Schmidt died July 26, 1957, succumbing to a heart condition after a lifetime of exceptionally good health. In addition to his long and effective service as manager of the St. Olaf Choir, Schmidt had other achievements of note. For example, he was elected to Phi Beta Kappa as a student at the University of Minnesota, from which he graduated in June of 1897. When St. Olaf College received its Phi Beta Kappa chapter in November of 1949, P. G. Schmidt became the first president of the local PBK society, Delta of Minnesota. Perhaps few realize that Schmidt was brought to St. Olaf to teach mathematics, or that he served the College as head of the mathematics department, treasurer, vice president, and in 1909-10 as acting president. Besides his work as manager of musical organizations, P. G. was chairman of the committee on public functions and had major responsibility for the Artist and Lecture series.

Luther College recognized P. G.'s extraordinary services to the church and education by awarding him the honorary degree, Doctor of Laws, at its commencement exercises May 28, 1945.[9] The citation included these words:

His systematic and efficient work as manager and singing member of the St. Olaf Choir since its inception, his vision and foresight in bringing the artistic excellence of the choir before music lovers in this country and abroad have been a vital factor in winning for St. Olaf College the acclaim which it enjoys in the world of music and in the contribution which the college has made to the spiritual and cultural heritage of our church and nation.[10]

That same month Schmidt was honored at the May Music Festival at St. Olaf when F. Melius directed several numbers and "in one of the longest and best speeches of his career" paid tribute to his long-time partner.[11] In warming to his subject, Christy entertained the audience by telling the story of the Choir all set to sing a number that began very softly, but P. G., thinking that the next piece was "Salvation is Created," boomed out all alone with "Sal...." After the concert Ruth Renden, one of the singers, tipped a porter to go about the hotel lobby and dining room crying out the message, "Calling Mr. Sal."

When the laughter finally died down, Christy continued with his remarks, describing the confidence he and the Choir members had in Professor Schmidt. "He always knows where to go, and we trust him and

The Fathers of the Choir
San Antonio, Texas, 1942

we follow him. He's been a wonderful manager, and I personally must say that I've had a wonderful boss on the Choir trips." In concluding, Christy addressed Professor Schmidt with these words: "We are trying our utmost to show you that we appreciate all you have done, for St. Olaf College, for St. Olaf Choir, and for me too! I thank you very much!"[12]

On Schmidt's death, Ella Hjertaas Roe wrote "A Colleague's Tribute to 'P. G,'" stating that it was his "high joy" to have a part in bringing to others through great music the things of the spirit for people to live by. Ella summarized the qualities that made P. G. a totally unique figure in the life of the St. Olaf Choir, loved and respected by all who knew him:

> For all the members of the St. Olaf Choir, down through the years from its very beginning, "P.G.," as he was affectionately called, set the highest standard of professional conduct and ethics. He loved the choir and the choir members loved him. They loved him for his ability, for his fine dignity, for his endearing sense of humor, for the wonders he seemed ever able to perform, for the understanding and the support he gave "F. Melius," and for making together with him that remarkable team. We were proud of him. [13]

"Ella Digs Ole Choir"

Another Ella, although unacquainted with the team, expressed her high regard for the St. Olaf Choir. One Friday night in the fall of 1957, St. Olaf student Dave Holland, a writer for the campus paper, the *Manitou Messenger*, made his way to Minneapolis to take in the Norman Granz show, "Jazz at the Philharmonic." Among the performers were Oscar

Olaf leading rehearsal

Steensland Library

Peterson, the Modern Jazz Quartet, and Ella Fitzgerald, the famous popular vocalist. Dave managed to meet Ella after the show and reported the following comment from their exchange: "You're from St. Olaf? I dig your choir."[14]

The St. Olaf Choir also made a favorable impression on a photo-journalism team sent to the campus by Look magazine to do a story on the Choir as part of a feature on Lutheranism in America. The Look team was on campus in January of 1958 with the story due to be published in April. The journalists followed Choir members through an entire day, observing and taking pictures of students in rehearsal in Steensland Hall, going to classes, relaxing, and having devotions.[15]

A dissenting note about the Choir was sounded in a *Messenger* editorial in December. The editor felt that the enormous investment of time in the Christmas Festival and the spring tour of the St. Olaf Choir ran counter to the Christian liberal arts philosophy of the College. While these extracurricular activities are of high quality, religious significance, and public relations value, maintained the editor, they remove the students involved from the academic scene.[16] Before long, a rebuttal came from a loyal alumna in a letter to the editor. She pointed out that in its early years St. Olaf College grew because of the Choir's appearances all over the country, that the Choir spreads the word of God through song to over 75,000 people annually, that 10,000 see and hear the Christmas program, and that

Studying on tour, 1959

Choir members have always maintained good scholastic records.[17] Regarding her last point, studies have confirmed that music students do better in their academic work than any other group.

In the meantime, the St. Olaf Choir went on with its regular touring program, setting out on January 30, 1959, to sing twenty-seven concerts in eleven midwestern and southern states. A Houston critic wrote of the concert in that city: "The whole occasion was of a beauty which inevitably suggests the word 'heavenly.' One cannot be sufficiently grateful to the spirit and artistry of those who made it available to a large and spellbound audience."[18] As usual, the singers remembered some of the lighter elements of the trip. A certain kind of dessert was always in evidence at the church suppers along the way: "lemon fluff with graham cracker crust and a delicate puff of whipped cream on top."

The Choir enjoyed the unique atmosphere of New Orleans and Bourbon Street, despite the fact that their visit fell on Friday, February 13th. During intermission at the New Orleans concert, the mayor presented a plaque and a gold key to the city to Olaf Christiansen and Fred Schmidt, and conferred upon them the degree of Honorary Citizens of New Orleans.[19]

Olaf and Fred could enjoy the fun of New Orleans in February, but should they take the Choir to Radio City Music Hall in New York for four weeks in March? The program director of Radio City theater had asked Fred Schmidt if the St. Olaf Choir could give four 15-minute appearances daily as part of a special Easter season series. Fred asked why he wanted the St. Olaf Choir when there were fine choral organizations such as the Westminster Choir closer to New York. The answer was that he wanted the finest choir in the country.

Fred told President Granskou about the offer, pointing out the extraordinary publicity to be realized in appearing before fifteen or sixteen thousand people every day. Fred also reminded the president of Olaf's high sense of purpose in wanting the Choir's message to make an impact on people's lives. "Well, let's call Olaf in," said Granskou. As soon as he made the connection between Radio City and the famous Rockettes who "go and kick their legs up in the air," Olaf settled the matter. "That's no place for the St. Olaf Choir," he said. Another obvious objection was that Choir members would miss another four weeks of classes not long after returning from a three-week tour.[20]

The Choir did not have to join the Rockettes to be subject to some good-natured spoofing on the campus. In 1949 a student-produced musical satire borrowed as its title the Northfield motto, "Cows, Colleges, and Contentment," in telling the story of how humble "St. Houston College" rose to national fame because of its traveling rodeo from "Kristy's Corral."[21] In 1960 another spoof took the form of an April First *Messenger* article about "St. Olaf's Big Choir" on its return from a good-will tour of Red China that had begun in 1957. "The Big Choir walked across the United States while chanting in unison." It walked through deserts and floods in long pink and green robes, crossed the Pacific on small wooden rafts, but spent only two weeks in China because the return journey would take at least two years. Once back, the director, Dr. Olaf Trygve Gunvald Rasmuss Jorsalfarsson, declared in a triumphant speech that the tour had been "very successful."[22]

Choir relaxing, ca. 1951

St. Olaf Choir in Boe Chapel, 1960

After Fifty Years

The St. Olaf Choir observed its Golden Anniversary in 1962, fifty years after the St. John's Church Choir adopted the name, "The St. Olaf Choir," as it set out on the 1912 Easter tour into Wisconsin and Illinois. The Golden Anniversary tour was to the east and south. Two of the cities visited, Madison and Chicago, had been host to the Choir on that first tour. In Chicago the Choir spent one day making recordings, and the next evening gave its official Fiftieth Anniversary concert in the Civic Opera House. The home concert took place in the gymnasium on the St. Olaf campus on Sunday, February 25, 1962, with a reunion of the 1912 Choir taking place before the concert.[23]

Members of 1912 Choir with Olaf Christiansen
Reunion, February 25, 1962
Front: Edith Glasoe Kildahl, Bessie Gulbrandson, Ella Hjertaas Roe, Mrs.
J. Arneberg
Back : Henry Tufte, O. M. Kleven, Mrs. G. W. Kirn, Anna E. Mohn, William
C. Benson, Olaf C. Christiansen

Issued in November of 1962 by Mercury Records, the new recording of the Choir's favorites was called, "Fifty Golden Years." Included were "Benedictus," "How Fair the Church," "God's Son Has Made Me Free," "Beautiful Savior," and three compositions by Olaf C. Christiansen: "Trumpets of Zion," "Prelude to Christmas," and "Son of Man Be Free."

Sales of a previous St. Olaf Choir album had been so successful that Mercury Records rushed to make the 1962 recording available ahead of schedule.[24]

The Golden Anniversary year elicited a backward look to the Choir's beginning and the high points of its history. Articles in campus publications, as well as tour reviews, touched on F. Melius Christiansen and the founding of the Choir, the 1912 Easter tour, the 1913 tour of Norway, and the entry of the Choir into American musical life in 1920 when it sang in such centers as Cleveland, Rochester, New York, and Philadelphia. [25]

Attention was also given to the more recent history of the Choir and its current director, Dr. Olaf C. Christiansen, who succeeded his father in 1943 and added "new lustre" to the rich choral tradition. The 1962 Choir of sixty-six voices presented concerts that year that began with works of the 16th and 17th century, including Jacob Handl's "Resurrection" and Francesco Durante's "Misericordias Domini." Handl

1962 Album Cover

1962 Tour Poster. Anna Odegaard '62 and Mary Gulbrandsen '62

(or Jacobus Gallus) was one of Olaf's favorite composers. Part II offered twentieth century settings of ancient texts, among them Olaf C. Christiansen's "Trumpets of Zion," based on Joel 2, and Hugo Distler's "Sing to the Lord a New Song" (Psalm 98). Part III presented old and new hymns, folksongs, and carols, including E. Paladilhe's "Benedictus," Olaf's "Son of Man Be Free," and Grieg's "God's Son Has Made Me Free."[26]

At one concert in the south during this tour, Olaf faced the not uncommon problem of an audience that dared not applaud in church. Not only did applause encourage the Choir, but it also gave time to get the pitch for the next piece. Both he and his father had been in the situation before, helping their listeners loosen up by quoting Psalm 47, "Clap your hands, all peoples! Shout to God with loud songs of joy!"[27] Indeed, F. Melius had based an anthem on this text. On this occasion, when total silence met the Choir after the first group and again after the second, Olaf turned to the congregation, gave them a long look, and said quietly, "Don't you believe? If you believe what we are singing, you must respond."

He went on as the Choir members stood, scarcely breathing, wondering what would come next. Said Olaf, "You can respond by putting one hand together with the other hand," and he demonstrated how this was done. Or you can say "Amen," he suggested, "but if you believe, then you must respond."

Then the response came. Not clapping, but a little stamping of the feet. It increased, and suddenly the church was filled with the thundering sound of hundreds of feet hitting the floor. [28]

The audience of 1,100 in the Mayo Civic Auditorium in Rochester, Minnesota, needed no coaching to applaud as the Choir sang there the night before returning to Northfield. Robert Oudal, Rochester reviewer, welcomed what he called the "feeling of dramatic abandonment" that was projected when the Choir sounded out the last three notes, "Free, Free, Free!" in the well-known anthem by Edvard Grieg. He also pointed out that of the eighteen numbers on the program, one-third were written or arranged by F. Melius and Olaf Christiansen, a fact that served to emphasize "the part these men have played in establishing and perpetuating this tradition."[29]

After fifty years the St. Olaf Choir had become a well-known and much-admired feature on the American choral music landscape. The fact that it had known only two directors, both of them Christiansens, added significantly to the reputation it enjoyed in the United States and abroad. What F. Melius Christiansen founded has endured in the work of the son, said a reviewer who heard the Jubilee concert in Chicago, noting that Olaf Christiansen built his program, as his father had done, around the chorale, Latin motets, and Scandinavian hymns and folk songs.[30] It may be noted, however, that Olaf made much more use of Latin motets than his father had done.

Critics and audiences everywhere knew what to expect at a St. Olaf Choir concert. The singers in their purple velvet robes entered briskly from the wings, mounted the risers in good order, and stood poised and alert. Thunderous applause always greeted F. Melius Christiansen when he made his appearance, and the same was true when Olaf Christiansen took the podium. Both directors were known for a dignified conducting style that avoided mannerisms. Both frequently employed the delayed attack, the first sound coming slightly after the conductor's initial entry cue.

As always, the entire program was sung from memory and without accompaniment. "Unaccompanied human voices raised in song can produce the most beautiful sounds on earth as Minnesota's justly famous St. Olaf Lutheran choir proved," wrote a reviewer for the *Atlanta Constitution*.[31] Although F. Melius was known to write choral pieces with instrumental accompaniment, both he and Olaf firmly committed the Choir to a cappella singing. If the St. Olaf Choir should be accompanied by instruments, wrote F. Melius, it "would change into something other than what it is."[32] In a 1968 article Olaf made the case for unaccompanied singing in these words:

> We try to sing with honesty, sincerity, with fullest understanding and in the most natural manner, avoiding any vocal gymnastics or embellishments. This is one reason why we sing without accompaniment. Subtle interpretations and spontaneous emphasis come best through a small, unaccompanied, alert and well-disciplined group.[33]

On the concert stage the St. Olaf Choir continued to be known for its "mysterious" way of getting its pitch (by pitch pipes blown unobtrusively during the applause), the "rich velvety quality" of the voices, clean attacks and releases, clear enunciation, faultless intonation, balance between sections, controlled dynamics, choral blend, sensitivity to the texts, and responsiveness to the director's every move. Thomas Willis, Chicago critic, held that the singing style of the Choir had remained constant. He wrote: "Discipline, precision of attack, and careful tuning of vowels build a rock solid sound which minimizes the individual voice."[34]

It was ever Olaf Christiansen's lot to be regarded as one who carried forward what had been begun by his famous father. Typical was the way critic Robert Oudal began his review after the Choir's appearance in Rochester on February 24, 1962:

> Lutheran choral music would not be what it is today if there had been no F. Melius Christiansen and his famous St. Olaf Choir. It was he who some 50 years ago began an a cappella choir belt of the nation. This tradition is now in the capable hands of one of his sons, Dr. Olaf C. Christiansen.[35]

In light of the fifty-year landmark, one could scarcely write about a St. Olaf Choir performance without recapping the father-to-son succession and underscoring the continuities. But the idea of the Christiansen tradition was often present in the minds of reviewers and the public, entirely apart from

Los Angeles Music Center

anniversary occasions. When the Choir appeared in The Music Center in Los Angeles in 1965, Albert Goldberg, music editor for the *Los Angeles Times*, was full of admiration for the Choir, its founder, the late F. Melius Christiansen, "a short, craggy man," and his son, Olaf C. Christiansen, "a tall, craggy man." As a veteran reviewer who had heard the Choir many times, Goldberg wrote of what had remained the same:

> Under both Christiansens it has maintained a notably high standard of a cappella singing. Despite the inevitable changes of personnel, it sounds like precisely the same group each time one hears it. There is no appreciable difference in basic style, in the concept of natural, unforced tone, in technical polish and purity of intonation.[36]

Such commendation is to be welcomed as part of a very affirmative review. The St. Olaf Choir brought a refreshing experience and was always a welcome visitor, said Goldberg. The other side of the compliment is an implication, probably unintended, that the Choir should remain what it was when led by F. Melius Christiansen.

In accepting the offer to come to St. Olaf, Olaf was conscious of the fact that his work would be linked to and compared with the contribution of his father. As Albert Rykken Johnson wrote on the basis of a 1970 interview with Olaf, "With the possible exception of the area of choral-vocal technique and a broader literature background, Olaf admits he will possibly

345

always be remembered in the shadow of the monumental achievements of his father, a step he knowingly took."[37]

All of which calls for a specific recognition of what Olaf achieved in leading the St. Olaf Choir into new musical territory. No one questions that he honored and confirmed his father's creative work, but he did more than maintain a tradition. What the memory of Olaf Christiansen deserves is a grateful appraisal of a musicianship and a choral leadership that was his own. He added distinctive elements to the life of the St. Olaf Choir.

Training the Choir

Olaf Christiansen was a singer and a voice teacher, which his father was not. Studying voice in New York, Olaf learned from Paul Parks that vocal clarity depends on knowing how to make the vowels sound pure. Hence the vocalizing exercises, along with the stretching and back rubs that all Choir members who sang for Olaf remember so vividly. The beginning of each rehearsal included the singing of different vowel sounds up and down the scale. Singers recalled the intensive work on achieving bright vowel sounds, such as the "ee's" and "aa's." They drilled by singing "bye-bye-bye-bye," "din-din-din-dee-dee-dee," and the ever-familiar "dickie-dickie-dickie-deee" to the

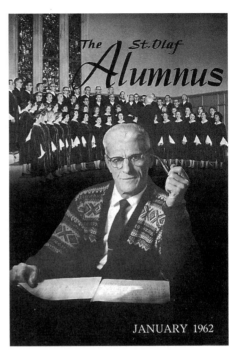

Dr. Olaf C. Christiansen
Director, St. Olaf Choir
Cover by Nels P. Isaacson, Choir
photo by Hoffman Studio, Northfield

Pre-concert back rub

346

point where a bemused yearbook writer observed, "Every day the St. Olaf Choir gets together to sing along with Olaf; its members massage, crane, um-hum, and dickeydee."[38]

Vocalizing with Olaf

Olaf himself wrote about the vocalizing procedure: "To achieve vowel unity, we vocalize every day on all the vowels. We listen and try to feel the rhythm as we vocalize. When we come to a vowel sound in a song that gives us trouble, we stop to correct the enunciation until we get the unified sound that gives us a clear and understandable word."[39] One anticipates the consonant so the vowel can be sung "on the beat." When this is done, "the words will be more clearly heard."[40]

In the margin of a piece of music Olaf wrote in bold red letters: "To vowel on pulse!" On the importance of getting the vowel on the beat, he once said, "Go with the vowel on the bounce of the ball."[41] Coaches Tom Porter and Charles Lunder of the St. Olaf Department of Physical Education recall that every fall Olaf stopped by the athletic office to borrow a soccer ball, always making sure it was well inflated. At Choir rehearsals he would use the ball to illustrate rhythm, quick response, and the exact sounding of the vowel. He constantly reminded his singers to avoid sliding into the vowel but hitting it right in the middle of the pitch. [42]

It goes without saying that Olaf followed his father in "dispensing with the tremolo voice" and controlling the sound, the purpose of which was to get everyone to sing in tune. Over the decades critics have cited the lack of vibrato as a feature of the St. Olaf Choir. In 1968, Olaf's last year as director of the Choir, one reviewer offered a brief historical note on the subject. He wrote:

> Over the last 50 years choral conductors throughout the United States have been waging war over the "right" tone to use. Many have lined up behind the wide-vibrato sound championed at Princeton's Westminster Choir school. Just as many others have copied the choir which presented a concert last night in Orchestra Hall—Minnesota's St. Olaf Choir.
>
> The St. Olaf, or "Christiansen sound"—started by F. Melius Christiansen in 1912 and sustained by his son, the choir's present conductor, Dr. Olaf C. Christiansen—is as straight as a dime, perfectly blended, and shuns all natural vibrato [or wobble] in the voice.[43]

As was suggested earlier, the "Christiansen sound" was a style of singing that was long practiced in northern Germany and the Scandinavian countries. F. Melius Christiansen made it known in the United States and Olaf indeed sustained it, but on his own terms.

Olaf put the Choir through vigorous warm-ups, stressing precise entrances and cut-offs, coaching the singers in breathing exercises, having them practice singing long notes, working on enunciation, and always aiming for the best ensemble sound. His father once began

Daughter and Father. Sigrid and Olaf Christiansen, ca. 1955

a letter to him with the statement, "Ensemble singing means to sing together, begin together, and end together."[44]

Yet Olaf did not accept the common view that he followed his father in demanding the so-called "straight tone." One year he made a recording of Choir member Ann Andersen's senior recital in order to demonstrate that a singer did not have to have a "straight tone" to be in the Choir.[45] To a student interviewer Olaf explained how his father, not being a singer, would use word pictures in instructing the Choir. "See that spot on the wall?" F. Melius would ask, "Well, sing straight to it." Said Olaf, "I fought that straight line type of singing. I believe in training voices to do what they are supposed to do. That's what is needed if they are to do all the music available." [46]

One type of music available that Olaf regularly worked into his programs was the polyphonic music of the 16th and 17th centuries. For such music, one reviewer noted, the "St. Olaf tone, a straight, flute-like sound most shown in the sopranos," worked very well. It helped the Choir make clear "the complex glories of Bach and Victoria."[47] Olaf would have agreed with the idea, but not with the vocabulary. He preferred to speak of a controlled vibrato rather than a straight tone.

In a 1965 article, "Solo and Ensemble Singing," Olaf expressed his views on vibrato and "straight tone." He wrote: "The wide vibrato is not tolerated in the *a cappella choir* because it is too earthy and sensuous for religious music—especially for 16th century polyphonic church music." All voices should have a natural vibrato. What one is after is to control or stabilize the vibrato, to limit the extent of deviation above and below the central pitch.[48]

With respect to the term, "straight tone," he wrote as follows: "What might sound like a straight tone is the result of listening to each other, thus getting in tune—making a pure *unison*." By controlling the vibrato, one is able to make a whole section sound like a single voice, as when a stranded wire cable wound together looks like a single wire. "There is no such thing as a *straight tone* among well-trained singers," he wrote. "I wouldn't have a STRAIGHT voice in my *a cappella* choir, but I demand trained voices, super-trained singers." Then he specified the aims of music teachers for both solo and ensemble singing. "Together we work toward producing pure vowels, sustained legato style, articulation, and declamatory style, controlled dynamics, expanding pitch and color range, flexibility, musicianship and listening habits."[49]

Such efforts with the St. Olaf Choir brought results, as Winthrop Sargeant recognized writing for the *New Yorker* after the Choir had sung in Philharmonic Hall, New York, in 1964. Sargeant wrote that he was especially appreciative in regard to one particular point: "The choir offered one of those comparatively infrequent opportunities to hear music performed in true pitch and with almost immaculate intonation. True pitch . . . gives a special glitter to the music in which it is used—a sort of heavenly purity of intonation, in contrast to the blurring often heard in our concert halls. It appears in the work of very well-trained *a-cappella* groups, like this one."[50]

An Arizona reviewer also recognized the thorough preparation when he heard the Choir the following year in Tempe, Arizona, in a concert held in Grady Gammage Auditorium, designed by Frank Lloyd Wright. Some choirs flat as the evening wears on, wrote William J. Nazzaro, "but when the choir is properly trained, as is the St. Olaf, you hear perfect intervals, fifths, sevenths, so that the

*Grady Gammage Auditorium
Tempe, Arizona, 1965*

349

harmonies sound sharper than usual," that is, right on pitch, "and this sharpness makes for a much livelier and dynamic kind of sound." It was a penetrating kind of sound that results from the combination of relatively little vibrato and pure intonation. The reason for the unusual sound is that "the St. Olaf Choir sings in exact pitch."[51]

The hours of training to control the vibrato, to sing in tune, to achieve purity of vowels, to breathe properly, and all the other measures had as their goal the delivery of the words of the text to the listeners. It has been said of Olaf that he brought to the St. Olaf Choir the two elements of "rhythmic precision and textual intelligibility."[52] He and the Choir worked to correct enunciation until they achieved a sound, as he said, "that gives us a clear and understandable word."

To a degree that went beyond the work of his father, Olaf Christiansen stressed clean articulation of the words for the sake of the message of the song. Believing, with his father, that sacred music bestows gifts of beauty and meaning upon those who hear it, he was inclined to emphasize the religious content more than his father did. And when it came to choosing what the Choir offered, Olaf found and introduced a new repertory that he combined with the old with impressive artistic skill.

New and Old Repertory

After the St. Olaf Choir had sung in Sacramento in February of 1965, the review in *The Sacramento Bee* the next day appeared under the headline, "Great Music Helps Make St. Olaf A Great Choir." The Choir sang with inspiration from three sources, said the reviewer, the Lord whom it glorifies, the composers, and the director. The virtues of the St. Olaf Choir were all in evidence: the quality of the music, the clarity and unity of the sound, the flexibility in phrasing, the projection of the music's emotions, the sense of pitch, and the dynamic style of the conductor. "Of all these virtues," wrote William C. Glackin, "the one which seems to me the most easily overlooked is also one of the most fundamental: Christiansen's abilities as a program builder."[53]

This critic was uncommonly sensitive to what Olaf Christiansen intended in the flow and contrasts of the program. The concert began with "Cantate Domino" by Heinrich Schütz followed by Jacob Handl's "Jesu dulcis Memoria," from the 17th and 16th centuries respectively. "Then, as if warmed up for a major effort, he [Dr. Christiansen] launched into the marvelous 'O Vos Omnes' of Tomas Luis de Victoria (still in the late Renaissance), a dark, passionately sorrowful work full of excruciating harmonic suspensions which were so tensely hung in the air by the choir as to wake vibrations in your very nerves and bones."[54]

Christiansen then "relieved this sorrow" with "Surrexit Pastor Bonus" by Orlando di Lasso, a contemporary of Victoria. "The dramatic effect was overwhelming," continued Glackin, "as it was a little later when the strikingly dissonant crucifixion scene by the 20th century Swedish composer Sven-Erik Bäck, "At the Cross 'Remember Me,'" was followed without pause by the optimistic message in the majestic Russian sonorities of Tschesnokoff's 'Salvation Is Created.'"[55]

Having begun with the Renaissance, Christiansen "did not hesitate to leap right into the 20th century with 'I Am The Lord' by the German Ernst Pepping, full of appealing modern surprises, and the lovely 'Prayer on Christmas Eve' by the Belgian Flor Peeters." After brief comments on the other parts of the program, Glackin concluded "that the St. Olaf reputation is grounded the way a great chorus must be grounded—on great music as well as technique."[56]

In program building, as in training the Choir in vocal technique, Olaf C. Christiansen continued features of his father's work but added new and distinctive touches. For F. Melius Christiansen, selecting numbers for the program was the most challenging part of his work. For Olaf Christiansen, the most difficult job was selecting the student singers who would constitute the St. Olaf Choir.[57] That did not mean that building a program was easy for Olaf, but his broader knowledge of musical literature enabled him to construct a richer repertory.

Olaf Christiansen's work in establishing a repertory from which he chose music for the annual concert tours can be described as following three tracks. Along one track he made selections from the compositions and arrangements that his father had contributed to choral literature. On a second track he added church music from the sixteenth and seventeenth centuries. The third track represented the finding and incorporating of new music of the twentieth century, including his own compositions, arrangements, and editions. By the time he retired in 1968, Olaf had published over 150 pieces.[58]

Former Choir members and veteran St. Olaf Choir concert-goers could easily list familiar works by F. Melius Christiansen that appeared repeatedly in concert programs during Olaf's tenure as

OCC at his desk

director. In 1950, for example, one finds "Wake, Awake," by Philipp Nicolai, arranged by F. Melius, "Hosanna," "Lost in the Night," Finnish folk song, "Be Ye Joyful, Earth and Sky," "The Christmas Symbol," and "Beautiful Savior."

It should be noted that Olaf Christiansen was unhesitant in making adaptations and editorial changes in choral compositions, even those written or arranged by his father. F. Melius Christiansen had tossed "The Christmas Symbol" aside, regarding it as too much of a "ditty," but Olaf took it up and reworked it, slowing the tempo, adding an introduction, filling out the chording, and setting the piece for soprano solo with hummed accompaniment. The result was an absolute gem and a concert favorite.[59] Olaf also made changes in "Beautiful Savior," raising the key a half step to D major and revising the score in certain details.

The 1954 program listed "How Fair the Church," arranged by FMC, "Psalm 50," Koenig's "This Night a Wondrous Revelation," also arranged by FMC, and "Lullaby on Christmas Eve." A glance at the 1964 program reveals "Praise to the Lord," from the Stralsund *Gesangbuch*, an arrangement by FMC and "In Dulci Jubilo," a fourteenth century German melody arranged by FMC. The program for Olaf's last tour has the F. Melius Christiansen arrangement of C. E. F. Weyse's "O Day Full of Grace." All the programs include "Beautiful Savior."[60]

Olaf made use of a total of thirty-five of his father's choral numbers. He never used his "Beauty in Humility" and several works of a more secular nature. Of the various compositions by F. Melius Christiansen based on words by Oscar Overby, Olaf included in his programs "Regeneration" and "Glorification," the third and fourth movements of a motet entitled *Celestial Spring*, and "Love in Grief," the second movement or "verse" of *From Grief to Glory*.

Among compositions or arrangements by F. Melius Christiansen that Olaf Christiansen used in his concert programs four times or more are the following pieces: "The Christmas Symbol," revised by Olaf C. Christiansen, "How Fair the Church," "Kingdom of God," "Lost in the Night," "O Day Full of Grace," "Praise to the Lord," *Psalm 50*, "Regeneration," Movement 3 of *Celestial Spring*, and "Wake, Awake." Absent from this list are such familiar pieces as "Dayspring of Eternity" and "From Heaven Above," both sung three times, and "Lamb of God," sung only twice under Olaf.[61]

The second track Olaf Christiansen followed in establishing a choral repertory was to identify and use sacred music selections from the sixteenth and seventeenth centuries. One is reminded that the time of Johann Sebastian Bach (1685-1750), whose motets F. Melius Christiansen used in his programs, was the late Baroque period. Several of the early composers favored by Olaf Christiansen, on the other hand, take one back a full century or more before Bach to the early Baroque or late Renaissance period.

Examples of these Renaissance composers and a few of their pieces selected for concert use by Olaf may be mentioned. Giovanni Pierluigi da Palestrina wrote "Hodie Christus Natus Est," edited by OCC. Giuseppe Corsi composed "Adoramus Te, Christe," a personal favorite of Olaf's which he also edited. Both of these numbers were sung by the Choir in eight concert tours. "O Magnum Mysterium" by Giovanni Gabrieli was sung in 1967 and 1968. Tomas Luis de Victoria also wrote a piece entitled "O Magnum Mysterium" as well as "O Quam Gloriosum" and "O Vos Omnes."

Familiar FMC choral pieces

Twice the Choir sang "Ave Verum Corpus" by William Byrd, and four times it offered Orlando di Lasso's "Surrexit Pastor Bonus."

Heinrich Schütz (1585-1672) provided "Cantate Domino," "I Am the Resurrection and the True Life," "Lord, if I but Thee May Have," "Psalm 97," and "Psalm 121." Four times in the fifties and again in 1966 the Choir sang Johann Hermann Schein's "Die mit Tränen säen." "Plorate Filii Israel" by Giacomo Carissimi and edited by OCC was sung by the Choir during three different years.[62]

In selecting this Renaissance music, Olaf Christiansen was also choosing a sound and a style of singing that was different from that of his father. The longer programs and the exacting technique required to achieve the exquisite clarity of these early works reflected his own vocal background. Rigorous vocal training, emphasis on clarity of diction and other techniques previously discussed laid the ground work for this extended repertory. The so-called "covered tone" employed by F. Melius Christiansen for his Baroque and Romantic repertory was not suitable for the Renaissance music introduced by Olaf who wanted a more brilliant tone.[63]

This brilliant, controlled sound worked well on the 16th and 17th

This brilliant, controlled sound worked well on the 16th and 17th century motets by Heinrich Schütz, Giovanni Gabrieli, William Byrd, and Giovanni de Palestrina, observed Chicago critic Kenneth Sanson. These composers had written for and used only boys' voices in the parts taken by women in modern mixed choirs; "thus the hooty St. Olaf sound made good sense historically."[64] Another reviewer found that "the pure, vibratoless tone that is quite suitable to most of their repertoire makes an unusually fine blend possible."[65]

Terms used by reviewers often need qualification. The "hooty" or flute-like sound applies to the sopranos in particular, whom Olaf trained to sing with a firm, controlled sound, but he disliked qualities described as "thin," "straight," and "white." Nor did he espouse "vibratoless" singing, although he was certainly known for insisting on the vocal discipline, purity, precise tuning, and accuracy of pitch that created much less vibrato.[66]

The third track along which Olaf Christiansen developed the repertory for the St. Olaf Choir was his successful effort to widen the scope of music from the twentieth century. Works by his father belonged to twentieth century music, of course, as did Olaf's own compositions, arrangements, and editions. But most striking was Olaf's achievement in bringing to the notice of the American public contemporary music that could have remained relatively unknown had it not been sung by the St. Olaf Choir.

A clear example is "Alleluia" from "Brazilian Psalm" by Jean Berger, introduced to American audiences by the St. Olaf Choir in 1949. A reviewer who heard it in 1965 described it as "rhythmically controlled and well articulated," and a delight to the audience.[67] Berger acknowledged that his attitude toward composing was changed when his piece became more

Composer Jean Berger

widely known. He wrote: "I have always composed. However, I never thought of becoming a professional composer until, indeed, the encouragement given me by Olaf Christiansen."[68] Berger, who is Jewish, once told Olaf that Christian choirs made his music known.[69]

About a year after presenting "Alleluia," Olaf placed Berger's "Vision of Peace" on the program. Robert P. Wetzler, whose "Sing Ye, Sing Noel" was on the 1967 program, recalled his reaction at hearing the "Vision" number at the first St. Olaf Choir concert he ever attended. He and a cousin, both avid Stan Kenton jazz fans, had never heard such singing before.

> What was most impressive was the way the choir sang modern sounds with such precision. Jean Berger's "Vision of Peace" was one of the numbers programmed. Here were sounds not too far removed from what Stan Kenton was doing in jazz at that time![70]

Other Berger compositions sung by the St. Olaf Choir were "The Eyes of All Wait upon Thee," "Glory be to God," "Psalm 13," "Thy Kingdom Come," and "Trust in the Lord."[71]

In selecting twentieth century works Olaf Christiansen did not seek to be among the avant-garde, but he knew the contemporary trends and at times moved ahead of them. When he had the Choir perform "Cantata of Peace" by Darius Milhaud in 1948 and 1949, he was venturing into new terrain. Hugo Distler and Ernst Pepping were regarded as doing advanced work for the time. The St. Olaf Choir sang Distler's "Psalm 98" and Pepping's "Come Unto Him," "Laud Him," and "Ich bin der Herr." At Pepping's request, Olaf edited the first two of these and had them published, thus bringing Pepping's name before American audiences. Other choirs began singing Distler and Pepping after the St. Olaf Choir had made their works known.[72]

Normand Lockwood, Olaf's colleague at Oberlin, wrote three Psalms that were published in the Oberlin Choir Series. One of them, "Psalm 117," was dedicated to Olaf and Ellen Christiansen. Four times in the fifties and again in 1961 the Choir sang "Psalm 134," the text beginning with the words, "Behold, bless ye the Lord, all ye servants of the Lord." In 1967 it sang Lockwood's Psalm 9, "I Will Give thanks."

Among Olaf's most unique programming choices were Adolf Brunner's very demanding "Come and Let Us Walk in the Light of God," the

Lockwood's "Psalm 117"

355

text of which Olaf translated, and Sven-Erik Bäck's "At the Cross, 'Remember Me.'" The latter piece represents a new wave Swedish choral style that demands perfect intonation, clarity, blend, and balance. Both numbers pose difficulties for any choir.[73] When the St. Olaf Choir sang the Bäck selection in Seattle in 1965, Louis R. Guzzo of *The Seattle Times* wrote as follows:

> Without question the peak of ingenuity of interpretation and perfection in intonation, dynamics and ensemble came with the halting, inspiring "At the Cross, 'Remember Me,'" by Sven-Erik Bäck.
>
> The St. Olaf Choir has no fear of dissonance or atonality when the cause is glorification of the Lord; its rendition of the "Remember Me" was ecstatic, profoundly moving and a rare experience in the concert hall. The work is recommended to all choirs—whether they are capable of solving its difficulties or not.[74]

The basic progression in a concert program as Olaf constructed it was from heavy to light, from "meat and potatoes" to "dessert." First came the early motets, then a Bach motet, "a stepping stone between the rather impersonal earlier music to a warmer, more intimate form," as Olaf put it. Music from the Romantic period could include Russian church music or the Lutheran chorales, with works by F. Melius Christiansen and by contemporary American and European composers. The final group consisted of lighter carols, folk songs, and solos, music which "children and those without a wide musical background can understand and appreciate."[75] Among the lighter selections that pleased listeners were Olaf's arrangement of "Deilig er den himmel blaa," the southern folk tune "I wonder as I wander," and Katherine Davis's "Carol of the Drum."

"Remember Me" in Swedish

Introduced to the public by Olaf and the St. Olaf Choir in 1954, "Carol of the Drum" became a seasonal favorite across the country.

In planning his programs, Olaf also liked to fit the music to historical, musical, or textual patterns. One of his favorites was the birth, life, death, and resurrection of Christ. Another was to move from the Classical Era, to the Romantic, and to the Contemporary. He would often group motets together, or Psalm settings, or "Three Songs of Prophecy" where he used Jean Berger's "Vision of Peace," Adolf Brunner's "Come and Let Us Walk in the Light of God," and his own "Trumpets of Zion."[76]

Olaf Christiansen divided the concert into four parts whereas his father used a three-part program, The singers would perform better, and be less apt to faint, if they were not on stage for such a long time. Going off stage three times was good for the Choir's vocal and physical health.[77]

The concert tour program for Olaf's last year as director, 1967-68, had the following four-part structure: Part I, Motets and Hymns; Part II, Twentieth Century Anthems; Part III, *Sing Ye to the Lord*, by J. S. Bach; Part IV, "Old and New Hymns and Carols." That final program included four works by Olaf C. Christiansen: "Son of Man Be Free," "Lift Up Your Heads," a processional arranged by Olaf, "The Song of Peace," and "Sing Nowell, Sing Gloria."[78]

Olaf's programming came in for critical appraisal. On the negative side, Doris Reno in Miami thought the 1966 program was narrow in scope and could be enriched by something from the Catholic liturgy, old English works, selections from Hebrew and Russian liturgies, and some Negro spirituals.[79] Actually, Olaf was both criticized and praised for introducing works from the Catholic liturgy into St. Olaf Choir concerts. One listener objected to the Choir's singing of "Ave Maria" while a reviewer credited him with conducting "a kind of musical ecumenical movement of his own," dipping into Catholic church music of the 15th and 16th centuries. "His singers perform the music of Vittoria and Palestrina just as sensitively as they sing the works of Bach."[80] Admittedly, Olaf did not use many spirituals, but in 1955 on the Norway tour he included "Deep River," arranged by H. T. Burleigh.

A more positive view of the 1966 program was voiced by Lorraine Nelson, an Indianapolis critic, who characterized it as a "who's who" in the history of choral music that left no period wanting.[81] Two years earlier Gerald Kloss of the Milwaukee Journal wrote: "It requires a masterful touch in the programing to keep the listener alert, and Dr. Christiansen obviously has it. He kept the pace varied, in moods and rhythms, displaying expert showmanship." Kloss thought that the processional, "Crown Him King of Glory," arranged by Olaf Christiansen, was especially effective.[82]

The Ultimate Goal

As director of the St. Olaf Choir from 1941 to 1968, Olaf C. Christiansen had an exceptionally clear vision of the Choir's purpose. While his father, F. Melius Christiansen, was sensitive to the beauty and appeal of the religious texts sung by the Choir, Olaf was more explicit in stating that the Choir had a religious mission. The tour program for 1963, the year following the Choir's Jubilee, stated the Choir's purpose as Olaf wanted it expressed:

> Throughout its fifty years the Choir, its members all St. Olaf students, has striven for perfection, not for its own sake, but to eliminate distractions from the music and text and to make the religious message the central purpose of the concert. Its lasting purpose is to reach perfection in singing the eternal music of the Christian faith.

When Olaf arrived at St. Olaf from Oberlin in 1941, he found among Choir members a preoccupation with reviews and recognition that disappointed him. One of his measures was to institute a devotional period before concerts, a practice that continues to the present.[83] Another was to train the singers in the techniques necessary to make the words of each song as understandable as possible. As noted earlier, Olaf gave special attention to the articulation of the vowels. "This unity of vowel sounds is the key essential in fulfilling our purpose of making the words of the text clear."[84]

And the texts chosen were choral works of religious content. In his own writings and in one interview after another, Olaf stated that the purpose of the St. Olaf Choir was to bring a specific religious message to the listeners.

Choir in Boe Memorial Chapel   STOARCHIV

As he neared retirement he told a reporter for the student paper, "The choir is a medium through which choir members and those who listen to us may experience the beauty and the joy of the Christian message."[85]

In order to get the message across, the Choir worked to remove all hindrances. Wrote Olaf, "We try to eliminate all distractions such as impurity of harmony, ragged rhythm, and distorted tone so that the religious message of the text can be paramount." Olaf hoped that Choir members would experience some memorable moments, some "passing reminders of God," whether in a great concert hall or in rehearsal. "When we have overcome the technical difficulties of a song, we can grasp the essence of the musical and verbal thought."[86]

But Olaf knew what it was to encounter discouragement and still find a way to continue the mission. He tells of calling his wife, Ellen, when the tour didn't seem to be going well. "We give our hearts and souls and energies," he said over the phone, "and it doesn't seem to make a dent." Said Ellen in response, "Who do you think you are, God?" As Olaf reflected on the experience, he commented, "We had tried to convert people. That is not our purpose. It's merely to sensitize them."[87]

A fuller statement of the Choir's purpose or goal appears at the end of an article Olaf wrote during his final year as director. Its title "A Little Like Love Letters," refers to Olaf's idea that songs, like love letters, carry additional meanings between the lines that are important to the interpretation of the text. The article discusses the program, the students and the work that goes on in rehearsals, and finally the goals, of which Olaf had this to say:

> We have many educational goals for the students, but the ultimate goal of the St. Olaf Choir goes beyond the members and includes both singers and listeners. We aim to sensitize people. We bring them a religious message—not necessarily to convert them, but to sensitize them. If our music can sensitize them, can reach into their emotions, then they will leave our concert with a different attitude toward themselves, toward others, and toward God. When this happens, we have reached our highest aspiration.[88]

Olaf Christiansen's dedication to the religious mission of the St. Olaf Choir was in evidence as the Choir made its final tour under his leadership in early 1968. On Friday, February 9th, the Choir sang in Philharmonic Hall in New York. As he was acknowledging a prolonged standing ovation at the conclusion of the concert, Olaf cupped his hands to his mouth and called out to the crowd, "Thank God, too!"[89]

It was a gesture befitting the spontaneity and nonconformity of a Christiansen, but it was also Olaf's personal declaration. As he told a

Philharmonic Hall, New York
February 9, 1968

student interviewer earlier in the year, "There is no better life than to lead people to God, and I enjoy nothing more than to find choir members who will help me."[90]

Before the Choir left New York, Carl Apone, a music editor from Pittsburgh, interviewed Olaf by phone for an article on the Choir and the director's approaching retirement. Olaf told Mr. Apone of a line from a review that was one of his happiest memories from his twenty-seven years of directing. An unknown reviewer had said: "No matter how grim the music, there was always a sense of hope in the way they sang." The editor

Choir members and poster
Lincoln Center, Philharmonic Hall

360

commented: "The choir sings religious works, and Dr. Christiansen views music as part of a missionary effort. His religious music has obviously reached and moved audiences the world over."[91]

The significance and emotion related to Dr. Olaf C. Christiansen's last tour with the St. Olaf Choir was well captured in a paragraph by Allen Hughes of *The New York Times* who wrote, "For most of the audience that filled Philharmonic Hall last night, the concert given there was more than a musical occasion. It was the leave-taking of a former mentor, friend and symbol of remembered joys in music when they were young." Hughes wondered if the tradition of unaccompanied singing would continue after Olaf Christiansen's retirement, but one thing was certain: "His own practice has left an indelible impression upon singers and listeners alike. This is no small achievement."[92]

To a retiring teacher, the most appreciated words are those coming from colleagues and students. At a recognition dinner given for Olaf C. Christiansen on the St. Olaf campus May 24, 1968, Kenneth Jennings, Olaf's younger colleague, former student, and successor, spoke some

Audience in Philharmonic Hall
Olaf's last New York concert

361

beautiful words in honor of a superb musician and a wonderful man:

Like your father before you, you have always believed that the finest choral art performed with exacting artistry was not enough; but that the purpose of this music was to work in a fundamental way on the inside of a person—performer as well as listener—to sensitize him, to move him to react and respond with new insight to his world, his neighbor, himself and to God. Your music, the concerts, the rehearsals where the magic first happens, have changed us, renewed us, and enriched us beyond measure. For some of the best times and most memorable moments in our lives, we thank you.[93]

On his retirement, Olaf Christiansen brought to a close a remarkable career in which high artistic attainment was placed in the service of a profound religious mission. Because of Olaf, his Choir members sang "always with a buoyant, beautiful quality and always with a musicianship born of joy and dedication."[94] As the son of a famous choral pioneer, as a musician of highest caliber, and as a man of exuberant faith, it was given to Olaf Christiansen to conduct the St. Olaf Choir in singing to the Lord a new song.

Olaf's final concert
Skoglund Auditorium, Spring 1968

Olaf C. Christiansen, ca. 1968

Notes for Chapter 11 SING TO THE LORD A NEW SONG

1. Letter from Helen Drovdal Larson to St. Olaf College Alumni/ae and Parent Relations Office, February 24, 1996.

2. *Minneapolis Star*, November 4, 1949.

3. Interview: Joseph M. Shaw with Alice T. Larsen '51, September 18, 1995; Joseph M. Shaw, *History of St. Olaf College* 1874-1974 (Northfield, Minnesota: The St. Olaf College Press, 1974), 408.

4. Jack Laugen, "Fifty Years a Chorister," *Lutheran Herald* XXXVI (April 29, 1952), 417.

5. *Manitou Messenger* (*MM*), April 6, 1956.

6. Clemens M. Granskou, "F. Melius Christiansen," Tribute at Memorial Service for Dr. F. Melius Christiansen, Boe Memorial Chapel, June 3, 1955.

7. Letter from Paul H. Christenson '56 to Bob Johnson, September 9, 1994.

8. *Minneapolis Morning Tribune*, June 1, 1955.

9. *The St. Olaf Alumnus*, October 1945, 31.

10. Citation prepared and read by O. W. Qualley, Luther College, May 28, 1945. STOARCHIV.

11. *St. Olaf College Bulletin*, October 1945, 31.

12. WCAL recording, May 1945.

13. *The St. Olaf Alumnus* 6 (September 1957), 4, citing "A Colleague's Tribute to P. G.," by Ella Hjertaas Roe.

14. *MM*, October 4, 1957.

15. *MM*, January 17, 1958.

16. *MM*, December 5, 1958.

17. *MM*, February 6, 1959.

18. Cited in *MM*, February 20, 1959.

19. *MM*, February 20, 1959; February 27, 1959.

20. *MM*, March 13, 1959; interview: Paul Benson with Fred Schmidt, July 14, 1982.

21. Shaw, *History of St. Olaf College*, 407.

22. *MM*, April 1, 1960.

23. *MM*, February 23, 1962.

24. *MM*, November 2, 1962; *The St. Olaf Alumnus* 10 (January 1962), 3.

25. *The St. Olaf Alumnus* 10 (January 1962), 3.

26. *MM*, February 23, 1962.

27. Letter from Phyllis Ensrud '48 to BJ, January 18, 1994.

28. Letter from Carole Lea Arenson '62 to BJ, January, 1994.

29. Robert Oudal, "St. Olaf Choir Presents Superb Concert," *Rochester Post-Bulletin*, February 26, 1962.

30. Thomas Willis, "St. Olaf Choir Marks Jubilee in Concert Here," *Chicago Daily Tribune*, February 24, 1962.

31. Alex Joiner, *Atlanta Constitution*, February, 1954, cited in *MM*, February 19, 1954.

32. F. Melius Christiansen, "The Choir," unpublished typescript, 1929.

33. Olaf C. Christiansen, "A Little Like Love Letters," *The St. Olaf Alumnus* 16 (May 1968), 5.

34. Thomas Willis, "St. Olaf Choir Marks Jubilee."

35. Robert Oudal, "St. Olaf Choir Presents Superb Concert."

36. Albert Goldberg, "St. Olaf Choir Holds High Note of Quality," *Los Angeles Times*, February 7, 1965.

37. Albert Rykken Johnson, "The Christiansen Choral Tradition: F. Melius Christiansen, Olaf C. Christiansen, and Paul J. Christiansen," A thesis submitted in partial fulfillment of the requirements for the degree of Doctor of Philosophy in the School of Music in the Graduate College of the University of Iowa, July, 1973, 313.

38. Interview: JMS with Paul E. Peterson '56, February 13, 1996; 1961 Viking, 136; *Minneapolis Star*, December 9, 1960.

39. Olaf C. Christiansen, "A Little Like Love Letters," 4-5.

40. Olaf C. Christiansen, "Solo and Ensemble Singing," *The National Association of Teachers of Singing Bulletin*, February 1965, 17.

41. Conversation: JMS with Paul Benson, June 19, 1996. Benson had interviewed Olaf Christiansen on July 9, 1982.

42. Interview: JMS with Kenneth Jennings '50, June 27, 1996.

43. Kenneth Sanson, "Hymns Top St. Olaf Concert," *Chicago's American*, February 17, 1968.

44. Letter from F. Melius Christiansen to Olaf C. Christiansen, n. d., ca. 1928.

45. Letter from Ann Andersen Hoven '53 to JMS, January 1, 1994.

46. Joel Andrews, "St. Olaf Choir — A Musical Tradition," *MM* 95 (November 6, 1981).

47. William C. Glackin, "Great Music Helps Make St. Olaf A Great Choir," *The Sacramento Bee*, February 15, 1965.

48. Olaf C. Christiansen, "Solo and Ensemble Singing," 17.

49. *Ibid.*

50. Winthrop Sargeant, "Pure Tone," Musical Events, *New Yorker*, February 22, 1964.

51. William J. Nazzaro, "Wright Structure And Great Choir Blend

Perfectly," *The Capital Times*, February 14, 1965. Reprinted from the February 5th edition of the *Arizona Republic*.

52. Paul Benson, "A Cappella Choirs in the Scandinavian-American Lutheran Colleges," *Norwegian-American Studies* 32 (Northfield, Minnesota: The Norwegian-American Historical Association, 1989), 228.

53. Glackin, "Great Music Helps Make St. Olaf A Great Choir."

54. *Ibid.*

55. *Ibid.*

56. *Ibid.*

57. Olaf C. Christiansen, "Choral Tradition Lives On," *Music Journal (March 1968), 36. This article was published in May 1968 in The St. Olaf Alumnus* under the title, "A Little Like Love Letters."

58. Willmar Thorkelson, "Christiansen Retirement. . . end of an era," *Lutheran Brotherhood Bond* 45 (May 1968), 10.

59. Letter from Sylvia Christiansen Buselmeier '50 to JMS, July 21, 1996; letter from Lyndon D. Crist to JMS, June 12, 1996.

60. "St. Olaf A Cappella Choir," Program, 1953-1954; "St. Olaf Lutheran Choir," Program, 1963-1964; "The St. Olaf Lutheran Choir in Concert— 1968."

61. Lyndon D. Crist, ed., "Yearly listing of programmed works: St. Olaf Lutheran Choir (1941 - 1968), Olaf C. Christiansen, Conductor." Lyndon Crist, B. M., M. M., M. A., former choral director and a meticulous student of the work of Olaf Christiansen, has also researched, compiled, and edited three other collections: "St. Olaf Lutheran Choir tour programs of the Olaf C. Christiansen era: 1941 - 1968," "Discography: St. Olaf Lutheran Choir (1941 - 1968), Olaf C. Christiansen, Conductor," and "Composer and publisher listing of programmed works: St. Olaf Luthean Choir (1941 - 1968), Olaf C. Christiansen, Conductor." These collections are invaluable for students who wish to do research on the musical contributions of Olaf C. Christiansen.

62. *Ibid.*

63. Letter from Paul G. Peterson '42 to JMS, March 15, 1994; letter from Lyndon D. Crist to JMS, August 1, 1996.

64. Kenneth Sanson, "Hymns Top St. Olaf Concert," *Chicago's American*, February 17, 1968.

65. *The Nashville Tennessean*, February 13, 1966.

66. Interviews: JMS with Kenneth Jennings, June 27, 1996, December 10, 1996.

67. D. R. McErven, "St. Olaf Choir Concert Shows Discipline, Control," *Albuquerque Tribune*, February 3, 1965.

68. Letter from Jean Berger to Kenyard E. Smith, cited in Smith's doctoral dissertation, "The Choral Music of Jean Berger," A thesis submitted in partial fulfillment of the requirements for the degree of Doctor of Philosophy in the School of Music in the Graduate College of the University of Iowa, May, 1972, 1. This thesis was called to my attention by Lyndon D. Crist, Iowa City, Iowa. In a phone conversation November 18, 1996, Mr. Berger told the writer, "My career as a composer of choral music in this country is almost entirely due to Ole's picking up 'Brazilian Psalm.'"

69. Conversation: JMS with Paul Benson. Based on Benson's interview with Olaf Christiansen July 9, 1982.

70. Robert P. Wetzler, "Contemporary Composers: Paul Christiansen," *Journal of Church Music* 11 (November 1969), 7.

71. Crist, ed., "Yearly listing of programmed works...Olaf C. Christiansen."

72. Letter from Lyndon D. Crist to JMS, June 12, 1996.

73. Crist letter, June 12, 1996; JMS interview with Kenneth Jennings, June 27, 1996.

74. Louis R. Guzzo, "St. Olaf Choir Thrills Soldout Audience Here," *The Seattle Times*, February 18, 1965.

75. Christiansen, "Love Letters," 3.

76. "St. Olaf Lutheran Choir," Program, 1958-1959; Lyndon D. Crist, ed., "St. Olaf Lutheran tour programs of the Olaf C. Christiansen era: 1941 - 1968."

77. Interview: JMS with Kenneth Jennings, June 27, 1996.

78. "The St. Olaf Lutheran Choir in Concert—1968," Program.

79. Doris Reno, "Choir's Singing Pure Music, But Program Narrow in Scope," *The Miami Herald*, February 18, 1966.

80. Herm Sittard, "St. Olaf College Choir Hailed in Triumphant Homecoming," *The Minneapolis Star*, February 24, 1964.

81. Lorraine Nelson, "St. Olaf Choir Sets High Standard," *The Indianapolis Star*, February 10, 1966.

82. Gerald Kloss, "College Choir Comes Up to Professional Standards," *The Milwaukee Journal*, February 21, 1964.

83. Willmar Thorkelson, "Christiansen Era to End at St. Olaf," *The Minneapolis Star*, April 2, 1968.

84. Christiansen, "Love Letters," 4.

85. Judy Olson, "Christiansen to retire after 27 years service," *MM*, January 26, 1968.

86. Christiansen, "Love Letters," 5.

87. Thorkelson, "Christiansen Era to End."

88. Christiansen, "Love Letters," 5.

89. Peter J. Laugen, "Olaf C. Christiansen Retires," *American Choral Review* X (1968), 116.

90. Olson, "Christiansen to retire."

91. Carl Apone, "St. Olaf Put On Map By Father And Son," *The Pittsburgh Press*, February 13, 1968.

92. Allen Hughes, "St. Olaf College Offers Concert," *The New York Times*, February 10, 1968.

93. Kenneth Jennings, Tribute at Olaf C. Christiansen Recognition Dinner, St. Olaf College, May 24, 1968.

94. Harriett Johnson, "St. Olaf Choir Returns to Philharmonic Hall," *The New York Post*, February 10, 1968.

CHAPTER 12

KENNETH JENNINGS

"St. Olaf 'Grad' to Lead Choir," was the heading on the fourth and final article in a series published by *The Minneapolis Star* in the spring of 1968. The College had announced a year earlier that Dr. Olaf C. Christiansen planned to retire in June of 1968. The "grad" appointed as the new director of the St. Olaf Choir was Dr. Kenneth L. Jennings, a younger colleague of Christiansen's on the St. Olaf College music faculty. The series, written by Willmar Thorkelson, commented on the St. Olaf Choir, the Christiansens and the Schmidts, and introduced Dr. Jennings.

Kenneth Jennings, ca. 1965

The first article was entitled, "Christiansen Era to End at St. Olaf." The second described Choir auditions and rehearsals and the third told of the two Christiansen-Schmidt teams that put the Choir on the map. The fourth article summarized Jennings' background and noted that he had been recommended by Olaf, who characterized his successor as "a thorough musician and a wonderful guy." When President Sidney Rand was asked if Olaf's retirement meant the end of the Christiansen tradition at St. Olaf, his answer was No. "The tradition is bigger than the name and individuals and we expect the same general emphasis to continue."[1]

Choice of a Successor

Largely through Olaf Christiansen's settled judgment and decisiveness, there was no opportunity for the question of his successor to assume grand, theatrical dimensions. No doubt there was speculation enough among alumni and professional musicians, but on campus the decision was arrived at quickly and with a minimum of fuss.

Olaf Christiansen reached the age of 65 in August of 1966, but he was under no obligation to retire at that time. In January of 1967 he informed President Rand that he had been interested in retiring that spring but was willing to continue through the next school year and retire in the spring of 1968.[2] Olaf linked his decision to step aside to a perceived loss of hearing. There was no hesitation in facing the matter of a successor. As Dr. Rand recalled the conversation, "Olaf was straightforward and said, 'It is not my business to pick my successor, but if you want my advice I believe it should be Jennings. He's an able musician and he has proved himself.'"[3]

Pres. Rand and bust of F. Melius Christiansen

In the meantime Kenneth Jennings, who had joined the music faculty in 1953, had been going about his work as classroom teacher, voice instructor, director of the Chapel Choir, and graduate student. In his view, the possibility that he might succeed Olaf Christiansen seemed remote. Within the department it was not clear when Olaf was planning to retire. Since Jennings would be 43 in the spring of 1968, it seemed prudent to look at openings elsewhere. He had been invited to interview for a position at the University of Southern California in 1961. Aspects of the California post were unappealing, however, so he turned it down. On his return to campus he told Olaf, chairman of the department, about the position and the interview, and went back to his duties.[4]

Kenneth Jennings, 1968

About six years later, as Christiansen and Jennings chatted in the music office, Olaf told his younger colleague that he was going to retire in the spring of 1968 and that he recommended that Jennings be his successor. It was "a bit of a shock" for Jennings, who asked if he could have time to think it over. Olaf replied that Jennings was to meet with the president the next day. Jennings met the appointment and informed President Rand that he would take the job. A phone connection had already been made between the president's office and Howell Skoglund, chairman of the Board of Regents. Rand handed Jennings the phone and Skoglund congratulated the musician on his new position.[5]

Howell Skoglund

On March 31, 1967, President Rand sent two memoranda about Christiansen's retirement and the decision to name Dr. Jennings as the new director of the St. Olaf Choir. One memo went to Dean Albert A. Finholt and key members of the music department; the other was sent to members of the Board of Regents.[6] An article announcing the change appeared April 19, 1967, in the *Minneapolis Tribune*.[7]

Looking back on the selection of a new director, Rand wrote it was not the difficult decision he had expected it to be. "As it turned out, we appointed a committee to advise the dean and the president, and with no difficulty Kenneth Jennings was the one recommended."[8] The process could be kept simple because the appointment took place before the days of national advertising, an exhaustive search, piles of dossiers, parades of candidates, interviews, and auditions. Clearly Olaf's support of Jennings carried considerable weight with the committee. When President Rand informed the Board of Regents that Jennings had been selected, he could say, "We are convinced we have made a proper choice."[9]

End Of An Era

With the appointment of Kenneth Jennings and the retirement of Olaf Christiansen, a unique era was coming to an end. Jennings and Anton Armstrong after him strongly maintained the rich choral tradition nurtured at St. Olaf College by the Christiansens. Nevertheless, when a musical genius and his highly talented son have given the world fifty-six years of exquisite music under the Christiansen name, one cannot but speak of the end of an era. The phrase was used again by Willmar Thorkelson as the title of another published article: "Christiansen Retirement . . . end of an era." The piece began with the statement: "Twenty-seven years of 'hard work' and 'joyous service' as director of the St. Olaf Lutheran Choir will end in late May for Dr. Olaf C. Christiansen." The article reviewed Olaf's career, told of the farewell tributes, and mentioned the hobbies Olaf would enjoy in retirement: golf, painting, and hybridizing day lilies.[10]

Throughout the first half of 1968 Dr. Christiansen and his wife Ellen were recipients of gifts and tributes by grateful alumni and friends during the choir tour and at the College. During the last intermission of the concert in Philharmonic Hall, alumni of the Greater New York area presented a pair of hand-wrought silver candlesticks to Dr. Christiansen. Another gift on the same occasion was a painting by Albert Christ-Janer '31, art dean of the Pratt Institute in New York, to show his gratitude to Olaf for the influence that led him into the field of art. In Chicago the Christiansens received an antique silver bowl from the alumni club, who had sponsored the concert and a reception in Orchestra Hall. The bowl was presented by Mary Ann Christensen Johnson '51.[11]

After the tour, Ellen and Olaf Christiansen expressed their gratitude to alumni and friends in the March issue of the *St. Olaf*

Olaf at his easel

The Christiansens receive a painting
Olaf and Ellen with Albert Christ-Janer

Receiving antique silver bowl
Olaf and Ellen with Mary Ann Johnson

Alumnus, thanking them for the warm reception given the St. Olaf Choir and themselves. They wrote:

> We treasure the heartwarming memories you have given us of generous hospitality, kind words of appreciation, and tangible reminders of your friendship and good-will. It has been a joy and a blessing beyond measure to have had these years of service and association at St. Olaf.[12]

More recognitions came later in the spring. In May Olaf received a citation from the Regents of the University of Minnesota. From Wisconsin Governor Warren Knowles, a Carleton graduate, Olaf received an executive citation. On June 7, 1968, in Northfield, Olaf was awarded the honorary degree, Doctor of Music, from Carleton College. He was the first faculty member, as opposed to retiring St. Olaf presidents, to receive an honorary degree from Carleton.

Honorary D. Mus. at Carleton

Another tribute with a Carleton connection was a framed cartoon, given by St. Olaf alumni but drawn by Carleton coach Jim Nelson whose sports cartoons were widely known in Minnesota.[13]

And Olaf was liberally honored on his own campus. The music department gave a dinner in his honor on May 17th. On May 24th, as part of Alumni Weekend, more than 500 persons, St. Olaf Choir alumni and spouses, gathered in the St. Olaf College dining room for the Olaf C. Christiansen Recognition Dinner that preceded a concert in his honor. Dr. Jennings spoke at both dinners. Some of his well-chosen words were cited earlier. On the May 24 occasion, Jennings promised Olaf that later in the evening the Choir would thank him by singing. He concluded with this fitting

Cartoon by Jim Nelson
Northfield News, June 13, 1968

373

tribute:

> To us insiders, as well as to your colleagues at St. Olaf and the musical world at large, you have been an example of the musical man and teacher, who has built a distinguished career based on strength of character, sensitivity, refined taste, and impeccable musicianship. Through the concentrated medium of choral music, your musical aims have been merged with spiritual realities into a distinctive musical vision uniquely your own.[14]

That Dr. Jennings was the right person to speak for the St. Olaf community in honoring Olaf Christiansen was implicit in his selection as the next director of the St. Olaf Choir. But it should also be said that Jennings possessed a broad and deep knowledge of the Christiansen musical philosophy. For many years he had enjoyed a close, working relationship with Olaf that began when Jennings first arrived on the St. Olaf campus as a student in the fall of 1946.

Kenneth Jennings and Olaf Christiansen Celebrating a new Choir recording, 1976

From Connecticut to Minnesota via Germany

Kenneth L. Jennings was born May 13, 1925, in Bridgeport, Connecticut, grew up in Fairfield, and finished high school in Westport. His father came from Puritan New England stock and his mother's family had roots in Germany. There was no special flair for music in the family, but Kenneth took piano lessons and enjoyed them. The two top students in his high school graduating class went on to become professional musicians. His friend David Hughes, valedictorian, went to Harvard as a student and continued his career there as professor of musicology. Kenneth Jennings, salutatorian, after an unusual Army experience that strongly

Kenneth Jennings, 1943

influenced his career, found his way to St. Olaf College and became the third director of the St. Olaf Choir.[15]

Jennings finished high school in the spring of 1943 and was drafted into the Army that fall. He was eighteen years old. After basic training and moving from one camp to another, he was eventually assigned to Fort Benning, Georgia, arriving in September of 1944. There he met Pfc. Luther Onerheim, chaplain's assistant, energetic musician and promoter, and a St. Olaf graduate, Class of 1937.

Everything in Onerheim's pre-war experience pointed toward a professional career in music. He first attended Luther College, then transferred to St. Olaf College where, in 1935, he founded and directed the Viking Chorus, a group of male students.[16] Onerheim was active in both the Band and the Orchestra. He also sang tenor in the St. Olaf Choir, then directed by F. Melius Christiansen. When the Choir stopped to see the Hollywood Bowl during its tour of the west coast in 1937, Christy asked Onerheim to conduct while he went out

Kenneth Jennings, U. S. Army

Luther Onerheim

St. Olaf Choir, 1937, Onerheim 3rd row, 1st on left

375

Luther Onerheim conducting St. Olaf Choir at Hollywood Bowl, 1937

among the seats to listen. F. Melius was "very pleased" with what he heard and the Choir was thrilled at having sung in the Hollywood Bowl, even though the occasion was not a regular concert.[17]

After leaving St. Olaf, Onerheim studied symphonic conducting at the New England Conservatory of Music in Boston. Before entering the Army he was music director in the public schools in Danbury, Connecticut. He entered the Army in the fall of 1943.

After meeting Jennings a year later at Fort Benning, Onerheim, whose preferred instrument was the trumpet, was delighted to have Jennings play the organ for chapel services. A man of great organizational drive, Onerheim persuaded his superiors to let him organize the Fifth Infantry Chorus. Thus what came to be called the Soldier Chorus was born in 1944 in the Fifth Army Chapel at Fort Benning, with Onerheim as director. Co-founders were two chaplains, Thomas O. Harrison and Leon R. Gorsline, and timely encouragement was received from Colonel Sidney C. Wooten, Commander of the Fifth Infantry Regiment. Jennings sang in the Chorus and assisted in various capacities, at the piano, as a member of a trio, baritone soloist, and section leader.

In January of 1945, the Soldier Chorus went to Europe with its outfit when the Fifth U. S. Infantry Regiment, Seventy-First Division, was shipped out. The Chorus held rehearsals and sang at several Sunday services aboard the "T. H. Bliss," which took the troops to Le Havre, France. During the short stay in France, the Chorus entertained troops in the "cigarette camps," named after American cigarette brands such as "Lucky Strike" and "Old Gold." Soon the Fifth Army was involved in the march across Germany, pushing the remaining enemy troops back and taking prisoners. When the fighting ended, the Fifth Army had reached Steyr, Austria, the farthest point east reached by any ground force of the Western Allies. The men of the Soldier Chorus survived the fighting. Three of them suffered wounds.[18]

After the V-E (Victory in Europe) celebrations, the forty members of Onerheim's Soldier Chorus were able to stay together by working up a show including a magician, a trio, and piano solos by Jennings in addition to choral numbers. Singing and the entertaining of troops was their main Army

Page from The Soldier Chorus

duty. In Steyr they soon performed for some high-ranking Russian military officers at a banquet given for them by American Army officers. Earlier, when the Russians had entertained the Americans, they had been proud of

The Soldier Chorus, 1945

their Cossack chorus, so Colonel Wooten had countered with, "I have a chorus too." The Soldier Chorus hurriedly put together a popular show called "Broadway Bound," but with the resourceful Onerheim looking ahead, they also learned a repertoire of sacred music to include in performances and to sing at church services.[19]

The singing and tours of the Fifth Army Soldier Chorus is a rather phenomenal story. The Chorus was in Steyr, Austria, for about a month, performing two or three times a day. Then it moved on to Augsburg and, assigned to the Special Service unit, spent the next six months performing at USOs, giving concerts, and singing at church services in many parts of Germany. Popular entertainers from the States and high-ranking Army officers in Germany were among the listeners. Paul Robeson and Raymond Massey had words of praise for the Chorus. In appreciation, Massey recited his well-known Lincoln's "Gettysburg Address" that he had given on Broadway. When General George S. Patton heard the Chorus, he fiddled with his four stars during the singing, but came up afterward to compliment the men for "fine music and excellent soldierly appearance."[20]

Thanks to Onerheim's determined negotiating, the Chorus was invited to participate in the first post-war Salzburg Music Festival

Rehearsing in Mozarteum

Augsburg Catheral

on September 2, 1945. Performing in the Mozarteum before a military audience, the Chorus sang fifteen selections, opening with "A Mighty Fortress is our God." Its presentation of "Lost in the Night," with Richard Eichenberger as soloist, was particularly well received. Someone recalled that "Colonel Wooten's approving whistle could be heard above the applause of the entire crowd." Director Onerheim received a bouquet of flowers and the Chorus was invited to return to the Festival the following year. The men of the Chorus were very disappointed, however, that an Army officer, overly zealous about non-fraternizing rules, would not admit a large group of Austrian civilians who were eager to attend the concert.[21]

With its base of operations in Augsburg, Germany, the Soldier Chorus had a very busy schedule of performances through the fall and the Christmas season. Rehearsals had to be squeezed in between many hours of guard duty. A dream was fulfilled when now-Sergeant Onerheim directed the Soldier Chorus before an audience of over 1500 German civilians in the Ludwigsbau auditorium in Augsburg on Sunday, January 13, 1946. It was Luther Onerheim's last concert. He was killed on January 16th when the jeep he was driving slid on an icy curve and crashed into an engineer truck.[22]

Included in the final concert under Onerheim were Bach's "Out of the Depths" and "Jesu Joy of Man's Desiring," Palestrina's "O Bone Jesus" and "Adoramus Te Christe," Grieg's "Landsighting," and as the two final numbers, the F. Melius Christiansen arrangements of the Finnish folk song, "Lost in the Night," and "Beautiful Savior." Given such a program, sung from memory, a cappella, and Onerheim's emphasis on covered vowels, staying on pitch, and unity of tone, one clearly recognizes that the choral principles of F. Melius Christiansen had found their way to war-torn Germany and Austria.

All that was remarkable enough, but from the standpoint of Kenneth Jennings and his future work, it was even more extraordinary that he should meet this musical St. Olaf graduate, a disciple of F. Melius Christiansen, and through him be drawn into the choral world that he would later come to know intimately at St. Olaf College. Jennings' acquaintance with Luther Onerheim had a direct bearing on his post-Army plans for college.

Luther Onerheim, January 1946

The Soldier Chorus continued for a time after Onerheim's death, but gradually broke up as the men became eligible to return to the

379

States. Jennings served as assistant to Chaplain Harrison in Germany until he returned to the U. S. and civilian life in May of 1946. He visited Onerheim's widow, Jane Onerheim, a pianist in nearby Danbury, and took some piano lessons from her. At her home he heard a recording of the St. Olaf Choir. They discussed St. Olaf College. Mrs. Onerheim encouraged him to apply for admission and wrote to people she knew at the College to recommend him.[23]

Dean Cully Swanson

When Jennings made his own contacts with St. Olaf College, he was told that because of the large number of veterans enrolling there was no more space. Knowing of Roy Harris, a composer of national reputation at Colorado College, Jennings applied and was accepted there. But he was still interested in St. Olaf. On his way west in the fall, he decided that since his train ticket took him only to Chicago, he would travel to Northfield to see what prospects there were of being admitted. Once on the campus, he met the Dean of Men, Carl "Cully" Swanson, with whom he discussed the possibility of enrolling. Swanson checked his credentials and said, "I guess you'll be a good enough risk."[24]

Jennings discovered that he was a week early because a polio scare had delayed the beginning of the fall semester. He was assigned a room in the one and only men's dormitory, Ytterboe Hall, the same building where F. Melius Christiansen had lived during his first year as a St. Olaf faculty member. Part of the week was spent searching the campus for a good piano. He found one in the lounge of Agnes Mellby Hall where he put in some hours of practice.

Student at St. Olaf College

Like F. Melius, Kenneth Jennings had other musical interests before he took up voice and choral conducting. His first intention as a student at St. Olaf College was to major in piano as a candidate for the Bachelor of Music degree. He went to Olaf Christiansen's office to audition for piano and to sign up for the Bachelor of Music program, but first was given a voice audition. Everyone auditions for the St. Olaf Choir, Olaf told him. As chair of the music department, Olaf kept a close eye on everyone showing musical promise and assigned them to music teachers. Jennings recalled that with Oscar Overby at the piano and Olaf listening, he was asked to sing a tune progressively higher until it went beyond his range. On the audition form Olaf wrote a number and "UNDEV," but told Jennings he was accepted for the Bachelor of Music program.

As Jennings left the office he assumed that he would not be selected for the Choir, but he was in the program he wanted and looked forward to his piano studies. A day or two later Lloyd Hustvedt, student head of the dormitory and later professor of Norwegian at the College, told him, "You're on the recall list." Of the forty men who showed up in Steensland Library to audition as baritones and basses, twenty-two of them were capable of singing a low C. Of that smaller group Olaf chose ten for the Choir.[25]

To his surprise, Jennings was called back as a tenor. He told Olaf that he had always sung baritone. Olaf tested his lower range and placed him in the middle of a line of tenors. Starting at one end, Olaf had each of the men sing a pattern until someone failed to remember it, then went to the other end to follow the same procedure. He never got to Jennings, standing in the middle and awaiting his turn. Jennings explained what happened next:

> There was one particular note, however, that no one could remember. Suddenly, he swung around and pointed at me. I sang it, and that's how I got into the St. Olaf Choir.[26]

Olaf was aware of Jennings' musical ability. He had been told about Luther Onerheim and the Soldier Chorus and knew that Jennings had been part of that experience. With respect to the shift from baritone to tenor, in voice classes Olaf offered some useful suggestions for developing a greater range. Jennings was one of the few, select students who are taken into the St. Olaf Choir the first year and sing in the ensemble all four years. In his case, the four-year Choir experience encompassed the period when war veterans and other able singers provided mature voices of richness and depth in the male sections of the Choir.

St. Olaf Choir, 1950

The post-war years also meant the resumption of the longer Choir tours. In two successive years, 1947 and 1948, the Choir went to the east coast. In 1949 it went to the west coast, "three and a half weeks of lugging suitcases, sleeping on trains, and singing successful concerts night after night in the largest music halls of the Pacific coast," as a student writer summarized the tour.[27] The tour of 1950, when Jennings was a senior and president of the Choir, was into midwestern states, Wisconsin, Illinois, Missouri, and Iowa.

Singing second tenor in the Choir, Jennings often stood next to the man with the extraordinary bass voice, P. G. Schmidt. While far from being the clown that tenor Wendell Wold was, Jennings was in the thick of Choir fun and frolic. A tour snapshot shows him in the middle of a pile of about eighteen laughing Choir members who are squeezing and jostling one another. Among them, with Ken at the bottom of the heap and Wendell at the top, are Lyle Iverson, Tom Anderson, Ruth E. Johnson, Dewey Brevik, Lois Jacobson, Stanley Nelson, Pauline Seim, Ida Marie Weinhardt, and John Thompson.

As a member of the Choir, Jennings had every opportunity to study the teaching and conducting techniques of Olaf Christiansen and to acquaint himself with the life and tradition of the Choir. He even conducted on occasion. Prior to a concert in the Midwest Olaf asked him, "Ken, do you know how to take a bow?" In the middle of a section, Olaf signaled Jennings to come forward to lead the Choir in the Norwegian Christmas song, "Jeg er saa glad hver julekveld."[28]

Jennings also applied his growing knowledge of music as leader of the tenor section. On one occasion, while he was rehearsing the tenors in the basement of Steensland Library, none other than F. Melius Christiansen appeared in the room and quietly sat observing the sectional.

Choir members cavorting, 1949   *Wendall Wold performing*

Jennings followed through on his desire to study piano, with Esther Woll as his teacher. Composition was another undergraduate interest. He studied voice first with Adolph Engstrom and later with Ella Hjertaas. In an important sense Olaf Christiansen was also one of his voice teachers since all music majors were required to take a voice class taught by Olaf. Jennings gave voice and piano recitals his junior and senior years. He had a reputation on campus as one of the finest pianists to come through the music department in several years.

Kenneth Jennings, pianist

Kenneth was a member of the Manitou Music Club. He was the recipient of the Agnes Skartvedt Glasoe Memorial Scholarship, named in honor of a woman who sang in the very first St. Olaf Choir, in 1912, and later served the College as preceptress and teacher of German and English. He belonged to the Honors Society and was elected to Blue Key, a national honorary fraternity that chose candidates on the basis of scholarship, leadership, service to the college, and character.[29] Always a bright student, he

St. Olaf graduate, 1950

graduated *magna cum laude* with the Bachelor of Music degree in the class of 1950.

Faculty Member at St. Olaf College

After graduation, Jennings received a scholarship that enabled him to attend the Oberlin Conservatory of Music where he received the Master of Music degree in 1951. Through Olaf Christiansen, who had taught there, he learned that Oberlin was building up its graduate program. His Master's thesis was a composition, "Prelude for Orchestra." Jennings then took a position as chair of the department of music at Mitchell College in Statesville, North Carolina, for two years, 1951-53. During that period he founded and directed the Statesville Oratorio Society and directed the Senior

Choir in the Associated Reformed Presbyterian Church. In the summer of 1952 he attended the University of Oslo, Norway, and directed the Summer School Choir.[30]

The invitation to return to St. Olaf College as a member of the music faculty came in 1953. Not only was there a position open in the department, but Olaf was looking ahead to the Choir's Norway tour in 1955 for which he would need an assistant conductor. One of Jennings' first assignments was to direct the Manitou Singers, a choir of first year women, and soon he was in charge of the Chapel Choir, which he directed until he was appointed to lead the St. Olaf Choir.

Kenneth Jennings
Oslo, 1952

After joining the St. Olaf faculty, Jennings used his summers for further study. In New York City in 1953, 1954, and 1956 he attended the School of Sacred Music at Union Theological Seminary and Columbia University, and took private voice lessons. In the summer of 1957 he attended the University of Minnesota, considering it as well as other schools where he might enter a doctoral program.

With the help of a Lutheran Brotherhood Faculty Fellowship, he began doctoral studies at the University of Illinois in 1958 and received the degree, Doctor of Musical Arts, on February 15, 1966. Prior to his candidacy, Illinois offered higher degrees only in musicology and composition. When Jennings expressed the desire to take work in choral music, he learned that his adviser, Professor Scott Goldthwaite, wanted to establish a new doctoral program in that area. Soon the program was in place, with the noted composer and pianist Jean Berger as the director. When Berger left for Colorado he was succeeded by Harold Decker. Jennings was the first to enter the program and one of the first to earn the Doctor of Musical Arts degree.[31]

Jennings' doctoral dissertation was entitled, "English Festal Psalms of the Sixteenth and Seventeenth Centuries." Characterized by Harold Decker as "a fascinating and enlightening thesis," it examined the primary sources of English psalmody, classified the festal psalms into four styles, and identified their common characteristics. Jennings spent some months in England completing his research. He was accompanied by his wife, the former Carolyn Henderson, piano instructor at St. Olaf College since 1960.

Kenneth and Carolyn were married in Boe Memorial Chapel on June 3, 1962. Fittingly, the St. Olaf Chapel Choir, which Jennings had been

Carolyn and Ken Jennings, June 3, 1962

directing, sang at the wedding. On this occasion it was conducted by Olaf Christiansen. Carolyn Jennings was a graduate of the University of Iowa, where she majored in music, and the recipient of the Master of Music degree from the University of Michigan. Carolyn's mother, Jeanette Donhowe, was a member of the St. Olaf Choir that traveled to the east coast in 1920. Decades later, as the Choir anticipated the 70th anniversary of that tour, an article in *Saint Olaf*, the alumni/ae magazine, carried a photo of Jeanette Donhowe Bakke with her granddaughter Lisa Jennings '89, both sopranos in the St. Olaf Choir.[32]

Arriving at St. Olaf College in 1919 as a transfer student, Jeanette Donhowe had already received some voice training. Her audition for the St. Olaf Choir took place at the Christiansen home. After she had sung for F. Melius, he said, "Vel, you may be too operatic for us." A day or two later, a friend told her, "Christy wants to see you again." Jeanette's reaction was to say, "He knows my voice. He's heard me." So she refused to go back. Apparently Christy admired the spunk as well as the voice. The next day Jeanette Donhowe was a member of the St. Olaf Choir.[33]

Jeanette Donhowe Bakke and Lisa Jennings

The Jennings family was as immersed in music as it was talented. The older son, Steven, graduated from Luther College and became a professional musician with special skills in percussion. Daughter Lisa Jennings, accomplished in violin and flute as well as voice, sang soprano in the St. Olaf Choir for four years. After receiving the M. A. in German at the University of Wisconsin, Madison, she taught at the University of Minnesota. The younger son, Mark, also sang in the St. Olaf Choir and after graduation studied music at Michigan State University where he received the M. M. in choral conducting.

Kenneth, Lisa, and Steven Jennings

Carolyn Jennings has had an unusually productive career as a professional musician, both at St. Olaf College and in circles beyond the campus. Beginning in 1970, she served as director of the Senior Choir at St. John's Lutheran Church in Northfield, the church where the St. Olaf Choir began. She has also coordinated the music program at St. John's. At the College, she was appointed chair of the music department in 1991. She is best known across the country for more than 100 published compositions, including some thirty commissioned works.[34] Her choral pieces are sung by youth and adult church choirs, by the St. Olaf Choir, and by other college choirs. Compositions, arrangements, and orchestrations by Carolyn Jennings are often heard at the annual St. Olaf Christmas Festival.

Composer Carolyn Jennings

In his work as director of the St. Olaf Chapel Choir, Kenneth Jennings was responsible for all the music provided at Sunday worship services in Boe Memorial Chapel, built in 1953 and used for worship services of the St. Olaf student congregation as well as for daily chapel exercises. It was understood that the Chapel Choir would

Boe Memorial Chapel
St. Olaf College

K. Jennings directing Chapel Choir
Boe Chapel, 1964

sing at the Sunday services, but Jennings wanted the other choral groups to participate, including the St. Olaf Choir.

As a college student and member of the St. Olaf Choir, Jennings had been part of the old practice whereby the Choir sang at St. John's each Sunday during the first semester, using the occasions to present anthems that would be sung on tour. But the situation changed when St. John's organized its own Senior Choir in 1950 and the students at St. Olaf founded their own congregation in 1952. Therefore Jennings suggested to Olaf Christiansen that the St. Olaf Choir participate in some of the Sunday services in Boe Chapel. From then on, the Chapel Choir sang at half of the services and other choirs provided the choral music for the rest of the services.[35]

The twelve and a half years as director of the St. Olaf Chapel Choir was more than an apprenticeship for the man who would be selected as the third director of the St. Olaf Choir in 1967. Perceiving the Chapel Choir as more than a "feeder" choir for what was often called the First Choir, Jennings had ambitious plans for the group that at that time was allotted only three 50-minute rehearsals a week. As a larger choral ensemble of 90 to 100 voices, with no binding commitment to a cappella singing or memorizing all of its music, the Chapel Choir was in a position to take on larger, longer works that could be performed with organ, piano, or full orchestra.

Jennings received supporting interest in a repertoire of symphonic pieces, oratorios, masses, and passions from colleagues Donald Berglund, Band and Orchestra director, Paul Ensrud, professor of church music and organ teacher, and G. Winston Cassler, music theory teacher and composer. Ernst Bloch's *Sacred Service* and Bach's *St. Matthew Passion* were among the first works the Chapel Choir performed.

One year the Chapel Choir under Jennings had an unusual opportunity that could have led to a tour abroad. With the assistance of actors and soloists, it had prepared Hugo Distler's *Totentanz*. Burr McWilliams of the

387

St. Olaf Music Faculty, 1966

St. Olaf music faculty narrated the part of Death. This work had been inspired by the uncovering of a mosaic depicting the "Dance of Death" in a chapel in Lubeck, Germany, where Distler was organist and music director. The Chapel Choir was invited to perform this 20-minute piece at a church music seminar in the large chapel at Valparaiso University in Indiana. In attendance were German conductors and other musicians from Europe, including some representing Dutch radio.[36]

On the basis of this performance, the Chapel Choir was invited to Holland the next year to do a repertoire that included the *Totentanz*. Its expenses would be paid. Jennings took the matter to Olaf Christiansen and to President Rand. The admin-istrative decision was that only the St. Olaf Choir should go on tour, although Jennings had taken the Chapel Choir on a short tour prior to the trip to Indiana. In any case, the connection made with Holland bore fruit for the St. Olaf Choir in 1970 when Fred Schmidt and Jack Laugen went to Europe and secured an invitation for the Choir to sing at the Heinrich Schütz Festival, being held that year in Breda, Holland.[37]

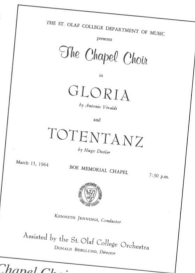

Chapel Choir program, 1964

When that time came, the St. Olaf Choir sang the *Totentanz* at Breda.

Under the direction of Kenneth Jennings, the St. Olaf Chapel Choir collaborated with the St. Olaf Orchestra over a period of a dozen years to perform annual concerts of larger works. Among these symphonic repertoire pieces the Choir and Orchestra presented Bach's *Magnificat*,

Cantatas No. 11 and 80, Passion According to St. John and *Passion According to St. Matthew*, Gabriel Fauré's *Requiem*, Honegger's *King David*, Mozart's *Requiem*, Poulenc's *Gloria*, Vivaldi's *Gloria*, and Stravinsky's *Symphony of Psalms*.

The experience Jennings had in preparing and conducting music of this type had much to do with his readiness to lead the St. Olaf Choir into a different repertoire when he became its director. As Jennings views choral programming, there are two kinds of repertoire: 1) the larger works discussed above, including oratorios, masses, and passions; 2) the smaller, art song-like repertoire, shorter pieces such as motets and anthems that take less time to perform. The St. Olaf Choir under the Christiansens had chosen the second type of music. Stanislaw Skrowaczewski, then director of the Minnesota Orchestra, had often urged Olaf Christiansen to take on larger projects but Olaf had declined. When Jennings became St. Olaf Choir director, he believed that the time had come to start performing the larger works.[38]

The First Year

It was not the singing of larger works that first caught the public's eye and ear when Kenneth Jennings assumed charge of the St. Olaf Choir. It was rather that the Choir had a new sound and a different repertoire. Another innovation was the occasional use of instrumental accompaniment in some of the numbers on the concert program. The move to employ instruments was less radical than perceived when one considers that F. Melius Christiansen had written pieces to be sung with organ. "Praise to the Lord" is an example.[39]

The first tour of the St. Olaf Choir with Kenneth Jennings as director began when the group left Northfield on January 30, 1969 and sang its first concert in the high school in St. James, Minnesota. The direction of the tour was south and west. Twenty-two concerts were given in a journey that included Denver, Phoenix, Los

"Praise to the Lord"

St. Olaf Choir, 1968-69, Jennings' first year

Angeles, Sacramento, Portland, and Seattle. The Choir flew from Spokane to Minnesota to present its home concert in Skoglund Center on Sunday, February 23, 1969.

Even before the Choir left Northfield the word on campus was that its program would offer a "first." Wrote John Cavert in the *Manitou Messenger*, "Formerly singing only 'a cappella', it will feature a number accompanied by flute and guitar." This number was Walter Pelz's "Who Shall Abide," based on Psalm 15:1-2. The article also stated that a "dramatically striking" twelve-tone piece by Arnold Schönberg would be performed.[40] "De Profundis" (Psalm 130), Schönberg's last composition, combines *sprechstimme*, spoken words, with singing. It received favorable comment during the tour.

Reviewers had much to write about as they heard the St. Olaf Choir under a new director offering a fresh repertoire. In general, they seemed more interested in repertory and sound than in the use of instruments. Thomas MacCluskey in Denver wrote: "Dr. Jennings has not only maintained and perhaps improved the group's widely known high standards of performance, but also he's added to its stature by means of greater depth in programming." This critic regarded the Schönberg work and Krzysztof Penderecki's "I will extol Thee" (Psalm 30) as the highlights of the program. As to the sound, MacCluskey did not find it as different as others would. In fact, he approved what he characterized as "the Christiansen-type tone which minimizes vibrato in ensemble singing." He also commended the singers for the beauty of their expressiveness.[41]

The latter idea was also on the mind of critic Walter Arlen, who heard the Choir in the Dorothy Chandler Pavilion in Los Angeles. He was impressed by the way the Choir fully invested itself in the singing. He wrote: "To top it all, there was genuine communication. The mixed chorus singing conveyed true feeling, unusual involvement, and a maturity of interpretation that belied the youth of the participants. Their age showed chiefly in the fresh sound of their voices."

Arlen, with others, recognized the significance of including works by Penderecki and Schönberg, but he was most thrilled by the first section of the program. "Nothing superseded the chorus' marvelously effective performance of Bach's gleaming 'Praise Ye the Lord,' or the deeply moving works by Hassler, Esquivel and Lassus that followed." The three latter works, sung in Latin, were "Verbum Caro Factum Est," by Hans Leo Hassler, "O Vos Omnes," by Juan Esquivel, and "Surrexit Pastor Bonus," by Orlando di Lasso.[42]

Comments on program, tone, and a touch of humor marked a piece by a San Francisco writer that appeared three days before the Choir gave its concert in Berkeley. Robert Commanday of the *San Francisco Chronicle* carried out a debate with himself between going to hear the St. Olaf Choir in the Berkeley Community Theater or attending another concert. In one of his "Pro-St. Olaf" paragraphs he wrote:

> In 1969, its new conductor, Kenneth L. Jennings, is departing from the old-fashioned Christiansen programs. Included will be works by Penderecki, Schönberg, Distler and Pepping.
>
> Maybe under a new conductor, St. Olaf's will break away from its habitual ice-blue tone and towards something humane and natural. This choir has a thrilling potential. The St. Olaf Choir stands at the center of a college tradition, older and prouder, than athletics at the Big Ten universities.[43]

As Commanday wrestled with his dilemma of two desirable events in conflict with one another, he considered the dire results if he attended a concert of a church-related group and wrote an unfavorable review. "The last time you criticized the St. Olaf Choir," he reminded himself, "one lady was simultaneously praying for you and heaping coals on your head."

Generous praise for Jennings and the Choir and recognition of changes did not mean that the Christiansen contribution was undervalued. Wrote a Bay area critic after the Berkeley concert: "Not changed in the Friday concert were the heritage of the choir from its founder F. Melius Christiansen, and its second director, the elder Christiansen's son, Olaf C. Christiansen. That heritage includes perfect pitch, perfect tone control and projection of religious conviction."[44]

Dr. Jennings at rehearsal

One way of recognizing the changes in the Choir was to speak of "a new and welcome humanity" that Jennings had achieved "by putting skirts on his sopranos," in the words of a San Francisco reviewer. This writer was glad that the boys' choir sound, "the Knabenchor ethereal quality," was gone. "It's nice to hear sopranos with flesh and blood, albeit with the same cool discipline," wrote M.K.T.[45]

After the concert in the First Congregational Church in Fresno, James Bort Jr. spelled out explicitly what he perceived as the difference in the Choir's sound. "The St. Olaf Choir in its first year under Dr. Kenneth L. Jennings has a new sound. Gone is the distinctive icy tone quality which marked the choir's singing under Dr. Olaf C. Christiansen. . . . Replacing it is a more vibrant, warm tone—a resonant, lively, brilliant sound that rings with vitality and conviction."[46]

Writing in *The Fresno Bee*, Bort noted also that Jennings had expanded the repertoire but retained the religious content. He felt that the Choir under Jennings "has lost none of its musical integrity nor the faultless intonation, the exceptional balance and the great precision. . . . The phrasing is superb and Jennings'—and the choir's—dedication to music is as impressive as the meticulous craftmanship which goes into their singing."[47]

Making its way north, the Choir performed in the Fine Arts Auditorium in Salem, Oregon. The reviewer, Stanley Butler, found it "stunning" that the

Choir sang Schönberg's "De Profundis" and exciting that "the audience responded to such a contemporary work with sustained applause." Butler observed the effectiveness of Jennings' conducting: "Dr. Jennings' authority with the choir showed itself in many ways, and always without exaggeration or self-consciousness about technique." The writer used the term, "an elegant naturalness" in speaking of the tone quality of the Choir[48]

The Choir arrived back in Northfield to give its home concert on Sunday, February 23, 1969. A discerning review by Paul Sorensen in the *Manitou Messenger* was headed, "Ole choir goes modern with wider repertory." Under the new director, wrote Sorensen, the Choir "has lost none of the clarity of line, exactness of pitch, attention to word declamation and precision of execution for which it has become famous." The new qualities apparent to the reviewer were "a livelier tone quality and an extension of the St. Olaf repertory formula." He regarded Schönberg's "De Profundis" as the high point of the concert, commenting on the good intonation and Jennings' masterful conducting.

Writing as a student, Sorensen had a pertinent remark about contemporary music at the conclusion of his review. He wrote, "The prospect of the choir's performing works written in a student's own lifetime and in a style applicable to the twentieth century is overwhelming, to be sure, but it's only right. It is *our* music."[49]

Later in the spring the St. Olaf Choir made its annual joint appearance with the Minnesota Orchestra in Northrop Auditorium on the University of Minnesota campus. Infrequent rehearsals since the tour plus poor acoustics in the hall may have accounted for a performance eliciting reviews that were less than generous. Peter Altman of the *Minneapolis Star* thought the Choir's singing "had more finish than power." He regarded the program as monotonous and the one piece that should have been an exception, Schönberg's "De

MAKING a JOYFUL NOISE

KENNETH L. JENNINGS, DIRECTOR

St. OLAF CHOIR

FREDERICK A. SCHMIDT, MANAGER, NORTHFIELD, MINNESOTA

PALM SUNDAY CONCERT

March 30, 1969
3:30 p.m.   NORTHROP AUDITORIUM

The ST. OLAF CHOIR
directed by Kenneth L. Jennings,
in a program of *a capella* religious choral music.

The MINNESOTA ORCHESTRA
conducted by Stanislaw Skrowaczewski,
performing the Bach Toccato and
Fugue in D Minor (arranged by Maestro
Skrowaczewski) and Beethoven's Symphony No. 7

ORDER YOUR TICKETS NOW ON THE TICKET ORDER BLANK BELOW

St. Olaf Choir at Northrop

Profundis," performed with lack of feeling. "Here was a work that should have been desperately angular, arid in tonality, choppy in line, anguished in mood, but the choir normalized its every anxiety."[50]

Allan Holbert of the *Minneapolis Tribune* also had some criticisms but described the Choir as "a musically sophisticated organization" that "sang a cappella with precise intonation, quick responsiveness and good college enthusiasm." He commented that Jennings "seems to be a most capable conductor." Altman, noting that the Choir was directed in Northrop for the first time by Kenneth L. Jennings, conceded that it "is an admirably trained and disciplined unit."[51]

The Minnesota Orchestra must have agreed with the positive assessments, because it joined in arrangements to appear with the St. Olaf Choir in four concerts in October of 1969. In Northrop Auditorium, in Rochester, and in Skoglund Center at St. Olaf, the Orchestra and Choir performed *Lelio*, an operatic work by Hector Berlioz. A modern dance company also participated in the performances. The fourth joint concert, in Minneapolis on October 31st, featured the St. Olaf Choir and the Minnesota Orchestra in Mozart's *The Magic Flute*.[52] Thus Dr. Jennings did not wait long in carrying out his intention to have the St. Olaf Choir prepare and perform larger works with an orchestra. It became evident over the next years that the music director of the Minnesota Orchestra, Stanislaw Skrowaczewski, had high regard for the musicianship of Kenneth Jennings and enjoyed collaborating with him and the St. Olaf Choir in many performances.

Stanislaw Skrowaczewski

By the end of his first year as director, Kenneth Jennings had demonstrated to all interested parties that he possessed the qualities needed to lead the St. Olaf Choir forward to new levels of excellence. A writer in Spokane gave this endorsement: "Those anxious about the Choir's change of leadership were quickly reassured—Kenneth L. Jennings is a superb choral conductor."[53] And a reviewer in Oregon wrote after the concert in Portland, "If Tuesday night was any indication, Dr. Jennings will carry on with distinction the international reputation of the choir established by the Christiansens."[54]

During the next twenty-one years Jennings upheld and extended the reputation of the St. Olaf Choir both at home and abroad. With modesty and grace he demonstrated that the tradition begun by the Christiansens was larger than the name of a family or an individual. For Jennings, it was never "Olaf's Choir" or "my Choir," but always "the St. Olaf Choir." In assuming his stewardship, Jennings faithfully preserved the basic principles of ensemble singing for which the Choir was known. At the same time, he injected a new freedom into the vocal expression, trained the Choir in a new repertory, and led it with a new style.

Notes for Chapter 12 KENNETH JENNINGS

1. Willmar Thorkelson, "St. Olaf 'Grad' to Lead Choir," *The Minneapolis Star*, April 5, 1968.

2. Letter from Sidney A. Rand to Olaf C. Christiansen, January 6, 1967. STOARCHIV.

3. Sidney A. Rand, *In Pleasant Places*: A Memoir (Northfield, Minnesota: St. Olaf College, 1996), 185.

4. Interview: Joseph M. Shaw with Kenneth Jennings, October 11, 1995.

5. *Ibid.*

6. Memo from President Sidney A. Rand to Dean Albert E. Finholt, Dr. Olaf C. Christiansen, Dr. David N. Johnson, Dr. Adolph White, Dr. Kenneth Jennings, March 31, 1967; Memo from President Sidney A. Rand to Members of the Board of Regents, St. Olaf College, March 31, 1967. STOARCHIV.

7. *Minneapolis Tribune*, April 19, 1967.

8. Rand, *In Pleasant Places*, 185.

9. President Rand to Members of Board of Regents, March 31, 1967.

10. Willmar Thorkelson, "Christiansen Retirement . . . end of an era," *Lutheran Brotherhood Bond* 45 (May 1968), 9.

11. "Olaf's Final Tour," *The St. Olaf Alumnus* 16 (March 1968), 11.

12. *Ibid.*

13. *Northfield News*, June 13, 1968.

14. Kenneth L. Jennings, Remarks at Olaf C. Christiansen Recognition Dinner, St. Olaf College, May 24, 1968. STOARCHIV.

15. Interview: JMS with Kenneth Jennings, June 27, 1996.

16. *Viking* 1936-37, 92.

17. *Ibid.*, 88; Robert A. Peck, *The Soldier Chorus*: An Illustrated History of the Great A Cappella Choir Built by Luther M. Onerheim in the Fifth U. S. Infantry Regiment, Seventy-First Division (Printed by J. P. Himmer, Augsburg, Germany, 1946), 62; letter from Jane Onerheim Hilton to Frances Anderson, October 25, 1996. The name of the author does not appear on the title page of *The Soldier Chorus*. According to Kenneth Jennings, the book was written by Robert A. Peck, a member of the Chorus who lived in Wyoming after World War II. Interview: JMS with Kenneth Jennings, July 23, 1996.

18. *Soldier Chorus*, 11-13.

19. Interviews: JMS with Kenneth Jennings, October 10, 1995; October 9, 1996.

20. *Soldier Chorus*, 17-19.

21. *Ibid.*, 21; JMS interview with Kenneth Jennings, October 9, 1996.

22. *Soldier Chorus*, 29-30.

23. Interview: JMS with Kenneth Jennings, October 10, 1995; Paul Benson, "The Empires of Song: A Cappella Choirs in the Scandinavian-Lutheran Colleges," unpublished typescript, n.d., 97. Used by permission.

24. Interview: JMS with Kenneth Jennings, October 10, 1995.

25. *Ibid.*

26. Bradley Ellingboe and Dennis Shrock, "An Interview with Kenneth Jennings On the Occasion of his Retirement as Music Director of the Saint Olaf Choir," *Choral Journal* XXX (May 1990), 6-7.

27. 1949 *Viking*, 79.

28. Letter from Ole Winter '51 to JMS, May 26, 1996.

29. William C. Benson, *High on Manitou*: A History of St. Olaf College, 1874-1949 (Northfield, Minnesota: The St. Olaf College Press, 1949), 292, 338; 1950 *Viking*, 98.

30. *The Ambassador Yearbook* (Oslo, Norway: University of Oslo Summer School for American Students, 1952), 25.

31. Interview: JMS with Kenneth Jennings, July 23, 1996.

32. Dan Jorgensen, "A Tour to Remember—And to Recreate," *Saint Olaf* 38 (November/December 1989), 6.

33. Interview: JMS with Kenneth Jennings, October 9, 1996.

34. "Composer Carolyn Jennings: An Interview," The Northfield Magazine 3 (Winter 1990), 41.

35. Interview: JMS with Kenneth Jennings, October 11, 1995.

36. *Ibid.*

37. *Ibid.; The St. Olaf Alumnus* 18 (July 1970), 9.

38. Interview: JMS with Kenneth Jennings, October 11, 1995.

39. "Praise to the Lord," arr. F. Melius Christiansen, *St. Olaf Choir Series* 11-0076, Augsburg Publishing House, 1957.

40. *Manitou Messenger* (*MM*), January 24, 1969.

41. Thomas MacCluskey, "St. Olaf Choir Offers Top Concert," *Rocky Mountain News*, Denver, Colorado, February 3, 1969.

42. Walter Arlen, "St. Olaf's Choir at Pavilion," *Los Angeles Times*, February 12, 1969; "The St. Olaf Choir," 1969 Concert Program.

43. Robert Commanday, "The Decisions A Critic Faces," *San Francisco Chronicle*, February 11, 1969.

44. Ruth Boots, "New Director for St. Olaf Choir," *Contra Costa Times*, February 20, 1969.

45. M. K. T., "St. Olaf Chorus' New Humanity," *San Francisco Chronicle*, February 17, 1969.

46. James Bort Jr., "St. Olaf Choir Sings With New Zeal, Traditional Skill," *The Fresno Bee*, February 14, 1969.

47. *Ibid.*

48. Stanley Butler, "St. Olaf Choir Gains Applause Of Big Audience," *Salem Statesman*, ca. February 21, 1969.

49. Paul Sorensen, "Ole choir goes modern with wider repertory," *MM*, February 28, 1969.

50. Peter Altman, "St. Olaf's Singers Lacked Feeling," *The Minneapolis Star*, March 31, 1969.

51. Allan Holbert, "St. Olaf Choir Appears at Northrop," *Minneapolis Tribune*, March 31, 1969; Altman, "St. Olaf's Singers Lacked Feeling."

52. *MM*, October 10, 1969.

53. Bob Hill, "St. Olaf Choir's Recital Praised," *Spokane Daily Chronicle*, February 24, 1969.

54. Martin Clark, "St. Olaf Choir Welcomed Warmly Here," *The Oregon Journal*, February 19, 1969.

CHAPTER 13

A NEW STYLE

"Art does not stand still," said Kenneth Jennings to the audience in Sacramento, California, as he introduced the contemporary works by Penderecki and Schönberg on the 1969 program. Wherever the St. Olaf Choir went during its first season of performances under Jennings, listeners and critics alike were alert to any new elements that would distinguish the Jennings style from that of his predecessors. In looking and listening for the new, they also found themselves acknowledging the familiar. One reviewer regarded Jennings' conducting style "remarkably similar to that of his predecessor, Olaf C. Christiansen."[1] Another even noted a physical similarity between Jennings and Olaf Christiansen, both appearing "tall and trim."[2]

Kenneth Jennings with Penderecki manuscript completed in Northfield, spring 1977

The aims of the St. Olaf Choir had not changed radically with the new director. Next to the picture of Dr. Jennings in the 1970 tour program was his statement of three purposes that suggested continuity more than innovation: "to create a choir of high musical purpose and achievement; to communicate a religious commitment; and to offer the audience as well as the Choir an enriching musical experience."[3] Reviewers rightly noted, however, that Jennings not only had "preserved the best of the Christiansen tradition," but also had "added a few new dimensions."[4]

Choir Tour Program, 1970

The New Sound

The first new dimension of the St. Olaf Choir often mentioned was the sound or tone, and how it differed from that of earlier days. When Nashville reviewer Werner Zepernick heard the Choir in Massey Auditorium in that city, he wrote: "There is less emphasis on austerity and straight tone singing and more stress on beautiful ensemble, flexibility, and consideration of the human voice," he wrote.[5]

The Choir's sound was not always judged to be a departure from the Christiansen vocal product. William Glackin of Sacramento, who had heard the St. Olaf Choir when Olaf Christiansen was the director and Jennings was a student member of the chorus, analyzed the tone:

> Choral buffs will be wondering if Jennings has continued one particular Christiansen tradition that is somewhat controversial: the use of a 'straight' choral tone with little or no vibrato. The

400

answer is yes, but he is also drawing from his choir singing of such personal warmth as to make the tones inescapably human; it is, in fact, the most beautiful St. Olaf tone I can remember, and I remember that concert of 20 years ago.[6]

Many would not agree that Jennings was continuing the so-called "straight" tone but most concurred with such descriptions as "warm," "human," and "natural." It is unfortunate that reviewers continued to ascribe a "straight tone" to the Christiansen choirs in light of the fact that Olaf Christiansen explicitly rejected that vocal concept and worked instead for a limited vibrato. The term "straight tone," if used at all, is better associated with the work of F. Melius Christiansen and the northern European style of singing that he introduced in this country.

Misleading as it was, critics persisted in using the term, either to say that the sound of the St. Olaf Choir led by Jennings was in contrast to the "straight tone" or a modification of it. Erving Covert in North Carolina thought that Jennings was continuing the earlier tradition of little or no vibrato, but with a difference. "But rather than lacking richness, as is often claimed, he is achieving a tone of great warmth and purity, an elegant naturalness. This fine tone quality is very definitely a distinguishing feature of this choir."[7]

After hearing the Choir at Louisiana State University, Anne Price of Baton Rouge praised the sound, but not necessarily as something new.

But the real distinction of the choir is its unparalleled intonation and precision. Jennings, in the long-standing tradition of the choir, treats the human voice like a fine musical instrument it is, and the young voices blend perfectly, with a pure, clear tone and perfect pitch.[8]

When Dr. Jennings took over leadership of the St. Olaf Choir, he wanted the ensemble to be less rigid vocally and to sing more freely. At one time he said, "I uncorked the vibrato bottle that first year and ever since have attempted to put it back."[9] He sought a more natural, less mechanistic sound, with less emphasis on creating a given effect and more on allowing the Choir some spontaneity in performing a given work.[10]

To the ear of Harold Decker, one of Jennings' professors at the University of Illinois, it seemed that Jennings had relaxed the Choir's tone considerably. By stressing intonation and "listening" within each section and in the total ensemble, he achieved "a more natural voice production" resulting in "a greater variety of tone colors from the choir."[11]

Robert Scholz, Choir member who sang under Olaf Christiansen and became a colleague of both Christiansen and Jennings on the St. Olaf music faculty, commented on how they differed. Christiansen's approach was

Robert Scholz '61, Professor of Music, St. Olaf College

more abstract than that of Jennings; he had an ideal sound in mind and trained the Choir to make that sound. The vowels had to be very clear and distinct for the sake of making the text understood. Jennings moved away from the abstract sound and worked to develop the tone through the music. His was the gift of building the wonderful musical phrase. He succeeded in achieving smooth lines and subtle, expressive phrasing with the text. If Olaf's hallmark was purity of sound, Kenneth's was sensitive phrasing.[12]

Louis Nicholas, Nashville reviewer, wrote in 1970 that it was "the most satisfying singing I have ever heard from a St. Olaf Choir in the almost 30 years I've been hearing them." He noted that Jennings, a St. Olaf product, had fresh ideas and a broad outlook gained from his studies elsewhere, as well as devotion to the musical excellence of his predecessors. Nicholas continued:

> The most notable improvement is in the tone quality which is now free and vital, with none of the rigid, held sensation which resulted from the insistence on a straight tone that has always characterized this choir in the past.[13]

The possibility of a freer tone also made a difference in solo work and in one soprano's personal outlook as well. Virginia Bergquist Bowles '70 recalled the spontaneous comment Dr. Jennings made to her one day on campus, "Ginny, I want to hear the sound *you* make." At first the remark was puzzling, but finally it was liberating. "Giving a person permission to be free and to sing their sound is truly the best gift of all," she wrote.[14] The result was evident when Bergquist sang the solo in Jean Berger's *Magnificat*

Virginia Bergquist

during the 1970 tour. One delighted reviewer called her "thrushlike" and another wrote: "Virginia Bergquist displayed a voice of ravishing beauty and timbre, well modulated and controlled."[15]

The new sound of the St. Olaf Choir may be summed up by borrowing the term "elegant naturalness," a phrase, incidentally, that first appeared in a review in Salem, Oregon, then turned up again in a review published the next year in Burlington, North Carolina. East and west, listeners were hearing a tone that was reminiscent of the earlier sound of the Choir but yet one with less rigidity, greater freedom and flexibility, and a new warmth.

Los Angeles Music Center, 1969

Expanded Repertory

On the first Choir tour under Kenneth Jennings, one of the concerts on the west coast took place in the Dorothy Chandler Pavilion in the Music Center in Los Angeles. After the February 1969 concert in the Music Center, critic Walter Arlen of the *Los Angeles Times* wrote of a new repertory along with the new leadership.

> The change in command seemed to have brought with it a spirit of renewal not only in the aesthetics and technique of tone production—the chorus has lost its 'romantic' quality—but also in the choice of repertory, as illustrated by Penderecki's 'I Will Extol Thee' and Schönberg's 'De Profundis.' Both exemplified solid (and curiously similar) essays in 20th century musical methods, good for introducing an audience to the rigors of the modern idiom."[16]

The selection of new pieces for the program was also good for the members of the Choir and their student generation. After a concert in Grand

403

Rapids in 1972, Dr. Jennings spoke about the inclusion of such pieces as Charles Ives' "Psalm 90," performed with organ and bells, and the "Collect for Peace" by the University of Michigan's Leslie Bassett, which included sounds by electronic tape. He said:

> This isn't a wildly contemporary program by any means. But I feel a responsibility to these students to explore these new avenues and not just do the tried and true. We must explore the artistic possibilities of our own century, too.[17]

The electronic tape heard with the Bassett "Collect" drew varied reactions. Boris Nelson of the Toledo *Blade* thought it "pretentious in its gurgly swashes of sound" and declared, "In the case of machine versus human voices, give me the latter any time."[18] Carmen Elsner in Madison, Wisconsin admired the way the electronic sounds moved in and out of the choral line and added, "The trick was in the timing, which was precisely perfect."[19]

Steve Aulie of Grand Rapids affirmed the use of tape to communicate in an unusual idiom, but felt that the effect, at certain points, "was more humorous than serious."[20] A positive reaction came from St. Olaf graduate Wilma Salisbury, writing for the *Cleveland Plain Dealer*. She regarded the Bassett number as the most satisfying of the new pieces. The St. Olaf Choir, "is ideally suited for singing with the synthesizer," she wrote, "and it gave to Bassett's skillfully-integrated piece a polished, moving performance."[21]

Other twentieth-century works receiving favorable reception in concerts from the early seventies were Jean Berger's *Magnificat* and "Vision of Peace." Olaf Christiansen had introduced Berger's music and also that of the Swedish composer, Sven-Erik Bäck. Jennings used Bäck's "Jesus, Remember Me" in 1972 and "Search Me, O God" in 1973. The 1971 program included the *Mass for Five Voices* composed in 1964 by Lennox Berkeley, Carl Nielsen's "Benedictus Dominus," and Kenneth Jennings' "Today, Heaven Sings." The programs for 1972, 1973, and 1974 included "Rimfrost" ("Winter Frost"), a piece written for flute, baritone solo, and male chorus by Erik Bergman, a contemporary Finnish composer.

Audiences could also enjoy more traditional offerings, J. S. Bach included. A "roar of approval" was heard in Coe Auditorium in Cedar Rapids, Iowa, as the Choir launched into the Bach double chorus number, *Sing Ye to the Lord*.[22] The 1972 program offered Bach's motet, *Jesus, Priceless Treasure*, not often done in its entirety. It was well received on the tour. And there was always a warm response to the F. Melius Christiansen arrangements of "Wake, Awake" and the closing number, "Beautiful Savior."

For Harriett Johnson of the *New York Post* the program showed "that Jennings has an ear for drama." His sense of timing, she wrote, was "the equivalent of the right kind of tension a first-class stage director produces in a play." Noted Johnson: "The works were superbly chosen for their contrasts in style, instrumental and vocal color and for the importance of nuance and climax."[23] For example, Sven-Erik Bäck's prayer of the thief on the cross and Jesus' response was followed by Bassett's "Collect" with the words, "We have put our trust in the world and refuge in instruments of violence." With others, she observed the range of the program, from the 16th century Englishman, Robert Stone, who provided a setting of the Lord's Prayer, to the 20th century American, Leslie Bassett, composer of the "Collect for Peace." Jennings "has built on the rock of the Choir's eminent traditions yet has given it offshoots of involvement with the contemporary scene," wrote Johnson. "The result is a more stimulating musical experience than formerly. The program expressed current trends and the creativity of living composers."[24]

Robert Sherman of the *New York Times* took note of the "heavier weighting of 20th century music in the repertory," commenting with appreciation on such contemporary Scandinavian music as the Danish "Jubilate" by Bernard Lewkovitch and "Rimfrost" by Erik Bergman, sung in Swedish. Sherman also observed that "percussion instruments added a happy bounce to the "Gloria" from the 'Creole Mass' by Ariel Ramirez and organ and bells provided a fascinating obbligato in Charles Ives's Psalm 90."[25]

In commenting on Jennings' expanded reportory, Harold Decker emphasized music by recognized contemporary composers, and also the inclusion of major choral works. Examples of such longer works are Bach's *Jesus, Priceless Treasure*, Berger's *Magnificat*, and Lennox Berkeley's *Mass for Five Voices*. Decker also credited Jennings with historical awareness. One could hear in the performances "an earnest resolve to be true to the composer's period as well as his individual style." With others, Decker also noted Jennings' use of instrumental accompaniment.[26]

Choir and instrumentalists, 1978

Sounding the bells for "Psalm 90"

Use of Instruments

Performing Bassett's "Collect for Peace"

In the light of Jennings' decision to include instruments, a comment by a reviewer in Olaf Christiansen's day was of "prophetic" relevance. In February of 1962, the St. Olaf Choir was in Mayo Civic Auditorium in Rochester, Minnesota, for its last concert before arriving back home in Northfield. Local critic Robert Oudal closed his thoughtful review with some comments on the a cappella tradition. Much as he respected a cappella singing, he longed for some accompanied works to create variety and free the emotions. Warning against perpetuating a tradition too long, he wrote: "The way is open now for the foundation of a new tradition which can embody the best of both a cappella and accompanied works."[27]

Kenneth Jennings pursued that way, continuing the a cappella practice but using instruments with some numbers for added dimensions of sound and color. In his view, while a cappella singing was prominent in the 19th century and carried over into the 20th, it was not the only way of performing choral music. Yet it was news among critics when the St. Olaf Choir incorporated instruments in its concerts. A review in the *Philadelphia Inquirer* in 1972 carried the headline, "St. Olaf Choir Has New Sound," in this case referring to the inclusion of instruments. "Having decided to use accompaniment," wrote Samuel L. Singer, "Jennings treads warily."[28] For the performance of Charles Ives' "Psalm 90," written for organ, bells, and chorus, the Academy of Music's organ was used to good effect. In accordance with Baroque continuo practice, organ, cello, and figured bass were added when the Choir performed Bach's *Jesus, Priceless Treasure*.

Jennings had no intention of slighting the a cappella style. He used instruments sparingly on a limited number of compositions. The Philadelphia reviewer, having mentioned the few instruments employed, including electronic tape, stated that the Choir upheld "its traditional standards of balance, clarity of line, and fidelity to pitch." The Choir still offered "many a cappella numbers" in which there was opportunity for "delicacy of nuance." As suggested earlier, how the Choir sounded and what it sang remained of first importance to listeners. The fact that some numbers were accompanied did not dominate the reactions.

The use of instruments in St. Olaf Choir concerts began very modestly. The first instance was the performance of Walter Pelz's "Who Shall Abide" with flute and guitar accompaniment on the 1969 tour. Most reviewers, including the person who reviewed the home concert, failed to mention the innovation. In the 1970 program, the two flutes used with Johann Cruger's "All My Heart" and the flute, tambourine, and triangle with Berger's *Magnificat* received much less comment than the electronic tape heard with Bassett's "Collect for Peace."

Nevertheless, the break with past practice had been made, and various instruments were taken into use. Examples included the rhythm section consisting of cello, string bass, and triangle, hidden among the men in the back rows, used in the "Gloria" from the *Creole Mass* by Ariel Ramirez.[29] During the 1974 tour, whenever a suitable organ was available, the Choir performed "Motet for the Archangel Michael," written in 1967 by the Swedish composer Bengt Hambraeus.[30] A Milwaukee reviewer found it to be the most exciting number on the program, creating "a compelling atmosphere of strength heightened by crashing organ punctuation."[31]

Inasmuch as St. Olaf College celebrated its centennial in 1974, the St. Olaf Choir's itinerary that year included Minnesota and Wisconsin towns and cities that had been visited by the Choir in 1912, its first year. In addition to new and exciting pieces such as the

Celebrating the Centennial

The
St. Olaf Choir
in concert

Kenneth Jennings, conductor

1874-1974 • FRAM • FRAM • KRISTMENN • KROSSMENN • 1874-1974

Centennial Year Program

Choir with instruments, 1990

Hambraeus motet just mentioned, the program offered works by F. Melius and Olaf Christiansen. The enduring appeal of the Christiansen heritage was expressed in the last sentence of the *Milwaukee Sentinel* review: "Two hymns, 'O Day Full of Grace,' and 'Beautiful Savior,' arranged by F. Melius Christiansen, the founder of the St. Olaf tradition, concluded the concert and brought the near capacity audience to its feet in appreciation."[32]

The determination of F. Melius and Olaf Christiansen that the St. Olaf Choir should sing unaccompanied is well known. For Olaf, a cappella singing was for the sake of proclaiming and interpreting the religious texts. For F. Melius, it was for the sake of the Choir's commitment to the chorale. In 1929 he said in a chapel talk:

> The St. Olaf Choir will end its existence as soon as it ceases to sing the chorale. If the choir should undertake to sing operas, it would lose its identity. And even if it should sing with accompaniment of instruments the choir would change into something other than what it is. The traditional chorale is the foundation of the St. Olaf Choir as it was the foundation of Bach's Choir in Leipzig.[33]

The Choir still sings the chorale. There has been a small taste of singing operatic music under Dr. Jennings. Of his use of instruments, Jennings has said, "I like the contrast of voices and instruments, and I think it sets off the a cappella literature in a special way."[34] In the sense of inevitable change, the

St. Olaf Choir indeed has become something other than it was in the time of F. Melius Christiansen, but its leaders and friends will insist that singing with instruments has not threatened its historic identity.

The Choir On Stage

A simple but effective measure of the Choir's enduring identity is its appearance and manner as it takes the stage to perform. The purple-robed singers display a poise and confidence that are not accounted for solely by practicing proper stage manners. Their demeanor conveys a quiet pride in the continuum in which they stand. After months of disciplined work under an inspired director, and with a clear sense of having a purpose that goes beyond their private concerns, they are ready to sing, knowing who they are, honoring who their predecessors were, and realizing that in due time others will replace them. By their faces and posture, the singers show that it is a privilege for them to share the gift of great music with the listeners.

Occasionally a reviewer takes the time to record the Choir's appearance and movements as seen from the audience. Erving Covert in Burlington, North Carolina, pictured the scene:

> In deep purple velvet robes with white collars and cuffs, 66 young singers made their entrance and with no delay launched into one of the most inspiring concerts this city and this state has heard. Their attire suited perfectly the deeply religious character of the music sung, while the brisk pace on and off the stage was the personification of youthfulness.[35]

The Choir brought "glowing warmth and animation" to the unadorned stage, Covert continued, observing that there was "not a note of music anywhere in sight" for singers or conductor. Covert, choral director of Williams High School where the concert took place, moved from these visual features to the performance itself. "With obvious concentration, but equally obvious ease, this most professional of choirs sang each challenging number with care, precision and beauty that actually achieved perfection!"[36]

A San Diego reviewer spoke of "the choreography of getting off and on stage . . . with speed and drill team exactitude." A writer for a Dayton, Ohio, paper commented on the "discipline" that marked more than the singing. "From the moment they entered one was impressed with their vitality, organization and control."[37] As Walter Arlen observed the St. Olaf Choir in action in the Pavilion of the Los Angeles Music Center, he saw a "clockwork-like precision" showing itself in the "brisk near-run" in which the Choir assembled and marched off. The precision was also evident "in the time-saving device of setting a composition's pitch while applause greeted conductor Kenneth Jennings as he entered."[38]

St. Olaf Choir on stage, 1969

As critics and other concert-goers used their eyes as well as their ears in enjoying the St. Olaf Choir on stage, it was only to be expected that they would watch every move of the conductor. Kenneth Jennings was like the two Christiansens in avoiding unnecessary gestures, but at the same time his conducting had a distinctive style. One critic admired the fine, flowing rhythmic sense Jennings displayed in contrast to the "stylized punching" of some directors. "In fact," wrote Louis Nicholas, "a sweet reasonableness and genuine sensitivity were hallmarks of every aspect of Dr. Jennings' direction."[39]

Jennings at rehearsal

An effective and vivid description of Jennings' conducting was written by a reviewer who heard the Choir in Great Hall at the University of Illinois. The hall was one of Jennings' favorites and the school was where he had earned the D.M.A. degree. Wrote Barbara Alice WeDyck in words that many admirers

Sculpting the sound

of Jennings would happily endorse: "Director Kenneth Jennings seemed to sculpt the sound with his hands, lifting, polishing, then gently setting it down as he communicated each nuance to the instrument before him. Every movement was reflected back in sound."[40]

Modest like the Christiansens before him, Jennings preferred to have people respond to the Choir and its music. He would have been pleased by the sentence in a New Orleans review, "The choir sang with more than beauty; it sang with joy."[41] The comment is in keeping with what Jennings himself has said: "At St. Olaf the emphasis has been on doing art rather than talking about it. The essence of the choir's activity lies in the joy of creating worthwhile music together."[42]

Under the leadership of Dr. Kenneth Jennings, the St. Olaf Choir was not preoccupied with matters of style in a self-conscious way. As always, the focus was on the responsibility and the privilege of creating a rich musical experience for itself and the listeners. Wrote Dr. Jennings in a note to Choir members: "Sing, think, feel your best so others may hear, respond, be filled, and renewed."[43]

With its new director, the St. Olaf Choir took its message of joy and renewal to concert halls and churches throughout the country. In 1970, 1972, 1975, and 1980, it found new opportunities for growth and discovered new audiences on a remarkable series of tours to Europe.

Making a Joyful Noise

411

1. Wilma Salisbury, "Choir is Polished at Concert," *Cleveland Plain Dealer*, February 7, 1972.

2. Harriett Johnson, "Jennings Leads St. Olaf Choir," *New York Post*, February 14, 1972.

3. 1970 Tour Program.

4. Werner Zepernick, "Choir Return Marked By Excellence," *The Nashville Banner*, February 7, 1970.

5. *Ibid.*

6. William C. Glackin, "New Conductor of St. Olaf's Choir Produces Stirring Effect," *The Sacramento Bee*, February 17, 1969.

7. Erving Covert, "St. Olaf Choir Gets High Praise," *The Daily Times-News*, Burlington, NC, February 16, 1970.

8. Anne Price, "St. Olaf Choir Has Unexcelled Tone," *Sunday Advocate*, Baton Rouge, LA, February 14, 1971.

9. Interview: Joseph M. Shaw with Kenneth Jennings, October 11, 1995.

10. Paul Benson, *The Empires of Song:* A Cappella Choirs in the Scandinavian-Lutheran Colleges," unpublished typescript, n.d., 98-99. Used by permission.

11. Letter from Harold A. Decker to JMS, February 7, 1995.

12. Interview: JMS with Robert Scholz, February 6, 1996.

13. Louis Nicholas, "St. Olaf Choir 'Free, Natural,'" *The Nashville Tennessean*, February 7, 1970.

14. Letter from Virginia Bergquist Bowles to Kenneth Jennings, January 1990. Retirement Book of Letters, 1990.

15. Dean Jensen, "St. Olaf Choir Performance Outstanding," *Milwaukee Sentinel*, February 5, 1970; Les Zacheis, "St. Olaf Choir Thrills Cedar Rapids Audience," *The Cedar Rapids Gazette*, February 22, 1970.

16. Walter Arlen, "St. Olaf's Choir at Pavilion," *Los Angeles Times*, February 12, 1969.

17. Steve Aulie, "St. Olaf choir is wholly satisfying," *The Grand Rapids Press*, February 5, 1972.

18. Boris Nelson, "65-Voice St. Olaf Choir Performs at Auditorium," *The Toledo Blade*, February 18, 1972.

19. Carmen Elsner, "Royal Family of College Choirs Upholds Professional Reputation," *Wisconsin State Journal*, February 21, 1972.

20. Steve Aulie, "St. Olaf choir is wholly satisfying."

21. Wilma Salisbury, "Choir is Polished at Concert."

22. Les Zacheis, "St. Olaf Choir Thrills Cedar Rapids Audience."

23. Harriett Johnson, "Jennings Leads St. Olaf Choir."

24. *Ibid.*

25. Robert Sherman, "65 in St. Olaf Choir Sing Sacred Music Of Several Periods," *The New York Times*, February 15, 1972.

26. Letter from Harold A. Decker to JMS, February 7,1995.

27. Robert Oudal, "St. Olaf Choir Presents Superb Concert," *Rochester Post-Bulletin*, February 26, 1962.

28. Samuel L. Singer, "St. Olaf Choir Has New Sound," *The Philadelphia Inquirer*, February 10, 1972.

29. Carmen Elsner, "Royal Family of College Choirs Upholds Professional Reputation," *Wisconsin State Journal*, February 21, 1972.

30. 1974 St. Olaf Choir Program, "Celebrating the Centennial."

31. Jay Joslyn, "St. Olaf's Choir Sings in Best Tradition," *Milwaukee Sentinel*, February 2, 1974.

32. *Ibid.*

33. F. Melius Christiansen, "The Choir," unpublished typescript, 1929. STOARCHIV.

34. Bradley Ellingboe and Dennis Schrock, "An Interview with Kenneth Jennings," *Choral Journal* XXX (May 1990), 11.

35. Erving Covert, "St. Olaf Choir Gets High Praise."

36. *Ibid.*

37. James B. Porter, "Modern Music Used By Choir," *Journal Herald*, Dayton, Ohio, February 19, 1970.

38. Walter Arlen, "St. Olaf's Choir at Pavilion."

39. Louis Nicholas, "St. Olaf Choir 'Free, Natural,'" *The Nashville Tennessean*, February 7, 1970.

40. Barbara Alice WeDyck, "St. Olaf choir fills Great Hall with perfection," *The Daily Illini*, February 7, 1974. Cf. the comment by former Choir member Debra Eckstrom '77: "I have always been amazed at how you were able to achieve the sound you wanted by painting such beautiful pictures with your hands." Letter from Debra Eckstrom to Kenneth Jennings, December 25, 1989, Kenneth Jennings Retirement Book of Letters.

41. Charles L. DuFour, "St. Olaf College Choir Puts Joy Into Its Music," *The States-Item*, New Orleans, LA, February 13, 1971.

42. Quoted by Joel Levy, "Direction in genre praised in St. Olaf Choir concert," *The Daily Reveille*, Baton Rouge, LA, February 16, 1971.

43. "From K. L. J.," 1970 Tour Book.

CHAPTER 14

EUROPEAN TOURS

"The St. Olaf Choir is invited to come back to the Strasbourg Festival every year. We have heard many choirs here, but we have never heard a choir like yours before." These gracious words were addressed to Dr. Kenneth Jennings and the St. Olaf Choir by Henri Lazare, chief administrator of the International Strasbourg Music Festival, after the Choir had sung before nearly 1,000 people in St. Thomas Church in Strasbourg, France, in June of 1970. Joining Mr. Lazare in the greeting was Paul Rouart, secretary general of the Strasbourg Festival.[1]

The St. Olaf Choir moved into high gear in the 1970s, making three trips to Europe between 1970 and 1975, and adding a trip to Norway in 1980. The annual domestic tours continued, and many special appearances were arranged, some with the Minnesota Orchestra. In 1974 the Choir participated in the centennial observances of St. Olaf College and joined the

St. Thomas Church, Strasbourg, France   *Choir in St. Thomas Church*

Minnesota Orchestra in the official opening of Orchestra Hall in Minneapolis. Two years later the Choir sang a new anthem written by Kenneth Jennings for the dedication of Christiansen Hall of Music, the new music building on the St. Olaf campus.

France, Holland, Germany in 1970

The International Strasbourg Festival was the first destination of the St. Olaf Choir when it embarked for Europe on June 1, 1970. The only non-professional group ever to be invited to the Festival, the Choir was one of three American groups participating; the other two were the Juilliard String Quartet and the New York Chamber Soloists.[2]

Securing a place for the St. Olaf Choir at the Strasbourg Festival required advance efforts by Fred Schmidt, who went to Europe in 1969 for the express purpose of securing engagements for the St. Olaf Choir at summer festivals. The summer before, Fred and Lenore Schmidt made contacts for the Choir's 1970 visits to the Heinrich Schütz Festival in Breda, Holland, and to the International Organ Week Festival in Nurnberg, Germany. In Holland and Germany they met persons who had heard the St. Olaf Chapel Choir, with Kenneth Jennings conducting, perform Hugo Distler's *Totentanz* in Valparaiso in 1964.[3] As noted previously, the contact with the St. Olaf Chapel Choir helped prepare the way for the St. Olaf Choir to visit the Heinrich Schütz Festival.[4]

Jennings and Choir members, 1970

416

At first, Henri Lazare in Strasbourg was skeptical about college choirs, since their personnel changes every year. Like other Europeans, he was accustomed to professional choirs with a more stable membership. But he was willing to listen as Fred Schmidt, armed with tape recordings and glowing reviews from leading papers in the United States, persuaded him of the high standing of the St. Olaf Choir in America. The invitation was extended. [5]

Choir tourists, 1970

As mentioned, the Choir gave its concert in the St. Thomas Church in 1970. Among the numbers sung were "Cantate Domino" by Jan Pieterzoon Sweelinck, two anthems by Heinrich Schütz sung in German, *Sing Ye to the Lord* by Bach, *Magnificat* by Jean Berger, "Gloria" by Ralph Vaughan Williams, "De Profundis" by Arnold Schönberg, "When Jesus Wept" by William Billings, and "Psalm 90" by Charles Ives. The response was overwhelming. Not only was the Choir invited back the next year, but it was asked to open the Festival. It was not possible for the Choir to return in 1971, but in 1972 it was back in Strasbourg where it would sing, not in the smaller St. Thomas Church, but in the large Strasbourg Cathedral.

In Holland the St. Olaf Choir performed in the Breda Cathedral at the International Heinrich Schütz Festival. With the assistance of Dutch narrators, it presented Hugo Distler's *Totentanz*, which was broadcast live on Dutch Radio. After the

Choir in Breda Cathedral, June 1970
International Heinrich Schütz Festival

Television filming of Totentanz

Breda concert the Choir spent two days in Bussem near Amsterdam, recording the *Totentanz*, with dancers and narrator, for later broadcast by Dutch National Television and Radio.[6]

Choir member David Engen '71, who sang bass but also served as organist when the Choir performed *Totentanz*, had reason to remember the rehearsal in the Cathedral with its enormous new organ. With Dr. Jennings and the Choir down on the church floor and David high up in the organ loft, seeing only Jennings' back through a tiny monitor and trying to cope with an unfamiliar, complex instrument, communication was difficult between Choir and organ. Finally, the director dismissed the Choir and stomped up the long spiral staircase for what seemed sure to be a fearsome confrontation.

Recalled Engen: "I was sitting alone in front of this huge console, surrounded by cameras, monitors, five keyboards and stop knobs all over the place, waiting for the boom to drop. His mouth dropped open and all he could say was, 'Big, isn't it?'" The tension broken,

Choir organist David Engen

Choir meets Dr. Wilhelm Ehmann, Church Music School, Herford, Germany

Marktkirche, Hanover, 1970

Jennings sent the church's organist up to show Engen how to find the stops he needed. The organist also arranged for Engen to stay after the concert to play the wonderful new organ for his own relaxed enjoyment.[7]

Moving on to Hanover, Germany, the Choir sang in the Marktkirche where rebuilt walls and the reused fragments of stained glass provided evidence of the heavy damage the church had suffered in the war. In that setting the Choir sang, among other numbers, Leslie Bassett's "Collect for Peace" for which the words are:

> Almighty, Eternal, before whom nations rise and fall, we have wandered from Thy ways. We have put our trust in this world and refuge in the instruments of violence. Have mercy upon us, O Lord! Renew our faith in Thy power, justice, peace, love. Lead us, forgive us, inspire us. Amen.[8]

The next stop was Nurnberg, Germany, the site of the International Organ Week Festival. In the impressive St. Sebald Church, following a contemporary organ-percussion composition, the Choir sang "Psalm 90" by Charles Ives and *Magnificat* by Jean Berger.

19.
Internationale Orgelwoche
Musica Sacra Nürnberg 70

Dienstag, 16. Juni 1970 · 20 Uhr · St. Sebald

St. Olafs-Chor, USA

Leitung: L. Jennings
Siegfried Fink, Würzburg, Schlagwerk
Joachim Widmann, München, Orgel

Choir Program, Nurnberg

At the Berlin Wall

Choir in St. Sebald Church

Both the Choir and the St. Olaf Band, which was also touring Europe in the summer of 1970, had the opportunity to visit West Berlin, to look at the wall then separating the two parts of the city, and to perform in the Kaiser Wilhelm Memorial Cathedral. Before the Choir's concert there on June 18th, Gunter Pohl, pastor of the Cathedral, greeted the Choir from the pulpit in these words:

If our city, surrounded and walled in as it is, wants to remain alive, friends and visitors have to come here to prove their friendship. Every visit from outside is a proof that we have not been forgotten—and we are grateful for such evidence. It is our request that you should tell at home how we appreciate such interest in our city. Music forms bridges between nations. Music brings them closer together.[9]

There were other concerts before the tour concluded. Taking a break from its schedule, Choir members went to Oberammergau to see the famous Passion Play on a day when the weather was curiously attuned to the drama. It rained when Jesus was before Pilate, it hailed during the crucifixion scene, and at the moment of resurrection the sun came out.[10] To temper miracle with meteorology, the locals in Oberammergau say that such afternoon weather patterns are quite frequent.

In the small town of Kreis Dieburg, outside of Frankfurt, the audience refused to leave after "Beautiful Savior" and continued to clap and stamp its feet for more. Jennings and the Choir obliged with two short anthems, closing the concert with the fully appropriate "Gute Nacht" by Robert Schumann.

Concert in Kreis Dieburg, Germany

**Der St. Olaf Chor
Konzert 1970**

The St. Olaf Choir in Concert - 1970

**Kenneth L. Jennings - Dirigent
Conductor**

Am Dienstag, dem 23. Juni, um 20.30 Uhr, in WILTEN
in der „BASILIKA"

Choir Program, Wilten, Austria

As every St. Olaf Choir member knows, there are also the disconcerting times when there is no applause. During the final concert of the 1970 European tour, at the Basilica in Wilten, near Innsbruck, Austria, it seemed that the listeners were frozen by the inhibition of being in a church. The first section of the concert, which opened with "Cantate Domino" by Sweelinck and closed with Bach's *Sing Ye to the Lord*, was received in total silence. The Choir came back to the chancel for the second part of the program and silence still prevailed. But one young man was not able to restrain himself, according to Frederick Gonnerman, St. Olaf's director of information services who traveled with the Choir that year. "He brought his hands together in one sharp clap," wrote Gonnerman. "It was as if a flood had been released. The applause built slowly until nearly everyone joined in the crescendo of appreciation as Director Jennings stepped to the podium."[11]

The appreciation did not diminish as the Choir returned to the United States and thrilled its audiences on two domestic tours and at a number of other concerts before the return to Europe in the summer of 1972. On the 1971 tour, which took the ensemble south into Texas and Louisiana, the Choir was

Wilten Basilica, Austria

421

praised in Baton Rouge as "a most remarkable choral ensemble with an unexcelled tone quality and power to reach the audience."[12] In New Orleans, Charles L. DuFour wrote: "No better guarantee of a warm reception from an audience exists than fine voices, admirably trained, being used with enthusiasm."[13]

The concert program for 1971 opened with Giovanni Gabrieli's "Jubilate Deo," sung in Latin. Two Bach pieces comprised the rest of the first section. Other numbers that year included Felix Mendelssohn's "Psalm Two," sung in German, Carl Nielsen's "Benedictus Dominus," sung in Latin, Lennox Berkeley's *Mass for Five Voices*, also sung in Latin, Bassett's "Collect for Peace," Kenneth Jennings' composition, "Today, Heaven Sings," "Sons of Eve, Reward My Tidings," a sixteenth century Spanish carol, and "Fife and Drum," a contemporary carol by Herbert Bielawa.

Since 1971 was the centenary of the birth of F. Melius Christiansen, founder and first director of the St. Olaf Choir, it was fitting that his arrangements of "Wake, Awake" and "Beautiful Savior" should appear on the program. At the home concert, the spirited singing of "Wake, Awake" brought a standing ovation from the audience as did the closing with "Beautiful Savior."[14]

Bands and choirs devoted a weekend in the spring of 1971 to mark the 100th anniversary of the birth of F. Melius Christiansen. At the St. Olaf Instrumental Festival on May 8th the St. Olaf Band played Christiansen's "Second Norwegian Rhapsody" and, joined by guest instrumentalists, a Christiansen march, "Manitou Heights." At the Choral Festival the next day, a massed chorus of more than 1,000 voices, made up of the St. Olaf Choir, three other campus choral groups, seven solo choirs, and other choirs sang four compositions by F. Melius Christiansen: "Immortal Love," "Offer Unto God," "Wake, Awake," and "Beautiful Savior." Among the solo choirs was the Senior Choir of St. John's Lutheran Church of Northfield, directed by Carolyn Jennings. The conducting of the massed chorus was shared by Kenneth Jennings and Olaf C. Christiansen.[15]

St. Olaf College
Fine Arts Festival

1971
Choral Festival
a Christiansen Centenary Event

Sunday, May 9, 4:00 p.m.
Skoglund Center Auditorium
Northfield, Minnesota

St. Olaf Choir
Campus Choir
Manitou Singers
Viking Chorus
Minneapolis Southwest High School Choir
White Bear Lake High School Choir
Harmony High School Choir
Elbow Lake High School Choir
St. Ansgar, Iowa, High School Choir
Central Lutheran Church Choir, Minneapolis
St. John's Lutheran Choir, Northfield
Massed Choir

1971 Choral Festival
Christiansen Centenary Event

The annual tour of 1972 was the Choir's first eastern tour with Kenneth Jennings as director. Another significant "first" was being the first college choir to appear on the concert stage of the Kennedy Center for the Performing Arts in Washington, D. C. The Kennedy Center had its opening night May 27, 1971, and less than a year later, February 14, 1972, the St. Olaf Choir performed in the Center's Concert Hall.

This distinction came about in large part through Fred Schmidt's personal acquaintance with George London, famous baritone whom Fred booked one year to perform in the Artists Series at St. Olaf College. After London completed his concert career, he became the manager of the Kennedy Center, and was receptive to Fred's request to schedule the St. Olaf Choir for a concert in the new facility.[16]

Kennedy Center for the Performing Arts

It was also through Fred Schmidt's efforts that the St. Olaf Choir was the first college choir to perform in Philharmonic Hall in Lincoln Center, New York, and was booked in the Dorothy Chandler Pavilion of the Music Center in Los Angeles.[17] These achievements were reviewed with gratitude during the 1972 tour because Fred was retiring from his position as manager of St. Olaf music organizations and director of public functions at the end of August that year. Fred was honored by the St. Olaf Alumni clubs in New York City and Chicago during the tour. When the Choir gave its concert in Orchestra Hall in Chicago, Fred was given a plaque of appreciation for his

twenty-four years of service by Carol Meyer Ptack '64, former member of the St. Olaf Choir, and Ernest Holman '53, president of the Chicago area alumni/ae group.[18]

The review of the New York concert in Philharmonic Hall by Robert Sherman of the *New York Times*, stated that it was rare to find such an intriguing program of sacred music and "even rarer

Fred Schmidt honored, Chicago, 1972

Choir faces, ca. 1971

to find an amateur ensemble with such secure professionalism." In his awareness both of new features and enduring qualities, Sherman noted the greater emphasis on 20th-century music and the departures from purely a cappella singing. "Unaltered, however, are the admirable performing standards: the skillful blend, accurate pitch, flexible dynamics and precise diction."[19]

Lawrence Sears, reviewing the concert in the Kennedy Center Concert Hall in Washington, said that Jennings was following the wise precepts of F. Melius and Olaf Christiansen, "the solid practices of Bach and the a cappella style," but going about them in a different way. For example, in the Bach motet *Jesus, Priceless Treasure*, the voices were accompanied by a portative organ, cello, and string bass to support the choral sound.[20] And by opening the program with Distler's joyful "Sing to the Lord a New Song," Jennings demonstrated "that these dissonant buoyancies could tune up a program as well as any Baroque work." According to Sears, the surprise of the evening was the "wistful tenderness" in Charles Ives' "Psalm 90" with antiphonal sets of bells and low C ground swell.[21]

After the Choir had sung in Bethel Lutheran Church in Madison, Wisconsin, on the homeward stretch, Carmen Elsner writing for the *Wisconsin State Journal* began with the statement, "In the Midwest and elsewhere, the St. Olaf Choir has been regarded for years as the royal family in collegiate choral circles as well as a bulwark of the Lutheran choral tradition." Elsner wrote that Jennings had brought the Choir into the second half of the twentieth century with an emphasis on contemporary composers such as Bassett, Ives, and Ariel Ramirez.[22]

At many points along the way, the Choir's appearances were benefit concerts to raise money for such projects as Pakistani Relief, hospital buildings, and children's homes. Choir members were moved by their visit to the Matheny School for children with cerebral palsy in Peapack, New Jersey. They were shown the facilities, joined the young residents for supper, and gave a short program for the children and the staff.[23]

During the same year of the Choir's tour to the east coast, the St. Olaf choral sound was heard in movie theaters where the film, "The Great Northfield, Minnesota Raid," was being shown. The movie, starring Cliff

Robertson and Robert Duvall, was issued in 1972, but the St. Olaf Choir heard in the film was probably from 1967, when Olaf C. Christiansen was director. One of the few members of the viewing public to notice the anachronistic touch of local color in the film was Lyndon Crist, an avid student of the music and career of Olaf Christiansen. Catching the spirit of the movie's tongue in cheek interpretation of the Jesse James bank raid of 1876, Crist wrote:

> Cole Younger (played by Robertson) and company unobtrusively ride into Northfield to reconnoiter the territory and prepare the groundwork for the projected bank heist. Enroute, this intrepid band passes a small frame church on the outskirts of town and from within its humble walls issues forth the strains of Palestrina's "Hodie Christus Natus Est," sung as only the St. Olaf Choir can sing it.[24]

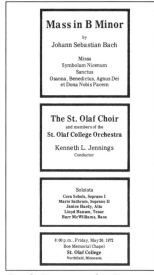

Ad for "The Great Northfield, Minnesota Raid"

France, Belgium, Switzerland in 1972

It was a unique and thrilling experience when the St. Olaf Choir opened the 1972 Strasbourg Festival by performing Bach's *Mass in B-Minor* with the Strasbourg Philharmonic Orchestra before an audience of 4,000 in the huge Strasbourg Cathedral. The opening of the Festival was set for June 9, 1972. The Choir left by chartered jet on June 2nd, allowing time first for a concert in Belgium and for rehearsals with the Strasbourg Orchestra and the soloists. To communicate with the Orchestra, Jennings had a St. Olaf student who was fluent in French do the necessary interpreting. The instrumentalists and the five soloists soon came to admire Jennings' thorough command of the music.[25]

Mass in B Minor
by
Johann Sebastian Bach

Missa
Symbolum Nicenum
Sanctus
Osanna, Benedictus, Agnus Dei
et Dona Nobis Pacem

The St. Olaf Choir
and members of the
St. Olaf College Orchestra

Kenneth L. Jennings
Conductor

Soloists
Cora Scholz, Soprano I
Marie Sathrum, Soprano II
Janice Hardy, Alto
Lloyd Hanson, Tenor
Burr McWilliams, Bass

8:00 p.m., Friday, May 26, 1972
Boe Memorial Chapel
St. Olaf College
Northfield, Minnesota

Bach Program for Boe Chapel, May 26, 1972

The Strasbourg Festival of 1972 observed its 34th season under the theme, "Bach and the 20th Century." The national significance of the occasion was underscored by the presence of Jacques Duhamel, French Minister of Cultural Affairs, who spoke to open the Festival. He was accompanied to the Cathedral by the prefect of Alsace and met by the bishop of Strasbourg, Monseigneur Elchinger. The international aspect was evident both in the presence of a choir from the United States and in the diverse origins of the soloists. Bishop Elchinger eloquently expressed

Cathedral in Strasbourg, France

the ecumenical dimension of the event by referring to the B-Minor Mass as "a monument of ecumenism."[26]

The performance itself fulfilled everyone's hopes and expectations. The Choir, the Orchestra, and the soloists were fired with enthusiasm under Kenneth Jennings' inspired conducting. The critics were powerfully impressed and pleased. One of them wrote, "The performance of the entire B Minor Mass by Bach put superhuman demands on all those involved, especially on the Choir. The ability to carry out the majestic choral arches until the 'Dona nobis pacem' without loss of tension is not given to every choir and conductor. . . . . The rich expressiveness and the almost chamber-music-like transparence of the singing of these young Americans was admirable."

St. Olaf Choir, Festival Orchestra
Strasbourg Cathedral, June 9, 1972

426

Another critic wrote: "The voices are young and true, the ensembles of an admirable homogeneity. One would look in vain for the slightest criticism to make of this international-class group."[27]

There was similar praise for the conductor. "Kenneth L. Jennings handled the baton with restraint and powerful expressiveness. Striving for a lean sound picture, he held the drums and trumpets back, but encouraged the singers and instrumentalists to penetrating musicality, without which Bach would remain dead notes."[28]

Kenneth Jennings conducting

Recalling the Strasbourg performance, Dr. Jennings praised the excellent singing of the five professional soloists, all of them established names in major opera houses.[29]

The triumph of the Choir at Strasbourg was the high point of the European tour of 1972, but the summer itinerary had just begun. The appearance at the Festival of Lorraine at Metz, France, called for three concerts June 10-12. On June 13 the Choir participated in the St. Denis Festival in Paris, singing in the largest cathedral in the country, named for the patron saint of France.

The Choir was in Lyon, France, on June 15 where it sang in the Basilica of Saint-Martin d'Ainay. A critic was enthused about "the exceptional quality of this ensemble: the voices are young, with good tone quality and well placed. Their pitch is impeccable, the section balance perfect, and all their interpretations, as concerns accents and shadings, reveal a profound understanding of the texts."[30]

Choir in St. Denis Cathedral, Paris

Last concert in Europe
Zug, Switzerland, June 19, 1972

The texts were those of a concert program very similar to the one used on the February 1972 eastern tour, the opening section consisting of Hugo Distler's "Sing to the Lord a New Song," Robert Stone's "Lord's Prayer," Sven-Erik Bäck's "Jesus, Remember Me," Bassett's "Collect for Peace," and Bernhard Lewkovitch's "Jubilate."

Two major works with accompaniment comprised the second and third sections. Bach's *Jesus, Priceless Treasure* was performed with cello, double bass, and organ. Charles Ives' "Psalm 90" was sung with organ and bells. The final section presented the "Gloria" from the *Missa Criolla* by Ariel Ramirez, Erik Bergman's "Rimfrost," and G. Winston Cassler's "The Godly Stranger," words by Naida Knatvold '34. Closing the program were two numbers arranged by F. Melius Christiansen, the second and third movements of *Psalm 50*, and "Beautiful Savior."[31]

After the Lyon concert the Choir had performances in Montpellier, France, Fribourg and Zug, Switzerland. The singers returned to the United States from Frankfurt, Germany, on June 22, 1972, while Dr. Jennings and his family remained in Europe for the remainder of the summer. In Stockholm, Sweden, Jennings spent time with Erik Erikson, famed conductor of the Swedish Radio Choir, who gave him access to the Radio Choir's library.[32]

St. Olaf College Centennial, 1974

The St. Olaf Choir was not yet in existence when St. Olaf College was founded, but it had its part to play in the centennial observances. St. Olaf College began with the signing of the Articles of Incorporation on November 6, 1874. The institution started as St. Olaf's School and achieved college status in 1889. Since its beginning, as the 1974 Choir tour program declared, the College was convinced "that the study and appreciation of music is an important part of education in the liberal arts." The keen interest in music present from

College Centennial Booklet

the earliest years provided the soil in which the instrumental and choral programs took root and flourished. F. Melius Christiansen joined the faculty in 1903, gave inspiring leadership to the musical life of the College, and founded the St. Olaf Choir in 1912.

Before the centennial year arrived, and after the accolades of the 1972 European tour had been savored, the Choir prepared for a tour to the west coast. It began with a concert in Hancher Auditorium in Iowa City, Iowa, on January 31, 1973. Concerts followed in Nebraska, Colorado, New Mexico, Arizona, and California. The Choir visited many of the places where it had sung in 1969, the first year Jennings was director. Two Choir members, Rebecca Nelson '73 and Deborah Schneider '73, spoke by phone with Howard Viken, host of a radio show at station WCCO in Minneapolis the morning after the San Diego concert.[33]

They could report that the tour had gone very well. Highlights included the presence of Jean Berger in Phoenix to hear the Choir sing his "Vision of Peace" in a concert hall designed by Frank Lloyd Wright. There was quiet reflecting about peace as the Choir sang the Berger number in Los Alamos, New Mexico, where the atomic bomb was perfected. On that same day, a large group of U. S. prisoners of war returned from Vietnam, reminding the

Choir of the prophet Isaiah's words in the "Vision of Peace": "And the ransomed of the Lord shall return, and come to Zion with singing; everlasting joy shall be upon their heads." (Isaiah 35:10).

Frederick H. Gonnerman

The tour had its usual share of zany happenings. After about five wearing days on the bus, some Choir members felt the need to purchase coloring books and crayons and hold coloring contests. Fred Gonnerman, appointed manager of the St. Olaf Choir and St. Olaf Orchestra in 1972, broke his toe while swimming in a pool in Los Angeles. Choir nurse Betty Schroeder turned cartwheels, without mishap. At the end of a concert in California, a member of the audience spoke up just as the Choir was set to sing one of its optional numbers. As the story appeared in the *Messenger*:

> We had taken our bows and Jennings walked back to his platform. He was poised and we were just ready to sing the first note, when some lady in the audience calls out, 'Beautiful Savior, please.' Tasteless, really tasteless.[34]

The Choir survived such moments with good humor and high spirits. On the return to the campus someone remarked, "One good thing that came out of tour was a four week vacation from choir practice." The home concert was well received despite the noise from the heating and ventilating system in Skoglund Gymnasium. The reviewer commended the Choir for its ability to make the music remain new, spontaneous, and alive for each performance. They could do this because of "the enthusiasm and musical sense of the choir members, as well as the remarkable leadership of Dr. Jennings."[35]

The same qualities were in evidence when the St. Olaf Choir set out on its tour in early 1974, the centennial year of St. Olaf College. In what was essentially a midwestern

St. Olaf Choir Program, 1974

tour, the Choir went to towns and cities in Minnesota, Wisconsin, Illinois, Missouri, Iowa, and South Dakota. The Choir's Centennial Tour Program included pictures of the Choirs of 1913, 1935, 1965, and 1972, pictures of the three directors, and a partial listing of communities to be visited where the Choir had given concerts in its early years. It also provided notes on the familiar and new numbers on the concert program.

Familiar to listeners were Gretchaninof's "Our Father," Georg Schumann's "How Great Are Thy Wonders," Gustav Schreck's "Advent Motet," and Bach's motet for double choir, *The Spirit Also Helpeth Us.*

"Sixteenth-century Latin motets have also been a part of the Choir repertoire, particularly since the days when Olaf C. Christiansen was director," stated the notes with respect to the first section of the program with works by Palestrina, Esquivel, and Byrd. From more recent times, but familiar since the Choir introduced it in the late 1940s, was Jean Berger's "Brazilian Psalm."

Among works new to audiences were the "Kyrie" and "Sanctus" from the *Mass* for double choir by Frank Martin, contemporary Swiss composer. When an appropriate organ was available, the Choir sang as an optional number the dramatic "Motet for the Archangel Michael" by Swedish composer Bengt Hambraeus. The Christiansen musical legacy was honored in the fourth section of the program with Olaf C. Christiansen's "Sing Nowell, Sing Gloria" and F. Melius Christiansen's "O Day Full of Grace" and "Beautiful Savior."

One of the Minnesota towns on the tour was Zumbrota, between Northfield and Rochester, where the Choir sang in the high school auditorium. After attending the concert, a reviewer summarized the experience: "Whether they were youngsters hearing one of the world's great choirs for the first time, casual listeners who came only on a whim, or nostalgic alumni dreaming of the 'good old days', the audience was treated to an evening of wonderful choral music."[36]

In light of the centennial year and the element of nostalgia in the Choir's program, Robert Oudal of Rochester, after the concert in the Mayo Civic Theater, credited Kenneth Jennings with keeping the tradition and improving its voice. The Choir still had good intonation while some "gentle vibratos" were allowed to warm the tone. Vowels must be stressed in a cappella work, but the Choir had also worked on achieving clear consonants. In all, wrote Oudal, the Choir had proven itself to be "a worthy musical ambassador of the school in its centennial year."[37]

Another of the 1974 tour appearances of the 65-voice St. Olaf Choir was in the Kiel Opera House in St. Louis, Missouri. A review had high praise for the sound "that at times resembles a perfectly tuned organ," for admirable diction, and acute sense of pitch. The conductor was described as "an excellent musician and a superb director who communicates his wishes unmistakably without ostentatious gestures." The Choir was "a perfectly balanced group," said the reviewer, with nearly equal numbers of sopranos, altos, tenors, and basses.[38]

In St. Louis the balance was threatened by a particularly powerful flu bug that swept through the Choir. The demands of the concert were met, but once the performance was over the hasty medications dispensed by nurse Betty Schroeder could not keep up with the needs of woozy Choir members. Tour manager Fred Gonnerman herded twenty or more of them into the bus and to the hospital. In Fred's memory is a vivid picture of twenty Oles sitting all in a row, each one with a thermometer in her or his mouth.[39]

The concert at Augustana College in Rockford, Illinois, prompted critic Bruce Johnson to issue a "Bravo!" at the beginning and end of his review. He liked "the sweep and power of the choir's emotional artillery—from the finest lustre of a 16th-century motet by Byrd to the soulful gusto of an American spiritual," namely, L. L. Fleming's arrangement of "Give Me Jesus." For Johnson, the most memorable highlight was "A Motet for the Archangel Michael" with its crashing tonal blasts depicting the strength of the forces of good. Johnson concluded with a cheery, "Happy trails to the St. Olaf Choir, happy 100th birthday to St. Olaf College and, again, bravo!"[40]

Music critic Michael Anthony issued the equivalent of another "bravo" when he reviewed the appearance of the St. Olaf Choir with the Minnesota Orchestra on April 11, 1974, in O'Shaughnessy Auditorium on the campus of the College of St. Catherine in St. Paul. With Stanislaw Skrowaczewski conducting, Choir and Orchestra presented Mozart's *Requiem in D minor*. Characterizing the work as "highly dramatic but also severely liturgical," Anthony stated that it required clear and precise choral singing. "And fortunately," he wrote, "the singers from St. Olaf came through splendidly in these matters and as well with strong, rich tone and even balance."[41]

The 1974 Centennial Tour Program included a brief article entitled, "The College and the Choir," in which this announcement appeared: "As a part of its Centennial celebration, St. Olaf College hopes to break ground for new music/theater facilities this year on Founders' Day, Nov. 6." Five million dollars of the Centennial Fund had been designated for the new facilities.

The plans were soon changed, however, because it proved less costly to build a separate music hall and renovate the women's gymnasium for a speech and theater building. Ground was broken for the new music hall September 5, 1974, and construction soon began. On November 6, 1974, exactly one hundred years after the birth of the institution, the date stone was laid for the Christiansen Hall of Music. Participating in the ceremony were Dr. Olaf C. Christiansen, former director of the St. Olaf Choir, Mrs. Gertrude Boe Overby, former voice teacher at the College and soloist with the Choir when it was directed by F. Melius Christiansen, Dr. Adolph White, chair of the music department, and Mr. David E. Johnson, Vice President.

Among the centennial festivities in which the St. Olaf Choir took part were worship services at Holden Lutheran Church near Kenyon, the church once served by the Reverend Bernt Julius Muus, founder of St. Olaf College, and St. John's Lutheran Church in Northfield, where generations of St. Olaf students worshiped before Boe Memorial Chapel was built. On both of these occasions, the St. Olaf Choir sang and Dr. Sidney A. Rand, president of the College, preached the sermon.

Groundbreaking for music hall, September 1974
Beatrix Lien, Charlotte Donhowe, Gertrude Overby with shovels

Filling the datestone, November 6, 1974
Johnson, Overby, Christiansen, White

In conjunction with the Centennial the St. Olaf Choir also went to Detroit in the fall where it sang before the biennial convention of the American Lutheran Church. Another special Choir appearance during the centennial year was in Minneapolis when it again joined the Minnesota Orchestra. Performing at the dedication of the new Orchestra Hall, the two groups presented Ravel's *Daphnis and Chloe*. Performances took place October 23, 24, and 25, 1974.

St. Olaf Choir in Orchestra Hall
Minneapolis, October 1974

Vienna and Rome in 1975

When the St. Olaf faculty adopted the 4-1-4 academic calendar in 1963, it opened new opportunities for study abroad, especially during the fall semester and the January interim. But for members of such music organizations as the St. Olaf Band and St. Olaf Choir, participation in terms abroad was nearly impossible because of rehearsing and performing schedules. A partial solution was found by designing interim programs abroad for the entire membership of a music organization. Donald Berglund took the St. Olaf Orchestra to Norway to study and perform during more than one January interim. Miles Johnson, director of the St. Olaf Band, organized and led Band interims to England. These were full credit courses on a par with interim study programs offered by other departments.

For the St. Olaf Choir, Kenneth Jennings planned three weeks in Vienna and a week in Rome for January of 1975. In Vienna there was a two-week lecture series on the *lied* and opera by an American teaching at the Vienna Conservatory of Music, tours to historic sites, attendance at operas in the evening, and two performances by the Choir.

Kenneth and Carolyn Jennings
Vienna, January 1975

434

Members enjoyed the quiet and order of Vienna, the parks, the beer, the chocolate, and hot chestnuts sold on street corners.[42]

After a sixteen-hour train ride through the Alps the Choir found itself in Rome, much different from Vienna in the noise of honking horns, screeching tires, and hordes of young people on the streets. In Rome Choir members quickly made contact with other Oles in the city, including about forty students enrolled in a St. Olaf religion course entitled "Christian Rome," supervised by Joseph M. Shaw, and Malcolm Gimse's interim group studying "The Arts of Europe" in Germany and Italy.

The presence of the St. Olaf Choir in Rome was significant for more than the obvious reason of a choir from a Lutheran college singing for His Holiness, Pope Paul VI, head of the Roman Catholic Church. The year itself was significant, because 1975 was a Holy Year. Since the fifteenth century, every twenty-fifth year was set aside as a Jubilee Year for pilgrimages, special masses, profession of faith, and prayers. Even the month was significant. As a result of the Vatican Council, churches in Rome observed the third week in January as the Week of Prayer for Christian Unity, a fact mentioned by Pope Paul VI at the papal audience attended by the St. Olaf students on Wednesday, January 29, 1975.

Oles in St. Peter's Square
In foreground: Mac Gimse, Sister Galema (in cape), Sister Elsbeth Klompé
(with purse), Joe Shaw

Modern papal audiences, in a spacious hall of contemporary design that accommodates 6,000 people, are informal if not frequently tumultuous affairs. The Choir did its singing from its place within the crowd before the Pope entered, as did other groups. It was also invited to sing after the Pope was on the

Walking to the papal audience, Sister Galema, Steve, Lisa, Carolyn, Mark, Kenneth Jennings

platform. The Vatican paper, *L'Osservatore Romano*, reported: "The choir of young students sang in polyphony, in Latin, and they won applause and satisfaction from the Pope and all those present."[43]

Speaking to the St. Olaf Choir during his address, Pope Paul VI said, "We know that you have come to Rome as pilgrims, that you are young people who have understood the 'signs of the times,' and whose hearts are open to the Holy Spirit and to his inspirations. On our part, we thank you

St. Olaf Choir at papal audience

for your presence, for your singing, for your sharing in the renewal and reconciliation of this Holy Year. And we assure you of our gratitude."[44]

Later in the papal audience, Dr. Jennings was invited to the stage to meet the Pope and to receive a commemorative medal that bore the Pope's likeness on one side and the Pentecost

Pope Paul VI and Dr. Jennings

scene on the other. The Jennings family, the Choir, and all the other Oles present that day were under the wing of a vivacious, cosmopolitan friend of St. Olaf College, Miss Leideke Galema, who led the group into the hall, showed them where to stand, gave them tips on holding their ground against the Pope's more frenzied fans, and escorted them out again. Sister Galema, who liked to be called "Miss Galema" and preferred smart clothes to religious habits, was the director of Foyer Unitas (Hearth of Unity), a small ecumenical foundation located near the Piazza Navona. Established and conducted by the Ladies of Bethany, an order of Dutch nuns, the Foyer Unitas had a special calling to extend hospitality to visitors and to introduce non-Roman Catholics to the sacred and classical monuments of Rome.[45]

The long and warm friendship between the Ladies of Bethany and St. Olaf College began through St. Olaf religion professor Ansgar Sovik and his wife, Muriel Sovik. In 1966 the Soviks came to Rome from Jerusalem where they had supervised a group of students on St. Olaf's first Term in the Middle East. Miss Galema and her associates gave them guided tours of Rome and arranged a private audience for the group with Pope Paul VI. From that connection many learning opportunities followed, including the cooperation of the Foyer Unitas with Dr. Sovik in organizing the St. Olaf interim course, "Christian Rome," which

Johannes Cardinal Willebrands, Miss Leideke Galema, Miss Josefa Koet Receiving sculpture by A. Malcolm Gimse

began in 1969 and for which the Ladies of Bethany conducted superb tours and lectures for more than twenty years.

Officially, the Choir's visit to Rome was arranged by the Secretariat for Christian Unity whose president was Johannes Cardinal Willebrands, 1976 recipient of the honorary degree, Doctor of Literature, from St. Olaf College. But the immediate contact was with Miss Galema. Through her efforts and connections, the Choir gave two concerts, participated in the papal audience, had a private tour of the Sistine Chapel, and sang at two ecumenical services.

The concerts, presented the evenings of Tuesday, January 28th, and Thursday, the 30th, took place in the Auditorio del Gonfalone, a sixteenth-century oratory dubbed "the Painted Box" by Choir members because of the Renaissance frescoes on every wall. Maestro Gastone Tosato, director of the Gonfalone, praised the Choir in his speech of welcome. A review in *Il Tempo* stated that "the splendid example of the St. Olaf Choir in its concert at the Gonfalone comes as an inspiration to all of us, as a lesson in discipline and high culture." With words of commendation for every piece, the review concluded that it was "a concert presented with a care, a competence and a love which was truly extraordinary."[46]

One of the rarest experiences ever known by the St. Olaf Choir was the privilege of spending a quiet hour and a half in the Sistine Chapel, free from

GONFALONE

AUDITORIO DI VIA DEL GONFALONE 32-a - TEL. 65.59.52

MARTEDI 28 e GIOVEDI 30 GENNAIO 1975 - Ore 21,15

CORO DI SAN OLAF

dell'UNIVERSITA' del NORTHFIELD (Minnesota)

direttore

KENNETH JENNINGS

Musiche di:

SWEELINCK - da PALESTRINA - BYRD - BACH - - LOCKWOOD - SCHONBERG
MESSIAEN - MARTIN - JENNINGS - GRETSJANINOW - FREED

Per informazioni rivolgersi alla segreteria del CORO POLIFONICO ROMANO vicolo della Scimia 1-b

Poster for Rome concerts, 1975

Concert in the Gonfalone
Rome, January 1975

the noise and bustle of tourists, on Saturday, February 1, 1975. Led by Miss Galema, the Choir members and the other two St. Olaf student groups ascended Bernini's Grand Staircase and were invited into the Chapel by Monsignor Jean Van Lierde, Vicar General for Vatican City. The Monsignor spoke a prayer for Christian unity and Miss Galema gave a brief talk on the Sistine ceiling, describing Michelangelo's art as depicting the love affair between God and the human family.

Then, in the stillness of the famous room where Popes are elected, under the Michelangelo ceiling frescoes and in the presence of the artist's powerful Last Judgment scene, the St. Olaf Choir sang "Sicut Cervus," sixteenth-century work by G. P. Palestrina, at one time the choir master of the Sistine Chapel. It was a moment for complete silence and tears. Professor Mac Gimse remembered:

> The Vicar General of the Vatican and the Rector of the Chapel wept for joy and offered a benediction. As the students and their professors left and fanned out onto the Piazza San Pietro, we knew we had experienced a profound spiritual and aesthetic event. We were transformed by the living spiritual unity between Michelangelo's 16th century masterpiece and the Choir's gentle accompaniment.[47]

Still under the spell of the Sistine Chapel, the Choir and the Rome interim group walked a short distance to participate in an ecumenical service at St. Ornofrio Church. The St. Olaf Choir sang and Professor Shaw gave the meditation.

A small historical footnote may be attached to the account of the St. Olaf Choir in Rome. After its tour of eastern cities in 1920 and during succeeding years, the Choir's reputation was growing. After it had sung in Chicago in 1924, Herman Devries, writing for the *Chicago American*, extolled the Choir, calling it "the greatest of its kind in America, and perhaps in the world." And he added: "If Mgr. Rella came all the way from Rome to show us the Vatican singers, we can safely send Christiansen and the St. Olaf Choir on a visit to Rome."[48]

Ken Jennings, Joe Shaw and host St. Ornofrio Church , Rome

Norway, 1980

Between its return from Rome in February of 1975 and its departure for Norway in the summer of 1980, the St. Olaf Choir followed an unusually heavy schedule. In addition to its annual tours, the Choir lent its presence to events related to the dedication of the new Christiansen Hall of Music and to the celebration of the 75th anniversary of the Minnesota Orchestra.

For its 1976 tour, when the nation was celebrating the Bicentennial, the St. Olaf Choir again made its way to music centers in the east. It gave concerts in such major halls as Orchestra Hall in Chicago, the Academy of Music in Philadelphia, Avery Fisher Hall in Lincoln Center, New York, the Kennedy Center in Washington, and Severance Hall in Cleveland.[49] The work that drew most comment was Aaron Copland's setting of the creation story, "In the Beginning," with Diana Reed '77 as mezzo soprano soloist. Another favorite was "A Motet for the Archangel Michael," by Bengt

Choir Reception in Washington, 1976. Al and Gretchen Quie, Sid and Lois Rand, Ken and Carolyn Jennings, and friends

Hambraeus. It was performed with organ accompaniment, ably provided by Jason Enquist.

When the $4.2 million music hall was dedicated on September 12, 1976, the St. Olaf Choir performed "Festival Alleluia," a composition by Kenneth Jennings written for the occasion. The building was named in honor of F.

Singing "Festival Alleluia"

Dedication of Christiansen Hall of Music, 1976
Howell Skoglund, Olaf Christiansen, David Preus, Sidney Rand

Melius and Olaf C. Christiansen who gave leadership in music to St. Olaf College for a period of sixty-five years. Olaf was on the platform for the rite of dedication performed by the Reverend David W. Preus, president of the American Lutheran Church.[50]

Present for the dedication and a look at the new music building were Mr. and Mrs. Henry M. Halvorson. Henry was one of Olaf's contemporaries from college days and a fellow member of the St. Olaf Choir that went to the west coast in 1924-25. Some of his snapshots from the tour appeared in an earlier chapter. Some fifty years later, he and Mrs. Halvorson made a different kind of contribution to St. Olaf music. Their generosity provided the music library for the new facility. The Halvorson Library, indispensable to the music program, is located in the west wing of the main floor of the Christiansen Hall of Music.[51]

The year of dedication of the Christiansen Hall of

Mr. and Mrs. Henry Halvorson, Pres. Rand

442

Christiansen Hall of Music

Music extended into 1977 and included the residency at the College of the Polish composer and conductor, Krzysztof Penderecki. The St. Olaf Choir joined other music organizations in performing four of Penderecki's works on campus, including "The Magnificat," conducted by the composer. Dr. Jennings hosted Penderecki, gave a symposium lecture on the "Magnificat," and prepared and read the citation for the awarding of the honorary Doctor of Music degree to the Polish musician on March 18, 1977.[52]

Joining the Minnesota Orchestra in celebrating its 75th anniversary, the St. Olaf Choir flew to New York to appear with the Orchestra at a concert in Carnegie Hall on January 10, 1978. As he did on other occasions when the Choir sang with the Minnesota Orchestra, Dr.

St. Olaf College Department of Music presents a

Program of Works by

Krzysztof Penderecki

Visiting Composer-in-Residence

Krzysztof Penderecki, *conductor*

Leroy Lehr, *bass-baritone*
John Goldsmith, *countertenor*
John Rudzinski, *countertenor*
Lloyd Hanson, *tenor*
Richard Steen, *baritone*
Michael Richardson, *baritone*
Burr McWilliams, *bass-baritone*

St. Olaf Chapel Choir
Robert Scholz, *conductor*
St. Olaf Choir
Kenneth Jennings, *conductor*
St. Olaf College Orchestra
Donald Berglund, *conductor*
St. Olaf Percussion Ensemble
Northfield Treble Chorus and members of the St. Olaf Manitou Singers
prepared by Mary Waller and Carolyn Jennings

7:30 p.m., Sunday, March 20, 1977
Boe Memorial Chapel

St. Olaf College

Program for Penderecki Concert

443

St. Olaf Choir and Minnesota Orchestra
Carnegie Hall, New York, January 1978

Jennings recruited additional singers from the voice faculty and the Northfield community. Conducted by the Orchestra's music director, Stanislaw Skrowaczewski, the Choir and Orchestra performed Ravel's *Daphnis and Chloe*.[53] Also on the program was Isaac Stern, playing with the Orchestra in the New York premier performance of Krzysztof Penderecki's *Concerto for Violin and Orchestra*, completed by the composer during his residency at St. Olaf the year before.

In her review of the concert, Harriett Johnson of the *New York Post* praised the Choir, "one of the

Concert in St. Paul Cathedral

444

world's greatest," for its part in the Ravel Suites. "Most notable was their singing in the long a cappella section of Suite No. 1 when they performed with ravishing tone, ending absolutely on pitch as the orchestra joined them."[54]

Entrance to Oslo Concert Hall

Two special concerts belonged to the upper midwest tour of 1978. On January 29 the Choir sang a dedicatory concert in the St. Paul Cathedral to help celebrate the completion of renovation work on the building. On February 9th, the Choir appeared in Minneapolis at the convention of the American Choral Directors Association.[55]

The St. Olaf Choir had last visited Norway in 1955 when Olaf C. Christiansen was director and Kenneth Jennings, then a recent addition to the St. Olaf music faculty, was assistant director. In 1980 the Choir was invited to perform at the International Music Festival in Bergen, Norway, one of the highlights of the 22-day, 17-concert tour. The tour was sponsored by *Nordmanns Forbundet* (the League of Norsemen).

Program for Norway Tour

Leaving Minneapolis the day after commencement, May 26, 1980, the Choir flew to Oslo for its first concert, in the new *Konserthus*. The Choir began by singing the Norwegian national anthem, "Ja, vi elsker dette landet," for King Olav, Crown Prince Harald, and Crown Princess Sonja.

During the intermission His Majesty Olav V greeted both the present and former presidents of St. Olaf College. Attending the concert was Dr. Harlan F. Foss, elected on March 21, 1980, as

Dr. Harlan F. Foss
Seventh president of
St. Olaf College

445

Dr. Rand becomes Ambassador
Sid and Lois with Vice President
Walter Mondale, February 14, 1980

His Majesty King Olav V of Norway

Mark Jennings meets Mayor of Oslo

Oslo Town Hall

seventh president of the College. His predecessor, Dr. Sidney A. Rand, had resigned on February 1st and was sworn in as United States Ambassador to Norway by Vice President Walter Mondale on February 14th. The day after the concert there was a reception for the Choir and a St. Olaf tour group at the Oslo Town Hall.[56]

One Oslo newspaper called the concert a "Choir Event." "We have missed the St. Olaf Choir for a quarter century," wrote Reimar Riefling. Of the current ensemble he observed: "Its special characteristic has been preserved, but its standards appear to me to have been heightened. Here we are faced with a discipline and vocal quality of highest order." Riefling was amazed that Choir and Director "mastered the entire program from memory."[57]

At 7:30 the next morning, May 29, 1980, the Choir left by bus for a concert in Kristiansand. At the lunch stop it was announced that Gay

446

Gay Gonnerman and Melissa Flynn

Gonnerman '81 and Melissa Flynn '81 were missing. They had overslept, but made every effort to catch up with the Choir. They took the afternoon train but missed the concert, making their guilty appearance at the reception. Dreading the inevitable meeting with Dr. Jennings, they were immensely relieved when he welcomed them. "We immediately felt his sense of relief at having the lost sheep returned to the fold."[58]

Among the choral numbers prepared for the Scandinavian tour were works by Heinrich Schütz and J. S. Bach, the latter represented by the motet *Singet dem Herrn*. Extremely well received by the Norwegian audiences were Edvard Grieg's setting of the folk tune, "Hvad est du dog skjøn" and the modern Norwegian composer Knut Nystedt's "O Crux." Of Nystedt's piece Johan Kvandal in Oslo wrote that it was "written with understanding of the text and done with brilliant utilization of choral possibilities." A Stavanger reviewer had just one word for the Nystedt composition: "fabulous!"[59]

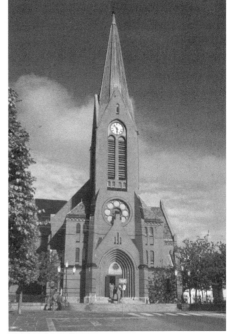

Our Savior's Church in Haugesund

447

Singing at Grieg's home
Dan Egan '80 conducting

The Choir also sang Richard Strauss's "Hymne," "The Exaltation of Christ," commissioned for the Norway tour and composed by St. Olaf faculty member Charles Forsberg, and Weyse's "O Day Full of Grace," arranged by F. Melius Christiansen, more familiar to Norwegians with the words, "God Bless Our Fatherland." The performance of "Brazilian Psalm" by Jean Berger was heard with great interest, one reviewer calling it "a fascinating piece."

On the program were two motets by Aaron Copland, "Help Us, O Lord" and "Sing Ye Praises to Our King." Commented reviewer Lage Robak in Aalesund, "Copland is seldom heard here which is a pity." The two spirituals always proved popular, "I'm Going Home," with baritone solo by Bradley Ellingboe '80, and "I Believe, this is Jesus."

On June 2nd the St. Olaf Choir sang in Grieg Hall at the Bergen International Music Festival. The reviewer commended each section: the low basses, the "round and warm altos," tenors "of the finest brand," and the "sparklingly bright sopranos." In his generous praise of the performance he was unashamed to acknowledge the powerful feelings that were generated. Anton Chr. Meyer put his finger on what the St. Olaf Choir and its directors have always aimed for when he wrote:

> Despite all that can be said for the choir's high technical standard, the most important praise remains, namely to acclaim its fulness of expression, its devotion and sincerity, warmth of feeling and the joy of singing which penetrated every number.

He even mentioned the "moist eyes" when the Choir wound up its four encores with "Norge mitt Norge" and commented on the "nearly perfect Norwegian." Meyer had high praise for the "remarkable, warm, and unstrained voice" of the "unnamed soprano soloist," who was Suzan Hanson '80.[60] At this important Festival concert in Grieg Hall in Bergen the recording was made that was issued under the title "Reflections of Norway."

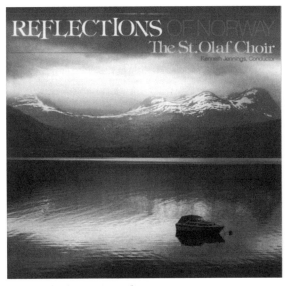

St. Olaf Choir Recording   Photo by Gay Gonnerman

Norway was celebrating "St. Olav Days" and the 950th anniversary of the Battle of Stiklestad when the St. Olaf Choir gave its concert in Nidaros Cathedral in Trondheim on June 8th. Hans Gaare headed his review with the emphatic statement, "The St. Olaf Choir was an experience." He took pleasure in the whole program, although he thought the Cathedral's acoustics worked against "the complete transparency of Bach's impressive polyphony" in the eight-part *Singet dem Herrn*. Gaare concluded his review with this paragraph:

> Last on the program was the legendary F. Melius Christiansen's treatment of the melody from 1665, "Praise to the Lord." The choral potentials of the arrangement were fully exploited by the St. Olaf Choir. The large audience in the cathedral rose in gratitude and admiration.[61]

The Norwegian critics tended to heap compliments on the St. Olaf Choir, but occasionally they expressed reservations on one point or another. For example, Dag Gjaerum characterized the Christiansen arrangements of "Praise to the Lord" and "Beautiful Savior" as "musical war horses," but conceded that the Choir made them sound more magnificent than he thought possible.

Reporting on a concert in the Kristiansand Cathedral, Amund Dahlen described "Praise to the Lord" as "pompous yet dignified." Dahlen felt that the audience could have been spared the two encores, "Norge mitt Norge" and "Deilig er jorden" ("Beautiful Savior"), reflecting the fairly common Norwegian view that the latter piece is a Christmas song, which is true of the Norwegian text.

Yet the review carried the heading, "Sterling Concert." And Dahlen had a number of good things to say about the Choir's rendering of Schütz, Bach, Grieg's "Hvad est du dog skjøn," and Berger's "Brazilian Psalm." Of the last-named piece he said "the performance was exquisite in every regard and the difficult rhythmic passages were sung with crispness and force."[62]

The concert in Larvik, the coastal town where F. Melius Christiansen grew up, came near the end of the tour, on Friday, June 13, 1980. "The applause never seemed to end in Larvik Church last night following the St. Olaf Choir concert," wrote Svend Einar Hansen. "The Choir verified its world class to the fullest, and the concert can hardly be described in words. A simple exclamation mark would be more fitting."[63]

Knowing full well the historic significance of Larvik, Choir members felt that they were singing for F. Melius Christiansen, a man, said Dr. Jennings, "to whom was given something few people get, the fact that he *changed* things."[64] It was a tribute packed with meaning, appropriate to the memory of F. Melius in its directness and brevity.

One of the Larvik reviewers had knowing comments on the Bach and Nystedt pieces, among others. Dag Gjaerum thought the performance of *Singet dem Herrn* was "an overwhelming experience." He wrote: "The eight-part choir sang brilliantly and the tenors, unstrained, soared to such heights that it was a joy to hear. In the forte portions the dynamics were always controlled so that there was no yielding to any temptation toward excess."

Three basses, one tenor
Jeffery Hanson, Brent Benjamin,
Todd Lines, Peter Narum

As to Knut Nystedt's "O Crux," the reviewer wanted his readers to understand its value. "For many, modern church music has unaccustomed sounds and structures, but this is a work of great power. A more 'daring' use of harmonics may at times better express certain moods in the texts than do customary choral arrangements. We were particularly taken with the interplay between the high sopranos and the deep resonant basses."[65]

As encores the Choir was prepared to sing Åhlén's "Sommersalm" in Swedish and, in Norwegian, "Norge mitt Norge" and "Deilig er jorden"

Relaxing at the Rand's

("Beautiful Savior"). In Larvik, the Choir sang "Beautiful Savior" in both Norwegian and English.

The 1980 St. Olaf Choir tour in Norway drew to a close with a final concert in Skien on June 14th. There were emotions of sadness for many members, especially the Seniors, as the Choir gathered for devotions before the concert in the Skien church. But it was a fine performance and the Choir arrived in Oslo the next day in high spirits. After getting settled in the hotel and doing some shopping, everyone dressed up and took the tram to the U. S. Ambassador's residence for "a tremendous party and dinner" hosted by Ambassador and Mrs. Sidney A. Rand.[66]

The food, drink, and desserts were delicious and in abundance. After dining, the group went out on the terrace for a variety of improvised, hilarious skits and acts. In borrowed plaid skirts and using their pitch pipes to simulate the sound of bagpipes, Steve Sandberg '81 and Doug Strandell '81 danced a jig and told jokes in their best Scottish accents. Moving indoors, the Choir heard tenor Stuart Jasper sing Gershwin's "Summertime," and enjoyed performances by others. Finally, the entire Choir sang "Norge, mitt Norge," "Och jungfrun," "Gute Nacht" by Schumann, and Erik Bergman's "Rimfrost." It had been a most memorable evening, wrote Choir journalist Steve Sandberg.[67]

Singing in Swedish, German, and Norwegian for its own entertainment, as well as in concert, was indicative of the Choir's adaptability to other languages and cultures. Latin motets, works by Bach and others performed in German, songs in French, Spanish, and other languages were commonplace. Singing in Norwegian was expected from the St. Olaf Choir; it had done so for decades. What at first had been a natural expression of an immigrant culture became a step toward achieving international recognition. The European tours of 1970, 1972, 1975, and 1980 enhanced the Choir's standing in the western world. Ahead was the opportunity to enter the wider and older world of the Orient. Within a few years after completing its Norway tour, the St. Olaf Choir would be singing in China, Japan, and Korea.

Notes for Chapter 14 EUROPEAN TOURS

1. Frederick H. Gonnerman, "Choir heartily welcomed," *Northfield News*, June 25, 1970, 12.

2. Frederick H. Gonnerman, "Europe, 1970," *The St. Olaf Aumnus* 18 (July 1970), 8. Gonnerman, who accompanied the Choir on its trip to Europe, was Director of Information Services and Editor of *The St. Olaf Alumnus*, later to be called *Saint Olaf*.

3. Memo: Frederick A. Schmidt to President Sidney Rand, Dr. Kenneth Jennings, Dr. Adolph White, Dr. Donald Berglund, Dr. Albert Finholt, Mr. David Johnson, August 30, 1968. STOARCHIV.

4. Interview: Joseph M. Shaw with Kenneth Jennings, October 11, 1995.

5. Fred Schmidt, "Christiansen surprises choir with athletic prowess less well known than musical talents," fifth segment in a five-article series on Schmidt's association with the St. Olaf Choir, *Northfield News*, March 25, 1992; interview: JMS and Betty Stromseth with Fred and Lenore Schmidt, December 26, 1994.

6. Gonnerman, "Europe, 1970," 9.

7. Letter from David Engen to Bob Johnson, January 10, 1994.

8. Cited in Gonnerman, "Europe, 1970," 11.

9. *Ibid.*, 14.

10. Gonnerman, "Choir heartily welcomed," 12.

11. Gonnerman, "Europe, 1970," 13.

12. Anne Price, "St. Olaf Choir Has Unexcelled Tone," *Sunday Advocate*, Baton Rouge, LA, February 14, 1971.

13. Charles L. DuFour, "St. Olaf College Choir Puts Joy Into Its Music," *The States-Item*, New Orleans, LA, February 13, 1971.

14. Bob Chamberlin, "A Very Sound Experience," *Manitou Messenger* (*MM*), February 26, 1971.

15. "Music fest to mark Christiansen centenary," *MM*, April 30, 1971.

16. Interview: JMS and Betty Stromseth with Fred and Lenore Schmidt, December 26, 1994.

17. Joseph M. Shaw, *History of St. Olaf College 1874-1974* (Northfield, Minnesota: The St. Olaf College Press, 1974), 526.

18. *Saint Olaf* 20 (Spring 1972), 13.

19. Robert Sherman, "65 in St. Olaf Choir Sing Sacred Music of Several Periods," *New York Times*, February 15, 1972.

20. The portative organ that the Choir took on tours was given to the College in memory of Dorcas Ensrud and in thanksgiving for the dedication to church music of her husband, Dr. Paul H. Ensrud, professor emeritus of music at St. Olaf College. *Saint Olaf* 20 (Spring 1972), 12.

21. Lawrence Sears, "St. Olaf Choir Voices Soar for New Leader," The *Evening Star*, Washington, D. C., February 15, 1972.

22. Carmen Elsner, "Royal Family of College Choirs Upholds Professional Reputation," *Wisconsin State Journal,* February 21, 1972.

23. *MM*, February 25, 1972.

24. Letter from Lyndon Crist to JMS, July 19, 1996.

25. Interview: JMS with Fred Schmidt, January 24, 1995.

26. Le "Nouvel Alsacien," June 10, 1972.

27. Cited in *Saint Olaf* 20 (Summer 1972), 12.

28. *Ibid.*

29. Conversation: JMS with Kenneth Jennings, December 16, 1996.

30. Cited in *Saint Olaf* 20 (Summer 1972), 13.

31. *Ibid.*, 11-12.

32. Interview: JMS with Kenneth Jennings, October 11, 1995.

33. *Northfield News*, February 8, 1973.

34. *MM*, March 2, 1973.

35. Tom Smith, "Magical Musical Tours," *MM*, March 2, 1973.

36. Dolph D. Bezoier, "The St. Olaf Choir Concert," *Zumbrota News*, January 24, 1974.

37. Robert Oudal, "St. Olaf Choir Tradition Lives—and Improves," *Rochester Bulletin*, January 31, 1974.

38. K. G. Schuller, "St. Olaf's Choir—a perfectly tuned organ," *St. Louis Globe-Democrat*, February 6, 1974.

39. Conversation: JMS with Frederick Gonnerman, August 18, 1996.

40. Bruce Johnson, "Choir Is Outstanding," *Times-Democrat,* Davenport-Bettendorf, Iowa, February 8, 1974.

41. Michael Anthony, *Minneapolis Tribune*, April 12, 1974.

42. Cindy Young and Dan Carlsen, "Choir, Jennings honored by Pope," *MM*, February 21, 1975.

43. Cited in *Saint Olaf* 23 (Winter 1975), 5.

44. *Ibid.*

45. Josefa Koet, Leideke Galema, Marion M. Van Assendelft, *Hearth of Unity*: Forty Years of Foyer Unitas, 1952-1992 (Rome: Fratelli Palombi Editori, 1996), 11. The Preface to this book was written by His Eminence Johannes Cardinal Willebrands.

46. Review in *Il Tempo*, Rome, February 1, 1975.

47. A. Malcolm Gimse, "The Sculpture, the Sculptor, the Creative Moment," Brochure prepared for presentation of Professor Gimse's bronze sculpture of the Triumphant Christ to the St. Olaf Associates. One of the limited edition sculptures was taken to Rome in January 1987 where it was given as an expression of thanks to the Foyer Unitas at an ecumenical service in the Pauline Chapel in the Vatican. Present at the service were His Eminence Johannes Cardinal Willebrands, and Miss Leideke Galema and Miss Josefa Koet of the Foyer Unitas. See *Saint Olaf* 35 (March 1987), 1; *Saint Olaf* 34 (March 1986), 15.

48. Cited in Leola Nelson Bergmann, *Music Master of the Middle West*: The Story of F. Melius Christiansen and the St. Olaf Choir (Minneapolis: The University of Minnesota Press, 1944), 132.

49. *MM*, February 13, 1976.

50. *Saint Olaf* 25 (Fall 1976), 1.

51. Dedication Brochure, "The Continuing Heritage," Christiansen Hall of Music, September 12, 1976; *Saint Olaf* 25 (Fall 1976), 4-5.

52. *Saint Olaf* 25 (Spring 1977), 15.

53. *Saint Olaf* 26 (Fall 1977), 20.

54. Harriett Johnson, "Minnesota's 75th diamond-studded," *New York Post*, January 11, 1978.

55. *Saint Olaf* 26 (Fall 1977), 20.

56. *Saint Olaf* 29 (Fall 1980), 9.

57. Reimar Riefling, "Korbegivenhet," unidentified Oslo newspaper, May 29, 1980.

58. Letter from Gay Gonnerman and Melissa Flynn in Kenneth Jennings Book of Retirement Letters, December, 1989.

59. Johan Kvandal, "Frisk og cultivert," *Aftenposten*, Oslo, Norway, Mary 30, 1980; Sigmund Hjorthaug, "Fabelaktig!" *Stavanger Aftenblad*, May 31, 1980.

60. Anton Chr. Meyer, "Korsang i toppklasse," *Morgenavisen*, Bergen, Norway, June 3, 1980.

61. Hans Gaare, "The St. Olafs Choir var en opplevelse," unidentified Trondheim newspaper, June 10, 1980.

62. Amund Dahlen, "Gedigen konsert," unidentified Kristiansand newspaper, May 30, 1980.

63. Svend Einar Hansen, "Applausen ville ingen enda ta i Larvik kirke i gaar," unidentified Larvik newspaper, June 14, 1980.

64. Letter from Robert Voelker '80 to Bob Johnson, January 19, 1994.

65. Dag Gjaerum, "St. Olaf Choir ga alle en enorm koropplevelse," *Posten*, Larvik, Norway, June 14, 1980.

66. Steve J. Sandberg, "St. Olaf Choir Log Book, 1977-1981," entry for June 15, 1980.

67. *Ibid.*

CHAPTER 15

TO THE ORIENT

Two unprecedented trips to the Orient by the St. Olaf Choir within a decade provide the chapter title. In 1986 the Choir celebrated its 75th anniversary by traveling to the Orient where it gave concerts in Japan, Taiwan, Hong Kong, and the People's Republic of China. Two years later, the Choir was one of five international choral groups invited to sing at the Olympic Arts Festival in August preceding the 1988 Olympic Games in Seoul, Korea.

As was the case in the 1970s, the extraordinary amount of travel abroad during the 1980s did not in the least reduce the pace of the Choir's commitments to performances in this country. It was an unusually full decade, beginning with a tour south in February of 1981 and ending with an eastern tour in 1990 that recreated the Choir's memorable first visit to eastern cities in 1920.

ST. OLAF CHOIR
MINNESOTA • U.S.A.

Ready for the Orient, St. Olaf Choir, 1986

Publicity for Ordway Concert, 1985

The decade was marked by new triumphs for the St. Olaf Choir, such as teaming up with the Minnesota Orchestra for concerts in Carnegie Hall in New York and the Kennedy Center in Washington in February of 1985. On the same tour the Choir had the further distinction of giving the first choral concert in the new Ordway Music Theatre in St. Paul, Minnesota. In the spring of 1985, as St. Olaf College observed the 300th anniversary of the birth of Johann Sebastian Bach, the Choir and other music groups on campus performed Bach's "St. Matthew Passion" under the direction of the famous guest conductor, Robert Shaw.

A major note of sadness was tolled in 1984 when Olaf C. Christiansen died after a long period of illness. The St. Olaf Choir sang at his funeral and dedicated its 1985 concert program to his memory. Another ending was in the picture as the decade of the 1980s drew to its close. Astonishing as it seemed to many, Kenneth Jennings announced that he would retire at the end of the 1989-90 school year, making the Choir's eastern tour of 1990 the last under his direction.

Kenneth Jennings, 1986

The Tour Book

Each year the members of the St. Olaf Choir compile and issue a tour book, a loosely-organized assortment of tour information and in-jokes distributed at the beginning of the annual tour. The predecessor of the tour book was a publication prepared and issued en route called *The Choir Scream*, which appeared as early as 1920 and was still seen in the fifties.

Eunice Rossing '23 explained its popularity as a source of entertainment during the long hours on the train.

> Mock trials, mock weddings, mock almost everything, puns, jokes and startling experiences were reported in the Choir Scream with touches for effect by the editor, till that paper was waited for with an eagerness often taxed beyond patience when the Screm came a day later than it had been expected.[1]

The more recent tour books reflect a similar spirit of student fun translated into the idioms of later decades. There are bus "do's" and "don'ts," quizzes (What is Montana's nickname?), rules for Big Hug Night, often planned for Valentine's Day, texts of "Songs Oles Love to Sing," limericks, games, "Trendy Reading for Tour," and columns of such distinctions as "Most Likely to bring entire wardrobe on tour," or "Most Likely to miss the bus," or "Cutest Sleeper" or "Biggest flirt."

Useful material such as advice from the director, itineraries, maps, and lists of Choir members was often included, but the humorous touch was always in evidence. The first

Tour Book for 1983

page of the 1970 tour book listed the names of key personnel in high style: "PRESENTING THE WORLD-FAMOUS SAINT OLAF CHOIR OF THE ORDER OF THE PURPLE SHEETS," beginning with THE GRAND DRAGON, KENNETH JENNINGS and THE IMPERIAL WIZARD, FRED SCHMIDT. Fred's usual tourbook title was "First National Freddie" since, like his father, he dispensed the meal allowances.

Director Jennings was the subject of much tour book humor, including being the model for cut-out clothes of the paper doll variety under the heading, "Dress The Conductor" (1983, 1984). And in more than

"Dress the Conductor" outfits, 1984 Tour Book

one tour book one finds a generous compilation of verbatim "K. J. Kwotes" that make irresistible reading. Here are samples from a few of the tour books:

From 1975:

"I'd like to hear the men." (Basses sing) "O.K.,
now the tenors." (Tenors hiss)
"Tenors, this note is very high, so if you can
sing it, uh, don't."

From 1978:

"'Praise' is not as effective when it's out of tune."
". . . 99 times out of ten."

From 1979:

"It's not a frivolous 'Hallelujah' — it's full and solid and
down-to-earth . . . full of *Lutheran* qualities!"
"Don't frown — only I'm allowed to frown!"
"'And around the wicked in Hell's abysses the huge flame
flickered. . .' Make more of those words. They're fun!!"

From 1983:

"Don't slurch—slurch, is that a word?"
"Hit the note right on the head—I don't want the
'Flight of the Bumblebee.'"
"The sopranos are too worldly and know too much."
"Altos, let your shapes show through."
"Sopranos, don't turn nice now."

From 1984:

"Altos, just think about the deceitful and unjust men
behind you."
"Tenors, what is your purpose?"
"Tenors, you're going to have to work to make
yourselves interesting."
"Don't slide on it like you're a cow sliding on
a wet barn floor."
"You second basses are still fuzzy."

From 1985:

"Let's take the men from 'violent excitement.'"
To the basses: "We need a nice singing sound, and
not a seal sound back there."
"That's too round, too mashed potatoes."

Entertaining as they were, the "K. J. Kwotes" also included gems that Choir members remembered for years. Well-known was K. J.'s disquisition on the gargoyles. The stone masons and carvers who created gargoyles for great European cathedrals, believing that they warded off evil spirits, took pains to carve not only the faces and the parts that would be seen by the people below, but also the unexposed backs and tops. The reason was that while human beings did not see the unexposed sides, God saw them. Applying the image to choral music, all parts of the Choir are important and need to be heard, also those that are not so obvious to the listeners. The aim is to achieve highest quality in the totality of the music.[2]

Returning to the lighter vein, Choir humor also embraced the manager. After Bob Johnson became the manager of the St. Olaf Choir in 1978, his name and caricature appeared regularly in the tour books. Like Fred Schmidt before him, Johnson was associated with money matters. Bob's image, in dark glasses, graced the Cut & Paste Page in the center of a special dollar bill, "One Beej Buck." To Choir members and many others, Bob Johnson was "Beej" or "B.J." As to the director, he was always addressed as

B. J. Legal Tender

B. J., Beloved Buck Broker

"Dr. Jennings," but often referred to as "K.J." When his wife Carolyn joined a tour the leadership contingent was "K.J.," "C.J.," and "B.J." Sometimes it was "Kaje" and "Ceej" in tune with "Beej."

An item congenial to tour book miscellany appeared in the *New York Times Magazine* issue for December 28, 1980. A clue in the Collegiate Collection crossword puzzle was "St. _____ College Choir." The only possible answer, of course, was "Olaf." In a letter to Dr. Jennings some years later, Dr. Martin E. Marty, well-known historian of religion and St. Olaf College Board of Regents member, commented on a similar crossword he had done in the *New York Times*. The clue was "Minnesota College Famed for Choir." Wrote Marty, "The answer was easy. The whole musical and collegiate world knows."[3]

The Early 1980s

Early in 1981 the Choir issued its new album, "Reflections of Norway," recorded in the Grieg Hall in Bergen during the 1980 Norway Tour.[4] In its home vicinity the Choir reflected on the Norwegian roots of St. Olaf College when it sang at the 125th anniversary of Holden Church in Goodhue County. It was founded in 1856 and served for forty years by Bernt Julius Muus, the Norwegian immigrant pastor who was the leading figure in the founding of St. Olaf College in 1874. St. Olaf President Harlan Foss preached the sermon at the anniversary service November 8, 1981.[5]

Holden Lutheran Church

St. Olaf Choir in Holden Church, 1981

Annual tours plus a variety of special appearances kept the Choir busy in the first half of the eighties while the Orient tours dominated the second half of the decade. The Choir traveled into the South in February of 1981, and to the Pacific Northwest in 1982. During the second semester of the 1981-82 school year, following the Choir tour, Dr. Jennings was on sabbatical leave. Working with the St. Olaf Choir during the semester was Alice Larsen '51, director of the Manitou Singers, and Knut Nystedt, Norwegian conductor, composer, and organist. Larsen was in charge of the Choir the first part of the semester and conducted its Alumni Weekend concert. Nystedt was in residence March 27 through May 3, 1982.[6]

Alice Larsen

Knut Nystedt at rehearsal

Nystedt conducted the massed choir of 1,000 singers at the Choral Festival held on the St. Olaf campus, May 2, 1982. In the evening he conducted the St. Olaf Choir in a concert that included "Missa Misericordiae" by Egil Hovland, another Scandinavian composer, and Nystedt's own "O Crux" and "Audi, The Day of the Lord," written for narrator, organ, and choir. Dr. Nystedt revealed a sly humor during a light number near the end of the program when he choreographed the singers in moving their bodies rhythmically left and right. To everyone's amusement, on the final note the entire Choir remained leaning to the left. Wrote Laura Beilfuss for the *Messenger*: "Knut Nystedt's music shimmers with unexpected chords, compelling melodies, inexplicably beautiful sounds." Nystedt said of the Choir: "They are easy to work with, kind, and disciplined. They follow my interpretation very well."[7]

Among the solo choirs performing at the May 2nd Choral Festival was the Ebenezer Tower Choir from Minneapolis, directed by Jeanette Donhowe Bakke, member of the St. Olaf Choir in 1920, mother of St. Olaf musician Carolyn Jennings and mother-in-law of Kenneth Jennings. Soloist in the Ebenezer Choir was Hagbarth Bue '11, who had attended every St. Olaf Christmas Festival since the first one in 1912. At the age of 96, he was present for the 72nd annual Festival in December of 1983.[8]

The extraordinary collaboration of the St. Olaf Choir with the Minnesota Orchestra begun in the late 1960s and continued through the 1970s became more frequent in the 1980s. When Dr. Jennings returned to the campus after his sabbatical in the fall of

Hagbarth Bue and President Melvin George

464

1982, the St. Olaf Choir joined the Icelandic Male Chorus, and the Finnish Tapiola Choir for two gala concerts in Orchestra Hall on September 11 and 12, 1982. Billed as "Tonight Scandinavia," the concerts were part of a Minnesota celebration of contemporary Scandinavian culture sponsored by the American-Scandinavian Foundation. At the climax of the program, the three choral groups and the Minnesota Orchestra, conducted by Sir Neville Marriner, gave a stirring performance of Jean Sibelius' *Finlandia.* "Tonight Scandinavia" was telecast nationally on the Public Broadcasting Service and distributed throughout Scandinavia.[9]

Sir Neville Marriner

The next appearances with the Minnesota Orchestra took place in the fall of 1984 when the St. Olaf Choir joined the Orchestra for three performances of Bach's *Magnificat,* two in Orchestra Hall and one in O'Shaughnessy Auditorium in St. Paul. Because their tours to the east coast coincided in February of 1985, the Choir and Orchestra performed the *Magnificat* again in Carnegie Hall in New York and in the Kennedy Center in Washington.[10] On September 14, 1985, the St. Olaf Choir was with Marriner and the Minnesota Orchestra to perform Handel's *Two Coronation Anthems* at the "British Festival of Minnesota" in Orchestra Hall.

"Tonight Scandinavia"

The St. Olaf Choir and its director gained a new kind of recognition in 1983 when the College announced the establishment of the Harry R. and Thora H. Tosdal Professorship in Music, endowed by a bequest of the late Mr. Tosdal.[11] The Board of Regents determined that the chair was to be held by the director of the St. Olaf Choir, thus making Kenneth Jennings the first to be named the Harry R. and Thora H. Tosdal Professor of Music.[12]

Harry R. Tosdal in the 1940's

Harry R. Tosdal, Class of 1909, a native of Estherville, Iowa, played clarinet in the St. Olaf Band that toured Norway in 1906. After graduate study abroad and at Harvard, he received the Ph. D. from Harvard and was appointed to the faculty of the Harvard Business School in 1920. He was named full professor in 1922, at age 33. During a distinguished teaching career, he pioneered in the field of sales management and authored seven books. In 1940 St. Olaf College awarded Tosdal the honorary degree, Doctor of Laws. Both Dr. Tosdal and his wife, Thora Helseth '15, maintained a life-long interest in music and the arts.[13]

The 1983 tour took the St. Olaf Choir to the Southeast, the most distant points being St. Petersburg and Sarasota, Florida. The tour book included a map of all the states where the Choir would sing between Minnesota and Florida and quoted more than one member's delighted anticipation of enjoying the warm Florida sun in February. In addition to the Tacky Postcard Contest and advice from Choir president Steve Schonebaum '83 about avoiding gaseous foods, editors Marie Spar and Shelley Kline '83 published essays by new members on "What Does St. Olaf Choir Mean To Me?" As expected, the writers waxed serious, poetic, and humorous.

David Robert Narum '85, whose father William H. K. Narum '43 and brother Peter W. Narum '82 had been Choir members, wrote that he loved to sing and enjoyed being part of "the continuing tradition of excellent a cappella singing which is the St. Olaf Choir." For Nancy Evert '84, the St. Olaf Choir meant "Purple velvet in which to frolic, a form-fitted halo to tame my cowlick" and "polished black pumps to deform my toes" balanced by the "Glory Hallelujahs" wherever the Choir goes.[14]

Ann Johnson '85 recorded her early hope of getting into the Choir. "To sing in THE CHOIR, to wear my own purple velvet robe, my own black pumps, to go to Florida in February, — alas, it was nothing more than a dream, a hope of glory." Why so? Because, while having the requisite blond hair, she was of *Swedish* ancestry. But perhaps she could conceal the fact. "I walked into auditions with every intention of lying about my heritage," she wrote. "But those penetrating blue eyes looked at me over the steel-rimmed glasses. 'Oh, you're the Svenska flicka, aren't you?' He knew! It was all over. I was washed up." But wait! She was able to pronounce and translate "Och jungfrun hon gar och ringen" correctly. There was hope. A dream was realized. She became a member of the Ole Choir![15]

David Lange '85 wrote that he had become obsessed by the color purple. When he first saw the purple robes he had to have one of his own, so he signed up for voice lessons. As a freshman member of the Viking Chorus, he was forced to sit in his tattered robe behind those wonderfully elegant purple robes at the Christmas Festival. Every night it was pure torture. Auditions were coming. He would try out. But what if he didn't make the Choir that wore "the soft velvet, so invitingly violet"? What if? It could not be! He devised a plan: "If I couldn't wear the sacred purple robe, no one would. I would sneak into their storage, kidnap one of the precious garments, and burn the rest, only to wrap myself in the one remaining robe in a state of ecstasy." Fortunately, David made the Choir.[16]

A somewhat unusual travel plan was followed by the Choir in 1984. It flew to Denver, went by buses to concert engagements in Colorado, New Mexico, Texas, Arizona, California, Nevada, and Utah, and flew home from Denver for the home concert on February 13. The San Francisco concert was given in St. Mary's Cathedral where the acoustics have troubled many choral groups. According to Marilyn Tucker of the *San Francisco Chronicle*, the St. Olaf Choir overcame the problem with its "absolute clarity of line and diction." The Choir was at its best in Healey Willan's "Hodie, Christus Natus Est," the "Sanctus" from Palestrina's mass, *Aeterna, Christi Munera*, and Liszt's "Ave Verum Corpus." Among other numbers receiving favorable comment were Jean Berger's *Magnificat*, Duruflé's "Ubi Caritas," and Schumann's "To the Stars." A musician in the audience was so moved by the Liszt number that she wrote to Jennings that it "broke my heart."[17]

The Passing of Olaf C. Christiansen

When the St. Olaf Choir returned to campus, reports were circulating that Dr. Olaf C. Christiansen was seriously ill with cancer. He died on April 12th.

The funeral was held in Boe Memorial Chapel on Monday, April 16, 1984.

In retirement, Olaf Christiansen consistently followed a policy of leaving all that pertained to the St. Olaf Choir in the hands of Kenneth Jennings. Never-theless, Olaf continued to be loved and recognized on the campus and in the wider musical world. At the Alumni Banquet in 1975, when his Class of 1925 was honored on its Golden Anniversary, Olaf led the

Christiansens at Sister Bay, 1975
Back: Sylvia, Julie, Sigrid, Fred
Seated: Ellen and Olaf

467

alumni in a number of college songs. That fall at the convention of the Minnesota State American Choral Directors' Association, Olaf received the F. Melius Christiansen Choral Award. On the same occasion he conducted a demonstration rehearsal that was videotaped for the ACDA state and national archives.[18]

Olaf at Alumni Banquet, 1975

As noted earlier, Olaf Christiansen was on hand in 1976 for the dedication of Christiansen Hall of Music. He was also present in 1979 when his portrait was unveiled by Mary Ann Christensen Johnson '51 who with her husband, James Johnson, had commissioned the oil painting by James Ingwersen and donated it to the College.[19] The portrait hangs in the Margaret Hoigaard Skoglund Reception Room where it joins the bust of Olaf's father, F. Melius Christiansen, carved by Arnold Flaten.

After the unveiling
From left: Mrs. James Johnson, Mr. and Mrs. James Ingwersen, Dr. and Mrs. Olaf Christiansen

Although his health was beginning to fail, Olaf was able to participate in a few campus activities in the early 1980s. His presence provided a thrilling moment at the 1980 Commencement concert as recalled by Choir member and historian Steve Sandberg '81. As is customary, former Choir members come forward toward the close of the program to join the St. Olaf Choir in the last two or three anthems. Steve wrote:

> After our program, the Alumni Choir formed and sang "Praise to the Lord" and "The Earth Adorned" by Åhlén. Then, before "Beautiful Savior," Jennings simply stepped off the podium and, to everyone's shock and delight, Dr. Olaf C. Christiansen stood up to conduct the last piece! He finally calmed down the riot of applause and held his hands out perfectly steady for the downbeat. He conducted with great precision and smoothness.

Sandberg concluded his report with an important observation: "The applause raged for several minutes as homage to a living tradition that has continued to change and grow under Jennings, not one that had stopped and died years ago."[20]

As the preacher at Olaf Christiansen's funeral April 16, 1984, it fell to the Reverend Clifford Swanson '42, former College pastor, to set forth the elements of Olaf's career for grateful reflection. He began: "We gather on an occasion of this kind to do two relatively simple things: to *remember* and to *give thanks*." Swanson continued: "We are sad but at the same time a strange kind of joy permeates our sadness for his was a good life—a relatively long life—but most especially because his life had the unique effect of blessing our lives." Swanson said it was hard to recall Olaf Christiansen without "a ready smile or a smile in the making."[21]

Clifford J. Swanson

Anthems by the St. Olaf Choir and hymns by the congregation made the service rich in the music of praise and thanksgiving. As a Choral Prelude the Choir sang Bach's *The Spirit Also Helpeth Us.* Following the Invocation the Choir sang F. Melius Christiansen's arrangement of "O Day Full of Grace." The congregation sang "Thine Is the Glory" and read responsively Psalm 145, which begins with the words "I will extol you, my God and King, and bless your name forever and ever."

The St. Olaf Choir also sang "O Light Everlasting," composed by Olaf C. Christiansen, and Olaf's arrangement of "Praise Him in Gladness," by Gastoldi. Choir alumni joined the St. Olaf Choir in the balcony of Boe Memorial Chapel to sing the Choral Postlude, "Beautiful Savior," arranged by F. Melius Christiansen.

469

Among the many thoughtful tributes to Olaf C. Christiansen spoken and written soon after his passing was the following paragraph in the obituary printed in the funeral service folder:

As he led the St. Olaf Choir on coast to coast tours for 27 years, Olaf expanded and added to the lustre of the a cappella choral tradition pioneered by his father. The tours included performances in the nation's leading concert halls as well as hundreds of small-town churches. Throughout the years, Olaf's main objective with the St. Olaf Choir was to present sacred music sung beautifully, with-

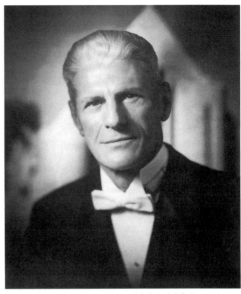

Olaf C. Christiansen, 1901-1984

out distraction, so the listeners would be sensitized to the Holy Spirit's message. This he saw as Kingdom work, and his calling on this earth.[22]

The concert presented by the St. Olaf Choir and the Alumni Choir on May 19 during Commencement Weekend was dedicated to the memory of Olaf C. Christiansen. Likewise, the 1985 concert tour of the St. Olaf Choir was dedicated to his memory. Olaf was buried at Little Sister Cemetery, Sister Bay, Wisconsin.[23]

The year before the first of its two visits to the Orient, the St. Olaf Choir had another annual tour with its own highlights. Mentioned above were the 1985 appearances in New York and Washington with the Minnesota Orchestra. The night after performing with the Orchestra in New York's Carnegie Hall, the Choir gave its own concert in Town Hall. Will Crutchfield in *The New York Times* took note of the "birthday cards" for Schütz, Bach, and Handel, namely, different settings of Psalm 98, "Singet dem Herrn" by Schütz and Bach, and Handel's *The King Shall Rejoice, Coronation Anthem No. 2.* These, he wrote, were "cleanly and clearly articulated." 1985 was the 400th anniversary of the birth of Heinrich Schütz and the 300th of J. S. Bach and G. F. Handel. The reviewer singled out as most enjoyable a series of short pieces by 20th-century composers,

Poulenc's "Exultate Deo," Duruflé's "Ubi Caritas," Penderecki's "Agnus Dei," and Knut Nystedt's "In Principio."[24]

After its concert in the Kennedy Center Concert Hall in Washington on February 11, 1985, Joan Reinthaler of *The Washington Post* declared the Choir "still among the best in the country." The Choir gave a

St. Olaf Choir in Kennedy Center, 1985

lesson, as she put it, "in what complete dedication to the basic choral virtues of intonation, rhythm, balance and diction can do."[25]

To lead the observance of the 300th anniversary of the birth of Johann Sebastian Bach, St. Olaf College invited Robert Shaw and Jaroslav Pelikan to the campus in May of 1985. Dr. Shaw, founder of the Robert Shaw Chorale, music director and conductor of the Atlanta Symphony Orchestra, and the most distinguished choral conductor in the country, received the honorary degree, Doctor of Music, and spoke on the topic, "The Conservative Arts" at a convocation in Boe Chapel on May 3rd. Dr. Pelikan, Sterling Professor of History at Yale

Jaroslav Pelikan

University, gave an evening lecture on "Themes and Variations" in the Bach *Passions*.

The climax of the Bach celebration was the performance in the Skoglund Center Auditorium of Bach's *The Passion of Our Lord Jesus Christ According to St. Matthew* on Sunday, May 5, 1985, with Robert Shaw conducting. Under Shaw's baton presenting the *Passion* were the St. Olaf College Orchestra, nearly 2,000 singers from all the choirs of St. Olaf College, the Northfield Children's Choir, many local choirs, and ten assisting artists, including soloists and continuo.[26]

Robert Shaw

To the Orient, 1986

"Choir to Warm Up in Texas for Orient," announced the November 1985 issue of *Saint Olaf*, the alumni/ae magazine. The itinerary for the 1986 winter tour into the South included five concerts in Texas as well as appearances in Iowa, Missouri, Illinois, Oklahoma, Kansas, and Nebraska. Anticipation of the tour to the Orient was building. Minnesota Governor Rudy Perpich issued a proclamation with suitable "whereases" naming the St. Olaf Choir "a cultural and educational representative of the State of Minnesota during its concert tour of the Orient May 26 to June 20, 1986."[27]

A long-standing interest in China at St. Olaf College fueled the tour to the Orient. Early in the 20th century St. Olaf graduates went to China as missionaries. In the 1960s, the first St. Olaf international study group went to Asia. By the 1980s, the St. Olaf Choir was eager to explore musical opportunities in a different part of the world, and it was important for the work of churches and missionaries in the Orient to have it come. The tour to the Orient marked the beginning of the 75th anniversary of the St. Olaf Choir, an observance that would continue into 1987.

Preparations for an anniversary tour abroad began in 1984 when Director Kenneth Jennings and Manager Bob Johnson requested a meeting with Frank and Jean Bencriscutto to discuss the St. Olaf Choir's tentative plan to make a concert tour to the Soviet Union in 1986. Frank Bencriscutto, often known as Dr. Ben, was the director of the University of Minnesota Wind Ensemble that had been in the Soviet Union in 1969 and in China in 1980. The experiences related by the Bencriscuttos of traveling with the Wind Ensemble in both areas and the changing political currents in the Soviet Union weighed heavily in favor of the eventual decision to plan a trip to the Orient.[28]

Bob Johnson made arrangements for a delegation from the Chinese Embassy in Washington to attend the St. Olaf Choir's concert in the Kennedy Center on February 11, 1985, and a reception prior to the concert. Soon thereafter the Choir was invited to tour China under the auspices of the All-China Youth Federation, the same entity that had invited the University of Minnesota Wind Ensemble to China in 1980. Johnson extended the plan by making arrangements in Japan, Taiwan, and Hong Kong for concerts to precede the China portion of the month-long tour.[29]

Dr. Jennings planned a repertoire that would include European choral masterpieces, American and English choral works of the 20th century, American folk songs and spirituals, and a section of the program called "Choral Music From Around the World" that included three French songs, two numbers in Chinese, two Japanese folk songs, and a text on Night and Morning sung in Hungarian. In all, the Choir would sing in ten languages.

World Theater Send-Off
St. Paul, May 22, 1986

At reception in Kyoto, Japan

Prior to leaving the States, the Choir gave a benefit and send-off concert in the World Theater in St. Paul on May 22, 1986.[30]

Departing from Minneapolis on May 26th for the tour, the Choir's first destination was Kyoto, Japan. Its first concert was in Kyoto Lutheran Church where the Reverend Ben Mori was the pastor. Also on the program was the Men's Glee Club from Kyoto University. At the post-concert reception, the Choir was divided into small groups to facilitate unhurried participation in the traditional Japanese tea ceremony. The next morning the tempo changed as the Choir traveled on the famous Shinkansen, the "Bullet Train," to Tokyo. There the concert was in Hitomi Hall at Showa Women's University. Sight-seeing in Tokyo offered the fish market, gardens by the Imperial Palace, a temple, and the Tokyo Tower. [31]

On the "Bullet Train"

Tea Ceremony, Kyoto

*Church members welcome Choir
Kumamoto, Japan, June 1986*

*Bob Johnson, Kenneth Jennings,
Kunihiro Sato, President, Japan
Evangelical Lutheran Church, Tokyo*

Kumamoto, the next stop on the itinerary, was the center of Lutheranism in Japan. In addition to presenting a concert in a large auditorium, where all the singers received flowers, the Choir split into five groups to sing at the five Lutheran churches in Kumamoto. Choir members stayed with host

Smiles for the Director

families where the hospitality was nearly overwhelming. Communication was not easy, but it took place through music, smiles, and bows. Terri Boyer '87 amazed her host family by playing catch with the boy in the family.

At Kyushu Gakuikin Lutheran High School, Kumamoto, Japan

Smile for Director's daughter
Lisa Jennings '89 surrounded

Richard Bodman, Bob Johnson,
Pastor Ellis

"They were so shocked that I could play catch that they went and got the neighbors," she recalled.[32] After the Choir gave a morning program at the Kyushu Gakuin Lutheran High School, the 1,000 boys of the school were totally unrestrained in their admiration of the female Choir members. The Choir's host and coordinator of events in Kumamoto was the Reverend Andrew B. Ellis.

When the Choir arrived in Taipei, Taiwan, the first impressions were of a military presence everywhere. On reaching Soochow University, however, it was welcomed by a bright red and white banner and friendly students. St. Olaf and Soochow had collaborated in academic programs for more than a decade. Also making pleasant the Choir's stay in Taiwan were Edward Yang, president of the University, St. Olaf graduate Tom Dedricks '62, who befriended every St. Olaf group coming to Taiwan, and the Reverend

Soochow University, Taipei, Taiwan

Truth Lutheran Church, Hong Kong

Stanley and Mrs. Sophia Tung. The concert took place in Sun Yat-sen Memorial Hall. In Hong Kong the Choir members did the obligatory shopping and gave their concert in Truth Lutheran Church where a striking feature of the decor was a double row of white doves descending from the balcony to the chancel.[33] In Hong Kong, Tim Ackerman '88, was quarantined for chicken pox and cared for by missionaries.

An agreement signed in 1984 between St. Olaf College and East China Normal University in Shanghai provided the St. Olaf Choir with a valuable contact in the People's Republic of China.[34] Discovering a radically different culture in the People's Republic, Choir members looked back on the ten days in China as more stressful than any other parts of the tour. They also reported that the experience drew them closer together.

President Mel George presents gifts

Flowers from Chinese students

Chinese audience behavior was disconcerting at first. Both singers and director were unprepared for the casual socializing and eating during the concert. But the Choir would have the audience's full attention when it performed the Chinese folk songs. There were spontaneous outbursts of appreciation at the Choir's skill in pronouncing the Chinese text so the listeners could understand the words. The crowd would cheer and clap along with the singing.[35]

The St. Olaf group was fortunate to have its own able interpreter in Dr. Richard Bodman, associate professor of Chinese at the College. Bodman expertly handled the language in Taiwan, Hong Kong, and on the Chinese mainland. The work of Betty Stromseth '53

Dick Bodman interprets for Mel George

Betty Stromseth   *Fred Gonnerman*

in cooperation with Bob Johnson was vital in planning and handling travel arrangements for an overseas tour of such complexity. Also contributing to the success of the tour was Frederick Gonnerman, St. Olaf's director of information services who traveled with the Choir and recorded its activities through hundreds of photographs and in published articles.[36]

The Choir could not avoid the issue of Chinese food, trying it, talking about it, and in one case, avoiding it. "The food was scary," some said.

Enjoying Chinese food

478

Mark Schowalter '87 agreed, and added: "We never knew what we were eating so we had a lot of fun guessing. One rumor had it that we were eating cat. But some of the food was great—one of the best meals I've ever eaten was in China. We did go to Pizza Hut as soon as we got back to Hong Kong, though!"[37]

Multi-course meal in China

There was no concert in Soochow (Suzhou), "the Venice of the East," but while sitting around a quiet pool in the Fisherman's Net Garden, Choir members sang "Go Tell It on the Mountain" at the request of a Chinese woman who identified herself as a Christian. In Nanjing the Choir saw the Yangtse River Bridge, a marvel of engineering, and climbed hundreds of steps to visit the Sun Yat-sen Mausoleum. A concert was given in the chapel of Nanjing Union Theological Seminary where Dr. Jennings presented a St. Olaf Choir record and other gifts to Chen Zemin, president of the Seminary.[38]

Awaiting a train in China

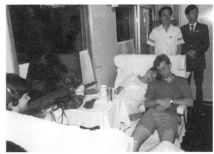

Aboard the train

Group photo on the Great Wall

The visit to Xian enabled the Choir to learn about the Terra Cotta Warriors, an army of 8,000 sculptured life-size clay figures created to guard the tomb of an ancient emperor. Spending June 16-19 in Beijing, the capital city, the Choir noticed modern features that distinguished it from other Chinese cities. It sang in a relatively new auditorium and took in the two best-known tourist attractions, the Great Wall and the Imperial Palace. During a stop in Hawaii on the way home, the Choir sang during Sunday worship services in Calvary by the Sea Lutheran Church. St. Olaf President Melvin D. George preached the sermon. The final concert of the tour was at St. Andrew's Cathedral in Honolulu.[39]

Walking on the Wall

Mel and Meta George

Kenneth and Carolyn Jennings
Imperial Palace, Beijing

Choir at Calvary by the Sea Lutheran Church
Honolulu, Hawaii

As the 75th anniversary carried over into 1987, the Choir made its annual visit to St. John's Lutheran Church in Northfield on January 11, 1987. During the worship services it sang six numbers, beginning with Sweelinck's "Cantate Domino" as a choral prelude. Other anthems sung were "Praise to the Lord," arranged by F. Melius Christiansen, "Walk as Children of the Light," by Randall Thompson, "How Fair the Church" and "Beautiful Savior," by F. Melius Christiansen, and as a postlude, "Ye Watchers and Ye Holy Ones," by Healey Willan. The sermon was preached by Dr. Melvin George. A special exhibit on view in the church basement depicted the historical ties between St. John's Church and the St. Olaf Choir. The exhibit was prepared by Joan Olson, St. Olaf archivist, who also served as St. John's historian.

The anniversary celebration included the 1987 Choir tour to the Pacific Northwest. In Billings, Montana, the 75-voice Choir "brought the audience to its feet with its strong, well-blended voices, impeccable pitch and moving interpretations of standard sacred literature."[40] St. John's Cathedral in Spokane provided the right setting and fine acoustics for such sacred numbers as Sweelinck's motet, "Cantate Domino" and Giuseppe Corsi's "Adoramus Te." The Spokane reviewer wanted Jennings to cast a little more fire into Knut Nystedt's *Missa Brevis*, but even so, the concert was "luminous and lovely."[41]

The review by Wayne Eastwood of Idaho Falls, Idaho, aptly expressed how a St. Olaf Choir concert can make listeners feel like participants. "When the St. Olaf Choir came onstage and joined their hands together, they in effect joined hands with their audience as well." The audience also shared in the Choir's past. Recognizing that "Today There is Ringing" was sung on the first tour in 1912 and that "Beautiful Savior" may be regarded as the Choir's theme song, Eastwood wrote: "We joined with maestro Jennings, the Christiansens, and the thousands of voices who have made up the history of the St. Olaf Choir in an evening of beautiful sound and uplifted spirit."[42]

As usual, Choir members overcame the weariness of eight-hour bus rides to enjoy the marvelous scenery of the Cascades, visit every McDonald's from

St. Olaf Choir rolls West

Graphic by Ward Sutton

Minnesota to British Columbia, observe their after-lunch "quiet hours," and belt out "Fram, Fram," "High on Manitou Heights," and "Um-Ya-Ya" with alumni/ae at every church supper along the way. They had a scare in Mitchell, South Dakota, when Dr. Jennings became ill during a concert and was removed on a stretcher.[43] To their great relief, he recovered quickly and led the Choir in the remaining concerts, at the World Theater in St. Paul, and at the home concert in Boe Memorial Chapel.

Jean Strohm '88

Before embarking for Korea in the summer of 1988, the Choir made another annual tour, the destination being the Southeast. In Atlanta the concert was in Glenn Memorial Auditorium, Emory University. Reviewer Jim Kopp thought the young singers "produced a well-blended and surprisingly mature sound" in Anton Bruckner's motet, "Christus Factus Est Obediens." The performance of Aaron Copland's *In the Beginning*, a 16-minute setting of the Genesis creation story, evoked this comment: "Rich-voiced mezzo-soprano Jean Strohm handled the extensive solo over the backing of the choir, whose singing was a tour de force of both memory and agility."

Kopp noticed that the Choir members held hands and asked about it. "A chorister explained after the concert that the clasping encourages feelings of solidarity and unity, both musical and spiritual."[44] The custom of holding hands was initiated by the Choir members themselves during Jennings' tenure as director; he neither endorsed nor discouraged the practice.

On the homeward stretch the Choir sang at Butler University in Indianapolis. Jay Harvey, critic for *The Indianapolis Star*, was impressed by the excellent diction in the performing of Copland's *In the Beginning*. "Every word stood out, as if being sung for the first time to hearers who had no other way to get the message." Harvey was pleased with the sustained soft volume in "As a Hart Longs for the Brooklet" and the depth of the male voices in Johann Kuhnau's "Tristis Est Anima Mea." Two spirituals, "Steal Away" and André Thomas's "Keep Your Lamps Trimmed," were also well received.

Knowing that the St. Olaf Choir had been invited to the Festival preceding the Summer Olympic Games in Korea the following August, Harvey observed that "this is an ensemble of Olympic-level powers." In that spirit he had placed his review comments under the heading, "College choir's performance demonstrates Olympic quality."[45]

An Olympic Choir: Korea, 1988

The St. Olaf Choir was the only choir from the United States invited to perform at the International Choral Festival of the "Seoul Olympic Arts Festival, 1988" held in Korea August 17-23. The invitation signified a most unusual distinction. And the Choir had the added honor of being asked to open the Festival with a solo concert on August 17, 1988.

The other international choral groups invited were the Tokyo Women's Choir, the Ars Nova from Brazil, the Stuttgart Kammer Chor from West Germany, and the Elmer Iseler Singers from Toronto, Canada. Each of these choirs also sang an individual concert and all of them, with the St. Olaf Choir, joined the five Korean host choirs in a massed choir performance with the Korean Philharmonic Orchestra to close the festival.[46]

News of the Choir's impending trip to Korea brought another proclamation from Minnesota Governor Rudy Perpich, an entry in the Congressional Record by Senator Rudy Boschwitz, and a letter of congratulations from President Ronald Reagan. From the White House August 5,

Sign at Olympic Arts Festival Seoul, Korea, 1988

Regents Concert, Orchestra Hall
Regents Chair Dean Buntrock '55 speaking

484

Embarking for Korea. KJ, Pilot Bob Matta, BJ

1988 President Reagan wrote:`

> The outstanding collegiate musical heritage that you embody will doubtless enrich, and be enriched by, the many cultural traditions you'll encounter in the Far East. And I know you'll take great pride in sharing with your peers from around the globe a special American treasure: "the St. Olaf sound."[47]

After singing for a very enthusiastic audience at the Regents Concert in Orchestra Hall, Minneapolis, the Choir was off to Korea. Pilot on their plane from Seattle to Kimpo Airport, Seoul, and donating his time for the flight was Robert Matta, father of Choir member Michelle Matta '90.[48] The much-anticipated opening concert in the new, shiny Olympic Festival Hall was a resounding success. The audience of 2,500 gave the Choir four standing ovations and called for four encores. The concert was seen on Korean National Television.

Sign of Welcome to Seoul

Choir in Festival Hall, Seoul   *Soloist Janis Hardy*

The mezzo-soprano solo in Aaron Copland's *In the Beginning* was sung by assistant professor of music Janis Hardy who had sung it several times before, including an occasion when Copland himself conducted. Hardy said that the piece is difficult to keep in tune. "It's really a tour de force for a choir and it really showcased the talents of the group."[49]

The Koreans were overwhelmed to hear the Choir sing so well in their language, and their delight only increased when they heard a Korean member of the Choir, Jin Kim '90, sing the solo in one of the Korean folk songs, "Arirang." In rehearsals, Jin had instructed the Choir in the difficult

Jin Kim with his father and Kenneth Jennings

Korean pronunciations. When the Choir began "Toraji," the second Korean song, the audience joined right in. President Mel George, who was at the concert, later described the response to Kim's singing as "a moment which crossed cultural boundaries, in which music brought together diverse peoples."[50]

The final night of the Festival was filled with music, emotion, and a sense of unity among the singers. The five international guest choirs and the five Korean host choirs came together for the closing event of the Festival on August 23. Before forming as a massed choir to perform the "Ode to Joy" from Beethoven's 9th Symphony with the Korean Philharmonic Orchestra, each visiting choir sang a folk song from its country. The St. Olaf Choir sang "Shenandoah." According to Choir member Tim Ackerman '88, the performance was "almost flawless" and Dr. Jennings was very pleased. "I've never felt so much energy and electricity in one song," said Ackerman.[51]

486

Massed Choir Olympic Festival Hall

After intermission all the choirs assembled for the Beethoven symphony and took their places by sections, the intermingling of robes creating "a sea of color." Reflecting on the brotherhood theme in the choral text, Janis Hardy was struck by "how wonderful it would be if we could all live in harmony like that."[52]

After the rare excitement of the Olympic Arts Festival, the Choir had appointments for concerts in some remarkably large churches in Seoul, Inchon, and Taegu. The fact that Korea is twenty-five per cent Christian was visible in the number of village churches and the enormous size of the city

St. Olaf Choir, Inchon, Korea
Inchon Soonghui Church

487

Sightseeing in Korea

churches. A crowd of some 5,000 packed Inchon Soonghai Church. The people refused to leave after the final number, and chanted for more until the Choir returned to the stage and sang three more songs. A visit was made to Luther Seminary, south of Seoul. Its president, Dr. Maynard Dorow '51, helped with arrangements for the tour. [53]

The last concert was given before 2,500 enthusiastic listeners in the auditorium at Hannam University in Taejon. Another 2,500 surged about outside hoping to get in. The over-capacity crowd was so dense that Choir members had to thread their way single file down the packed aisle and literally step over persons occupying every foot of floor space as they made their way to the platform. The air was also dense with extraordinary heat and humidity. The Choir produced wonderful music and several gallons of perspiration that went back to Northfield with the purple robes.

The Choir carried from Korea warm memories of the welcome and friendship it had experienced. Despite media reports of anti-American protests, Choir members reported friendly treatment from audiences, cab drivers, and students. Beth McDowell '90 said that students came up after concerts to ask for autographs and to practice English. Tim Ackerman said, "The people on the whole were incredibly nice."[54]

At the first rehearsal in the Olympic Festival Hall, Dr. Jennings was greeted and embraced by Dr. Hakwan Yoon, director of the Daewoo Chorale who had extended the invitation to the Choir from the Choral Association of Korea. Kenneth and Carolyn Jennings received gifts from the pastor of

488

Jungang Lutheran Church and the bishop of the Lutheran Church in Korea. Solveig Nilsen '89, president of the Choir, was presented with a bouquet of flowers during the final performance at Taejon. These gestures of friendship were recorded by David Gonnerman '90, official tour photographer, who provided a report in photos and text of the Choir's highly successful visit to Korea.[55]

Kenneth Jennings Retires

After its triumphs in Korea, the St. Olaf Choir characteristically went back to work, preparing for its tour to the Southwest in January and February of 1989. Before leaving Minnesota the Choir sang a benefit concert for Choir member Lynn Dornfeld '90 in Fergus Falls. Lynn had suffered a serious injury in a train accident in Germany the previous October. The story about the Choir and the benefit for the Dornfeld family was broadcast over National Public Radio.[56]

Lynn Dornfeld

Two concerts were given in Colorado, one each in New Mexico and Texas, three in Arizona, and seven in California, ending with the performance in St. Mary's Cathedral in San Francisco before the flight home.[57] In Los Angeles Mayor Tom Bradley proclaimed February 9, 1989, to be "St. Olaf Choir Day." At its concert that evening in the Dorothy Chandler Pavilion, the Choir's special guests included the cast of the popular television show, "The Golden Girls."[58]

That Dr. Jennings planned to retire in 1990 was known by the press at the time of the 1989 tour. On the basis of a phone interview with Jennings, Bruce Burroughs of the *Los Angeles Times* wrote about the Choir's history, its methods, and Jennings' thoughts on his work with the Choir. The interview moved between the new and the traditional. Burroughs asked Jennings to comment on the changes he had introduced during his twenty-two years with the Choir and quoted him as follows:

> I brought in more contemporary music—we just gave the Midwest premiere of Dominick Argento's 'Te Deum' in October—and more early music, too, more Palestrina in addition to the Lutherans [Bach, Schütz]. Also, we expanded into larger works as well. For instance, on this tour we are doing a Mozart Mass with small orchestra. That wouldn't have been done under Olaf Christiansen.[59]

Giving his article the title, "Well-Respected Traditions of St. Olaf Choir," Burroughs noted the respect for tradition and continuity at St. Olaf College emphasized by Conductor Jennings, only the third director in an

Choir members Terri Boyer '87, Mark Schowalter '87, Karen Spong '87, Kenneth Waisanen '87, and Dr. Jennings

organization with a 77-year existence. What Jennings said about continuity is an instructive commentary on the sound and style of the St. Olaf Choir:

> The original ideals haven't changed. We still produce what some call a Northern European sound, closely in tune, unisons as nearly perfect as possible. We don't use an operatic style, but more of an art-song style, one could say. The singers are all undergraduates and we stay right with the style of what students can do at this age. If we had graduate students, or singers with more developed voices, it might be different, but we are traditionally identified as a youthful sound.[60]

Did Dr. Jennings have any advice to his successor? "Just enjoy it thoroughly," he replied. "It's a marvelous experience working with such talented young people."

But the Kenneth Jennings era was not over. The 1989 tour had to be completed and another year of Choir leadership carried out. The items receiving special praise as the Choir sang before audiences in the West were Mozart's *Missa Brevis in B-flat Major*, Anton Heiller's "O Rex Gentium," Georg Schumann's "How Great Are Thy Wonders," and Jean Berger's "Canticle of the Sun," text by St. Francis of Assisi.

One reviewer declared the Canticle the highlight of the concert. The viola solo by Charles Gray of the St. Olaf music faculty was praised repeatedly. Wrote the critic for *The Arizona Republic: "Canticle* was

490

performed with violist Charles Gray, an outstanding instrumentalist who played the solo part, including a number of difficult double-stops, with warmth and accuracy."[61]

The Arizona critic, Dimitri Drobatschewsky, began his review by characterizing Mozart's *Missa Brevis*, as "a musical jewel of matchless beauty." He wrote that it was given "a sparkling performance by the St. Olaf Choir." Regarding encores, Drobatschewsky stated that Carolyn Jennings' arrangement of the Christmas carol, "O Come, Little Children," and "Beautiful Savior," as arranged by the founder, "allowed the patrons to leave in a mood of spiritual elation that only the serenity of beautiful music can help one achieve."[62]

After the St. Olaf Choir completed its 1989 tour, Kenneth Jennings went on sabbatical leave for the rest of the semester and Alice Larsen '51, professor of music, was in charge. As on Jennings' previous leave, Larsen rehearsed the Choir and prepared it for a visiting conductor. Her selection on these two occasions indicates the high regard Jennings and the music department had for her. As a student, Alice Larsen was a member of the St. Olaf Choir for four years and on occasion sang the solo in "Beautiful Savior." Larsen's outstanding work as director of the Manitou Singers and as a voice teacher won the admiration of her colleagues and hundreds of students.

Invited to be acting director of the St. Olaf Choir from April 3 through May 7 was Simon Preston, conductor, concert organist, and church musician from England. Among the positions he had held were those of organist and tutor in music at Christ Church, Oxford, and organist and master of choristers of Westminster Abbey. As assistant to Neville Marriner for the movie *Amadeus*, Preston had played the music heard and seen on the film as performed by Salieri and Mozart. [63]

During his final year with the St. Olaf Choir Dr. Jennings was given a special honor

Simon Preston

by the Minnesota chapter of the American Choral Directors Association. At its meeting in November 1989, Bruce W. Becker, president of ACDA of Minnesota, conferred on Jennings the F. Melius Christiansen Award for significant life-long contributions to choral music in Minnesota. As Becker recalled the presentation, "The response of the convention audience was overwhelming." In a letter Becker thanked Jennings for his loyal support of ACDA, his leadership, artistry, and pursuit of excellence.[64]

The 1990 tour begins
Bob Johnson and Kenneth Jennings

The final concert tour led by Kenneth Jennings as director of the St. Olaf Choir was a journey eastward to sing in such major halls as Hill Auditorium in Ann Arbor, Michigan, Carnegie Hall in New York, the Kennedy Center in Washington, and Orchestra Hall in Chicago. The 1990 tour marked the 70th anniversary of the 1920 tour to the east coast that won national recognition for the Choir. Fittingly, the program included F. Melius Christiansen's arrangement of "Wake, Awake," which had been sung in 1920.

After the performance in Milwaukee's Uihlein Hall of the Performing Arts Center, critic Nancy Raabe's response was an assertion: "St. Olaf Choir concert beyond most superlatives." What sets the St. Olaf Choir apart from its peers, she maintained, was, first, that it does not seek to impress but rather pursues the simple purpose of offering musical expressions of religious faith. Second, it makes the text paramount, which accounts for "the remarkable clarity" that has been its trademark.[65]

Choir members at Ann Arbor

492

On February 5, 1990, the Choir ventured into Canada, singing in St. Matthew's Lutheran Church in Kitchener, Ontario. The reviewer wrote of the "dynamic St. Olaf Choir," its "daring music," "flexibility," and "a program of unusual variety and uncommonly high quality." Emphasized was Jennings' confidence in himself and his singers to present fresh interpretations, for example, of Palestrina's "Sicut Cervus" and Esquivel's "O Vos Omnes."[66]

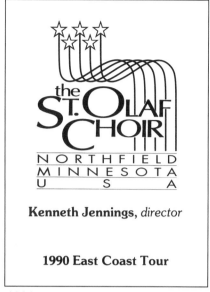

Kenneth Jennings, *director*

1990 East Coast Tour

1990 Tour Schedule

The Choir's Washington concert in the Kennedy Center for the Performing Arts was a benefit for the Lutheran Social Services of the National Capital Area. The reviewer for the *Washington Post* was impressed by the prayerful interpretation of Palestrina's "Sicut Cervus," the joyful rhythms in Lasso's "Surrexit Pastor Bonus, the "singers' light, pure tone" in the Bach selections, the balance and power of Gretchaninov's "Holy, Holy," and the beauty of Penderecki's "Song of Cherubim" in which "a bass chant underscored a high haunting melody."[67]

On its return to Minnesota, the Choir gave a concert in Orchestra Hall at which Dr. Jennings was honored on his retirement after twenty-two years as director. Michael Anthony of the Minneapolis *Star-Tribune* wrote that Jennings had introduced more contemporary music, examples on the program being works by Penderecki, Avshalomov, and Berger. Another change was in the use of accompaniment. An 11-piece instrumental ensemble was used with some of the Bach selections and solo instruments at other points in the program.

Selections of particular merit mentioned by Anthony were "Song of the Cherubim" by Penderecki, where the resonance of the bass voices was impressive, Juan Esquivel's "O Vos Omnes," with "a smoothly tapered *pianissimo* at the end," and the power heard in the "Gloria" from Vaughan Williams' *Mass in G minor.* "The St. Olaf sound was thrilling," wrote Anthony, in such works as Gretchaninov's "Holy, Holy, Holy, Lord of Sabaoth" and in the well-known arrangement of "Beautiful Savior."[68]

On February 17, 1990, the evening before the Orchestra Hall concert, Dr. Jennings and his family were guests of honor at a recognition banquet

Choir and Instrumentalists
1990 Tour

held in the Hyatt Regency Hotel in Minneapolis. Among the many tributes and gifts of appreciation, mention should be made of the unique bronze sculpture designed and executed by Paul T. Granlund, and the large and ornate bound "Book of Letters" containing letters of tribute to Kenneth L. Jennings from present and former choir members, friends, colleagues, associates, and other well-wishers. The Granlund sculpture is called "Double Chorus." When Marie Biorn Sathrum '56 unveiled the sculpture and presented it to Dr. Jennings at the banquet, she read what Granlund had written about the piece:

Artist Paul Granlund and
"Double Chorus"

"Double Chorus," Granlund Sculpture

494

I have fashioned a group of singers—the four inside figures form more of a circle while the outside four complete a square. These two elements, plus the fact that they sing to each other and interconnect, symbolize some of the structure and lyricism of music.

Only at the time of presenting the sculpture for approval did I learn that the St. Olaf Choir had its origin within the framework of an octet and that the choir now sings with their hands linked. While I hadn't intended these additional layers of symbolism, I welcomed them in the same spirit in which I receive the beauty of music.[69]

On the front cover of the "Book of Letters" were the logo of the St. Olaf Choir, the name KENNETH L. JENNINGS in large letters, and the dates of his service: Music Director 1968-1990, and St. Olaf Music Faculty 1953-1990. Prominent among the letters was a greeting from President George Bush recognizing the 70th anniversary of the first national tour and including the "sad note" that it was the last tour under the direction of Dr. Kenneth Jennings. "He will be greatly missed, but I am confident that the beautiful sounds of your choir will continue to captivate audiences for years to come."[70]

One after the other, the letters reveal the profound respect, admiration, and affection Jennings' friends and associates had for him. More than one former choir member wrote in touching terms of how Dr. Jennings affirmed and encouraged them, often helping them set a direction for the rest of their lives. Wrote one, "More than any other single individual, you taught me the value of standards—perhaps the most important lesson a musician can ever learn."[71]

Among the prominent musicians who sent Dr. Jennings their congratulations and good wishes were Sir Neville Marriner, Stanislaw Skrowaczewski, Dale Warland, and Weston Noble. Sir Neville wrote, "Your work has encompassed many happy memories for me, and countless other colleagues—not to mention thousands of young people you literally introduced to music—a wonderful legacy."[72] Unique to the Jennings legacy were the St. Olaf Choir's performances of great musical literature with the Minnesota Orchestra, a significant change from earlier years when the two groups performed separately on joint programs.

A letter from Doug Norquist '84, former Choir member, eloquently described an unforgettable episode from a rehearsal. The Choir had just finished Gretchaninoff's "Holy, Holy, Holy." There was a pause before the director said, "You see how beautiful it is when you people sing in tune!"

The Choir knew what he meant, wrote
Norquist, and continued:

> It was one of those magical
> moments when the chords line
> up perfectly and the piece
> receives a glimmer of sonic
> light you never knew existed
> before. Some of us were
> experiencing this for the first
> time, but even Dr. Jennings was
> moved to give one of the most
> beautiful sermons I've ever
> heard on how we can only use
> what the Creator has given us to
> make beauty happen—in this
> case by unlocking the laws of
> harmony.[73]

Kenneth Jennings

The strengths of Kenneth Jennings as director of the St. Olaf Choir
embraced a host of personal and musical qualities. His students were in awe
of him, but they knew him as a humble and compassionate man, selfless and
patient. They remembered his uncanny ability to convey to them the effect
he wanted without labored verbal instruction. Former Choir members and
colleagues viewed him as a master of phrasing, unexcelled in painting the
elegant musical line. He was also admired for his gift of programming.
Jennings introduced more contemporary music and occasional secular
works, used instrumental accompaniment, and had a sure instinct for what
young singers could do and how the one piece should flow into the next.

To summarize Jennings' contribution to the life of the St. Olaf Choir,
one could choose from many laudatory statements. In an interview, former
colleague Alice Larsen said of the Choir that "under Kenneth they suddenly
just started to soar."[74] Harold Decker, one of his professors at the University
of Illinois, wrote a tribute expressing what many would wish to say:

> With the St. Olaf Choir you have created your own distinctive
> musical tradition, built on that of the Christiansens who preceded
> you. You have brought their expertise, enthusiasm, and devotion
> to the choral art to even greater heights. Your choirs and music
> making have been a model for college choral conductors to
> emulate and your influence has been nationwide.[75]

Dale Warland '54, St. Olaf alumnus who established his own nationally-
famous choral group, the Dale Warland Singers, wrote as former student,
professional musician, and St. Olaf alumnus. First he stated his gratitude for

Jennings' thoughtful and generous support when Warland as a student was just learning to conduct. Next he marveled at the "awesome responsibility" Jennings inherited when he was appointed Music Director of the St. Olaf Choir. Warland wrote: "You took it, sailed with it in a brilliant, exciting manner and made all of us who are alumni of St. Olaf and 'Minnesota choral people' very happy and very proud. You have made a significant contribution to the choral art . . . and we are all grateful."[76]

Kenneth Jennings was a good steward of his opportunity. He inherited a treasured musical tradition from the Christiansens, respected it and let it sing, and added his own musical artistry to the growth and enrichment of the St. Olaf Choir. What he accomplished will live on through his compositions, recordings of the St. Olaf Choir under his direction, and especially through the hundreds of students whom he inspired. Among them was a young man from West Hempstead, New York, who sang baritone in the St. Olaf Choir from 1976 to 1978. His name was Anton Armstrong.

Dr. Kenneth Jennings, St. Olaf Choir Director, 1968-1990

Notes for Chapter 15 TO THE ORIENT

1. Eunice Rossing, "Eastern tour of the Choir 1922," *The 1922 Viking, 138.*

2. Letter from Daniel Egan to Joseph M. Shaw, September 9, 1996.

3. *Saint Olaf* 29 (Spring 1981), 21; Kenneth Jennings Retirement Book of Letters: Martin E. Marty to Kenneth Jennings, November 30, 1989.

4. *Saint Olaf* 29 (Winter 1981), 13.

5. Saint Olaf 30 (Fall 1981), 16.

6. "Norse musician interim director of St. Olaf Choir," *Northfield News,* April 1, 1982.

7. Laura Beilfuss, "Norwegian composer Nystedt directs St. Olaf Choir," *Manitou Messenger (MM),* April 8, 1982.

8. *Saint Olaf* 30 (Spring 1982), 11; *Saint Olaf* 32 (November 1983), 9.

9. *Saint Olaf* 30 (Summer 1982); "Tonight Scandinavia" Program, September 11, 12, 1982.

10. *Saint Olaf* 32 (August 1984), 9.

11. *Saint Olaf* 31 (Winter 1983), 10.

12. Minutes, St. Olaf College Board of Regents, Executive Session, December 3, 1982.

13. *Saint Olaf* 31 (Winter 1983), 10.

14. 1983 Tour Book.

15. *Ibid.*

16. *Ibid.*

17. Marilyn Tucker, "The St. Olaf Choir Is Clearly a Winner," *San Francisco Chronicle*, February 8, 1994; conversation: JMS with Kenneth Jennings, January 24, 1997.

18. *Saint Olaf* 23 (Spring 1975), 7; *Saint Olaf* 24 (Spring 1976), 20.

19. St. Olaf College News Release, December 18, 1979; *Saint Olaf* 28 (Spring 1980), 12.

20. Steve J. Sandberg, Journal of St. Olaf Choir Activities, 1977-1981.

21. "Olaf C. Christiansen, 1901-1984, A St. Olaf Giant in the World of Music," *Saint Olaf* 32 (June 1984), 9.

22. Service folder for the funeral of Olaf C. Christiansen, April 16, 1984.

23. *Saint Olaf* 32 (June 1984), 9.

24. Will Crutchfield, "St. Olaf College Choir in Concert at Town Hall," *The New York Times*, February 12, 1985.

25. Joan Reinthaler, *The Washington Post*, February 13, 1985.

26. Bach Commemoration Program, St. Olaf College, May 5, 1985; *Saint Olaf* 33 (June 1985), 15.

27. Cited in *Saint Olaf* 34 (November 1985), 14.

28. Memo: Bob Johnson to JMS, November 7, 1996.

29. *Ibid.*

30. *MM*, April 11, 1986; "The St. Olaf Choir In Concert," Orient Tour Program, 1986.

31. *Saint Olaf* 34 (August 1986), 16-17.

32. *MM*, September 12, 1986.

33. *Saint Olaf* 34 (August 1986), 20.

34. *Saint Olaf* 33 (November 1984), 13.

35. Cf. Jennifer Arndt and Barbara Biegner, "Choir Explores the Orient Through Music," *MM*, September 12, 1986; conversation: JMS with Carolyn Jennings, February 10, 1997.

36. Frederick H. Gonnerman, photography and narrative, "Orient Tour Creates Mountains of Memories," *Saint Olaf* 34 (August 1986), 15-26.

37. Arndt and Biegner, "Choir Explores the Orient."

38. *Saint Olaf* 34 (August 1986), 22-23.

39. *Ibid.*, 24-26.

40. Christene C. Meyers, *The Billings Gazette*, February 1, 1987.

41. Harvey Hess, "St. Olaf Choir concert is luminous and lovely," *The Spokesman-Review*, Spokane, Washington, February 3, 1987.

42. Wayne Eastwood, "Choral perfection St. Olaf's heritage," *The Post-Register*, Idaho Falls, Idaho, February 11, 1987.

43. Anne Christenson, "Music, mountains create choir tour highs and lows," *MM*, February 20, 1987.

44. Jim Kopp, "Traditional St. Olaf Choir gives stirring performance at Emory," *The Atlanta Constitution*, February 11, 1988.

45. Jay Harvey, "College choir's performance demonstrates Olympic quality," *The Indianapolis Star*, February 12, 1988.

46. St. Olaf News Release, March 1988; cf. *Saint Olaf* 36 (March 1988), 17.

47. Quoted in *Saint Olaf* 36 (August/September 1988), 23.

48. *Saint Olaf* 36 (August/September 1988), 23.

49. Ann Sorebo, "Ole Choir returns from tour of Seoul, Korea," *MM*, Sepember 23, 1988.

50. *Saint Olaf* 37 (November/December 1988), 21.

51. Sorebo, "Ole Choir returns."

52. *Ibid.*

53. St. Olaf News Release, August 1988; *Saint Olaf* 37 (November/December 1988), 4.

54. Sorebo, "Ole Choir returns."

55. David Gonnerman, photos and text, "Honor Tinged with Emotion: The St. Olaf Choir in Korea," *Saint Olaf* 37 (November/December 1988), 1-4.

56. *MM*, February 17, 1989.

57. *Saint Olaf* 37 (November/December 1988), 34.

58. *MM*, February 17, 1989.

59. Bruce Borroughs, "Well-Respected Traditions of St. Olaf Choir," *Los Angeles Times*, February 9, 1989.

60. Quoted in Borroughs, "Well-Respected Traditions."

61. Dimitri Drobatschewsky," Choir's lofty standards deserve praise," *The Arizona Republic*, Phoenix, Arizona, February 8, 1989.

62. *Ibid.*

63. *Saint Olaf* 37 (November/December 1988), 34.

64. Kenneth Jennings Retirement Book of Letters: Bruce Becker to Kenneth Jennings, January 2, 1990.

65. Nancy Raabe, "St. Olaf Choir concert beyond most superlatives," *Milwaukee Sentinel*, February 2, 1990.

66. Colleen Johnston, "Dynamic St. Olaf Choir makes the difficult seem easy," *The Kitchener-Waterloo Record*, February 6, 1990.

67. Jeanne Spaeth, "St. Olaf Choir," *The Washington Post*, February 15, 1990.

68. Michael Anthony, "Departing director's work reflected by St. Olaf Choir," *Minneapolis Star-Tribune*, February 19, 1990.

69. Paul T. Granlund, comments regarding his sculpture, "Double Chorus," read by Marie Biorn Sathrum '56 at Recognition Banquet for Jennings family, Minneapolis, Minnesota, February 17, 1990.

70. Jennings Retirement Letters: President George Bush to the St. Olaf Choir, January 23, 1990.

71. Jennings Retirement Letters: Allen Borton '79 to Kenneth Jennings, January 1, 1990.

72. Jennings Retirement Letters: Sir Neville Marriner to Kenneth Jennings, December 12, 1989.

73. Jennings Retirement Letters: Douglas Norquist '84 to Kenneth Jennings, December 1989.

74. Interview: JMS with Alice Larsen, September 18, 1995.

75. Jennings Retirement Letters: Harold Decker to Kenneth Jennings, December 5, 1989.

76. Jennings Retirement Letters: Dale Warland '54 to Kenneth Jennings, February 8, 1990.

CHAPTER 16

ANTON ARMSTRONG

In the August 1989 issue of *The Choral Journal* a notice appeared announcing a position available at St. Olaf College: "Music Director - The St. Olaf Choir." It was the first time the College had advertised the position of director of the St. Olaf Choir. The first paragraph of the ad was as follows:

> St. Olaf College is seeking applicants for the position of Music Director for the St. Olaf Choir, a 72-voice choral ensemble which tours both nationally and internationally. The position will also include teaching conducting classes and/or other coursework, depending on the qualifications and experience of the candidate.[1]

Anton Armstrong, 1989

The decision by Kenneth Jennings to retire at the end of the 1989-90 school year was totally a matter of his desire and judgment. He could have continued had he chosen to do so. His health was good and the quality of his work remained in top form. After a concert on Jennings' last tour, a reviewer observed that those attending "had the opportunity to

Entrance to St. Olaf Campus Highway 19, Northfield, Minnesota

experience the artistry of this gifted conductor and musician at the height of his career."[2]

Born in 1925, Dr. Jennings reached his 65th birthday in May of 1990. "The time had come," he said. Jennings was equally unassuming when asked what he planned to do in retirement. "Be a retired person, I guess."[3] In fact, he took on more than one demanding task of teaching and conducting as a retired person. He spent an entire school year teaching full-time and conducting choirs at the University of Arizona in 1992-93, and in the winter of 1994-95 he directed the Gustavus Adolphus Choir and led it on a tour to Germany, Finland, Sweden, and Poland.

In an interview published in *The Choral Journal* in May of 1990, Jennings was asked what advice he might have for young conductors. He responded that while one might learn how Robert Shaw or Erik Erikson do their work, the main learning is the result of one's own study and digging. And he offered a perceptive comment on the human aspect of music performance.

> You have to learn how to deal the best way you can with the very imperfect human instrument housed completely within real human beings. There are no props or mechanical aids. It's this "humanness" that reaches into people's hearts and deepest needs. Choral music is able to do that.[4]

Kenneth Jennings

Selecting the New Director

When Olaf Christiansen decided to retire, he suggested to the president of the College who his successor should be. His preference carried significant weight with the committee, and in short order Kenneth Jennings was chosen. There was no national search nor the interviewing of several candidates.

By the time Kenneth Jennings retired, the academic world had developed new procedures for

Music directors receiving checks from Neil A. Kjos, Jr. Dean Jon Moline, Neil Kjos, Kenneth Jennings, Miles Johnson, Steven Amundson, January 1987

finding and hiring new faculty. The process was especially thorough when it came to filling key leadership positions in music, such as band, choir, and orchestra directors. In addition to the advertising in national journals, the application itself, the dossier, the references, and the interviews, there was the requirement of a trial performance with the specific group the successful candidate would be conducting.

The first step in finding a replacement for Kenneth Jennings was the formation of a search committee. The chairperson was Dr. Kenneth Graber, professor of music and chair of the department of music at St. Olaf College. Dr. Jennings himself was not a member; he took no part in the procedures nor did he recommend any candidates. The committee discussed the kind of person they were looking for, announced the position, and read through more than sixty applications as they came in between August and October 15, 1989.

Kenneth Graber

Among those who read the announcement in *The Choral Journal* was Dr. Charles K. Smith of Michigan State University who discussed it with one of his recent doctoral students, Anton Armstrong, then teaching at Calvin College. Armstrong told his mentor that Kenneth Graber had informed him that his name had been submitted to the committee as a potential candidate. In effect, Armstrong was being asked to apply. Smith then urged Armstrong to reply by submitting an application, which he did.[5]

By December of 1989 the search committee had reduced the number of candidates to five, with Armstrong among them. They were interviewed by the committee, President Mel George, Dean Jon Moline, and a representative group of students. Each candidate was asked to conduct the St. Olaf Choir in Jean Berger's *Magnificat*, Johann Kuhnau's "The Righteous," and a third piece of the candidate's choosing. The try-out took place in the presence of the search committee and a fairly large number of observers.

Dr. Armstrong remembered vividly his try-out on December 7, 1989, at the end of a long, exhausting day of interviews. He stood before the St. Olaf Choir in the Fosnes Rehearsal Room and led some warm-up exercises. Since all the previous candidates had taken the Choir through Berger's *Magnificat*, it was agreed that Armstrong would conduct only two pieces, omitting Berger. When he announced the Kuhnau piece, a groan went up from the ensemble. He conducted and the Choir sang dutifully but without inspiration. It seemed best to move on.

Armstrong then handed out copies of Ralph Manuel's "Alleluia" and had the Choir begin. The piece was unfamiliar and the Choir had difficulty with the sight reading. The singing was not going well and Armstrong wondered if the audition was heading toward a failure. He stopped and asked an alto what the word "Alleluia" means. "A word exuding praise and joy," she answered. "Well, you could have fooled me by the way you all are singing this!" said the candidate. It was a critical moment.

The situation demanded a better connection between Choir and candidate. Armstrong spoke a few candid words to the Choir to this effect: It's been a rough week. I know you're tired. But this may be the only time I get to conduct you. If it is I'm going to have the best time I can, and I want you to summon up full energy, sit up, and sing! If this is a song of praise then I need you to sing it that way. Let's have a good time and let's sing! With that little pep talk, the tide was turned. The Choir took hold of the piece, and it leaped off the page. Afterwards, Armstrong could return to Grand Rapids free of regrets, knowing that he had given his best in the audition.[6]

There were more contacts between the search committee and Dr. Armstrong. Before long he learned that he was the unanimous choice of the committee. The official offer came in a letter from President Melvin D. George shortly before Christmas.[7] Accepting the position was not an automatic decision. Armstrong had to weigh the professional opportunities and personal satisfactions he was enjoying in Grand Rapids against the contribution he might be able to make at St. Olaf College. He decided to accept the St. Olaf offer.[8] On January 2, 1990, Dr. Kenneth Graber announced that Dr. Anton Armstrong, a 1978 graduate of St. Olaf College and a former member of the St. Olaf Choir, had been selected to succeed Dr. Kenneth Jennings as Music Director of the St. Olaf Choir. Wrote President George to Dr. Armstrong: "We are all delighted and excited that you have decided to come to St. Olaf."[9]

Kenneth Jennings congratulates Anton Armstrong, January 1990

West Hempstead Years

Anton Eugene Armstrong was born April 26, 1956, in West Hempstead, Long Island, New York. His mother, Esther, was a nurse who later worked in retail sales. His father, William Armstrong, was a tailor. The family's home church, the Lutheran Church of the Epiphany, operated a parish day school that Anton attended and where, as a kindergarten pupil, he sang his first solo, "Thou Didst Leave Thy Throne and Thy Kingly Crown." Later he sang in the Church's Junior Choir and played the piano by ear for the morning devotions at the parochial school.

Anton Armstrong, 1st Grade

Seeing these musical gifts in evidence, the teachers and the pastor, the Reverend Dr. Herbert Gibney, urged Anton's parents to provide music lessons for him. With both parents working, the Armstrong family was comfortable financially, but not wealthy enough to pay for music instruction if it was only a child's passing whim. But the talent and interest were genuine, and soon Mr. and Mrs. Armstrong agreed to let Anton, then age ten, take piano lessons from Mrs. Amelia Samuel. Since there was no piano in the Armstrong home, Mrs. Samuel went with the Armstrongs to find and buy an upright piano. Her generosity was also shown in that she gave back to the local church any fees received from her piano students.

Anton took piano instruction from Mrs. Samuel for eight years, from 1966 to 1974. Under her tutelage, he was introduced to a fine range of musical literature. As a traditional piano teacher, Mrs. Samuel felt it her duty to lead Anton away from playing by ear to the reading of music. Hers was a significant influence. She constantly encouraged him, and as he moved through the grades and went to different schools, she gladly adjusted the lesson times to his changing schedule.

Two members of the Lutheran congregation to which Anton and his parents belonged, Carl and Carol Weber, graduates of Westminster Choir College, often took young people to a one-week vocal music camp at the College in Princeton, New Jersey. Also located in Princeton was the American Boychoir which, with the Westminster Choir College, had roots in Ohio, having been founded by a student of Westminster founder John Finley Williamson. In 1950 the former Columbus Boychoir moved from Ohio to

Princeton and located its campus on the grounds of the former Gerard Lambert estate. In 1962 the Boychoir's summer camp was also brought to Princeton. The ensemble changed its name in 1980 to the American Boychoir, to reflect more fully the identity and mission of the group.

On one of its tours, the American Boychoir came to Long Island for a concert in the spring of 1967. The Webers, eager for their son and Anton to hear the choir, took the two boys and Anton's parents to the concert. Anton recalled that when the Boychoir came out on stage and opened the concert with a double chorus Renaissance piece, "I was just blown away!" He wanted to be in that choir! After the concert he auditioned and was invited to the summer camp, which he attended in 1968.

After further voice testing by Donald Bryant of the American Boychoir, Anton was invited to attend the boarding school in Princeton, but his parents said No. Therefore his next school was Nassau Lutheran School, a school closer to home operated by the Lutheran Church, Missouri Synod. Anton still longed to be in the American Boychoir and to attend its boarding school in Princeton, but his parents could not afford to send him.

By this time he was 13 years old and in the seventh grade. His voice would be changing soon so there was no time to lose if he were ever to sing in the American Boychoir. He tried every stratagem he could think of to get around his parents' decision. The Boychoir school had invited him and offered a very generous scholarship. After more family discussion, it was agreed that Anton could attend the boarding school in Princeton and sing in the American Boychoir.

From September 1969 to June of 1971, Anton spent his middle school years, eighth and ninth grade, as a member of the American Boychoir and its school. At that young age, he had unusual musical and cultural opportunities. The American Boychoir made extensive tours. It sang in Rome, for example, and in the White House

Singer in Boychoir, 1970

for President Nixon and his family. The Boychoir joined the Toronto Mendelssohn Choir and Toronto Symphony Orchestra in presenting the Canadian premiere of Penderecki's *St. Luke's Passion* under the baton of Elmer Eiseler.

To earn money for the 1971 Italian tour, Anton worked at the Boychoir summer school. In 1972 he became a junior counselor and in 1974 a regular

508

counselor. His association with the American Boychoir School continued for many years. He served as assistant director of the summer camp, called ALBEMARLE, and from 1980 to 1993 as director of the summer program. He was elected to the institution's Board of Trustees in 1994.

After two years in the American Boychoir and attending its school, Anton and his parents had to decide on the next phase of his education. A local public school had been plagued with ugly racial incidents. Anton's parents were determined that he should continue to get a good education. They settled on the Cathedral School of St. Paul, a private boarding and college preparatory school for boys in Garden City, New York, where Anton took his tenth through twelfth grades.

At St. Paul's Anton received good academic preparation but musical opportunities were very limited. When he jammed his fingers playing baseball, he incurred the disapproval of Mrs. Samuel, his faithful piano teacher, so he quit baseball. St. Paul's was a small school, with a senior class of only 32 students. Anton was one of four blacks and there were two Asians, all of them leaders in student activities. Anton was editor of the school newspaper in his senior year.

Soon he exerted leadership in music. St. Paul's students took coeducational classes with nearby St. Mary's, a girls' school. Anton took organ lessons and played the organ at both schools. During his senior year, as the annual Christmas pageant was approaching, Anton felt that the St. Mary's Glee Club could be supplemented by a mixed chorus. He organized a mixed glee club and conducted it in performances at Christmas and through the rest of the school year.

In the spring of 1974, Anton Armstrong graduated from the Cathedral School of St. Paul. The three years at St. Paul's had built his self-confidence and prepared him intellectually for college. Graduates of St. Paul's regularly went on to prestigious colleges. As Anton began to think about colleges, music was a prominent but not an exclusive interest. He also wanted to study anthropology, political science, and theology.[10]

Anton Armstrong, 1974
At Cathedral School of St. Paul

Student at St. Olaf College

How Anton Armstrong from West Hempstead, New York, eventually enrolled at St. Olaf College in Minnesota is an unlikely story, but it happened. His piano teacher had some knowledge of St. Olaf College. In 1972 when the St. Olaf Choir sang in Lincoln Center, New York, the Reverend Robert Hawk took him to the concert. Pastor Hawk, a graduate of Thiel College, another Lutheran institution, told Anton that he would enjoy the pure a cappella sound of the St. Olaf Choir. But when they reached the concert hall, they saw instruments on stage, an organ and a string bass, signs that changes were taking place in the ensemble from Minnesota. Anton was fully absorbed in the Choir's singing throughout the concert.

With his parents and his older brother Garry, Anton began to consider what college to attend. He ruled out state universities at once, with the exception of Indiana University. Also under discussion were Westminster Choir College, Capital University, and the New England Conservatory of Music in Boston where he could live with Garry. A visit to Lutheran College Night in New York in the fall of 1973 provided information about Wagner, Gettysburg, Muhlenberg, and St. Olaf. "Where is this school again?" he asked Director of Admissions Bruce Moe as he came back to the St. Olaf table. "Minnesota?"

Minnesota indeed. It was a winter wonderland and bitterly cold in February of 1974 when Anton and his brother flew to Minneapolis, rented a car, and drove for what seemed to be miles and miles through the snowy countryside to reach Northfield and the St. Olaf campus. "Everything was white! The snow, the buildings, the people," recalled Anton. He met the admissions staff, had an interview with Kenneth Jennings, and sang for him. Jennings mentioned that the St. Olaf Choir was preparing Mozart's *Requiem* and invited him to the rehearsal. Time did not allow it, but on the way back across the campus they stopped by Boe Chapel where the Chapel Choir under Robert Scholz was rehearsing Bach's *St. Matthew Passion*. As Anton listened, he thought to himself: "This

*St. Olaf campus scene
Winter, 1973-74*

*Robert Scholz
Director, Chapel Choir*

510

is incredible, and it's not the touring choir!" He felt that if he decided to come to St. Olaf, failed to get into the St. Olaf Choir but sang in the Chapel Choir, he could be a very happy man.[11]

Snowshoes by Rølvaag Library

The decision for St. Olaf was not an easy one. Northfield was half-way across the country. Indiana, Capital, and the New England Conservatory remained in the running, but St. Olaf seemed to show the greatest interest in Anton. In the family conferences, Garry put in good words for St. Olaf but his mother was not at all sure it was the right place. His high school friends teased him about snowshoes, the Minnesota Vikings, and Mary Tyler Moore. Nevertheless, St. Olaf was the choice and Anton arrived on campus in the fall of 1974 when the College was celebrating its centennial year.

Anton Armstrong's first two years at St. Olaf College brought both triumphs and disappointments. He exercised leadership in music by directing the Liturgical Choir for three years. He tried out for the St. Olaf Choir in the spring but was only named an alternate. As a member of the Chapel Choir, he became a section leader. During his sophomore year he took the initiative in forming a small chamber choir that provided the choral music for art professor Mac Gimse's exhibit of a variety of cruciforms. That year he carried worries about a problem in his father's business at home. At the same time, he was working to improve his vocal technique. He entertained thoughts of transferring to Oberlin.

Anton Armstrong
First year at St. Olaf

Prospects in the St. Olaf milieu became brighter the second half of his sophomore year. In January of 1976 he did a music education interim in New York. Hearing the St. Olaf Choir in New York when it came through on its tour and seeing close friends who were in the Choir gave him second thoughts about leaving St. Olaf. That spring, he was invited to join the St. Olaf Choir.[12]

The last two years at St. Olaf were happier than the first two. As a candidate for the Bachelor of Music degree, Armstrong pursued a vocal performance major but concentrated on vocal pedagogy. He took instrumental conducting from Donald Berglund and Miles Johnson and choral conducting from Kenneth Jennings. Alice Larsen, director of Manitou Singers, gave him an opportunity to conduct that group. One of Larsen's singers, Solveig Benson Mørkeberg '81, remembered having Armstrong as student conductor. "We thought he was so cool," she wrote. "He was a *senior*."[13] For Anton, these experiences, added to his work with the Liturgical Choir, fostered a growing interest in conducting.

St. Olaf Choir, 1976
Armstrong in third row

Singing baritone in the St. Olaf Choir, Armstrong participated in the 1977 and 1978 tours. At an informal party during the Choir's 1978 tour of the Midwest, Anton, Don Lee, the tour manager, Paul Andress, Steve Christenson, and Marilyn Galstad put on their purple robes to entertain the other Choir members in the style of "Gladys Knight and the Pips." Anton and Don had the natural "Afros" to go with the act while blond Paul and Steve had their heads styled with pincurls.[14]

Donald Berglund, 1978
Director, St. Olaf Orchestra

Miles Johnson, 1978
Director, St. Olaf Band

A picture in the *Manitou Messenger* shows Anton next to his college roommate Ralph Johnson at the home concert at the conclusion of the 1978 tour. The caption said that "a tired but joyous St. Olaf Choir performed superbly in its home concert." Among the numbers on the program were "Singet dem Herrn" by Heinrich Schütz, "Adoramus Te, Christe," by Corsi, Bach's *Cantata No. 150*, accompanied by a small orchestra, works by Mozart, Schumann, and Ligeti, and Jennings' "Today, Heaven Sings."[15]

Important as music was for Armstrong during his student days, he had time for other activities. In the spring of 1977 he was a candidate for Political Activities Coordinator in the Student Senate. A letter of support in the *Manitou Messenger* described him as "a person who is very sensitive to the needs and feelings of everyone, and is aware of the issues on St. Olaf campus." Another supporter wrote that as a candidate Armstrong "unveiled a very creative approach by dealing with specific themes for next year and by asking for greater student involvement in planning."[16]

Despite these warm endorsements, Anton lost the election by eighteen votes.[17] But he was not deterred from political activity. The next fall he and Lula Isom, representing the Black Action Committee, announced the first of a series of forums on racial issues. The first topic was "Affirmative Action: Reverse Discrimination," an especially relevant issue because of a publicized court case in which a white applicant to a law school claimed that he had been rejected because of his race.[18] In his senior year Anton won the Leadership and Service Award given by the Black Student Affairs office at St. Olaf.

Armstrong speaking in Chapel

As a music major, Anton gave voice recitals his junior and senior years. He recalled being commended for his "good stage presence." He also remembered that both recitals were attended by St. Olaf President Sidney Rand and Lois Rand. For student participants, the annual St. Olaf Christmas Festival is often a source of special memories. In Anton's case, he had the privilege of a visit by his mother and his brother Garry for the Festival his senior year, December 1977. This first visit to St. Olaf College convinced his mother that his choice had been a good one. "Now I know you were right," she said.[19]

Anton Armstrong graduated from St. Olaf College with the Bachelor of Music degree in the Class of 1978. Both his father and mother, as well as his brothers Garry and Billy, were present for his graduation.

Anton Armstrong
Senior picture, 1978

Graduate Study

During the second semester of his senior year at St. Olaf, Armstrong was a candidate for a Danforth Foundation Fellowship. He was selected as a finalist and was interviewed at the University of Chicago. While he did not receive a fellowship, he took satisfaction in having his abilities recognized by the Foundation.

Anton Armstrong, Bachelor of Music Congratulated by President Sidney Rand

After graduation Anton was accepted as a candidate for the Master of Music degree at the University of Illinois. To earn his way he took a job as resident head in a university residence hall and directed a choir for two years at St. Matthew's Lutheran Church in Urbana, Illinois.

Armstrong had two good years at Illinois, receiving the Master of Music in Choral Music in 1980. He developed a friendship with another promising young musician, André Thomas, composer and conductor who later became director of choral activities at Florida State University. At St. Matthew's, Armstrong's responsibilities grew to include senior choir, handbell choir, and a children's choir. From that experience, added to his Boychoir background, he gained a lasting interest in doing music with children.

André Thomas

As Armstrong's second year at the University of Illinois was drawing to a close, he was looking for a job. Kenneth Jennings had given Armstrong's name to a private school. Robert Scholz, director of the St. Olaf Chapel Choir and Armstrong's voice teacher, had told Howard Slenk, choral conductor at Calvin College, about Armstrong. At Calvin some people still remembered another St. Olaf musician who had taught summer sessions there in 1956 and 1960 and had made a strong impression. His name was Olaf C. Christiansen.

In 1980 Calvin College offered Armstrong a sabbatical leave replacement position that led to a full-time three year contract. Calvin had a robust music program with as many as six choirs, numerous music courses, and private music lessons. From 1980 to 1983 Anton Armstrong was involved in a busy and satisfying round of work at Calvin College.

In 1983 Armstrong received a call from Charles Smith at Michigan State University informing him of a competitive fellowship for minority candidates in the Doctor of Musical Arts program. Armstrong applied, received the fellowship, and began commuting between Grand Rapids and East Lansing to take the courses required for the doctor's degree.[20] Although he resigned from the Calvin faculty in order to do graduate work, Armstrong retained certain conducting positions in Grand Rapids. As a graduate teaching fellow at Michigan State, he taught choral conducting and literature and conducted the M.S.U. Women's Glee Club.

Armstrong received the Doctor of Musical Arts degree in the spring of 1987. The topic for his doctoral dissertation was the St. Olaf Choir. The thesis was entitled, "Celebrating 75 Years of Musical Excellence: The Evolution of the St. Olaf Choir."[21] In his summary Armstrong stated that the mission of the St. Olaf Choir has been to proclaim a religious message and to celebrate musical art as a gift from God.[22] He had no inkling at the time that one day he would become the next steward of the mission.

At Calvin College

Anton Armstrong's doctoral studies at Michigan State took place between two teaching stints at Calvin College, the first as visiting instructor of music. His first year he conducted Calvin's concert choir, The Capella. Other duties over three years included conducting men's and women's choruses and teaching voice, choral conducting, music history, and introductory music theory.

During his graduate study at Michigan State University, Calvin College kept in touch with Armstrong. Hope College in Holland, Michigan, was keenly interested in securing Armstrong for its faculty. In the end, he accepted an offer to return to Calvin where he served from 1986 until 1990, attaining the academic rank of Associate Professor of Music.

Returning to St. Olaf College as an alumnus to celebrate the 10th anniversary of his graduation in May of 1988, Anton was asked to lead the singing at the banquet attended by 1,000 alumni/ae and parents. The same weekend Anton and two other black alumni were interviewed about the recruitment and support of minority students and faculty at their alma mater. Armstrong '78, Ken Brown '38, and Isaiah Harriday '63, agreed that St. Olaf needed a comprehensive, well funded strategic plan in order to become a multicultural campus where students from diverse backgrounds can not only survive but grow and thrive. Armstrong cited the positive results of such a plan recently implemented at Calvin College.[23]

In examining the Calvin College part of Anton Armstrong's career, one has to point out that Grand Rapids, Michigan, where the college is located, is unique among cities of comparable size for the scope and quality of its musical culture. In addition to the full musical program of Calvin College and the choirs of the many Grand Rapids churches, the city has the Grand Rapids Symphony Orchestra with its 125-member Symphony Chorus, the Schubert Club, the St. Cecilia Music Society that sponsors Singers, Youth Chorale, and Junior Orchestra, the Chamber Choir, and other groups.

Anton Armstrong's duties while at Calvin College included both college and community musical responsibilities. At Calvin he taught choral conducting, vocal-choral methods, and music appreciation. He was conductor of the Campus Choir, a mixed ensemble of 75 voices. One of two touring choirs, it was Anton's favorite.

Calvin College Alumni Choir, 1985

Members of the Campus Choir were primarily first and second year students.[24]

He was also music director and conductor of the Calvin College Alumni Choir, founded in 1977 and enthusiastically supported by the alumni. A small group to start with, the Alumni Choir grew to a semi-professional choral ensemble of more than forty voices. Members were Calvin alumni who lived within a 90-minute drive from Grand Rapids. After its Christmas and Epiphany program in Grand Rapids in early 1985, a reviewer noted that the young conductor "achieves some of the characteristics of the famous St. Olaf Choir in his work," specifically the blend and the diction.[25] The writer could have added that the Choir also concluded each concert with the singing of "Beautiful Savior."

Alumni Choir rehearsal, 1986

516

Calvin College Alumni Choir
Conducted by Anton Armstrong

In March of 1985 the Alumni Choir was honored by an invitation to sing at the national convention of the American Choral Directors Association meeting in Salt Lake City, Utah. Letters of high praise from the officers of the organization were received at Calvin. Colleen Kirk, Vice President, called it an outstanding performance and a highlight of the convention. "This sensitive choral ensemble, under the able direction of Anton Armstrong, delighted the audience which was comprised of 3,000 choral conductors."[26]

Two other interesting performances may be mentioned. On April 21, 1985, Armstrong and the Calvin College Alumni Choir shared a program with the American Boychoir of Princeton, New Jersey, directed by John Kuzma. It was a unique pleasure for Armstrong who had sung with the American Boychoir in his early teens.[27]

The following year, on March 15, 1986, the Calvin College Alumni Choir performed at a music festival at Hope College with the Holland Chorale and the Western Michigan University Brass and Percussion Ensemble. Guest conductor was British composer John Rutter who led the Alumni Choir in two of his works. With Armstrong directing, the Alumni Choir sang five other pieces, including two numbers by Jean Berger and a lively spiritual called "Rockin' Jerusalem." A reviewer wrote, "The Choir continues to grow in stature under Armstrong's skillful direction. Its singing was certainly a highlight of this program."[28]

Another indication of the stature of the Calvin College Alumni Choir was the fact that when Armstrong went to St. Olaf College, his successor was Charles K. Smith, professor of music and director of choral activities at Michigan State University and Armstrong's doctoral adviser.[29] Concerning

Armstrong's selection as director of the St. Olaf Choir, Professor Smith said: "It's important that St. Olaf has hired someone comfortable on the world stage, someone capable of producing world class ensembles. And Anton is that man."[30]

One of the several vigorous music organizations in Grand Rapids is the St. Cecilia Music Society, founded in 1883. Armstrong became the conductor of the St. Cecilia Youth Chorale in 1981 and artistic director of the Society in 1986, a position he filled without pay. This chorus of 75 treble voices is made up of boys and girls ages 10 to 14. During the time Anton was conductor, it performed with Opera Grand Rapids, the Grand Rapids Symphony Orchestra and Symphony Chorus, the Detroit Symphony Orchestra, and in New York with the American Symphony Orchestra. The St. Cecilia Music Society dedicated its May 20, 1990, concert to Anton Armstrong "with love and appreciation for his outstanding leadership in the choral music program for children in our organization."[31]

In 1982, Armstrong was appointed conductor of the Grand Rapids Symphony Chorus of 100 voices. The Symphony Chorus performed with the Grand Rapids Symphony Orchestra and in its own concerts. In February of 1987 Armstrong led the Orchestra and Chorus in four performances of Mendelssohn's *Elijah*.[32] On Armstrong's call to St. Olaf, Peter Smith, executive director of the

ST
CECILIA
MUSIC
SOCIETY

PROGRAM
1989-90

1986-87 Season

Grand Rapids Symphony

Catherine Comet, Music Director

Volume 3

Grand Rapids Symphony Orchestra, said, "I'm happy for him and proud of him and delighted for him—no matter what that might mean for us."[33]

As word spread of Armstrong's appointment at St. Olaf College, the popularity he enjoyed in Grand Rapids and at Calvin College was recognized in articles in the *Calvin College Chimes*, student newspaper, in the *Grand Rapids Press*, and in reviews of his last concerts. The Fine Arts Center Auditorium at Calvin was packed for the two performances by the Calvin College Alumni Choir at its spring concert, May 19 and 20, 1990. At the close of the last concert there were standing ovations and encores. The Choir gave Anton a gift and the alumni association made him an official "Honorary Alumnus" of Calvin College. Another spirited ovation rolled across the hall when Armstrong's parents were introduced. The applause subsided, but instantly broke out again with renewed force and delighted laughter when everyone heard Anton's mother as she shouted out, "THAT'S MY BOY!!"[34]

Music Director - The St. Olaf Choir

When Anton Armstrong's selection as Music Director of the St. Olaf Choir was announced on January 2, 1990, Dr. Kenneth Graber, chair of the music department and of the search committee, issued this statement:

> We are very pleased to have Anton Armstrong join the music faculty at St. Olaf. We look forward to his leadership in continuing and building the

Bob Johnson, Anton Armstrong, Kenneth Jennings

St. Olaf Music Faculty

tradition of musical excellence of the St. Olaf Choir that has been achieved through the work of Kenneth Jennings and his predecessors, Olaf and F. Melius Christiansen.[35]

In his letter of application, Armstrong wrote of his love and respect for the St. Olaf choral tradition. While writing his doctoral thesis, he stated, he gained "a deeper understanding and appreciation for this tradition."[36] Bob Johnson, manager of St. Olaf music organizations who would be Armstrong's partner on the tours and other Choir activities, gave his version of the appointment:

> We were looking for a consummate musician, for a person with strong Christian convictions. And we were looking for a person who would carry on the ideals the Choir has had over the years, to maintain and enhance a great choral tradition—and we think he's the right person to do that.[37]

The St. Olaf Choir rehearses in the Fosnes Rehearsal Room on the second floor of the Christiansen Hall of Music. One of the Choir members, Ann Oldfield '92, recorded her memory of the moment in the fall of 1990 when Dr. Armstrong took his place for the first time on a rectangle of green carpet directly in front of the singers. With a huge grin on his face he said, "I still can't believe I'm standing here."[38]

Anton Armstrong, 1991

If the spontaneous remark conveys a bit of boyish enthusiasm, one should take into account that Anton Armstrong was 34 years of age at the time, the youngest director the St. Olaf Choir had ever had. F. Melius Christiansen was 41 when he founded the Choir; Olaf Christiansen was 40 when he was appointed to succeed his father; Kenneth Jennings was 43 when he took the position in 1968.

The young director was quickly caught up in the varied musical events of the new school year. At the opening chapel service, the St. Olaf

Choir audition, 1990. Michael Engelsgjerd with Dr. Armstrong

Choir under Armstrong's direction sang a South African hymn, "Haleluya! Pelo Tsa Rona." The same number was performed when the Choir participated in worship at the Norwegian Lutheran Memorial Church in Minneapolis on October 7, 1990. Also sung on that occasion was an arrangement of an old Norwegian folk tune, "My Heart is Longing to Praise My Savior."

Armstrong let it be known that he intended to broaden the scope of the Choir's repertoire without laying aside the traditions on which the College was built. For him, singing African as well as Norwegian music, as two examples, could help the College become a more multi-national community. Each person has his or her own ethnic mix to understand and celebrate. The better one understands one's own mix of traditions, he said, the better one can appreciate someone else's.[39]

The same idea of maintaining old traditions and introducing new ones would be evident in the 1990 Christmas Festival, for which Dr. Armstrong as director of the St. Olaf Choir had the leading responsibility. "We're not out to shake the house," he said. "There will be a variety of traditional carols, hymns, and anthems including the beloved Norse carol, 'Jeg er saa glad.' We will also be incorporating new repertoire for this event such as the African-American spiritual, 'Keep Your Lamps Trimmed and Burning.'"[40] The spiritual, arranged by André Thomas, was very effective as a rhythmic processional at the opening of the Christmas Festival concert.

The first tour of the St. Olaf Choir led by Anton Armstrong was into ten states of the Midwest and the South, including Louisiana and Texas. Seeing his role as the "ultimate steward" of the Choir, Armstrong defined its mission on the tour as taking the "wonderful hope" of the Gospel to people with a wide range of musical interests. One of the first reviews from the 1991 tour carried the headline, "St. Olaf Choir lives up to tradition of excellence," a felicitous choice of words given the title of Armstrong's doctoral dissertation on the St. Olaf Choir, "Celebrating 75 Years of Musical Excellence."

The reviewer, Donald Callen Freed, who heard the Choir in Lincoln, Nebraska, described the musicianship of the St. Olaf tradition: "The group sings as a cohesive unit, with command of pure vowels and flowing legato, precise pitch and diction, balance, blend, clarity, and a sense of complete control." More than that, he continued, was the Choir's expressive sense: "The text is given life and color and one can choose to listen to the smallest detail or the musical whole."[41]

Armstrong and the Choir presented a five-part program. One part was devoted to two motets by Mozart in honor of the 200th anniversary of the composer's death. The final section paid tribute to the previous directors of the St. Olaf Choir, eliciting from a reviewer the comment, "The St. Olaf tradition is still alive and still a pleasure to hear."[42] The numbers by previous directors were "Spirit of God, Descend Upon My Heart," by Kenneth Jennings, "Light Everlasting," by Olaf C. Christiansen, and "O Day Full of Grace" by F. Melius Christiansen.

One of the more difficult yet rewarding numbers on the program was Krzysztof Penderecki's avant-garde "Stabat Mater." Scored for three choirs, it included shouts, whispers, and chants. The text conveyed the pain of the grieving Mother as she stood, "tear-filled by the cross where hung her son," followed by the whispered prayer, "Make my heart burn in loving the Lord Christ that he may delight in me."[43] The impact of the piece caused one reviewer to observe, "I saw Mary weeping at the sight of her son hanging on a cross as if it were in Brown Auditorium."

Another contemporary work on the program that required concentration and control on the part of the singers was *The Lamentations of Jeremiah*, by Alberto Ginastera. In its performance of this dramatic, three-movement piece, the Choir was lauded for its sense of rhythm, diction, vocal range, and ability to handle contrasts.[44]

After the Choir's appearance on Valentine's Day in Rammelkamp Chapel at Illinois College in Jacksonville, Illinois, reviewer Karl Knudston Jones gave his response to what he heard: "It was immediately evident that the audience would be treated to an exhilarating yet highly controlled choral sound, characterized by an impeccable uniformity of vowel production, consistently energized consonants and articulation and nearly perfect intonation. These factors, along with the exquisite blend and outstanding balance of the voice parts in the ensemble, represent the hallmarks which have distinguished the St. Olaf Choir as a leader in the widely respected Midwestern choral tradition of a cappella singing."[45]

Following the lead of Kenneth Jennings, Anton Armstrong supplemented the a cappella numbers with select use of a few instruments. An oboe accompanied the singing of "Evening Meal" by Ralph M. Johnson, and conga drums were played with the South African "Haleluya! Pelo Tsa Rona."

The Choir completed its tour and gave its home concert on Sunday, February 17, 1991. Senior members said that the tour was one of musical and spiritual growth. One of them, *Concert Program, 1991*

Charles Gray   *John Ferguson*

Amy Walter, said that "of my three tours with the choir, this was by far the most consistent and exciting." The singers reported being pleased with the new director, crediting him with good work in handling the pressures of daily performances. One of them commented, "He was conscious in making sure we did our best and the message got across."[46]

In 1992 the St. Olaf Choir took its message to the Pacific Northwest. True to his intention, Armstrong included in the program more 20th century works and folk music from the United States and third world countries. Among the classical choral numbers were Sweelinck's "Cantate Domino," Lotti's "Crucifixus," and "Jauchzet dem Herrn" by J. S. Bach. An unusual modern work was John Leavitt's "Kyrieleis." Charles Gray, associate professor of music at St. Olaf, played violin and viola obbligatos on three numbers, one of them a setting of "Ah, Holy Jesus" by St. Olaf music professor and organist John Ferguson. According to one reviewer, Gray "plays with a beautiful sense of phrase expressiveness."[47]

The expansion of the repertoire was illustrated by two South African folks songs, "Singabahambayo" and "Freedom Is Coming." A Portland reviewer was impressed by the Choir's ability to sing these songs "with just the right supple phrasing and relaxed rhythmic feel."[48] The same reviewer reported how the Choir looked as it took the stage:

> This is a group with confidence. Everything about them, including the way they walked—call it the "St. Olaf Stride"— proclaimed a sense of purpose and the promise of good things to come. Fortunately, they delivered.[49]

Another reviewer saw fit to comment on the distinctive "St. Olaf sound." Wrote Travis Rivers in Spokane after hearing the Choir in St. John's Cathedral, "It takes only a few notes for any attentive listener to identify this choir. The combination of a light tone without vibrato with precise intonation gives the sonority a purity that rings even at the softest levels."[50]

Not mentioned in any review was the story of Manager Bob Johnson's mishap early in the 1992 tour. When the Choir arrived in Alexandria, Minnesota, Bob's home town, the manager slipped on the ice and broke his left leg. He spent the rest of the tour in a wheelchair. After the Choir reached the airport in Seattle, Ron Pechauer, College director of church relations, did the honors of pushing Bob (B. J.) in the wheel chair. All went well for a few minutes until Ron spotted an old friend and rushed over to greet her, leaving the manager, leg-in-cast extended, helpless and unattended in the wheelchair that began rolling down an incline straight toward a heavy steel post. B. J. attempted braking action with his other foot, but the painful crash could not be avoided. With characteristic grit and good humor, however, he carried on and guided the Choir successfully through the rest of the tour.[51]

Manager Bob Johnson

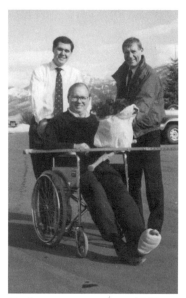

B. J. on western tour, 1992

In May of 1992 the Choir and the College received a visit from Betty White, well-known television actress who played the part of Rose Nylund from the mythical town of "St. Olaf" in the successful television series, "The Golden Girls." As noted in a previous chapter, the cast of the show had been the guests of the Choir at the Los Angeles concert in the Dorothy Chandler Pavilion. The Choir also went to see "The Golden Girls" and taught the cast "Um-Yah-Yah!" Dan Jorgensen, director of public relations, invited Betty White to St. Olaf College and eventually worked out a date for the visit.

During her two days on campus, White saw the women's softball team win first place in the conference, went to a St. Olaf Choir concert, attended Chapel and signed autographs, was interviewed by President Mel George on the College radio station, WCAL-FM 89.3, was made a member of Theta Alpha Phi, theater honor society, and spoke with theater classes about acting and television. During the discussion White recalled the Choir's visit to the television show in Los Angeles:

> Wouldn't you know it, the day they were there was my birthday? After Rue and I stood up and sang, "We come from St. Olaf," the choir sang "Happy Birthday" in this full, glorious, as-only-your-choir-can-do-it "Happy Birthday," and Rue and I crawled off the stage. It was such fun. And anything Rose said that night, bad joke, good joke, was hysterical![52]

Bob Johnson, Betty White, Mary Auge
At the real St. Olaf, May, 1992

Everyone who met Betty White was charmed by her graciousness, including Choir members, Anton Armstrong, Bob Johnson, and Mary Auge, secretary for music organizations. When White first met the St. Olaf Choir, it was directed by Kenneth Jennings. In May of 1992, Armstrong was at the helm, then completing his second season as director.

On the first tours under Armstrong's leadership, with audiences seeing him in action for the first time, close

Anton Armstrong and Betty White
Choir warm-up, Boe Chapel

attention was given to his conducting style as well as to the other aspects of the performance. One observer singled out "the ease of musical communication of director and choir to the audience." One commented that the group remained "absolutely focused while performing," a mark of the tradition of superb training, now carried on by the new director. "Throughout the concert the St. Olaf vocalists were riveted to Armstrong's every move, their attention never wavering." Travis Rivers wrote, "Though Armstrong's platform manner is unostentatious, he's clearly in control."[53]

Members of the St. Olaf Choir who met for rehearsals day after day in Fosnes Rehearsal Hall were treated to sides of Armstrong's style and personality that were not always on public view. He worked them hard and charmed them, instilling in his singers his own love for music and joy in living. Ann Oldfield '92, the Choir member quoted earlier, saw Armstrong's working style at close range and recorded her observations.

Ann Oldfield

When she described how he demonstrated his response to the music by "the bend of an elbow, the raising of an eyebrow, the lift of his chin," she could have been writing about any one of the four directors of the St. Olaf Choir. Similarly, of his predecessors too it could have been said: "He creates new music every time the choir sings a piece" and "He is willing to push us to the limit emotionally and physically, and we are willing to give him everything we've got." Choir members who had sung under the Christiansens and Jennings had the same experiences.

Yet Anton Armstrong brought to the task his own unique background, skills, and personality traits. As expected, he had a gift for preparing the Choir to sing African freedom songs and American spirituals, but he was equally effective with light Norwegian folk songs. While conducting the livelier numbers in the repertoire, his true personality would often shine through the most, wrote Oldfield, who continued with this description:

> His knees would be bouncing, his shoulders would be grooving, his neck would be jiving, and he was never afraid to tell the choir his opinion about our posture or expression. He would say, "Altos, time for a little Aretha here," or "I want more Motown," or "I'm getting white M & Ms here. We need Godiva chocolate."[54]

It would seem that a young black director who could call for "molto con blasto" and characterize former president Lars Boe as "an ecumenical sort of dude" was, in his mannerisms and vocabulary, generations removed from the buttoned-up dignity of F. Melius Christiansen. Certain differences from earlier leadership are obvious, but it should not be forgotten that "Christy" was known for strikingly original metaphors and earthy humor, that Olaf Christiansen, in addition to wielding the pithy phrase, more than once showed his singers what he wanted by graceful dance movements, and that Kenneth Jennings employed a rich set of colorful expressions as he urged the Choir to loosen up and sing with a free, natural tone.

The director relaxes

With good reason one would regard Anton Armstrong as one who brought fresh new impulses to the St. Olaf Choir. He was selected with the expectation that he would widen the global paths that Kenneth Jennings had opened. At the same time, it is also evident that he stood solidly within the creative pattern that formed his predecessors. They were free, talented persons whose devotion to great music made them work to make it come alive for their generation, and always to move forward. They strove to be true to the mission of the Choir, true to the art of music, and true to themselves.

After his first two seasons as director of the St. Olaf Choir, Armstrong had shown himself equal to the task. He and the Choir had known some faltering moments here and there, so the disciplines of concentration would have to continue. But the overall results had been favorable. Dr. Armstrong had won the approval of the key constituencies: listeners in concert halls and churches, the critics, his colleagues at St. Olaf and in the music profession, the College community, and the members of the St. Olaf Choir.

Armstrong and St. Olaf singers

Notes for Chapter 16 ANTON ARMSTRONG

1. *The Choral Journal* (August 1989), 34.

2. Colleen Johnston, "Dynamic St. Olaf Choir makes the difficult seem easy," *Kitchener-Waterloo Record*, February 6, 1990.

3. Rita Hoffmann, "Vitae: Kenneth Jennings," *Minnesota Monthly* (May 1990), 47.

4. Bradley Ellingboe and Dennis Schrock, "An Interview with Kenneth Jennings On the Occasion of his Retirement as Music Director of the Saint Olaf Choir," Choral Journal XXX (May 1990), 12.

5. Interview: Joseph M. Shaw with Anton Armstrong, June 21, 1996.

6. *Ibid.*

7. Letter: Melvin D. George to Anton Armstrong, December 22, 1989.

8. Letter: Anton E. Armstrong to Melvin D. George, December 27, 1989.

9. News Release, St. Olaf College News Service, January 2, 1990; letter: Melvin D. George to Anton Armstrong, January 3, 1990.

10. Interviews: JMS with Anton Armstrong, June 20, 1996; December 17, 1996.

11. JMS interview with Anton Armstrong, June 20, 1996.

12. *Ibid.*

13. "President's Report: Seven Alumni Profiles," *Saint Olaf* 39 (November/December 1991), 10.

14. Letter: Joan Pechauer '79 to Bob Johnson, January, 1994.

15. *Manitou Messenger (MM)*, February 23, 1978.

16. *MM* 90 (March 25, 1977), 6.

17. *MM* 90 (April 8, 1977), 1.

18. *MM* 90 (October 27, 1977), 1.

19. *Saint Olaf* 36 (August/September 1988), 1.

20. *Saint Olaf* 31 (August 1983), 20.

21. Anton Eugene Armstrong, "Celebrating 75 Years of Musical Excellence: The Evolution of The St. Olaf Choir," A thesis submitted in partial fulfillment of the requirements of the Doctor of Musical Arts degree from Michigan State University, May, 1987.

22. *Ibid.*, 84.

23. Frederick H. Gonnerman, "Loyalty, Concern Voiced by Returning Alums," *Saint Olaf* 36 (August/September 1988), 1-3.

24. Letter: John D. Witvliet to JMS, September 21, 1996.

25. Richard DeVinney, "Calvin Alumni Choir gives fine performance," *The Grand Rapids Press*, January 14, 1985.

26. Letter: Colleen J. Kirk to Howard Slenk, March 20, 1985.

27. Richard DeVinney, "Boychoir joins Calvin Alumni in fine concert," *The Grand Rapids Press*, April 22, 1985.

28. Richard DeVinney, "Rutter and His Music Make a Grand Finale," *The Grand Rapids Press*, March 16, 1986.

29. Julie Ridenour, "MSU choral head tabbed as Calvin College Alumni Choir director," *The Grand Rapids Press*, June 14, 1990.

30. Quoted from *The Grand Rapids Press* by Sarah Koops, "Armstrong to leave for renowned St. Olaf choir," *Chimes*, Calvin College, Grand Rapids, Michigan, January 12, 1990.

31. Julie Ridenour, "GR's Armstrong will direct St. Olaf Choir," *The Grand Rapids Press*, January 3, 1990; *The Grand Rapids Press*, May 13, 1990; St. Cecilia Music Society, Program 1989-90.

32. Program, Grand Rapids Symphony, 1986-87 Season.

33. Julie Ridenour, "GR's Armstrong will direct St. Olaf Choir," *The Grand Rapids Press*, January 3, 1990.

34. Letter: John D. Witvliet to JMS, September 21, 1996.

35. St. Olaf College News Service, Press Release, January 2, 1990.

36. *Ibid.*

37. Bob Johnson, quoted in Julie Ridenour, "GR's Armstrong will direct St. Olaf Choir," *The Grand Rapids Press*, January 3, 1990.

38. Ann Oldfield, "Ceremonial Speech," St. Olaf College, Spring 1991.

39. Louis Lystig, "Armstrong preserves tradition while exploring new ideas," *MM* 104 (October 5, 1990), 10.

40. *Ibid.*

41. Donald Callen Freed, "St. Olaf Choir lives up to tradition of excellence," *The Lincoln Journal*, February 1, 1991.

42. *Ibid.*

43. Richard Olsen, "St. Olaf Choir rated 'superb,'" *Albert Lea Tribune*, February, 1991.

44. Cf. 1991 reviews by Karl Knudtson Jones, Jacksonville, Illinois, Rick Rogers, *The Sunday Oklahoman;* Donald Callen Freed, *The Lincoln Journal*, Richard Olsen, *Albert Lea Tribune*.

45. Karl Knudstson Jones, unidentified paper, Jacksonville, Illinois, ca. February 15, 1991.

46. Emily Blejwas, "St. Olaf Choir returns from tour," *MM*, February 22, 1991.

47. Rolf Anderson, "St. Olaf College Choir was a listening pleasure," unidentified paper, Willmar, Minnesota, January 19, 1992.

48. Kip Richardson, "St. Olaf Choir bridges centuries, continents," *The Oregonian*, Portland, Oregon, February 8, 1992.

49. *Ibid.*

50. Travis Rivers, "St. Olaf Choir sets tone beautifully," unidentified paper, Spokane, Washington, February 10, 1992.

51. Cf. *Saint Olaf* 40 (March/April 1992), inside front cover.

52. So July/August 1992, 13.)

53. Richardson, *The Oregonian*, February 8, 1992; Rivers, Spokane, February 10, 1992.

54. Ann Oldfield, "Ceremonial Speech," Spring 1991.

CHAPTER 17

FOCUS ON THE FUTURE

When Dr. Anton Armstrong was appointed Musical Director of the St. Olaf Choir in January of 1990, the news release noted how the candidate viewed the new position. Armstrong related the choral art to the liturgical proclamation of the Word of God and characterized St. Olaf College as a leader in worship and music for the Evangelical Lutheran Church in America and in the larger ecumenical community. He also registered his own love and respect for the St. Olaf choral tradition, having grown in his understanding of it through preparation of his doctoral dissertation. Continuing, Armstrong made this important affirmation:

Anton Armstrong

> Yet, I also realize that while the past has laid a firm foundation, the focus for this tradition must be to the future as we seek to serve others through the choral art.[1]

Since any responsible leader must plan and act toward the realization of future goals, the statement might seem routine. But in this case, the focus on the future had particular relevance for the St. Olaf Choir and the College. F. Melius Christiansen once said that "the St. Olaf Choir is an expression of the spirit of the institution."[2] And that spirit is captured in the Norwegian motto of St. Olaf College: "Fram, Fram, Kristmenn, Krossmenn." "Forward, Forward, Men of Christ, Men of the Cross." Both College and Choir define themselves by looking to the future.

From its earliest years, the St. Olaf Choir applied itself to moving forward, working to make each performance better than the last. The

533

Choir's founder said in the late twenties: "The choir has improved steadily through a period of nearly 20 years. We know that perfection can never be reached, but we have to work toward that goal nevertheless."[3] Anton Armstrong's statement in 1990 revealed his understanding of a choral tradition that does not allow itself to stand still but prepares for future service.

Renewing the Repertory

To move forward in choral work requires an ongoing search for new music. "It is necessary for us to realize that musical expression, if it is sincere, must change to a certain extent with changes in the thought and outlook of succeeding generations. We cannot

Motto of King Olaf Haraldsson, source of College motto

expect the young people of today to rest contented with singing exactly what was being sung two centuries ago, if it has been outmoded in spirit and manner."[4] So said F. Melius Christiansen in a 1925 interview.

Being young and attuned to "the thought and outlook" of the student generation, Anton Armstrong introduced into the St. Olaf Choir's repertory a musical literature that gave a new flavor to the concerts. In doing so, he was consciously guided by the College mission statement in which being "rooted in the Gospel" is paired with cultivating "a global perspective." Moreover, Armstrong saw himself as following in the footsteps of Kenneth Jennings who had already given the Choir a larger global awareness by introducing music of eastern Europe and the Orient.[5]

Asked about specific areas he intended to investigate, Armstrong named African-American choral influences, music of South America, Africa, Asia, and countries of the eastern European bloc. He also stated an interest in rediscovering both sacred and secular American folk songs. Again, one thinks of the first director of the St. Olaf Choir who loved the folk melody. When explaining the search for appropriate compositions, F. Melius Christiansen had told a reporter: "We must go back every once in so often and refresh our inspiration at its very fountain—folk music." Many Lutheran chorales, he said, can be traced back to secular songs familiar to the people. "They owe their beauty to simple sincerity of spirit and the fact of a spontaneous expression of honest human feeling."[6]

Like his predecessors, Armstrong put the main emphasis on the classical choral repertoire, but as his programming the first two years indicated, he soon had the St. Olaf Choir singing South African hymns, African-American spirituals, American hymns and folk songs, and folk songs from other cultures. When he took the Choir to Grand Rapids in 1993, the reviewer said it was no surprise that Armstrong and the Choir were greeted by sustained applause, shouts, and whistles as he returned to his former home. But what was unexpected, wrote the reviewer, "was Armstrong's already evident global sense of musical evolution," ranging from the ancient Latin mass to "O Sifuni Mungu," arranged by David Maddux and sung in both Swahili and English as a translation of the text, "All Creatures of our God and King."[7]

In addition to the Maddux piece and the folk numbers mentioned in the previous chapter, the Choir explored ethnic diversity during the next few years with such songs as "Hush! Somebody's Callin' My Name," arranged by Brazeal W. Dennard, "I Open My Mouth," arranged by André Thomas, the Norwegian "Pål på Haugen," arranged by Bradley Ellingboe, and "Ngana" ("Songs of Passage") by Australian composer Stephen Leek.

Choral pieces from various countries and in different languages were often part of the regular concert program, as was "O Sifuni Mungu," for example, and not confined to the category of Optional Selections. A spiritual called "John Saw Duh Numbuh," arranged by Robert Shaw and Alice Parker, appeared in the fifth part of the 1993 program. That same year "Go Where I Send Thee," arranged by André Thomas and "Jamaican Market Place," arranged by Larry Farrow, were among the optional numbers. In 1994, "African Noel," arranged by André Thomas, was in the fourth part while "Halle, Halle, Halle" arranged by Marty Haugen, and the Korean song, "Arirang," arranged by Kenneth Jennings, were optional.

In building a more multinational and multicultural program, Armstrong drew upon new or familiar folk songs or contemporary anthems by younger composers. On the 1995 concert tour, for example, listeners heard the premiere performances of "Vanity of Vanities," by Peter Hamlin, born in 1951, a member of the music department at St. Olaf, and

Peter Hamlin

"Psalm 96," by Ralph M. Johnson, Armstrong's St. Olaf classmate, born in 1955. The program also included "Magnificat," composed by the Estonian Arvo Pärt, born in 1935. Out of African culture came the text for "Kasar Mie La Gaji" ("The earth is tired!"), composed by Alberto Grau, a Venezuelan born in 1937, sometimes performed with spoken parts emphasizing perils to the environment and sung in a dialect of the African Sahel. "Prayer Before Sleep," translated from the

Ralph M. Johnson

Babylonian Talmud by Sid Robinovitch, born in 1942, was sung in Hebrew.[8]

Following Kenneth Jennings in the use of instruments, Armstrong planned programs incorporating the sounds of strings, woodwinds, percussion, piano, and organ. In 1995 a small orchestra performed with the Choir in some of the opening numbers and Charles Gray, associate professor of music at St. Olaf, played the viola on two pieces. In 1996 St. Olaf professor John Ferguson, organist, traveled with the Choir and performed in a section devoted to music for choir and organ.[9]

Choir and instrumentalists
Rehearsal in Carnegie Hall, 1995

536

As stated, the Choir's tradition of singing classical sacred music continued under Anton Armstrong. In 1994, for example, the concert opened with William Byrd's "Sing Joyfully Unto God," Palestrina's "Sicut Cervus," and Johann Pachelbel's "Jauchzet dem Herrn." Later in the program came Movements 2 and 3 of F. M. Christiansen's *Psalm 50*. The 1995 tour program presented Johann Michael Haydn's "Laetatus Sum," William Byrd's "Ave Verum Corpus," and Johann Sebastian Bach's *Singet dem Herrn ein neues Lied*. In 1996 opening numbers were "The Lord's Prayer" by Robert Stone, "Exsultate Deo" by Palestrina, "Coenantibus Autem Illis" by Juan de Lienas, and "Psalm 98: Singet dem Herrn" by Heinrich Schütz.[10]

Anthems by the Christiansens and Kenneth Jennings appeared on programs year by year. Olaf Christiansen's "Light Everlasting" was sung in 1991, "Easter Morning" by Paul J. and "Praise to the Lord" by F. Melius in 1992. "My Song in the Night," arranged by Paul J. Christiansen, and the last two movements of F. Melius's *Celestial Spring* were performed in 1993. The 1994 program offered Jennings' arrangement of "Arirang." On the 1995 tour to the east coast, the first standing ovation at nearly every concert came after the F. Melius arrangement of "Wake, Awake," by Philipp Nicolai. The program in 1996 included Kenneth Jennings' "All You Works of the Lord, Bless the Lord," and F. Melius Christiansen's arrangement of "O Day Full of Grace."[11]

G. Winston Cassler

Programs during the nineties presented compositions by other composers from the St. Olaf music faculty. Works by G. Winston Cassler and Charles Forsberg were sung in 1991. A setting of "Ah, Holy Jesus" by John Ferguson and an arrangement of "What Wondrous Love" by Robert Scholz were sung in 1992. Peter Hamlin's "O God of Our Salvation" was on the 1993 program and his "Vanity of Vanities" was sung in 1995. Ferguson's arrangement of "Lord of the Dance" was performed in 1996.[12]

The multicultural impulse in Anton Armstrong's choice of music gave a fresh basis for the singing of Norwegian songs. An

Charles Forsberg

optional piece on the 1992 program, as reported, was Bradley Ellingboe's arrangement of "Pål på Haugen." The 1993 tour program listed two numbers by Edvard Grieg in the opening section, "Hvad est du dog skjøn" and "God's Son Has Made Me Free." The spring and summer of 1993 gave the St. Olaf Choir further opportunities to sing the music of Edvard Grieg. In mid-April St. Olaf College hosted "Edvard Grieg: A Musician for Today," a symposium marking the 150th anniversary of the famous Norwegian composer's birth. The St. Olaf Choir joined the St. Olaf Band and St. Olaf Orchestra in a

Poster for Grieg Symposium

Grieg concert at the celebration. On April 30, 1993, the Choir sang with the Minnesota Orchestra in a performance of Grieg's *Peer Gynt* in Orchestra Hall in Minneapolis.[13]

With Grieg's music on the 1993 tour program and a celebration of his work on the campus and in Orchestra Hall in April, the St. Olaf Choir was getting tuned up for a tour to Norway. In June, the Choir would join other groups in the festive observances to be held in Bergen, Norway, the city of Grieg's birth.

To Norway in 1993

The St. Olaf Choir was the only non-Norwegian performing group invited to participate in the opening ceremonies of the Bergen International Festival in June of 1993. Flying first to Copenhagen, where it gave a concert in Trinity Church, the Choir made its way to Bergen by way of Larvik, the Norwegian town where F. Melius Christiansen spent most of his youth before emigrating to America. For the Larvik arrangements the Choir was indebted to Odd

Bob Johnson and Odd Terje Lysebo At St. Olaf College, 1991

538

Terje Lysebo, local musician and band director who had been at St. Olaf College several times as instructor and guest conductor of the St. Olaf Band.

The significance of singing in the Larvik church made a strong impact on members of the Choir. It came home to them that its roots as a singing institution were embodied in that very place. For Anton Armstrong, it was a moving experience to direct the Choir in the home church of its founder and first director and to consider again the high privilege of being the steward of what F. Melius Christianen had begun. David Fuller, the Choir's tour journalist, reflected on the concert from the singers' standpoint:

Anton Armstrong at Larvik Church

Photo by Betty Stromseth

> As sunlight streamed in the window and bathed different portions of the choir in majestic purple luminescence and profound happiness, we captivated the audience with radiant songs from the many languages of our diverse repertoire. It was odd to realize that for the first time we were singing the Grieg set in the native tongue of most if not all of those listening![14]

St. Olaf Choir, Larvik Church, 1993

Photo by Alicia Small

Two causes for wonder marked the bus trip from Larvik to Kristiansand. First was the skill of Sven and Ove, the two drivers who safely negotiated the sharp curves, the black tunnels, and the rocky terrain. Second was the incredibly beautiful scenery. The vast fjords highlighted by the morning sun moved Choir members to rejoice in the grace and majesty of God's creative power. Mark Tiede, Choir chaplain, coined a new liturgical expression: "Way to go, God!"[15]

Walking on stilts, Kristiansand

Photo by Alicia Small

For the visit in Kristiansand the Choir had two former Oles as guides, Aashild Watne and Sigbjørn Sødal, who showed them the harbor and took them to a picnic at the Vest-Agder Fylke Museum. In the pleasant outdoor setting the Choir had fun stilt-walking and singing American, African, and Norwegian folk songs. The concert was performed in the Kristiansand Cathedral with its wooden arches and pillars. In Stavanger the concert was in the ancient stone Cathedral dating from the 12th century.

Stavanger Cathedral

Going on to Bergen, the Choir was just beginning to enjoy the history and charm of the city when it received the sad news from Northfield that St. Olaf associate dean of students Dan Cybyske had died of a heart attack. Spontaneously, the singers gathered for a memorial hour, recalling Cybyske's warm-hearted concern for the well-being of the

Gordon Hafso '52 and Armstrong Hafso's choir from Canada sang in Stavanger the previous night.

students he served. In recording the solemn evening, David Fuller quoted from an anthem by Knut Nystedt: "Cry aloud to the Lord! Oh children of Zion! Let tears stream down like a torrent day and night. Pour out your heart like water before the presence of the Lord."

King Harald V and Prime Minister Gro Harlem Brundtland were in the audience in Grieg Hall on the afternoon of June 2, 1993, when the St. Olaf Choir made its contribution to the opening ceremonies of the Bergen International Music Festival. It was an honor for the Choir to sing before His Majesty on the 150th anniversary of the birth of Edvard Grieg, born in Bergen in 1843.

Bradley Ellingboe in Urness Recital Hall, St. Olaf College

For its two numbers, the Choir had the assistance of St. Olaf alumnus and former Choir member, Bradley Ellingboe '80, professor of vocal music at the University of New Mexico. Ellingboe, a specialist in the music of Grieg, gave a lecture at the festival on how foreign singers can best pronounce Grieg's vocal music. With the Choir, he sang the solo in Grieg's "Hvad est du dog skjøn" ("How Fair Thou Art"). And it was his arrangement of the Norwegian folk song, "Pål På Haugen," that was the Choir's second number at the festival. The song, a favorite with children, tells of a farm boy who is afraid to go home after accidentally letting the chickens out of the coop. The delighted audience soon caught on to the musical joke Ellingboe had worked into the arrangement, at one point having the basses boom out the opening theme from "In the Hall of the Mountain King" from Grieg's *Peer Gynt* suite. [16]

That evening the Choir was part of an outdoor gala, performing on a large platform floating on a man-made lake in downtown Bergen. The Choir shared the stage with two bands and a grand piano that nearly slid into the lake as performers left the platform after rehearsal. Members of the Choir enjoyed the brisk, clear evening, the enthusiastic crowd, and the chance to turn two percussionists loose on the conga drums in the performance of "O Sifuni Mungu."

Outdoor concert, Bergen   Photo by Alicia Small

The next day the Choir went up the hill from Bergen's central business district to the stately brick *Johanneskirke* where it gave a full concert. Grieg's "God's Son Has Made Me Free" was sung in the first part of the program. Bradley Ellingboe sang the solo in the Norwegian anthem, "Den Store Hvide Flok," known in English as "Behold a host." In the performing of Penderecki's "Agnus Dei," Choir members noticed that during the final chord, an open fifth, they would hear the resonant third echoing up in the rafters.[17]

The Choir left Bergen and entered fjord country, traveling along the Sognefjord to Balestrand and Skei where they bought hand-knit sweaters and enjoyed an evening's entertainment by local folk dancers. Everywhere they saw high mountains, blue fjords, sheer cliffs, and real glaciers. Like St. Olaf Choirs before them, they traveled down the beautiful Geirangerfjord and viewed with awe the "Seven Sisters" waterfall and the "Bridal Veil." It was only natural that the English text of "O Sifuni Mungu" should come to mind:

Folk dancing, Skei   Photo by Alicia Small
Chris Aspaas '95 to the right

542

Let all things their Creator bless,
And worship God in humbleness!
O, praise the Father, praise the Son,
And praise the Spirit, three in One!"[18]

A St. Olaf Choir visit to Trondheim usually calls for a concert in the stately Nidaros Cathedral, but in 1993 the concert was given in Olavshallen, a modern auditorium where the acoustics were good but the crowd not commensurate with the large dimensions of the hall. During a wreath-laying ceremony at the grave of Bernt Julius Muus, founder of St. Olaf College, the Choir sang "My Heart is Longing," the College song, "Fram, Fram, Kristmenn, Krossmenn," and "Beautiful Savior." St. Olaf President Melvin George gave a brief talk and offered a prayer, and the Dean of the Cathedral recounted the significance of Nidaros in the history of Christianity.[19]

In Snåsa, birthplace of B. J. Muus, the Choir received a warm and enthusiastic welcome, receiving standing ovations at the concert in the ancient church where Muus worshipped as a young boy. After every encore, someone presented a gift to Dr. Armstrong. And even as the Choir finally started to leave, the mayor of Snåsa ran down the aisle to catch the director and hand him yet another gift, a clock decorated with a picture of

Walking to Muus's grave, Trondheim
Tom Adcox, Mark Pearson with flowers
Photo by Alicia Small

Prayer at founder's grave   Photo by Alicia Small

Snåsa Church   Konserthus, *Oslo, Norway*

the Snåsa church.[20] In many gestures of friendship, the Snåsa community showed its pleasure at the visit of another St. Olaf group, having hosted the St. Olaf Band, for example, on earlier occasions.

On the way to Oslo a concert in Lillehammer was given in Maihaugen Concert Hall, built for cultural events related to the 1994 Winter Olympics. The final concert was in Oslo's *Konserthus* on Thursday, June 10, 1993. Singers and listeners agreed that it was the finest performance of the entire Norway tour. Dr. Sidney Rand, former president of St. Olaf and former ambassador to Norway, and his wife Lois, were among the many American friends of the Choir who attended the Oslo concert.

Sid and Lois Rand, Walt and Betty Stromseth, Oslo, Norway, 1993
Betty assisted Bob Johnson in coordinating travel.

After two days of pleasant sight-seeing in and around Oslo, the Choir sang several numbers at Sunday worship services of the American Lutheran Church. Dr. Rand delivered the sermon. Later that day the Choir assembled for group photographs near the royal palace followed by a fond farewell gathering with speeches and gifts, laughs and tears. Manager Bob Johnson received help from others in the group as he reviewed the tour from

St. Olaf Choir, 1993. Near Royal Palace, Oslo

beginning to end. He said it was a privilege to facilitate the activities of a choir so "dedicated to moving the human spirit."[21]

Practicing the Choral Art

At the beginning of this chapter Anton Armstrong was quoted as placing the focus of the St. Olaf Choir tradition on the future "as we seek to serve others through the choral art." From its founding to the present, Choir wisdom has been that directors and singers serve others only if they remain servants of art. "In Anton Armstrong," wrote the Grand Rapids reviewer, "we have a craftsman in true obeisance to his utmost art."[22] It was a precept with F. Melius Christiansen that the choir director is only a servant of the spirit of the music. Another was the importance of being true to art. "The spirit of art is very much like the spirit of Christ."[23]

Early in his career as fourth director of the St. Olaf Choir, Anton Armstrong invoked the image of "steward" with respect to his role and that of the members of the Choir. The student newspaper elaborated:

> He feels the pressure of upholding the high standards of the choir, but he is confident that the choir will succeed. It is his challenge to motivate the choir to do its very best, but the final result is in the hands of the choir members. He believes the choir will put forth a team effort as ambassadors for the college and the wider church by taking full responsibility for communicating their message.[24]

A clear example of serving through the choral art was the benefit concert given by the St. Olaf and Luther College Choirs in Austin, Minnesota, on November 16, 1993. The event, the first time the two choirs had ever performed together, raised $18,500 for residents of Iowa and southern Minnesota who had suffered from the summer floods. Regarding the purpose of the concert Anton Armstrong said, "We want to generate financial and prayer support for the victims. This is a message of love—to reach out and ease some of the pain."[25]

As the St. Olaf Choir headed west on its annual tour in the early part of 1994, the memory of the flood benefit concert equipped Armstrong and the singers with the empathy needed to feel the pain of earthquake victims in California. Audiences were touched when Dr. Armstrong, at the close of a concert, expressed sympathy to those who had suffered major losses. Later he received notes from listeners: "Thank you." "What you said meant so much." "I lost my home in the earthquake."[26]

It was not just the spoken words that conveyed comfort. The program that year included F. Melius Christiansen's arrangement of *Psalm 50*, Movements 2 and 3. Listeners drew strength from the text that had once ministered significantly to F. Melius himself. As noted earlier, following the death in 1921 of his ten-year-old son Carl in a car accident, he turned to Psalm 50: "Offer unto God the sacrifice of thanksgiving. . . . Call upon me in the day of thy trouble; I will deliver thee, and thou shalt glorify me. . . . Whoso offereth praise, glorifieth God."[27]

On its way west in 1994 the Choir first flew to Colorado for concerts in Boulder and Colorado Springs. Travel was by bus for the concerts in New Mexico, Texas, Arizona, and California. The Choir flew back from San Francisco for its home concert February 14, 1994. The program that year began with William Byrd's "Sing Joyfully Unto God," Palestrina's "Sicut Cervus," and Pachelbel's "Jauchzet dem Herrn." The second part included Berger's "Alleluia," Richard Marlow's "Veni, Creator Spiritus," and "Laudate," by Kirke Mechem. Music from other cultures included "African Noel," arranged by André Thomas, "Halle, Halle, Halle," arranged by Marty Haugen, and "Arirang," a Korean song arranged by Kenneth Jennings.[28]

Choir members' personal memories from the 1994 tour have the usual mix of oddities, hilarious and sad. A second alto passed out during the Boulder concert, recovered enough to retreat behind the risers, had her fingers stepped on by one of the basses, but finally made it off stage. It was snowing in New Mexico as the buses moved across that state. In California one of the sopranos received belated word of the death of her grandfather and, because of the constant rain, was trapped inside the hotel when she wanted to be alone in her grief.[29]

The most frequently told story from tour 1994 has to do with Jeff Wright '97, then a first-year student traveling with the Choir to sell records. Jeff became a member of the Choir his sophomore year and sang the next three years. In San Diego the Choir was staying at a resort consisting of small bungalows, a miniature golf course, and a number of small lagoons that added beauty to the setting.

Selling St. Olaf Records, 1994
Megan Movold, Jeff Wright, Mel and Meta George, Kurt Lothe, Melita Anderson

Returning from a walk down to the beach late one night, Jeff spotted his roommate, Aaron Fullen '96, across the way. With all the bungalows looking the same in the dark, Jeff thought Aaron might be having trouble finding the right one, so he called out, identified himself, and ran across to intercept him.

Picking up speed as he quietly rounded one bungalow, he moved into high gear and raced forward. Suddenly he was no longer running, but was thrashing around in water over his head. As he recovered his bearings and climbed out, he realized that what had seemed to be one of the greens of the golf course was, to be sure, one of the lagoons. By the time Jeff boarded the bus the next morning, everyone knew the story. The next year's tour book named Jeff Wright as "most likely to fall in the New York harbor."[30]

As the Choir looked forward to the 1995 tour, when it would celebrate the 75th anniversary of the significant eastern tour of 1920, it prepared for additional performances during the rest of 1994. On April 17, 1994, the Choir joined the St. Olaf Orchestra, directed by Steven Amundson, and the St. Olaf Band, directed by Miles "Mity" Johnson, in a special concert in Orchestra Hall, Minneapolis, in honor of Band Director Johnson's retirement. Johnson had compiled a distinguished record in thirty-seven years of conducting the Band, having joined the St. Olaf faculty in 1957. The event marked the first time the three

Steven Amundson
Director, St. Olaf Orchestra

organizations appeared together on the stage of Orchestra Hall. A high point of the concert came when all three groups joined in the performance of selections from Carl Orff's *Carmina Burana*.[31]

Added to Anton Armstrong's schedule in the fall of 1994 was the invitation to present the first of the two Mellby Memorial Lectures on November 3, 1994. In the Mellby Lecture series faculty members reflect on their own scholarly work within their chosen fields. Armstrong took the title of his address from a Quaker hymn: "How Can I Keep From

Miles Johnson
Director, St. Olaf Band, 1957-1994

Singing?" He told of the place of music in his early life and commented, "My life flows on in endless song, blessed by the training I received in my youth." At St. Olaf he found the same values he had grown up with: striving for excellence, serving others, being called to make the world a better place. The integration of faith and learning makes St. Olaf a distinctive community. The religious perspective enriches students; it nurtures the human soul. The St. Olaf Choir, he said, is a reflection of the mission of the College.[32]

Each fall the St. Olaf Choir participates with visiting choirs and with the other choral groups at the College in the annual Choral Festival. Once held

The 13th Annual **Carl A. Mellby Memorial Lectures**

Anton Armstrong,
Associate Professor of Music, Conductor of the St. Olaf Choir:

"How Can I Keep From Singing?"

Thursday, 3 November 1994, 8:00 p.m.
Urness Recital Hall
St. Olaf College
Northfield, Minnesota

Brochure for Mellby Lecture

in the spring as part of a weekend May Music Festival, in 1984 the Choral Festival was moved to the fall. At the 92nd annual Choral Festival, Sunday, November 6, 1994, forty-one church and high school choirs met at Skoglund Center Auditorium with the St. Olaf Choir, the Chapel Choir, Viking Chorus, Manitou Singers, St. Olaf Cantorei, and the St. Olaf Brass Quartet.

Directed by Anton Armstrong, the Festival Chorus sang "Sicut locutus est" from the *Magnificat* by Johann Sebastian Bach, "In the Bleak Midwinter" by Harold Darke, "Praise the Lord," an arrangement by Ralph M. Johnson, and "Festival Alleluia," a composition written by Kenneth Jennings for the dedication in 1976 of the Christiansen Hall of Music. Performing as a solo choir, the St. Olaf Choir sang "Lord Hosanna" from the Advent Motet by Gustav Schreck, "Alleluia," by Peter Mathews, and the vigorous "Elijah Rock," arranged by Moses Hogan. The last piece had a rousing effect, bringing everyone to their feet, cheering and clapping.

Following the Choral Festival the St. Olaf Choir was soon immersed in preparations for the 1994 Christmas Festival. The austere-sounding theme, "In the Bleak Midwinter," was taken from Harold Darke's anthem based on a poem by Christina Rossetti, who died in 1894. Orchestrated for the concert by Robert Scholz, its place in the program, surprisingly yet appropriately, was in the portion called "Hope Renewed." Another musical setting of the Rossetti poem, Stephen Paulus's "Snow Had Fallen; Christ Was Born," was sung by the St. Olaf Choir during the concert. Also offered by the Choir was "Mary's Little Boy Chile," arranged by Jester Hairston, a piece that became a popular optional selection during the Choir's 1995 tour.[33]

After the four performances of the St. Olaf Christmas Festival, December 1-4, 1994, the 500 or so student musicians readied themselves for semester examinations, took their finals, and rushed home for Christmas. Members of the St. Olaf Choir, as usual, returned to campus earlier than the others for intensive rehearsals prior to the annual tour. Inasmuch as hard work accounts for much of the success of the St. Olaf Choir in furthering the choral art, it is fitting to look in on its rehearsal routines.

The Choir rehearses every day, Monday through Friday, from 4:30 to 6:00 p.m. On two or three of those days there are sectional rehearsals, led by students, from 4:30 to 5:00. In accepting membership in the St. Olaf Choir, a student commits a minimum of seven and a half hours per week to rehearsals. For many Choir members, the dedication of those hours has a settling effect on their campus lives. Said Allison Wedell '96: "What I like about the schedule is that it's something I can depend on. Everyday no matter what's going on I know I'll be in that choir from 4:30 to 6:00 and I'll have all my choir buddies to eat dinner with afterwards."[34]

Time for the backrubs

The daily rehearsal takes place in Fosnes Rehearsal Hall on the second floor of Christiansen Hall of Music. Choir members are expected to be there by 4:25 in order that backrubs can begin precisely at 4:30. Everyone turns and massages the neck and shoulders of the person to the right; then the whole Choir turns the other way and administers the backrub to the person on the left. The procedure takes only two or three minutes, but in addition to relaxing the singers, it also helps them leave other cares aside and concentrate on music. Jeff Wright '97 explained the effect: "Okay, it's choir time and I'm going to sing and I'm going to forget everything else that's happening and making me tight in the outside world."[35]

Next are the vocal warmups. The Choir is still standing and Dr. Armstrong is at the piano, sounding the few notes and chords necessary to get the vocalizing started. The Choir will hum for a while, then sing nonsense syllables up and down the scale, changing from one vowel to another. Heavy use is made of the singing exercises in "Sing Legato," a book prepared by former director Kenneth Jennings.[36] The short songs have appropriate words to teach and practice legato, staccato, marcato, flexibility, and so on. Warmup continues with

Armstrong leads vocal warmups

repetition of such sung phrases as "I sigh to sing," "I love to sing," and "I wander through the lovely woods."

The warmup over, the Choir members sit down and take out their music. On a chalkboard in front of them are listed the pieces that Dr. Armstrong plans to rehearse that day. The singers begin. The director stops them, makes a comment, and has them begin again. There is much repeating and polishing. The director often asks one section to sing alone, ironing out some problem of tone quality, pitch, or enunciation.

Rehearsal continues

The inexperienced observer thinks the sound is perfect, and is surprised that the director is not satisfied. A visitor to rehearsal is also impressed by the discipline of the group. When the Choir is suddenly stopped by the director, no one talks. The director has everyone's attention and respect, yet the atmosphere is not heavy. Singers take a quick sip from their omnipresent plastic water bottles.

Dr. Armstrong knows how and when to loosen things up. Now and then he joins in the goofiness of a funny moment, but quickly it is back to the business at hand in a concentrated effort that lasts until 6:00 p.m.

Like his predecessors, Dr. Armstrong is lovingly and humorously quoted by his singers. Each year the tour book contains a fresh batch of the sayings of "Dr. A." Naturally the compilers seize on the funnier comments and are not averse to choosing some for their double meanings. A few selections, avoiding the egregiously risqué examples:

Tour Book, 1997

"Don't start singing like a bunch of cows in a China shop."
"You guys will be able to sing Penderecki like row, row,
    row your boat by January."
"Give me a P so I can hear it."
"I need that sweet honey Earth-Mama tone; you know what I
mean, altos."
"It's like a paratrooper tryin' to boogy."
"That way you're not hung up there naked."
"He gives you an unadulterated triadic entity."
"Ladies, this piece needs that earthy sensuousness."
"We'll do the Johnson; I'm not going to mess with the Schreck."
"It's a shame that we're almost to the end of the century and
    people still do not adequately appreciate the music of this
    century."[37]

The production of a tour book is one of the many functions carried out by the St. Olaf Choir through its own organization. Officers are elected each year to carry out certain responsibilities. The president acts as liaison between the director and Choir members and works with the manager on numerous tasks. The vice president is in charge of robes, which often require attention and a ready supply of pins. The secretary-treasurer collects the $10 dues from each member early in the year and dispenses money for the tour book and parties. The chaplain makes sure that before each concert the volunteer is ready to conduct the devotions, shortened in recent years to "devos." If not, the chaplain will tell a story or offer a prayer. In addition to these four elected officers there is a student manager, appointed by Bob Johnson for a two-year term, and a choir librarian, appointed by Dr. Armstrong.

The practice of the choral art takes the Choir on the road to the concert halls. The audience shares in the performance, but important things outside the public view take place before and after the concert. When the buses reach the concert venue, the director and student manager immediately look over the hall and make decisions regarding the shell, risers, lights, instruments, and dressing spaces. One of the two rotating crews brings in the needed equipment. All or some of the risers are usually called for but the shell is not always needed. Together the director and student manager work out how the Choir will enter and leave the stage.

When the concert hall has been set up, the Choir assembles for a warmup and short rehearsal. Then the group is taken to a local church for the evening meal. The sameness of church suppers is legendary, but it will also happen that the cooks have prepared a delicious meal that cannot be savored adequately because of too little time. At the conclusion of the meal, the Choir president thanks the hosts and leads the Choir in its harmonized song: "Thank you for the food so great. Thank you cooks, you really rate! A hearty meal, we all admire. Thank you from the St. Olaf Choir."

Prior to the concert, while Dr. Armstrong is getting into his formal concert attire with the assistance of a valet, Choir members are putting on their purple robes. They quickly learn to adapt to odd or inadequate spaces. Often the women get the more choice room while the men have to manage in hallways or crowded bathrooms. While everyone is dressing, Manager Bob Johnson or the Choir president will announce where the Choir

Concert flyer, 1995

should assemble for "devos." If there are Orchestra members along on the tour, they join the singers in the pre-concert quiet time.

Choir members who sign up to lead "devos" give considerable thought to what they want to say or read or even sing. The "devo" might be the learning of a perky camp song; someone might play the guitar and sing; one night the leader commented on what it means to sing "Beautiful Savior." Quite often a poignant experience is related, as when an alto told of the total destruction of their farm house by fire. All attempts by friends to console them seemed futile, until their pastor said, "You've lost your house, but you haven't lost your home."[38] When the speaker is finished, there are two or three minutes of complete silence. The desired effect of "devos" is to achieve quiet, unity, and focus.

While it is the same program each night, each concert is different. The performance is affected by the mental and physical alertness of the singers, the director's energy, the acoustics in the hall, and the response of the audience. As Choir members know, sometimes there is no applause when the performance is in a church. When the response was hesitant and tentative in Philadelphia in 1995, Dr. Armstrong turned to the audience and

Carnegie Hall, February 3, 1995   Photo by Chris Lee
Dr. Armstrong, Choir, Orchestra

said, "This is music of the Spirit, so if the Spirit moves you to respond, do so." From then on, applause filled the church.

On tour and at the home concert, Armstrong frequently had a few words for the audience right before the final number. For him, it was a moment of profound personal meaning when he stood in front of the St. Olaf Choir and faced the audience in Carnegie Hall in New York on February 3, 1995. It was an overwhelming experience for the Choir, he said, and for "this kid from West Hempstead." He paid tribute to the Lutheran Church of the Epiphany in Long Island where he had grown up and expressed gratitude to members of his family who were in the audience.

A heavy, wet snow was falling in New York at the time of the concert. Armstrong, now transplanted to the Midwest, was ready with a good Minnesota comment: "No, we didn't bring the snow. But we know how to deal with it!" The crowd laughed, and he went on to say that the music of faith sung by the Choir is based on what makes us human; it says who we are. "The glory, honor, praise, and adoration belong to the Creator," he said, and turned to conduct the Choir in "Beautiful Savior." There was a standing ovation after the final notes of "Now and forevermore be Thine."

Immediately after the conclusion of a concert, the Choir

Conductor and parents, Carnegie Hall
William, Anton, and Esther Armstrong

554

disappears from public view for a few minutes. The practice has developed over the years of having a private post-concert moment of thanksgiving in the form of two anthems of praise. The women sing one stanza of "Praise to the Lord, the Almighty, the King of Creation." The men then sing the well-known Doxology, "Praise God from whom all blessings flow." All join together in the "Amens" at the close of these numbers.

On the homeward stretch of the 1995 tour the Choir sang in Stetson Chapel on the campus of Kalamazoo College, Michigan. The review in the Kalamazoo Gazette provided another impression of the Choir's exercise of the choral art. The many languages were noted: Latin, German, French, English, Swahili, Hebrew, and an African dialect. The reviewer observed that the repertoire included works by contemporary composers and music from Eastern Europe, Africa, and South America. She had this comment on the musicianship of the ensemble:

> The St. Olaf Choir takes all the elements of a good choir—
> perfect vowel production, crisp diction, seamless phrasing,
> flawless intonation—and hones them with precision.[39]

Among numbers from that year's program that elicited special mention were the Bach motet, *Singet dem Herrn*, accompanied by a small orchestra, Gabriel Fauré's "Cantique de Jean Racine," with viola solo by Charles Gray of the St. Olaf music faculty, Peter Hamlin's "Vanity of Vanities," premiered on the tour, and Estonian composer Arvo Pärt's "Magnificat," characterized by the reviewer as the most demanding piece on the program. As to the performance of David Maddux's African-inspired arrangement of "O Sifuni Mungu," with Swahili and English text and animated percussion, it "created an almost irresistible urge to get up and start dancing down the aisles of the chapel."[40]

The spirituals, "Elijah Rock" and "My Lord, What a Mornin'" were also very well received. In his remarks at the close of the concert that evening, Dr. Armstrong said that the members of the Choir receive a greater gift in performing for their audience than they are able to give. The reviewer sensed this graciousness of spirit throughout the evening.

Back to FMC; Forward to New Zealand and Australia

The forward motion of the St. Olaf Choir is fueled in part by anniversaries. The Choir launched the celebration of the 75th anniversary of its founding by making a tour to the Orient in 1986. Anton Armstrong's first trip with the Choir to the east coast marked seventy-five years since the 1920 tour. The following year, 1996, the Choir had more than one occasion to observe the 125th anniversary of the birth of its founder and first director, F. Melius Christiansen, born April 1, 1871.

The program for the annual tour included Christiansen's arrangement of the hymn by C. E. F. Weyse and Nikolai F. S. Grundtvig, "O Day Full of Grace," and his beloved "Beautiful Savior." An article in the tour program reviewed in words and pictures the history of the Choir from its beginnings under F. Melius Christiansen through the work of the subsequent directors, Olaf C. Christiansen, Kenneth Jennings, and Anton Armstrong.

Mentioned briefly above was the inclusion of five numbers for Choir and Organ on the 1996 tour. Dr. John Ferguson, professor of music and College organist at St. Olaf College, played the organ part on such numbers as "Behold, O God Our Defender," by Herbert Howells, "Praise the Lord, O My Soul," by Ned Rorem, and "All You Works of the Lord, Bless the Lord," by Kenneth Jennings. The program also included Ferguson's arrangement of "Lord of the Dance."[41]

One of the pieces in the third part of the program hinted at what lay ahead for the St. Olaf Choir. It was "Ngana," the first of five *Songs of Passage* by the contemporary Australian composer Stephen Leek. As explained in the program, the song "captures the driving energies, rhythms, and vivid colors of the island seascape that is to be found in the northeastern tip of Australia."[42] In January of 1997 the St. Olaf Choir traveled to New Zealand and Australia for a four-week concert tour.

Before its attention shifted to the great continent Down Under, the Choir prepared for the most important event in the F. Melius Christiansen anniversary year. On the weekend of November 15-17, 1996, St. Olaf College was the site of the 22nd annual state convention of the Minnesota chapter of the American Choral Directors Association. The convention theme was "F. Melius Christiansen: The Man, The Legacy."

Setting a tone of partnership in the choral legacy was the Friday morning convocation when St. Olaf College conferred the honorary degree of Doctor of Fine Arts on the beloved veteran choir and band leader, Weston H. Noble, professor of music and director of choral activities at Luther College and director of the Luther College Nordic Choir. St. Olaf President Mark U. Edwards Jr. presided. The citation was read by Anton Armstrong. Assisting with the hood were Carolyn Jennings, chair

ACDA of Minnesota

presents:

**F. Melius Christiansen
The Man · The Legacy**

F. Melius Christiansen
The Man · The Legacy · 1871-1955

**The 22nd Annual State Convention
on the campus of St. Olaf College,
Northfield, Minnesota**

ACDA Convention Program

President Edwards and Carolyn
Jennings congratulate Dr. Noble

Anton Armstrong and Weston Noble

of the St. Olaf department of music, and Steven Amundson, director of the St. Olaf Orchestra and a graduate of Luther College. The St. Olaf Chapel Choir, directed by Robert Scholz, sang the prelude and the anthem.[43]

Friday and Saturday were filled with performances, interest sessions, panels, and the premiere showing of the video, "Now and Forevermore," on the life and legacy of F. Melius Christiansen. Participants in a panel on "The F. Melius Christiansen Choral Tradition and Legacy" were Kenneth Jennings, Leland Sateren, Harold Decker, Curtis Hansen, and Diana Leland, moderator. The centerpiece of the convention was an extraordinary

Hansen, Decker, Sateren, Jennings
November 15, 1996

557

anniversary concert presented by five college choirs from the Upper Midwest: the Augsburg Choir, the Concordia Choir, the Gustavus Adolphus Choir, the Luther College Nordic Choir, and the St. Olaf Choir. Enthusiastic crowds poured into Skoglund Center Auditorium for the performances on Saturday evening, November 16, and Sunday afternoon, November 17, 1996, filling the bleachers and the main floor to capacity.

Each choir performed separately, singing three or four numbers, one of which was a composition or arrangement by F. Melius Christiansen. Appearing in alphabetical order, the choirs sang the following FMC anthems: Augsburg, *From Grief to Glory*, Verse II; Concordia, "Wake, Awake"; Gustavus, "Praise to the Lord"; Luther, "Lost in the Night"; and St. Olaf, "O Day Full of Grace."[44] A surprise for the audience was the playing of a tape that sent the voice of F. Melius Christiansen himself out across the hall. The recording was of a talk given by F. Melius in 1945 in which he paid tribute to Gertrude Overby and P. G. Schmidt.

The rich, widespread impact of the influence of F. Melius Christiansen was most vividly displayed at the climax of the concert. All five choirs assembled on the risers, the colors of their robes gloriously mixed, to form the Festival Choir. Directed by Kenneth Jennings, Conductor Emeritus of the St. Olaf Choir, they sang *Psalm 50, Movements II and III*, by F. Melius Christiansen, and two well-known FMC arrangements: "O Bread of Life from Heaven" and "Beautiful Savior," which Dr. Jennings dedicated to the memory of F. Melius and Olaf Christiansen and in honor of the Christiansen family, many of whom were present for the concert.

Festival Choir and Concert Conductors
L. to R.: Weston Noble, Luther; Peter Hendrickson, Augsburg: Gregory
Aune, Gustavus Adolphus; René Clausen, Concordia; Anton Armstrong,
Kenneth Jennings, St. Olaf

The superb singing, evoking the spirit of the one whose music still stirs the heart, drew a powerful emotional response from the audience. It was stunning to see on the Skoglund platform a living symbol of the extent and fellowship of the choral community. The art of sacred music to which F. Melius Christiansen devoted his life and talents now engages students, directors, voice teachers, and other musicians in many different places, not just at one institution.

After the mid-November choral event, the St. Olaf Choir plunged into preparations for the St. Olaf Christmas Festival, scheduled for December 5-8, 1996. As noted, after Christmas the St. Olaf Choir always returns to campus early to begin rehearsals for the annual tour, but in January of 1997 an academic component was added to their routine. Choir members began two weeks of lectures and readings for an interdisciplinary course called "The Society and Culture of New Zealand & Australia," planned jointly by Dr. Armstrong and Dr. Walter Stromseth, professor emeritus of philosophy, principal lecturer and coordinator.

The first two weeks of January was an intensive period of rehearsals, studies, and pre-tour concerts. On January 10th the Choir sang at morning convocation in Skinner Chapel at Carleton College. Out-of-town concerts were given in Appleton, Wisconsin, and Faribault, Minnesota, January 11 and 12. Choir members took an exam on the campus unit of their course on Tuesday morning the 14th, sang a full concert in Boe Chapel Tuesday night, and left the campus for the Minneapolis-St. Paul airport and the flight to Los Angeles at 9:00 a.m. on Wednesday, January 15, 1997. From Los Angeles the group flew to Auckland, New Zealand, arriving there at 6:00 a.m., January 17, 1997.

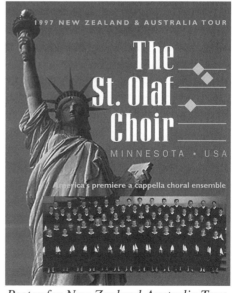

The idea of a tour to New Zealand and Australia went back to 1989 when Kenneth Jennings was invited to bring the St. Olaf Choir to Perth, Australia. Another foreign tour was not feasible at that time, but interest was renewed in 1993 when the Chorale of St. Peter's Lutheran College from Brisbane, Australia, came to St. Olaf. Manager Bob Johnson made contacts with the

Poster for New Zealand-Australia Tour

Lutheran Church of Australia and its New Zealand District in 1994 and visited the two countries in June of 1995 to solidify plans.

In the meantime, Dr. Armstrong was in Brisbane, Australia, in July of that year as conductor-in-residence at St. Peter's Lutheran College. He returned to the country in August of 1996 to present a session at the Fourth World Symposium on Choral Music held in Sydney. After the symposium, Armstrong and his St. Olaf colleague Sigrid Johnson, director of the Manitou Singers, *Sigrid Johnson* gave a series of workshops for choral directors in Adelaide, Melbourne, and Brisbane. These contacts helped build interest in the coming visit of the St. Olaf Choir.[45] To work with him as travel consultant for the trip, Bob Johnson secured the services of Betty Stromseth, who had previous experience in planning international tours for both the St. Olaf Choir and the St. Olaf Band.

The New Zealand and Australia tour moved from one high point to another, remarkably free of the emotional strains often met with on domestic tours, according to Bob Johnson. A healthy balance was achieved between the concert schedule and the academic aspect. The two weeks of study on campus prepared the students to examine the intersection of the Western settler culture with the two indigenous cultures, specifically, that of the Maoris in New Zealand, descendants of the first inhabitants, who now comprise about 15% of the population, and the Aborigines in Australia. The spectacular natural beauty of the two countries and the sunny warmth of the southern hemisphere added immeasurably to the experience.

Immediately on arrival in Auckland, the group was taken up to Mt. Eden, a lovely grass-covered crater from where they could look out across the harbor and enjoy the beautiful sunrise. That afternoon the Choir company was aboard a large sailing ship,

Auckland, New Zealand   Photo by Betty Stromseth

560

the "Søren Larsen," sometimes serving as part of the crew, on a delightful cruise out in Auckland harbor. Asked to sing by the regular crew, the Choir performed the Maori lullaby, "Hine e Hine," arranged by New Zealander David Hamilton. The crew responded with its own song. Besides telling their friends about the St. Olaf Choir, crew members of the "Søren Larsen" turned up in the audience for the Auckland concert in Holy Trinity Cathedral.[46]

A reviewer praised the Choir's "clarity of diction and pinpoint accuracy in intonation" in its repertoire ranging from Henry Purcell's "Hear My Prayer, O Lord," from the 17th century, to

On the "Søren Larsen"
Photo by Betty Stromseth

Australian composer Sarah Hopkins's contemporary "Past Life Melodies," described as "an eerie and memorable piece that was magnificently interpreted." The reviewer thought the Choir was more in its element with such new music as Hopkins, David Hamilton's "Lux Aeterna" and Knut Nystedt's "O Crux," and she enjoyed the tenor solo by Albert Jordan in the spiritual, "City Called Heaven."[47]

In the judgment of St. Olaf College Pastor Bruce Benson, who traveled with the Choir, the turning point in the concert was the presentation of Nystedt's "O Crux," a difficult but magnificent piece of music that moved the

Holy Trinity Cathedral, Auckland
Photo by Taunya Schueler

audience and won it over.[48] At the conclusion of the concert, the Choir received a standing ovation.

Pastor Benson was with the Choir earlier that day at the Auckland Museum and observed how wariness turned to welcome when the dark-skinned Maoris heard the mostly white American students singing a lullaby in the Maori language. A demonstration of Maori dancing and singing began with a traditional rite of challenge and welcome when Dr. Armstrong, the "chief" of the choir "tribe," well-coached for the ceremony, stood firm without flinching during a threatening dance by a local "warrior." By bending down to grasp the stick, a symbol of peace, he assured the Maoris that the visiting "tribe" was not hostile, and all was well.

Challenge and Welcome   Photo by Josh Carlyle
Maori ceremony, New Zealand

At the conclusion of the ceremony, the Maori singers requested a song from the Choir, which responded with the Maori lullaby. Benson described what followed:

> Thus began the continuing series of spur-of-the-moment concerts by the choir. Since then they have sung on buses, at a festive Maori-style dinner, in a Maori park and village, and in a museum again. In every case their singing has magically pulled Maori people away from cash registers, offices, souvenir counters, security posts, tractors, kitchens, and dining rooms. Their faces beam, their eyes shine as they listen, rapt with attention. Ah, sweet music! It makes so many friends.[49]

With Maori performers, Auckland
Rebecca Plante and Marit Johnson

It was astonishing to New Zealand residents that the Choir received standing ovations at its concerts in Auckland, Wellington, and Christchurch. Audiences were less accustomed to religious music and reviewers were not uncritical. Two New Zealand reviewers admired the Choir's "technical virtuosity" but decried the "tonal sameness" of the first half of the program. On the whole, however, they heard much to praise. Lindis Taylor, Wellington, stated that the 74-member Choir from America's Midwest

At Auckland home of Neil Lindstrom, New Zealand host and facilitator
Back: Bruce Benson, Bob Johnson, Kristen Lindstrom, Neil Lindstrom
Front: Walt and Betty Stromseth, Sigrid Johnson, Mrs. Jenny Lindstrom

"filled summer's musical drought with an eclectic concert of uncommon richness." Conductor Armstrong, she wrote, had maintained excellence in religious music and in contemporary and non-Western music.[50]

Timothy Jones, the Christchurch reviewer, speculated that the perfect choir in a perfect world would sound much like the St. Olaf Choir. He appreciated the Choir's ability to handle difficult contemporary music. Both critics seemed more responsive to the ethnic music in the second part of the program, regarding the first part as demonstrating "impeccable technique" and establishing credentials in intonation, balance, and subtle dynamics.[51]

When the Choir reached Australia, local musicians said that audiences there were not inclined toward enthusiastic responses, but standing ovations continued. In Melbourne, Choir members met their host families for a well-organized two-night home stay. The Choir gave a public concert before a packed house at Luther College on January 30th and sang at chapel the next morning. Interest ignited by these appearances carried over to the concert that evening in St. Paul's Cathedral. Melbourne reviewer Jeremy Vincent reported: "In true American fashion, the choir inspired the fastest standing ovation I have seen in Australia."

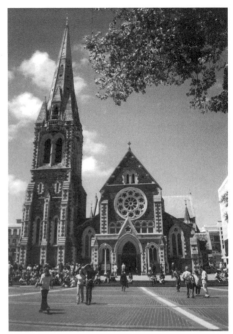

Christchurch Cathedral, New Zealand
Photo by Dara Kirchofner

St. Paul's Cathedral
Melbourne, Australia

564

The piece drawing the biggest applause was Sarah Hopkins's "Past Life Melodies," depicted as "a haunting journey told through deft vocalizing and beautifully sustained mood." But Vincent also had an appreciative ear for F. Melius Christiansen's setting of Psalm 50. "For this work alone," he wrote, "the concert was worth hearing."[52]

The next night, February 1st, the concert was in the Adelaide Town Hall. The reviewer, Raymond Chapman Smith, characterized the performance as "nearly two hours of singing that was close to flawless—unerring in ensemble, intonation, and diction." Smith welcomed the "courteous inclusion" of the two pieces from Down Under, Sarah Hopkins's composition and David Hamilton's "Lux Aeterna." Unlike the New Zealand critics, Smith regarded as musically most satisfying the sacred music in the first half, such as "Alleluia, I Heard A Voice," by Thomas Weelkes, "Hear My Prayer, O Lord," by Henry Purcell, "Nun Danket Alle Gott," by Johann Pachelbel, and Felix Mendelssohn's "For God Commanded Angels To Watch Over You."[53]

Especially memorable was the concert at the Queensland Performing Arts Center in Brisbane on February 10th. That morning the Choir had sung at a chapel service at St. Peter's Lutheran College, an academy. Among the 1200 listeners at the evening concert were the Choir's student hosts from St. Peter's, dressed in their school uniforms. Adding to the success of the Brisbane concert was the presence of the Australian composer, Sarah Hopkins, who also attended the afternoon rehearsal and spoke to the Choir. She gave her hearty approval to the Choir's performance of her extraordinary piece, "Past Life Melodies," which fascinated audiences throughout the tour.[54] In this wordless composition, inspired by Australian

Chapel at St. Peter's, February 10, 1997
Brisbane, Australia

Queensland Performing Arts Center
Brisbane, Australia

Aboriginal music, the voices produced a steady droning sound, melodic chants, and flute-like harmonic overtones.

Of the many cultural experiences the Choir had in the two countries, certain to be remembered was the gripping lecture by a young Maori man, tatooed in face and body, who described his search for a distinctive cultural identity in New Zealand society. His story made graphic the focus of the academic course: the shaping of equitable multicultural societies in our ethnically divided world.[55] Other highlights included the Maori performance at the Auckland Museum, the evening of Maori dining, singing, and dancing in Rotorua, the walk to the Franz Josef Glacier, and the visit to

At the Franz Josef Glacier, New Zealand   Photo by Jeff Wright

the International Antarctic Center just before the flight from Christchurch, New Zealand, to Australia.

After giving its concert in the Adelaide Town Hall in Australia, the Choir had some free days to spend with host families, many of whom took them to the beach. The homestays were regarded as significant cultural experiences, along with visits to the Tandanya National Aboriginal Cultural Centre, the South Australia Museum, the Barossa Valley, and the Warrawong Sanctuary famous for the sunset nature walk where, with the aid of flashlights, visitors can see indigenous nocturnal animals safe from predators.[56]

From Adelaide a full day of travel by air brought the Choir entourage to Cairns, northernmost point of the Australian itinerary where the group experienced rain for the first time. The main recreational attraction was the

International Antarctic Center   Photo courtesy Taunya Schueler
Leigh Ann Mock, Taunya, Stephanie Phelps

Playing the didjeridoo   Photo by Taunya Schueler
Calvin Chong, K. Tyler Wycoff, Dan Nass

Jeff Wright and kangaroo   Photo courtesy Jeff Wright
Warrawong Sanctuary, Adelaide

Great Barrier Reef. The group was transported by hydrofoil thirty miles out to sea where scuba diving, snorkeling, and boating began from a huge floating platform well equipped to take care of all tourist needs. Through a glass-bottomed boat one could view all kinds of underwater wonders, the fabulous variety of exotic fish, and of course the beautiful, living coral. Those who chose scuba diving descended to the ocean floor where among other creatures and shapes they observed a giant clam with its fascinating movements.

The next day B. J. incurred disfavor when his promised "10 or 15 minute walk" to Trinity Lutheran Church for a lecture turned out to be a strenuous hike that had everyone soaked with perspiration. In the afternoon the group went to Kuranda, a city in the Queensland rain forest where they also visited the Tjapukai Aboriginal Culture Park. It was interesting to have a demonstration of how the musical instrument, the didjeridoo, is played. A different and sobering matter, however, was the film depicting the realities of murder and bondage that belonged to the history of the white settlement of Australia. The concert in Cairns on February 7th was at the Civic Theatre before a disappointingly

Leaving for Cairns   Photo by Jeff Wright

Ready for scuba diving   Photo by Jeff Wright
Ingela Eilert and Anton Armstrong

Aboriginal dancers   Photo by Carl Schoenborn
Cairns, Australia

Rehearsing in Sydney Town Hall   Photo by Jeff Wright

small but enthusiastic audience. Happily, the concert in Brisbane three days later, attracted the largest crowd of the tour.[57]

The final concert before leaving Australia was in the Sydney Town Hall on Wednesday, February 12th. The crowd was small and there was no standing ovation, but the Choir gave its best for those who were there. On Thursday, Choir members and Professor Stromseth wrapped up the academic part of the program. Group presentations were given on such

Choir officers present gift to director
L. to R.: Lea-ann Dunbar, Heather Beggs, Leigh Ann Mock, Jeff Wright,
Dr. Armstrong, Bob Johnson

569

topics as race relations, health care, gender roles, environmental issues, and political practices in New Zealand and Australia. That evening everyone enjoyed a farewell dinner aboard a cruise ship on Sydney Harbour, sailing past the Opera House and under the famous Sydney Harbour Bridge. Departure from the Sydney Airport was on the

Sydney Harbour Bridge

afternoon of Friday, February 14, 1997. Many were still writing their final essays, handing them in while boarding the plane. The group was in the air for more than fifteen hours, crossing the date line, regaining the day lost on the trip out, and reaching Minneapolis late that night.[58]

For many, the long flight home provided time to reflect on the concertizing, the people they had met, the academic and cultural learnings, the beauties of nature, and the profound sense of oneness that had drawn them all together during the tour. Two moments in particular stood out in Choir memories. At the Franz Josef Glacier in New Zealand, the awesome grandeur of the scene called for an impromptu worship service. Pastor Benson spoke briefly on a Gospel text in which Jesus goes off by himself to

Singing "Beautiful Savior"
Franz Josef Glacier, New Zealand

Photo by Walt Stromseth

570

pray. Spontaneous prayers were offered and the Choir, facing the Glacier, joined hands and sang:

> Fair are the meadows, fairer the woodlands,
> Robed in flowers of blooming spring.
> Jesus is fairer, Jesus is purer,
> He makes our sorrowing spirits sing.[59]

The second unforgettable moment was related to a need to sorrow with and for others. Choir members had been thinking of the recent death from non-Hodgkins lymphoma of St. Olaf student Christian A. Green, and of Choir tenor Tom Larsen, Chris's longtime friend and classmate, who had flown back to Iowa to serve as pallbearer at the funeral and would rejoin the Choir at Cairns. On a day tour out from Adelaide, the group stopped for lunch and reassembled at a local church before boarding the buses. Pastor Benson and Choir member David Halvorson said a few words. Prayers were invited for the Green family, for Tom, and for others suffering pain and loss. Several responded. Some simply mentioned the needs of a dear one, a friend, a cousin, an aunt, a grandmother. Again, the communal bond sought expression in music: Felix Mendelssohn's "For God Commanded Angels To Watch Over You." After the singing came the tears and hugs, signs of the closeness and respect that moved the group as it came together in the little stone church in Australia.[60]

The home concert took place in Orchestra Hall, Minneapolis, on Sunday afternoon, February 16th. The hall was filled with an enthusiastic gathering

Orchestra Hall, Minneapolis, February 16, 1997
Al Jordan singing the solo on "City Called Heaven"

of friends, family, and other well-wishers. The tumultuous applause that greeted the Choir as it stepped out on the stage left no doubt as to the warmth of the welcome home. It was as if currents of electricity flowed between singers and audience. By the time the concert was over, there had been four standing ovations, one of them after the mesmerizing Sarah Hopkins piece, "Past Life Melodies."

Addressing the listeners before the final number, Dr. Armstrong said of the tour, "It was an incredible experience." He was liberal in extending thanks to the many members of the team, on the campus and on the tour, who made the trip possible. As part of the community effort Armstrong mentioned President Mark Edwards, Carolyn Jennings, chair of the music department, other colleagues in music, Manager Bob Johnson, Walter and Betty Stromseth, Sigrid Johnson, associate conductor for the 1997 tour, and Pastor Bruce Benson. His final tribute was to the members of the St. Olaf Choir. In the spirit of F. Melius Christiansen, they had worked hard. They gave as well as received during the tour. They had seen in a new light the oneness and glory of God's creation and their place in it as stewards. Meeting old human cultures and hearing new human stories had validated the purpose of their St. Olaf education as preparing men and women for lives of service.

Anton Armstrong
Punakaiki, New Zealand

Photo by Jessica Springer

572

The long experience of the St. Olaf Choir indicated that any tour, no matter how unusual or climactic, was always the springboard to new adventures ahead. The historic tour to New Zealand and Australia, with its combination of concerts and course work, was an experiment that could serve as a model for future tours abroad. In the meantime, domestic tours were no less important. A few days after the Orchestra Hall concert, Manager Bob Johnson was at his desk in the Christiansen Hall of Music, reviewing the tour Down Under. In the middle of the conversation, he reached into a folder and brought out a neatly printed paper with the heading, "The St. Olaf Choir 1998 West Coast Tour." Planning was already underway for next year's tour. New opportunities awaited the St. Olaf Choir to share the choral art with others. The focus is on the future.

Notes for Chapter 17 FOCUS ON THE FUTURE

1. News release, St. Olaf College News Service, January 2, 1990.

2. F. Melius Christiansen,"The Choir," unpublished typescript, 1929; cf. "Dr. Christiansen Speaks on Choir, Band in Chapel," *Manitou Messenger* (*MM*), April 23, 1929.

3. *Ibid.*

4. Frances Boardman, "Ideals of St. Olaf Lutheran Choir Explained," *St. Paul Pioneer Press*, July 5, 1925, 6.

5. *MM* 104 (October 5, 1990), 10.

6. Boardman, "Ideals," 5.

7. J. Alfred Thigpen, "Armstrong proves you can go home," *The Grand Rapids Press*, February 1, 1993.

8. "The St. Olaf Choir," 1995 Tour Program.

9. "The St. Olaf Choir," 1995 and 1996 Tour Programs.

10. "The St. Olaf Choir," 1994, 1995, and 1996 Tour Programs.

11. "The St. Olaf Choir," 1991-1996 Tour Programs.

12. "The St. Olaf Choir," 1991-1993, 1995-1996 Tour Programs.

13. *Saint Olaf*, November/December 1992, 4; *Saint Olaf*, March/April 1993, 4.

14. David Fuller, "St. Olaf Choir 1993 Tour of Denmark and Norway," unpublished typescript: entry for May 29, 1993.

15. Fuller, May 30, 1993.

16. Ann Nordby, "Grieg expert Brad Ellingboe '80 teams with choir in Norway, Denmark to bridge international gap," *Saint Olaf*, July/August 1993, 26.

17. Fuller, June 3, 1993.

18. Fuller, June 5, 1993.

19. Fuller, June 7, 1993.

20. Interview: Joseph M. Shaw with Nikki Johnson '95, March 7, 1995.

21. Fuller, June 12, 1993.

22. J. Alfred Thigpen, "Armstrong proves you can go home."

23. F. Melius Christiansen, "To Choir Directors," *Lutheran Herald* XXIII (January 3, 1939), 31; letter: F. Melius Christiansen to Lars W. Boe, February 10, 1927.

24. *MM*, February 15, 1991.

25. *Saint Olaf*, March/April 1994, 6.

26. Interview: JMS with Beth Baumgartner '96, May 9, 1995.

27. Interview: JMS with Rebecca Lowe '96, March 29, 1995; Leola Nelson Bergmann, *Music Master of the Middle West*: The Story of F. Melius Christiansen and the St. Olaf Choir (Minneapolis: The University of Minnesota Press, 1944), 130.

28. "The St. Olaf Choir," 1994 Tour Program.

29. Interviews with Beth Baumgartner and Rebecca Lowe.

30. Interview: JMS with Jeff Wright '97, March 8, 1995; Tour Book: "East Coast Tour '95"; Beth Baumgartner interview.

31. *Saint Olaf*, March/April 1994, 9.

32. *MM* 108 (November 11, 1994), 1.

33. "In the Bleak Midwinter," Festival Program, Christmas at St. Olaf College, 1994.

34. Interview: JMS with Allison Wedell '96, March 16, 1995.

35. Jeff Wright interview, March 8, 1995.

36. Kenneth Jennings, *Sing Legato*: A Collection of Original Studies in Vocal Production and Musicianship (San Diego, California: Neil A. Kjos Music Company), 1982.

37. Tour books, 1993, 1995

38. Beth Baumgartner, pre-concert devotions, Willmar, Minnesota, January 22, 1995.

39. Julie Scrivener, "St. Olaf Choir still stellar at 75 years," *Kalamazoo Gazette*, February 10, 1995.

40. *Ibid.*

41. "The St. Olaf Choir," 1996 Tour Program.

42. *Ibid.*

43. "A Program Honoring Weston H. Noble," St. Olaf College, November 15, 1996.

44. "The 125th Anniversary Celebration Concert," St. Olaf College, November 16, 17, 1996.

45. Memo: Bob Johnson to JMS, November 10, 1996.

46. Interview: JMS with Bob Johnson, February 20, 1997.

47. Tara Werner, "Wholesome and heavenly choir," *New Zealand Herald,* Auckland, New Zealand, January 20, 1997.

48. Interview: JMS with Bruce Benson, February 27, 1997.

49. Fax: Bruce Benson to Dan Jorgensen, "News from Benson," New Zealand, January 28, 1997.

50. Lindis Taylor, "St. Olaf's an oasis in musical drought," *The Evening Post*, Wellington, New Zealand, February 5, 1997.

51. Taylor, "St. Olaf's an oasis"; Timothy Jones, "Minnesota's St. Olaf Choir," *The Press*, Christchurch, New Zealand, January 29, 1997.

52. Jeremy Vincent, "Vocal artists weave rich fabric," *The Australian*, February 3, 1997.

53. Raymond Chapman Smith, "St. Olaf shines on," *The Advertiser*, February 3, 1997.

54. Interview with Bob Johnson, February 20, 1997.

55. Interview: JMS with Walter and Betty Stromseth, March 14, 1997.

56. Bob Johnson interview.

57. *Ibid.*

58. Stromseth interview.

59. Interview: JMS with Bruce Benson, February 27, 1997.

60. Interview with Bruce Benson, February 27, 1997; interview: JMS with Jeff Wright, February 27, 1997.

CHAPTER 18

BEAUTIFUL SAVIOR

Wherever the St. Olaf Choir appears, it is expected to sing "Beautiful Savior," and usually does. On one occasion, however, Dr. F. Melius Christiansen displayed a curious reluctance to sing the beloved anthem. The Choir was in Rochester, Minnesota, where it had sung an extra concert in the chapel of the Sisters of St. Francis at St. Mary's Hospital. During the intermission, a group of nuns, nurses, and patients sent a request to the director through one of the doctors that the Choir sing "Beautiful Savior."

No, said Dr. Christiansen, they couldn't do that song. When urged to reconsider, he still declined. There was something about the setting that inhibited him from leading the Choir in "Beautiful Savior." At the moment, he and his host, Dr. Donald Balfour,

Jesus the Shepherd
Window in Boe Memorial Chapel

were standing in a doorway looking out at the hospital lawn, fresh and green in the May sunlight. "There!" said F. Melius. "We'll sing it out there."

Quickly the word was spread throughout the hospital. Windows were thrown open; patients were wheeled or carried out on balconies overlooking the lawn. Leola Nelson Bergmann, who tells the story in *Music Master of the Middle West*, concludes the account:

> When the chapel concert was finished, the choir and its audience moved outside for the encore. Christiansen's impulse had been right. Some of the listeners have heard the choir sing "Beautiful Savior" many times, but never, they say, with such unearthly beauty as that morning under the trees on the hospital lawn.[1]

From the days of F. Melius to the present, concert goers have looked forward to hearing the St. Olaf Choir sing "Beautiful Savior." This favorite song has been regarded as "practically synonymous with the St. Olaf Choir," its "trademark" and "signature." In 1945 a reviewer stated that it was "still one of the most completely effective arrangements to come from his pen," referring, of course, to F. Melius Christiansen.[2]

"Beautiful Savior" consistently wins a warm response from listeners. Sung as an encore in Springfield, Illinois, in 1930, it drew "a most enthusiastic burst of applause from the audience." At its singing in La Crosse,

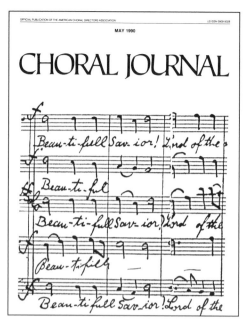

Portion of F. Melius ACDA Used by permission.
Christiansen's manuscript of
"Beautiful Savior"

Wisconsin, in 1945, with Dorothy Wommeldorf as soloist, "the audience burst into the most spontaneous applause of the evening." In St. Paul, "the audience refused to go home without hearing 'Beautiful Savior,' which seemed as lovely and touching as ever."[3]

More than any other anthem, "Beautiful Savior" has the effect of forging ties among the singers and between them and the listeners. As Anton Armstrong once commented, the piece is beautifully crafted and provides "a wonderful bonding for everyone."[4] After hearing the Choir in 1966, a Columbus, Ohio, reviewer wrote this about the experience: "It is difficult to listen to this nationally famous choir without coming away with the feeling that you have been more than a part of an audience."[5]

Choral music has the capacity to foster a sense of participation, similar to a satisfying theater experience. In the case of a choral concert, however, there is the added feeling on the part of listeners that they themselves could be doing the singing. The idea was expressed well by another Ohio writer, who observed that the chance to sing hymns, Christmas carols, and the like is available to all, and therefore: "Deep down we have the feeling that choral music is not foreign or impossible to us; that we might have participated, that we, too, might have helped to make that music."[6]

Those Who Help Make The Music

Figuratively speaking, the St. Olaf Choir travels in a big bus. That is, there are many besides the singers on the stage and the director who contribute to making the music, beginning with the audience. Also assisting in the process are local committees, alumni/ae and parent groups, churches and other sponsoring organizations, the manager and other colleagues in the music faculty, the other choral groups on campus and their directors, the administration, and the College community itself.

St. Olaf Choir
Boe Chapel, 1989

The audience is never to be taken for granted, as Choir and director know from repeated experience. That is why Choir members, when they meet concert goers backstage, in a hallway, in the lobby, or out by the waiting buses, invariably respond to the thanks and compliments with the simple but sincere, "Thank you for coming." The Choir draws energy and inspiration from the listeners. Its performance is animated measurably by the welcome sound of lively applause in the church or concert hall.

There are touching stories of the time and exertion patrons have expended to hear the Choir, such as the depression-era widow who laundered a pair of curtains for her neighbor to earn the price of a ticket to a St. Olaf Choir concert.[7] Audiences have often shown extraordinary patience awaiting the Choir's arrival when some travel problem caused a delay.

The presence of an audience means that local forces have done their work of publicizing the concert and selling tickets. Choir members on tour observe the hard work done by committees to provide food and housing. A dinner is served before the concert and often there is a reception afterwards. A familiar scene after many concerts is the friendly milling about as the manager matches Choir members with their host family for the night. The next day Choir members regale one another with accounts of the overnight stay and the hospitality enjoyed, and no doubt leave their hosts with a few choice stories to tell.

579

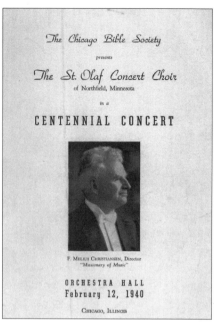

Concert at Capital University, 1936   *Concert in Chicago, 1940*

A variety of sponsoring organizations have contributed to the success of St. Olaf Choir concerts. A portion of the proceeds from the concerts is earmarked to benefit the non-profit sponsor or another charitable cause. Sponsors in earlier years included such groups as a Lutheran hospital association in Brooklyn, a community hospital auxiliary in San Diego, the Chicago Bible Society, the Milwaukee Federation of Lutheran Laymen, the Lutheran Inner Mission Society of Pittsburgh, the Kiwanis Club of Eastern Columbus, the Kern County Music Educators Association, Bakersfield, California, and the Greater Miami Council of Churches.

Changing circumstances also require finding new sponsors. St. Olaf alumni/ae and parent clubs, always loyal to the Choir, have become even more important as sponsorships have expanded throughout the country. Today there are more than 80 St. Olaf clubs active in such key places as Chicago, Milwaukee, Phoenix, Denver, San Francisco, and Portland. They have presented the Choir in major concert venues with proceeds of the events helping offset tour expenses, as well as providing scholarships or travel funds for St. Olaf students from those areas. In smaller as well as larger cities, clubs have supported local social service organizations or causes such as community foodshelf, AIDS awareness, and youth ministries with concert proceeds.[8]

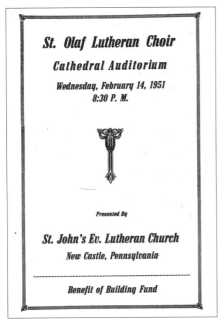

St. Olaf graduates, parents, and friends infuse extra enthusiasm into the concert event as listeners, committee members, overnight hosts, and participants at social functions. The dinners and receptions are of value in College outreach and are pleasant social occasions. Frequently the president of St. Olaf is on hand to speak on the state of the College, and other officials are often present to greet Oles and facilitate the renewing of friendships. On these occasions, a common affection for the College and a store of similar memories create an instant bond between Oles of different generations. For Choir members the experience takes on special meaning as they meet Oles who sang in the Choir two, five, ten, twenty, thirty, or more years ago.

Concert in Pennsylvania, 1951

Reception at Norwegian Embassy
Washington, D. C., 1956

As the alumni\ae network has widened, the audience base for St. Olaf Choir concerts has grown. College and university artist series where strong choral programs are in place have solicited concerts by the Choir. Having begun with a concert in Northfield's Congregational Church in 1912, the Choir has continued its ecumenical ways by singing in numerous Baptist, Methodist, Presbyterian, Roman Catholic and other non-Lutheran churches. First Presbyterian Church in St. Petersburg, Florida, represents churches that

St. Olaf Choir in St. Mary's Cathedral
San Francisco, 1977

have requested concerts by the St. Olaf Choir as part of their music ministry. Anton Armstrong's visibility at state, regional, and national choral conventions has brought increased requests for the Choir's appearances.[9]

Lutheran connections have continued, including countless churches and other institutions. In the greater New York area the Choir has collaborated with such agencies as the Wartburg Home and the Eger Foundation. Lutheran Social Services in New York, Washington, D.C., and Milwaukee, and other social service organizations have received its support. Bethel Lutheran Church in Madison, Wisconsin, and Zumbro Lutheran Church in Rochester, Minnesota, are among the long-time friends and sponsors of the Choir. Westwood Lutheran Church in St. Louis Park, Minnesota, sponsored concerts of the St. Olaf Choir in 1991 and 1994, with part of the proceeds going to the Lutheran Volunteer Corps. In April of 1997 the Choir led a joint worship service as a local benefit with the Gustavus Adolphus College Choir at Christ the King Lutheran Church in Bloomington, Minnesota. Singing benefit programs has been an important way by which the St. Olaf Choir serves the wider society.

Beginning with the excellent work of P. G. Schmidt, the St. Olaf Choir has been assisted in making beautiful music by a series of able managers. Each concert is preceded by numerous arrangements and decisions, and at the performance itself the manager has to be ready to meet any exigency. Planning two or three years ahead is necessary in order to secure concert sites, be it a local church or a prestigious concert hall. Where P. G. Schmidt preferred to travel by train, Fred Schmidt, who succeeded his father in 1949, saved time by flying to the cities where future concerts would be held. Foreign tours make additional demands on the Choir manager who

Benefit Concert, April 13, 1997

usually makes a personal visit to each of the concert sites to inspect concert venues and confer with local sponsors.

For a few years after Fred Schmidt's retirement in 1972, there was no manager of music organizations. Adding to their other duties, Frederick Gonnerman, director of information services, managed the Choir and the St. Olaf Orchestra, and Bob Phelps, director of the news bureau, managed the St. Olaf Band. Working with the St. Olaf Choir from 1972 to 1975, Gonnerman also devoted his considerable photography and writing skills to producing handsomely illustrated articles on Choir tours.[10] When the St. Olaf Choir went to Vienna and Rome in January of 1975, Professor Sigurd Fredrickson, voice teacher in the music faculty, was acting manager. Don Lee was part-time tour manager in 1976 and 1977.

In 1978, at the suggestion of Kenneth Jennings, the music department decided to appoint a full-time resident manager who would also serve as assistant to the chair of the department. Several inquiries brought forward the name of Robert C. Johnson, then on the administrative staff at the University Musical Society at the University of Michigan. Johnson accepted the position and began work as manager of music organizations at St. Olaf College on September 1, 1978.

A native of Alexandria, Minnesota, Johnson attended Concordia College, Moorhead, Minnesota, graduating in 1971. He sang in the Concordia Choir under Paul J. Christiansen all four years plus an additional year to do practice teaching and to court Sigrid Nelson, talented soprano from Bismarck, North Dakota. Bob and Sigrid were married June 12, 1971.

Johnson was student manager of the Choir for three years, gaining valuable experience in tour managing under the tutelage of Kurt Wycisk '42, manager of the Concordia Choir. After leaving Concordia, "B. J.," as he is known to his colleagues and associates, spent three years as junior/senior high choral director in Monticello, Minnesota. Sigrid had transferred to St. Cloud State University where she received the Bachelor of Music degree. The Johnsons moved to Ann Arbor, Michigan, in 1974 where Sigrid studied for the master's degree in voice performance at the University of Michigan and Bob served on the staff of the University Musical Society.

Johnson's position with the Society included that of manager of the University Choral Union, a town and gown organization of 400 voices. The Musical Society had the largest classical concert series of any college or university in the country and a long tradition of artist presentation. Johnson's diverse responsibilities included meeting many famous artists at the Detroit Metro Airport and bringing them to the University for their performances.[11]

In his St. Olaf position as manager of music organizations and assistant to the chair of the music department, B. J. was responsible for planning and coordinating the concerts and tours of three major musical ensembles, the

Band and Orchestra as well as the Choir. As all three organizations grew both in personnel and number of concert appearances, the manager's work increased in scope. In 1988, the College added the position of assistant manager of music organizations, appointing Jim Erickson that year. He was succeeded by Sally Sawyers '64, who served from 1992 to 1995, and Richard Erickson '66, appointed in 1995. As noted earlier, Johnson secured the services of Betty Stromseth '53 as travel consultant for several Band and Choir tours abroad.

Bob Johnson has oatmeal
Ole Store, April 1, 1996

When the St. Olaf Choir goes on tour, the manager literally rides one of the buses, with the director of the Choir on the other. In keeping with the symbol of the big bus, many of their music colleagues at the College are among the invisible passengers. Since every Choir member takes private voice lessons, a large segment of the music faculty contributes directly to the training of individual singers. One must also count the instrumental instructors whose students often travel and perform with the Choir.

In many cases, a student who is admitted to membership in the St. Olaf Choir will have previous choral experience in the Manitou Singers, directed by Sigrid Johnson; the Viking Chorus, directed by Robert Scholz; the

Manitou Singers, Christmas Festival, 1989

Viking Chorus, ca. 1987

Chapel Choir, 1987

St. Olaf Cantorei, 1988

Chapel Choir, also directed by Scholz; or the Cantorei, directed by John Ferguson. The value for the student of learning choral literature and technique through singing in one or another of these groups cannot be overestimated. Moreover, students profit from the collegiality they

586

experience in the musical culture on the St. Olaf campus represented by the several vocal and instrumental ensembles and their able directors. Members of the St. Olaf Choir pursue their music in the awareness that their efforts are acknowledged and appreciated not only by audiences on the road, but by a supportive community at the College.

The Choir and the College

F. Melius once said that the St. Olaf Choir is an expression of the spirit of the institution. He referred to the religious background of St. Olaf College and a student body that constantly imbibes "the spirit of the strong and majestic music of the Lutheran Church by the singing of these traditional melodies in chapel and in church."[12] From these comments some might conclude that only at St. Olaf College were the conditions right for Dr. Christiansen to produce such a choir. The Norwegian Lutheran students at the school had the religious, social, and cultural background that were congenial to the director and his

Boe Chapel window honors M. B. Landstad, Norwegian poet and hymnist

aims. In short, one might asssume, they were just the material Christiansen needed to build a good choir.

Against such a view, Christiansen reportedly rejected the idea that he needed Norwegian Lutherans to make a good choral organization. In her book, *Music Master of the Middle West,* Leola Nelson Bergmann contended that Christiansen could have fashioned an even better choir at a larger school with more students to choose from, whether the institution happened to be Lutheran or not. When Christy was offered a more lucrative position at the University of Minnesota, he elected to stay in Northfield. Bergmann's view was that he remained at St. Olaf, not because he thought that only there could he create a great choir, or that "he felt a holy call to deliver the musical souls of Norwegian Lutherans from the bondage of bad church music," but simply to give his children a healthy small town environment in which to enjoy a safe and happy childhood.[13]

The question of the importance of the St. Olaf ethos for the birth and development of the St. Olaf Choir remains of interest. It was discussed in November of 1996 when the Minnesota Convention of the American Choral Directors Association met at St. Olaf College to honor the memory of F. Melius Christiansen on the 125th anniversary of his birth. Panel members agreed that F. Melius would have succeeded at any institution, but felt that one could not ignore the features of the St. Olaf environment that encouraged the cause of choral music. Said Leland Sateren, former director of the Augsburg Choir, F. Melius was "the right man at the right place at the right time."[14]

Former St. Olaf Choir director Kenneth Jennings said that "undoubtedly" Christiansen would have achieved excellence in another place, but certain favorable conditions converged at St. Olaf: young, college-age people who loved to sing; a culturally and religiously homogeneous community; provision for generous rehearsal time; the matchless contribution of P. G. Schmidt, both in singing and in management; the solo and ensemble singing of a professional soprano, Gertrude Boe Overby; a supportive faculty and administration; and finally, the genius of the man who could seize all these elements and weld them into the St. Olaf Choir.[15]

Choral School brochure, 1951

588

Another panelist, music publisher Curtis Hansen '41, itemized several historical factors that supported what Christiansen achieved at St. Olaf. In the early part of the century the Norwegian-American Lutheran Church provided concert opportunities for choirs, octets, and quartets, and in Christiansen's arrangements of hymns and folk tunes they had music that could be sung in their native language. St. Olaf sent out various singing groups to publicize the College and to make known the Lutheran chorales. The Choral Union, in which F. Melius was an early leader, also paved the way for the development of the St. Olaf Choir. The Christiansen Choral Schools, with expert managerial and promotional help from Neil Kjos, Sr., influenced as many as 6,000 choral directors from 1935 to 1962. Finally, said Hansen, there has been at St. Olaf a sense of camaraderie and support for the Choir in the student body.[16]

The factors emphasized by Kenneth Jennings and Curtis Hansen are to be given due weight, even though it is agreed that F. Melius Christiansen could have achieved great success in some other place. In a related thought, Esther Tufte Rian '36, a former Choir member, stressed the debt that the Choir owed to the College and the Church. She wrote, "It goes without saying that the Lutheran Church and St. Olaf College, with its goals and its standards, were essential to the life of the Choir. Without them, even with 'Christy,' there could have been no Choir."[17] In effect, she agreed with Christy's theme that the Choir is an expression of the spirit of the institution.

Similarly, former Choir member Charlotte "Shoonie" Hartwig '57 stated that what the St. Olaf Choir has been and continues to be is an expression of the College. The story of the Choir, she suggested, is a metaphor of the College at work. It brings together, in a discipline, young people in their formative years who learn from different cultures, time periods, and languages, what it means to live in community and to praise the Creator. The medium of music provides a dynamic of mystery that cannot be related to an equation, and the use of words by the human voice can express spirituality in a way that instruments cannot.[18]

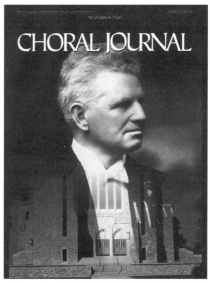

Commemorating   ACDA Used by permission.
F. Melius Christiansen

From time to time others have offered thoughts on how College and Choir serve a common purpose. In 1922 a Michigan reviewer wrote: "Indeed, St. Olaf College has done a significant thing. In a remarkable degree it has developed music as a means of the spiritual expression of its students."[19] A *Viking* editor in 1962 wrote of what the Choir has done for the College:

St. Olaf Choir members, 1983

> The St. Olaf Choir has given St. Olaf both tradition and an international reputation. It characterizes a fundamental quality of the spirit that is St. Olaf College. By representing unity, strong purpose, and artistic appreciation and accomplishment the choir embodies the spiritual and cultural ideal St. Olaf presents to its students.[20]

After hearing the St. Olaf Choir in its home concert in 1965, President Sidney Rand wrote to Director Olaf Christiansen to express, on behalf of the College, "our sincere appreciation for the way in which the Choir continues to impress its hearers and to sing the Christian message with force and effectiveness wherever you go." Rand also commented on the perennial importance of the Choir for the College: "I suppose there is no single piece of our work here at the College which has over the years been as well received as that which the Choir represents."[21]

Since it is the oldest and most prestigious choral group on campus, and has generated its own independent income through ticket and record sales, the St. Olaf Choir is seen as receiving favored treatment by some segments of the College. Some professors have been irritated when the tours have caused Choir members to miss classes. Other music organizations would like to receive as much publicity, budget, and touring opportunity as the St. Olaf Choir enjoys. Nevertheless, the entire music program at the College benefits from the fine reputation of the Choir. All the musical forces, including both faculty and students, have applauded the success of the St. Olaf Choir and have given it enthusiastic support. For some years now it has been evident that the other musical groups have won their own prestige, making striking progress in artistic competence through superb performances and highly successful, if limited, off-campus appearances.

With few exceptions, members of the St. Olaf Choir avoid putting on airs and feeling superior. With the help of director and manager, they learn to see themselves as servants of the community, not lords. A maxim for the Choir from its early years and stated in the 1920 constitution is that Choir members must possess "a spirit of willingness to sacrifice self-interests for the general welfare of the choir."[22] The model of that spirit was P. G. Schmidt. Said F. Melius Christiansen in a tribute to his modest friend and co-worker: "Happy is the man who is not an egoist." Schmidt was such a man, continued F. Melius: "He has done well with his talents. The talents that God gave him he has used, and they have multiplied through his life."[23]

To this day, the leaders and members of all the performing groups at St. Olaf College consciously affirm the idea of talents as gifts to be used for the benefit of the community. At home concerts, or at the annual Christmas Festival, for example, the thrill of offering the gift of great music to enthused and grateful listeners burns away any notion of using talents to impress others. Because they have been blessed with certain musical gifts, it is the privilege of performers to create the sounds through which the entire gathered family of God can express its corporate thanks and praise to the Creator and Redeemer.

St. Olaf Christmas Festival, 1984

The St. Olaf Christmas Festival

At the annual St. Olaf Christmas Festival, members of the St. Olaf Choir discover in a unique way the realities of collegiality, service, and community. In their rich purple robes they are easily identified. By their preparation and discipline, as well as their voices, they set a standard among the several performing groups. The Christmas event, often one of the Choir's first public appearances, impresses on the new members especially a vivid sense of the unity of the St. Olaf Choir. At the same time, it gives them the experience of a larger unity, blending their voices with those of the other talented choirs and with the sounds of the superb St. Olaf Orchestra in the great songs of the Advent and Christmas season.

The St. Olaf Christmas Festival began as a "Christmas Program" given by the St. Olaf Choral Union on December 17, 1912, in Hoyme Memorial Chapel. The program was directed by F. Melius Christiansen, assisted by a tenor soloist, a pastor who gave a speech, a violinist, a pianist, and a quartet that sang "Holy Night." The Choral Union sang three numbers in Norwegian at the beginning of the program and closed the evening with J. P. Sweelinck's "O Lord God to Thee be praise."[24] The program was for the College family, given on a Tuesday evening "shortly before school closed for the holidays." The *Messenger* account makes no mention of the St. Olaf Choir, which had taken its first tour the previous spring. No doubt its members on that occasion sang in the Choral Union.

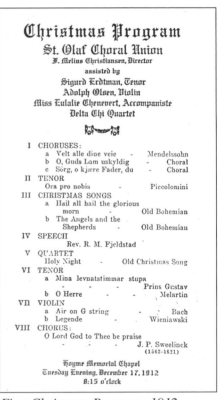

First Christmas Program, 1912

Participants listed in the 1914 program were The First Choir, that is, the St. Olaf Choir, directed by F. Melius Christiansen, The Second Choir, directed by J. Jørgen Thompson, tenor Carsten Th. Woll, violinist Adolph Olsen, and accompanists Eulalie Chenevert, organ, and Esther Erhart Woll, piano. The first time the program named the St. Olaf Choir as such in the

Hoyme Memorial Chapel
Site of first Christmas Programs

program was in 1915, with J. Jørgen Thompson as director since F. Melius Christiansen was on leave that school year. In 1920 the St. Olaf Choir was listed as one of two choirs, the other being the Choral Union. The audience joined in singing "Joy To The World" before an address by President Boe, and also sang "Holy Night, Peaceful Night" at the end of the program. The St. Olaf Choir sang four numbers and joined the Choral Union in Wagner's "Pilgrim's Chorus."[25]

Audience participation was not a feature of the program in the early years, but became a regular practice in the late twenties. Early programs reveal little use of the organ in Hoyme Memorial Chapel. Choral singing was unaccompanied, and there were often violin solos. The Christmas program was moved to the gymnasium in 1922, apparently to accommodate a growing audience since Hoyme Chapel, destroyed by fire in 1923, was still standing.

The first year in the gymnasium, 1922, marked the first participation by the St. Olaf Orchestra. Also performing were the St. Olaf Choir and a Ladies' Quartet that sang "Silent Night, Holy Night." Gertrude Boe was one of the soprano soloists. In 1924 the St. Olaf Choir was joined by a group called The Choral Society, successor of the Choral Union; the following year it appeared on the program as The St. Olaf Church Choir, directed by Oscar Overby.[26]

The move from Hoyme Chapel to the College gymnasium made possible more decorations, with Christmas trees, special lighting and art work, but always the enchanting music. Students eagerly helped in the preparations. In 1930, Ruth Paysen '32 (Halvorson) found herself with the job of preparing decorations for the gym. All she was promised on the depression budget was "two tall skinny fir trees for either side of the stage." One wing of Mohn Hall, the women's dormitory, was put to work cutting out 2 1/2 inch stars from old white cotton sheets and starching them.[27]

St. Olaf Gymnasium
Site of Christmas Festivals 1922-1966

In an article entitled "Christmas Festival at St. Olaf," Lois Rand captured some of the memories from the old gym:

> Thousands still recall occasions during the 44 years the old gym housed the festival when choir singers robed in white descended improvised stairs from the running track, singing, "From heaven above to earth I come." They remember Gertrude Boe Overby's

Christmas Program in the Gym, 1933

594

voice like a single golden thread spinning its way from some-where up under the roof, "This little child of lowly birth shall be the joy of all the earth," and, floating back from another secret corner, a contralto echo, ". . . of all the earth." And they speak of manger scenes with angels and shepherds, and sometimes faculty children coming to peer down at a real baby.[28]

Rand's article names several of the campus stalwarts who took part in the planning in that earlier time. F. Melius Christiansen and Oscar Overby shared ideas on texts and music, and Overby, as coordinator of the planning committee, made careful notes each year on both performance and logistics. P. G. Schmidt oversaw the many support functions and of course sang with the Choir. John Berntsen, head of grounds and buildings, found creative ways to implement Arnold Flaten's artistic concepts.[29]

A few days before the Christmas program in 1934, F. Melius Christiansen suddenly decided that he wanted a choral version of the Norwegian "Vuggesang om Julekvelden" ("Cradle Song on Christmas Eve") that he had arranged as a solo. As he so often did, he phoned Oscar Overby, played and sang his choir setting of the piece, and asked for a translation of

Christmas Festival planners at work, 1946
From left: F. Melius Christiansen, P. G. Schmidt, John Berntsen, Knute
Leidal, Oscar Overby, Arnold Flaten, Olaf Christiansen

Christmas Festival, 1963
Donald Berglund directing audience

the text into English *at once*. Overby was in bed with the flu and a temperature of 102, but he went to work as soon as he could. In short order the anthem, music, and English text was written, copied, and placed in the hands of the St. Olaf Choir for its next rehearsal. The Choir sang "Lullaby on Christmas Eve" from memory at the festival with Gertrude Boe Overby as the soloist.[30]

Christiansen, Overby, and their successors not only composed and arranged choral music for the Christmas Festival, but also had to prepare orchestrations of the hymns and carols sung by the audience. Without an organ in the gym, congregational singing was led by the Orchestra. G. Winston Cassler, St. Olaf professor of music and teacher of music theory and composition, assiduously produced orchestrations for opening numbers and hymn accompaniments when the Festival was in the gym and later when it was held in Skoglund. Professor Charles Forsberg, Cassler's successor, frequently wrote orchestral arrangements of hymns for Festivals in Skoglund Center Auditorium, and other music faculty have provided orchestrations as well as original compositions. One year six present and past St. Olaf faculty members were represented on the program by compositions or arrangements.[31]

A familiar feature from 1922 until the early fifties was the closing of the program by a ladies' quartet, concealed behind the risers, singing F. Melius's fine arrangement of "Holy night! peaceful night!" The audience was invited to repeat each stanza after the quartet. From 1933 and on, the text of this carol became the more familiar words, "Silent night! Holy night!"

The first time "Beautiful Savior" appeared on the program was in 1924, but it was not the closing number. It was sung by the St. Olaf Choir just before the quartet sang two stanzas of "Holy night." The same was true the next two years. In the 1929 program the St. Olaf Choir sang "Beautiful Savior" as the last of its three numbers, presented in the middle of the program. The other two were "Clap Your Hands" by F. Melius Christiansen and "Mary's Cradle Song" by Georg Schumann.[32]

Christmas Program

GYMNASIUM, ST. OLAF COLLEGE

Sunday, December 14th, 1924

8:15 P. M.

1. The Magic Flute . . . . *Mozart*
   ST. OLAF ORCHESTRA

2. a) Sing, O Heavens . . . . . . *Tours*
   b) My God, How Wonderful Thou Art . *Scotch Psalter*
   ST. OLAF CHORAL SOCIETY

3. a) The Three Kings . . . . . . *Romeu*
   b) In Dulci Jubilo . *Melody of the 14th Century*
   ST. OLAF CHOIR

4. Christmas Gospel
   REV. NILS KLEVEN

5. Song by the Audience

   Joy to the world! the Lord is come;
   Let earth receive her King;
   Let every heart prepare Him room,
   :,:And heav'n and nature sing:,:

   Joy to the world! The Savior reigns;
   Let men their songs employ,
   While fields and floods, rocks, hills and plains,
   :,:Repeat the sounding joy:,:

   He rules the world with truth and grace,
   And makes the nations prove
   The glories of His Righteousness,
   :,:And wonders of His love:,:

6. a) Vision of Christ . . . . . . *Folk Song*
   b) Christmas Night . . . . . *Overby*
   THE CHORAL SOCIETY

7. a) Welcome Again . . . . *Christiansen*
   b) Beautiful Savior . . . . *Pilgrim Song*
   CHOIR

8. LADIES' QUARTET AND AUDIENCE

   Holy night! peaceful night!
   Through the darkness beams a light,
   Yonder, where they sweet vigils keep
   O'er the Babe, who in silent sleep,
   :,:Rests in heavenly peace:,:

   Silent night! holiest night!
   Darkness flies, and all is light!
   Shepherds hear the angels sing:
   "Halleluja! hail the King!
   :,:Jesus the Savior is here!":,:

Christmas Program, 1924

Although "Beautiful Savior" did not appear on the printed programs from 1930 to 1940, all or a part of it was included, sometimes sung from the back of the gym after the recessional. On a copy of the program for 1930 is a penciled note in F. Melius Christiansen's hand giving instructions for singing it after the lights were dimmed. In 1941, the year Olaf C. Christiansen joined the faculty, after "Silent Night! Holy Night!" sung by ladies' quartet and audience, the last stanza of "Beautiful Savior" was used as the recessional, the words printed in the program for the audience to join in the singing.[33] The same procedure was used from 1943 through the rest of the forties. After 1950, "Beautiful Savior" came at the end of the program but not always as the recessional. Contrary to the assumption that it became an absolute fixture, there were a few festivals during the sixties and seventies when "Beautiful Savior" was not included. In 1976, for example, the program ended with "Nunc Dimittis" by A. Gretchaninoff.[34]

The familiar pattern of the Christmas program that was set in the mid-twenties has continued. It included the St. Olaf Choir and other choral groups, the Orchestra, an address or the reading of the Christmas Gospel by the College president or another clergyman, and one or more hymns for the audience to sing.[35] Since the move to Skoglund, the Orchestra's role has been enlarged, the College pastor usually reads the Gospel, and on a few occasions dancers have taken part in the program.

Through the twenties and into the thirties the event was still the "Christmas Program," although it was called "Annual Christmas Song Service" in 1929 and "Christmas Concert" in 1930 and 1931. From 1936 through 1940, the term used was "Commemoration of Christmas." In 1941 the observance was first called "Christmas Festival at St. Olaf." For the past few decades, "Christmas Festival at St. Olaf College" or "Annual Christmas Festival" have been the usual designations.

The year 1936 marked the giving of two performances on successive evenings. In 1941, three performances were offered. During a rehearsal for this Christmas festival in the old gym on Sunday, December 7, 1941, the student musicians first heard the news of the attack on Pearl Harbor.[36] War conditions reduced the Christmas Festival to one night in 1942 and 1943. But in 1944, there were two performances, and three from 1945 to 1948. In 1949 the Festival was presented on four evenings, but on three again in 1950.

When Olaf Christiansen took charge of the Christmas Festival, he gave it more cohesiveness by organizing the music around a theme. There had been themes in 1938, "The Morning Star," and again in 1939, "Seek and Ye Shall Find," but Olaf and his colleagues sought to make the program a spiritual and artistic whole. Examples of themes in Olaf's time as director were "How Shall I Receive Thee?" in 1948, "Come Unto Him" in 1949, "Thy Kingdom Come" in 1950, "From darkness into light," used in 1954 and again in 1961, and "He Has Done Wonders," chosen for the 1968 Festival.[37]

Program cover, 1936

598

Christmas Festival tableau, 1951
Theme: "Spreading the light of the World to All Nations"
Students in native costumes approach the manger

The first year the Festival was televised, 1975, when Kenneth Jennings was overall director, the theme grew out of an apparent misprint. Jennings came across a published copy of "Praise to the Lord" in which the phrase, "Wonder anew," appeared instead of the expected "Ponder anew." After considering the less familiar "Wonder Anew," he and the other planners adopted it as a very appropriate theme. The 1985 theme was "Joy of Heaven, To Earth Come Down." In 1990, the first year Anton Armstrong coordinated the preparations, the theme chosen was "Arise, and set the captive free."[38]

"Wonder Anew," 1975 theme
Cover of record album

Christmas Festival, 1959
First use of Maakestad art work

The director of the St. Olaf Choir serves as the overall artistic director of the annual Christmas Festival. F. Melius Christiansen, Olaf Christiansen, Kenneth Jennings, and Anton Armstrong have worked with the directors of the other choral groups and the Orchestra in planning the Festival. Assistance and advice is sought from colleagues in other departments such as art, dance, drama, speech, and religion. Following Arnold Flaten, John Maakestad of the art department designed sets and backdrops, annually devoting his Thanksgiving break to festival preparation. Local and student artists have given their ideas and time to the decorating of Skoglund Center. Perry Kruse '69, assistant director of facilities, and his student crews put in hundreds of hours at the lighting control center. The skills of carpenters, electricians, and others from the physical plant have been put to use every year.

Artist John
Maakestad

Perry Kruse at work   *Dancers, 1975 Festival*
Christmas Festival, 1975

From 1922 to 1966, the Christmas Festival was held in the College gymnasium, a building converted in 1977 to the Speech and Theater Building. With about 2,300 packed in each of the four nights, the gym could accommodate nearly 10,000 persons. For some, the joy of the occasion was tempered by worry that the balcony might collapse or the building catch fire, though it was inspected for safety each year. When the Festival moved to the new Skoglund Athletic Center in December of 1967, the new worry was that the larger space would deprive the program of the warmth and intimacy experienced in the old gym.

Needless to say, the St. Olaf Christmas Festival only grew in popularity, becoming a multi-media production with no loss in the quality of the music. As artistic director, Kenneth Jennings insisted that the original purpose of the Festival was to present a Christmas concert for the campus community that it shared with others. With the bigger facility, he believed that three

Skoglund Athletic Center
Site of Christmas Festivals since 1967

Christmas Festival dress rehearsal
Skoglund Center, 1992

performances should suffice, but before long the Thursday evening dress rehearsal virtually became an unofficial fourth performance. On the basis of the three regular performances, about 12,000 people could attend. As four performances became the rule, estimates of the total number rose to over 15,000.

With the large number of visitors, the involvement of 500 student performers, and the enormous effort of many people, the Festival is indeed, and long has been, an all-college event, not just a project of the music department.[39] A wide range of persons on campus do publicity, send out tickets, clean and decorate, prepare and serve food, supervise parking, clear the walks and roads, manage the crowds, arrange seating and lighting, take tickets, usher, and carry out other supporting functions. Even so, it is primarily the high quality of the music that brings national attention to this observance.

The Festival receives much publicity across the country. The Sunday performance is regularly broadcast live over the College radio station, 89.3 WCAL. The station also produces a 90-minute version that is distributed by satellite for use within the season by public radio stations, and a 30-minute version on compact discs to some 500 radio stations the following year.[40] In 1996 the 90-minute concert was distributed internationally by the European Broadcasting Union. According to the *New York Times*, the St. Olaf

602

The Christmas Festival according to Cartoonist L. K. Hanson

Christmas Festival Concert is "one of the ten Christmas events in the United States not to be missed" and the *Los Angeles Times* places it among the world's 30 top events and festivals in December.[41]

"...see, we get to hear the choirs tonight, then when KTCA shows the concert on television we get to see them..."

From Northfield Times, *December 22, 1975*

When the Festival was televised for the first time in 1975, with the theme, "Wonder Anew," it was video-taped by KTCA-TV in the Twin Cities and shown on stations of the Midwest Television Education Network. On Christmas Day in 1978 a 45-minute version was shown on Norwegian National Television.[42] When a one-hour special of the 1975 program was telecast nationwide by Public Broadcasting Service in 1976 and 1978, the College received scores of letters of thanks from all parts of the country. A California viewer wrote: "Thank you for 'Wonder Anew.' It was superb technically and spiritually moving in its beauty." From Alaska: "Thank you all for the beautiful Christmas music on educational TV this evening. I enjoyed the voices, the faces, the music, the directing, and everything. Beautifully done!" From Florida: "I delighted in every moment of the hour, and I realize what tremendous organization and rehearsing was required to produce it. It's the highlight of my Christmas. Thank you all!"[43]

Festival Faces!

Choirs and Orchestra, 1983 Festival. Steve Amundson directing

In preparing to video-tape the 1983 festival, "What Child Is This?" the KTCA-TV crew designed the set with painted backdrop, a huge star, and large fabricated beams to suggest the feeling of a stable. An edited one-hour special was shown on Public Broadcasting Service stations throughout the country. That year as usual, despite a blizzard and ten-inch snowfall that closed down the entire campus the weekend before, more than 12,000 persons were on hand to celebrate the beginning of the Christmas season.[44]

It was probably a rebroadcast of the 1983 Festival that prompted a viewer in New York City to send the president of the College the following hand-written letter, dated December 19, 1986:

Festival Program Cover, 1983

Manitou Singers, 1983 Festival

> *Dear Mr. President,*
>
> *Last night after our staff Christmas reception I happened to tune in to the last half of a program by the St. Olaf's College choir & orchestra. It was **superb**.*
>
> *In these days when there is so much trivial trash on T.V. it was heartwarming & inspirational to listen to fine music so expertly produced for the television audience.*
>
> *All who were fortunate enough to hear the program are in your debt.*
>
> *Sincerely,*
>
> *Richard Nixon[45]*

When televised in 1989, the Festival was presented as "A St. Olaf Christmas: Go Tell It On The Mountain." In 1993, a one-hour special entitled "Christmas at St. Olaf: What Wondrous Love" was prepared by KTCA-TV and distributed to PBS stations for broadcast. In 1994 the program was seen in 40 states and the District of Columbia and was sent to

606

Festival dress rehearsal, 1989

Armed Forces Radio and Television. In 1995 it was distributed in Australia and other countries.[46] These rebroadcasts one or two years after the original video-taped performance enabled viewers in distant places to enjoy a version of the Christmas Festival almost every year.

A small but sensible change in the time of the Sunday performance took place in 1993. It was moved from 7:30 in the evening to 3:30 in the afternoon, giving the 500 or so student musicians some welcome additional hours to prepare for classes and final exams.[47] The change also allowed visitors from out of town to get home earlier on a wintry December night.

For the public, the first concern is to get a ticket. Most of the tickets, which are free, are spoken for and distributed to students, parents, alumni, staff, and faculty months before the Festival. Those willing to wait in line for a returned ticket the day of the

Fred Schmidt with Festival tickets

607

concert invariably seem to get one. The College offers a beautifully decorated campus with wreaths in abundance and colorful displays in the windows of residence halls. For some years students in Agnes Mellby Hall created a mood of peace and good will with the warm glow of more than 140 candles placed in the windows. In 1991 the residents of Kildahl Hall used strings of Christmas lights in the windows to send forth the all-season message in huge letters, UM YAH YAH.[48]

Stirring the fløte grøt

The custom of serving a bountiful holiday smorgasbord began in 1940. It featured such Norwegian food items as fruit soup, fløte grøt, lutefisk—the debatable dried cod delicacy—baked spare ribs, Norwegian meat

Getting the lutefisk ready

balls, lefse, jule kake, rosettes, fattigmann, and krum kake. For many years, the candlelight at these meals was furnished by candles made by melting down the ones used at previous Christmas Festivals.[49]

When the Minneapolis *Star Tribune* did an article on the twelve months of preparation for the Festival in 1994, it noted that the bleachers are checked for splinters since someone had complained "that he had picked up a souvenir in a vulnerable area." And of course the lutefisk drew a comment. Wrote staff writer Peg Meier, "Ten years ago, St. Olaf diners ate a ton of lutefisk. Now the order is half that. The lutefisk eaters are dying off. (No, *not* cause-and-effect.)" For the record, as early as 1962 lutefisk consumption had dropped to 1,850 pounds, and in 1973, St. Olaf food director Mike Simione reduced the lutefisk order to only 1,000 pounds.[50]

For the St. Olaf Choir and the other student participants, preparation for the Festival begins in the fall, with intensive rehearsing taking place right after

Kenneth Jennings and Donald Berglund

Christmas Festival directors
Scholz, Ferguson, Armstrong, Johnson, Amundson

Thanksgiving. The music directors have spent twelve months thinking about a theme and appropriate music to express it. When Kenneth Jennings directed the Festival, he conferred with Donald Berglund, David O'Dell, and Steven Amundson, successive directors of the St. Olaf Orchestra, Robert Scholz, director of the Chapel Choir, Campus Choir, and Viking Chorus, Alice Larsen and Sigrid Johnson, directors of the Manitou Singers, and John

Pastor Bruce Benson

Ferguson, College organist and director of the St. Olaf Cantorei, a group that evolved from the earlier Campus Choir. Since Anton Armstrong became conductor of the St. Olaf Choir and artistic director of the Christmas Festival, he has worked with Steven Amundson, Robert Scholz, Sigrid Johnson, and John Ferguson.

According to Ferguson, the first question in the planning is: "What should the theme be this year?" The themes are not arrived at easily. The directors and College pastor Bruce Benson exchanged some misgivings about the theme for 1994, "In the Bleak Midwinter," but decided to use it.[51] The

609

1995 theme, "With Grace Unbounded," fittingly included the massed chorus singing F. M. Christiansen's arrangement of "O Day Full of Grace." Each year Pastor Benson reads the Christmas Gospel and other Bible passages related to the theme.

The theme for the 1996 Festival, "And the desert shall blossom," based on Isaiah 35:1-2, was proposed by Judy Seleen Swanson '57, Northfield artist, who designed a set in purple and pink shades, suggestive of the desert with the sun reflecting upon it. Having worked with Pastor Benson and the musicians in discussing the theme, Swanson was impressed by the "fantastic body of musical

Back cover of 1996 Festival program

literature" the directors have in their minds. "And they work together so well," she added. "They have this wonderful working relationship."[52]

Anton Armstrong, who coordinates the planning, agreed. "My colleagues and I have a good time together, and in the end we make something more beautiful than we could make individually," he said. Armstrong has fostered the same principle among members of the St. Olaf Choir. They give up a bit of individuality, but gain much in the ensemble. Each singer is part of something larger. "We're part of an ongoing tapestry," Armstrong once said. The philosophy effectively describes the cooperation among the several music groups who sing and play at the Christmas Festival.

Making beautiful music

Processional, 1987

The student performers extend themselves physically and emotionally through the several rehearsals and four concerts. Many find themselves crying during the final performance. It is a wearing but fulfilling time. Said Mark Pearson '93, president of the St. Olaf Choir his senior year, "We enjoy making beautiful music. It's gratifying to know that people are benefitting from what we put into the festival."[53] In the words of Dr. Armstrong, "It's part of their service. It's a chance to share this college's talents with the larger community, which is why the students are so willing to sacrifice their time during a very busy time of the year." Dan Jorgensen, director of public relations for the College, described the Festival concert as "our gift to the community."[54]

Dr. John Ferguson, director of the St. Olaf Cantorei, reflected on the meaning of the festival as a "spiritual gift." It is more than just a concert to

Pre-concert backrubs

St. Olaf Choir Album, 1976

611

Telling the story

enjoy, he wrote. From the podium where he directs the audience in a hymn, Ferguson can see from the faces that people come not only to listen, but also to participate in the re-telling of the story that in the Christ Child God comes to earth to be with the human family. Music, he wrote, is a gift from God that can lead people out of their winters of despair to a rebirth of hope. Ferguson continued with this important thought:

> The spiritual dimension of each festival concert is evidenced in at least one other way for me: the dedication and diligence of the performers, the delight in being servants, not just to our recreative art as performing musicians, but also to the telling of a story of promise and hope.[55]

Ultimately it is the simple story of the Child that brings thousands of people to the St. Olaf College campus every December. Mindful of the contrast between the simple beginnings and the modern scale of the Festival, Frederick Gonnerman, former director of information services at the College and editor of

Christmas Album, 1979

612

Saint Olaf, the alumni/ae magazine, wrote that "despite the larger numbers, the sophistication of the music, and the national attention through the media, today's concerts still portray the simplicity, grandeur, peace, and joy of the birth of Jesus Christ."[56]

Many graduates of St. Olaf are among those who attend the Festival every year if possible. Alumna Linda Strandemo Schroeder '70 wrote of making her "annual trek" to Northfield: "Attending the St. Olaf Christmas Festival is like taking a long, deep, serene breath before the hustle of the holiday season begins."[57] Stating what thousands of others have felt, Schroeder described her experience as the concert ended:

> As the Festival service draws to a close with F. Melius's "Beautiful Savior," the spirit lingers—the warmth, the joy, and the belief that we have indeed been blessed with "the gift of love divine." I return home, and I take with me the true spirit of the holiday season.[58]

Christian conviction, not simply fond tradition, has led to the custom of closing the Christmas Festival concert with the beloved anthem. Those who have sat enthralled in Skoglund Center Auditorium for close to two hours know that the holy season has come when they hear the quiet then soaring words of "Beautiful Savior," and an awed silence settles over the hall.

Christmas Festival, 1975

Beautiful Savior

The custom of singing "Beautiful Savior" at the close of the Christmas Festival and as the final piece at concerts of the St. Olaf Choir required several years to become a tradition. As the practice of closing the Christmas program with "Silent Night" sung by a quartet diminished, the use of "Beautiful Savior" gradually became more prominent. Occasionally its use was related to the recessional. In the early years, the St. Olaf Choir alone sang "Beautiful Savior," but from Olaf Christiansen's time and on, others participated. Typically, the other choirs might remain on stage singing the hymn while the St. Olaf Choir recessed and, at the appropriate moment, sang alone on the Coda: "Now and forevermore be Thine!"[59]

In 1962, "Beautiful Savior" was the recessional hymn with everyone singing the words of the first stanza: "Beautiful Savior, King of Creation, Son of God and Son of Man! Truly I'd love Thee, Truly I'd serve Thee, Light of my soul, my joy, my crown." Another year, in 1975, Kenneth Jennings had the St. Olaf Choir sing the above text beginning with "Son of God" as an "Epilogue" from the back of Skoglund Center.[60]

The St. Olaf Choir and the other choral groups divided the singing of "Beautiful Savior" in different ways. Sometimes the St. Olaf Choir sang the last stanza as well as the Coda from out in the foyer. Sometimes Kenneth Jennings, from the back of Skoglund Center, directed all the choirs in "Beautiful Savior" as they surrounded the audience on all sides. Often the audience was invited to join in the singing of a familiar hymn such as "Joy to the World" used as a recessional, leaving "Beautiful Savior" as the final

Kenneth Jennings directing, 1983

piece. The recessional in 1996, for example, was "Crown Him With Many Crowns," everyone singing, with Anton Armstrong conducting. The Chapel Choir remained on the stage as the other choirs took positions at the rear and along the sides of the auditorium. After the closing narration, Armstrong directed all of the choirs in "Beautiful Savior," with the women singing the stanza frequently done by a soloist: "Fair are the meadows, Fairer the woodlands, Robed in flowers of blooming spring; Jesus is fairer, Jesus is purer, He makes our sorrowing spirit sing."[61]

The St. Olaf Choir's use of F. Melius Christiansen's arrangement of "Beautiful Savior" at the close of its concerts is a topic distinct from its place in Christmas Festivals. The current practice at concerts of the St. Olaf Choir is that the first stanza is hummed in eight parts with the melody in the first altos and baritones. A soprano or alto soloist sings the second stanza, supported by the humming of the men in four parts. In the third and final stanza, the melody is sung by all the women's voices while the men, the "male chorus," also sing the words plus the Coda in eight parts, which repeats the melody of the final phrase in the first tenors.

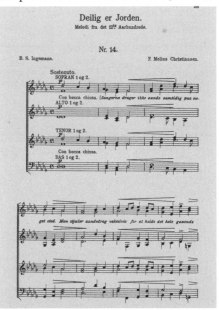

"Deilig er jorden," 1919 version

The first step in Christiansen's development of the well-known arrangement of "Beautiful Savior" was his publication of "Deilig er jorden" ("Lovely is the earth"), with words by B. S. Ingemann, in 1910. This anthem, sung to the same tune as "Beautiful Savior" and known as a Christmas song in Norway, appeared in the third of the Song-Services (*Sang-Gudstjeneste*) prepared by St. Olaf President J. N. Kildahl and F. Melius Christiansen, beginning in 1907. The motif of the Savior's birth is explicit in the third stanza. The angels sing to the shepherds: "Peace on earth! Humankind rejoice! For us today a Savior is born!"

There is no humming or solo in this early arrangement, but there are unmistakable similarities to later versions. "Deilig er jorden" begins with women's voices in four

1976 Festival
Kenneth Jennings conducting

parts on the first stanza, the melody with the first altos. The second stanza is sung by men only in four parts using the same harmonization. On the third stanza, the women have the melody while the men sing in four parts, as is also the case in Christiansen's 1919 arrangement. Of special interest is the fact that the anthem ends with a coda. The final words, "Os er idag en frelser fød" ("For us today a Savior born"), correspond to "Now and forevermore be Thine!" at the end of "Beautiful Savior."[62]

Christiansen reworked the piece between 1910 and 1919 when he published "Deilig er jorden" in Norway and "Beautiful Savior" in the

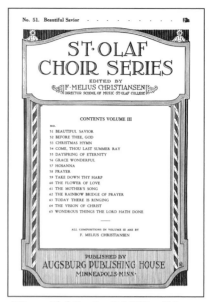

"Beautiful Savior," 1919 edition

St. Olaf Choir Series, Augsburg Publishing House, in this country.[63] The earliest reported use of a soloist was one evening during the first Norway tour, in 1913, when F. Melius Christiansen pointed to Mrs. William Benson and told her to sing solo on a stanza of "Deilig er jorden."[64] F. Melius added the solo and humming by both men and women in his 1919 arrangement.

Both F. Melius and Olaf introduced minor changes from time to time. F. Melius originally set the anthem in the key of D-flat. The 1919 arrangement in the St. Olaf Choir Series is also in D-flat. When Olaf C. Christiansen revised the piece for publication by Augsburg in 1955, he moved the key up one-half step to D major. The Norwegian association of "Deilig er jorden"

F. Melius Christiansen

Olaf C. Christiansen

616

with Christmas has never inhibited the St. Olaf Choir from singing it at any time of year, whether in Norway or on special occasions in this country, such as the 1941 concert in Washington, D. C. attended by the Crown Prince and Princess of Norway.

Revised edition, 1955

The English words for "Beautiful Savior" are not a translation of the Norwegian "Deilig er jorden." They are rather a translation of the German "Schönster Herr Jesu" by Joseph A. Seiss, a Moravian born in Maryland in 1823, who studied for the ministry with Lutheran clergymen in Pennsylvania and served as a Lutheran pastor in Philadelphia. Seiss's translation was published in Philadelphia in 1873 in the *Sunday School Book for the use of Evangelical Lutheran Congregations*.[65]

The melody is from Silesia in eastern Europe, published in Leipzig in 1842 in a collection of sacred and secular folksongs. An older view designated it as "Melody from the 12th Century." The 1955 re-issue of "Beautiful Savior" in the St. Olaf Choir Series correctly identified the melody as a Silesian folk tune, dispensing with the "entirely unfounded" designation of "Crusaders' Hymn" that appeared on many St. Olaf Choir programs. On the 1952-53 tour program it appeared as "Silesian Folksong." Later programs usually had the words, "Arr. F. M. Christiansen" after the title of the song.[66]

The St. Olaf Choir gave concerts for many years before "Beautiful Savior" became the usual closing number. On the first tour, in 1912, the Norwegian "Deilig er jorden," sung to the same tune, was the second number on the program. When the Choir went to the east coast in 1920, "Beautiful Savior" was sung just before the closing number, "Wake, Awake." It was not listed at all from 1922 to 1928, but was available as an encore. The first time it appeared on the printed program as the final number was in 1929. The next times were in 1931, 1934, and 1937.[67]

Choir programs began listing "Optional Numbers" in 1935, when "Beautiful Savior" was third of three options. From the thirties through most of the sixties, this anthem was an option more often than it was listed as the final number on the program. At the discretion of F. Melius or Olaf Christiansen, "Beautiful Savior" could be placed at the end of the program as an "Optional Number." Through Olaf's years "Beautiful Savior" was the last number on the program nine times; otherwise, it was the last of the optional numbers. Following the Christiansens, Jennings and Armstrong placed "Beautiful Savior" on the program as one of two or three "Optional Selections," and rather consistently used it as the final optional or encore piece.

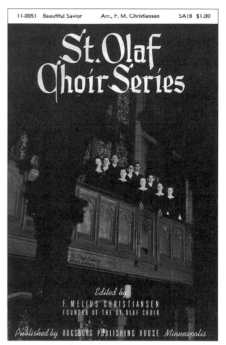

Cover of 1955 edition

The ongoing story of the St. Olaf Choir is bound up with the sounds of "Beautiful Savior" echoing through the years. When the Choir sang the corresponding Norwegian hymn in Norway in 1913, a reviewer said, "Particularly 'Deilig er jorden' was of overwhelming effect, with the bell-pure and glorious soprano solo."[68] Twenty-five years later, a Massachusetts reporter became intrigued by one of the encores and wrote:

> "Beautiful Savior" was unusually effective in its presentation. It opened with the humming of one stanza by the entire choir. Then followed a verse sung as a solo by Gertrude Boe Overby, soprano, to a continued accompaniment of humming from the rest of the choristers. Against that background Miss Overby's voice rose clear and sweet, and when it was over the young woman had to acknowledge again and again the prolonged applause.[69]

Under the direction of Olaf Christiansen, the St. Olaf Choir sang in Allentown, Pennsylvania, in January of 1947 when Winnifred Greene was a soloist. A writer for *The Morning Call* had this comment: "This final encore, 'Beautiful Savior,' is so beautifully performed by the choir that it sends an audience away from a St. Olaf Choir concert with the strains lingering in memory—the first chorus hummed by the choir, the second sung by Miss Greene against a background of humming which sounds like the string section of an orchesra, and the third sung by the choir in full

618

voice." Many years later a reviewer in Cleveland wrote: "The moving finale, 'Beautiful Savior,' projected qualities of fervor and faith that were unspeakably beautiful."[70]

Throughout the Jennings years, listeners continued to respond warmly to "Beautiful Savior." When the Choir went to the Southeast in 1988, Jim Kopp of *The Atlanta Constitution* described the impact of the familiar anthem in these words: "And with Christiansen's half-hummed, half-sung setting of the much loved 'Beautiful Savior,' they reduced the near-capacity audience to silence, then brought it to its feet."[71] When interviewed in 1990, Jennings said, "People wonder how we can sing *Beautiful Savior* so many times, but when we reach that climax, it's a great refreshment to me."[72]

For Anton Armstrong, who has incorporated a wider multicultural dimension in the Choir's programs, "Beautiful Savior" has stood the test of time. "It is still the foundation for what we do. This is why it becomes refreshment."[73] And it is the one song that binds the generations of St. Olaf Choir members together, as Tim Schmidt '96 said when he led the Choir in its pre-concert devotions in Carnegie Hall in 1995. Present members honor those who preceded them and invoke a blessing on those who will come after. As the first stanza of "Beautiful Savior" is being hummed, singers have a profound sense of being joined by the legendary figures of the past. "It is something that has spanned time and remains an integral thread in the tapestry we weave as the tradition of the St. Olaf Choir continues," said Schmidt.[74]

To listeners, the singing of "Beautiful Savior" brings musical pleasure and a simple Christian message. Art and theology come together

Anton Armstrong directing

in the song's title. The capacity of humans to create beautiful sounds is a gift from God. The Spirit moves human voices to declare the beauty of the One who lived, died, and rose again for the redemption of the world. For the St. Olaf Choir and all others who join the song, it is a duty and delight to offer glory, honor, praise, and adoration to the Lord of the nations, Son of God and Son of Man, the Beautiful Savior.

Jesus doing mighty works
Window in Boe Memorial Chapel

Notes for Chapter 18 BEAUTIFUL SAVIOR

1. Leola Nelson Bergmann, *Music Master of the Middle West*: The Story of F. Melius Christiansen and the St. Olaf Choir (Minneapolis: The University of Minnesota Press, 1944), 137.

2. Norman Houk, *Minneapolis Morning Tribune*, February 27, 1950; *La Crosse Tribune*, April 5, 1945.

3. *La Crosse Tribune*, April 5, 1945; Frances Boardman, *St. Paul Pioneer Press*, March 25, 1945.

4. Pauline Walle, "Armstrong enriches St. Olaf Choir history," *Rochester Post-Bulletin*, January 28, 1993.

5. *Citizen Journal of Columbus*, cited in *Manitou Messenger (MM)*, February 18, 1966.

6. D. H., "Choral Singing in Oberlin," Oberlin *Alumni Magazine*, January 1932.

7. "Your Troubles," by Mary Lane, unidentified newspaper, February 1930. News clipping in Elizabeth Day Wee scrapbook, St. Olaf Choir Southern Tour, January-February 1930.

8. Memo: Bob Johnson to Joseph M. Shaw, March 27, 1997.

9. *Ibid.*

10. An outstanding example was Gonnerman's narrative of the tour to the Orient in 1986. See *Saint Olaf (SO)* 34 (August 1986), 15-26.

11. Memo: Bob Johnson to JMS, December 10, 1996.

12. F. Melius Christiansen, "The Choir," unpublished typescript, 1929. STOARCHIV.

13. Bergmann, 123-24.

14. Leland Sateren, Panel, "The F. Melius Christiansen Choral Tradition and Legacy," ACDA of Minnesota Convention, St. Olaf College, November 15, 1996.

15. Kenneth Jennings, *idem.*

16. Curtis Hansen, *idem;* letter from Curtis Hansen to Joseph M. Shaw, December 10, 1996.

17. Letter from Esther Tufte Rian to Bob Johnson, February 18, 1994.

18. Interview: JMS with Charlotte "Shoonie" Hartwig, November 10, 1995.

19. *The Dearborn Independent*, August 19, 1922.

20. *Viking* 1962, 50.

21. Letter from Sidney A. Rand to Olaf C. Christiansen, February 24, 1965.

22. Eugene E. Simpson, *A History of St. Olaf Choir* (Minneapolis: Augsburg Publishing House, 1921), 29; Paul G. Schmidt, *My Years at St. Olaf*, A Centennial Decade Publication (Northfield, Minnesota: St. Olaf College, [1967]), 110.

23. Tape recording from May Music Festival, St. Olaf College, May 1945. Courtesy of 89.3 WCAL.

24. "Christmas Program," Hoyme Memorial Chapel, December 17, 1912. STOARCHIV; *MM* XXVI (January 1913), 327-28.

25. "St. Olaf College Christmas Program," Hoyme Memorial Chapel, December 13, 1914; December 19, 1915; December 12, 1920.

26. "Christmas Program," St. Olaf Gymnasium, December 17, 1922; December 14, 1924.

27. Ruth Paysen Halvorson, "Remembering Christmas at St. Olaf in 1930," Class of 1932 Newsletter, 1995, edited by Genevieve Severtson Odegaard.

28. Lois Rand, "Christmas Festival at St. Olaf," in Randolph E. Haugan (ed.), *Christmas: An American Annual of Christmas Literature and Art,* Volume 50 (Minneapolis: Augsburg Publishing House, 1980), 58.

29. *Ibid.,* 57-58.

30. Oscar R. Overby, *The Years in Retrospect*, Unpublished Typescript (Northfield, Minnesota, 1963), 74; Rand, "Christmas Festival," 57-58.

31. Conversation with Kenneth Jennings, April 8, 1997; John Ferguson, "Hymnody and St. Olaf: I. The Hymn in the St. Olaf Christmas Festival," *The Hymn: A Journal of Congregation Song* 38 (October 1987), 33.

32. "Christmas Program," Gymnasium, St. Olaf College, December 14, 1924; "Annual Christmas Song Service," St. Olaf College, At the Gymnasium, December 15, 1929.

33. F. Melius wrote the following on the cover of the 1930 program folder: "Lights on. Lights dimmed - Beautiful Savior. Go downstairs during the ff singing. All march as soon as one chord is struck on the piano." "Christmas Concert," St. Olaf College, Gymnasium, December 14, 1930; "Christmas Festival at St. Olaf," December 13, 14 and 15, 1941.

34, "Christmas Festival St. Olaf College," Skoglund Center Auditorium, December 3, 4, 5, 1976.

35. Joan Olson, "The Lasting Legacy of the St. Olaf Christmas Festival," *MM,* December 2, 1994.

36. Letters to Bob Johnson from Violet Wekseth Risch, January 20, 1994; Harold Heiberg, January 23, 1994; S. R. Saterstrom, n.d.

37. "Program Analysis," St. Olaf College Christmas Festivals. Chart with information on Christmas Festivals from 1912 to 1978. Columns record Year, Theme, Audience Participation, Spoken Content, Use of "Beautiful Savior," and Special Instruments.

38. Conversation with Kenneth Jennings, April 8, 1997; L. Rand, "Christmas Festival," 58; *SO* 38 (July/August 1990), 28.

39. Cf. Sara Wagner, "The Magic of the St. Olaf Christmas Festival," *Aerial* (December 1996), 5.

40. *Ibid.,* 4.

41. *Northfield News*, November 22, 1996; "89.3 to air The 84th Saint Olaf Christmas Festival Concert," *Aerial* (December 1995), 3.

42. *SO* 27 (Winter 1979), 4-5.

43. *SO* 25 (Winter 1977), 1; *SO* 27 (Winter 1979), 4-5.

44. *SO* 32 (November/December 1983), 1.

45. Copy of Nixon letter and memo from President Melvin D. George to Kenneth Jennings, Steve Amundson, Bob Scholz, Sig Johnson, John Ferguson, December 29, 1986.

46. Joseph M. Shaw, *Dear Old Hill*: The Story of Manitou Heights, the Campus of St. Olaf College (Northfield, Minnesota: St. Olaf College, 1992), 204-05, 267; Minneapolis *Star Tribune*, November 27, 1994; *Northfield News*, November 22, 1995.

47. Jennifer Thielbar, "Christmas Festival draws crowds and cameras," *MM* 107 (December 3, 1993), 1.

48. *MM*, December 7, 1956; Shaw, *Dear Old Hill*, 255.

49. *MM*, December 9, 1955; Pat Arnold, "Staging Festival Feast," *SO* 21 (Winter 1973), 6; *MM*, December 7, 1956.

50. Peg Meier, "The Twelve Months of Christmas," Minneapolis *Star Tribune*, November 27, 1994; Pat Paul, "Festival Time," *MM*, December 14, 1962; Pat Arnold, "Staging Festival Feast."

51. Meier, "The Twelve Months of Christmas."

52. *Northfield News*, November 22, 1996.

53. *MM* 107 (December 3, 1993), 1.

54. Michael Cooper, "Behind the scenes at the Christmas Festival: thousands of hours of hard work," *SO*, November/December 1992, 9; Peg Meier, "The Twelve Months of Christmas."

55. John Ferguson, "Choir director shares meaning of festival's 'spiritual gift,'" *MM*, December 2, 1994, 9.

56. *SO* 34 (November 1985), 15.

57. Linda Strandemo Schroeder, "'STO POSTMARK': The tradition continues," *SO*, March/April 1992, 28.

58. *Ibid.*

59. Interview: JMS with Kenneth Jennings, July 23, 1996.

60. "Christmas Festival at St. Olaf College," programs for 1962, 1975.

61. "St. Olaf College Christmas Festival," program for 1996.

62. *Sang-Gudstjeneste Nr. 3*, Tale ved J. N. Kildahl, Musik ved F. Melius Christiansen (Minneapolis: Augsburg Publishing House, 1910), 21-23.

63. As editor of the St. Olaf Choir Series, which began in 1919, F. Melius devoted the first pieces, in the first two volumes, to works by other composers. The next fifty, in Volume III, are his own arrangements and compositions. No. 51 is "Beautiful Savior."

64. Letter from Mrs. Oscar Lyders to JMS, February 14, 1997; cf. Simpson, 103.

65. Marilyn Kay Stulken, Hymn 518 "Beautiful Savior" ("Schönster Herr Jesu"), *Hymnal Companion to the Lutheran Book of Worship* (Philadelphia: Fortress Press, 1981), 532.

66. *Ibid.*, 531; "St. Olaf Lutheran Choir," Annual Tour 1951-1952, 1952-1953, 1964. Oddly enough, even though the "Crusaders' Hymn" designation was declared to be false in a program note for a concert of the Choral Union, conducted by F. Melius Christiansen, on June 8, 1923, St. Olaf Choir programs continued to use the description occasionally for more than forty years. See program, "The Fourth National Convention of the Choral Union of the Norwegian Lutheran Church of America," June 7 and 8, 1923, St. Paul, Minnesota, 10.

67. St. Olaf Choir concert programs for 1912, 1920, 1922-1937.

68. Simpson, 103.

69. Tyra Lundeberg Fuller, *Worcester Daily Telegram*, February 5, 1938.

70. *The Morning Call*, Allentown, PA, January 1947; Ethel Boros, unidentified Cleveland paper, February 3, 1964.

71. Jim Kopp, "Traditional St. Olaf Choir gives stirring performance at Emory," *The Atlanta Constitution*, February 11, 1988.

72. Lois Rand, "A Conversation with Kenneth Jennings," in "The St. Olaf Choir," Concert Program, 1990.

73. JMS conversation with Anton Armstrong, December 17, 1996.

74. E-mail from Tim Schmidt to JMS, November 10, 1996.

ACKNOWLEDGMENTS

It is a pleasure to present the names of persons who have helped in the preparation of this book and to extend my thanks to all of them. As a non-musician and one who did not sing in the St. Olaf Choir, I would not have taken on this task without the confidence that I would receive assistance from musicians, former St. Olaf Choir members, and many others.

Two early interviews were held with distinguished musicians Paul J. Christiansen, former director of the Concordia Choir, and Leland Sateren, former director of the Augsburg Choir. Paul J. was joined by his wife, Eleanor, former member of the St. Olaf Choir, in the interview held in the Stillwater home of their son Erik, a third generation Christiansen musician. They had vivid personal memories of F. Melius Christiansen and pertinent observations on his work and that of Olaf Christiansen. Leland Sateren, like Paul J. Christiansen, had long experience as a choral leader, and he too related memories from his association with F. Melius Christiansen. I thank them for their time and courtesy.

Other members of the Christiansen family were also generous in responding to my requests for information about both F. Melius and Olaf C. Christiansen. My contacts with Elsa Christiansen Wycisk, Sylvia Christiansen Buselmeier, Sigrid Christiansen Ostrem, and Julianne Christiansen were primarily by phone, but through Sylvia and Sigrid I also had access to a number of letters from F. Melius Christiansen to members of his family. I had an interview with Fred and Mary Christiansen, and from them received the loan of choice family pictures that appear in the book. I am grateful to the Christiansens for their assistance and encouragement.

In Northfield and on the St. Olaf College campus I was able to confer several times with Kenneth Jennings, director emeritus of the St. Olaf Choir, and Anton Armstrong, present director. With their help I reviewed a large segment of Choir history stretching back to Jennings' student experience as a member of the St. Olaf Choir and forward to the Choir's most recent appearances under Armstrong. Both gave me tape-recorded interviews, numerous informal comments, and careful responses to drafts of many chapters. Both helped me understand the particular genius of their predecessors, Jennings on the basis of personal contacts with F. Melius and Olaf Christiansen, Armstrong through his own Choir membership under Jennings and preparation of his doctoral thesis. Carolyn Jennings as chair of the department of music approved the project and supplied data and helpful suggestions relevant to certain chapters. She and Kenneth also provided a number of photos. My sincere thanks to Kenneth, Carolyn, and Anton.

Thanks are also extended to two of their colleagues who granted me interviews. Robert Scholz, director of the Chapel Choir and Viking Chorus, and a former member of the St. Olaf Choir, had special insights into the musicianship of Olaf Christiansen and Kenneth Jennings. Alice "Dolly" Larsen, former director of the Manitou Singers, told of voice production, tours, rehearsals and other Choir experiences with Olaf Christiansen and as his colleague in the department of music. Larsen directed the St. Olaf Choir during two separate periods when Kenneth Jennings was on leave. I also thank Dolly for making available two scrapbooks with valuable tour materials.

Special thanks go to Bob Johnson, "B. J.," manager of music organizations, who invited me to write this book. He and Mary Auge, his able secretary, acted promptly and effectively in providing whatever was needed at each stage of the writing process. Thanks to B. J. and the music department, I had the privilege of traveling with the St. Olaf Choir on its tour to the east coast in January and February of 1995.

To assist in the project, B. J. engaged the services of Betty Johnson Stromseth, who had worked with him on travel plans for Choir and Band tours abroad. Betty brought diverse abilities to this task. Her help was invaluable in archival research, locating and contributing photos, and reading drafts of chapters. Betty also joined me in conducting a few interviews. She and I were always able to count on the knowledge and willing spirit of Joan Olson, St. Olaf archivist, and a number of well-trained student workers who helped us find materials in the College archives. Forrest Brown, archivist for the Norwegian-American Historical Association, directed me to documents in that special collection.

B. J. also secured Carolyn Nitz to prepare the index and Jeff Wright to compile the two appendices. Thanks to Carolyn and Jeff for their careful work. Nancy Ashmore, director of publications at St. Olaf College, and Holly Welch, assistant publications director, designed the book cover. Thanks are expressed to them.

A number of former Choir members agreed to be interviewed about their experiences in the St. Olaf Choir, including the directors mentioned above. I also wish to thank Winnifred Greene Alberg, Frances Williams Anderson, the late James Coates, A. B. "Bud" Engen, Edwin and Louise

Horchler Gass, Stewart Govig, Charlotte "Shoonie" Donhowe Hartwig, Marilyn Swanson Haugen, William H. K. Narum, Lois Jacobson Nelson, Ronald and Betty Lou Oleson Nelson, Paul E. Peterson, Frederick and Lenore Swenson Schmidt, Genevieve Hendrickson Sovik, and June Anderson Swanson.

Fred and Lenore, who cheerfully responded to further inquiries, also made available to me "Bits from 'Christy,'" a unique collection of impromptu, verbatim remarks by F. Melius Christiansen compiled and sent to them by Lillian Bengston Eliasen. I take this opportunity to extend thanks to Mrs. Eliasen. Thanks are also due to Opal Bollenbach Wolf for an interview and the loan of her notes from the course, "Choir Conducting," which she took from F. Melius Christiansen in 1939-40.

While the book was in preparation, I interviewed members of the St. Olaf Choir, all of whom have graduated. My thanks to the following persons: Beth Baumgartner, Sarah Boe, Nikki Johnson, Kevin Kienbaum, Rebecca Lowe, Carrie Opheim, Angela Schum, Allison Wedell, and Jeff Wright. Tim Schmidt and Christine Meyer sent me notes on pre-concert devotional talks they had given. Jeff Wright shared additional Choir experiences through conversations and pictures. Other present or recent Choir members who supplied pictures were Josh Carlyle, Jason Etten, Dara Kirchofner, Carl Schoenborn, Taunya Schueler, Alicia Small, and Jessica Springer.

Permission to examine Choir scrapbooks, diaries, or journals was granted by the following, to whom I express appreciation: Winnifred Greene Alberg, Frances Williams Anderson, Jerry Evenrud, David Fuller, Edwin and Louise Horchler Gass, Marilyn Swanson Haugen, Ramona Halverson Jacobsen, Signe Ramseth Johnson, the family of Ida Hagen Kirn, Alice Larsen, Mary Anne Lyders Felker, daughter of O. Matthew Lyders, Boral R. Biorn and Marie Biorn Sathrum on behalf of the family of Gladys Edwardson Rice, Steve Sandberg, Norma Lee Simso, and Elizabeth Day Wee. In the St. Olaf Archives I perused scrapbooks compiled by A. Sophie Boe, Henry Halvorson, Edward Jacobson, Gerhard Mathre, Ella Hjertaas Roe, and Paul G. Schmidt, and the Gerhard Peterson collection of photos.

In the fall of 1993 Manager Bob Johnson sent letters to St. Olaf Choir alumni/ae asking for stories, anecdotes, diaries, recollections about rehearsals, concerts, tours, and other Choir activities. The letters received in response were turned over to me; others reached me through direct correspondence. On behalf of Bob as well as myself, I express thanks to the following for their letters: Mildred Hoff Anderson, Trudy Roe Anderson, Ethel Honaas Anthonisen, Boral R. Biorn, Beatrice Boe, Charles F. Bolton on behalf of Grace Riggle Bolton, Sanford Egge, Jean B. Ellison, June

Haugner Gerber, Howard J. Glenn, Curtis E. Hansen, Jane Onerheim Hilton, Olive Okdale Kildahl, Paul S. Lavik, Lydie Rice Marquart, Willis H. Miller, Clare Bruns Moore, Sigrid Horneland Quello, Rudolph A. Ramseth, Esther Tufte Rian, Margaret Bestul Russell, Jean Malmquist Schuler, Margaret Lunder Sloane, Conrad Thompson, Hazel Baker Tudor, and Ruth Mellby White. These former Choir members sang while F. Melius Christiansen was director.

Another group of respondents sang under both F. Melius and Olaf in the early forties. Thanks is hereby expressed to Phyllis Hardy Blodgett, Harold Heiberg, Neal S. Johnson, Violet Wekseth Risch, S. R. Saterstrom, Mary Reiter Sherman, and Keith Textor. Also in the Choir in this period were Paul G. and Harriet Finsand Peterson with whom I had personal correspondence including anecdotes, reflective comments, clippings, and pictures. Choir members who sang under Olaf Christiansen later in the forties and who submitted letters or other items were Lois Simen Brooke, John A. Elliott, Phyllis Ensrud, Donald G. Flom, Ronald A. and Betty Lou Oleson Nelson, Marie Weinhardt Pooler, Martha Row Roberts, and Ruth Sanden Thorson. I thank them for their help.

Thanks to the following letter writers who sang under Olaf Christiansen in the decade of the fifties: Louis W. Banitt, Nordis Evenson Christenson, Paul H. Christenson, Donald Colton, Marilyn L. Droebel, Rodney Eichenberger, Jerry L. Hanson, Ann Andersen Hoven, Ramona Halverson Jacobsen, Lars Kindem, David A. Lee, Jerry Narveson, Ellen Clark Olson, Tom Twaiten, and Ole Winter. Some of these persons provided materials in addition to a letter. Those who sang in the Choir in the sixties and sent letters were Carole Lea Arneson, Tom Erickson, Vera Ryen Gregg, Florence Stroebel Kahn, Michael E. Miller, Richard S. Munsen, David W. Olson, Warren K. Olson, Linda Grundahl Stauffacher, Diane Steen-Hinderlie, and Naomi Quam Wagenknecht. Their letters were received with gratitude.

During the seventies and eighties Kenneth Jennings was director of the St. Olaf Choir. Those who sang in that period and submitted letters are the following, to whom I express my appreciation: Ellen Doerrfeld Coman, David P. Engen, Martha Bolin Frank, Robb Hiller, Kevin Horsted, Joan Pechauer, Jane Stamstad, and Robert Voelker. By phone and through personal correspondence I also heard from the following persons who sang under Kenneth Jennings: Bradley Ellingboe, Daniel Egan, Ralph Johnson, David Narum, Jean Strohm Parish, and Mark Schowalter. Sincere thanks also to them.

Students who have sung under Anton Armstrong have contributed to this project largely through interviews and other on-campus communications. Ann Oldfield provided a copy of a speech about Anton Armstrong she had given in an advanced speaking course. I am grateful to her and all the other recent and current students who have passed along observations about life in the St. Olaf Choir with Armstrong as director. After the St. Olaf Choir returned from New Zealand and Australia in the early part of 1997, College pastor Bruce Benson and Walter and Betty Stromseth, who traveled with the Choir, provided valuable observations about the tour. My thanks to them.

Here I also wish to acknowledge with gratitude communications from Armstrong's colleagues in other places. Bradley Ellingboe, Ralph Johnson, Darlene Meyering, André Thomas, and John Witvliet offered information on earlier phases of Armstrong's career and insights regarding his current work. Anton's mother, Esther Armstrong, kindly sent pictures of her son from his school years.

Thanks are expressed to a number of other persons who have shared knowledge, materials, and stories with me as I have gathered data about the St. Olaf Choir. Harold Decker, now of Wichita, Kansas, who headed a new doctoral program at the University of Illinois when Kenneth Jennings studied there, had a professional, overarching grasp of the entire St. Olaf choral tradition. Lyndon Crist of Iowa City, former choral director, has singled out the particular choral contribution of Olaf C. Christiansen for sustained research and publication. I am indebted to Lyndon for important information and insights conveyed in conversations and correspondence. Through phone calls and written materials, Paul Benson of Dallas, Texas, shared the results of his research into a cappella college choirs.

Frederick Gonnerman provided pictures from St. Olaf Choir tours in addition to those he had included in published articles. Gay and David Gonnerman also made slides and pictures available. Esther Lyders of Minneapolis had information about the Choir's 1913 tour to Norway. Former Choir member Tom Erickson of Red Wing forwarded a unique set of college term papers written in the late twenties and early thirties by St. Olaf Choir members who were required by Professor Edward Ringstad to write "make-up" papers because of their absence from psychology class. The papers had come into Erickson's possession from his mentor in Rock Island, Illinois, the late Linden Lundstrom, St. Olaf Class of 1939, who as a student served as secretary to Professor F. M. Christiansen. My thanks to these persons.

Odd Terje Lysebo, a musician who lives in Larvik, Norway, where F. Melius Christiansen received his early training, kindly gave me and my daughter Margaret a tour of Larvik when we visited there in September of 1995. Lysebo, a friend of St. Olaf College for many years, was the Choir's host when it sang in Larvik in 1993. My inquiries about the period F. Melius Christiansen spent in Wisconsin brought me in touch with Andreas

Jordahl Rhude of Minneapolis, who provided documents about Our Savior's Lutheran Church, Marinette, Wisconsin, where F. Melius was organist and choir director, the Lindem family, and the church's record of the marriage of F. Melius Christiansen and Edith Signora Lindem. I express my thanks to Mr. Lysebo and Mr. Rhude.

The St. Olaf Choir takes pride in its appearance on the concert stage, thanks in no small part to the diligent work of "the robe lady" who makes sure that all robes are exactly the same length from the floor. I thank Ethel Green, former robe lady, for an interview in which she explained all that was involved in keeping the robes in good condition. Thanks also to her successor, Becca Coates, who agreed to appear in a photo showing how the hemming is done.

It is a pleasant duty to express my appreciation to Northfield Printing, Inc., Alan Marks, president, for producing the book, and to Gloria Heinz, who did the layout and design and with whom I conferred regarding text and illustrations for each chapter. Jody Greenslade, secretary for the Department of Religion, provided valuable assistance in preparing chapters for printing. Special thanks are due to her and to the Department of Religion for the time devoted to this book.

In these pages I have tried to name all who have contributed to the writing of the book about the St. Olaf Choir. To my regret, some choice materials could not be included. My sincere apologies to anyone whose name unwittingly was omitted. Thanks to friends and colleagues who, in passing, offered a useful comment, story, or bit of information, and to those I had hoped to interview. The Acknowledgments represent the scope of the vast company participating in the life of the St. Olaf Choir. The singers, directors, and managers form the core of the choral caravan that has traveled through the decades, but many others along the way have been caught up in the joyful mission of the St. Olaf Choir.

APPENDIX A

ST. OLAF CHOIR TOUR ITINERARIES
1912-1997

1912-Minneapolis, MN; Eau Claire, Madison, Mt. Horeb, Milwaukee, WI; Chicago, Ottawa, IL; Albert Lea, MN; June tour: Fargo, ND; Moorhead, MN; Hatton, Mayville, Grand Forks, ND; Crookston, Ada, Warren, Fertile, Fergus Falls, Alexandria, MN

1913-Tour of Norway, Sweden, Denmark- En route to New York: St. Paul, MN; Eau Claire, Madison, Milwaukee, WI; Niagara Falls, Brooklyn, NY. Sailed on the "Christianiafjord" to NORWAY: Bergen, Christiania, Drammen, Christiania, Fagerness, Gjøvik, Lillehammer, Hamar, Trondheim, Stenkjaer, Levanger, Stiklestad, Trondheim, Kristiansund, Veblungsnaes, Molde, Ålesund, Florö, Bergen, Haugesund, Stavanger, Flekkefjord, Mandal, Kristiansand, Arendal, Skien, Larvik, Christiania, Eidsvold, Moss, Fredrikstad, Sarpsborg, Fredrikshald; SWEDEN: Gothenburg, Malmö; DENMARK: Copenhagen

1914-Rushford, Lanesboro, Spring Grove, Harmony, Preston, Spring Valley, MN

1915-Minneapolis, Montevideo, Milan, Sacred Heart, Granite Falls, Hanley Falls, Cottonwood, Clarkfield, Madison, Boyd, Dawson, Minneota, Canby, MN

1916-Ellsworth, Spring Valley, Baldwin, Menomonie, Eau Claire, Black River Falls, WI; Winona, Zumbrota, Ellendale, Blooming Prairie, MN

1917-Northwood, Mason City, Belmond, Eagle Grove, Badger, Fort Dodge, Huxley, Des Moines, Stanhope, Ellsworth, Jewell, Roland, Marshalltown, Clermont, Decorah, Osage, IA; Dennison, Nerstrand, MN

1918-Austin, Adams, Hayfield, Faribault, MN. Storms canceled concerts in Grand Meadow and Oakland, MN.

1919-"Owing to the conditions brought about by the World War, when a great many St. Olaf students were in their country's service, the choir did not sing outside of Northfield." Simpson, Eugene, *A History of St. Olaf Choir*, Augsburg, Minneapolis, MN, 1921, p. 187

1920-Chicago, IL; Fort Wayne, IN; Columbus, OH; Pittsburgh, PA; Washington, D.C.; Baltimore, MD; Philadelphia, PA; Brooklyn, NY; Baltimore, MD; Paterson, NJ; New York, NY; Lancaster, York, PA; Albany, Rochester, NY; Youngstown, Cleveland, Akron, Canton, Springfield, Dayton, Cincinnati, Toledo, OH; Fort Wayne, IN; Detroit, MI; Minneapolis, MN

1921-St. Cloud, Willmar, Montevideo, Canby, Madison, MN; Watertown, Brookings, Madison, Sioux Falls, SD; Sioux City, Des Moines, IA; Omaha, Seward, NE; Kansas City, St. Louis, MO; Detroit, MI; Glenwood, Duluth, MN

1922-Milwaukee, WI; Chicago, IL; Toledo, Akron, Cleveland, OH; Allentown, PA; Camden, NJ; New York, NY; Washington, D.C.; "eastward from Chicago to New York through Ohio, Pennsylvania, Missouri, and Indiana back to St. Olaf College." *Viking* Yearbook 1922-1923, p.137

1923-La Crosse, Wausau, Green Bay, Racine, Appleton, Janesville, WI; Indianapolis, IN; Springfield, IL; St. Louis, MO; Omaha, NE; Winona, MN

1924-Detroit, MI; Indianapolis, IN; Chicago, IL; Cleveland, Toledo, Dayton, Cincinnati, Springfield, Canton, Youngstown, OH; Allentown, Pittsburgh, PA

1925-Aberdeen, SD; Miles City, Great Falls, Missoula, MT; Moscow, ID; Spokane, Everett, WA; Vancouver, British Columbia; Tacoma, Seattle, WA; Portland, OR; Sacramento, Los Angeles, Pasadena, San Diego, CA; Tijuana, Mexico; Los Angeles, CA; Salt Lake City, UT; Denver, Colorado Springs, CO; Lindsborg, St. Joseph, KS; Kansas City, St. Louis, MO; Des Moines, Cedar Falls, IA; Northfield, MN

1926-Chicago to Pittsburgh- Superior, WI; Detroit, Flint, Saginaw, Ann Arbor, MI; Milwaukee, WI

1927-Toronto, Ontario; New York, NY; Cleveland, OH; Boston, MA; Chicago, IL; Summer: St. Cloud, Fergus Falls, Crookston, MN; Fargo, Grand Forks, Devils Lake, Bottineau, Minot, Williston, ND; Havre, Great Falls, Missoula, Kalispell, MT; Spokane, Everett, Mt. Vernon, Bellingham, Seattle, Tacoma, WA; Portland, Silverton, OR

1928-St. Louis, MO; Grand Rapids, Ann Arbor, MI; Dubuque, IA; Rockford, IL; South Bend, Valparaiso, IN; Muskegon, MI; Ohio and Pennsylvania, Washington, D.C.

1929-Milwaukee, WI; Chicago, IL; Detroit, MI; Oberlin, Cleveland, OH; Buffalo, Syracuse, Utica, Schenectady, NY; Worcester, Boston, MA; Portland, ME; New Haven, CT; Elizabeth, NJ; Baltimore, MD; Brooklyn, New York, NY; Allentown, Reading, York, Altoona, PA; Toledo, OH; Chicago, IL

1930-St. Louis, MO; Atlanta, GA; Nashville, TN; Joliet, IL; Springfield, OH; Chattanooga, TN; Jacksonville, FL; Savannah, GA; Charleston, Columbia, SC; Charlotte, Greensboro, NC; Washington, D.C.; Wheeling, WV; Columbus, Dayton, OH; Rockford, IL. Tour to Europe- En route to New York: St Paul, MN; Eau Claire, Madison, Janesville, WI; Elgin, Oak Park, Chicago, IL; Grand Rapids, Lansing, MI; Mansfield, Cleveland, Canton, OH; Jamestown, NY; Oil City, Kane, Altoona,

Clearfield, PA; Binghamton, Syracuse, NY; Scranton, Wilkes-Barre, PA; New Haven, CT; Brooklyn, NY. Sailed on "Stavangerfjord" to NORWAY: Trondheim, Melhus, Christiania, Drammen, Eidsvold, Hamar, Moss, Larvik, Risør, Arendal, Kristiansand, Stravanger, Haugesund, Bergen, Ålesund, Åndalsnes, Molde, Kiristiansund, Levanger, Trondheim, Christiania, Moss, Sarpsborg; SWEDEN: Gothenburg, Malmö; DENMARK: Copenhagen; GERMANY: Nordlingen, Augsburg, Eisenach, Stuttgart, Nuremberg, Frankfurt, Naumburg, Leipzig, Wittenberg, Berlin, Hamburg

1931-Kansas City, MO; Fort Worth, Houston, Austin, San Antonio, TX; New Orleans, LA; Omaha, NE

1932-Chicago, IL; New York, NY; Washington, D.C.; Baltimore, MD; Philadelphia, Allentown, Reading, PA

1933-Duluth, Brainerd, Two Harbors, MN; Eau Claire, Rice Lake, Superior, WI; Detroit Lakes, Ortonville, Mankato, MN; Sioux Falls, SD; Fargo, ND; Moorhead, Worthington, MN; Spencer, Fort Dodge, IA

1934-Chicago World's Fair

1935-La Crosse, Beloit, WI; Aurora, Chicago, IL; Grand Rapids, Lansing, MI; Toledo, OH; Detroit, MI; Cleveland, OH; Erie, PA; Buffalo, Schenectady, NY; Worcester, MA; Portland, ME; Cambridge, MA; New York, NY; Princeton, NJ; Philadelphia, Reading, Allentown, Huntingdon, PA; Springfield, OH; Indianapolis, IN; Chicago, IL

1936-Eau Claire, Wausau, Madison, Milwaukee, WI; Holland, MI; Fort Wayne, IN; Columbus, Dayton, OH; Bloomington, IN; Champaign, IL; Lafayette, IN; Chicago, Rockford, IL; Dubuque, Cedar Rapids, Des Moines, Ames, Waterloo, IA

1937-Fargo, Grand Forks, Minot, ND; Kalispell, MT; Moscow, ID; Spokane, Bremerton, Seattle, Everett, Tacoma, WA; Portland, OR; San Diego, Los Angeles, Long Beach, Pasadena, Santa Barbara, Oakland, San Francisco, CA; Kansas City, MO

1938-La Crosse, Milwaukee, WI; Kalamazoo, Grand Rapids, Flint, Detroit, MI; Sandusky, Cleveland, OH; Buffalo, Rochester, NY; Providence, RI; Hartford, CT; Worcester, MA; East Orange, NJ; Brooklyn, NY; Hagerstown, MD; Lancaster, Allentown, Philadelphia, PA; Mansfield, OH; Chicago, IL; Madison, WI

1939-Minneapolis, St. Paul, Granite Falls, MN; Watertown, Brookings, SD; Sioux City, Des Moines, IA; Kirksville, Columbia, MO; Waverly, Charles City, IA; Rockford, IL; Racine, Appleton, Wausau, Eau Claire, Superior, WI; Hibbing, Duluth, MN

1940-Fargo, Bismarck, ND; Miles City, Billings, Bozeman, Missoula, MT; Spokane, Tacoma, WA; Portland, Eugene, Klamath Falls, OR; Sacramento, Oakland, Long Beach, Van Nuys, Pasadena, Los Angeles, CA; Denver, CO; Omaha, NE; Fort Dodge, Dubuque, IA; Chicago, IL

1941-Milwaukee, WI; Saginaw, Grand Rapids, Detroit, MI; Cleveland, Canton, OH; Oil City, PA; Buffalo, Syracuse, NY; Boston, MA; Philadelphia, PA; Washington, D.C.; New York, NY; Williamsport, Johnstown, Pittsburgh, PA; Cincinnati, OH; Chicago, Evanston, IL

1942-Sioux City, Council Bluffs, IA; Omaha, Lincoln, NE; Kansas City, MO; Oklahoma City, OK; Dallas, TX; Shreveport, LA; Waco, Austin, San Antonio, Corpus Christi, TX; New Orleans, LA; Jackson, MS; St. Louis, MO; Memphis, TN; Ottawa, Chicago, IL; Minneapolis, MN

1943-"Due to wartime transport difficulties, a scheduled tour of the East had to be canceled. A short tour, however, was arranged by manager Paul G. Schmidt, and in January the group presented concerts in Milwaukee, Evanston, Chicago, Oshkosh, Madison, La Crosse, and Rochester." *Viking* 1943

1944-Twelve day tour of the midwest highlighted by concerts at Great Lakes and Orchestra Hall in Chicago (*Viking* 1944). Appleton, Manitowoc, Milwaukee, WI; Chicago, Rockford, IL; St. Paul, MN

1945-Rochester, Albert Lea, MN; La Crosse, Madison, Milwaukee, WI; Chicago, IL; Fort Dodge, IA; Minneapolis, MN

1946-Appleton, Milwaukee, WI; Elmhurst, Decatur, Springfield, Champaign, IL; South Bend, IN; Austin, Minneapolis, MN

1947-Detroit, MI; Cleveland, Toledo, OH; Allentown, Lancaster, Philadelphia, Pittsburgh, PA; Syracuse, New York, Utica, Troy, NY; Minneapolis, MN

1948-Milwaukee, WI; Battle Creek, Detroit, Monroe, MI; Cleveland, OH; Niagara Falls, Utica, Troy, NY; Boston, MA; New Haven, CT; Philadelphia, PA; Wilmington, DE; Reading, Bethlehem, PA; New York, NY; Harrisburg, PA; Washington, D.C.; Pittsburgh, PA; Chicago, Champaign, Bloomington, Sterling, IL

1949-Fergus Falls, MN; Fargo, Grand Forks, Minot, ND; Spokane, Seattle, Parkland, WA; Portland, Salem, Klamath Falls, OR; Sacramento, Oakland, San Francisco, Fresno, La Jolla, San Diego, Los Angeles, Pasadena, CA; Salt Lake City, UT; Denver, CO; Cheyenne, WY; Omaha, NE; Des Moines, IA

1950-Superior, WI; Duluth, MN; Milwaukee, WI; Ishpeming, MI; Green Bay, Sheboygan, Wausau, Madison, Racine, WI; Decatur, Springfield, IL; St. Louis, Kansas City, MO; Sioux City, Webster City, Waterloo, IA; Montevideo, MN; Sioux Falls, SD; Spencer, IA; Evanston, Chicago, Rockford, IL; Dubuque, IA; Rochester, MN

1951-Janesville, WI; Princeton, IL; Saginaw, Detroit, MI; Cleveland, OH; Buffalo, NY; Boston, MA; New York, NY; New Haven, CT; Wilmington, DE; Philadelphia, PA; Atlantic City, NJ; Williamsport, Harrisburg, York, PA; Havre de Grace, MD; Washington, D.C.; Pittsburgh, New Castle, PA; Toledo, OH; Goshen, IN; Grand Rapids, MI; Champaign, Joliet, Chicago, Zion, IL

1952-Fargo, Grand Forks, Minot, Williston, ND; Great Falls, Kalispell, MT; Spokane, Tacoma, Seattle, Everett, WA; Portland, Salem, Eugene, OR; Davis, San Francisco, Long Beach, Los Angeles, Pasadena, San Diego, CA; Salt Lake City, UT; Denver, Pueblo, CO; Newton, KS; St. Louis, MO; Des Moines, IA; Northfield, MN

1953-La Crosse, Madison, WI; Rockford, IL; Hammond, South Bend, IN; Muskegon, Battle Creek, Saginaw, Grand Rapids, MI; Fremont, Oberlin, OH; Meadville, PA; Akron, Canton, Findlay, Springfield, Dayton, OH; Fort Wayne, IN; Chicago, IL; Manitowoc, Green Bay, Appleton, Milwaukee, WI; Northfield, MN

1954-Brainerd, Detroit Lakes, Fergus Falls, Glenwood, MN; Eau Claire, Neenah, WI; Indianapolis, IN; Louisville, Lexington, Corbin, KY; Chattanooga, TN; Atlanta, Macon, GA; Jacksonville, FL; Savannah, GA; Charleston, Spartanburg, SC; Charlotte, Winston-Salem, NC; Lynchburg, VA; Charleston, WV; Elkhart, IN; Chicago, Sterling, IL; Cedar Rapids, Waterloo, IA; Albert Lea, Northfield, MN

1955-Mason City, IA; Rock Island, IL; Winona, Red Wing, MN; Chippewa Falls, Beaver Dam, Portage, Wisconsin Rapids, WI; Ottawa, IL; Dubuque, IA; Marshall, St. Joseph, MO; Fremont, NE; Sioux City, IA; Sioux Falls, Canton, Watertown, Brookings, SD; Jamestown, Bismarck, ND; Moorhead, MN; Grand Forks, ND; Bemidji, Montevideo, Northfield, MN. Tour to Europe, June, 1955- En route to New York: Lanesboro, MN; Whitewater, WI; Cicero, Park Forest, IL; Kalamazoo, Monroe, MI; Youngstown, OH; Wheeling, WV; Hagerstown, MD; Johnstown, Altoona, Williamsport, Harrisburg, Lancaster, PA; Wilmington, DE; Bethlehem, PA; Newark, NJ; Brooklyn, NY. Sailed on "Stavangerfjord" to NORWAY: Kongsberg, Drammen, Oslo, Sarpsborg, Fredrikstad, Larvik, Skien, Kristiansand, Sandnes, Stavanger, Haugesund, Bergen, Førde, Volda, Ålesund, Trondheim, Lillehammer, Oslo; SWEDEN: Lund; DENMARK: Copenhagen; GERMANY: Hamburg, Hanover, Nuremburg, Munich, Augsburg, Stuttgart, Frankfurt, Dusseldorf; NETHERLANDS: Amsterdam; New York, NY

1956-Marshfield, Madison, Milwaukee, WI; Joliet, Chicago, IL; Toledo, OH; Detroit, MI; Cleveland, OH; Erie, PA; Buffalo, NY; Kitchener, Ontario; Rochester, Schenectady, NY; Providence, RI; New York, NY; New Haven, CT; Havre de Grace, MD; Washington, D.C.; Huntington, PA; Great Lakes, IL; Austin, Northfield, MN

1957-Des Moines, IA; Omaha, NE; Denver, CO; Salt Lake City, UT; Los Angeles, Long Beach, Pasadena, San Francisco, Oakland, Davis, CA; Eugene, Salem, Portland, OR; Seattle, Bellingham, Tacoma, Richland, WA; Kalispell, Havre, MT; Williston, Minot, ND; Northfield, MN. Spring tour to Iceland

1958-La Crosse, WI; Mt. Sterling, IL; Evansville, IN; Nashville, TN; Atlanta, Milledgeville, GA; Jacksonville, St. Petersburg, Miami, Orlando, FL; Savannah, GA; Charleston, Columbia, Spartanburg, SC; Hickory, Winston-Salem, NC; Corbin, Berea, KY; Indianapolis, IN; Wooster, Westerville, OH; Goshen, IN; Decatur, IL; Milwaukee, WI

1959-Mankato, MN; Sioux City, IA; Fremont, NE; Hesston, KS; Tulsa, Oklahoma City, OK; Dallas, Fort Worth, Waco, Austin, San Antonio, Houston, TX; Shreveport, LA; Jackson, MS; New Orleans, LA; Memphis, TN; Fulton, St. Louis, MO; Peoria, IL; Davenport, Cedar Rapids, IA; Austin, Northfield, MN

1960-Eau Claire, Janesville, WI; South Bend, IN; Kalamazoo, Grand Rapids, Detroit, MI; Cleveland, OH; Niagara Falls, Schenectady, NY; New Haven, CT; Malverne, NY; Bernardsville, NJ; Annapolis, MD; Washington, D.C.; Pittsburgh, PA; Fort Wayne, IN; Chicago, Joliet, Rockford, IL; Madison, Milwaukee, WI; Northfield, MN

1961-Ames, IA; Omaha, NE; Pueblo, Denver, CO; Salt Lake City, UT; San Diego, Los Angeles, Pasadena, Long Beach, Fresno, San Francisco, Oakland, Sacramento, CA; Eugene, Salem, Portland, OR; Parkland, Seattle, Bellingham, Richland, WA; Missoula, Glendive, MT; Valley City, ND; Northfield, MN

1962-Waterloo, IA; Madison, WI; Springfield, IL; Evansville, IN; Nashville, TN; Atlanta, GA; Anniston, AL; Valdosta, GA; Jacksonville, St. Petersburg, Miami, Orlando, FL; Augusta, GA; Columbia, Spartanburg, SC; Winston-Salem, NC; Huntington, WV; Bluffton, Painesville, OH; Chicago, IL; Rochester, Northfield, MN

1963-Watertown, SD; Sioux City, IA; Fremont, Hastings, NE; Salina, Winfield, KS; Tulsa, Oklahoma City, OK; Fort Worth, Waco, Dallas, Austin, San Antonio, Houston, TX; Lafayette, Shreveport, LA; Jackson, MS; Memphis, TN; St. Louis, MO; Davenport, IA; La Crosse, WI; Northfield, MN

1964-Sparta, WI; South Bend, IN; Detroit, MI; Cleveland, Canton, OH; Buffalo, Syracuse, Albany, Huntington, NY; Danbury, CT; New York, Malverne, NY; Washington, D.C.; Philadelphia, Pittsburgh, Greenville, PA; Toledo, OH; Chicago, IL; Milwaukee, Madison, Eau Claire, WI; Northfield, MN

1965-Des Moines, IA; Omaha, NE; Denver, CO; Albuquerque, NM; El Paso, TX; Tucson, Tempe, AZ; Los Angeles, Long Beach, San Diego, Pasadena, Bakersfield, Fresno, San Jose, Sacramento, CA; Salem, Portland, OR; Seattle, WA; Cut Bank, MT; Williston, Minot, ND; Northfield, MN

1966-Kalamazoo, MI; Kokomo, IN; Grand Rapids, Saginaw, Detroit, Trenton, MI; Fort Wayne, IN; Columbus, OH; Indianapolis, IN; Murray, KY; Nashville, Oak Ridge, TN; Winston-Salem, NC; Spartanburg, SC; Jacksonville, Miami, St. Petersburg, FL; Northfield, MN

1967-Sioux City, IA; Fremont, Hastings, NE; Hesston, KS; Oklahoma City, OK; Dallas, Austin, Abilene, San Antonio, Victoria, Houston, TX; Baton Rouge, LA; Memphis, TN; St. Louis, MO; Carbondale, Harvey, IL; Ames, IA; Austin, MN

1968-Madison, Kenosha, WI; South Bend, IN; Mansfield, Kidron, OH; Detroit, MI; Buffalo, Albany, NY: Danbury, CT; Malverne, New York, NY; Philadelphia, PA; Cumberland, MD; Oakland, PA; Cleveland, OH; Chicago, IL; Winona, Northfield, MN

1969-St. James, MN; Wayne, Grand Island, NE; Cheyenne, WY; Denver, CO; Albuquerque, NM; El Paso, TX; Tucson, Phoenix, AZ; Long Beach, San Diego, Los Angeles, Pasadena, Bakersfield, Fresno, Berkeley, San Jose, Sacramento, CA; Roseburg, Salem, Portland, OR; Bellingham, Seattle, Parkland, Spokane, WA; Marshfield, WI; St. Louis Park, Minneapolis, Northfield, MN

1970-Viroqua, Milwaukee, WI; Evansville, IN; Nashville, TN; Atlanta, GA; Jacksonville, Miami, St. Petersburg, Orlando, Lake City, FL; Columbia, SC; Burlington, NC; Annapolis, MD; Reading, PA; Dayton, OH; Indianapolis, IN; Chicago, IL; Cedar Rapids, IA; Northfield, MN. Tour to Europe- GERMANY: Strasbourg, Nuremberg, Frankfurt, Stuttgart, Weisenhorn, Hartford, Berlin, Hanover; CZECHOSLOVAKIA: Prague; AUSTRIA: Vienna, Klagenfurt, Innsbruck

1971-Worthington, MN; Fremont, NE; Lindsborg, KS; Tulsa, Oklahoma City, OK; Dallas, Austin, Houston, TX; Lafayette, New Orleans, Baton Rouge, LA; Jackson, MS; Memphis, TN; Springfield, IL; Ames, Dubuque, IA; La Crosse, WI; Northfield, MN

1972-Eau Claire, WI; Rockford, IL; Grand Rapids, Detroit, MI; Cleveland, OH; Houghton, Albany, NY; Philadelphia, Allentown, PA; Somerville, NJ; New York, NY; Washington, D.C.; Selinsgrove, PA; Shepherdstown, WV; Toledo, OH; Chicago, IL; Madison, WI; Northfield, MN. Tour to Europe- BELGIUM: Tongeren; FRANCE: Strasbourg, Metz, Paris, Lyon, Montbeliard; SWITZERLAND: Freibourg, Zug

1973-Osseo, WI; St. Paul, MN; Iowa City, IA; Omaha, Grand Island, NE; Sterling, Denver, Colorado Springs, CO; Albuquerque, Los Alamos, NM; Snowflake, Phoenix, AZ; Los Angeles, San Diego, Riverside, Bakersfield, Sacramento, San Francisco, San Jose, CA; Northfield, MN

1974-Rochester, Spring Grove, MN; Milwaukee, Mt. Horeb, WI; Ottawa, Urbana, IL; St. Louis, MO; Rock Island, IL; Des Moines, Mason City, IA; Minneapolis, Albert Lea, Montevideo, MN; Aberdeen, SD; Grand Forks, ND; Duluth, Brainerd, Northfield, MN

1975-Appleton, Washburn, WI; Hutchinson, MN. Interim travel/study in VIENNA and ROME.

1976-Forest City, IA; Owatonna, Golden Valley, MN; La Crosse, WI; St. Charles, Chicago, IL; Indianapolis, Fort Wayne, IN; Columbus, OH; Harrisburg, Philadelphia, PA; New York, NY; Washington D.C.; Pittsburgh, PA; Cleveland, OH; Detroit, Kalamazoo, Grand Rapids, MI; Madison, WI; Northfield, MN

1977-Fairmont, Virginia, MN; Omaha, Lincoln, NE; Denver, Colorado Springs, CO; Taos, Santa Fe, Albuquerque, NM; Fort Huachuca, Phoenix, Yuma, AZ; San Diego, Beverly Hills, Los Angeles, Fresno, San Jose, San Francisco, CA; Minneapolis, Northfield, MN

1978-Burnsville, Willmar, Minneapolis, St. Paul, Rushford, MN; Glen Ellyn, IL; Milwaukee, Wausau, Neenah, Eau Claire, Madison, WI; Arlington Heights, IL; East Lansing, Mt. Pleasant, Auburn Heights, MI; Archbold, OH; Janesville, WI; Owatonna, Northfield, MN

1979-Lakeville, MN; Hayward, Stanley, La Crosse, WI; Oak Brook, IL; Richmond, IN; Fort Knox, KY; Oak Ridge, TN; Athens, Savannah, GA; Lakeland, Fort Myers, Tampa, St. Petersburg, FL; Montgomery, AL; Searcy, AR; Bridgeton, MO; Des Moines, IA; Minneapolis, Northfield, MN

1980-St. Paul, Edina, MN; Viroqua, WI; Evanston, Urbana, IL; Dayton, Ashland, OH; Cumberland, MD; Washington, D.C.; York, PA; Hartford, New Haven, CT; New York, NY; Allentown, Pittsburgh, PA; Detroit, MI; Fort Wayne, IN; Decorah, IA; Northfield, MN. Tour to Scandinavia- NORWAY: Oslo, Larvik, Skien, Kristiansand, Stavanger, Haugesund, Bergen, Molde, Kristiansund, Ålesund, Trondheim, Tønsberg, Fredrikstad, Lillehammer, Gjøvik, Hamar

1981-Mountain Lake, Mankato, White Bear Lake, Owatonna, MN; Ames, Davenport, IA; Godfrey, IL; Little Rock, AR; Shreveport, LA; Austin, Corpus Christi, San Antonio, Dallas, Amarillo, TX; Norman, OK; Wichita, Topeka, KS; Sioux City, IA; Sioux Falls, SD; Northfield, MN

1982-St. Cloud, Thief River Falls, MN; Dickinson, ND; Bozeman, MT; Blackfoot, ID; Walla Walla, WA; Portland, Salem, OR; Seattle, Spokane, WA; Great Falls, Billings, MT; Bismarck, ND; Moorhead, Minneapolis, Northfield, MN

1983-Beloit, WI; Danville, IL; Cincinnati, OH; Salem, VA; Hickory, NC; Clemson, SC; Charlotte, NC; Charleston, SC; Savannah, GA; Orlando, Sarasota, St. Petersburg, FL; Valdosta, Atlanta, GA; Brevard, NC; Oak Ridge, Nashville, TN; Decatur, IL; Milwaukee, WI; Rochester, Northfield, MN

1984-LeSueur, Willmar, MN; Pueblo, CO; Albuquerque, NM; El Paso, TX; Tucson, Tempe, AZ; Pasadena, San Diego, Santa Barbara, San Luis Obispo, San Francisco, Sacramento, CA; Reno, NV; Salt Lake City, UT; Grand Junction, Fort Collins, Denver, CO; Northfield, MN

1985-Austin, Winona, MN; Decorah, IA; Rockford, IL; Fort Wayne, IN; East Lansing, Kalamazoo, MI; Warren, PA; Rochester, NY; Worcester, MA; New York, NY; Washington, D.C.; Sunbury, Pittsburgh, PA; Holland, MI; Chicago, IL; Madison, WI; St. Paul, Northfield, MN

1986-Duluth, Brainerd, MN; Marshalltown, Iowa City, IA; Hannibal, MO; Jacksonville, IL; Kansas City, MO; Oklahoma City, OK; Canyon, San Antonio, Houston, Austin, TX; North Newton, KS; Lincoln, Omaha, NE; Sioux Falls, SD; Northfield, MN. Tour to the Orient in May- JAPAN: Kyoto, Tokyo, Kumamoto; TAIWAN: Taipei; HONG KONG; CHINA: Shanghai, Suzhou, Nanjing, Xian, Beijing; Honolulu, HI

1987-Chippewa Falls, WI; St. Cloud, MN; Bismarck, ND; Billings, Missoula, MT; Spokane, WA; Vancouver, British Columbia; Seattle, WA; Portland, Eugene, Bend, OR; Boise, Idaho Falls, ID; Gillette, WY; Rapid City, Mitchell, SD; Mankato, St. Paul, Northfield, MN

1988-Edina, MN; Wausau, Janesville, WI; Urbana, IL; Oak Ridge, TN; Charlotte, NC; Savannah, GA; Gainesville, Sarasota, St. Petersburg, Jacksonville, FL; Atlanta, GA; Nashville, TN; Indianapolis, IN; St. Charles, IL; Green Bay, WI; Northfield, MN. Tour to Seoul Olympic Arts Festival- KOREA: Seoul, Inchon, Pusan, Taegu

1989-Willmar, Fergus Falls, MN; Colorado Springs, CO; Albuquerque, NM; El Paso, TX; Sun City, Tucson, Phoenix, AZ; San Diego, Palm Desert, Los Angeles, Fresno, Santa Barbara, San Luis Obispo, San Francisco, CA; Northfield, MN

1990-Duluth, MN; La Crosse, Milwaukee, WI; Fort Wayne, IN; Ann Arbor, Grand Rapids, MI; Kitchener, Ontario; Buffalo, Rochester, NY; Springfield, MA; New York, NY; Washington, D.C.; Lewisburg, Pittsburgh, PA; Indianapolis, IN; Madison, WI; Chicago, IL; Minneapolis, Northfield, MN

1991-Hudson, WI; Marshall, Worthington, MN; Sioux City, IA; Lincoln, NE; Wichita, KS; Oklahoma City, OK; Irving, Austin, San Antonio, Houston, TX; New Orleans, Baton Rouge, Monroe, LA; Little Rock, AR; Memphis, TN; Edwardsville, Jacksonville, IL; Des Moines, IA; Albert Lea, Northfield, MN

1992-Willmar, Long Lake, Alexandria, MN; Minot, ND; Miles City, Bozeman, Great Falls, Helena, MT; Lewiston, ID; Walla Walla, WA; Portland, OR; Seattle, Spokane, WA; Missoula, Billings, MT; Dickinson, ND; Moorhead, Northfield, MN

1993-Brainerd, Grand Rapids, Rochester, MN; Janesville, WI; Grand Rapids, MI; Columbus, OH; Charleston, WV; Durham, NC; Greenville, Charleston, SC; Brunswick, GA; St. Petersburg, Tallahassee, FL; Atlanta, GA; Nashville, TN; Terra Haute, IN; Cedar Rapids, IA; Northfield, MN. Summer tour to Europe- DENMARK: Copenhagen; NORWAY: Larvik, Kristiansand, Stavanger, Bergen, Trondheim, Snåsa, Lillehammer, Hamar, Oslo

1994-Red Wing, LeSueur, Duluth, MN; Boulder, Colorado Springs, CO; Albuquerque, NM; El Paso, TX; Phoenix, Tucson, Rio Verde, Sun City, AZ; Riverside, Thousand Oaks, San Diego, Los Angeles, Santa Barbara, San Luis Obispo, Palo Alto, San Francisco, Sacramento, CA; Northfield, MN

1995-Benson, Willmar, Winona, MN; Madison, Milwaukee, WI; Richmond, IN; Weirton, WV; Philadelphia, PA; New York, NY; Washington, D.C.; Selinsgrove, PA; Parkersburg, WV; Indianapolis, IN; Kalamazoo, MI; Urbana, Evanston, IL; Northfield, MN

1996-Hastings, MN; Washington, D.C.; Richmond, VA; Iowa City, IA; Lincoln, NE; Hesston, KS; Oklahoma City, OK; Dallas, San Antonio, Austin, Corpus Christi, Houston, TX; Arkadelphia, AR; Springfield, MO; Belleville, IL; Kansas City, MO; Sioux Center, IA; Sioux Falls, SD; Northfield, MN

1997-Appleton, Stevens Point, WI; Faribault, Northfield, MN. Interim tour to New Zealand and Australia- NEW ZEALAND: Auckland, Wellington, Christchurch; AUSTRALIA: Melbourne, Adelaide, Cairns, Brisbane, Sydney; Minneapolis, MN

Appendix A is a listing of all tour itineraries of The St. Olaf Choir from 1912 to 1997. The state abbreviation follows the last city in each state. Several sources were used to create this list: the *Saint Olaf* magazine; *Viking* yearbooks; St. Olaf Choir scrapbooks; archived tour itineraries; the *Manitou Messenger*; Simpson, Eugene, *A History of St. Olaf Choir*, Augsburg, Minneapolis, MN, 1921; St. Olaf College archival materials.

APPENDIX B

ST. OLAF CHOIR TOUR PROGRAMS
1912-1997

1912

Der ringes paa jord	F. Melius Christiansen
Deilig er jorden	Folk Melody, arr. F. M. C.
Song Cycle	A. Søderman
a. Lamb of God	
b. He is Blessed	
c. Hosanna	
I Know That My Redeemer Liveth	From Messiah by Handel, arr. F. M. C.
Jeg saa ham som barn	Norwegian folk song, arr. F. M. C.
O Jesus, se	Shop, arr. F. M. C.
O hoved høit forhaanet	Hassler, arr. F. M. C.
Som sol gaar ned i havet	F. M. C.
Det ringer fra alle taarne	Kjerulf, arr. F. M. C.
Lover den Herre	Søhren, arr. F. M. C.

1913

Der ringes paa jord	F. Melius Christiansen
Moderens Sang	F. M. C.
Hvad est du dog skjøn	Edvard Grieg
Lover den Herre	Søhren, arr. F. M. C.
Still, Still with Thee *(Ladies' Quartet)*	Franz Abt
Alone with Thee	J. G. Conradi
O Bread of Life	Heinrich Isaac
Song Cycle—Hear Us Lord	A. Søderman
The Lord is Full of Compassion *(Ladies' Quartet)*	F. M. C.
I Know That My Redeemer Liveth—from Messiah	Handel
Wake, Awake	Nicolai, arr. F. M. C.

1914

Der ringes paa jord	F. Melius Christiansen
O Jesu, se min Skam og Ve	Arr. F. M. C.
Lover den Herre	Søhren, arr. F. M. C.
Holy Spirit, Dove Divine	Gottschalk
Den store hvide flok	Grieg, arr. F. M. C.
Still, Still with Thee *(Ladies' Quartet)*	Franz Abt
Built on a Rock	Lindeman, arr. F. M. C.
Kun dagligdags	F. M. C.
Herre, hvor laenge?	Handel, arr. F. M. C.
Deilig er jorden	Folk melody, arr. F. M. C.
Retirement	F. M. C.
Domine Exaudi	Grieg
O Bread of Life	Isaac, arr. F. M. C.
Wake, Awake	Nicolai, arr. F. M. C.

1915

Cherubic Hymn	Gretchaninoff
O Bread of Life	Heinrich Isaac
Nunc Dimittis	Gretchaninoff
Lover den Herre	Søhren, arr. F. M. C.
Still, Still with Thee	Franz Abt
One Sweetly Solemn Thought	R. S. Ambrose
Som sol gaar ned	F. Melius Christiansen
Two Christmas Songs	F. M. C.
Pilgrim-song	Folk melody, arr. F. M. C.
Jesus, Savior, Pilot Me	Gould
Lead, Kindly Light	Folk song
Cherubim Song	Glinka
Tænk naar engang	Folk song
Wake, Awake	Nicolai, arr. F. M. C.

1916

Op dog, Sion	Ludv. M. Lindeman
Fred til bod	Hartmann
O Bread of Life	Isaac, arr. F. Melius Christiansen
Lover den Herre	Søhren, arr. F. M. C.
Deilig er Jorden	Folk melody, arr. F. M. C.
Julen har Engle Lyd	Ih. Fenger
Guds Engle i Flok	Ludv. M. Lindeman
Bedre kan jeg ikke fare	
Lord, to Thee I Make Confession	
Oh, Come Let Us Worship	M. Hauptmann
I Praise for This Day	
Wake, Awake	Nicolai, arr. F. M. C.

1917

In Heavenly Love Abiding	Mendelssohn
My God, My God (Psalm 22)	Mendelssohn
How Blest Are They	Tschaikowsky
Violin solo: Miss Alma Rasmussen	
Second Movement from D-Minor Concerto	Wieniawski
Souvenir	Drdla
O hoved høit forhaanet	Hassler, arr. F. Melius Christiansen
O Bread of Life	Isaac, arr. F. M. C.
In Heaven Above	Lindeman, arr. F. M. C.
Lover den Herre	Søhren, arr. F. M. C.
Violin solo: Miss Alma Rasmussen	
Air for the G String	J. S. Bach
Romance	Svendsen
Deilig er jorden	Folk melody, arr. F. M. C.
Som sol gaar ned	F. M. C.
Tænk naar engang	Folk melody, arr. F. M. C.
Wake, Awake	Nicolai, arr. F. M. C.

1918

In Heavenly Love Abiding	Mendelssohn
Cherubim Song	Glinka
In Heaven Above	Lindeman, arr. F. Melius Christiansen
Christmas Song	arr. Rimsky-Korsakoff
O Praise Ye	Arensky
The Nightingale	Tschaikowsky
Song Cycle	Søderman
Moderens Sang	F. M. C.
Som sol gaar ned	F. M. C.
Wake, Awake	Nicolai, arr. F. M. C.

1919

Der ringes paa jord	F. Melius Christiansen
Jeg saa ham som barn	Norwegian folk song, arr. F. M. C.
Deilig er Jorden	Folk melody, arr. F. M. C.
Song Cycle	A. Søderman
Still, Still With Thee	F. Abt
Gracious Spirit, Dove Divine	Gottschalk
In Heavenly Love Abiding	Mendelssohn
Tænk naar engang	Folk song
Autumn	A. Gretchaninoff
Sunshine Song	Grieg
By the Rivers of Babylon	S. Pantchenko

1920

Blessing, Glory, and Wisdom	Georg Gottfried Wagner
Praise to the Lord	Søhren, arr. F. Melius Christiansen
Built on a Rock	Lindeman, arr. F. M. C.
A Mighty Fortress Is Our God	Luther, arr. F. M. C.
The Word of God	Grieg
Savior of Sinners	Mendelssohn
O God, Hear My Prayer	Gretchaninoff
Father, Most Holy	Crüger
Hosanna	F. M. C.
Beautiful Savior	Folk melody, arr. F. M. C.
Wake, Awake	Nicolai, arr. F. M. C.

1921

The Spirit Also Helpeth Us	J. S. Bach
Truth Eternal	Gustav Schreck
Song Cycle	Søderman
O Praise Ye God	Tschaikowsky
Bless the Lord	Tschesnokoff
Agnus Dei	Kalinnikof
O How Shall I Receive Thee	Gustav Schreck
The Morning Star	Nicolai, arr. F. Melius Christiansen
Built on a Rock	Lindeman, arr. F. M. C.
All My Heart	Ebeling, arr. F. M. C.
A Christmas Song	F. M. C.
In dulci jubilo	14th century melody, arr. F. M. C.

1922

The Spirit Also Helpeth Us	J. S. Bach
O Sacred Head Now Wounded	Hassler, arr. F. Melius Christiansen
How Fair the Church of Christ Shall Stand	Chorale from Schumann's Gesangbuch, arr. F. M. C.
It Is a Good Thing (Psalm 92)	Georg Schumann
Yea Through Death's Gloomy Vale (Psalm 23)	Georg Schumann
Lord, How Long? (Psalm 13)	Georg Schumann
O How Shall I Receive Thee	Gustav Schreck
Praise the Lord, O My Soul	Gretchaninoff
A Christmas Song	F. M. C.
In dulci jubilo	14th century melody, arr. F. M. C.
Praise to the Lord	Søhren, arr. F. M. C.

1923

Be Not Afraid	J. S. Bach
O Darkest Woe	Shop, arr. F. Melius Christiansen
This Is the Sight that Gladdens	Crüger, arr. F. M. C.
Magnificat	Stanley Avery
The Morning Star	Nicolai, arr. F. M. C.
Earth, in Singing	Schumann
In dulci jubilo	14th century melody, arr. F. M. C.
Advent Motet	Gustav Schreck
Nunc Dimittis	Gretchaninoff
How Fair the Church of Christ Shall Stand	Chorale from Schumann's Gesangbuch, arr. F. M. C.
Psalm 50	F. M. C.

1924

Come, Jesu, Come	J. S. Bach
O Wondrous Type	Latin chorale, arr. F. Melius Christiansen
A Crown of Grace	Brahms
Make Me, O Lord God, Pure in Heart	Brahms
Our Father	Gretchaninoff
Come, Thou Savior of Our Race	Latin chorale, arr. F. M. C.
O Sacred Head Now Wounded	Hassler, arr. F. M. C.
Hosanna	Gustav Schreck
Who Can Comprehend Thee?	Peter Lutkin
Glory Be to God	Rachmaninoff
The Three Kings	Catalonian Nativity Song, arr. Romeau
Wake, Awake	Nicolai, arr. F. M. C.

1925

Sing Ye	J. S. Bach
O Sacred Head	H. L. Hassler
O Wondrous Type	Chorale from Pre-Reformation Source
Hosanna	F. M. C.
Savior of Sinners	Felix Mendelssohn
In dulci jubilo	14th century melody, arr. F. M. C.
Glory Be To God	S. Rachmaninoff
The Three Kings	Catalonian Nativity Song, arr. Romeau
Our Father	Gretchaninoff
As Sinks Beneath the Ocean	F. M. C.
In Heaven Above	Norwegian folk melody
Advent Motet	Gustav Schreck

.ıg Ye	J. S. Bach
Misericordias domini	Durante
Benedictus qui venit	Franz Liszt
Put Up the Sword	F. Melius Christiansen
Yea Through Death's Gloomy Vale	Georg Schumann
Come, Guest Divine	Georg Schumann
From Heaven Above	Chorale from Schumann's Gesangbuch, arr. F. M. C.
Whence, Then, Cometh Wisdom?	Gustav Schreck
O Sacred Head Now Wounded	Hassler, arr. F. M. C.
Deck Thyself, My Soul, With Gladness	Crüger, arr. F. M. C.
From Heaven Above	Lindeman, arr. F. M. C.
Praise to the Lord	Søhren, arr. F. M. C.

1927

The Spirit Also Helpeth Us	J. S. Bach
Cherubim Song	M. Glinka
Deck Thyself, My Soul, with Gladness	Johan Crüger, arr. F. Melius Christiansen
Benedictus qui venit	Franz Liszt
Now Sinks the Sun	Horatio W. Parker
From Heaven Above	Lindeman, arr. F. M. C.
Two Norwegian Sacred Folk Songs	Grieg
Hvad est du dog skjøn	
Guds Søn har gjort mig fri	
O Gladsome Light	Alexander Gretchaninoff
Two German Christmas Songs	Arr. Kranz
Heiligste Nacht	
Geistliches Wiegenlied	
Advent Motet	Gustav Schreck

1928

Jesu, Priceless Treasure (from the motet)	J. S. Bach
How Fair the Church of Christ Shall Stand	Chorale from Schumann's Gesangbuch, arr. F. M. Christiansen
Go, Song of Mine	Edward Elgar
Hosanna	F. M. C.
May Our Mouths Be Filled with Thy Praise	Rachmaninoff
Salvation is Created	Tschesnokoff
From Heaven Above	Chorale from Schumann's Gesangbuch, arr. F. M. C.
The Morning Star	Nicolai, arr. F. M. C.
So Soberly	Norwegian folk melody, arr. F. M. C.
Marienlied	Arr. C. A. Fischer
Wake, Awake	Nicolai, arr. F. M. C.

1929

Sing Ye	J. S. Bach
Misericordias Domini	Durante
The Morning Star	Nicolai, arr. F. Melius Christiansen
Go, Song of Mine	Edward Elgar
Be Thyself My Surety Now	Max Regar
Mary's Cradle Song on the Twelfth Day	Georg Schumann
Ihr Kinder Zion freuet euch	Arnold Mendelssohn
Glory Be to God	Rachmaninoff
So Soberly	Norwegian folk melody, arr. F. M. C.
Clap Your Hands	F. M. C.
Beautiful Savior	Folk melody, arr. F. M. C.

1930 Winter Tour

Sing Ye	J. S. Bach
Cherubim Song	Glinka
Benedictus qui venit	Liszt
Misericordias domini	Durante
Two Sacred Songs	Folk songs, arr. F. M. C.
What Joy to Reach the Harbor	
So Soberly	
Guds Søn har gjort mig fri	Edvard Grieg
How Fair the Church of Christ Shall Stand	Chorale from Schumann's Gesangbuch, arr. F. M. Christiansen
Lost in the Night	Finnish folk song, arr. F. M. C.
Clap Your Hands	F. M. C.
Advent Motet	Gustav Schreck

1930 European tour

Sing Ye	J. S. Bach
Cherubim Song	Glinka
Benedictus qui venit	Liszt
Nu runden er den saele Stund	F. Melius Christiansen
O Hoved, høit forhaanet	Hassler, arr. F. Melius Christiansen
Savior of Sinners	Felix Mendelssohn
Deilig er jorden	Folk melody, arr. F. M. C.
Advent Motet	Gustav Schreck
I Himmelen, i Himmelen	Lindeman, arr. F. M. C.
Lost in the Night	Finnish folk song, arr. F. M. C.
Wake, Awake	Nicolai, arr. F. M. C.

Not Afraid	J. S. Bach
All Creatures of Our God and King	Armstrong Gibbs
Come Holy Spirit	Georg Schumann
O Praise Ye God	Tschaikowsky
Agnus Dei	Kalinnikof
Regeneration	F. Melius Christiansen
A Snow Mountain	F. M. C.
Psalm 50	F. M. C.
Motet zum Weihnachtsfest	Arnold Mendelssohn
Salvation Is Created	Tschesnokoff
Hosanna	F. M. C.
Marienlied	Arr. C. A. Fischer
Beautiful Savior	Folk melody, arr. F. M. C.

1932

Agnus Dei	Kalinnikof
This Is the Sight That Gladdens	Crüger, arr. F. Melius Christiansen
Be Not Afraid	J. S. Bach
Be Jubilant My Spirit	Heinrich Schmid
When God Paints the Sunset	Norse folk melody, Overby, arr. F. M. C.
Celestial Spring	Overby-F. M. C.
I. The Spirit's Yearning	
II. Exaltation	
III. Regeneration	
IV. Glorification	
Das Geläut zu Speir	Ludwig Senfl
O Praise Ye God	Tschaikowsky
Two German Christmas Songs	Arr. Kranz
Praise to the Lord	Søhren, arr. F. M. C.

1933

Our Father	Gretchaninoff
Glory be to God	S. Rachmaninoff
Three Sacred Songs	Georg Schumann
Yea, Through the Vale	
Behold, How Good	
How Long Wilt Thou Forget	
Hvad est du dog skjøn	Grieg
Celestial Spring	Overby-F. Melius Christiansen
Magnificat	Stanley Avery
Creator of Beauty	F. M. C.
All My Heart This Night Rejoices	F. M. C.
Advent Motet	Gustav Schreck

1934

O God Our Great Jehovah	Richard Kountz
Here Leave Your Sorrow	Danish folk melody, arr. F. Melius Christian.
Misericordias Domini	Durante
Sing Ye	J. S. Bach
Our Days Are As a Shadow	J. S. Bach
It Is a Good Thing to Give Thanks	Schvedof
Hosanna	F. M. C.
Regeneration	F. M. C.
Savior of Sinners	Felix Mendelssohn
Beyond the Haze	Paul Christiansen
So Soberly	Folk song, arr. F. M. C.
Lullaby on Christmas Eve	F. M. C.
Beautiful Savior	Folk melody, arr. F. M. C.

1935

Ascendit Deus	Jacobus Gallus
Angels Made an Arbor	Overby-F. Melius Christiansen
Hvad est du dog skjøn	Grieg
Sing Ye	J. S. Bach
Yea, through the Vale of Death	Georg Schumann
Behold, How Good	Georg Schumann
Psalm 50	F. M. C.
Kingdom of God	16th century chorale, arr. F. M. C.
Heiligste Nacht	Arr. Kranz
O Heart Attuned to Sadness	Swedish folk song, arr. F. M. C.
Vistas of Song	F. M. C.
Sunbeam Out of Heaven	F. M. C.
Lullaby on Christmas Eve	F. M. C.
Beautiful Savior	Folk mleody, arr. F. M. C.

1936

Be Not Afraid	J. S. Bach
Come, Soothing Dove	J. S. Bach
Song of Praise	J. S. Bach
Wake, Awake	Nicolai, arr. F. Melius Christiansen
Kingdom of God	16th century chorale, arr. F. M. C.
From Grief to Glory	Overby-F. M. C.
I. Decadence	
II. Love in Grief	
III. Spring Returns	
IV. Life	
Rock of Refuge	Swedish folk melody, Overby, arr. F. M. C.
Vistas of Song	Overby-F. M. C.
From Heaven Above	Chorale from Schumann's Gesangbuch, arr. F. M. C.
Advent Motet	Gustav Schreck

.rom "Apostrophe to the Heavenly Hosts" Healey Willan
.pirit Also Helpeth Us J. S. Bach
.ic Dimittis Gretchaninoff
.utumn Woods Paul Christiansen
When God Paints the Sunset Norse folk melody,
  Overby, arr. F. Melius Christiansen

Exaltation (Part II, Celestial Spring) Overby-F. M. C.
Regeneration (Part III, Celestial Spring) Overby-F. M. C.
Easter Bells Overby-F. M. C.
In excelsis gloria Breton melody, arr. Morten Luvaas
Thanksgiving Motet Arnold Mendelssohn
Lost in the Night Finnish folk melody, arr. F. M. C.
Beautiful Savior Folk melody, arr. F. M. C.
Lullaby on Christmas Eve F. M. C.
From Grief to Glory F. M. C.
Snow Mountain F. M. C.

1938

Sing Ye J. S. Bach
Hvad est du dog skjøn Grieg
Misericordias Domini Durante
Finale from "An Apostrophe to the Heavenly Hosts" Healey Willan
Cherubim Song Glinka
We Have No Other Guide Schvedof
The Twenty-Third Psalm Gustav Schreck
Autumn Woods Paul Christiansen
Lo, How A Rose E'er Blooming Rhenish folk melody,
  arr. F. Melius Christiansen
Beauty in Humility F. M. C.
Lost in the Night Finnish folk melody, arr. F. M. C.
Praise to the Lord Søhren, arr. F. M. C.
Beautiful Savior Folk melody, arr. F. M. C.
The Three Kings Catalonian Nativity Song,
  arr. L. Romeau

652

1939

Be Not Afraid	J. S. Bach
Tenebrae Factae Sunt	Palestrina
Psalm 50	F. Melius Christiansen
O Thou Gladsome Light	Gretchaninoff
Unto the Lord	Paul Christiansen
Magnificat	Paul Christiansen
Benedictus	E. Paladilhe
O Be Joyful, All Ye Lands	Gretchaninoff
Clap Your Hands	F. M. C.
Aspiration	Norse folk melody, Overby, arr. F. M. C.
Wake, Awake	Nicolai, arr. F. M. C.
Lullaby on Christmas Eve	F. M. C.
Beautiful Savior	Folk melody, arr. F. M. C.
Lost in the Night	Finnish folk song, arr. F. M. C.
Longing for Home	Halfdan Kjerulf
Cradle Hymn	F. M. C.

1940

O Praise Ye God	Tschaikowsky
Tenebrae Factae Sunt	Marc Antonio Ingegneri
Restoration	Benjamin Edwards
Advent Motet	Gustav Schreck
Benedictus qui venit	Liszt
As a Flower	Paul Christiansen
Sing to God	Paul Christiansen
From Grief to Glory	Overby-F. Melius Christiansen
From Heaven Above	Chorale from Schumann's Gesangbuch, arr. F. M. C.
Beauty in Humility	F. M. C.
Lost in the Night	Finnish folk melody, arr. F. M. C.
Wake, Awake	Nicolai, arr. F. M. C.
Beautiful Savior	Folk melody, arr. F. M. C.
The Song of Mary	Fischer-Kranz
Longing for Home	Halfdan Kjerulf
Benedictus	E. Paladilhe

1941

O Savior, Throw the Heavens Wide	Brahms
O Sacred Head	Hassler, arr. F. Melius Christiansen
We Have No Other Guide	Schvedof
The Lord Reigneth	Paul Christiansen
Savior of Sinners	Felix Mendelssohn
Thanksgiving Motet	Arnold Mendelssohn
Come, Guest Divine	Georg Schumann
Faith Victorious	Gretchaninoff
When Curtained Darkness	F. M. C.
Beauty in Humility	F. M. C.
Sing Unto Him	Morten Luvaas
Lullaby on Christmas Eve	F. M. C.
Doxology	Bourgeois
Beautiful Savior	Folk melody, arr. F. M. C.
Lo, How A Rose E'er Blooming	Rhenish folk song
Wonders Are Wrought	Norse Christmas Song

1942

America (Audience and Choir)	
Born Today (Hodie Christus Natus Est)	J. P. Sweelinck
O Magnum Mysterium	Tomás Luis de Victoria
The Spirit Also Helpeth Us	J. S. Bach
Finale from "An Apostrophe to the Heavenly Hosts"	Healey Willan
Our Father	Gretchaninoff
O Darkest Woe	J. Shop, arr. F. Melius Christiansen
Psalm 50	F. M. C.
Born Anew	Overby-F. M. C.
Lost in the Night	Finnish folk song, arr. F. M. C.
Marienlied	Arr. Carl Aug. Fischer
Heaven and Earth	F. M. C.
Beautiful Savior	Folk melody, arr. F. M. C.
Wonders Are Wrought	Norse Christmas song, arr. F. M. C.
Praise to the Lord	Peter Søhren, arr. F. M. C.

1943

America (Audience and Choir)

Adoramus te, Christe	Giuseppe Corsi
O Nata Lux	Thomas Tallis
Prayer to Jesus	George Oldroyd
Jesu, Priceless Treasure	J. S. Bach
Our Father	Gretchaninoff
Nunc Dimittis	Gretchaninoff
Praise the Lord, O My Soul	Gretchaninoff
Advent Motet	Gustav Schreck
Built on a Rock	Lindeman, arr. F. Melius Christiansen
O Darkest Woe	J. Shop, arr. F. M. C.
From Heaven Above	Chorale from Schumann's Gesangbuch, arr. F. M. C.
Beautiful Savior	Folk melody, arr. F. M. C.

1944

America (Audience and Choir)

Surrexit Pastor Bonus	Orlando di Lasso
Christus Factus Est	Felice Anerio
Bénédiction Avant le Repas	Claude le Jeune
Come, Soothing Death	J. S. Bach
Wake, Awake	Nicolai, arr. F. Melius Christiansen
The Trumpets of Zion	Olaf C. Christiansen
Only Begotten Son	Gretchaninoff
Prayer to Jesus	George Oldroyd
An Apostrophe to the Heavenly Hosts	Healey Willan
Dayspring of Eternity	Freylinghausen, arr. F. M. C.
Regeneration (Part III, Celestial Spring)	F. M. C.
Rock and Refuge	Swedish folk melody, Overby, arr. F. M. C.
O Day Full of Grace	Weyse, arr. F. M. C.
The Christmas Candle	Roberta Bitgood
My Psalm	F. M. C.
I Wonder as I Wander	Appalachian Carol, arr. John Jacob Niles

1945

Sing Ye to the Lord	J. S. Bach
Father Most Holy	Johann Crüger, arr. F. M. Christiansen
O Savior, Throw the Heavens Wide	Johannes Brahms
Gloria	Martin Shaw
Nunc Dimittis	Alexander Gretchaninoff
Tenebrae Factae Sunt	Marc Antonio Ingegneri
O King of Glory	Olaf C. Christiansen
Salvation is Created	Peter Tschesnokoff
Rock and Refuge	Swedish folk melody, arr. F. M. C.
I Sat Down under His Shadow	Edward C. Bairstow
Birthday Greeting	Zoltán Kodály
The Song of Mary	Fischer-Kranz
The Trumpets of Zion	Olaf C. Christiansen
Hark Now, O Shepherds	Moravian melody, arr. F. M. C.
A Cradle Hymn	F. M. C.
Beautiful Savior	Folk melody, arr. F. M. C.
Lamb of God	arr. F. M. C.

1946

Sing Ye to the Lord	J. S. Bach
Tu Es Petrus	Giovanni Pierluigi da Palestrina
Adoramus Te, Christe	Giuseppi Corsi
Praise the Lord, O My Soul	Alexander Gretchaninoff
Kingdom of God	arr. F. Melius Christiansen
How Fair the Church	arr. F. M. C.
Fiftieth Psalm	F. M. C.
Light of God	Heinrich von Herzogenberg
A Spotless Rose	Herbert Howells
A Joyous Christmas Song	arr. Margrethe Hokanson
Advent Motet	Gustav Schreck
Clap Your Hands	F. M. C.
Beautiful Savior	arr. F. M. C.
I Wonder As I Wander	arr. John Jacob Niles
Gloria In Excelsis	Martin Shaw

1947

Sing Ye to the Lord	J. S. Bach
Adoramus Te, Christe	Giuseppi Corsi
Two Psalms	Heinrich Schütz
Psalm 97	
Psalm 121	
Wake, Awake	Nicolai, arr. F. Melius Christiansen
Trumpets of Zion	Olaf C. Christiansen
Psalm 92	Georg Schumann
How Fair the Church	arr. F. M. C.
Praise the Lord, O My Soul	Alexander Gretchaninoff
Our Father	Alexander Gretchaninoff
A Spotless Rose	Herbert Howells
A Joyous Christmas Carol	arr. Margrethe Hokanson
The Song of Mary	Fischer-Kranz
Finale from "An Apostrophe to the Heavenly Hosts"	Healey Willan
O Day Full of Grace	C. E. F. Weyse, arr. F. M. C.
Beautiful Yuletide	F. M. C.
Beautiful Savior	arr. F. M. C.

1948

The Spirit Also Helpeth Us	Johann Sebastian Bach
Plorate Filii Israel from "Jephtah"	Giacomo Carissimi
Praise to the Lord	arr. F. Melius Christiansen
Cantata of Peace	Darius Milhaud
Come Unto Him	Ernst Pepping
Laud Him	Ernst Pepping
An Apostrophe to the Heavenly Hosts	Healey Willan
Awake (chorale from "Die Meistersinger")	Richard Wagner
Psalm 92	Georg Schumann
As a Flower of the Field	Paul Christiansen
My Heart is Longing	Sune Carlson
Advent Motet	Gustav Schreck
From Heaven Above	arr. F. M. C.
The Christmas Symbol	F. M. C.
Joyous Bells of Christmas	arr. Morten J. Luvaas
Beautiful Savior	arr. F. M. C.
Gloria In Excelsis	Martin Shaw
In Dulci Jubilo	Traditional carol, arr. F. M. C.
A Joyous Christmas Song	arr. Margrethe Hokanson

1949

Hodie Christus Natus Est	G. P. Palestrina
Adoramus Te, Christe	Giuseppi Corsi
The Spirit Also Helpeth Us	Johann Sebastian Bach
Cantata of Peace	Darius Milhaud
An Apostrophe to the Heavenly Hosts	Healey Willan
Fiftieth Psalm	F. Melius Christiansen
Advent Motet	Gustav Schreck
Kingdom of God	F. M. C.
Alleluia, Christ is Born	Morten J. Luvaas
Benedictus	E. Paladilhe
We've Been A While a-Wandering	Yorkshire carol, arr. O. C. Christiansen
Beautiful Savior	arr. F. M. C.
Salvation Is Created	Peter Tschesnokoff
A Joyous Christmas Song	arr. Margrethe Hokanson
God's Son Has Made Me Free	Edvard Grieg

1950

Hodie Christus Natus Est	G. P. Palestrina
O Magnum Mysterium	Tomás Luis de Victoria
How Fair the Church of Christ Shall Stand	Schumann's Hymnbook
Wake, Awake	Nicolai, arr. F. Melius Christiansen
Jesus, Priceless Treasure	J. S. Bach
Hosanna	F. M. C.
Psalm 23	Georg Schumann
Lost in the Night	Finnish folk song, arr. F. M. C.
Brazilian Psalm	Jean Berger
Be Ye Joyful, Earth and Sky	F. M. C.
The Three Kings	Healey Willan
The Christmas Symbol	F. M. C.
A Joyous Christmas Song	arr. Margrethe Hokanson
Beautiful Savior	arr. F. M. C.
Lullaby on Christmas Eve	F. M. C.
We've Been a While a-Wandering	Yorkshire Carol, arr. Olaf C. Christiansen

1951

Hodie Christus Natus Est	G. P. Palestrina
O Magnum Mysterium	Tomás Luis de Victoria
Die mit Tränen säen	Johann Herman Schein
Praise to the Lord	arr. F. Melius Christiansen
Jesus, Priceless Treasure	J. S. Bach
Vision of Peace	Jean Berger
Brazilian Psalm	Jean Berger
Our Father	Alexander Gretchaninoff
The Cry of God	Morten J. Luvaas
All My Heart This Night Rejoices	J. G. Ebeling, arr. Olaf C. Christiansen
Happy Bethlehem	Spanish Carol, arr. Padre Donostia
Sing Unto the Lord	Paul Christiansen
While Stars Their Vigil Keep	Morten J. Luvaas
Beautiful Savior	arr. F. M. C.
God Be Merciful Unto Us	Sven Lekberg
O How Beautiful the Sky	Danish carol, arr. Olaf C. Christiansen

1952

Sing Ye to the Lord	J. S. Bach
Die mit Tränen säen	Johann Herman Schein
Plorate Filii Israel from "Jephtah"	Giacomo Carissimi, arr. Olaf C. Christiansen
O Nata Lux	Thomas Tallis, arr. Olaf C. Christiansen
Hodie Christus Natus Est	J. P. Sweelinck
Vision of Peace	Jean Berger
Laud Him	Ernst Pepping
Our Father	Alexander Gretchaninoff
The Cry of God	Morten J. Luvaas
O God, Thou Faithful God	Johannes Brahms, arr. Winfred Douglas
Sing a Song of Joy	Harold E. Darke
Psalm 23	Georg Schumann
In Heaven Above	Norse folk song, arr. F. Melius Christiansen
Alleluia	G. Winston Cassler
Make We Joy Now in This Fest	William Walton
The Song of the Angels	F. M. C.
Brazilian Psalm	Jean Berger
Guiding Star Carol	Danish Carol, arr. Olaf C. Christiansen
O Soul, Why Grievest Thou	J. S. Bach
From Grief to Glory	F. M. C.
Beautiful Savior	arr. F. M. C.

1953

Hodie Christus Natus Est	J. P. Sweelinck
Adoramus Te, Christe	Giuseppi Corsi
Ascendit Deus	Jacobus Gallus
Dayspring of Eternity	Freylinghausen, arr. F. M. C.
Wake, Awake	Nicolai, arr. F. Melius Christiansen
The Righteous	Johann Christoph Bach
Supplication	Johann Christoph Bach
O Soul Why Grievest Thou	Johann Sebastian Bach
Sing Ye to the Lord	Johann Sebastian Bach
Vision of Peace	Jean Berger
Praise the Lord, O My Soul	Alexander Gretchaninoff
Grief to Glory	F. M. C.
Regeneration	F. M. C.
Glorification	F. M. C.
God's Son Is Born	John Bergsagel
When Christmas Morn Is Dawning	German, arr. Morten J Luvaas
God's Son Has Made Me Free	Edvard Grieg
Alleluia	G. Winston Cassler
Beautiful Savior	arr. F. M. C.
The Song of Mary	Fischer-Kranz
O God, Thou Faithful God	Johannes Brahms, arr. Winfred Douglas

1954

Sing Ye to the Lord	J. S. Bach
Misericordias Domini	Francesco Durante
How Fair the Church	arr. F. Melius Christiansen
An Apostrophe to the Heavenly Hosts	Healey Willan
Psalm 134	Normand Lockwood
Psalm 13	Jean Berger
Psalm 23	Georg Schumann
Psalm 50	F. M. C.
This Night a Wondrous Revelation	König, arr. F. M. C.
Sing Nowell, Sing Gloria	Olaf C. Christiansen
Silesian Cradle Song	arr. Albert Kranz
Carol of the Drum	arr. Katherine Davis
Entrance Scene	Gustav Schreck
Lullaby on Christmas Eve	F. M. C.
A Joyous Christmas Song	arr. Margrethe Hokanson
Salvation Is Created	Peter Tschesnokoff
Beautiful Savior	arr. F. M. C.

1955

Sing Ye to the Lord	J. S. Bach
Die mit Tränen säen	Johann Herman Schein
Plorate Filii Israel	Giacomo Carissimi
Death, I Do not Fear Thee	J. S. Bach
Our Father	Alexander Gretchaninoff
Psalm 92	Georg Schumann
Hvad Est Du Dog Skjøn	Edvard Grieg
God's Son Has Made Me Free	Edvard Grieg
Vision of Peace	Jean Berger
How Fair the Church	arr. F. Melius Christiansen
Deep River	arr. H. T. Burleigh
Alleluia	G. Winston Cassler
Auf dem Berge	German, arr. Albert Kranz
Deilig er den himmel blaa	Scandinavian, arr. Olaf C. Christiansen
Lowly Shepherds	Polish, arr. Kozinski
Jeg er saa glad	Norwegian, arr. Margrethe Hokanson
Carol of the Drum	Czech, arr. Katherine Davis
Beautiful Savior	Silesian, arr. F. Melius Christiansen
Wake, Awake	Nicolai, arr. F. M. C.
While Stars Their Vigil Keep	Morten J. Luvaas

1955 European Tour (Norway)

Sing Ye to the Lord	J. S. Bach
How Fair the Church	arr. F. Melius Christiansen
Plorate Filii Israel	Giacomo Carissimi
Death, I Do Not Fear Thee	J. S. Bach
Vision of Peace	Jean Berger
The Kingdom Come	Jean Berger
Hvad Est Du Dog Skjøn	Edvard Grieg
Guds Søn Har Gjort Mig Fri	Edvard Grieg
Wondrous Love	Sydstat-hymne U. S. A.
Deep River	African American Spiritual, arr. H. T. Burleigh
Deilig Er Den Himmel Blå	Skandinavisk, arr. O. C. Christiansen
Lowly Shepherds	Polsk, arr. Kozinski
Jeg Er Så Glad	Norsk, arr. M. Haakansen
Carol of the Drum	Tsjekkisk, arr. K. Davis
Wake, Awake (Sions vekter hever røsten)	Phillip Nicolai
Alleluia	G. Winston Cassler
Our Father	Alexander Gretchaninoff
Til Norge	Edvard Grieg, arr. O. C. Christiansen
Ja Vi Elsker	arr. O. C. Christiansen
Beautiful Savior	Schlesisk, arr. F. M. C.

1955 European Tour (Germany)

Singet dem Herrn	J. S. Bach
Die mit Tränen säen	J. H. Schein
Plorate Filii Israel (Aus dem Oratorium Jephtah)	Giacomo Carissimi
Vaterunser	Alexander Gretchaninoff
92. Psalm	Georg Schumann
Wie bist du so schön	Edvard Grieg
Gottes Sohn hat mich befreit	Edvard Grieg
Wie hoch wird sein der Kirche Stand (Choral 1539)	Vertonung: F. Melius Christiansen
Tiefer Fluß	Vertonung: H. T. Burleigh
Hallelujah	G. Winston Cassler
Auf dem Berge	Deutsch, Vertonung, Kranz
Herrlich ist der Himmel blau	Skandin., Vertonung, O. C. Christiansen
Ich bin so froh	Norwegish, Vertonung, M. Haakansen
Schönster Heiland	Schlesisch, Vertonung, F. M. Christiansen
Wachet, erwachet	Phillip Nicolai
Wenn die Sterne ihre Wache halten	Morten J. Luvaas

1956

Hodie Christus Natus Est	G. P. Palestrina
I Am the Resurrection and the True Life	Heinrich Schütz
Ave Verum Corpus	William Byrd
The Shepherd Has Arisen	Orlando di Lasso
The Spirit Also Helpeth Us	J. S. Bach
Psalm 134	Normand Lockwood
Thy Kingdom Come	Jean Berger
Regeneration	F. Melius Christiansen
Finale from "An Apostrophe to the Heavenly Hosts"	Healey Willan
Lost in the Night	Finnish folk song, arr. F. M. C.
The Godly Stranger	G. Winston Cassler
Songs of Joy to Heaven Raise	Jacob Handl
O Day Full of Grace	C. E. F. Weyse, arr. F. M. C.
Sing Ye to the Lord	J. S. Bach
Carol of the Drum	Czech, arr. Katherine Davis
Beautiful Savior	Silesian, arr. F. M. C.

1957

A Star is Moving Across the Sky	Harald Fryklöf
O Magnum Mysterium	Tomás Luis de Victoria
Adoramus Te, Christe	Giuseppi Corsi
Wake, Awake	Nicolai, arr. F. M. C.
The Spirit Also Helpeth Us	J. S. Bach
Psalm 134	Normand Lockwood
Come, Let Us Walk in the Light of God	Adolf Brunner
Glory Be to God	Jean Berger
Advent Motet	Gustav Schreck
Kingdom of God	F. Melius Christiansen
This Night a Wondrous Revelation	König, arr. F. M. C.
Christmas Symbol	F. M. C.
Come and Adore	Basque carol, arr. Donald Malin
Carol of the Drum	Czech, arr. Katherine Davis
Beautiful Savior	Silesian, arr. F. M. C.
Nunc Dimittis	A. T. Gretchaninoff

1957 Iceland Tour

Psalm 97	Heinrich Schütz
Adoramus Te, Christe	Giuseppi Corsi
The Spirit Also Helpeth Us	J. S. Bach
Kingdom of God	F. Melius Christiansen
How Fair the Church of Christ Shall Stand	Schumann's Hymnbook
Advent Motet	Gustav Schreck
Passion Chorale	Páll Isolfsson
Wake, Awake	Nicolai, arr. F. M. C.
Psalm 134	Normand Lockwood
O Brother Man	Olaf C. Christiansen
Glory Be to God	Jean Berger
This Night a Wondrous Revelation	König, arr. F. M. C.
Christmas Symbol	F. M. C.
Come and Adore	Basque carol, arr. Donald Malin
Carol of the Drum	Czech, arr. Katherine Davis
Lofsønger (The Icelandic National Anthem)	arr. O. C. Christiansen
Beautiful Savior	Silesian, arr. F. M. C.

1958

Be Not Afraid	J. S. Bach
Misericordias Domini	Francesco Durante
Sing a Song of Joy	Harold E. Darke
Babylon	Darius Milhaud
O Wondrous Night	Flor Peeters
Son of Man Be Free	Olaf C. Christiansen
Psalm 50	F. Melius Christiansen
Our Father	Alexander Gretchaninoff
Hosanna	F. M. C.
Psalm 23	Georg Schumann
Praise to the Lord	arr. F. M. C.
The Sun Has Gone Down	Norse folk song
Brazilian Psalm	Jean Berger
Beautiful Savior	Silesian, arr. F. M. C.

1959

All They from Saba	Jacobus Gallus
Die mit Tränen säen	Johann Herman Schein
Be Not Afraid	J. S. Bach
Vision of Peace	Jean Berger
Come and Let Us Walk in the Light of God	Adolf Brunner
Trumpets of Zion	Olaf C. Christiansen
Praise the Lord O My Soul	Alexander Gretchaninoff
From Grief to Glory	F. Melius Christiansen
An Apostrophe to the Heavenly Hosts	Healey Willan
Processional: At the Name of Jesus	Vaughan Williams, arr. Olaf C. Christiansen
Break Forth, O Beauteous Heavenly Light	J. S. Bach
The Song of Mary	Albert Kranz
Carol of the Drum	Czech, arr. K. Davis
We've Been a While a-Wandering	Yorkshire Carol
Beautiful Savior	Folk melody, arr. F. M. C.

664

1960

A Star Shall Rise	Jacobus Gallus
Adoramus Te, Christe	Giuseppi Corsi
Surely He Hath Borne Our Griefs	Karl Graun
Let All the Peoples Praise the Lord	Gallus Dressler
Lord, If I but Thee May Have	Heinrich Schütz
We Need Thee O Lord	J. S. Bach
Be Not Afraid	J. S. Bach
Jubilate Deo	Bernhard Lewkovitch
Dayspring of Eternity	Johnann Freylinghausen, arr. F. Melius Christiansen
Regeneration	F. M. C.
Glorification	F. M. C.
Three Introits for Advent	
To Thee, O Lord	Vassily Kalinnikof
Daughter of Zion	Olaf C. Christiansen
Drop Down, Ye Heavens	G. W. Cassler
Godly Stranger	G. W. Cassler
Guest From Heaven	Spanish carol, arr. O. R. Overby
Lo, How a Rose	M. Praetorius
Advent Motet	Gustav Schreck
Fear Not	J. G. Schicht
Beautiful Savior	arr. F. M. C.

1961

Hodie Christus Natus Est	G. P. Palestrina
Lord, If I but Thee May Have	Heinrich Schütz
Tenebrae Factae Sunt	Marc Antonio Ingegneri
Christ Jesus Lay in Death's Strong Bands	Wittenberg: 1524
Resurrection	J. Gallus
Jesus Priceless Treasure	J. S. Bach
Jubilate Deo	Bernhard Lewkovitch
The Eyes of All Wait Upon Thee	Jean Berger
Psalm 134	Normand Lockwood
Psalm 23	Georg Schumann
Psalm 98	Hugo Distler
Processional: At the Name of Jesus	Vaughan Williams, arr. Olaf C. Christiansen
Annunciation and Magnificat	Olaf. C. Christiansen
Drop Down, Ye Heavens (Introit for Advent)	G. W. Cassler
Holy Manger	Arnold F. Keller
Guest From Heaven	Old Spanish carol, arr. Oscar R. Overby
Song of Simeon	Alexander Gretchaninoff
O Day Full of Grace	C. E. F. Weyse, arr. F. Melius Christiansen
The Song of Peace	Olaf C. Christiansen
Patapan	Old French
In Bethlehem (Congaudeat)	12th century carol, arr. Olaf C. Christiansen
Beautiful Savior	arr. F. M. C.

1962

Let All the Peoples Praise the Lord	Gallus Dressler
Misericordias Domini	Francesco Durante
Christ Jesus Lay in Death's Strong Bands	Wittenberg: J. S. Bach
Resurrection	Jacob Gallus-Händl
Jesus Priceless Treasure	J. S. Bach
Trumpets of Zion (Joel II)	Olaf C. Christiansen
How Fair the Church of Christ Shall Stand	arr. F. Melius Christiansen
How Great Are Thy Wonders	Georg Schumann
Sing to the Lord a New Song	Hugo Distler
Benedictus	E. Paladilhe
Three Carols	
Come and Adore (Basque)	arr. Donald Malin
The Song of Mary (German)	Fischer-Kranz
What Child is This (English)	Greensleeves
Son of Man Be Free	Olaf C. Christiansen
God's Son Has Made Me Free (Norwegian)	Edvard Grieg
Whoso Offereth Praise (Ps. 50)	F. M. C.
Lost In the Night (Finnish Folk song)	arr. F. M. C.
Beautiful Savior	arr. F. M. C.

1963

Hodie Christus Natus Est	G. P. Palestrina
O Come, Let Us Sing	Jan Sweelinck
O Quam Gloriosum	Tomás Luis de Victoria
Surely He Hath Borne Our Griefs	Karl Graun
If By His Spirit	J. S. Bach
Psalm 50	F. Melius Christiansen
Trust In the Lord	Jean Berger
At the Cross "Remember Me"	Sven-Erik Bäck
Laud Him	Ernst Pepping
Advent Motet	Gustav Schreck
From Heaven Above to Earth I Come	Schumann, arr. F. M. C.
Sing Nowell, Sing Gloria!	Olaf C. Christiansen
I Wonder as I Wander	Appalachian Carol, arr. John Jacob Niles
Jeg er saa glad	arr. Margrethe Hokanson
O Little Town of Bethlehem	Kenneth Jennings
Carol of the Drum	arr. Katherine Davis
The Song of Peace	Olaf C. Christiansen
Praise Him in Gladness	Gastoldi, arr. O. C. Christiansen
Beautiful Savior	arr. F. M. C.

1964

Hodie Christus Natus Est	G. P. Palestrina
O Quam Gloriosum	Tomás Luis de Victoria
Alas, They Have Taken The Lord	Thomas Morley
Surrexit Pastor Bonus	Orlando di Lasso
Praise to the Lord	Stralsund Gesangbuch, arr. F. Melius Christiansen
Be Not Afraid	J. S. Bach
We Need Thee O Lord	J. S. Bach
An Apostrophe to the Heavenly Hosts	Healey Willan
Vision of Peace	Jean Berger
All Men Draw Near	Zoltán Kodály
Agnus Dei	V. Kalinnikof
Christus Factus Est	Anton Bruckner
Sing to the Lord a New Song	Hugo Distler
Crown Him King of Glory	arr. Olaf C. Christiansen
Resonet in Laudibus	arr. Olaf C. Christiansen
Auf dem Berge	arr. Albert Kranz
In Dulci Jubilo	arr. F. M. C.
Christmas Symbol	F. M. C.
Praise Him in Gladness	Gastoldi, arr. Olaf C. Christiansen
Bless the Lord, O My Soul	Isadore Freed
At the Cross "Remember Me"	Sven-Erik Bäck
Beautiful Savior	arr. F. M. C.

1965

Cantate Domino	Heinrich Schütz
Jesu Dulcis Memoria	Jacob Händl
O Vos Omnes	Tomás Luis de Victoria
Surrexit Pastor Bonus	Orlando di Lasso
Ich bin der Herr	Ernst Pepping
Prayer on Christmas Eve	Flor Peeters
At the Cross "Remember Me"	Sven-Erik Bäck
Christus Factus Est	Anton Bruckner
Salvation is Created	Peter Tschesnokoff
Brazilian Psalm	Jean Berger
Jesus Christ from the Law Hath Freed Us	Johann Schelle
Be Not Afraid	J. S. Bach
Crown Him King of Glory (processional)	Olaf C. Christiansen
Now Is Born Emmanuel	arr. Olaf C. Christiansen
Babe Divine	Olaf C. Christiansen
Glad Tidings Bringing (Polish Carol)	arr. Theron Kirk
In Dulci Jubilo (XIV Century German)	arr. F. Melius Christiansen
Praise Him In Gladness	Gastoldi, arr. Olaf C. Christiansen
Beautiful Savior	arr. F. M. C.

1966

Cantate Domino	Heinrich Schütz
O Magnum Mysterium	Tomás Luis de Victoria
Lamb of God	Johann Spangenberg, arr. F. Melius Christiansen
Die mit Tränen Säen	Johann Herman Schein
Wake, Awake, for Night is Flying	Nicolai, arr. F. M. C.
Hail the Dawning Day	Johann Franco
As the Flower of the Field	Paul Christiansen
Hope in the Lord	Olaf C. Christiansen
Two Introits	
Drop Down, Ye Heaven	G. Winston Cassler
With a Voice of Singing	Kenneth Jennings
Glory Be to God	Jean Berger
Brazilian Psalm	Jean Berger
Advent Motet	Gustav Schreck
Crown Him King of Glory	Olaf C. Christiansen
Glad Tidings Bringing	Polish, arr. Theron Kirk
Guiding Star Carol	Danish, arr. Olaf C. Christiansen
Jeg er saa glad	Norwegian, arr., Margrethe Hokanson
Carol of the Drum	Czech, arr. Katherine Davis
God's Wondrous Love	Southern U. S., arr. Olaf C. Christiansen
Praise Him in Gladness	Gastoldi, arr. Olaf C. Christiansen
Beautiful Savior	arr. F. M. C.

1967

Hodie Christus Natus Est	G. P. Palestrina
O Magnum Mysterium	Tomás Luis de Victoria
Adoramus Te, Christe	Giuseppi Corsi
O Jesu Christe	Jachet van Berchem
O Beata et Gloriosa Trinitas	G. P. Palestrina
Ich bin der Herr	Ernst Pepping
God Is My Salvation	Olaf C. Christiansen
I Will Give Thanks	Normand Lockwood
The Cherubic Hymn	A. Gretchaninoff
Jubilate	Bernhard Lewkovitch
Jesus Priceless Treasure	J. S. Bach
Rejoice (Advent Hymn)	Adam Gumpeltzhaimer
A Great and Mighty Wonder	Melchior Vulpius
Sing Ye, Sing Noel	Robert Wetzler
Lo, How a Rose	arr. Hugo Distler
While Stars Their Vigil Keep	Morten J. Luvaas
All My Heart	F. Melius Christiansen
The Mystery	Arthur Benjamin
Praise Him in Gladness	Gastoldi, arr. Olaf C. Christiansen
Beautiful Savior	arr. F. M. C.

1968

Cantate Domino	Heinrich Schütz
O Magnum Mysterium	Giovanni Gabrieli
Ave Verum Corpus	William Byrd
Ave Maria	Giovanni Pierluigi da Palestrina
Rejoice (Advent Hymn)	Adam Gumpeltzhaimer
Our Father	Alexander Gretchaninoff
How Great Are Thy Wonders	Georg Schumann
Son of Man Be Free	Olaf C. Christiansen
O Day Full of Grace	Weyse, arr. F. Melius Christiansen
Advent Motet	Gustav Schreck
Sing Ye to the Lord	J. S. Bach
Lift Up Your Heads	arr. Olaf C. Christiansen
The Song of Peace	Olaf C. Christiansen
Lo, how a Rose E'er Blooming	Hugo Distler
Sing Nowell, Sing Gloria	Olaf C. Christiansen
O Little Town of Bethlehem	Kenneth L. Jennings
God's Son Has Made Me Free	Edvard Grieg
Beautiful Savior	arr. F. M. C.

1969

Praise Ye The Lord (from Sing Ye)	J. S. Bach
Verbum Caro Factum Est	Hans Leo Hassler
O Vos Omnes	Juan Esquivel
Surrexit Pastor Bonus	Orlando di Lasso
The Spirit Also Helpeth Us	J. S. Bach
Mass in G Minor	Ralph Vaughan Williams
Sing to the Lord a New Song	Hugo Distler
Bow Down Thine Ear	Ernst Pepping
I Will Extol Thee	Krzysztof Penderecki
De Profundis	Arnold Schoenberg
With a Voice of Singing	Kenneth Jennings
Who Shall Abide	Walter Pelz
The Gift Carol	Spanish carol, arr. Lloyd & Debby Pfautsch
From Out of a Wood (Carol of the Birds)	Arnold Freed
Praise To the Lord	F. Melius Christiansen
Sanctus	Ralph Vaughan Williams
Beautiful Savior	arr. F. M. C.

669

1970

Cantate Domino	Jan Pieterszoon Sweelinck
O Lord, Creator of All Things	Heinrich Schütz
I Am the Resurrection and the Life	Heinrich Schütz
Viri Galilaei	Jan Pieterszoon Sweelinck
Sing Ye to the Lord	J. S. Bach
Magnificat	Jean Berger
Gloria	Ralph Vaughan Williams
Collect for Peace (for choir and tape)	Leslie Bassett
Trust in the Lord	Knut Nystedt
De Profundis	Arnold Schoenberg
All My Heart	Johann Cruger
A Spotless Rose	Herbert Howells
Hacia Belén Va Un Borrico	Traditional Spanish Carol, arr. Parker-Shaw
When Jesus Wept	William Billings
Wake, Awake	Nicolai, arr. F. Melius Christiansen
Ride On, King Jesus	Spiritual, arr. Parker-Shaw
Beautiful Savior	arr. F. M. C.

1971

Jubilate Deo	Giovanni Gabrieli
Come, Jesus, Come	J. S. Bach
Praise Ye The Lord (from Sing Ye)	J. S. Bach
Psalm Two	Felix Mendelssohn
Benedictus Dominus	Carl Neilsen
Mass for Five Voices Kyrie-Gloria-Agnus Dei	Lennox Berkeley
Collect for Peace	Leslie Bassett
Lord's Prayer	Robert Stone
Today, Heaven Sings	Kenneth Jennings
Nunc Dimittis	Rachmaninoff
Sons of Eve, Reward my Tidings	16th Century Spanish Carol
Wake, Awake	Nicolai, arr. F. Melius Christiansen
There Is No Rose of Such Virtue	John Joubert
Bow Down Thine Ear	Ernst Pepping
Fife and Drum	Herbert Bielawa
Beautiful Savior	arr. F. M. C. *

1972

Sing to the Lord a New Song	Hugo Distler
The Lord's Prayer	Robert Stone
Jesus, Remember Me	Sven-Erik Bäck
Collect for Peace	Leslie Bassett
Jubilate	Bernhard Lewkovitch
Jesus, Priceless Treasure	J. S. Bach
Psalm 90	Charles Ives
Gloria (from Missa Criolla)	Ariel Ramirez
Rimfrost	Erik Bergman
The Godly Stranger	G. Winston Cassler
Psalm 50	F. Melius Christiansen
Beautiful Savior	arr. F. M. C.

1972 Tour of Europe

Mass in B Minor	J. S. Bach
(See also 1972 Winter Tour Program)	

1973

Hodie Cristus Natus Est	G. P. Palestrina
O Lord, Creator of All Things	Heinrich Schütz
Search Me, O God	Sven-Erik Bäck
I Am The Resurrection and the Life	Heinrich Schütz
Wake, Awake	Hugo Distler
Vision of Peace	Jean Berger
The Evening-watch	Gustav Holst
Jubilate	Bernhard Lewkovitch
Sing Ye To The Lord	J. S. Bach
Hacia Belén Va Un Borrico	arr. Parker-Shaw
September	Wilhelm Stenhammar
Rimfrost	Erik Bergman
Easter Morning	Paul J. Christiansen
Ye Watchers and Ye Holy Ones	Healey Willan
Christmas Symbol	F. Melius Christiansen
Beautiful Savior	arr. F. M. C.

1974

Hodie Cristus Natus Est	G. P. Palestrina
Sicut Cervus	G. P. Palestrina
O Vos Omnes	Juan Esquivel
I Will Not Leave You Comfortless	William Byrd
The Spirit Also Helpeth Us	J. S. Bach
Our Father	Alexander Gretchaninoff
How Great Are Thy Wonders	Georg Schumann
Advent Motet	Gustav Schreck
Kyrie, Sanctus from Mass for Double Choir	Frank Martin
September	Wilhelm Stenhammar
Rimfrost	Erik Bergman
Brazilian Psalm	Jean Berger
Sing Nowell, Sing Gloria	Olaf C. Christiansen
The Gift Carol	Spanish Carol, arr. Lloyd Pfautsch
Give Me Jesus	Spiritual, arr. L. L. Fleming
O Day Full of Grace	arr. F. Melius Christiansen
Beautiful Savior	arr. F. M. C.
A Motet For the Archangel Michael for Choir and Organ	Bengt Hambraeus
Sanctus (from the Mass)	Leonard Bernstein

1975

Cantate Domino	Jan Pieterszoon Sweelinck
Sicut Cervus	G. P. Palestrina
Ave Verum Corpus	William Byrd
Non Vos Relinquam Orphanos	William Byrd
Sing Ye to the Lord	J. S. Bach
Psalm 134	Normand Lockwood
De Profundis	Arnold Schoenberg
O Sacrum Convivium	Olivier Messiaen
Sanctus (from Mass for double chorus)	Frank Martin
With A Voice Of Singing	Kenneth Jennings
Our Father	Alexander Gretchaninoff
From Out of a Wood (Carol of the Birds)	Arnold Freed
Psalm 50	F. Melius Christiansen
The Lord's Prayer	Robert Stone
Kyrie (from Mass for double chorus)	Frank Martin
Give Me Jesus	Spiritual, arr. L. L. Fleming
Beautiful Savior	arr. F. M. C.

1976

Cantate Domino	Jan Pieterszoon Sweelinck
Sicut Cervus	G. P. Palestrina
Die mit Tränen säen	Hermann Schein
Be Not Afraid	J. S. Bach
A Motet For the Archangel Michael	Bengt Hambraeus
How Great Are Thy Wonders	Georg Schumann
O Sacrum Convivium	Olivier Messiaen
Gloria (from Mass in G Minor)	Ralph Vaughan Williams
In the Beginning	Aaron Copland
Three American Hymns	arr. Alice Parker
Come, Ye That Love The Lord	
God Is Seen	
Hark, I Hear the Harps Eternal	
How Still He Lies	Brent Pierce
Go Pretty Child	Jack M. Jarrett
Alleluia	Randall Thompson
Praise to the Lord	arr. F. Melius Christiansen
Beautiful Savior	arr. F. M. C.

1977

Laudate Dominum	Claudio Monteverdi
Singet dem Herrn	Heinrich Schütz
Hear My Prayer, O Lord	Henry Purcell
Sanctus	J. S. Bach
Stabat Mater	Krzysztof Penderecki
Psalm 116	Roberto Caamaño
Psalm 130	Heinz Werner Zimmermann
Neue Liebeslieder, Op. 65	Johannes Brahms
Three American Hymns	arr. Alice Parker
Come, Ye That Love The Lord	
God Is Seen	
Hark, I Hear	
A Spotless Rose	Herbert Howells
Wake, Awake	Nicolai, arr. F. Melius Christiansen
Carol of the Drum	Katherine K. Davis
Beautiful Savior	arr. F. M. C.

1978

Singet dem Herrn	Heinrich Schütz
Adoramus Te, Christe	Guiseppe Corsi
Praise Ye The Lord (from Sing Ye)	J. S. Bach
Cantata No. 150	J. S. Bach
Venite Populi	Wolfgang Amadeus Mozart
Songs for Double Choir, Op. 141	Robert Schumann
An Die Sterne	
Gottes ist Der Orient!	
Gottes ist Der Occident!	
Night/Morning	Gyorgy Ligeti
Praise the Lord, O My Soul	Alexander Gretchaninoff
Today, Heaven Sings	Kenneth Jennings
Set Me As A Seal Upon Thine Heart	William Walton
Easter Morning	Paul J. Christiansen
Praise to the Lord	arr. F. Melius Christiansen
Beautiful Savior	arr. F. M. C.

1979

Praise Ye The Lord	J. S. Bach
O Jesu Christe	Jachet van Berchem
I Will Not Leave You Comfortless	William Byrd
The Spirit Also Helpeth Us	J. S. Bach
How Great Are Thy Wonders	Georg Schumann
O Crux	Knut Nystedt
God's Son Has Made Me Free	Edvard Grieg
Hymn to St. Cecilia	Benjamin Britten
Night/Morning	Gyorgy Ligeti
I Gondolieri, La Passeggiata	Gioacchino Rossini
Hacia Belén Va Un Borrico	arr. Parker-Shaw
I'm Going Home	African American Spiritual, arr. Undine Smith Moore
Celestial Spring	F. Melius Christiansen
King Of Love	Irish folk tune, arr. Paul J. Christiansen
Beautiful Savior	arr. F. M. C.

1980

Cantate Domino	Heinrich Schütz
O Lord, Creator of All Things	Heinrich Schütz
I Am The Resurrection and the Life	Heinrich Schütz
Sing Ye to the Lord	J. S. Bach
A Hymn of the Nativity	Kenneth Leighton
Hvad Est Du Dog Skjøn	Edvard Grieg
O Crux	Knut Nystedt
The Exaltation of Christ	Charles Forsberg
Hymne (Friedrich Ruckert) Op. 34, No. 2	Richard Strauss
Gloria	Jeffrey H. Rickard
Two Motets	Aaron Copland
Help Us, O Lord	
Sing Ye Praises to Our King	
O Day Full of Grace	arr. F. Melius Christiansen
Rimfrost	Erik Bergman
Beautiful Savior	arr. F. M. C.

1981

Exultate Deo	Hans Leo Hassler
Vere Languores Nostros	Tomás Luis de Victoria
Surrexit Pastor Bonus	Orlando di Lasso
Sing to the Lord a New Song	Hugo Distler
Dilexi, quoniam exaudiet Dominus	Roberto Caamaño
An Apostrophe to the Heavenly Hosts	Healey Willan
Missa Brevis Sancti Johannis de Deo	Joseph Haydn
90th Psalm—Prayers and Declamations!	Charles Ives
Three Anthems	Jean Berger
Alleluia (from Brazilian Psalm)	
The Eyes of All Wait Upon Thee	
O Give Thanks Unto the Lord	
Psalm 50	F. Melius Christiansen
I Believe This Is Jesus	Spiritual, arr. Undine Smith Moore
Och Jungfrun hon går i ringen	arr. Hugo Alfvén
Beautiful Savior	arr. F. M. C.

1982

Cantate Domino	Richard Deering
Call to Remembrance	Richard Farrant
O Beatum et Sacrosanctum Diem	Peter Philips
Two Motets, Opus 29	Johannes Brahms
Sing Praise To God Who reigns Above	
Make Me, O Lord God, Pure In Heart	
Lamentations of Jeremiah	Alberto Ginastera
Creator Spirit, Heavenly Dove	Komm, Gott Schöpfer, setting Kenneth Jennings
Advent Motet	Gustav Schreck
Friede auf Erden	Arnold Schoenberg
Three American Hymns	arr. Alice Parker
Come, Ye That Love The Lord	
God Is Seen	
Hark, I Hear the Harps Eternal	
How Still He Lies	Brent Pierce
Wake, Awake	Nicolai, arr. F. Melius Christiansen
From Heaven Above	arr. F. M. C.
If I Flew To The Point Of Sunrise	Jean Berger
Beautiful Savior	arr. F. M. C.

1983

Gaudete Omnes	Jan Pieterszoon Sweelinck
O Domine Jesu Christe	Sweelinck
Viri Galilaei	Sweelinck
The Righteous	Johann Christoph Bach
Jauchzet dem Herrn (Psalm 100)	Johann Pachelbel
O Glorious King of Martyr Hosts	Otto Olsson
Min Sjel er stille for Gud alene	Bernhard Lewkovitch
Gloria	Lars Edlund
Our Father	Alexander Gretchaninoff
Glory Be to God	Jean Berger
Neue Liebeslieder, Opus 65	Johannes Brahms
Gloria	John Rutter
Lord, Thee I Love	Ralph Johnson
Give Me Jesus	Spiritual, arr. L. L. Fleming
I Believe This Is Jesus	Spiritual, arr. Undine Smith Moore
Praise to the Lord	arr. F. Melius Christiansen
Hear Us, O Father	arr. Knut Nystedt
O Come, Little Children	arr. Carolyn Jennings
Beautiful Savior	arr. F. M. C.

1984

Hodie, Christus Natus Est	Healey Willan
Sanctus from Missa "Aeterna, Christi Munera"	G. P. Palestrina
Ave Verum Corpus	Franz Liszt
Judge Me, O God	Felix Mendelssohn
The Spirit Also Helpeth Us	J. S. Bach
Magnificat	Jean Berger
Four Double Choruses Opus 141	Robert Schumann
To the Stars	
Uncertain Light	
Assurance	
Talismans	
Ubi Caritas	Maurice Duruflé
Praise The Lord, O My Soul	Alexander Gretchaninoff
O Day Full of Grace	arr. F. Melius Christiansen
Go, and Tell John	L. L. Fleming
Salvation is Created	Peter Tschesnokoff
Beautiful Savior	arr. F. M. C.

1985

Psalm 98: Singet dem Herrn	Heinrich Schütz
For God So Loved the World	Heinrich Schütz
I am The Resurrection and the True Life	Heinrich Schütz
Singet dem Herrn	J. S. Bach
The King Shall Rejoice	George Frideric Handel
Exultate Deo	Francis Poulenc
Ubi Caritas	Maurice Duruflé
Agnus Dei	Krzysztof Penderecki
In Principio	Knut Nystedt
All That Have Life and Breath Praise Ye The Lord	René Clausen
Yea, Though I Wander	Georg Schumann
Sing Nowell, Sing Gloria!	Olaf C. Christiansen
Wake, Awake	Nicolai, arr. F. Melius Christiansen
Go, And Tell John	L. L. Fleming
Nunc Dimittis	Alexander Gretchaninoff
Beautiful Savior	arr. F. M. C.

677

1986

Hodie Christus Natus Est	G. P. Palestrina
Sicut Cervus	G. P. Palestrina
Super Flumina Babylonis	Orlando di Lasso
Factus Est Repente	Gregor Aichinger
Lobet den Herrn, alle Heiden	J. S. Bach
Venite Populi	Wolfgang Amadeus Mozart
Mass In G Minor (Kyrie, Gloria)	Ralph Vaughan Williams
Lamb of God	Vassily S. Kalinnikof
Laudate	Kirke Mechem
All You Works of the Lord	Kenneth Jennings
Trois Chansons	Claude Debussy
Dieu! Qi'il la fait bon regarder	
Quant j'ai ouy le tabourin	
Yver, vous n'estes qu'un villain	
A Feast of Lanterns	Carolyn Jennings
Kangding qingge	A Kangding folk song, arr. Shi Weiliang
Ejszaka/Reggel (Night/Morning)	Gyorgy Ligeti
The Promise of Living	Aaron Copland
Go Tell It On The Mountain	Spiritual, arr. Carolyn Jennings
Gloria from Missa Criolla	Ariel Ramirez, arr. J. G. Segade
King of Love	Irish folk tune, arr. Paul J. Christiansen
Celestial Spring (Exaltation, A New Hosanna)	F. Melius Christiansen
Auf dem Berge	Silesian folk tune, arr. Albert Kranz
Nunc Dimittis	Sergei Rachmaninof
Beautiful Savior	arr. F. M. C.

1986 Tour of the Orient

Hodie Christus Natus Est	G. P. Palestrina
Sicut Cervus	G. P. Palestrina
Lobet den Herrn, alle Heiden	J. S. Bach
Venite Populi	Wolfgang Amadeus Mozart
Gloria (from Mass in G Minor)	Ralph Vaughan Williams
Laudate	Kirke Mechem
All You Works of the Lord	Kenneth Jennings
Trois Chansons	Claude Debussy
A Feast of Lanterns	Carolyn Jennings
Kangding qingge	A Kangding folk song, arr. Shi Weiliang
Chin Chin Chi Dori	Japanese folk song, arr. Hikaru Hayashi
Hangasa - ordori	Yamagota folk song, arr. Kiyoshige Koyama
Ejszaka/Reggel	Gyorgy Ligeti
The Promise of Living	Aaron Copland
Gloria (From Missa Criolla)	Ariel Ramirez, arr. J. G. Segade
Go Tell It On The Mountain	Spiritual, arr. Carolyn Jennings
My Lord, What A Morning	arr. Harry T. Burleigh
Every Time I Feel The Spirit	arr. William Dawson
Celestial Spring (Exaltation, A New Hosanna)	F. Melius Christiansen

1987

Cantate Domino	Jan Pieterzoon Sweelinck
Adoramus Te, Christe	Guiseppe Corsi
Die mit Tränen säen	Herman Schein
Be Not Afraid	J. S. Bach
"Alleluia" from Brazilian Psalm	Jean Berger
O Sacrum Convivium	Olivier Messiaen
Walk As Children of Light	Randall Thompson
An Apostrophe to the Heavenly Hosts	Healey Willan
Missa Brevis	Knut Nystedt
Songs of Redemption	Charles Forsberg
Today There Is Ringing	F. Melius Christiansen
How Fair the Church	arr. F. M. C.
The Godly Stranger	G. Winston Cassler
Praise to the Lord	arr. F. M. C.
I Believe This Is Jesus	Spiritual, arr. Undine Smith Moore
This Night	arr. F. M. C.
Beautiful Savior	arr. F. M. C.

1988

Cantate Domino	Richard Deering
As a Heart Longs for the Brooklet	Louis Bourgeois, arr. Claude Goudimel
Tristis Est Anima Mea	Johann Kuhnau
Dearest Lord God, Waken Us Now	Johann Christoph Bach
Praise Ye the Lord	Johann Sebastian Bach
Christus Factus Est Obedians	Anton Bruckner
Jesus, Remember Me	Sven-Erik Bäck
Alleluia	Randall Thompson
All You Works of the Lord	Kenneth Jennings
In The Beginning	Aaron Copland
Gloria	Jeffrey Rickard
Steal Away	Spiritual, arr. Andrew Carter
Psalm 50	F. Melius Christiansen
Keep Your Lamps!	Spiritual, arr. André Thomas
Beati Quorum Via	Charles Villiers Stanford
Beautiful Savior	Silesian folk tune, arr. F. M. C.

1988 Seoul, Korea

Singet dem Herrn	J. S. Bach
I Saw a Stranger Yestere'en	Jacob Avshalomov
Vision of Peace	Jean Berger
Collect For Peace	Leslie Bassett
Alleluia	Randall Thompson
All You Works of the Lord	Kenneth Jennings
In the Beginning	Aaron Copland
I'm Going Home	Spiritual, arr. Undine Smith Moore
Keep Your Lamps	Spiritual, arr. André Thomas
Psalm 50	F. Melius Christiansen
Arirang	Korean folk song
Toraji	Korean folk song
Shenandoah	arr. James Erb

1989

Sanctus	Giovanni Pierluigi Palestrina
Hodie Christus Natus Est	Palestrina
O Lord, Creator of All Things	Heinrich Schütz
I Am The Resurrection and the Life	Schütz
Singet dem Herrn	J. S. Bach
Missa Brevis in B-flat Major (K. 275)	Wolfgang Amadeus Mozart
O Rex Gentium	Anton Heiller
How Great Are Thy Wonders	Georg Schumann
It's A Saying Surely True	Hugo Distler
Lord Hosanna	Gustav Schreck
Canticle of the Sun	Jean Berger
Love in Grief	F. Melius Christiansen
Praise to the Lord	arr. F. M. C.
O Come, Little Children	arr. Carolyn Jennings
Thy Bountiful Care	Kenneth Jennings
Keep Your Lamps!	Spiritual, arr. André Thomas
Beautiful Savior	arr. F. M. C.

680

1990

Hodie Christus Natus Est	Giovanni Pierluigi Palestrina
Sicut Cervus	Palestrina
Verbum Caro Factum Est	Hans Leo Hassler
O Vos Omnes	Juan Esquivel
Surrexit Pastor Bonus	Orlando di Lasso
The Righteous	Johann Kuhnau, J. S. Bach
Jesus, Source of Every Blessing	J. S. Bach
The Holy Spirit Helpeth Us	J. S. Bach
Magnificat	Jean Berger
I Saw A Stranger Yestere'en	Jacob Avshalomov
Song of Cherubim	Krzysztof Penderecki
Gloria (from Mass in G Minor)	Ralph Vaughan Williams
Holy, Holy, Holy, Lord of Sabaoth	Alexander Gretchaninov
How Still He Lies	Brent Pierce
Hacia Belén Va Un Borrico	arr. Alice Parker, Robert Shaw
Wake, Awake	Nicolai, arr. F. Melius Christiansen
Go Tell It On The Mountain	arr. Carolyn Jennings
Justice, O God	Felix Mendelssohn
Beautiful Savior	arr. F. M. C.

1991

Hosanna to the Son of David	Thomas Weelkes
Hear My Prayer	Henry Purcell
Nun Danket Alle Gott	Johann Pachelbel
Ave Verum Corpus	Wolfgang Amadeus Mozart
Venite Populi	Wolfgang Amadeus Mozart
Alleluia	Ralph Manuel
Evening Meal (The Lord's Supper)	Ralph M . Johnson
Stabat Mater	Krzysztof Penderecki
My Soul Waiteth for the Lord	G. Winston Cassler
The Exaltation of Christ	Charles Forsberg
The Lamentations of Jeremiah	Alberto Ginastera
Haleluya! Pelo Tsa Rona	Traditional South African
Hush! Somebody's Callin' My Name	arr. Brazeal W. Dennard
Spirit of God, Descend Upon My Heart	Kenneth Jennings
Light Everlasting	Olaf C. Christiansen
O Day Full of Grace	arr. F. Melius Christiansen
Keep Your Lamps	arr. André Thomas
My Heart Is Longing to Praise My Savior	arr. Leland B. Sateren
Beautiful Savior	arr. F. M. C.

1992

Cantate Domino	Jan Pieterszoon Sweelinck
Crucifixus	Antonio Lotti
Jauchzet dem Herrn	J. S. Bach
How Great Are Thy Wonders	Georg Schumann
Talismane	Robert Schumann
A Hymn of the Nativity	Kenneth Leighton
I Saw A Stranger Yestere'en	Jacob Avshalomov
Lord, Thee I Love	Ralph M. Johnson
Ah, Holy Jesus	Setting by John Ferguson
Kyrieleis	John Leavitt
Set Me as a Seal	René Clausen
Canticle of the Sun	Jean Berger
Singabahambayo	Traditional South African folk song
Freedom Is Coming	Traditional South African folk song
Hombe	arr. Laz Ekwueme
I Open My Mouth	arr. André Thomas
What Wondrous Love	arr. Robert Scholz
Easter Morning	Paul J. Christiansen
Praise to the Lord	arr. F. Melius Christiansen
I Believe This Is Jesus	arr. Undine Smith Moore
Pål på Haugen	arr. Bradley Ellingboe
Beautiful Savior	arr. F. M. C.

1993

Gaudete Omnes	Jan Pieterszoon Sweelinck
Agnus Dei	William Byrd
Hvad est du dog skjøn	Edvard Grieg
God's Son Has Made Me Free	Edvard Grieg
Coronation Anthem No. 4	George Frideric Handel
Vinea Mea Electa	Francis Poulenc
O Sacrum Convivium	Peter Mathews
Agnus Dei	Krzysztof Penderecki
Kyrieleis	John Leavitt
Salvation is Created	Peter Tschesnokoff
Sing for Joy	Peter Hamlin
Water Under Snow Is Weary	Harri Wessman
O Sifuni Mungu	arr. David Maddux
My Song in the Night	arr. Paul J. Christiansen
John Saw Duh Numbuh	arr. Shaw/Parker
Celestial Spring II Exaltation/Glorification	F. Melius Christiansen
Go Where I Send Thee	arr. André Thomas
Jamaican Market Place	arr. Larry Farrow
Beautiful Savior	arr. F. M. C.

682

1993 Scandinavian Tour

Gaudete Omnes	Jan Pieterszoon Sweelinck
Agnus Dei	William Byrd
Easter Anthem	William Billings
Fürchte dich nicht	Johann Sebastian Bach
Salvation is Created	Peter Tschesnokoff
The Steadfast Love	Knut Nystedt
O Sacrum Convivium	Peter Mathews
Agnus Dei (Polish Requiem)	Krzysztof Penderecki
All That Have Life and Breath	René Clausen
Pinsesalme: "Velsignede morgen" Peer Gynt	Edvard Grieg
Den Store, Hvide Flok	Edvard Grieg
Dona Nobis Pacem	Edvard Grieg
Hvad est du dog skjøn	Edvard Grieg
Guds Søn har gjort mig fri	Edvard Grieg
O Sifuni Mungu	arr. David Maddux
My Song in the Night	arr. Paul J. Christiansen
John Saw Duh Numbuh	arr. Robert Shaw and Alice Parker
Å at jeg kunne min Jesus prise	arr. Leland Sateren
O Day Full of Grace	arr. F. Melius Christiansen
Norge, Mitt Norge	Alfred Paulsen
Jamaican Market Place	arr. Larry Farrow
Siyahamba	Traditional South African
Pål På Haugen	arr. Bradley Ellingboe
Witness	arr. Jack Halloran

1994

Sing Joyfully Unto God	William Byrd
Sicut Cervus	G. P. Palestrina
Jauchzet dem Herrn	Johann Pachelbel
Alleluia (Brazilian Psalm)	Jean Berger
Veni, Creator Spiritus	Richard Marlow
Cantate Domino	David Conte
Laudate	Kirke Mechem
Gloria (Missa Criolla)	Ariel Ramirez
O Schöne Nacht	Johannes Brahms
Heart We Will Forget Him	James Mulholland
Rise Up, My Love, My Fair One	James Mc Cray
Trois Chansons Bretonnes	Henk Badings
A Spotless Rose	Herbert Howells
African Noel	arr. André Thomas
Every Time I Think About Jesus	arr. L. L. Fleming
Psalm 50 (movements II and III)	F. Melius Christiansen
Halle, Halle, Halle	arr. Marty Haugen
Arirang	arr. Kenneth Jennings
Beautiful Savior	arr. F. M. C.

1995

Laetatus Sum	Johann Michael Haydn
Ave Verum Corpus	William Byrd
Singet dem Herrn ein neues Lied	J. S. Bach
Lord Hosanna	Gustav Schreck
Cantique de Jean Racine, Op. 11	Gabriel Fauré
Vanity of Vanities	Peter Hamlin
Psalm 96	Ralph M. Johnson
Ubi Caritas	Maurice Duruflé
Magnificat	Arvo Pärt
Alleluia	Peter Mathews
Kasar Mie La Gaji	Alberto Grau
O Sifuni Mungu	arr. David Maddux
Prayer Before Sleep (Talmud Suite)	Sid Rabinovitch
Elijah Rock	arr. Moses Hogan
My Lord, What a Mornin'	arr. Larry Farrow
Wake, Awake	arr. F. Melius Christiansen
Mary's Little Boy Chile	Jester Hairston
Danny Boy (Londonderry Air)	arr. Joseph Flummerfelt
Beautiful Savior	arr. F. M. C.

1996

The Lord's Prayer	Robert Stone
Exsultate Deo	Giovanni Pierluigi da Palestrina
Cœnantibus Autem Illis	Juan de Lienas
Psalm 98: Singet dem Herrn	Heinrich Schütz
I Was Glad	Sir C. Hubert H. Parry
Behold, O God Our Defender	Herbert Howells
Praise the Lord, O My Soul	Ned Rorem
Canticle: The Hungry Angels	Robert A. Harris
All You Works of the Lord, Bless the Lord	Kenneth Jennings
Salmo 150	Ernani Aguiar
Dilexi, quoniam exaudiet Dominus	Roberto Caamaño
Our Father	Alexander Gretchaninoff
Ngana (Songs of Passage)	Stephen Leek
Lord of the Dance	arr. John Ferguson
Shenandoah	arr. James Erb
Worthy to be Praised	Byron J. Smith
Deep River	arr. Carol Barnett
O Day Full of Grace	C. E. F. Weyse,
	arr. F. Melius Christiansen
Halle, Halle, Halle	arr. Marty Haugen
Beautiful Savior	arr. F. M. C.

1997

Alleluia, I Heard A Voice	Thomas Weelkes
Hear My Prayer, O Lord	Henry Purcell
I Am The Rose of Sharon	William Billings
Nun Danket Alle Gott	Johann Pachelbel
For God Commanded Angels to Watch Over You	Felix Mendelssohn
O Crux	Knut Nystedt
Teach Me, O God, The Way	Kenneth Jennings
Lux Aeterna	David Hamilton
The Exaltation of Christ	Charles Forsberg
How Great Are Thy Wonders	Georg Schumann
Past Life Melodies	Sarah Hopkins
Kasar Mie La Gaji	Alberto Grau
Sigalagala (Let There Be Ululation!)	arr. S. A. Otieno
City Called Heaven	arr. Josephine Poelinitz
Rockin' Jerusalem	arr. André Thomas
Psalm 50 (movements II and III)	F. Melius Christiansen
Siyahamba	Traditional South African song
Hine E Hine	arr. David Hamilton
Advance Australia Fair	arr. Stephen Leek
Beautiful Savior	arr. F. M. C.

Appendix B is a listing of all tour programs of The St. Olaf Choir from 1912 to 1997. Optional selections are listed with the tour programs when available. Several sources were used to create this list: Bergmann, Leola Nelson, *Music Master of the Middle West*: The Story of F. Melius Christiansen and the St. Olaf Choir, Minneapolis, ©1944; Crist, Lyndon, Tour programs of the Olaf C. Christiansen era: 1941-1968; Armstrong, Anton, "Celebrating 75 Years of Musical Excellence: The Evolution of the St. Olaf Choir," May 1987; archived tour programs; the *Manitou Messenger*; St. Olaf Choir scrapbooks; St. Olaf College archival materials.

INDEX

Note: References to Choir indicate the St. Olaf Choir
Bold page numbers indicate photographs

A

a cappella singing, Choir's commitment to, 345
Aaker, Marie, 70, 71
Aasgaard, J.A., 167, **168**, 174, 181
    dedication of Rølvaag Library, 259
Aasgard, Dr. & Mrs. J.A., 178
Abrahamson, Carl, 263
Ackerman, Tim, 486, 488
Adams, Charles, 239
"Adoramus Te, Christe" (Corsi), 352, 512
"Advent Motet" (Schreck), 297, 431
"Adventure in Faith" historical pageant, 333
Aeterna, Christi Munera (Palestrina), 467
"African Noel" (arr. Thomas), 535, 546
Agnes Mellby Hall, **261**
Agnus Dei (Penderecki), 471, 542
"agonizing," 151
Agony Hall, 147
"Agony Quartette," 128
"Ah, Holy Jesus" (arr. Ferguson), 523, 537
Alberg, Winnifred Greene, **276**, 295, 300, 618-19
"All My Heart" (Cruger), 407
"All You Works of the Lord, Bless the Lord" (K. Jennings), 537, 556
"Alleluia" (Berger), 353, 546
"Alleluia" (Cassler), 314
"Alleluia, I Heard A Voice" (Weelkes), 565
"Alleluia" (Mathews), 26, 549
"Alleluia" (Thompson), 618
"Alone with Thee" (Conradi), 107, 115
alumni/ae clubs, 580-83
American Boychoir, 507, 508, 517
American Choral Directors Association, 445, 491, 517, 556, 588
Amundson, Steven, **504**, 547, 557, **609**
Andersen, Ann, 348
Anderson, Gertrude Roe, **215**
Anderson, Janet, 296

Anderson, Mildred Hoff, 232
Anderson, Tom, 382
Andress, Paul, 512
Andrews, J. Warren, 49
Annual Christmas Song Service, 598
    See also Christmas Festival
"Apostrophe to the Heavenly Hosts" (Willan), 184, 267, 279, 297
applause in church, 343, 553-54
Arirang" (Korean folk song) (arr. K. Jennings), 486, 535, 546
Arizona Republic, 490
Armstrong, Anton E., **503, 506-509, 511, 513, 514, 516, 519, 520, 525, 527, 528, 533, 539, 540, 550, 551, 554, 557, 558, 562, 568, 569, 572, 619**
Armstrong, Anton E., youth and student years, 507-09
    American Boychoir, 508-09
    graduate study, 514-15
    student at Cathedral School of St. Paul, 509
    student at St. Olaf, 497, 510-13
Armstrong, Anton E., at Calvin College, 514-19
    conducting and directing responsibilities, 516, 518
    musical culture in Grand Rapids, 516
    reviews, 517-18
    teaching responsibilties, 515
Armstrong, Anton E., director of St. Olaf Choir
    appointed director 519-20
    selection process for director, 504-06
    Choir tours, 17
        1995 concert in Carnegie Hall, 554
        Australia/New Zealand, 526-27, 560, 562
        See also Choir tours 1991-1997

"Jubilate Deo" (Gabrieli), 422
"Jubilate" (Lewkovitch), 428
Jubilee Singers, 161
Juilliard String Quartet, 416

K

Kaiser Wilhelm Memorial Cathedral, 420
Kalamazoo Gazette, 555
"Kasar Mie La Gaji" (The Earth is Tired)
   (Grau), 536
"Keep Your Lamps Trimmed and Burning" (arr.
   Thomas), 483, 521
Kennedy Center for the Performing Arts, 423,
   440, 458, 465, 492
Kildahl, Edith Glasoe, **341**
Kildahl, H.B., 109
Kildahl, John N., **57**, 58, 59, **66**
   1912 Choir tour, 108-09
   purposes of choir tours, 10, 11, 48
   requests music director for St. Olaf, 68
   song services, 97, 615
   supports improvement of St. John's Choir,
   106
Kim, Jin, **486**
Kindem, Lars, **322**
King David (Honegger), 389
King Haakon VII, **114**, **119**, 170, 174
King Harald V, 17, 445, 541
King Olav V, **114**, 170, 174, 445, **446**
King Shall Rejoice, The (Handel), 470
Kirn, Mrs. G.W., **341**
"K.J. Kwotes," 460
Kjerulf Club, 54, 55, 84, 85, **86**
Kjerulf, Halfdan, 85
Kjerulf Octet, 85, 86
Kjerulf Quartet, 85
Kjos, Clarence, **237**
Kjos Music Company, 234-36
Kjos, Neil A. Jr., **504**
Kjos, Neil, Sr., 234, **236**, 589
Kleinhans Music Hall (Buffalo), 301
Kleven, Nils, 18, 108
Kleven, O.M., **341**
Kline, Shelley, 466
Klüver, Birgitte Muus, 70, **168**, 169
Knatvold, Naida, 428
Koet, Josefa, **437**, 454
"Kong Kristian," 245, 257, 259
Konserthus, Oslo, **544**
Korea Philharmonic Orchestra, 484

Koren, Lina, 74
Kruse, Perry, 600, **601**
Kunze, William, 181
Kuzma, John, 517
Kyoto Lutheran Church, 473
Kyoto University Men's Glee Club, 473
"Kyrieleis" (Leavitt), 523

L

Lace, Pat, **297**, 307
Lachmund, Carl V., 49, 79
Ladies of Bethany, 437, 438
Ladies' Chorus, 86-87, **100**, 104
Ladies' Hall, **74**, 147
Ladies' Octette, 87
Ladies' Quartet, **145**, 593, 597
"Laetatus Sum" (J.M. Haydn), 537
"Lamb of God" (F.M. Christiansen), 106, 219
"Lamb of God" (Söderman), 108
Lamentations of Jeremiah (Ginastera), 522
Lange, David, 466-67
Langen, L., 71
Langum, Henry, **96**
Larsen, Alice, 264, **297**, **463**, 491, 496, 512
Larsen, Ditman, **79**, 88
Larsen, the Reverend and Mrs. G.A., 97
Larsen, Tom, 571
Larson, Martha, 79
Larson, Ole, 128
Larvik Band, **35**
Larvik Trinity Church, **36**
"Laud Him" (Pepping), 354
"Laudate" (Mechem), 546
Lazare, Henri, 415, 417
Lee, Don, 512
   acting Choir Manager, 584
Lee, Ingebret, 82
Lee, Norma
   See Simso, Norma Lee
Leidal, Knute, **595**
Leland, Diana, 557
Lelio (Berlioz), 394
liberal arts, philosophy of, 337
Lien, Beatrix, **262**, 263
Lilje, Bishop Hans, 320
Lincoln Center, 290, 423
Lindaas, Alpha, **134**
Lindem, Jacob and Serine, 43
Lindstrom, Andrew, **261**
Lindstrom, Mr. and Mrs. Neil, **563**

St. Olaf Choir in Concert

St. Olaf Choir in rebuilt Marktkirche Hanover, Germany, 1970

St. Olaf Choir at Holden Church, 1971

St. Denis Cathedral, Paris, 1972

St. Olaf Choir at Strasbourg Festival, Strasbourg Cathedral, 1972

Orchestra Hall, Minneapolis, 1977

St. Olaf Choir on stage at Kennedy Center, Washington, D.C., 1980

St. Olaf Choir in Wellington Cathedral, New Zealand, 1997

St. Olaf Choir singers, Boe Memorial Chapel

Asian Tour, 1986

Saying good-bye at Kyushu Jogakuin Junior College for Girls, Kumamoto, Japan

Kyushu Gakuin Lutheran High School Kumamoto, Japan, June 1986

Lisa and Kenneth Jennings Mt. Aso, Japan, 1986

Students welcome the Choir Soochow University, Taipei, Taiwan

Director Jennings receives flowers Sun Yat-sen Memorial Hall, Taipei

At the Chiang Kai-shek Mausoleum, Tai L. R. standing: Guide, Ingrid Johanson ' Kim Bowman '88, Amy Saxum '86, Mai Jennings, Lisa Jennings '88, Dr. Jenning Sitting: Karen Spong '87, Elizabeth McCabe '86, Bryan Hanson '88

Choir at Truth Lutheran Church, Hong Kong, June 7, 1986

On the Great Wall outside Beijing, China

Singing at East China Normal University (ECNU), Shanghai, where St. Olaf has an exchange agreement

Choir, Chinese dignitaries, and St. Olaf delegation on stage in Xian, Shaanxi Province, China. In front row are Richard Bodman, translator, Vice President Dennis Griffin, Kenneth Jennings and Bob Johnson, manager.

Buying hats at the Great Wall Geoffrey Knight '86 and Paul Jensen '88

St. Olaf Choir in Korea, 1988

Signs of Welcome

Massed Choir and Orchestra at Olympic Festival Hall, Seoul, August 23, 1988

Post-concert hug
Jill Swenson '89 and
Margaret McClure '90

Recessing with a smile
Elisabeth Lindland '90
and Valerie Drum '89

Sightseeing in Korea, 1988
L. to R.: Todd Benjamin '89, Hans
Peterson '90, Lisa Anderson '89,
Paul Jensen '88, Laurie Rapp '91,
Lora Sampson '87, Sara Condit '88

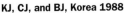

KJ, CJ, and BJ, Korea 1988

Families reacquainted
in Korea
Back row, L. to R.: Hee
Sung Keel, Lisa Jennings,
Mrs. Keel. Front row, L. to
R.: Mark Jennings, Jane
and Ellen Keel, Carolyn
and Kenneth Jennings.
Dr. Hee Sung Keel taught
in the St. Olaf Religion
Department from 1977 to
1982. Mrs. Keel worked
in the St. Olaf Library.
Ellen took piano from
Carolyn Jennings.

St. Olaf Christmas Festival, 1989
Photo by Mitch Kezar

Choir scenes 1990s

Quartet in impromptu Oslo concert, 1993
L. to R.: Dean Niquette '93, Mark Tiede '93, William Heim '94, Thomas Adcox '93

St. Patrick's Day, 1996
Bob Johnson, bust of FMC, Anton Armstrong

St. Olaf Choir in Carnegie Hall, Friday, February 3, 1995

Kennedy Center for the Performing Arts

Anton Armstrong meeting with young people
Kennedy Center lobby, Washington, February 5, 1995

New Zealand & Australia 1997

Touring a farm in New Zealand

On the Franz Josef Glacier
New Zealand, January 26, 1997

Concert in St. Paul's Cathedral
Melbourne, January 31, 1997

Concert at Luther College Chapel
Melbourne, Australia, January 30, 1997

Big Hair Night, Cairns, February 7, 1997
L. to R.: Karin Rooney '98, Matt Schwinghammer
'97, Sharon Fennema '98, Manda Helmick '98

St. Olaf Choir in Adelaide Town Hall
Adelaide, Australia, February 1, 1997

Sydney Opera House and Harbour Bridge

St. Olaf Choir, February 16, 1997
Orchestra Hall, Minneapolis

Anton Armstrong at Christiansen grave
Oak Lawn Cemetery, Northfield, April 1, 1996

Seal of St. Olaf College
Boe Chapel window